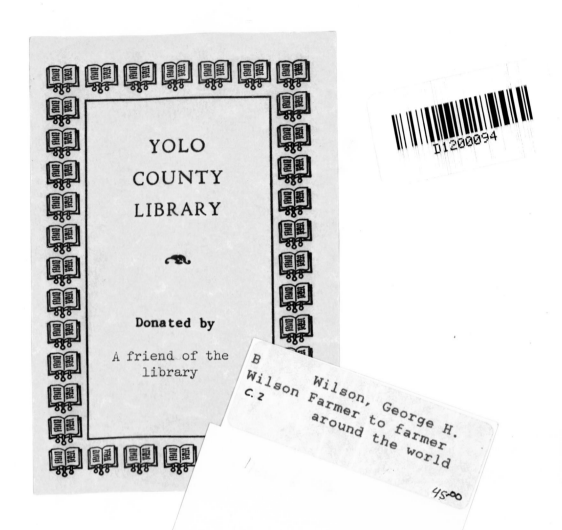

D1200094

B
Wilson   Wilson, George H.
C.2   Farmer to farmer around the world.
              Univ. of the Pacific, 1987.
                  407 p.   photos.

              1. Wilson, George H., 1892-. 2. Yolo
              County - Biography. 3. Clarksburg -
              Biography. I. Title.

450   45.00/687
                                        6-87

Farmer to Farmer Around the World

by George H. Wilson

Director, AFBF 1938 to 1958
President, CFBF 1951 to 1955
President, Transworld Agricultural Development Corp. 1967-1977

Bella and Me

Printed by
University of the Pacific
3601 Pacific Avenue
Stockton, California 95211

Cover design by Patricia Forseth
Graphic production by Robin Suzanne Vincent

DEDICATION & ACKNOWLEDGEMENTS

I wish to dedicate this book to my wife Isabelle (Bella) in recognition of her devotion and dedication to our family. So many times I have been away, and the household and family duties were well handled by her. At other times, in Mexico, Iran, and India, she has been with me, living under trying conditions, similar to an early pioneer, yet ever cheerful and helpful.

Our children, David, Dick, Patricia and Dorothy, had less paternal support than they may have hoped for during my busiest years, but all have done well. I have often thanked our Creator for such a fine, healthy family, with good minds and good works.

Our grandchildren are the ones who urged me to leave this record, and they have been a great satisfaction and inspiration to me. I hope some of the experiences and thoughts in this book will be helpful to them.

I wish to give special thanks to a Clarksburg neighbor, Patricia Forseth, who helped edit and organize the book, plus typed it for publication.

The events in the book are true, the conversations as true as I can remember them. Where I have had success in my life, the credit must be shared with many (too numerous to mention here). . . but I must claim my failures as my own.

Our home in Clarksburg.

Above left, my father, George W. Wilson, Chaplain from 1905-1922 at National Soldier's Home; at right, Mother Wilson. Below left, Isabelle and Father Mack; right, Mother Mack in our living room.

Above left, David, Dick, and our first Buick, right, Isabelle with David, Dick, and Pat.
Below, our family in the 50s in our yard, l-r Isabelle, Erma, David, Dick, Patty, Dorothy.

Top left, Patty's wedding 1949, Pastor Elliott Fisher; right, David and Erma. Ctr, Dorothy Ann's wedding 1957. Bottom left, granddaughter Sandra playing ball with her brothers (c 1962); right, a typical Christmas at our home — the boat was purchased in Japan, was self-propelled, and made a big hit!

CALIFORNIA FARM BUREAU FEDERATION

GEORGE H. WILSON
President

LOUIS A. ROZZONI
First Vice President

ROY R. McLAIN
Second Vice President

RICHARD W. OWENS
Secretary - Treasurer

FRANK S. PIERCE
General Secretary

2223 FULTON STREET
BERKELEY 4, CALIFORNIA
TELEPHONE THornwall 3-9600

Retirement from Farm Bureau in 1955.
        . . . . I would like to believe I've helped to achieve my life goal represented
by my Farm Bureau stationery — improved education and production with freedom as the issue.

FREEDOM IS THE ISSUE

TABLE OF CONTENTS

1

FAMILY HISTORY

My father, George W. Wilson, was born March 25, 1853, at New Ross in the south of Ireland. My mother was born July 9, 1856, in Lawrence County, Ohio, eligible to be a daughter of the American Revolution.

My father's father, John Wilson, was a sea captain living at New Ross and sailing out of Waterford Harbor. Most stories of the old sailing ships describe crews only a short step removed from the pirate gangs of those days, with officers picked from the toughest of the tough. I expect in real life they were people willing to meet the hardships of nature but otherwise much like the rest of us.

A captain was responsible for his ship, his men, and his cargo. Principally he was a merchant. He would ship out of port with a cargo which he and the ship owners felt could best be sold in the ports of call or used to purchase or trade for other commodities for resale.

The rough, tough image did not seem to fit John Wilson. His letters indicate a very gentle person interested in the welfare of his wife and twelve children, his brothers, sisters, and friends. He also showed a real concern as to whether the sales and purchases of the voyage would show the ship owners a reasonable profit.

On one of these trips off the northeast coast of South America, the ship ran into a hurricane which broke the masts. John took several crew ashore to cut timbers to repair the damage. Somehow his leg was cut. The masts and spars were replaced and the voyage continued, but he contracted erysipelas and was buried at sea.

John's death was a terrible blow to his wife, a very gentle woman left with twelve children, of whom my father was the youngest. She had plenty of friends and work to keep her busy, but without the companionship and counsel of her husband she seemed lost and weak and gradually withered away.

George was 13 years old when he was left an orphan. He had two brothers in America, so he set sail to live with brother William, in or near Buffalo, New York. George worked on farms and in a print shop. He attended some night classes and managed to get some education. His penmanship was almost an art for style, uniformity, and clarity. His grammar and spelling were almost perfect, possibly because he was an avid reader and fairly early in life began writing books.

His brothers William and John were Methodist ministers, and George decided to follow their calling. He moved to southern Illinois, where he married in 1875. From

1

this marriage came three children, Carrie, Nellie, and Walter.

On September 20, 1877, my father was appointed a deacon of the Methodist Episcopal Church and declared a proper person to administer the ordinance of baptism and marriage, the burial of the dead in the absence of an elder, and to preach.

On January 31, 1880, at Pinchneyville in Perry County, Illinois, he received his naturalization papers as a U.S. citizen. In September that year, at Fairfield, Illinois, he was elected an Elder of the Methodist Episcopal Church with authority to administer sacraments and ordinances of the church.

His first wife passed away in 1880, and in 1882 he married Mary Elma Boggs of Urbana, Illinois, my mother.

My father was very successful in his ministry. In those days a young minister in the rural areas was a circuit rider with three or four local churches, often preaching at one on Sunday morning and another Sunday afternoon or evening, then one or two others the next Sunday, with prayer meetings in between either in churches or in homes. My father was enthusiastic about his work and an effective speaker, so he soon devoted most of his time to evangelistic work.

He always retained his affiliate membership in the local Methodist Conference, attending the annual conference and the general conferences held each four years. He became rather widely recognized as the historical authority in the Methodist Episcopal Church.

Most of his revival services were held in a Methodist church, but he always insisted he would not go to a community unless several denominations joined in the services and he had the assistance of their ministers. He often took his own organist and always his own soloist and song leader. Most of his meetings were in the Midwest, but he also covered the far West and the East.

In the fall of 1885 he took a trip to Deadwood City with his close friend, Bishop Ninde. He described the trip as follows.

††† An Exciting Trip to Deadwood, Dakota Territory

It was the fall of 1885. Weary from excessive labors, Bishop Ninde requested me to accompany him to the Black Hills Mission.

In the rickety station at Omaha we were safely quartered in a "Burlington" sleeper, where we fell in company with Mr. W of the firm of F&W, New York. Nothing unusual occurred as we slipped across the plains of Nebraska. After delays common to those days in a new country, we reached Chadron, Nebraska, at that time the end of the rails.

Chadron was a town of about two-hundred tents with an occasional board house. The Bank was a boxed frame with a tent roof; the word Bank was painted on canvas fastened near the battered door. A drugstore made of boards graced a prominent corner. Gamblers carried on their work in broad daylight. Indians stood around watching them, when not engaged in selling a few of their trinkets or begging of the newly arrived passengers. Saloons furnished "firewater" from counters made of baled hay.

Early in the afternoon we left for Deadwood on the stage, a two-seated convey-

ance with leather springs running parallel with the coach, which was covered with sail cloth. A latticed platform behind was held up by large leather straps for trunks and baggage. The express and mail were at the feet of the driver, who wore a belt of revolvers. With a bottle of whiskey in his big coat and fur robes wrapped around, he was ready for his long, cool drive. An admiring host saw us off, a motley collection of all sorts and conditions of men and one woman. With one loud crack of the driver's whip, we commenced our journey.

Five persons were in the coach: Bishop N, Mr. W, a printer and his wife, and myself. We made reasonable headway, leaving eight miles behind us each passing hour. Occasionally we crossed a rut in the road which threw us forward into the laps of those opposite us, who returned the compliment before either party had time to apologize.

The next morning we ate our first meal "out." The place where we changed horses was a shanty too low to stand up in. The table was bare boards, and the knives were furnished by ourselves. As we drove up, a short man stood in the doorway, with sleeves rolled above his elbows. He enquired, "How many?" The driver answered, "Five." Dough covered his hands up to his wrists, which were of several colors, but hunger from incessant jostlings made us forget who made the biscuits. We were only thankful that out on the mountains we could get a meal with canned foods, fresh biscuits, and black coffee. Canned-food boxes served for chairs, our pocket knives for service, and seventy-five cents for price.

Some of the scenery was magnificent. Our horses ran down some of those roads with canyons a thousand feet below, where a misstep would cost us our lives. How often we saw a narrow passage, where we could neither turn, return, or escape from the "hold-up man"! Sometimes a shadow would materialize, by the aid of an expectant imagination, and we thought of slipping our money into our shoes. Occasionally we met men on horseback wearing belts of revolvers, and we held our breath until they had passed with merely a courteous word or a question.

The second night we had commenced to nap when my attention was caught by the printer. He was a small, wiry man, crouched in the corner opposite me with his knees pressed against mine. Now his eyes were like a wildcat and fastened on me.

Thoroughly aroused, I thought my hope was in a pleasant conversation, without showing a single sign of fear. We had a crazy man on our hands. With my first word, keeping that awful stare, he began to implore our protection. By now we were all thoroughly awakened. His wife commanded him, implored him, threatened him, to no purpose. Fortunately, we came to another stop. We alighted and discussed our plans while he ran out in the darkness. We found him shivering with fear that he was going to be murdered, and, partly by persuasion, partly by force, we landed him in the coach and started for Deadwood City.

I had anticipated a high pulse and possibly mountain fever, so I had placed in my vest pocket a small bottle of Bryonia. With the aid of the others, I succeeded in giving him a dose, which put him into a restful sleep until the grey dawn of the morning.

We had awakened from a doze and were congratulating ourselves that we would reach the city, four hours away, when suddenly the printer aroused, struck out in every direction, pleading not to be murdered. Then he leaped out the window, lighting on his back, sprang to his feet, and swift as a deer ran ahead of us for about a mile. Hoping he would become exhausted, we drove on. Suddenly he turned and ran swiftly past us in the other direction and disappeared. Satisfied that we could do nothing, and urged on by the driver who was anxious to deliver the express and mail, we hastened on toward the city to report his case and have the authorities and friends find him. We consoled his wife, and wondered what the end would be for a man in those mountains without food, water, shelter, and surrounded by wild beasts.

At first his wife seemed to take the matter calmly. She told us they had traveled second-class from New York, and had not slept since leaving, four days before, except as they napped in a seat; that they had not tasted a warm meal since leaving; that he had been drinking excessively for some time past, and the higher altitude finished what a diseased condition had begun. While thinking and wondering about him, as suddenly she cried out, "Please don't. Don't murder me and my husband!" And, leaving her hand-satchel on the seat, she went out the same window, falling on her breast. We were passing a fenced pasture, and she ran right through the barbed-wire fence as though it were made of string, tearing her clothing to shreds and fearfully lacertaing her body.

On our arrival, we notified the landlord at the hotel. The driver notified the crowd which always gathers to see the stage arrive. Weary from loss of sleep and excitement, we retired to our rooms for sleep.

I had just settled into a fine sleep when a thundering knock woke me. I called, "Who is there?" I was told to get up, as some serious business was on hand. I did so. A plain looking man stood in the doorway and said, "A rumor is in town that three men drugged a man and his wife in the stagecoach, and her father and brothers are arranging for a hanging bee." I sought to explain and was asked for the bottle of Bryonia for analysis. Fortunately, some of its contents was left. Taking the bottle, he said, "I will report later."

Immediately I dressed and rapped on the door of Bishop N's room. I told him to dress and prepare for the worst, perhaps "to be sent over the range with our boots off." Presently the plain man appeared saying, "I have satisfied the men as to who you are, and had I been there myself I would have administered as you did having

4

nothing else with you. I am a physician and it is all explained."

The sheriff and friends took a team and wagon and went after the printer and his wife. They found her in tattered garments, shoeless and hatless and nearly naked, torn in body and wild. They had to handcuff her and chain her on a chair to the wagon, to bring her in.

The news quickly spread of the arrival. Instead of taking her to some private place, she was brought up the main street and stopped opposite a drugstore. Bishop N and myself (Mr. W had gone on to Sturgis) went to see her. No more lovely man ever graced the office of bishop; I never met a man with a sweeter face. I was somewhat fearful that she would identify me, and perhaps say some things to the crowd that would incense them, though they saw she was crazy. As soon as the bishop appeared she recognized him and turning toward him, said, "That is the one that did it. When I get out of here I will settle him."

Instantly, all eyes were turned on us, but the father, who had heard the explanation and was satisfied, ordered her to be still. A word from him would have endangered our lives. We spoke to the father and confirmed the statement of the doctor. The following day the man was found and after proper care and treatment they were both restored.

Such things are not possible in a trip to Deadwood now. The Pullman Coach leaves you in the center of a thriving town untouched by crazy passengers, but, dear reader, after twenty-two year's reflection, we would not care, after all, to leave this thrilling chapter out of our lives. Bishop N was always a friend, and our travels and interviews were frequent. Never was our trip to Deadwood City brought up that it did not furnish amusement and entertainment. I promised him I would willingly accompany him when possible on his episcopal tours, but that hereafter he should guarantee me immunity from crazed passengers if they fell to our lot. However remote the cause that brought it about, he must be willing to accept the verdict even of a crazy woman, "That is the one that did it."

In 1889 Bishop Ninde asked my father to accompany him on a trip around the world, which was far more of an adventure then than today. However, he stopped off first to see his relatives in Ireland. Finding them in great difficulty, he stayed until it was too late to accompany the Bishop. As he had used most of his money on his family in Ireland, he stopped only in Paris and then returned home.

My sister Jenny Ethel was born July 1, 1885, in Illinois. Celia Bernice was born November 24, 1888, and I, George Harold, was born at 4 a.m. March 26, 1892, at 1024 South Clay Ave., Jacksonville, Illinois. Soon the family, now with six children, moved to Des Moines, Iowa, where we stayed two years, then moved to Moulton, Iowa. My recollection of Moulton was a few acres of land, a large square two-story house with lots of rooms, lots of shade and fruit trees, and a large Newfoundland dog. After two years we moved again to 81 Providence Street, Providence, Rhode Island.

I remember the heavy snowfalls in Providence. In winter it was getting dark when school closed. I remember the northern lights bouncing all over the northern sky.

There were nine years of grammar school and four years of high school. Each morning we started with the pledge of allegiance and our national anthem, a prayer, a chapter of the Bible or a repeating of the twenty-third or some other Psalm, a song or two, and a lecture on etiquette. If a teacher saw you on a streetcar and you didn't give a girl or woman your seat, or if you didn't properly tip your hat or say Sir or Maam to an elder, it was just as much a punishable offense if committed off the school ground as if on the grounds. Sometime during this ritual, if your hands were dirty or your hair ruffled, you went to the rear of the room and corrected the matter. Punishment was sitting on a dunce stool, one-half hour in the cloakroom, writing on the blackboard 100 times, staying after school, or so many strokes on your open palm with a rattan rod. Maybe the long opening program had something to do with the nine years instead of eight, but it was worth it.

We had a small summer cottage in a very small community, Riverside, on Narragansett Bay. Offshore was Pomham lighthouse and next door was Pomham Club House, quite elegant with band concerts on all occasions. Every evening at 9 p.m. the *S.S. What Cheer* went south to New York. Along the way, many residents often would light colored flares or other fireworks, and the ship's whistle gave us a toot.

We had a rowboat with a keel and a sail. It was a great sport. I was out on the Bay one day when a big blow came up. Of course, I cut for home, but the waves got bigger and started coming over the stern. Sailing and baling was quite a chore, and I wasn't getting ahead. The lighthouse keeper saw me and came out in a whale boat and got me into the lighthouse until the storm was over.

We enjoyed unlimited clams, short neck as I recall. As you walked along the beach at low tide many fine fountains of water would shoot up a foot high. You dug with a fork spade and could fill a 3-gallon pail in a very short time. They were delicious. We also got lots of eels and lobsters in traps. That was before laws bothered you.

While we lived in Providence, I saw the most of my father's family. They would arrive soon after noon, put on a big pot of tea, and start telling all the old family stories. The more they were told, the funnier they seemed to get. I never heard the end of them, for they and the tea lasted far into the night.

My mother often spoke of joining the DAR—Daughters of the American Revolution—which was a very active organization in my youth. She could trace her family to the time of the landing of the Mayflower and always thought with a little more effort she would be eligible for the Daughters of the Mayflower.

Our earliest family record of my mother's family is of her great grandparents, Robert Armstrong and Mary Boyan Armstrong, to whom was born a son, James Loudon, on 5 April 1801, in Frankfort, Kentucky. James Loudon Armstrong married Elizabeth Neal on 21 July, 1825. Elizabeth was born February 17, 1807. One of their eight children was Mary Jane, born November 29, 1835.

On 20 December 1853 Mary Jane Armstrong married Benjamin Franklin Boggs (born July 2, 1832). They lived in Lawrence County in southern Ohio. The first of their eleven children, a daughter, was born 9 July 1856, named Mary Elma. Nine of the children lived to maturity and were all well known by myself. My mother was small, about 105 pounds. She enjoyed good health most of her life and was always alert. She went shopping the day before her passing on 13 February 1951 at age 94 in Los Angeles.

When the Boggs family had grown to include four children, and during the Civil War, they moved from Ohio to Champaign County in Illinois in a covered wagon.

They were to farm with relatives who had moved to Illinois four years earlier. My grandfather had accumulated land a little at a time until he had a very nice farm on the southern border of Champaign County and also in Kansas.

Our family inherited 80 acres of the farm, which we sold about 25 years ago. It had been a great aid to my mother in supplying our living, educating my sisters Ethel and Bernice, and caring for them in their retirement years. We sold it to a gas company who sent me the title search going back to 1860. This furnished a record of the times and the family fortunes. We saw how often grandfather had borrowed a few dollars to live on, buy hogs, or a few more acres of land. Sometimes it was paid back on time or ahead of time, and sometimes only after quite a struggle.

Both a church and a school were near the large two-story home of the Boggs family. I always thought of those early schools as grammar schools, But Mary Elma studied latin, algebra, geometry, and logic! She had an excellent teacher, but he got to drinking heavily and the school board let him go. They put my mother, a student, in as teacher, and she continued teaching until she was 19 when the family moved to Urbana.

They bought a block of land on Illinois Street and built a large, two-story house on one corner. Later Uncle Frank built a nice home on another corner. Their object in moving to Urbana was so the children could attend the University of Illinois. My mother went to the university for three years and then taught school until she married my father on October 18 1882, in Illinois. (All the other children were University of Illinois alumni.)

The three children of my father's first family were Carrie, Nellie Lind, and John Walter. Nellie made her penmanship a work of art. Rather late in life, about 1923, she married Arthur Lindley, an architect in Los Angeles. They had no children. Walter was a machinist in Rhode Island. He married Emma rather late in life; they had no children.

Carrie married Warren Scott in Rhode Island. Warren was a graduate of Massachusetts Institute of Technology. He was an estimator. They had six children, Walter, Dwight, Gilbert, Raymond, Allan, Louise They moved to California about 1913.

Warren worked for the largest contracting firm in southern California, taking specifications for a job, estimating every bolt, screw, window, board, hours of labor needed on the job, and its cost as the basis for the bid. As the boys grew, they thought it would be well to move to a farm in Kern County. After several years they returned to Los Angeles. Warren's old job was filled and there was not another construction firm big enough to warrant an estimater, so he induced the county of Los Angeles to hire him on the grounds that he could save them money. It is hard to realize that there was only one construction company in Los Angeles forty years ago large enough to hire an estimator. The children's marriages and their children are listed in Appendix 1.

The children of George W. Wilson and Mary Elma Boggs were Jenny Ethel, Celia Bernice, George Harold, Ralph Emmit.

Ethel graduated in Education, then went back to Columbia University in New York to get her Masters in kindergarten teaching. Ethel joined the Nazarene Church and was very dedicated. She taught for many years in the Nazarene University in Pasadena. She never married. One of her very close friends was a Nazarene missionary who went with her husband to Peru. The friend died in Peru, leaving two boys and a girl. Ethel adopted and raised the girl Esther and the younger boy. After Ethel retired, she lived for several years with Esther, who was then married and a mother. Ethel was the epitome of kindness and thoughtfulness for others. It is too bad she didn't have a family of her own.

Bernice graduated from Santa Monica High School in 1909, then went back to Urbana, Illinois, graduating in Home Economics in 1914. She went with several young men, but never married. She taught Home Economics and ran the school cafeteria in Rockford, northwest of Chicago, then signed up in the YMCA for duty in Europe during the war and was assigned to Russia. Her group got to Constantinople (Istanbul) when the Armistice was signed. They moved to Bucharest, where she was entertained several times by the famous Queen Marie of Rumania. Returning home Bernice taught school in Los Angeles until her retirement. She liked people and had many friends. She and my mother lived together until mother's death, then Bernice moved to a first-floor apartment. She was very active until she passed away during an afternoon nap.

Ralph married Rachel Kimball, a school principal in Los Angeles. They had two children, Ronald and Barbara. Ronald manufactures and sells many ornamental and useful objects made of plastic and has been very successful. Ralph had a farm machinery store in Exeter for many years. He was active in the Lions Club. He was also a councilman, city mayor, and then Exeter City Manager. Ralph's second wife was a school teacher named Corrine. They retired and moved to Pacific Grove where they have lived very comfortably for years.

George Harold married Margaret Isabelle Mack in 1921. Their children are George David, Richard Mack, Patricia Jane, Dorothy Ann.

One of those stories over the Wilson family teapot concerned my Irish cousin Nan. At that time Queen Victoria had been on the throne a long while, and Prince Edward was just waiting. He enjoyed slipping over to Ireland for its fairs and festivals. Nan was young, beautiful, lively and looking her best when Prince Edward came by. He made a pass, and Nan turned quickly and slapped him in the face. This reached the height of ambition for the Wilson family and was one of the highlights of our past. It probably still brings satisfaction and much merriment to her progeny.

††† Early Days

By 1901, my mother's parents were getting along in age. She was the oldest of the eight children. They would like her to be close and my father had lots of Midwestern demands, so we moved to Urbana, Illinois, 81 Orchard Street. Many of our Providence friends were quite concerned as to our future and our chances of being scalped by wild Indians away out on the Illinois frontier.

Urbana was the county seat. It had about 5,000 people, had two railroads, and was the site of the University of Illinois. I started school in the fourth grade. They had just added the eighth grade to grammer school; before that it was only seven followed by four of high school. The school openings were similar to Providence except there was no etiquette, and teachers felt no responsibility for your actions after you left the school grounds.

8

It was a typical Midwest town, mostly white houses, nice green lawns, principal streets all paved with brick, the others dirt but sprinkled in the summer to keep down the dust. Crystal Park had a nice lake with boats. In summer, there were band concerts in town every Saturday night, and everyone came.

Everyone in Urbana had a horse and buggy, but I had my first automobile ride here. The Olds was built something like a buggy, the driver using a steering rod. The back of the front seat was also the back of the back seat, the occupants facing backward seeing what was past. Often that was the most pleasant. Horses were scared, often running away. I also rode in a Moline, the first to come out with back-seat passengers facing forward. It had doors on each side entrance to keep out the wind and cold. No autos then had front doors; those came in about 1910.

We played baseball in season, spun tops, rode bikes, played Indians, hide and seek, charades, fished, swam, skated, whipped tops, rode our sleds, and hunted rabbits in the wintertime. We all wore long black cotton stockings, knee-length pants, and black sateen shirts to school.

We had a character who would come to school or the public square and give us a talk on Abraham Lincoln. We could well use him all over America today. He was called the immortal J. N. Free. He had been a railroad lawyer. The story about him was that he had once had an important murder case. He was convinced that his client was innocent, and he gave all he had to win the case, which he did. His client thanked him, then told that in fact he did kill the man. J. N. brooded over it and never was the same again. He was still young, vigorous and a great student of Lincoln, as were most Illinois lawyers in that day. As a railroad lawyer he had a free pass on all railroads. He traveled all over the Midwest lecturing on Lincoln. The railroad passes lasted one year, and he went to Chicago yearly to get a new one. But J. N. finally told them he couldn't spare the time to come for it each year; he wanted one to last as long as his mortal body lasted. He got his permanent pass and was known henceforth as the immortal J. N.

He didn't charge for his lectures, and he didn't pay for his hotels, his meals, or his clothes. Once he got a suit from a clothier he didn't know and started to walk out. The clothier wanted his money. J. N. was quite astonished and said he never paid for his clothes. Finally the clothier agreed to be generous and knock off one half the price. J. N. expressed appreciation of the generosity, but no one was more generous than himself, said he, so he would knock off the other half, and he walked out. His speeches on Lincoln were masterpieces. I hope they, too, are immortal.

My father bought a flat in Chicago in 1904, 6117 Drexel Blvd. I suppose today it is six apartments in a three-story brick building with a basement for furnace and storage. We were about two blocks south of the midway developed for Chicago World's Fair of 1893, two blocks from the sixty-third street elevated railroad into the city, several blocks from Washington Park, and not too far from Jackson Park on the lake front where the principal fair buildings were located. It was a pleasant residence area then. For years now it has been all black, not a slum but not good unless it has improved lately. The Chicago park system was one of the finest in the world. They were pleasant in summer with good boating and various games, in winter they provided wonderful skating and had marvelous toboggan slides. If the kids would build small levees around the empty lots, the fire department would flood them for ice rinks.

9

My father did a good deal of home repair work and had a good set of tools. We had a shop in the basement with plenty of room to work. A friend and I spent many long hours in that shop building wooden model locomotives, trains, and battleships. Our model locomotives were copies of Lake Shore and Michigan Southern. It seems impossible, but we two seventh- and eighth-grade kids had the run of that round-house. We were there at least once a week. Our mentor was Mr. Stuckey. He was in charge of being sure the locomotives were ready for the road, so he and we were crawling all over them. We would take one out for a short run to be sure everything was working all right, then spot it on the track where the crew was to pick it up for its run of 100 miles to Elkhart, Indiana. We boys could study and measure an original of the model we were working on. My friend's last name was Tate. I wish I knew what became of him, for he surely seemed set for a productive life.

The basement was the highlight of our two years in Chicago. In addition to the shop, the furnace room was large and warm. I really do not know where he came from or why, but each fall a small-time pro boxer would show up with gloves, and we would get eight or ten local kids to come in and practice under his direction. If you were a kid in Chicago at that time, you better know how to defend yourself. Some of the kids got pretty good. I am sure I learned something of the manly art of self-defense, but I never got good. Another feature of the basement was each fall we got in two wooden barrels of apples, several cases of honeycomb, and a good supply of honest pure maple syrup and maple sugar.

Each community in Chicago had its gang and each knew just about where it stood. Maybe our gang was tougher than some but the Grove Street gang was still tougher, and the top of the list was the Stock Yards gang. They were in walking distance from us.

Halloween is recognized all over the country, but in Chicago it lasts three nights. The first is Corn night, the second, I believe, Pumpkin night, and the third Halloween, all the same except in intensity. They have a delightful custom; all the kids get a long black cotton stocking, the kind we wore, and fill it with soot out of the chimney, of which we had plenty. Then they walked around after dark and wrapped it around their victim's neck with a big swing and a fast getaway! If word comes that another gang has entered your territory, you decide whether to stand and fight or retire. If word comes that the Stock Yard gang is on its way, you just seek the closest way home. It was always a wonder to me that all the kids raised in Chicago didn't turn out to be Al Capones.

I think that in the seventh and eighth grades in Chicago I had two of the best teachers I had anywhere, but morale and discipline were unbelievably bad. It was open warfare between the teachers and the principal, Mr. Van Der Water. But I did not stay long enough to be greatly affected one way or another. As usual, it was soon time for father to move on.

My father loved the evangelistic work he was in. He enjoyed the satisfaction and stimulation of knowing he had helped get thousands of people to accept Christianity as the dominant force in their lives. He kept lists of the names of the people who under his ministry professed acceptance of Christ as their savior. He knew of course that some were only emotional and short-lived, but I have met so many people who have told me how years before they had been converted under my father's ministry that I know there were thousands whose lives were really changed. This is a great tribute to any man.

The extensive travel and high tension work took its toll, and he was thinking of a smaller pastorate and slowing down a little. He went to Los Angeles for revival services, and some folks wanted him to stay. The Chaplaincy was vacant at the Soldier's Home. He could fill that position and still be active in the Los Angeles Ministerial Association. He tried it out for a few months, then came back in April, 1906, to pack up and move the family out to southern California. In addition to evangelistic work, my father had by this time written five religious books besides many magazine articles. He also read extensively. He had a very large religious library, so packing was a major operation. By May 1, we were on our way to the train for California. The newspaper boys were crying the headlines, "Los Angeles Rocking Like A Boat." I wondered why we were so anxious to get there. This was two weeks after the San Francisco holocaust.

We pulled out of the Chicago station with a solid train of eighteen Pullman sleepers. Our family was alone in our car, and, in fact were alone on the train until the next morning, when an Ohio brickmaker and contractor joined us in St. Louis, and a woman going to San Francisco to bring her mother-in-law back East. All the rest of the cars were empty, going to return refugees from San Francisco.

That evening we stopped because a freight train full of canned goods and food for San Francisco was rolling too fast and left the track on a curve, so we sat still until the wreckage was cleared next morning. The next night we slept well again, as the train didn't move. We got to Salt Lake City. The Conductor said they wouldn't leave without us, so we all went to a picture show and left the next morning. Coming across we often sat on sidings when we could get out and pick flowers or just walk out on the prairie. Several times we saw deer and antelope. We saw a few buffalo. In Salt Lake and Ogden and on West we saw six or eight camps set up by the army or Red Cross for refugees from San Francisco. We passed several trains filled with children, separated from their folks in San Francisco, going East to the camps where they could be identified and reunited with their parents or otherwise cared for.

We had a large basket of prepared food for the trip. Chickens, everything for 3 or 4 days. We had plenty of time to fill up at stops and twice our contractor friend fed us in style in the diner.

No one was allowed in San Francisco, so we went down the east side of the Bay to Palo Alto. We spent a few days at Stanford University with Aunt Florence, my mother's sister, and Uncle Oliver and their children Winifred, Florence, and Oliver. Uncle Oliver Johnston was head of the Romance language department at Stanford, and their house was on the campus. The destruction of buildings was probably worse at Stanford than in San Francisco, but without fire. The cracks in the ground were in places several feet wide and quite deep. The Johnston's wooden home was cracked, but they were living inside.

Finally we got to Los Angeles and our new home just built for us on the grounds of the Soldiers Home. Los Angeles in 1906 was a city of 100,000 people. Broadway Department Store, Third and Broadway, was the largest building, three stories high and I do not remember any higher. The Pacific Electric cars ran out to the Soldiers Home and past four miles to Santa Monica. West Lake Park was on the west boundary

11

of Los Angeles, and all the land was in grain or beans to the Soldiers Home excepting the Los Angeles Country Club on the north side of the road.

We camped in our new house for a month or more. There was not a furniture store in Los Angeles with furniture to sell. You could go in and look at a few samples of more popular tables, chairs, beds, etc., but only single samples. Then you could browse through the catalogs, pick what you wanted, and order from North Carolina or wherever it might be made and wait for it to arrive.

We had a comfortable home, big front porch, living room, parlor, dining room, large kitchen, and work porch in back. The yard was much like living in a park.

The salary here was $125. per month. We bought our horse and carriage, but the Home fed and cared for them. We bought most of our staples at the commissary at a little above wholesale.

We had to get used to the coyotes. They howled and sometimes cried like children. They sounded like they were legion, sometimes in the day but always in the evening.

At the ranch just above us in Sepulveda Canyon they caught several bobcats every year and sometimes a mountain lion in their corrals.

The exciting annual event was the Santa Monica road races. I am not sure how long it was, maybe one or two hundred miles, but the course was a sort of triangle about 12 miles around. Barney Oldfield, Teddy Tetzloff and all the old-time great drivers were in it. The most exciting turn was about a block from our house. On the turn, the mechanic got his center of gravity out just as far as possible to keep the car on four wheels, while the driver fought for all he was worth to either turn or slide the car around the turn. Those old race cars, supposed to be standard models, were surely heavy, and no hydraulics. It was a grueling race for man and car, but especially for tires. The practice runs in early morning were the best, as they didn't spare man, car, or tires. The winner of the race itself was often the fellow who stopped least often for tire changes or oil leaks.

Bernice and I went to Santa Monica High School. We usually rode the four miles on bikes. In real bad weather we put the side curtains on and went horse and buggy.

Santa Monica High School would not accept my transfer from Chicago, as I quit in April to move West, so I never did graduate from grammar school. But I could take two units grammar school work and two units of high school during my freshman year, then make up later and finish high school in 3½ years, which I did as Valedictorian. I played basketball in high school; it was a rough game then with few rules. They gave me the lead part in our senior play, ' "She Stoops to Conquer." I got through two years of Latin because my sister Bernice had been good in Latin, and the professor felt he shouldn't spoil her record by giving me a bad time, so I made it too.

My closest friend was George Paulin, who was a year behind me in high school. He lived in a very large new house in Brentwood Park. He had an older sister Ollie and an older brother Hal. Our families enjoyed many happy times together. George and I entered Berkeley together and roomed together through college.

I attended the first air meet held at Dominguez field. This was a big, open field, with pylons like power poles placed in an oval about a mile around like a horse race track. The idea was to fly the planes around this course. Few got higher than the maybe 40'-high poles, and few got all the way around even once. Some did better,

12

and a Frenchman named Paulin took most of the honors. He flew well above the poles and several times around. They were all light bi-planes.

The Brentwood area where the Paulins lived was developed by Janss Development Company. They built a few modest but good homes, and sold them. About 1912 they built a nicer home in about the center of the development, and couldn't find a buyer. After several years it was offered and given as a prize by the L.A. Examiner to the person who secured the most new subscriptions to the paper. I enter this note as a reminder that real estate prices can fall to a point where demand almost ceases to exist. Of course, most economists say we will never have another depression like the 30's, but I am not that sure of it.

Another pleasure in high school days was tennis. We had a court near our house, and all the young people played a good deal. Another was swimming in the ocean. After school the boys would go to an old vacant barn about two blocks from the ocean, climb up the ladder to the hayloft, and change clothes. Santa Monica was a great beach. It was very steep, so it was easy to run along the beach, take only a step or two in the water, and dive directly into the large breakers; immediately you were in water deep enough for good swimming. After swimming we would practice walking on the beach on our hands, handsprings front and back, flips, and all sorts of tumbling acts.

The money was a new experience to us also. Nickels, dimes, quarters, halves, and dollars, then fives, tens, and twenties in gold. There were practically no pennies and no paper money at all. Pennies existed; the street car conductor would let you ride for five pennies but throw the coppers out on the street. The bath houses and many other places would not accept them as legal tender. Sometimes the silver and gold was heavy, but it sure felt good and solid.

Santa Monica was definitely known as a small, quiet residence town with a good many Englishmen, generally called remittance men, as their families saw fit to send them remittances every month or quarter so they would stay in America and not interfere in family affairs at home. They played a good deal of tennis and had their own social life.

The big school event was the annual picnic in Topango Canyon. We rented an old Talley-Ho and four horse teams and drove up the ocean front to Topango Canyon, then up the canyon for games and campfire and fun. It was wild.

One morning three of us boys got saddle horses and went up over the hills back of Brentwood for the day. The hills were covered solid with chaparral and dense brush. Deer, coyotes, cats, and mountain lions had made a few trails, but they were not easy to follow. By afternoon, we knew where we were but couldn't find a trail back, so we decided the safest thing to do was go west to the ocean and have a road back. We could not phone our folks to tell them where we were. We traveled all night and came out at the old Japanese fishing village near Long Wharf. They were just getting up at about 3:30 a.m., so they gave us some breakfast and we set out for home. About 5:30 a.m., three miles from home, we met my father out looking for us. It seemed like a long day's trip. We never dreamed then that it would be filled with houses in our lifetimes. Today it is difficult to visualize that trip without sight of a house, a light, or a person.

By now Ethel was going to Columbia University in New York, training as a kindergarten teacher. Bernice was at the University of Illinois in Urbana, living with our grandmother and majoring in home economics. Before my graduation from high school in May 1910, my father had located a job for me in a machine shop in L.A. But I had decided long before that I wanted to be a farmer like my grandfather Boggs, and that I wanted to go to Agricultural College. I needed farm experience, but even more important I needed money. My father contacted the Methodist minister in Lompoc in Santa Barbara County. He got me a job with a Mr. Carter a few miles out of Lompoc on the Santa Ynez River. Right after graduation I bought some blankets and took the train for Lompoc. I had worked in a hardware store in Santa Monica during summer vacation and Saturdays for $1. per day, but this was my first real venture into the world.

On the farm, we got up early, went to the barn to feed and curry horses, then in for a big breakfast of hot mush, meat and potatoes, etc. We were well fortified for a day's work. Most of the plowing was with a single moldboard walking plow, though we also had a riding plow with a steel seat. The disc had a seat. We heard of harrow carts with a seat but never had one.

That winter the river got pretty high. I went out to plow the field by the river, and made my first round or two in good shape, but the next time I got to the river my last furrow was gone, caved into the river. I stayed back a little with a new furrow, but the next time around it was gone. I went to the house for further advice.

On the farm at Lompoc we raised potatoes and beans. Mr. Carter also had a farm out about 10 miles at Santa Rita where we raised mustard seed, hay, and beans. This ranch was larger and was in two pieces, in two valleys with steep winding roads between them. Here I was introduced to driving a four-horse team, sometimes with a trail wagon.

Here I also learned about rattlesnakes. I am sure that with a six or eight man crew, we would often kill 40 rattlers a day. We were close enough to the ocean to have a good deal of fog, and fortunately it was fairly cool so the snakes were pretty docile until disturbed. The hay, beans, and mustard were all shocked, then loaded on wagons to be hauled to the threshing sheets. Often as we lifted a shock, we would uncover a rattler or sometimes he rode up with the shock and then slid down the fork or landed on your shoulder. Several dogs had enlarged heads from snake bites. Mr. Carter called me down one day for using a pitchfork to kill a snake for fear I might break the pitchfork.

All the crops were spread on big canvas sheets, 30' or 40' square. The beans or mustard were spread in a circle on the sheet, then rolled by teams pulling wooden rollers until the pods opened and the seed released. The stems were beaten with forks until the seed was on the sheet, then the straw was thrown off the sheet. The seed and chaff were rolled up into a pile and put through the hand-powered fanning mill to be cleaned and sacked. The process might take several rollings, but that was it. It took lots of time and men, but we got the job done.

One of my partners there was a Mexican, a fine fellow. Many of them were called early Californians. One day we went to lunch and sat down to eat, but there were no chili peppers on the table. He asked for the peppers, but the cook was out of peppers. Pedro grabbed his hat and went down the road. I rushed out to beg him to stay. He said he could not get by one meal without peppers, and it showed the "Padron" had

14

no real respect for him or he would never run out of peppers. I finally got him back by promising the cook would go ten miles to town that afternoon to have peppers for supper.

At Santa Rita we had a typical rural church. The minister preached in Lompoc in the morning and got to Santa Rita about 2:30 p.m. for another sermon.

We finished the harvest and I went to work for Bill Cooper of the old Santa Rosa Ranch, one of the old Spanish grants. It was one of the smaller grants, 13,500 acres, but excellent land and very productive. On the dryland rolling hills we would get forty 100-lb sacks of barley per acre, and the grass was excellent.

Bill's father had driven cattle and sheep overland from Ohio, and they still had both cattle and sheep, plus hogs. The Coopers lived in a well-preserved original adobe which sat on a hill above the bunkhouse and corrals.

I remember my introduction to the Santa Rosa Ranch. All farm workers, often called bundle stiffs, had their own bedrolls. When you took to the road, your meager personal effects were rolled up in blankets and you traveled light. I walked the four miles from Carters to Coopers. It was a beautiful day, about sunset on a winding road at sheep-shearing time. I gradually picked up the bleating of the sheep and then the melodious sounds of the sheep shearers singing as they worked, the sounds getting more distinct as I walked along. The oak trees, the green grass, the melody of the sheep and the shearers, and the rays and shadows of the setting sun gave me a romantic introduction to an old Spanish grant.

I went right up to a good dinner in the low-lying adobe. The kitchen supplied the family on one side and the mess hall on the other. After dinner I was introduced to a wool sack made of cotton about 30" wide and 7' long. You could put that between you and the 1 x 12's you slept on, or you could take it to the barn and fill it with straw for a mattress to soften the plank bunk. There was a 1 x 6 on the edge of the bunk to hold you in. The room where I bunked was about 10' x 12'. As you came in the door you faced six bunks, three high against the 12' wall. To the right was the old-time mule skinner's army cot; to the left was the stove, and the 10 x 12 space was taken up. A lantern furnished the light.

Every day of the year on the ranch they killed a sheep, and every day we had mutton, except during cattle roundup twice a year they killed a steer to feed the roundup crew. I still like lamb.

Bill Cooper was a graduate of U.C. Berkeley in Chemistry. He took more interest in me because I was going to go to Cal. He encouraged me to take two years of Engineering as good education and good preparation for farming. I followed his advice.

The Coopers had a young son, "Billito" (little Bill), and a daughter. The ranch belonged to the estate. A few years later they sold part to settle the estate. Bill kept the part on the north side of the river and Billito, when he returned from U.S.C., farmed it. I was first introduced to sugar beets here. There was a field of about 15 acres which they planted to sugar beets; in the fall they would plow a few rows at a time and turn in the hogs and some cattle to feed. I had the job of thinning the beets, but about 2 p.m. each day Mrs. Cooper and the children would come by in their Chalmers Detroit car and ask me to join them to crank the car or change tires if need be. It was a welcome sight for me to see them coming down the road.

The barley on the ranch was planted in the fall. They would drive the bands of sheep over the new planting to firm the ground around the seed. It seemed a real help. They harvested it with a header consisting of the reel, sickle, draper, and elevator out in front, with four horses pulling or pushing it from the rear. Then there was a wagon header box with the side by the header about 18" high and the far side about 5' high and flaring out to hold lots of grain. A rope net was fastened on the low side and laid across the floor and up the high side of the bed. There was a header loader—that was me—with a fork to place the barley as it flowed as an almost continuous ribbon into the box, always placing it so the butts of the stalks faced out so it could be stacked higher in the bed.

In a light to normal crop, the job was easy, but in a heavy crop it was real work and took real skill. Going up the steep hillsides, we would chain the header box to the header to keep the box from tipping over. Going down, both teams would be on the run and you hoped you were still on your feet and not buried in the barley rolling out of that elevator. It was stimulating and exciting; that is why you got $2. per day for feeding header.

Header box loaded, you went to a level stack area. A team of horses on a rope was hooked into a ring on the net in the bed, a 4 x 4 was placed vertically under each corner of the low side of the bed to take the weight of the load and prevent the wagon tipping over. The team then rolled the load out of the bed on the ground, you returned your net, and went for another load.

Next, a stationary harvester came, the barley was fed into the harvester with a jackson fork, and the barley was returned to you all sacked up. When delivery time came, two grain wagons would be loaded up with sacked grain to drive the 14 miles to Lompoc. Six or eight horses with a jerk-line skinner would set out at about 4 a.m., get to the warehouse about 8:20, hope to be unloaded by noon and get back to load up by 4 or 4:30 p.m. ready for the next morning.

A good deal of the conversation on the ranch was about hunting wild boars, and there were a good many of them. The cowboys would go every so often. The object was to rope the boars, but that was difficult. However, they would take strong wooden cages to hold any they got. Occasionally they would get home with two or three and turn them loose in the corrals with plenty of water and feed, but always they were dead by morning from running all night.

I learned a little about sheep. One time the herder was taking a band across the river when the water was a little high. He used the dogs; he tried to lead the sheep across; he did all he could think of, but no luck. Several of us were sent out to help. We worked, but to no avail. The next day we set out early to try again. Ten to twenty were drowned in the river, but no sheep went across. The next morning we went out again, and they all jumped in like they loved it and went across without wear or tear or excitement. It just depends.

The foreman was a Mexican, probably third-generation Californian. He couldn't understand me because I read and wrote letters and didn't drink or smoke.

One day Bill Cooper was on his horse bringing in some sows from a field of high grass. He went after a sow he was following when his horse stumbled over another sow laying low in the grass and Bill went over the horse's head and broke his collarbone. He decided to take the evening train to San Francisco to see his doctor, and his wife would go along. As the nights were cold, and the car quite open, his wife took a heavy, full-length fur coat to wear into Lompoc. I was to go with them, drive the car to a garage in Lompoc, and the next morning the foreman would come in with the team of snappy mules and the buggy to take me and the fur coat back to the ranch. He came into town about 10 a.m., but said he would not be going out until 2 p.m. If I came back at 2:00, that would be fine. I got back about 1:30, and the stable man said he left at 1:15. I asked around, and he had been seen going out the road toward the ranch. I bundled up the fur coat as best I could and set out on foot; the weather and the coat were both hot. Probably two miles out a friend from Santa Rita over-took me and gave me a buggy ride to Santa Rita, four miles from the ranch, still hot and getting late for supper. I borrowed a bicycle and pumped as hard as I could the four miles and delivered the fur coat. My Mexican friend had gotten there well ahead of me and told all the others how he had left me, and I wouldn't be in that night but would have my tail between my legs when I did come. I stayed near the adobe, and when the supper bell rang I was at the top of the hill waiting for the rest. After that we were good friends and no pressure.

The University of California opened in early August those years. About mid-July, my mother and father drove up in a new Saxon to take me home. The Saxon was six cylinders and had front doors as well as back; it seemed pretty snappy. In 14 months I had saved $440., that being $1. per day regular and $2. per day for harvest work. Lompoc prospered little by what I spent there—one haircut and 10¢ worth of candy per month. My father helped me some also, and I worked the next summer on the Santa Rosa ranch again. Those earnings carried me almost through the sophomore year. The next summer, 1913, I worked on a hay press for Mr. Cotton out of Davis. It was an old Junior Monarch 5-wire press, and I made an unbelievable $4. per day. The junior and senior years I got some scholarship assistance, was fraternity house manager for which I received free meals, and I worked at campus jobs to get through.

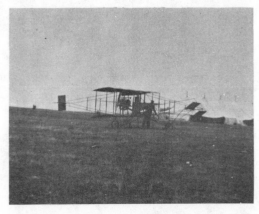

At left, Ralph and I, Providence, Rhode Island, about 1897.

Below: First International Air Meeting, Dominguez Field near Los Angeles

Above, Professor True
At right, President Taft
Below, Rowing crew and
the Greek Theatre

2
A YOUNG MAN MAKES HIS WAY, 1912-1917

College Days

The first two years at Berkeley, George Paulin and I roomed together in the Berkeley YMCA. Other special friendships were developed there with Dutch Hartranft, Reuben Hallner, and George Cable. Cable was in engineering, the other four in agriculture. Reuben and I went out for freshman crew. Reuben was tops, I just squeezed in. The next year Rube was securely in the Varsity, I rowed Sophomore. That meant a street-car ride to Oakland, another car to the Estuary boathouse, and repeat that to get home. We were late for supper, but it was great training. Our other principal activity was the Agriculture Club.

Our junior year we joined the Hilgard Club, a house club of all students in the College of Agriculture. In the fall of 1913 we went down to the Berkeley S.P. station to greet Professor B. H. Crocheron, the new director of the agricultural extension service of U.C.

From then on Paul Dougherty, Roy Hagen Carl Williams, and I worked after-noons and evenings in a basement office of the Ag building doing anything we could to help establish Ag Extension. One of the first decisions by B. H. Crocheron was that before a farm advisor entered a county, there must first be a County Farm Bureau made up of, I believe, 10 percent of the farmers of the county, with a minimum in any case of 50. The counties were then divided into centers, usually eight to sixteen centers per county, often similar to school districts, and meetings were held in the schools, or sometimes a store or church. It was felt the farm advisor must have a group to work with. The Grange was considered as such a group, but was rejected as its meetings were open to grangers only.

Youth groups were set up almost as soon as a county was organized. There were Boys Agricultural Clubs or Pig Clubs or Calf Clubs before 4H Clubs. They were origi-nally set up because it was believed the easiest way to teach a parent was to demon-strate through the children. It has worked in a big way for children, parents, and leaders

The big prize of club work was a train trip East for winners, under the leadership of B. H. Crocheron, winding up in Washington D.C. About thirty boys were selected to go.

The Agriculture Club at Berkeley decided to help finance the trip, so we planned a Flower and Fruit Mart to be held for two or three days in the Greek Theatre on the campus. I was selected as chairman of the event in the fall of 1914. We got authorization to hold the event in the Greek Theatre with dates approved, and set in to plan it in a big way.

We got farmers and shippers to send in boxes of fruit from all over the state. We arranged with a cold storage company in Oakland to hold them for us. The club kids around Santa Cruz cut three freight-car loads of redwoods, some 10 to 20 foot trees, and lots of smaller branches. The railroad contributed the hauling cost. The trees were used to decorate around the stage. The branches were tied to wires running from the walls behind the stage to the rear of the theatre. The wall at the rear of the stage was divided into ten large panels from top to floor. We used chicken wire to support a solid background of red geraniums in each panel, with a big letter in white geraniums to spell out CALIFORNIA. We constructed a waterfall and stream on the stage, and had a beautiful display of gladiolas, chrysanthemums, and other flowers.

We had posters and publicity all around the Bay Area, and big banners advertising the Flower and Fruit Mart, its time and place, on the ferry boats and in the ferry building in San Francisco. We spent quite a little money and an awful lot of time. We were to sell the fruit and flowers, and the big money was to be a nickle dance, 5¢ each dance.

All was ready, and the day before the opening two of us went up to officially invite President Benjamin Ide Wheeler of the University to head the official parade we were having from California Hall to the Greek Theatre. He apparently was just waiting for us, and he tore us to pieces. He was exceeding proud of the Greek Theatre, and to think of desecrating the theatre with a 5¢ dance was more than he could stand. Under no circumstances could we have a dance in there, and if we questioned it at all, he would call the whole thing off. As we left, his secretary said if we would keep a taxi in front of Cal Hall, he would try to get the President to find time to go up and see our show.

Showers were forecast, and no dance. We surely had no money for a taxi. We got the fruit all delivered and made nests of straw on the rows of seats, filling each nest with a neat display of fruit. The day had arrived. We had the opening parade. The place was fantastic. Prof. Crocheron went down to Cal Hall, invited the President, and they walked back up to the Greek Theatre at 10:30 a.m. Pres. Wheeler didn't leave for lunch; he stayed just looking around until 2:30. He was amazed at the size and grandeur of the Greek Theatre. It was too late for the dance. We paid all our bills and had a very few dollars left to buy buttons badges, and a few things for the trip. But from then on, any time the College of Agriculture had a workday or any other event, Pres. Wheeler was always there and became a great friend of agriculture.

I have sat in the Greek Theatre several times since and visualized the solid wall of geraniums, the canopy overhead of redwood branches, the flowers and redwoods on the stage, and wondered how we did it.

The College of Agriculture was then the largest college in the University. Each spring semester about ninety juniors and seniors in animal husbandry, soils, irrigation, and other majors went up to the university farm at Davis. At that time the campus at

Davis had a two-year, year-around program for nondegree students; there were about 400-500 of them.

It was one big family at Davis, very informal in dress and we knew the faculty well. There were very few distractions, everybody studied. The UC Varsity football team, or rugby as it was then, were mostly registered in agriculture. Some were better players than students in the fall semester, so most of them went to Davis in the spring and studied to become eligible to play rugby again in the fall semester. The entire campus was much smaller then. The buildings, all of wood construction, were mostly located around the present quadrangle, which was planted in barley.

The town of Davis, or Davisville as it was often called, was a long block running north and south. It had rather wide wooden sidewalks on the west side of the street, and a short block of narrower wooden sidewalk running west. A block or so to the west, the Lillard dairy barn provided a central feature of the town.

The summer of 1914, my sister Bernice was to graduate from the University of Illinois at Urbana, and I was elected to represent Cal at the Alpha Zeta conclave at the University of Missouri in Columbia, so my mother and I went East together for the summer. We stopped at Phoenix, Arizona, still a cow town. There were some nice homes, but the town was small with mostly dirt streets.

We arrived in New Orleans Saturday evening and went to the Methodist Church Sunday morning. My mother said she had heard a great deal about the singing of anthems in colored churches, so as we left the morning service she asked the minister where we might go that evening to hear some good colored singing. He apparently had never heard that question before, but he finally said there was a colored Baptist group meeting in a large formerly white church building. We might not be welcome, but we could try.

We did. He thought they met at 8 p.m. We got there about 8:00 and stood in the door. There were several groups in for earlier meetings. The preacher was with a Christian Endeavor group in front, as busy as they could be. He looked up and saw us, settled all the young folks down, came back to greet us, and was happy to be so honored. He showed us to a seat, then announced it was time for church to start. They all got their seats. The young good-looking ones mostly sang in the choir, and the service started quite apparently earlier than usual, as most of the congregation came in late, taking time to speak to friends along the way as they found their seats. Choir members drifted in, too, and leisurely made their way to the choir.

The minister preached his best sermon and closed the regular service, then intro-duced Mr. and Mrs. Wilson from California with quite a welcome, then asked us to say a few words. My mother told how she had always wanted to hear some good Southern colored singing and she had been gratified by what she had heard. That was it. The minister wrung his hands and told how happy he was to be thus honored, and how he loved to receive the flowers while he was still here to enjoy them, then he preached another whole sermon just for our benefit. He then turned to the choir and asked them to sing a few songs in our honor. They sang a hymn or two, then really cut loose on their real Negro melodies. That was really something, just what we had wanted to hear. During the regular service there were no books. They lined the songs. The preacher would read a line, and they would sing it; he read the next line, and they sang it with full voice. It was a great evening.

In Urbana I went with my mother to her thirty-fifth class reunion (class of

1879). There were many well-known people there, but my impression was, "What a gang of old cripples." My sixtieth was two years ago. It all depends on where one sits.

The conclave in Missouri was quite an experience for me, meeting with the delegates from all over the U.S. and discussing all the problems. Alpha Zeta is a national honorary fraternity for students in agriculture. The appropriate summer dress then was white shirt and white woolen slacks, so I wore them, but in the heat and humidity of Columbus, Missouri, they were not appropriate; if you sat awhile in a solid-seat chair, a pool of perspiration spoiled the look of the slacks.

Several days were spent campaigning with Uncle Frank for Judge. It was my first experience in practical politics.

Several relatives in Urbana had bought some land in a new reclamation project in Idaho. They gave me a cashier's check and asked me to stop off on the way home and look at it for them. I got into Ogden, Utah to transfer to Pocatello, and there transfer to Burley to look up the property. I thought a cashier's check solved all problems, so I went into a bank in Ogden to get it cashed. The check was good, but they didn't know I was G. H. Wilson. I had enough to get to Pocatello, and I thought it would be easier in a small town like Pocatello, but they didn't know me either. I wasn't quite so cocksure that I could get the money now, and I was about broke, so I bought a ticket to the first station out of Pocatello. When I got that far, I spent my time in the men's room, or with my head out the window, or asleep, and rode on through to Twin Falls. Here I surely looked innocent, handed the check to the cashier, and got the money without a word. Then I got a train back to Burley, went to the stables, and got a two-horse team and buggy to see the property, probably ten miles south.

Several miles out, off to the west was a rolling black cloud right on the ground. It was black! I decided it must be fire on that sagebrush desert. We made good time for awhile, until it got close enough for me to recognize my first black dust storm. At the project headquarters, I got the flow sheets on the stream supplying the project reservoir. With great confidence, I announced that they didn't have water enough to supply the whole project. I was then less-than-enthusiastically received. They said I was wrong. I expect Uncle Frank felt the same when I told him. Several years later the Reclamation Service announced they were reducing the size of the project for lack of water.

The following day, on the train going home, I heard that war was being declared in Europe. It was of passing interest; it seemed of little concern to me. That fall I was house manager for the Hilgard Club at UC in Berkeley. That of course meant being responsible for the cook and the meals. We ate an awful lot of beef heart and tongue. They were cheap, all meat, easily cut, good flavor if properly done. You learn to take all the gripes and get your meals free. I recommend it as a part of any education.

One of my professors was Dr. John Gilmore, an agronomist. He had traveled and worked in many countries of the world. His courses were quite elementary, but he was a great fellow. I dropped into his office one day to ask a question. He slowly turned to his card file, picked out the right one, and looked up the answer. I commented on his filing system. He said "Well, I find in life that if I keep room in my head for good thoughts, I don't have much room left for all these details I can care for in the file." I am not sure his agronomy altered production much, but he was a great counselor and an inspiration to lots of young folks.

The Picnic Days at Davis in April were great days in 1914-15, as they are now. The two-year students had dances and other social events, but the degree students had little social activity in Davis. However, some of the principal social events in Berkeley were geared to the dates the Aggies came down from Davis. Two or three times a semester we would get half-fare rates on the railroad and all go down for a weekend. The big dances in Berkeley were set for those dates and also the fraternity and sorority parties.

Professor and Mrs. Gordon H. True at Davis were great folks; they said we should have a dance at Davis for the degree fellows, including Babe Salter's sister who was there. We set the date and made all the arrangements for the dance in the dining hall. Girls around Davis were at a premium, but most of our fellows got dates all lined up. Bob Yelland was to take Myrtle Rowe, and I asked Ruth Lillard. But a week or ten days before the big event, word went out from the two-year fellows, "Who are you going to dance with in the fall when the university fellows aren't there?" Word went out to the mothers that the Berkeley boys were city slickers and really not nice boys, so overnight Bob and I were about the only ones who still had a date. We had to line up the two cars available and get a driver and chaperone for each car; then we lined up a group of girls in Woodland and in Sacramento and made two trips each way to get the girls back and forth.

We got good live music. We decorated the place in style. We even got a couple of pounds of good chocolates put in the girls dressing room, and punch and cookies—the works.

About 10 p.m., the lights went out, the switches pulled by the two-year fellows. We got them going again, but out they went an hour later. This time the wires were cut outside the building, and weren't easy to fix. We had candles enough by now, so it just added zest to the dance from then on. There were no casualties on the campus, but the next Woodland Democrat had headlines: "Woodland Society Cut Assunder." The division was between the girls who came to the Davis dance and those who didn't.

One Sunday Bob Yelland and I rented a surrey and team. We picked up Myrtle Rowe and Ruth Lillard and drove over to Myrtle's sister's house on the campus. John Rodgers was farm manager, handling all the farming on the campus. They were not home, so we sat down on the lawn and talked. A hen went running across the lawn, and Bob said we ought to catch that chicken for supper. The girls dared us to do it. We thought they wouldn't cook it even if we caught it. They said they sure would, so what could two poor innocent fellows do? We caught it and put it under a crate and went back to the conversation.

About 4 p.m., the girls said, "Well, if we are to have chicken you have to wring its neck." Again, we thought they wouldn't cook it, but they assured us they would, so its neck was wrung, its feathers picked, and in the oven it went. We were not sure whether it would all seem funny to Punk Rodgers and his wife or not, so we got a good meal for six hoping that would help a little. We had a real banquet prepared when they came in. We weren't congratulated at all, but we enjoyed a pleasant evening.

While we were busy in the house, our college friends were busy outside. When we went out, we found the surrey with the front wheels in back and the back in front. Then we had to search for the reins. The ride home was another new experience. Try it sometime.

Bob and I thought we had had quite an afternoon and evening, but it wasn't quite over. Early the next morning, one of our fellow Alpha Zeta friends came bursting into my room, all excitement. What was Alpha Zeta going to do about one of our members being involved in chicken stealing? It was a disgrace to Alpha Zeta and he might be expelled.

Of course I, still in bed, asked what he proposed we do about it. He didn't know. That was why he came to see me. After considerable stalling, I asked what he knew about the case. It seems two of the Davis town boys had a buggy and decided it would be fun to go out to the Farm, as the campus was called then, and swipe a couple of chickens to have a feed. They figured it would take two to get the chickens, as they needed someone to look out and hold the horse while the other did the dirty work. Our Alpha Zeta brother was picked up to hold the horse, so he was involved.

There were several meetings, but I never could be quite sure that I should get involved, so I didn't. Of course these chickens were very special, part of a very import- ant research project and now that was all spoiled. It became quite a test case. It was near the end of the semester. I didn't know the Alpha Zeta member very well. He was sent home to San Diego. What credit he got for the semester I do not know.

My trips back and forth between Los Angeles to Berkeley were about divided between the railroad and the *S.S. Harvard* or *Yale*. As I remember, the ships left Los Angeles harbor about 4 p.m. and arrived San Francisco about 10 a.m. They were fast ships for their day, and on account of their speed, were used for troops crossing the English Channel, hoping the speed would save them, and it did. They later wore chevrons on their funnels for each six months of war service. They were modern ships and made the trip quite pleasant. There would usually be a good many students aboard. The first year George Paulin came up by car with his parents. It was a full four-day trip from Los Angeles, and they came in with blown-out tires all over the inside and outside of the car.

While we roomed at the YMCA, we were bid into the Delta Upsilon fraternity. It was the one we liked best, but we decided not to join any at that time. The Delta Upsilons are one of the best nationally. We attended church at the Methodist Church near the campus. We went to some university YMCA meetings and taught classes in English to foreigners in YMCA classes. We attended sorority teas on Sunday evenings occasionally. Crew took a lot of time the first two years. It is a spring sport, but we worked at it all year long. We went to musical programs occasionally, and to the Orpheum for musical comedies such as "Abie's Irish Rose," but these evenings out were rather rare. I do not believe I went to any dance until my junior year.

Occasionally I would take a girl home from the library. The rule then was that no fellow and girl ever walked together on the campus in daytime. During our junior year, George Paulin was going some with Virginia Ballaseyus, and she had a sister, Hedwig, who was quite musical and wrote the music for the Junior Prom. The com- poser and escort always lead the Grand March at the Prom. Two weeks before the Prom, Hedwig had not yet been invited. Knowing my poor dancing, and knowing the girl very little, I still invited her. She accepted, and we led the Prom.

During the senior year I was asked on several occasions to help in the office of Dean Thomas Forsyth Hunt of the College of Agriculture. I enjoyed several dinners

24

and very pleasant evenings at the Dean's home. In college his wife had been a room-mate of my mother's sister, which seemed to create a common bond. But all seniors, in groups of about six, were invited to the Dean's home for dinner and an evening, a memorable occasion for them. Along with all other male students, I took cadet military training the first two years. I seriously felt that was a part of my contract with the government. They would give me an education, which I considered a very valuable gift, and I would prepare to return military service if called upon. I think that is the way it still should be. An education at the expense of the State is a gift, not a right.

Another extracurricular activity was going up to Gridley and several other high schools, where they called the boys to a special assembly to hear about setting up a Boy's Agricultural Club. I spoke to the boys, but I saw all the girls, as every last one showed up to see what was going on for boys only. The clubs were organized. It was interesting for me. Lots of land in the Gridley and Biggs area could have been bought for $5. per acre at that time. It was later very valuable rice land.

In early May, 1915, graduation was over. I had my sheepskin. I needed a job and money, so I started right in feeding the Carnation Dairy herd of Holstein cows at the 1915 San Francisco World's Fair. I fed the cows and kept the place neat. It was May, but damp and cold. Early Monday morning I went to a Jewish merchant in the second-hand district. I bought a beautiful full-length, double-fold, woolen Army overcoat for $3. It was my best friend until Uncle Sam gave me a poor imitation two years later. The best thing about the job was the laughs we got from the silly questions and comments we got from the city folks about the animals.

In a corral near us were a half-dozen Texas longhorn steers; real, live, and original. They got loose several times, and then the chase was on.

On July 1, 1915, Paul Dougherty, Carl Williams, and I became Assistant Farm Advisors at $83.33 per month and the promise of a motorcycle to get around on. I was soon sent to San Diego County to help organize a Winter Vegetable Union to sell winter vegetables for the members.

††† Farm Advisor in a Flivver

Seeing the San Diego area today, it is very difficult to visualize the San Diego of 1915. The Farm Advisor, H. A Weinland, had planned the Coop effort, and I was to help sign up members.

The farmers were certainly in need of help. Many did not wear shoes on their plots of several acres, not because they were Hippies or just liked it that way. They had shoes only for very cold weather or for wearing in town.

Much of the irrigation was done with garden hoses. On an early trip to a farm where the water was coming rather leisurely from a garden hose, I commented that he didn't have much water. I got right back, "What do you mean? I have a wonderful water supply." That issue was never again raised. The husband and wife usually worked together on ground preparation, seeding, weeding, etc. During harvest time it would be necessary to be up at 4 a.m. or so, feed and harness the horse, get breakfast, and usually the husband would drive to San Diego to be there at 5 or 5:30 a.m. for the day's sales. They sold what they could from the wagon at retail or to smaller buyers. By noon or so, they would sell any remainder wholesale or at the best price they could get, usually quite low, then drive home, prepare the next day's sales, and have the wagon loaded up by the cool of the evening ready to take off in the cool of early morning. In the meantime, the wife was doing all necessary to keep the operation going at home, with the help or hindrance of the children.

It cost $5. to join the Association. No one parted with it readily, a few wanted desperately to join but wanted to pay $1. down and $1. per month. Several times I would have liked to put up the $5. myself out of my $83.33 per month, but I had been told I must not do that. They were set up in business and doing fairly well when, several years later, a big flood came down through the principal area and washed them out, both the land and the Association.

The first week or so I was tied to work in the office or going out with Henry Weinland in his car for day visits and night meetings. I was sure champing at the bit to be out on my own on my new motorcycle. I finally sat down and wrote B. H. Crocheron a letter telling him that if the motorcycle wasn't available the next morning, I would go rent one and bill his office. It didn't arrive, so I rented the motorcycle. I had used George Paulin's a good deal in high school and thought I was on good terms with them. I got several miles out and a push rod fell out of this 2-cylinder bike. It fell out again a little later but, by pushing it up hills, sometimes I did O.K. on one cylinder.

Next the tire went flat. By filling the tire with weeds and refilling it a time or two, I did fairly well. Then, going down a hill in late afternoon, a push rod dropped out again, but just ahead of me was an interurban track and a garage just across the track. I pushed the bike over to the garage and told them the shop from which I rented it would pick it up next day. I rode the interurban into town.

Next morning I told the shop where the cycle was. They weren't the least bit interested. I then went straight to the office, telling B.H. "no motorcycle for me." It had to be a Model T. I expect he was just waiting for that letter before he ordered a motorcycle. In two or three days a letter came telling me to go to the Ford Agency and pick up the Model T. I did, and set right out on farm calls. I pulled into a barnyard and talked to the owner a while. He said "just back around and go out the way you came in." I tried first one of the three pedals and then the other, but none seemed to back up. Then one started the car ahead. I went with it around back of the barn. The barn doors were open on both ends so I went right through the barn and out the gate. As I passed him, I heard him say, "I thought I told you to back out," but I was on the road by then and kept going until out of sight. Then I stopped and found out for sure what those three pedals were and how to use them.

The Association formed, I went to Humboldt County to help Andy Christenson introduce alfalfa growing to the cattlemen and dairies in the Humboldt hills. As rainfall was over 100 inches a year there, water was not a limiting problem. Humboldt was the first California county to have Farm Bureau and Extension. Andy Christenson had been there two years. It seemed a long time then. He had introduced burning lime and applying it to their acid soil and so had developed quite a reputation.

I didn't get a room there until shortly before I left. I had a cot in the back of the Farm Advisor's office in Eureka, but most of the time I was on the road in the hills with my bedroll in the back seat of the Model T. But even that was often not used as, if you arrived at a ranch after 2:30 p.m., they would do all possible to see that you stayed all night, and they were very pleasant occasions. Any traveler was the bearer of news, and they lived on the news of the world and their neighbors.

World War I was in progress. The "intelligentsia" of Berkeley knew a war had started in the Balkans, but in the hills of Humboldt County the folks voraciously read the "Review of Reviews," a sort of U.S. News and Reader's Digest all in one. They knew where the Balkans were, which countries were included, and just how the battles were going, and they wanted to know more.

I did have one problem. I followed Marcus A. W. Lee on the job up there. He was a year ahead of me at Cal. He was the tennis champ on campus, the swimming champ, the Adonis, the socially sought after. I do not know how much he resisted the charms of the coeds, but he hadn't succumbed.

The Humboldt County Farm Bureau had a picnic planned for Ferndale, and Marcus planned to drive to the picnic, then on down to Berkeley. They had a soloist lined up, but the singer needed an accompanist who couldn't leave Eureka until about noon. They asked Mark to bring her down to Ferndale with him.

That afternoon Mark decided to go to Berkeley by the boat from Eureka, so the young lady might as well ride back to Eureka with him. He saw her again at breakfast, then he sailed off on the ship to San Francisco.

About ten days later, on Tuesday, he drove into Eureka. Wednesday he had dinner with several of his male friends and announced that he was thinking of matrimony, so his friends took over. The girl agreed, didn't she? Yes. He loved her, didn't he? Sure. Then why not get married tonight? He called her. O.K , but she was pianist at the church this night for prayer meeting—just right, the preacher and lots of witnesses would be there at 9 p.m. So Mark's friends rousted out the county clerk and got him to the office to issue a marriage license. By 9:30 p.m., Humboldt County had lost one of its well-known daughters. Understandably, after this incident, my reception was often, "Ha, is this another Marcus Lee? I do not know whether I should let you into my house or not."

Many people in the hills did not have a car, so their needs were often filled by itinerant salesmen in cars or small trucks. I pulled into a ranch one afternoon, and here was a salesman with all his wares spread out to be seen and fully appreciated. A lady visitor was there whom I hadn't met. She just couldn't wait to buy, but she was on horseback and couldn't carry much. Finally she asked me if I would drop her purchases off at her house. My job was to be helpful, so I said "Sure." But she didn't want just a few items of food, cosmetics, medicine, trinkets, or kitchen ware. She put on about all the Model T would hold. She said she would cut across the canyon on her horse and get to her house before I did. I thought it quite interesting and amusing, but as I hit the road, I wondered what her husband might think, so I gave her plenty of time to arrive first. I drove in cautiously, with some concern. When he came out and saw it, I thought he would never quit laughing. He thought it was about the funniest thing he had ever seen. This made for a very pleasant night under that roof.

One of my jobs was to help gather some money for the Boy's Clubs, both potato and calf clubs, and to see that the two boys from our county got on the train for the trip to Washington D.C. This was the same trip we had the Flower and Fruit Mart for. One boy had raised potatoes. He was no problem. Neither was the small Italian boy who had raised a dairy heifer. Both he and his parents thought the trip was wonderful, but could see many hazards in the young boy being so far from home. He was a great boy. I was in Ferndale the morning the train pulled out, and it did seem like it was swallowing up a very small boy, with all his needs for the trip folded up in a big bandana handkerchief. B. H. Crocheron told me after their return that he had sat with the boy on the trip home and asked him what he thought of the trip. He said when he got to San Francisco and saw those streetcars and high buildings, he was about scared to death, but when he got to New York he just stood and looked up at those high buildings and said to himself, "You can build them as big as you want to, you can't scare me." I would like to meet him someday. I am sure he has made a success of life.

The railroad from San Francisco to Eureka had just been completed and put in service. Before, the only transportation was by boat. Travel was quite an experience for everyone. I have rarely ever enjoyed myself more than when spending an evening at a home or a Farm Bureau meeting and the men got to telling the stories and thrills of their trip on the new railroad to see the 1915 World Fair in San Francisco. That was humor at its best.

The dances should not be forgotten. I have been on my rounds at ten in the morning and met girls on horseback on the way to the dance. If they got there by noon, they would fix lunch, then start cleaning up and maybe decorating the hall. Next was supper and preparing the dinner to be eaten at midnight. People dropped in on horseback or buggies all afternoon and evening. Sometimes there was a little meeting, then the live orchestra struck up for the square dance, the waltz, the schottische, or two-step. Young and old filled the benches around the sides of the hall, with babies under the benches or wherever convenient. At midnight or a little after, tables were set for a real dinner made of every woman's best, and plenty of it. Then the dance proceeded. About 2 a.m. I would sneak out for an hour or two of shut-eye in the back seat of the Model T, for I knew I had to be on the job that day.

About a half-hour before sunup, things broke up a little and the fellows went out to saddle up or harness the horses. I especially remember one such dance. The music had stopped. I had danced with all the girls there but one I had never met. I asked her where she lived. She said "Over on Bear Creek. We'll stop at Uncle Ben's tonight and go on home by noon tomorrow." It looked to me like it would not take a young couple many dances like that to get acquainted.

It seemed to me then that the older women were spryer, danced better, and lasted longer than the young ones, but when I was only 23 I am not sure just how old a woman had to be to be "older."

There were lots of hills. One day I came up over one in the Ford into a farmyard. The farmer came out and said he had seen several autos go down that hill, but it was the first time he had seen one come up it. By now I knew just what it took to do it besides luck. You see the hill, and you know the gas will not flow into the carburator at that angle, so you remove the seat cushion, break the head off a match, get down on your knee, and blow as hard as you can into the little hole in the gas tank top. While you have the pressure on the tank, you shove the wooden match into the hole in the top, and replace the seat cushion. Then you back up if need be to be sure you have room to get all the speed you dare before hitting the hill. If you come fairly close, take out all your baggage, the seats, the jack, and everything else. Put them on the ground and try it again. If in luck, you make it, then go back and get all your baggage, carry them to the top, load up, and you are on your way. When you've gone a few miles, happy to be there, and your motor sputters, remove the seat cushion again, pull out the match to let air into the tank, and you are on your way again.

In 1915 few of the redwoods had been cut. The dirt roads were narrow, so one had the feeling of actually being in the forest. The fern breaks and rhododendrons were beautiful, especially as the shafts of sunlight came through the trees. I still enjoy some of those fantastic views which got to be commonplace.

Dairies seemed to be at their best in Humboldt County, and many advances in production and manufacturing, as well as leaders in those fields, came from Humboldt County. We got a number of improved pasture demonstrations going in the county and came back to the Berkeley office of BHC to help compile county reports, work on new bulletins, etc.

Maybe this is the time to tell a little about B. H. Crocheron, or B.H. as he was known. He was born in New Jersey in 1882, ten years ahead of me. He spent part of his youth on a New York farm. From 1900 to 1904 he managed a large orchard in Maryland, then went to Cornell University for his BS and MS in agriculture.

He was thoroughly dedicated to the improvement of rural life. Following Cornell he organized, built, and directed an agricultural high school in Maryland open country as a new experiment in rural education to serve students, farm homes, the whole community, hoping to instill in its students a love of rural life and a dedication to its welfare. B.H. had a young lady friend to whom he was quite devoted, but he moved into the Adirondack Mountains to study the rural mountain people and see if he could suggest a plan for their benefit. He wrote often, and sent flowers to his lady friend every Saturday, but she felt if he really loved her he would return in person each weekend, so the relation cooled. He was asked by Dean Hunt to come to the University of California to organize and head the Agriculture Extension Service. He and his girl friend had often discussed a honeymoon at Lake Louise in Canada, so he decided he should see it alone on his way to California. When he arrived at the hotel, there on the broad steps was his potential fiancée. They rented a rowboat, spent most of the night on the lake, maybe seeing if the romance of the lake would be effective, but he came to Berkeley and she went her way, and I never heard of his having any further love except his work.

He was a new figure and a new type on the Berkeley campus: tall, slender, attractive, with what I believe was called an eyelash mustache. His clothes appeared to have been pressed daily, he was a perfectionist in every detail. At least weekly he had his barber come to his home for a haircut, shave, shampoo, massage, the works. This was all very strange, both to his fellow faculty and the students. His dedication, however, was not to himself but to his work. He thought his plans through in every detail and insisted that every plan must specify by whom, what, when, and where the work was to be done, and all projects must be planned locally in the state, county, community, or farm on which they were to be carried out. He was adamant that the purpose of extension was education, and it must never be involved with the police powers of government. He called his county men Farm Advisors to be sure they gave only advice, not direction.

In January, 1939, B.H. reviewed twenty-five years of work to his annual Extension Conference. I will include some excerpts and comments. He pointed out there were many extension services in the world, but, although they were directed by departments of agriculture and did educational work, they also enforced laws and represented the "voice of authority." The American system was the extension of education, the teacher in the countryside to disseminate the research from colleges and accumulated experience of other farmers. The federal extension act required no cooperation with the federal department other than "mutual agreement" by the Secretary of plans and projects developed in the state. Congress appropriated funds to the colleges, not to the U.S. Department of Agriculture. The need for a local county group for the Extension agent to work with and through was early recognized, so the nationwide Sears, Roebuck Foundation put up one million dollars, one thousand dollars to any county that would form a Farm Bureau and provide an agent.

"Despite all its shortcomings, the Extension work in agriculture and home economics in America is the greatest single adult educational effort in the world. To all those who engage in educational work, the development of the individual is of the utmost importance. The people trained by Extension to see a larger vision are its real glory."

"If country people have the ability to sift the plans and proposals which come before them, it is in part because of the natural sense of values that comes from life out of doors. But in part, also, it is because of the teaching done by Extension agents during the past generation. . . . Whatever may be held in the hand of the future, this we see clearly: The Extension Services of America were established as educational agencies, and as a part of the state colleges. Their real contribution during the last quarter-century has been to enrich the lives of millions by developing the knowledge and the thinking of the men, women, and children who live on the land."

Two years later, in January 1941, B.H. spoke to the Extension Conference on "What of the Future." I find much in this talk which expresses my thinking as follows:

"Perhaps the most disconcerting element in the present situation is the apparent spread of belief in the power of machines over men. By this we do not mean in particular the power of destructive machines, but rather the increasing belief that the peoples of the world move ahead by power not of themselves, but of the mechanistic processes that serve them. Such belief presupposes that the importance of man as an individual, or of a people as a whole, is not so much vested in their ability, their integrity, their will to work, or their cooperative spirit, as in their possession of material resources. It leads to the assumption that peoples, nations and individuals, are successful in proportion to the materials they command. It is a belief in the power of things as the deciding force on the earth rather than the power of men over things. Such a belief or emphasis reaches the inevitable conclusion that the most important problem of the world is the equitable distribution of materials, goods, and machines, and that all else must and therefore shall be subservient to the division of these overpowering, god-like resources. Ultimately—in this philosophy—the final welfare of individuals is determined by what they possess. This philosophy is the doctrine of

30

materialism. It finds its expression in socialism and in its logical conclusion, communism. If the possession of goods is the most important thing in life, and if it is these possessions or the lack of them that determine human welfare and happiness, then, in these philosophies, their possession becomes of supreme importance. Believers in these doctrines declare that material possessions are the things for which all men strive and toward which all actions of the human race are consciously or unconsciously directed. They believe that all humanity is motivated by economic ambitions, and that spiritual and idealistic impulses have no real force whatsoever; that, like the beasts of the field, it is food and shelter for which men really struggle.

This materialistic philosophy has taken an increasing hold as goods and materials become more abundant. The bigger the ships, the larger the factories, the higher the skyscrapers, the more evident are the results of technological advancement. Men are dwarfed beside the results of their own accomplishments and are prone to conclude that it is not *men who are important, but rather the goods that they have created.* People come to judge others—whether as individuals or as nations—by such details as the number of enameled steel bathtubs they possess or by the speed, size, and date of their automobiles. Enlightenment is judged by the size of public and private buildings, and human happiness is estimated by stores of food and clothing. In the materialistic philosophy, the word 'housing' becomes a measure of the successes or failures of democracy, as though the shell in which people live were a measure of people themselves.

From ancient times to modern days the story of mankind has been filled with his revolt against materialism. All experiences of the human race point to the conclusion that man does not live by bread alone, and that within the human mind there is the conviction that material things are not, after all, the most important objectives in life. Brought square with the issue, the human race has hitherto decided that ideals transcend ideologies. Where and when peoples did not so decide, they went down to disaster and disappeared from the earth. If materialism is to become dominant, then all observers throughout the ages have drawn the wrong conclusions. If the most important problem of society is to see that goods and materials are divided among the members of the human race, if other needs of men are of less importance, then all that has gone before us has been a mistake.

From time immemorial the farmer has been an example of independent thought. How does the farmer and his family look at the modern materialistic philosophy? America was founded by those who here sought a respite from the regimentation of European governments. It was not to gain riches or an easy life that the early pioneers of America journeyed in small ships across the tempestuous Western ocean. The civilization of Europe was in an age of flower. World trade and world conquest had brought to those nations more luxury than they had ever known. Life was easy as compared with ancient days. Leaving all this behind, those who came to America risked life itself in an effort to gain something that European life then withheld.

Except for the demands of church and state, there was no reason to leave a world of plenty for a new world of peril or want. But, in the old world, labor guilds held men in a static life, governments drove them into conscript armies, and the established church held their spirit in its control. The force that drove the early settlers to the shores of America was not a hope for more material possessions. It was a conviction that freedom of mind and spirit were of more importance, and that a dignity of soul could here be enjoyed. Amid all the want and privation, all the death and disaster of the early days, the written testimony which they have left is a hymn of thankfulness that they had been guided into a new world where the soul and the spirit of men were free.

When the exactions of the European order again closed upon the descendants of the first settlers, they revolted. It was 'life, liberty, and the pursuit of happiness' which they insisted should be theirs. It is true that among the long list of grievances they mentioned unjust taxes and unjust restrictions of trade. But it was neither the worth of the trade nor the value of the taxes to which they objected. It was injustice from which they revolted, and it was the struggle for freedom to which they said they were willing to pledge their lives, their fortunes, and their sacred honor Again, the importance of material possessions passed away in the face of a revolt of the spirit. Democracy was a spiritual philosophy. It taught that man as an individual, as an independent being, was the supreme concern; that man must be master of government, not government master of man. Democracy said that to this principle all material conceptions must be subservient.

Later generations moved Westward. They encountered hardships similar if not equal to those who landed on the Atlantic shores. In letters and in diaries, they left the message that privations and perils were gladly offered to find a home where men could live as they pleased and could face the sky with uplifted head.

The same spirit prevails among farm folk Farmers admit that life on the farm is hard; that the combat with weather rain, sun, pests and diseases is a lifelong struggle, but they have no real desire to retreat from it. Their fear is that they may lose the farm and have to move to a city. They admit that in town, for the same labor, they would have more protection from the elements, more clothes, and perhaps even more food; but they will forfeit, they fear, some things which they value even more highly. It is evident the chief reason people stay on the farm is that they desire to escape from the overwhelming oppressions of materialism. It is not more contact with the blessings of the materialistic age, but less, that they seek.

So overwhelming is the desire to escape to the land that lands sell for higher prices than will pay a decent return. The pressure for land increases in precise proportion to the rise of socialism. The pressure for land is in itself ample testimony that the intangible values of farm life are those for which people cling to the soil. Even though intangible these values are real. The blind materialist cannot see them; the socialist and communist do not admit their power; but they rule rural life as surely today as in the past.

It is to sustain the principles of freedom and of democracy that farmers and farm families are invaluable. This is seen more clearly today than ever before. When the towns and cities are disturbed with agitation and strikes, when industries are paralyzed by the eternal dissensions between employer and employee, when the doctrine is preached that by less work you can have more and that by producing less we may become more prosperous, the farmer remains now, as heretofore, the evident balance-wheel in our national life and the most stable factor in the republic. Perhaps there is an ingrained perception of the worth of the intangible things of life in an environment where storms and sunshine, frosts and droughts, mean success or failure. Perhaps here is a realization that man must be greater than his environment.

The constant clamor by press and radio—all of which is written from the towns—is a chorus screaming for more materialism as a remedy from materialism itself. Fallacy is piled upon fallacy in an effort to correct fallacies. If the older generation is discouraged and soured by the rise of materialism and by the dominance of those who deify materialistic theories, then, among this new generation who live in the country, there is an opportunity to develop the ideals for which America has striven. If the native values of rural life are to be rescued for human society then the young people are those who must and will have the largest part in such an undertaking.

Men have always been led by those to whom ideals were paramount. Today, no less than in ancient times the spiritual values of life in the country make possible the leadership of rural people over the nation. If democracy is to continue, it will be largely the farm people who will maintain it. If the native values of rural life are rescued, it must be the young people of the farms who will save them In these times of dishonest dallyings and incessant demands for more leisure, we can show the rewards that come to those who stand on their own feet and do their own job."

It was a great privilege for me to have worked with B.H. in his normal office routine as well as observing in public. How many of my present ideas originated in things he said or did I do not know, but as I look back I feel sure some came from his keen mind and personal inspiration.

Before I started with Extension my real desire was to farm, and about this time George Paulin asked me to come to Imperial Valley to manage a farm for him. B.H. was very understanding when I told him, and he said that would fit in just right. I should go to Imperial County on 1 December 1915 to represent him and the Extension Service in helping organize the Imperial County Farm Bureau. I would work with Walter Packard, Director of the Meloland U.C. Experimental Station. Walter was reported to know every man, woman, and child in the valley by their first name. Then there was Dr. Cady, DVM from Washington D.C., representing the USDA. We usually met in school houses in the various areas of the county selected for farm centers. Of course, a good deal of preliminary work had already been done. We met, each of us added our selected words of wisdom. They moved to organize a center there, give it a name, sign up members, elect officers, select a once-a-month meeting date, have some coffee and cake or pie, and say goodbye. I was elected secretary of a center three miles south on Brawley Main from 8th Street, Imperial.

On 1 January 1916, I started as manager of the 80-acre farm one mile west of Imperial on the east side of Brawley Main. We had 200 sows and of course lots of pigs. We had 40 acres of alfalfa, mostly for pasture, and 40 acres of milo for feed. Milo was then quite tall and uneven in height. To harvest it we had a sharp blade that fit onto the finger to cut the stalk off near the head. One dropped the heads into a cotton bag hung from your neck, then when it was full, dumped it in the wagon nearby. The wagon loaded, the heads were dropped onto a canvas or burlap sheet to dry, then run through an engine-powered grinder for pig feed. We also took the wooden tank wagon to town every day to get skim milk or buttermilk from the creamery. It was wonderful feed for the pigs.

In the corral was a lane with farrowing pens on each side. There was an open roof in back for shade in summer, or protection in winter. We lived in a frame house. I had a couple to help; he helped me outside, she did the cooking and housework. The summers were hot; rainfall was only an inch or two per year. I slept on a cot under the tree where we had a little breeze. We were far better off than the town folks, as the buildings and some sidewalks would hold the day's heat into the night, and they got very little breeze, even on the screen porches.

The skies at night were beautiful, clear as could be. The stars were so bright that they gave light, but on full-moon nights, one could easily sit out and read the paper without other light.

The Imperial ranch job was my first real job after college where I was located with any idea of permanence. I believe my salary was $125. per month, but that was of secondary importance. I was just interested in working, getting good crops and lots of good, fat hogs. I well remember when I got a bid of 8¼¢ a pound for four carloads of fat hogs. I was so delighted that I decided to go up to Los Angeles to deliver them to the packer. We loaded up and left Imperial in the evening. They had a coach on the rear of the train. In those days, you also got a free ticket back if you were accompanying livestock. We would all get out at each stop to see how our animals were coming. We stopped above Indio, and cattle were down in several cars, so I helped get them on their feet The train took off while we were in the cattle car, so when we got done, we climbed up on top of the car to ride to the next stop. It was beautiful moonlight, but it soon clouded up, then the wind came up followed by snow. It was great for a little, but we soon climbed back into the cattle car to get the warmth of the animals. It was good to get back into the coach in San Bernardino. We were in Los Angeles at daylight.

George Paulin was living in Imperial running the Imperial Valley Investment Co. (IVI), handling real estate, principally the land and lots, of the company owned by his father. Imperial Valley had fewer problems then than later with alkali, poor drainage, and water shortages. But even in 1916 there was some water shortage and it seemed each year some farmer would sell out. George would buy the crop of milo, and we would finish the crop and harvest it for feed for the hogs.

The I.V. Irrigation District each year built a brush dam across the Colorado River to divert the water through Mexico to the valley. I suppose building the brush dam to get just the right amount of water diverted was quite a delicate operation, and, as it came through Mexico, the volume might fluctuate a good deal, and so did the water delivered to the valley. If things went well, production was high, but somehow the hazards were high also.

In summer most of the women went to the hills toward San Diego. The cars were fewer and subject to overheating, blowouts, etc., and the roads outside the irrigated area were terrible.

Most of the roads inside the district were quite wide those days, with a levee down the middle and each side. They flooded one side and used the other until the dirt and ruts got impossible, then they reversed the process.

I visited the Imperial High School to form an Agricultural Club and spoke at a general assembly. Looking down on the front row I saw a nice-looking little blonde girl; nice to look at, but of course too young for me, a college grad. A few looks later, after meeting in church, Epworth League, and other places she didn't look so young, and I saw more of her.

34

That high school drew its students from quite a distance; they would pay one student who had a car to bring in other students who lived along the way. Finally, they decided to buy busses just for that purpose, and I understand that was the beginning of school bussing in California; it may have been first in the U.S.

They also had a number of private passenger cars, from **Model Ts to Pierce** Arrows and Packards, hauling passengers to Brawley, El Centro, Calexico, and other valley towns for a nickel or a dime. This paid, of course, if you could fill your car, so the competition got pretty keen. Several times I saw one car full of people speed over to clip a competitor and try to scare the life out of him. Finally, I am told, some of the winners got together and formed the company which grew into Greyhound.

Politics was a rather rough game there, too. Mr. Paulin, George's father had owned all the townsites in the valley except El Centro and one-half of Holtville. He had put a provision in all bills of sale or deeds for the lots that no liquor could be sold on the property at anytime. Something was wrong in the deeds for the Imperial lots, according to the judge some years later, so by 1919, there were saloons in Imperial to meet the needs of the entire valley. Every so often there would be a proposal to outlaw liquor in Imperial, as most of the citizens wanted it dry. The county and the transients wanted the source of supply retained.

George's older brother, Hal, had the Overland Auto Agency, and his family lived in town, as did George. They owned the hotel and several of the rooming houses and had owned or financed many of the other buildings. Some months before the election, they employed a private detective to come to town to look out for fire threats or other damage, but also to check on registration. All the rooming places had three or four times as many names registered to vote as there were rooms.

A new hog grower moved in across Brawley Main Canal from us. One of his boars came across the canal to our farrowing area. One of our dogs chased the boar. It was a hot day, and he just went down dead. The owner came over the next day, walked through the farrowing pens, and said we had also stolen two of his sows. I knew the sows, and knew we had them long before he moved there, but I went to the house and got the individual cards on each sow. The cards showed her ear notches, just where the white spots were on her body, her farrowing date, and the date she farrowed pigs. There was no question of their being our sows. George had the best attorney in the valley on a retainer basis. He went over the case and felt there were no problems. Our neighbor, however, got a new attorney who had just arrived in the valley. I feel sure this case meant nothing to him except a chance to defeat the ranking attorney in the valley and be recognized overnight.

The trial date came. They requested a jury trial. Our attorney wasn't really prepared for that. The opposing attorney eliminated every juror he thought was dry, so, when they were selected, they were almost all wet. It seemed like the line of witnesses would never end. The question from the opposing attorney was, "You have driven up the road from Imperial to Brawley?" Answer, "Yes, sir " "Did you see some black and white sows on the right-hand side of the road?" "Yes, sir." "Do you think two of them were the black and white sows under question here?" "Yes, sir I sure do." No judge or juror ever saw the sows in question, but the questions and answers were good. The jury found us guilty on one count. We had to pay a little, not much, so we weren't hurt much. The Wets won, and the attorney, Phil Swing, won immediate standing in the valley. Not too long after that, he was elected to the U.S. Congress and, with Senator Hiram Johnson, sponsored the legislation to build Hoover Dam. I saw him about twenty years ago in San Diego at a Rotary meeting.

On Sundays, I always got the feeding done in time to get a bath, shave, and get to the Methodist Church, where I was usher much of the time. After church, I enjoyed the day with friends, then went to Epworth League and church at night. Isabelle Mack, the blonde girl on the front seat in high school, played the piano in church, so I would see her there. We enjoyed evenings at her home as well as at church and some other occasions.

We had a University Club which met a few times at the Barbara Worth Hotel in El Centro. There were about six grads from Berkeley during my time who were farming in the valley.

The war in Europe was, of course, news, but it seemed still far away and our oceans seemed adequate insulation. Both the English and the Germans were interfering with our merchant ships at sea. German submarines had sunk the "Lusitania," and when a German sub sank the "Sussex," sentiment turned more anti-Kaiser. President Wilson was reelected in November 1916 on the grounds that he had kept us out of the war. About 2 April 1917 we declared a state of war, and we were in it. It seemed still far off, but things heated up rapidly. All the early talk was that food was essential and farmers should stay on the farm and produce to the maximum. Still, one wondered what he should do. The draft boards were set up, and in Imperial most of the young men were farmers, so my name was in the first draft.

George Paulin had raised some cotton that did very well, so one day he said to me that he and his brother, Hal, would like me to join them in putting in forty acres. We would rent the land and hire all the work done. I told him I did not have any money. That was OK. I didn't have any time to look after it. That was OK, too, so they borrowed the money, they hired all the work done, they harvested and sold the cotton, and the next spring, in Camp Lewis, I got a check for over $3000. for my one-third share clear. The next year, my one-third share was $550. That was like manna from heaven. I was in France then, so they decided we had our fun and had better quit.

Early in the summer of 1917, one of the men on the ranch borrowed my saddle horse to ride into town, tied it to the hitching rack, and went his way. He came back and no horse. A number of horses had been rounded up and driven across the border. We were very busy. I thought I had to have a saddle horse, so I got a three-year-old from the pasture, never ridden, threw the saddle on and took off. She was fat and round. After a few runs and bucks, which went OK, the saddle went over one side and I with it, but I thought it had gone well except the cinch coming loose, so I tightened the cinch up good and threw my leg over the saddle again. I never could quite get my right foot into the stirrup so never got well seated. Every lunge her head was coming back as mine went forward. I slid off as best I could. My face looked like a new potato, all skinned up, and my collar bone was broken when her head hit it, so it wasn't a good day.

My draft notice came, and my folks suggested we take a trip to Yosemite Valley, so I went home. We had the Saxon car, and it was loaded: mother, father, Bernice,

36

Carrie, and Walter. We packed the car the night before, and left Los Angeles at 5 a.m. The roads were dusty and rough. The old ridge route was started then, but not far along. I was just starting to use my right arm. At breakfast, my left hand started to hurt. By noon I couldn't use it. We reached the Bakersfield Hotel about 5:30 p.m. and called in a doctor. He took me to his office, said I had blood poisoning, and he would have to lance my hand. He had had quite a few drinks. He told me he was an army doctor in the Philippines, and he never would operate unless he was drunk, dead drunk, then another swipe with the scalpel and drunk, dead drunk, another swipe and drunk, dead drunk. I remember Doc Hayes, a vet, always told us to cut plenty deep and clean it out thoroughly. This he did, and it felt better.

We were off again in the morning before six. We got into the higher country, arriving at Tuolumne Meadows Hotel that evening, a beautiful country, then on into the valley the next evening to tents in Camp Curry. School opened then in August, so the big crowd was past. The "fire fall" was really spectacular. They had an entertainment program each evening using talented guests. It was delightful. Next morning I went to the hospital. The doctor there had a disinfectant sent to him for trial. It not only helped me, but it really felt good.

We climbed Half Dome and Cloud Rest and all the others, and were heading out Big Oak Flat Road the third morning when the rear end of the Saxon went out, so back we went to the garage and a two-day wait for parts. I was happy, as it gave me two more days of the doctor's care, and a far better time in the valley. We went home via Stanford University and down the Camino Real, now 101, but it was then four days from Stanford to Los Angeles. We came up that road several months ago at 60 mph and I remembered all those gullies going down by the Kings River and how, in 1917, sixty years earlier, we had driven to the bottom and back up to the top of every one of them.

Above left, Batallion officers, Battery F, 316 Field Artillery, George Wilson on left
Above right, at Camp Lewis, Washington
Below, 316th Field Artillery, 81st Division

3

WORLD WAR I

Training Camps

My family and I had returned from a very pleasant trip to Yosemite, even though I was a little handicapped with a bad hand. I got back to Imperial to meet my date with Uncle Sam. The send-offs were rather gala occasions in World War I El Centro was all decorated. We had to be sworn in and that night there was a big street dance. Two blocks of Main Street were cleaned up and sealed off, and we had quite an evening. Bella and I went down in the Model T, but when we decided to come home there was no Model T. Fortunately, we were able to get home with George and Dorothy. The next morning, George and I got out early and found the Ford out in the desert, abandoned below the border west of Mexicali. We got it and us home in time to board the train for Camp Lewis, near Tacoma, Washington, the afternoon of September 17, 1917. Imperial had become my home and I hated to leave.

Our first stop was Los Angeles, where we took on several more cars of embryo troops from downtown Los Angeles. My mother and father were at the station and the stop gave us an hour or so to visit. I think they hated to see me leave, but they were realists, so the visit was very pleasant, though there was lots of weeping around us. I still feel especially for young married folks and others whose farewell must be very serious. People were out at every railroad station where we stopped with coffee, doughnuts, and best wishes, so it was a rather gala trip. We had a fellow who always sang "The Long, Long Trail," or "Tipparary" or "Smiles," and others.

Camp Lewis was a beehive of activity, all new barracks, mess halls, etc., in various stages of construction. We were among the first to arrive. We soon found we were Company F 316th Engineers of the Ninety-First Division. Our captain was Captain Lavelle, a great fellow, who seemed quite mature and experienced, probably twenty-eight years old. He went to the first officer training camp at Plattsburg, N.Y., then, on his own time and expense, he drove all the way across Canada, visiting every military camp he could find to see how the Canadians did their training. He had graduated from college as a mining engineer and had already made quite a success and a good deal of money when the war was declared. He was very confident, not cocky, but well prepared and knew that any captain of engineers outranked any infantry colonel in the army.

39

We had no uniforms, no rifles or other equipment to use, so we just drilled all day with plenty of sitting-up exercises and double time to get hardened up. There were no showers yet, hot or cold, so right after breakfast, frost still on the ground, the captain marched us to a lake out in the woods and told us to strip and get in. The officers kept track of the hesitation period to help pick the privates, first class, and corporals.

One day at the 5 p.m. formation, the captain announced that they were organizing the regimental fights, so anyone wishing to represent the company could step three paces forward and the sergeant would take the names. About five men stepped out. Then, "Anyone who is afraid to fight, step three paces to the rear, and the sergeant will take the names." No one dared. Maybe ten days later, we were marched to a big clearing, a meadow in the timber. The captain followed in his Cadillac full of footballs, baseballs, and boxing gloves.

The order was, "Now you men who stepped three paces ahead to represent the company, fall out and use the baseballs, football, or do as you please. The rest of you weren't afraid to fight, so pick your partners." What a day! Most of the time there were several fights going on. The last two really didn't want to fight, but the whole company had them circled, calling for blood. Finally a punch was solid enough to make the recipient mad, so he was going to kill his assailant in one blow. To give all he had, he threw his arm back so far he dislocated his shoulder and we had to take him to the hospital to get it back in the socket. The captain decided there wasn't time for "sitting up" exercises after breakfast, so our reveille blew twenty minutes early to have them before breakfast, until orders came direct from the War Department to cease that irregularity.

The commanding general of Camp Lewis issued orders that all companies would have Wednesday afternoon off, if they were caught up with their work. Captain Lavelle read the order to us, then said, "No one is caught up until the war is over. We continue as usual Wednesday afternoons." So every Wednesday we saw the rest of the camp come and go by us.

Combat engineers are supposed to equal the best at combat, and still be engineers all night. Washington has rain, so, if the downpour was good, our captain would burst into the barracks at 2 or 3 a.m. to announce, "This is a great opportunity to drain water around some infantry barracks." We all slid into boots and rain equipment with shovels and picks to control water running wild any place in the camp.

In December, I was recommended to go to officer's training camp there in Camp Lewis. I wanted engineering, but the engineers wouldn't look at you if you didn't have a B.S. degree or better in engineering. But, being an engineer, they assigned me to field artillery, which was second choice.

Officers training started January 5. I was assigned to divisional guards duty January 2-3, so was away from our barracks. Word came to me to stay away as our company was quarantined for scarlet fever. I hated to leave Company F, but I was selected to go to officers training and wanted to do that too. I was sitting outside on a log when word came that I should report to the doctor's office. The doctor's question was, "Have you ever had scarlet fever?" "Me? No sir, Doc." "You sure you have not had scarlet fever?" "Yes, sir." "Have you ever had scarletina?" "Oh, yes sir." "OK, report directly from here to training camp this afternoon." I was like the mule—it took a couple of bats over the head with a 2 x 4 to get my attention, and then I cooperated. It took several experiences like this before I realized that help can come from most unexpected places.

Our artillery company was 150 men from all over the Western states. Its objective was to teach field artillery and the duties of an officer, but also to break down your nerves, if possible, so they wouldn't waste time training officers only to have them break down under stress and strain. Several months under Captain Lavelle was good training for that.

After Company F 316 Engineers got out of quarantine, I went back to get my things. I found the captain had told the company that war was no daylight game, it was day and night, so he had divided the company in three sections, each on an eight-hour shift and changing shifts each two weeks so one third were always at work, day or night, wet or dry, hot or cold, building bridges, digging trenches, handling explosives, or just moving to a new location, or in simulated battle. He was sure getting them tough. I wondered if I should have left, for Company F was the only one in the camp on such a schedule.

Every two weeks in artillery training, we were seated on hard benches for roll call. A group of names were read slowly, and you were never sure whether they were the ones to continue or the ones to return to their old outfits.

By graduation on April 19, 1918, we had about fifty left in our artillery group. We were declared eligible for 2nd Lieutenant Field Artillery and awarded seven days leave. Some went home, several of us went to Seattle, but the third day we were called back to leave for Camp Jackson, South Carolina. Here we found 3600 field artillery officers not yet assigned to regular outfits, and other groups like ours not yet commissioned.

My recollection of Camp Jackson was hot, humid, button your blouse (coat), and salute the officers. We would drill, then come in and strip and perspire on our bunks. If you went to Columbia, the city, you spent all your time dodging or saluting officers. After a few days, an officer asked if I wanted to go to France. I sure did, so he told me they would pick a group at drill next day to go to France. I snapped into it, and was picked. We were told we would take our exam the next day in arithmetic, geometry, trigonometry, and calculus. I went to the library, got books on these subjects, and actually stayed up all night studying. I had never had calculus.

We took the examination, and I passed number one out of 400. The first day or two of May, we were secretly moved at night up to the New York area. Three-hundred of us were on the road at midnight, marching to the pier in New York to get the "Leviathan" for France, but they had never heard of us and wouldn't take us, so we got to the "Chicago," a French ship in civilian service. The captain said he had never heard of us and had no food for us, but if we wanted to go, get aboard, and we did.

††† "Over There"

Our bunks were in the hold. Our first meal out was classic. We went down a steep, winding stairway into the galley where we got the fumes of rabbit stewing in wine. Only the strong got beyond that, then we got mess kits and a ladle of stewed rabbit, which exposed rabbit parts that usually do not show up on the plate. Then appeared a chunk with not only the skin but the fur on the skin. That saved the ship a number of meals the next few days.

In the ship with us were regular civilian passengers and 1000 Poles from Chicago who had volunteered for service. We didn't see much of them. There were 300 U.S. soldiers who had been gathered up from guard houses around New York, marched down under armed guard, and put aboard. They had good rooms on the top decks of the ship, so some of our group complained that army regulations said our group ranked second class passage. Of course, the guard house boys didn't, so finally we moved up where we got better air anyhow.

Also on board was a navy chaplain, a fine fellow and a quartermaster captain. I presume he was to deliver the guardhouse men, but he had had no troop command experience.

The captain of the good ship *Chicago* was right. He did not have any food for us. The civilians were eating OK, so after meals they would come just above us and throw fruit, bread, or what they had down to us to help a little. At night we crawled out of our bunks and went down a ladder to the cook's quarters. We woke one up. He would push us into a closet while he got a sandwich fixed up, collected a dollar— lots of money then—and back up the ladder we went.

About the fourth or fifth day out, the guardhouse group revolted. The quartermaster captain walked around with his 45 in his hand all day. Finally the ship captain agreed to putting cooks from the guardhouse group into the galley, and we did better after that. We also had aboard French marines who manned the antisubmarine rifles and stood watch for submarines.

The sailors, however, said they had seen the subs, but had never been bothered as the *Chicago* carried Swiss mail, and the Germans used it all the time so had orders not to molest us. Of course, most troops went in convoys with naval escort and were fairly fast ships. We were slow, 11 days, and alone.

On Sunday afternoon, the American chaplain was holding services when suddenly the ship changed course several times. It seemed torpedos must have been sighted and we were zigzagging to miss them. Everyone rushed to the rail to see them. The rudder mechanism had stuck first one way, then the other, until they got it back in adjustment.

The eleventh day, we saw France. It looked good. It was a long, slow trip up the Garrone River to Bordeaux, but calm, quiet, and beautiful. Wine barrels everywhere. We went to an American debarkation camp not far out. No one there had ever heard of us, but they assigned us tents. Again, there was little food in our mess hall, so we got about a week's experience on living off the country. The camp food was free game wherever we found it, so we had lots of fun and really ate very well. Then the camp quartermaster showed up, apologizing for not knowing of our arrival. He was sure we had had little food, but we would have a big meal that evening. He had lined up a first-class passenger train to take us to the army artillery training camp at Saumur. The train was luxury, and the country in mid-May was beautiful.

Saumur was in the Chateau country on the Loire River. It had long been a Protestant stronghold and was now the Protestant center of France. They said before the religious wars in the sixteenth and seventeenth centuries, it had a population of 24,000 people, but the wars cut it to 12,000, where it was then in 1918. It was said to be the area where people spoke the most perfect French. It was the home of the French Cavalry Military Academy, comparable to West Point Academy, except that in France the cavalry, infantry, and artillery academies are separate. The young men of ordinary French families went to infantry; the engineers, mathematicians, etc. to artillery; and the aristocracy to cavalry. Saumur was considered the finest cavalry school in the world. In taking over the academy as an American artillery school, Pershing had asked that some of the horses and several top instructors be retained for our instruction. Some artillery were still horse-drawn.

Our principal instructors were all French artillery officers wounded in the first battle of the Marne. They were outstanding men. We were divided into sections of twenty who bunked together and had all classes together. The hour of equitation was exercise and diversion as well as instruction. The rest was all dead serious. We had one fellow, Al Albert, the District Attorney from Vandalia, Illinois. He was unpredictable and irrepressible; clothes always looked like he had slept in them, and his drawl didn't fit in with any military maneuver. The French colonel had very meticulously explained a problem in ballistics, going over it several times to be sure we had it, then asked for questions and answered several with detailed explanation. Then up goes Al's hand, and he says, "Now, Colonel, I wonder if you would mind just starting in again at the beginning. I don't believe I got it." He was the Court Jester and gave us most of our laughs.

Equitation was three days a week, the best hour of the afternoon, always with a flat French saddle, much like a flat English saddle with no stirrups, far more difficult than bareback, and every day a different horse. It was a great experience and a real privilege. We had fairly simple jumps and other obstacles. Several times, near the end, we went out several miles to the steeple chase course at Verry, considered the finest and most difficult anywhere. Of course, we took only the easier ones. At one jump, we were pretty well bunched. I was near the front and we went over all right, but my horse stumbled on landing. His nose hit the dirt and I went right on over beside his head, but, as I looked up, here were the front feet of other horses coming over, looking as big as elephants. When I see a movie of a steeple chase, I know just how the rider feels amid all that horse flesh when he hits the ground. The problem was that, during the war, they didn't have anyone to fill in the depressions where the horses front feet had been landing.

We had little social contact. I did go to the Protestant church quite often. They had a sermon in French and one in English. The old customs were retained, and if you saw a young couple out walking, her parents would be following close behind. We visited a number of the chateaux, some unfurnished, some still lived in and beautifully furnished.

In the last of August we took our final exams. We each had thirty minutes of artillery fire under a French Major. I snapped to attention and saluted, then it went like this:

Your name: George H. Wilson
Where are you from?   California
Your education: University of California
Your business: Farming

A quizzical look, then, "Your name...your education...your business?" Then all was repeated.   Finally, he said, "You stand here a minute." He went over to an American officer and told him he had a man lying to him. "He says he is a graduate of the University of California and that he is farming." The officer told him that was OK, so he came back and we went through it again. He looked at me awhile, then gave me the best discourse on California wines that I have ever heard. He was sure I was lying to him. He didn't let me get a shot away. The thirty minutes was up.

We had an afternoon for our final in topography. We worked in pairs and went out to a new area to work out our problem. The day was beautiful, the berries were ripe, we were through with training. Nothing was as important as the scenery, the sunshine, the berries. We didn't get far with the problem, but we had a good day.

I still have an old slip of paper with my grades; I was sixth in a class which finished with 158 out of over 200 starting. An interesting note is that, of the five ahead of me, one was Charles Taft, son of President Taft, brother of Senator Robert Taft. In 1958 I had lunch in Washington with Charles Taft. One was the son of Charles Hughes, Chief Justice of the Supreme Court, who barely missed being President of the U.S. at that time because he lost California by a small margin. One was Charles Schwab, son of Charles Schwab, President of Bethlehem Steel Company, the heaviest producer of steel for World War I.

My commission as 2d Lieutenant had come through, but they did not tell us as they thought we would make better students as noncoms than as officers. New groups were coming to Saumur while we were there, all commissioned, some 1st Lieutenant already, but we got the commission on graduation.

During the course of our training we were joined by Teddy Roosevelt, son of President Theodore Roosevelt, and his wife; so far as I know, the only wife in France. He had joined the British forces early in the fighting—they allow wives—then he transferred to the U.S. forces and came to Saumur to get horsemanship and some artillery.

We broke up quickly to get to our new assignments. I was sent to Battery F, 316 F.A. of the 81st Division, North and South Carolina and Tennessee. My first outfit was Company F, 316 Engineers, 91st Division. This new outfit was located at Valdoun, near the Swiss border northwest of Geneva in the lower Alps. They had just arrived in France so all the officers were sent immediately to a school for final artillery training. I found myself the only Officer-in-Charge of the company, responsible for their training all day and censoring their outgoing letters at night, with a little help from the Doctor—when he was sober. Of course, the sergeants did most of the training in the daytime, but I had records to keep to be sure we were getting the job done.

My best break was that most of the boys could not read or write, at least very little, so there were not as many letters as might be. At first some letters told how many boys had frozen to death on the decks of the ship coming over, and tales of all sorts. Of course, those were homesick boys wanting sympathy and feeling they should make it sound interesting. As time went on, more letters contained pathetic appeals to send the other kids of the family to school, telling how important it was to have some schooling. The chaplain helped in what time he had to teach the boys to write a letter home. I am sure the war was a great stimulant to education in the South.

There was an airfield near us and we heard a good deal of the American Aces who had brought down five American planes. The 316th Regiment of six batteries were stationed together. The officers and the two YMCA girls of the battalion of three batteries ate together. Our Major was Barnard Manning. His father was governor of

44

South Carolina, and he had four brothers, all in the service. One had already been shot down at Verdun.

I was appointed liaison officer to maintain all communications between the infantry ahead of us and the battalion headquarters and regimental headquarters. I also acted as battalion adjutant a good deal of the time. The best job of all was mess officer for the battalion officer's mess. It was my job to pick the house where the kitchen and officer's mess would be located, to pick the cook and help to get utensils, tablecloths, etc., and to provide the food. Most of the food could be purchased at the commissary, of which some were good and well-stocked. But usually the vegetables, eggs, and often all the meat had to be secured from French farmers, so I had regular routes to go to pick these up. All this ranked a motorcycle sidecar and driver. Jeeps and staff cars were very scarce, as was gasoline. When gas was rationed, I had to go to the colonel's office several times a week to get the use of the sidecar; he finally gave me a permanent permit to keep me out of his hair. I knew many of the farmers in the area and had almost every Sunday dinner with some one of them. Wild boar was the best meat we could get occasionally, and a few times we had venison. If bought in shops, the most common meat used by local folks was "chaveau," horsemeat. It was lighter colored and coarser grained than beef. I never tried buying it for the table, but it may have been there sometimes. For months, the only meat we could get from the commissary was five-gallon cans of fat soft bacon. It was terrible. I found early that, regardless of your position in the organization chart, there would be lots of other jobs to be done. You could speak up quickly and volunteer for the jobs you might like, or sit back and hear the captain announce you had volunteered for a job you didn't want. I always had enough jobs on hand, so I never had to take one. This I recommend.

The infantry of the 81st Division had been on at least two active engagements, with other artillery for support. We were now about ready to join them for the big push on Metz, planned for November 15. We, of course, all knew it, and so did the Germans. After several false rumors, the Armistice was signed 11 a.m. on November 11. We got the news as we got up. At breakfast, there was hardly a word spoken. That was true most of the day. We had just finished a week of day-and-night simulated action, moving a lot of artillery positions, laying down barrages, and moving on or firing on a fixed object until it was demolished. This was good for me, for the sidecar and I had covered most of the hills and valleys in the area, and I knew where the good gun enplacements were.

We had trained, planned, and dreamed military success for fourteen months, six months in France, and it seemed like we had lost our chance to prove our training. That evening the airfield nearby put on a good air show. We had seen little of the Frenchmen of the town, but after the 9 p.m. formation, the cheering started, and the boys went from door to door and dragged out the Frenchmen, mostly pretty well "liquidated" by then, and had a big night of it.

Immediately, we broke camp and moved to St. Blin near Chaumont, General Pershing's headquarters. It was back about sixty miles from Metz where we were to have been part of the big offensive.

We were not positive that the war was over. Word came down that it might be temporary, so keep on training; if it started up again, it could be worse. Our outfit was located in wooden barracks on the edge of town. Another officer and I were billeted in a stone and heavy timber house near the edge of town. There was a good deal of snow by November. We would go on hikes with our 155 mm 6-inch Howitzers, set up our gun enplacements, camouflage and all, then run the communication wires to the simulated infantry location and to battalion or regimental headquarters. We usually would take the ovens along and eat on location, then get back about 3 p.m. About ten of us would go to Mademoiselle Marie Vourins across from our billet. Four, I believe, were billeted at her place. She would have hot tea ready and some cake, if we had gotten her flour, chocolate, sugar, etc. Then we either sat around and talked or played bridge for ¼ centime a point. I do not remember now how much that was, but it didn't matter.

The job now was to keep the men happy, which meant occupied. We had school classes in almost anything. Many of the boys learned to read and write, or at least get started at it. An agricultural school was set up at Bonn, Germany. I got orders to report there as an instructor, but it meant delaying return home by at least six months, so the Major asked that the order be rescinded as they needed me there. I learned later that the school was set up and run for a year or more by Knowles Ryerson, a good friend of university days, and it would have been interesting to work with Knowles awhile. He was later Chancellor at Davis.

From St. Blin, I often went to Chaumont to the commissary. We could usually get chocolates there. I heard many stories of General Black Jack Pershing. He often said enlisted men don't make mistakes. The smaller mistakes are made by the lower officers, and the big ones by the higher officers. He was unmerciful in demanding that the higher officers do their homework and leave nothing to chance. Fundamentally, that is a most important approach to success in almost any project, and he wanted to be sure the officers knew every detail of any plan.

We traveled all day with 55 mm guns on tractors to join the rest of the 81st Division for a review next day by Pershing. It was winter, wet and muddy. Captain Icky Bowen was a perfectionist. The rest of us got out in the morning and washed off the mud, but Icky kept his company up all night cleaning and then painting the Howitzers and equipment. They, too, still had to rush all morning without sleep, and they showed it.

The troops were drawn up for inspection. **Pershing** arrived at Icky's company and started his drumbeat of questions. "What did you men have for breakfast? Who is your best pitcher, catcher, left fielder? What is the name of the company show? Who is your lead man? Who is your comedian? Do you have a quartet? What kind of shoeshine do the men use? How many attended your last show? How many are attending school? How many teachers?" Captain Bowen had worn his long overcoat all night and somehow he got a smear of black paint on it. Pershing's parting comment was, "Captain, your men look pretty sloppy and it looks to me like they get it from their captain." Poor Icky was never the same after that. He just tried too hard. I expect Pershing knew the story. Another of Pershing's demands was, "Never plan an attack without an adequate plan of retreat." I have often remembered that, but haven't always lived up to it.

The Mayor of St. Blin was a young fellow, and most people felt he should be in the army. He also lived in the house in which we were billeted. He came in about 11 one night. All the rooms were heated by fireplaces, the only heat. He took his shovel to another room, got some live coals, and took them to his room to start his fire. He may have dropped some coals in the hallway. About 2:30 a.m. he smelled smoke, rushed out into the hall filled with smoke, opened all the doors and cried, "Fue-fue-fue" (fire). This let the oxygen into the fire and set it burning. We took our time, as there was no real danger in our room, then went out the window to a ladder. We were second floor. I remember well the picture in our school history books of the fire engine ascribed to Franklin and the Philadelphia fire department. It had handles on each end which were pumped up and down like a railroad handcar, and the fire equipment of St. Blin looked just like it.

Many of the troops were manning the pumps on the fire engine, and a long line passed buckets of water from the hand pump a block away to the open tank in the fire pump; then a hose took it to the fire. Everyone was having lots of fun; the Americans were working the operation and the Frenchmen watched them. About daylight, the GI's decided this was all wrong—let the Frenchmen do the work, it was their fire. So the GI's used all pressure necessary to keep up the water pressure with French manpower. Since the construction was of stone and heavy timbers, it never did break into a raging fire.

Speaking of fires and fireplaces, the French had great firescreens. I never could figure why we do not have them. All my life I have harbored a hope to sometime manufacture them. The screen of metal fills the entire opening. The better ones we used in 1915 looked and operated a good deal like the old wooden rolled-up desks we used to have. When you go to bed at night, your regular fire is going. You pull the screen all the way down to the hearth. This cuts off all the oxygen, and practically no fuel is used during the night. At reveille, you sneak out from under that thick down comforter, raise the screen about two inches to let in the oxygen, it goes POOF as you jump back into bed! In three minutes there is a nice warm dressing area in front of the fireplace. Raise the screen up, and all is set for the day. You have used hardly any fuel during the night, and in the morning the room is warm before you need more fuel. With all our conveniences, when we roll in at night, we leave fuel in the fireplace and, by morning, it is all gone and you have to set a new fire before you get heat. Further, if you have furnace heat that comes on at 5 a.m., a good part of that heat may go up the chimney until you are sure the fire is all out so you will not be smoked out when you close the damper.

On a later trip to France, I looked a number of places in Paris and found cheap imitations of those screens, but didn't find a good one to bring back. Maybe a reader will finish one of my planned projects.

One day I was walking down the sidewalk with a fellow officer. A labor detail came shuffling up the street with shovels, picks, etc. As they came opposite, the sergeant called attention. They straightened the picks and shovels over their shoulders and the sergeant saluted; all OK. A block further, another group came along with a colored fellow in the lead. They straightened up, but no salute. My companion called the leader over. "Don't you salute officers?" "Yes, sir. Yes, sir. If there is anything I like to do in this army, it is to salute the officers." "Then why didn't you salute?" "Sir, I'se not allowed to salute. I'm with that outfit up there. All's the matter with me is I'se not closed up."

I had no idea that the feeling against the North was so strong, or that the control of blacks so tight. Every officer in the battalion was North and South Carolina or Tennessee, except one from New York City. He was a Northerner, and I from California was neutral, so all the disputes were put up to me. I have had good, sober men, in all seriousness, come up and ask, "If you had a sister and one of these Northern boys came down and they wanted to get married, who would you shoot, the Northern boy or the sister?" I know that is extreme, but I had many questions only a little more reasonable.

The 92d or 93d Division was a colored division. They were in France quite a little while. They got the divisional croix de guerre citation, so every member could wear it and, of course, they did.

By April or May, our fellows were getting letters from home about how these black boys were showing off the croix de guerre citations, so they had to take them out in the woods and eliminate them, for that couldn't be permitted. I didn't pay much attention. I thought it was loose talk, a long way from home. Governor Manning of South Carolina and his wife had five sons in the service, one our Major. Two were fatalities so, soon after the armistice, President Wilson gave the parents authority to come over, and they spent a week with us, eating at our mess. While they were there, "shooting niggers" was about the only subject of discussion. He told them not to expect to be discharged right away on their return. He needed them to round up fresh "niggers."

We moved, for a short time, to another town. A colored labor battallion had been there for some time, and the French girls did not draw the color line, so they were on the streets together all the time. This led to arguments from our fellows, who just couldn't take it. I was called up as Officer-of-the-Day in charge of the troops on guard duty. As I relieved the outgoing officer at 10 a.m., he said the colonel's orders are, "If you see a white man and a 'nigger' in an argument, ask no questions, shoot the 'nigger.'" Without thinking, I guess I said, "I am not shooting any 'niggers,'" and never gave it a further thought as I went about my duties. Pretty soon an orderly came up, all out of breath, snapped a salute, and said the colonel wanted to see me immediately. I still had no idea why. I got there and he sure gave me his best scowl and barked, "I understand you said you weren't shooting any 'niggers.' The orders are Shoot the 'niggers,' ask no questions, shoot the 'nigger.'" I left and went to my room to make sure I didn't see any argument of any kind, but the orders were clear.

It was winter, and we decided to throw a dance. We had our YMCA girls, a few others, and from a hospital in another town we got probably six or seven nurses. I had heard of Southern chivalry, and it was an education to me to see the finesse and delicacy with which they handled the girls. But I noticed one girl not too beautiful or graceful, not much of a dancer although probably better than I, but I felt I should ask her to dance, so I did and we spent a good deal of the evening together. Not a single Southern gentleman came near. The good dancers and good lookers had a great evening. When the evening broke up, I was elected to take the nurses back to the hospital. Others said they would get the car so we could have a good car, and out came the colonel's new staff car, just delivered to him that morning. All was going well. Our driver had just finished "runner up" in the all-AEF competition between drivers. The roads were winding. We came to a forest on the right which shaded the roads, so it was solid ice. We skidded, but he had it well in hand when we hit another. It seemed to pick up speed as we skidded. In France they often have small piles of gravel along the roadside. We would hit one and bounce back on the icy road, then hit another and bounce off it. Then we came to a sudden stop, wrapped around a roadside tree. We were picked up and taken to the hospital. One girl had a pretty sore head; it had bumped on the wooden bow over the top. The next morning, the driver and I got a car and went out to see the wreckage—a new car just delivered, all four wheels broken off. We lifted the hood and the motor was broken off the frame. These were basically White trucks with heavy semi-armored bodies.

The next day the colonel called me in, asked a question or two, and then, "How fast was the driver going?" I told him I thought about 25-30 miles per hour. He told me to get out. He wasn't going to learn anything from me. In a few days he had a new car. A Major on his staff was the brother of the General in charge of all motor transport in France.

I am not critical of the Southern chivalry. They have a technique far superior to the North or West. The same is often said of the French men, and it is true, but with either group, if a girl gets in their way or is not attractive for any reason, she can be completely ignored or roughly handled in a way Western courtesy would not tolerate. There seems to be compensations for almost all things.

By Christmas, of course, all the fellows were raring to be at home, but that was out, so they did second best and all sorts of programs were set up to raise money for toys, or to make them. This was to be the fifth Christmas of war for French children; many knew no other state of living. Some of the sergeants were elected to handle the program. They had a big supply, it seemed, when the Priest heard of it and ordered all the toys delivered to his place. This almost started a new war. The sergeant told him off, and the French loved it. Really, it only added new interest to the occasion. The program was a great success, with happiness for all, and probably more for the homesick Americans than for anyone else.

The artillery range we used had been used by many units on their way up front, so it was well covered with duds which needed cleaning up before we left. I got to pick a squad of men to do the job. We had heard so much of the danger of moving a dud that it seemed it might be a long assignment. An experienced demolition squad came from Third Army headquarters to instruct us in just how to do it. It was winter, so the first thing was to build a little fire to warm us up and heat the coffee. Half our squad was getting its first instruction on how to explode duds when a number of shell fragments came tearing into the ground around us, the closest we ever came to a casualty. At first, as we came to a dud, we dug a little hole beside it, placed a detonator in the hole, lit a long fuse, and ran plenty far. Then we cut the fuse a little shorter; then we piled several shells on each other near a tree, cut the fuse fairly short, ran behind the tree, and heard the shell fragments go whistling by. We had 75mm (3-inch) shells, 155mm (6-inch) regular powder or high explosive. Each had its own habits, and we learned the characteristic sounds and habits. One day we had a dozen or more in the pile and had lit the fuse when a small plane came over fairly low. Just as he flew maybe 1000 feet above, the explosion occurred. He immediately rolled over and fell like a falling leaf to maybe 300 feet, then shot off on his way and out of sight. I, at least, was really scared. Whether the air disturbance flipped him over and out of control for a bit, or he was just putting on a show for us, I will never know.

We were about done with the job when one day a bent old Frenchman came down a little road through the range. His face was lined with streaks of blood and his clothes were tattered. I guessed we had a casualty and maybe real trouble.

A six-inch high-explosive shell is quite heavy, and the explosion of the detonator and shells around it may break it in many parts without exploding the powder inside it. As this happened, the heavy base of the shells might land and slide along the ground with quite a little yellow, high-explosive powder still in ti, leaving a streak of powder on the road as it slid along and still more explosive in the base of the shell. This was the story. As he walked along the road, he saw the yellow powder streak. He leaned over to examine it, and his pipe fell out of his mouth and lit the powder trail. It, of course, sped right up to the shell base and exploded the powder still in it. The shell was almost like a gun, so it picked up the small gravel on the road and spattered his face and tore his clothes. It had happened early in the morning, and he was traveling the road to show all his neighbors that he was a wounded veteran of the war.

When we left Saumur, my friend Al Albert came with me. He was assigned to regimental headquarters. He was the only Officer-in-Charge there, as all the others went to a school for further training. He never marched or even walked along. He just shuffled. He might show up on time or five minutes late; it was of no concern to him. His uniform was always rumpled. We wore wrapped leggings then. One might be wrapped from the top down and the other from the bottom up. His first command would be, "All right now, you fellows, fall in," and then maybe that would be followed by a funny story he had just thought of. The outfit ranked dress and order right at the top, and the officers came back for a weekend midterm in their training, saw Al, and about died of chagrin, so they immediately started procedure to have him charged with inefficiency and transferred out of the outfit. I told them they would like him when they got to know him, and I thought they were going to add my name to the charges. After two weeks the officers were all back, and they didn't bother him either. The colonel sent him to our battalion. He soon was the jester and the life of the group.

Just when everybody was getting to know Al so they could enjoy his humor, orders came for his appearance before court-martial. The Major and two captains had signed the charges, so they went with him. They told him they didn't know what this was all about. He told them they didn't need to explain it to him. He understood it all perfectly. In the court-martial, he told them that he got along fine with the troops when he was alone with them, but when all these brilliant experienced officers came back, they were just so much more able than he that there was nothing for him to do. About two weeks later, word came that the court-martial wanted further information and for all, Al and the officers, to return. By now the officers felt it was all a mistake, but they couldn't stop it. The court was called to order by the presiding colonel, and Al said, "Colonel, before we start this procedure, could I ask you a personal question?" The colonel said, "Certainly." Al said, "Colonel, I wonder if you would tell me about how I should answer these questions so that I will be sent back to the U.S." The colonel turned to the reporter and said, "Take that down, take that down." Al said, "No, Colonel, don't take that down; that was just a personal question for your personal advice." The hearing was completed. The presiding colonel said, "Lieutenant, there are three things we can do with you. We can send you to a labor battalion, or we can give you another trial with the regiment, or we can send you to Blas for return to the U.S." Al said, "Well, Colonel, its just like I told you. They got plenty of smart and capable officers in the outfit. They don't need me, and I don't want to go to the labor battalion, so it looks to me that all you can do with me is to send me back to the U.S."

All officers reassigned to the U.S. were sent to the camp at Blas, where they were almost like being in a guardhouse and might wait months to get sailing orders. Shortly, Al got orders for immediate return to the U.S. Al went to Blas. He went to the camp commander and said, "Colonel, I am here, but you know how it is, my papers will be weeks getting here. I have been in France nine months without a leave. There is no need to feed and house or bother with me here. I want a two-week leave to Nice and I will be back before my papers get here." The 316th FA had by now just been in France a little over six months, so leaves were starting. Several of our group went to Nice. They came back with a great story of how they met Al having the time of his life, and they were convinced that the Major had court-martialed the smartest man in the outfit.

Field artillery is divided in three groups with many variations. The mortars are short-barrelled for throwing a shell high in the air for a short distance, one to three miles; they were used a good deal in World War I against trench warfare. Then we had howitzers 155mm, or 6 inches, in diameter. They are for intermediate range, three to eight miles. The howitzer has a medium length barrel, so is much more mobile than the rifles. The rifle has a long barrel; a 6-inch rifle would be used in a range of six to twelve miles and is used mostly with high explosive shells for demolition of fortifications, etc. Many of the howitzers were horse-drawn, and we had some horse-drawn at Saumur with which we trained. The artillery uniform included boots and spurs, but in fact we used what we called 8-ton tracklayers. They were heavy for their power but had wide tracks and were speeded up above ordinary field working speeds. We had trouble having them run off the tracks if we weren't careful, but they gave us a good deal more maneuverability than horses. Then we used the same 8-ton tractor to pull a large spool of wire mounted as a cart. This was no real load, so we would go about any place the tractor could go empty. Most of our work was over rolling hills. The biggest concern was adequate grease and lubrication.

My real job was to locate the batteries and the command post, or actually to scout out, with the sidecar, the positions which looked best to me and then suggest them to the Captain and Major. The best land formations are the ones that best protect you from enemy fire and where you can best use natural or artifical camouflage to make you more difficult to locate from land or air. Of course, probable mud, floods, or blowing sands were all considered. Getting the phone lines in was next, then our signalmen were to send signals in case the lines went out. Four to six runners were used as a last resort to maintain communications. We had men located in the front lines with the infantry to notify the battery commander when the infantry wants artillery support, and to let the battery know if shells are falling short or long, and help better identify the target and stay on it.

By Armistice Day, I had been in France for six months, so was qualified to wear the chevron on my sleeve and to have a leave of absence. They didn't come immediately, but by December 7 I had the leave and was all ready. I wanted to see what I could of what the front really looked like. It was pretty hard for the other officers to see me, an outsider, leave while they stayed behind, so we got up a party. Major Manning's brother had been shot down and buried out of Verdun, so he had good reason. All had some reason for a weekend, so we set out in a White staff car with a chauffeur on Satuday noon, December 7. Also with us were Major Sheriet, Captains Brown and Craig, and Chaplain Currie. We went through Nancy on to Pont-à-Mousson—quite a wartorn country. Eight miles out of Metz, we ran out of gas. We found a little, and were only out about two miles when we were dry again. By now, it was getting dark, so I took off afoot to get hotel rooms while the chauffeur looked for gas. I made my way way on to the Hotel de Europe, which was full of light and gaiety. Young officers were everywhere. I went up to a rotund old fellow and asked for a room. He directed me. I went up to see if they were OK for my majors and captains. As I came down the stairway, some English officers called me over and asked if I knew the first man I spoke to, my hell hop. He was the ranking Admiral in the French Navy.

At 10:30 p.m. our party dragged in. We had a delicious cold meal and a good night's sleep.

Still being junior officer, I knew I had to roll out early and find a tank full of gas, so I got the chauffeur and car and set out. The streets were jammed—lots of girls dressed in Alsatian and Lorrainian costumes of many colors. We had one of the biggest cars in town and loaded it up with girls as we went. No gas anywhere. Finally we went to the old fortification which had been German headquarters. They had none, but the quartermaster had some in the next courtyard. We drove right up and filled up. As we were pulling the hose out, a sergeant came up, mad enough to eat us. It was all the gas they had, and the closest was over 100 miles away, but we had it. The M.P. officers came out and wanted to know who we were, where we came from, and how we got into Metz. This was the day the Allies were officially taking over Metz, and because Metz was such a sentimental victory for France, Pershing had agreed that the day would belong to France and no Americans would be seen in Metz that day. All roads were closed by MPs, but he sais, "My orders say, keep them out, not put them out, but leave as soon as you conveniently can."

We got our officers. The French had been on parade since 7 a.m. About 10 the big celebration was held in the Esplanade with President Poincre, P. M. Clemenceau, Marshal Foch, General Pershing, Lloyd George, and all the brass of all the allies. It was surely a colorful occasion. I exchanged salutes with General Pershing, and he looked like he was delighted to see an American. We left again about noon for Verdun. The maps showed all forest around Verdun. There were broken tree trunks, but no trees. The ground was all turned over just as if plowed. Underneath the central city, on a large hill, was a complete town all tunneled out, electric lights and small streetcars, stores and all, as I remember, for about 3500 people, and they lived there.

We located the Manning grave and Quentin Roosevelt's close by. Then the car and the party left for camp, and I spent that night with two 313th Infantry men.

On Monday I visited Verdun and a few citizens living in back of town. I went north and west of Verdun; along the front, equipment, rifles, clothes, were just as they had been left. Horses lay where they fell. Human bodies were all removed, though sometimes it appeared they were only inches under the soil. For relaxation, one could sit and fire rifles as long as you wished, with shells in easy reach.

On Tuesday I went down into the headquarters of Prince Maximillian of Baden. It was under heavy concrete and dirt, with electric lights, shower, bath, wainscoted walls, operating room for the doctor, bay windows for light and view, all very nice.

Wednesday was just one month after Armistice Day. I left Buzancy toward Méziers. Still desolation. On this whole trip I saw very few people. Some of the German camps here were built for good, with mission-type houses for the officers— exposed beams, electricity, water. There were movie theaters, pool halls, everything.

It had rained all day and I was soaked. I stayed this night in a YMCA hotel in Charleville; good bed, good supper, but the Germans had taken all the bedding with them. Charleville is practically on the Belgium border; it was as far as the allies had advanced on November 11. I bought a pair of socks in an open store on Thursday morning. It was about all they had for sale. As I worked south toward Reims, I passed many people on foot, occasionally a pony carrying all their goods back to their homes to start over again. I got to Reims about 1:30 p.m. I was hungry, but the only place to eat was a soup kitchen in a basement, served by the YMCA with no service after 1:30.

The streetcar tracks were cut every few feet by shell fire, and the streets were all torn up. They were sweeping out the cathedral. Part of it stood and parts hung. The stained glass windows were partly blown out early, so they took the rest out to preserve them. Fourteen 15-inch shells had entered the cathedral and thousands of small ones.

The town seemed more alive on Friday morning, and we had a good breakfast. I met a Lieutenant I had seen before. We went up to the chateau, a beautiful sight, and then off to see Belleau Woods. The woods around Belleau are very thick; there are openings planted to wheat with clumps of trees all through, and the higher ground on the sides is covered with big boulders just right to dig under for machine gun nests. The whole area is perfect for defense. How our boys ever got through is fantastic, but the U.S. graves were many. I stayed at Chateau Thierry, at the Hotel de Guerre. I woke up early Saturday to get a train to Paris.

I had spent fifteen months in the army training for one purpose, not to be used by me. I wanted to know what a war-torn country looked like. For a week, I had seen it. I did not get the action; I did get the desolation, silence, devastation of life, homes, and forests. Many small villages had nothing left but a road sign to mark its site. Tanks by the hundreds were battered and burned out, trucks were blown to bits or stuck in mud holes. One could almost feel every bit of the drama as you came on a battery of howitzers just like ours. They tipped over, and the horses lay still in harness just as they fell, the result of a direct hit. The horror was all about; maybe about as impressive to one totally alone, the silence broken only by the patter of rain, as it might have been in the crowd, with the noise, excitement, and reality of imminent death.

We got to the railroad station early. It was crowded. The train for Paris arrived and it was crowded. We heard the news that President Wilson was to arrive in Paris that day. Here we saw the French courtesy in reverse. Women actually got up on the car platform, and men behind grabbed their dresses and pulled them down to the ground. We rushed a door to the compartment where there was still standing room. Our French occupants talked only of throwing us out at the next stop. As soon as that idea calmed a little, I casually pulled out a package of cigarettes and passed them around. They were accepted with the statement that, if they let us stay on, they were paying very dearly for the cigarettes. The second time I passed the cigarettes, two men got up and gave us their seats, and we rode in the seats into Paris, arriving about 8 a.m.

The streets were packed. I saw President Wilson marching down the Champs-Elyseés. The crowd was wild. I went to a comic opera in the afternoon, then found a room in the Hotel Normandy. The evening was a celebration such as I had never seen before or since. You had to keep your overseas cap, and everything else loose, in your pocket if you wanted to keep it. German 77 artillery were parked on all the squares. The girls would pile all over the guns, and the fellows dragged them all over the place, singing all the French war songs. The Star Spangled Banner and the Marsiellais always drew a crowd. Dancing was everywhere. It was President Wilson whom they adored then, but it was also the first night of street lights in four years. This all went on until daylight. I didn't see much excessive drinking, no Americans, but everybody knew everybody and enjoyed it.

On Sunday I got to the railroad station at 7:30 a.m. for a train to Le Havre to see if I could find Ralph. He was located near the railroad with a truck transport company. We spent the afternoon seeing Le Havre, then I got a room at an officer's YMCA. Ralph and I had breakfast together on Monday, then I left for Paris, where I again saw President Wilson in parade. On Thursday, my leave was over. I returned to Nancy by train and on to St. Blin.

I had another leave about April, when I went to Marseille. I walked in the lower part of the city until I came to the cathedral started by Napoleon. It is still under construction, and the plans called for at least a hundred more years to complete, largely mosaic work now. I found myself a rare visitor, as the whole area was off limits to Americans. It was beautiful. They were preparing for the ordination of a new bishop in several days. They said, if I would stay, they would reserve all of one wing for me as representative of the U.S. The French government and military were to occupy the other wing. I wished I could have—maybe I should have.

I met some other Americans, and we went up to Grasse, the center of the perfume industry of France. Large areas were solidly planted to flowers. They were spectacular and gorgeous. The perfume there was the pure essence of the flowers. I remember they put a drop on us in each area of the factory. It was very nice but, when we left in an open car, the scent was oppressive so we had to take our coats off. I went on to Nice and found it beautiful. The French went wild over a loud American band.

We went to a YMCA reception. Two sisters asked us to come to a reception dance at their home the next afternoon. The YMCA man then told us we should surely go. These were the Curtis sisters of Curtis Publishing Company fame (the publisher of the *Saturday Evening Post*). Their father was American consul at Nice. The girls told me to take a streetcar; the orchestra and a group of other officers would be on board and would know where to get off. It was southeast of Nice on a hillside overlooking the bay. My friend and his entire outfit were called back to camp during the night, so I was the only officer on the car with the orchestra. They got off, so I did too.

The home and its setting were beautiful. As you entered the home, a wide stairway led down to the living room. On the wall before you was a life-size portrait of Mrs. Curtis, by Sargent, who was often a house guest. In the garden, it looked like the vistas ran almost to eternity. We talked, we danced; two gals for one man. They were planning a trip to the U.S. soon. They had never been there, but they had marvellous books and pictures of the U.S. They knew personally many of the leaders of the U.S. business, government, social, and entertainment world. General Pershing had spent several rest periods of a few days, staying with them, as had other top military men. They told me a few guests would be dropping in for tea at five o'clock, and I should surely stay. The guests came at five, but they were all major generals or better, so before long I excused myself and returned. The mother was indisposed that afternoon, but she and the girls had spent all their time during the war feeding and entertaining soldiers. I sometimes wonder where they are now.

Spring was bursting into bloom, and everyone was getting anxious to get home. Many of the outfits had arrived in New York with money left in the mess fund, so the obvious thing was to throw a big dinner party, with plenty of entertainment to celebrate homecoming and use up the mess fund.

This was great at first, but it was getting out of hand, so orders came out that all mess funds would be commandeered by the army before arrival in New York. There was only one course for us, and that was to use it up in France. This was the GI mess, not the officers. We paid for our own mess, so there was never a surplus. We sent out jeeps to get vegetables, eggs, meat, fruit, anything for sale that looked good to eat.

One day I got a letter from Pershing's headquarters to explain fully the "enclosed letter." It was to a boy's family stating, "Here it is Easter, and I am over here all alone. You will have Easter eggs; I haven't seen an egg for months." Then a homesick boy let his mind and pencil wander. His mother sent the letter to General Bliss in Washington D.C. Bliss sent it to Pershing for immediate explanation, and Pershing sent it to me, operation officer of the battalion. I called the boy in. "Was he happy?" "Sure." "Was he getting enough to eat?" "Yes, sir." "Did you get up for breakfast on Easter morning?" "Yes, sir." "Were there any eggs on the table when you left?" "Yes, sir." Then I opened the letter, and he realized the reason for the questions. He said he was just homesick and didn't know what to write; he just wanted to tell them he missed them and home. His relatives probably told friends how the boys were underfed in France. Many sad stories in life are true, but many are fantasy.

Maybe I should say a word about cigarettes. I have never been seriously tempted to use them. In my high school days I had a friend several years older who was a chain smoker, Bull Durham, roll-your-own. His fingernails and finger tips were always brown; I guess from nicotine. He was always nervous and, if he wanted a cigarette, he just had to have it. I decided I would never let myself get in the shape he was in. By army days, cigarettes were cleaned up a good deal. I had no desire for them, but someone often wanted one, so I carried them. I got to buying them by the carton, then I found that often, as I came in, a new carton would be on my bunk, so I had those to give away. My friends could always get cigarettes from me, and everyone was happy. In France, however, or almost any other country, people want not only a cigarette but an American cigarette. What the difference in taste was, I do not know, but it must be considerable. In many cases, a cigarette will unlock doors or grant privileges where pleading, or even money, would have little effect.

Finally the drilling, the school classes, the officer's mess, the shows, the leaves were all over, and we moved to Brest for embarkation home—the true objective of all we had done in France. We arrived at Brest but found there was not room on the ship for all of us, so I was assigned to another ship about five days later. It was a disappointment, but they were interesting and full days. I looked up a friend, Polly McVey; she was Hal Paulin's sister-in-law. I had met her at Hal's wedding and had heard a good deal about her. She was YMCA and stationed in Brest. Much had been said of the proportion of time some of the "Y" girls spent with officers, so she had sworn to revise the trend. I looked her up at the "Y" Club. Like everyone, she was delighted to see someone from home, but she shoved me through a door so fast I first thought I was in a closet. She explained to the boys why she was going to talk to an officer, then we had a good talk of all our mutual friends and what we had been doing. The next day we saw some of Brest together. I met a "Y" executive I knew who had a car, so the next day we took a ride all around the Brittany Coast country. It was beautiful, the women were still dressed in their native dress.

By this time, President Wilson was in Paris on his second trip, drawing up the essentials of the Peace Treaty and advancing his famous fourteen points. His passenger ship, the *George Washington*, was in the harbor at Brest waiting his return. We were invited to a reception and dance on board, so I took Polly to that. It was quiet, formal for those with formals, with fancy invitations and programs, but all felt at ease; a good American orchestra and a good evening for a farewell to France.

I was assigned to the *Leviathan* for my return voyage. It formerly had taken a week to turn it around in port, but the U.S. army and navy took on the job, so she was really only in port a little over two days. She used coal, all put from barges into wheelbarrows and wheeled into the bunkers. The barges were lashed to each side of the ship as soon as it hit reasonably calm waters, the army on one side and the navy on the other, with a bonus each trip for the winner. They shoveled day and night; the last shovel went in when they hit rough water again. The minute they got into smooth water, troops and supplies started leaving from one side and boarding from the other. All was lightered from shore to ship.

We had over 12,000 military aboard beside a crew of 2500 navy men. The bunks were five high where I was, and two men could not pass between bunks. Every inch of space was used. The galley was at the head of my bunk, and men were being fed continuously from 6 a.m. to 7 p.m., getting two meals a day. I am not sure of the time for the return trip, but I know it was a record.

Officers mess was on an upper deck. We sat down at tables for three meals. I remember I had been ribbed a good deal for having lots of prunes for our officer's mess, and on the *Leviathan*, we had them for dessert. But no one was worrying about the food. We were going home!

One of the pleasures was that we had on board my old captain, now Major Lavelle, 316th Engineers. He had a fantastic record. They were in seven major engagements. The regiment got seven D.S.C., six of them in Company F. They did not lose a man in action; only one was permanently disabled and he was out against orders.

Captain Lavelle was the only person I saw written up in the news columns of Stars and Stripes for personal bravery. When I met the fellows at home in Imperial, they told me the same story. This was a most remarkable demonstration of the effect of discipline and thorough, intensive training.

After the Armistice, Lavalle was put in charge of all public utilities in the occupied area of Germany. He was surely one of the greatest men of the war. I sometimes regretted I ever left him.

We landed in New York. Everyone felt good. We had several days waiting for travel orders. My mother was there visiting Ethel, and we saw some of New York for a day, then took the boat trip up the Hudson to West Point, where we had several hours before picking up the ship on its return.

I remember a small incident at West Point. We were taking the regular tourist tour, and I was glad to feel like one of them. We came to one small building, and the guide announced that all would stand by a few minutes while he took the lieutenant through this building which was off limits to civilians. I started to stand by until he took my arm, and we went in. That was probably the first time I had thought of rank as separating people. It was of little importance in France in social relations. It wasn't generally the insignia you carried, but the job you held. My commission was granted two months before I even knew it. My job of liaison officer and of battalion adjutant ranked a captain's commission, but it never bothered me or anyone else that I didn't have a commission as captain. It was quite a shock to us when we learned of all the bickering over, and for, rank that went on here in the U.S., but I guess that is normal. Busy people have far less time for nonessentials.

We went on to Camp Lewis about June 20, I thought to be mustered out, but it was only to clear records and be granted 15 days home leave to return to San Francisco for termination. As I recall, we were given $300.00 to get new clothes, to get home, and get a new job. By July 10, 1919, I was a civilian again.

Trip to Durham Colony by Australian students 1919 (in Davis)

George Wilson in uniform in France

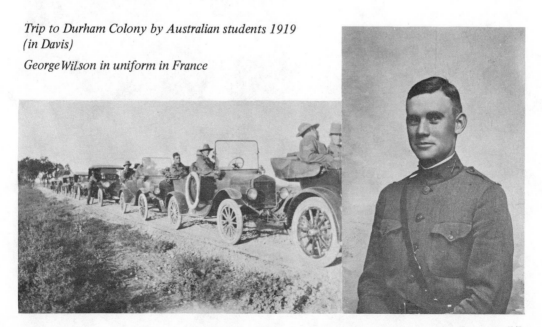

Above, Isabelle in 1916
At right, Isabelle graduating 1918

Ctr right, our wedding party, 1921

Below left, our wedding;
bottom center, Isabelle
Bottom right, George and Isabelle 1924

4
HOME AGAIN 1919-1941

Part of my fifteen day leave was used to return to Imperial and renew my friendship with Isabelle Mack, with whom I had corresponded all during the twenty-two months absence, and to whom I brought a small gift. It was a pleasant reunion. I also looked at possible ranch leasing or management opportunities. The valley itself did not look as good as when I left, and cotton prices had dropped disastrously. It was just as hot; no air conditioning yet. Wages sounded good, but it hardly seemed the place to start all over again.

I made several trips up and down the central valley and the coast area. I had about $4000 available, but the opportunity to rent or buy cheap was nil. Each trip I would stop and talk to Tommy Thompson of the AH Department in **Davis**. Professor True was in the East. The change from Lieutenant FA in France to job hunter in California was pretty sudden. Things had changed a good deal in two years, so I expect I was a little confused.

On one trip, I stopped in Berkeley to see Dean Hunt and ask his advice on some issues. He said, "Well, what is your life plan for the future?" I hadn't been asked that question before and wasn't sure of the answer. He said, "Well, if you will first settle that question, then as these problems come along, the main issue will have already been settled, and all you will then have to do will be to settle the details, but that is difficult until the main question is decided." I haven't fully followed his suggestion, but I have worked at it and it helps. I recommend it to others.

Finally, I received a wire from Professor Thompson asking if I would accept an appointment as instructor to set up a Range Cattle Experiment Station and operate it. I sent back a wire as follows:

Professor Thompson: You know that I do not really want the job. I want to farm, but I haven't found what I want so, if you wish to accept me under those conditions, I will accept.
— George H. Wilson

I got one back:

You can be sure you are not the man we want, but we have looked all over for him without success, so if you want to accept the job under those circumstances, you are hired.
— J. I. Thompson

So I went to Davis to start in my new job at $183.33 per month. I rented a bedroom on the second floor of Professor Thompson's home. They had two young boys. I was told to get ready to start right out with a course in swine management, one in feeds and feeding, and a section in livestock judging. I was assigned charge of the cattle on the U.C. Davis farm. The herdsman was Alex McDonald, the top herdsman and cattle feeder and judge in the U.S., so my responsibility was minimal in that area.

Then, in spare time, I was to plan the Range Cattle Experiment Station, locate one, lease it, and then operate it. We visited ranches in Fresno County which looked good. Then the Barrett ranch in ElDorado County at Shingle Springs was available. It was fairly close to Davis, and Dean Hunt, who went with me to see them, wanted to be sure we had a ranch that was rough enough so we would not be accused of selecting one too easy to show results. We picked the Barrett ranch of 3500 acres, in two parts, for the winter range. The home place on French Creek, two miles south of Shingle Springs, and the Meader place on the Green Valley road. The mountain (summer) range was private patented land surrounded by the El Dorado National Forest on which we were permittees. It ran from about twenty miles east of Placerville to the Silver Creek Camp 25 miles further east, then northeast of Wright Lake to the summit at 9,000 feet.

We leased the ranch for seven years, because the university economists told us you could always figure on seven good years price—wise after a war. We bought all the cattle, 555 head, cows, calves, and bulls.

The Barrett brothers, Ernest and Phil, had been partners for many years. They had married sisters and their homes were across the road from each other. They still ran their cattle together, but they didn't speak to each other. All communication was through the children.

As soon as the lease was completed, Phil and his family moved out. Ernest and his wife stayed, and I lived in their house and boarded with them. Ernest was pretty well crippled with rheumatism, but he was a great help to me, advising me in many ways. His wife was very motherly by nature, and she was quite solicitous to see that I was well cared for.

The ranch house was about 40 miles from Sacramento, 55 miles from Davis, and about 12 miles west of Placerville. Shingle Springs once had a shingle mill, but it was better known in the mining days as the end of the railroad. They said that, in the early days, the railroad freight sheds were four-hundred feet long, and they kept one-hundred stage teams at Shingle to take passengers and equipment back up into the mines. It was a lively place then, and many of the relics of those days were still around in 1920. Mrs. Barrett used to tell me that, when she was young, she could stand on the front porch of the house we lived in and call 3000 miners from there. On the ranch were the remains of quite a few old houses, often with the old chimney still standing.

The ranch had a great deal of brush, small oak and other trees on it. There were many remains of old ditches to carry water to the mines, but there were also, on the bushy hillsides, still furrows showing the land had been plowed, probably for wheat. Wheat was used locally by the miners, but also hauled by eight-mule teams to Sacramento. The records show that there were more acres farmed in California in the

60

active mining days than were farmed any time later up to about 1940.

Grapes grew on a hillside near the house, and there was also a winery. One of the vats had about two feet of wine turned to vinegar; it was excellent vinegar.

The state highway from Sacramento to Placerville was the first one built under the original highway bond issue. It was made of macadam with some experimental stretches of concrete. It must have been about fourteen feet wide, as two small cars could pass with slow speed and caution. Turnouts were scattered along for the cautious to use. The highway engineers cut down a few of the sharpest curves and deepest dips in the road, but a minimum of grading and dirt-moving was practiced, so every trip over the road warranted considerable caution, not always practiced.

On the Davis campus were one-hundred Australians still in uniform who were assigned to a year's instruction in agriculture enroute home from France. I was assigned to help them make the adjustment to American ways and customs. I took a group of them to visit Woodland, then much larger than Davis. We passed an undertaker's office on Main Street. A couple rushed back to see if they saw what they thought they saw, a large window full of flowers. An undertaker's office was supposed to be sad and gloomy, but here it was bright with flowers. They laughed and laughed. It was a new idea. As it was hot, we went into an icecream parlor and ordered sundaes. The ice cream parlor was a new and delightful experience, but ordering a *sundae* was a whole new experience. We returned to that spot several times, partly because the environment was delightful, but mainly for the fun of ordering a sundae. That was a special pleasure for a long time.

By 1919, Cal was playing football again rather than rugby, but our Australian friends wanted me to get up a rugby team for them to play against. They knew we didn't play rugby, but maybe I could get three or four Americans so we would call it the American team, and they would fill the team out to get up a game. I told them not to be in such a hurry; I would get a rugby team to play them. I saw Bob Lockhart and Babe Slater, who were running sheep on the Conway Ranch. They got a team together, and the day arrived with a good crowd. After about 15 minutes of play, I noticed hardly any leaders of the group were actually playing, so I went over to their benches and said, "I thought you wanted to play rugby." They pointed to Babe Slater and said, "Play against that fellow! We have seen and played rugby all over the world, but we have never seen anything like that. We don't want to play against him; we want to *watch* him!"

Babe had played in the Olympics twice, being team captain the second time, and winning the gold medal each time. I enjoyed the Australians very much, but I didn't always accompany them. About fifteen of them married American girls; about half of these returned and lived in the Sacramento area.

Jim Wilson came from Wyoming as a wool expert at the same time I did. He had several years of university research and teaching. We were in the office talking when he said he had to go home and get ready for next day's class. I asked him what he did to get ready. He had taught the subject for several years and knew what he was going to say. Jim said, "Yes, but to be a good teacher, you must be a good actor and be just as well prepared in how you say it as in what you say, so I need time to practice my act." It seemed more humorous than instructive at the moment, but I have never forgotten its truth.

61

The military had been a good experience in instructing, still I often thought, here I am teaching university classes with no preparation in the field of education. It takes a four-year education major to teach grammar school, but no such training to teach university classes, and nobody ever came into one of my classes to see how I was doing. I would have welcomed advice and counsel in the art of instruction. I understand and agree with academic freedom for a teacher to teach the truth as he or she sees it, but I could never understand freedom from accountability for the quality of the performance. The idea of academic freedom and control of the university by academic senate was getting its start while I was a student.

The matter was brought to a head somewhat by Dean Hunt, who sent a communication to all the faculty of the College of Agriculture, saying that, if a farmer came to the campus seeking assistance or advice, they should arrange to see him as soon as possible and take time to help solve his problem. Students should have access to faculty members when convenient, but faculty should post on their doors some definate hours each week when they would be available to see students.

Professors Lipman and Bird wrote to the dean that they had no intention of ever visiting with any farmers coming to the office, nor of posting definite hours to see students, and they wanted no more interruptions of their day's work, so they were having the phones taken out of their offices. These two men were dedicated and diligent workers. The dean's suggestion may not have been entirely appropriate in their cases, but they became the heroes of the campus with the academic senate group. I later saw the ultimate outgrowth of that independent spirit.

Professor True had come from Nevada to Davis. He and Dean Hunt realized that California had a great deal of rough land above 3000 feet elevation which was given little thought by the state or by the university, but which some day would be very important to the state. They brought Professor Pat Kennedy from Nevada, a botanist and specialist in plants above 3000 feet elevation. They gave him five years of uninterrupted study to come up with a proposal for the best uses of those lands. He seemed delighted with the opportunity and challenge. He wanted first to inventory and develop an herbarium of all the plants in the area. Our summer range ran 3000 to 9000 feet. We furnished him camps, cook, and camp tender, horses, Graflex camera, bedding, all he asked for to carry out his work and, of course, checked in with him often. He collected quite a large herbarium, but it was only a start. The following year he submitted a budget calling for camera, camp outfit, cook, all for his exclusive use. The university had all these things to be requisitioned for special use, so they cut them out of his budget. I went to see him about the next summer's work. He said he wasn't going out. He had notified the university he didn't move until he had all he needed for his exclusive use. I asked if what we had last summer was OK. He said, "Sure, but I have to have my own." I asked "Well, can't you work on the university range until you want to go elsewhere?" "No, I don't move until I get all I requested for myself." He didn't go out that year, or the next or ever. He didn't have a class or a research project. He didn't do a thing for the university, and he did give away the entire herbarium he had collected the first year, which certainly belonged to the university. Yet he collected his full salary. He lived at the faculty club, on the Berkeley campus, as a living example of academic freedom. I saw him there 25 or 30 years later, so I suppose he stayed until retirement or death, demonstrating his academic freedom to use his time as he saw fit.

Academic freedom, as such, wasn't very active in Davis in my student years, nor did I see it in Davis as an instructor. There was, however, a very active debate and division between the applied science group and the "anything which adds to the sum total of human knowledge is worthwhile" group. The politics of these two groups was just as active and disruptive on the campus as was the politics of the sixties. The Davis faculty was not initiating this division. It came from Berkeley, but it was virile in Davis, wasting a good deal of the time and energy of the faculty and interfering with the volume and quality of teaching and research.

One day Dr. W. W. Robbins and another professor put up notices that at 4 p.m. each Tuesday in the Pomology auditorium, there would be a seminar on "How to Instruct." They waited with fear and trembling to see who would show up. The place was about filled. They discussed how to prepare and present a lecture or a research problem. The series was completed, and the Davis faculty settled down.

While my Range Cattle Experiment Station project was under the Animal Husbandry Division in Davis, it was also under the Experimental Station. At first, the director was Dr. Webber, a citrus specialist from southern California. He divided the Davis staff into four groups. Livestock included irrigation and Ag engineering. We would meet at night at least monthly. Any new proposed projects were described with samples of data sheets to be kept, etc. Then we had questions and answers. Often, knowledge of similar work came from unexpected sources. Irrigation people might say, ' We want information in this area and would like you to add one more column to keep data for us." The comments from other departments were often very helpful, and greatly increased interest in other work going on. Progress reports were made as time permitted. I found these evening meetings very helpful to me, but I guess it smacked a little of administration direction of a faculty effort and Berkeley soon sent us a new director of the experiment station who didn't get you out at night or give any counsel on the research work.

Professor Gordon H. True believed in fundamental research, but he also believed the university should be helping livestock men with their current problems. He was transferred to Berkeley to teach animal husbandry from a book, without animals. J. I. Thompson, with thoughts similar to Professor True, found it more agreeable to go to San Luis Obispo. Dr. W. W. Robbins, for similar reasons, was passed up as Chancellor of the Davis campus.

In 1919 and 1920, cars had individual characteristics. There were still many medium-sized and small manufacturers building cars they had designed and built. For rough roads and durability, Dodge was the leader, and that was what I wanted. But so did everyone else, which meant many months of waiting, so I got the imitation Dodge, the Dort, in exchange for some of my liberty bonds, which I had bought with my cotton windfall from Imperial.

I enjoyed teaching and working with the students and was pleased to be initiated into the Phi Alphs-Iota fraternity as faculty honorary member. They are now the SAEs in Davis.

Harold Wadsworth was instructor in irrigation. He planned to devote his life to university teaching, but he wanted to have a piece of land so he would always feel a little independent. I wanted land to farm, so, one day, we drove down to see the Holland Land Company land which was being subdivided. We looked at land priced from $250 to $325 per acre. We selected a 106-acre lot along a main canal and bought it together, 10 percent down and 10 percent a year. The land was in barley. There was a house for the tenant and a row of corn cribs along the south side, as it had been in corn. I had to borrow most of the $1800 down payment from my father, but I felt more prosperous; I had started on my way.

The harvest was abundant for that time, 6000 pounds per acre and at harvest $3.25 per hundred pounds. But the economists at Davis, as well as grain buyers, all said the price had to go up as the demand was almost unlimited. One day in the spring, Mr. Otten of the Holland Land Company called and recommended I take the current price of $2.25, which fortunately I did. The price slid on down to .65 and didn't get back up to $1.00 until next season.

The first year on the range cattle experiment was one of getting acquainted with the land, the cattle, the cattlemen, and what was most needed. We started by ear-tagging, using aluminum tags for each animal, large or small, and preparing an identity card for each showing age, color, markings, weight, calving date, etc.

We set a one-ton scale in the cattle chute, so we got individual weight before they left for the mountains. We later got a scales at George A. Wilson's mountain camp, so we could weigh them as they left the mountains in the fall and again as they arrived at the home ranch after the drive. This gave us the gain on the summer mountain range and the shrink on the trip home. With the 555 head, we would miss some or err in reading a tag, but with each marked individually, we got good figures on how the calves, the yearlings, the mature cows, and the bulls did. These figures were very helpful in moderating the proposed Forest Service grazing fee increases. They were the only such figures in the country. It was a shame they were not continued after I left.

Practically all the cattle in that area were shorthorn blood. (There was one Hereford herd.) We bought one white and two roan shorthorn bulls, purebred and big. They had been raised on level land around Davis and were fat. As I rode the range in the winter, I carried part of a sack of rolled barley with me and, as I would come to one of them, I put out a little pile of barley. I told this to Fred Bixby as I was driving him to Sacramento. He was then president of the California Cattlemen's Association and one of the most prominent cattlemen in the U.S. He told the story in several cattlemen meetings about how this ridiculous young university professor was feeding barley to range bulls. I am sure it helped those bulls make the adjustment and helped us get more calves.

For branding, weighing, etc., I would have a small group of students come up from Davis. Irene Scheiber, a Barrett daughter, came home for a visit and suggested I bring up a group of boys from Davis and have a barn dance some night. We went down French Creek and arranged to use the Bowman barn with the dance to be in the hayloft. There was a little hay and farm equipment in the loft. We went down to clean it up and found a hardwood floor which polished up beautifully by pulling a bale of hay back and forth. It had been a dance hall in mining days.

About ten boys came up from Davis. The girls and old folks all turned out, we had good live music, and a big dinner at midnight. The boys had a big time, and it comes up for discussion every time I go up to El Dorado County. A fire took the barn some years ago.

Teaching and starting the Range Cattle Experiment Station kept me pretty busy,

64

but I still had time to write a few letters to my Imperial friend, Isabelle Mack; just nice friendly letters. I went out some with Pearl Newkirk, a nurse at the Woodland Clinic. We talked some of engagement, but I guess I wasn't quite ready for that. Then I went with Ernestine Bates of Davis. Her father was the Davis doctor and also the doctor for the university. They lived on the south side of the street going from the railroad station to the campus. She had finished high school in Sacramento, so had many friends there as well as in Davis. She was a very capable and fine girl, and I was beginning to think maybe she was the one, though we never talked of engagement. But I could see it might be imminent, so I decided I better go down to Imperial and see again how it felt to be out for a walk with Isabelle Mack. I went down in the fall of 1920 and stayed in the home of my old friends, George and Dorothy Paulin. I went over to Bella's that evening. We took a walk down some of the quiet streets of Imperial. It just felt *good*, so finally I said, "Why don't we just quit fooling around and decide to get married?" It seemed to hit a responsive chord and so, as soon as I could get up my courage, I asked Mr. Mack, and it was OK all around.

The letters to Imperial were a little more regular now. I went down to Los Angeles in the winter and got a diamond ring. I went to the principal jeweler there and looked at many stones. I didn't have much money, so I had to stay with the smaller ones, but I wanted the brightest, clearest, most perfect stone I could get. They may have been all alike, but I bet I had the best. There were no credit cards in those days. I went on down to Imperial, got the ring on the finger, and felt she was at least partly mine. The date was set for April 17, 1921. That was largely because on March 31 she would be 20 years old, a more reasonable age for marriage. The year before, Bella had gone to college at Whittier, majoring in music, but this year she worked in the bank in Imperial.

Ernestine Bates became secretary to Roy Hagen, then manager of the California Cattlemen's Association. Roy and I had worked a great deal together in college, in Alpha Zeta, the Ag Club, the Cal Ag Monthly, and the small group who worked with B. H. Crocheron. Roy then became president of Union Ice Company of Los Angeles, a subsidiary of Standard Oil Company of California. About 1938, I sent Roy several crates of green asparagus to try freezing it for the market. He sent up samples. It wasn't very good, but it was the beginning of frozen asparagus.

About the same time, I was on the train going to Los Angeles and met Ernestine Bates. She was still Roy's secretary and loved it. She was quite an accomplished horsewoman and prominent in the arts and club life of Los Angeles, quite the successful professional woman. I admired her, but I was comfortable and happy with my helpmate.

Back at Shingle Springs, the winter of 1920-21, we organized the French Creek Farm Center. I was elected secretary, so I got into the swing of Farm Bureau again. There was heavy brush on much of the range and some snow with much freezing, so the grass started late. We fed hay all winter, and still the cows were thin; we also found several aborted calves. It may have been accident or nutrition, and there was a chance it was contagious. The calf crops in the area were lower than optimum so, with Dr. Hayes of Davis, we set up a study to see if we could determine the cause and a solution.

The cattle got pretty thin in the winter, improving as the grass grew in the spring and most getting pretty fat in the summer, being in good shape as they came out of the mountains in the fall. The cows calved in the later winter and spring so, if cows were fat in the fall and didn't calve but were thinner in the spring, we had lost a good deal of meat and money—and no calf. We tried to see if, by feeling inside the cow, we could determine pregnancy and, if not pregnant, sell them while fat in the fall. Of the pregnant ones, we could sometimes determine a good idea of the calving date. This also helped in studying abortion. If they had a calf coming in the fall, it must be accounted for. Thirty cows in which we could not feel any fetus were sent down to Davis for closer attention. Most of them calved, as it turned out. But it was a start, and if it had been continued after I left, we would have been further along in pregnancy determination today.

For the cattle drive, we left the ranch by daylight in May to make the drive to the mountain, about 35 miles. We went up the old road to El Dorado, then to Diamond Springs, and over the hill into the west end of Placerville, arriving about 7:30 a.m. As we entered Placerville, there was always a woman waving her apron and shouting to keep the cattle off her place. She just excited them and us, as we were about to enter the main street of town and drive the full length, stores just opening, and especially the bulls walking up the sidewalks looking in the windows, sometimes seeing their reflection and wondering what to do, while we sat quietly and wondered too. At the top of the hill, five miles above Placerville, we would stop and rest the cattle. There was always good grass and good clear water in an irrigation ditch for them. People were just beginning to put up fences then.

We would drive on to Pacific House and corral the cattle for the night. We then went on to Riverton, 23 miles above Placerville across the American River, up the Icehouse hill to the McConnell place for grazing until about July 4 to 15, when we gathered again and went on up to Silver Creek and up to the summit northeast of Wright's Lake.

We had good water for the cattle in that area, but still some of the campers, for fear or fun, I do not know, would feel they had to drive the cattle off if they came near and often have their dogs chase them. People may need a little jogging if they are getting fat, but not cattle.

One of our projects was to work out with the Forest Service a statement on the back of all campfire permits, saying there was plenty of room on the forest lands for both cattle and people if everyone was considerate. Do not let children or dogs chase the cattle, do not camp at a water hole, etc. It was a little thing but it was very helpful for a number of years.

In all that big country, the cattle were turned loose. We just had a few drift fences to keep them from straying too far. The fences would be across a natural travel route. They were two- or three-wire. We put a staple in the post just above and below where each wire went. The staples stuck out about ½ inch, then a nail was dropped through the two staples outside the wire. As we left in the fall the nails were pulled out, the wire dropped to the ground, and the nail dropped back in place for next spring. The process is reversed on return. If fences were left up, the frost and snow would break some wires, and trees or branches could fall across the wires and break them, so it was better to drop them.

When we leased the Barrett ranch and bought the cattle, we also bought the brand, meaning all cattle carrying the brand. Several years before, coming out of the mountains, someone had shot a yearling steer in one eye. It became quite wild and took off from the herd near Diamond Springs and they could not get him back. He just stayed there alone, grazing where the grass was good, eating hay around the lumber company corral in the winter. He was now five years old, big, fat, horned and wild, so people became afraid of him and wanted him out. We got about five fellows with pistols and rifles and left early one morning to get him. He was pretty cagey, but after covering the area on foot, horseback, and pickup, we finally located him and dropped him. We had a tackle to hang him in a tree, and cleaned him so we could get him in the pickup. We skinned him at the ranch and took one side down to Davis to the university dining room. The other half we kept, using some fresh, but corned all the rest in a big, wooden barrel. Mrs. Barrett knew just how to do it and season it. Corned beef is usually made of brisket, flanks, and all the cheaper cuts of cow meat, and can still be good. This corned beef was made out of prime steer meat and was wonderful. Judging from the side we weighed in Davis, he was about a 1350 pound steer. We also cured our own bacon, ham, and olives while we were there. Some of those were excellent, some not so good.

††† The Farmer Takes a Wife

Our wedding date was getting closer, and I hadn't panned near enough gold for a wedding ring. I decided to go up on the hill on the ranch and see a miner, Mike Ryan, so I at least could have gold mined on the ranch. He was happy to cooperate. He moved out the wood behind his stove, opened a little trap below the wood pile, pulled out his chamois bag of gold nuggets, and weighed out what he thought was right. He said I must have the ring made of pure gold. He said I should save my money and pay him after the wedding. I told the jeweler to make the ring as near pure as he possibly could. When we returned to the ranch with both the wife and the ring, Mike came down the hill to see them. He said he was very much pleased by both and insisted the gold be a gift so, really, another Irishman furnished my wife's wedding ring.

Going to my wedding, I set out for Los Angeles in the Dort, went to the life insurance company, and borrowed $300, saw my folks, and went on down to Imperial by way of San Diego, which was the only way then. It was a two-day trip. On my way over from San Diego, I stopped at Jacumba at a motel, reserved a room for Sunday night, and paid a boy to be sure and have some wild flowers in the room to make it look cheery.

We had a very nice wedding in the Imperial Methodist Church on Sunday, April 17, 1921, at 4 p.m. My father performed the ceremony. Brother Ralph was best man, and Bella's brother Bill and Ernest Machey were ushers. George Paulin sang the solos. We went over to Bella's sister's house, Eleanore and Dee Anderson's, for the reception, then back to Bella's home to dress for our trip north. The whole crowd, it seemed, followed us over to Mack's.

I looked the situation over. My car was in the alley. I thought I could just turn right across the yard to the street and lose them before they got reorganized. Outside of town in Imperial all was open desert. By the time we left, it was dark, and I could go any way I wanted. I thought I had left all of them, then a headlight or two would show up. Ours were not on. We would lose them again, and then they would catch up.

It was full moon, and it shone on our windshield like a lighthouse, and they would see us and catch up again. Finally, we took off for Jacumba and got maybe ten miles out when BANG—BANG—BANG went our connecting rods. Fortunately, George Paulin and Dot followed us and pulled us back to El Centro to the Barbara Worth Hotel. We left the car in the garage to be repaired by noon next day, and we spent the night in the Barbara Worth—without wild flowers.

We went over the lawn and into the street at Bella's home all right, but in doing it, the oil pan hit the curb and knowcked the oil plug out and drained all our oil. We spent the next night in San Diego, Bella not feeling too well. Then we went up to the Mission Inn in Riverside. It was about 8 p.m. when we got there, but they gave us a good dinner. One of the staff came to the room with hot water bottle and probably aspirin, as Bella's throat was getting quite sore by then, not the way she had planned the honeymoon.

The Mission Inn was considered by many to be the finest hotel in the world. The art, the chapel, the whole place was beautiful. It was too bad we couldn't fully enjoy it. I had reserved the room on university stationery, so it was $5.00 per day for each one for room and meals. We had a five-course dinner; eight dollars was the regular rate.

We spent several days at my folks in Los Angeles seeing the sights. We spent a night in Santa Barbara, then, as we were going over the twisting, hilly, dirt roads to Santa Maria, a bearing began to bang again. An oil pipe had not been put in right at El Centro. We took it easy and got to a garage, but more of that $300 stopped there. Santa Maria Inn was a very nice stop, as was Paso Robles Inn. Next was the old Del Monte Hotel at Monterey. As we drove in, the Dort looked awfully small beside all the Packards, Pierce Arrows, Cadillacs, Peerless, Locomobiles, etc. We had a beautiful, big room, large fireplace, davenports, lovely original paintings, but Bella was not feeling well so she went right to bed. The grounds were large and beautiful. The next mroning, we took the 17-mile drive and had lunch at Pebble Beach Lodge. Then we drove to Palo Alto to see Aunt Florence, Uncle Oliver, and Winifred, Florence Mary, and Oliver Jr. on the Stanford campus. There Bella went to the doctor. He said she had a quinzy sore throat and painted it with silver nitrate, so it very soon got better. Fortunately, she was feeling better by the time she was introduced to the U.C. Range Cattle Experimental Station.

††† A "Home on the Range"

The house had a large kitchen, dining room, living room, and two bedrooms. On the back porch was a wooden sink with a faucet for running water and a hand pump, if need be. At the end of the porch was a bathroom with a bathtub. The other now-customary bathroom fixtures were located out back with a new moon cut out on the side. The water came from a close-by spring. In the kitchen was a restaurant-size stove which could really use up fire wood. It did have coils and a tank for hot water if there was a fire.

I heard the community planned a proper charivari, but I didn't know when. I told the groceryman to provide ice cream, cakes, and plenty of food for the occasion, but unfortunately, we went to Davis for a weekend and heard of a great party at the house on our return. Everything and about everyone was there except the "charivaried." We received a nice welcome from our university friends in Davis and then settled down to business as married folks.

In May, we decided to take a ride up the road we would drive the cattle over. On the old, dirt road, you went right through the big pines, firs, and cedars, and the rain came down with plenty of lightning and thunder. I am sure Bella felt a long way from home, not only in miles but hills, mud, timber and lightning—all foreign to Imperial. We went to church every Sunday we could at the old Methodist Church right at the head of the main street of Placerville, the road dividing on each side. Sunday School was downstairs. Church was upstairs, a fine large chapel. The Minister would see before him twenty-three to twenty-nine people, mostly women and elderly. It is too bad it wasn't restored as a landmark.

††† Dr. Barrows

Dr. David Prescott Barrows was the president of the University of California. He sent word he would like to camp with his family on the summer range on Silver Creek. He would like to see it first, so, in May, we drove up in the Ford pickup to the Chimney, about 43 miles above Placerville. Here we parked the car about a half-mile off the highway and walked six miles into camp. We got to Silver Creek, the snow about a foot deep on the land and the creek high. The road crossed the creek, or we could have followed the creek over rough land without crossing. He just peeled off to to the waist, tied it all up in his shirt, and jumped right in. I was right with him but, BOY, it was cold! Of course, we had to cross the creek a second time going in, and it was colder. We shoveled the snow away from the camp door, went in and stoked up the fire, cooked a good supper, and got the camp dried out and warmed up a little for a good night. Coming out, we took the rougher way. It was a great experience.

When his vacation time came, he put his horse on the steamer for Sacramento. He was to come up to Sacramento, get the horse and ride it up to Shingle Springs, spend the night with us and then ride on about 60 miles up to the camp. The day came but he didn't arrive at our place, so I looked everywhere I could think of that night and next morning. Then the phone rang and he was in Placerville. He left Sacramento OK and rode to Folsom, then up the Green Valley Road to a little store about five miles northwest of our place. They had no bed for him, but told him he could sleep in the hayloft. He asked for dinner, but they sold him some soda crackers and told him how their folks had come around the Horn. He figured they had brought the soda crackers with them. They didn't have a phone, so he rode into Placerville and called us. I took a man to ride his horse on up while Dr. Barrows rode with me. They had Bella and me over to dinner a time or two when we were up there. It was a delightful family. He rode the horse a good deal in the mountains, then he put his family on the Stage and he rode sixty miles down to the ranch, stopping at night and just rolling up in a saddle blanket and one extra blanket and sleeping along the road. He then took the Stage to Berkeley for a regents meeting, though being also a major general in the California National Guard, he was quite disappointed that he wasn't heading for a national guard camp starting at that time in Yosemite Valley.

He left the horse with us, saying his son, Tom, would be up soon to ride the horse down to Berkeley. Several weeks later, Tom arrived. A fine fellow, and he was enjoying it and stayed several days with us, which we enjoyed also. Then he set off, probably 6:30 a.m. one morning, but he was back about 10 a.m. saying that might be fine for his Dad but not for him. Later, Butch Powers, a student at Davis, visited us and he rode the horse back to Davis. Butch was later Senator and then Lieutenant Governor of California.

Dr. Barrows had a great life. He was director of education in the Philippines. He spent a good deal of World War I in Russia with the U.S. Secret Service. He was a great horseman and student of horses. While his family was in camp up there on the range, he would see Tony Lowmiller start out every morning on an old buckskin mare with a few good jumps and a run before she settled down. I think she was 23 years old and had nineteen colts.

Dr. Barrows was much impressed by the stamina, longevity, and productivity of this mare. He had seen many finer animals, but felt that in our concentration on a few characteristics such as speed, style, size, color, etc., we were missing some of these fundamentals like stamina and fertility in the bloodlines, and we should preserve these qualities too.

We had a breeding program at Davis sponsored by the U.S. Cavalry. They sent to the university at Davis a son of Man of War, who himself had an impressive track and show record. He was for breeding selected mares to improve the bloodlines in this area.

Dr. Barrows wanted the stallion to mix his highly successful genes with the buckskin mare's for stamina, longevity, and productivity. Carol Howell, in charge of horses at Davis, saw the mare and said he wouldn't even allow her on the campus. Dr. Barrows was surely not using rank to get privilege. I expect he intended to give the mare and colt to the university. Sometimes a great mind meets a weaker one and a great idea is lost.

††† The Strange Life of a Professor on a Mountain Ranch

Bella made several trips with me to the mountains. Sometimes we made beds of fir boughs and slept on them for a mattress. We had plenty of blankets and a tarpaulin over the top, so it was warm, but sometimes the tarp would be covered with a heavy frost.

Going to McConnell Camp, which was the lowest of three mountain camps, required quite a winding climb over an old lumber road. But coming back, if in a hurry or with a guest who needed a thrill, we came to a turn where we could get out and cut a small tree, tie a rope around the top of the tree to the rear bumper and then go straight down the hill pulling the tree against the branches. It was a sure thriller for any tenderfoot from Davis.

I took Dean Hunt up to see the summer range one day. We were driving along an old road when we came to a few cattle. He asked me to stop the car so he could watch them. He said he had written several books on the nutritional needs of cattle, and according to any book he wrote or had read, there just wasn't enough feed on the ground to maintain a cow, to say nothing of fattening her. The cattle up there get some browse, some grasses, some legumes, etc. It has to be very strong feed. The browse called birch has a berry covered with a honeylike ooze which is very fattening. The same was true of the cactus, grasses and shrubs on the Viscaino Desert in Mexico.

Gathering the cattle in the fall was an interesting operation. About one-third of the cattle were belled, so there was usually a bell or two in any group. As we put salt in the salt logs during the summer, we would call the cattle to come get the salt. At the end of the summer we would withhold the salt. At the first snowfall, usually in September, they tend to move down to the lower areas. We would go out and call them, and, being salt-hungry, a good many come in. We would have a holding field with good feed to hold them until we had a good bunch to drive. We weighed them at Wilson's corrals if possible, then drove them down the road to the home place. Some were always left behind. Most were fairly easy to gather during the ten days or two weeks before the next snow but, if we had good weather after that, they seemed to want to scatter out and get as high as possible. Finding them then and getting them out was a real job.

The fall of 1921-22 was a bad one, and we were short thirty or more head. The snows were early and heavy. We went up to the upper camp, 7,200 feet, near Barrett Lakes. The cabin was cold, and a fire didn't seem to warm it much so the nights were cold. We would get out early, go out and break the ice on the spring for a bucket of water, build up a good fire in the cook stove, and get breakfast. If we left a bucket of water on the floor near the stove, it would be covered with ice by the time breakfast was over. We would put on all the clothes we had, chaps and hooded stirrups, and then tie a barley sack around each shoe to keep them drier and warmer. We found all the cattle and were driving down the trail from camp. The new snow was heavy, and the cows would actually nudge the calves out in the lead to break the trail, and if the calves hesitated, the cows would force those or some other calves into the lead. Somebody was thinking.

We had the last of our cattle on the road home when we met Burt Granlies going up to get his last cattle out. We sent ours on with our cowboys and I went back with Burt to his camp northeast of Ice House. I had never been there before, and Ernest Barrett said the mare I was riding had never been there. It was late in the year, all the telephone lines were down, and the rangers were out for the winter.

We rode out early in the morning to a crossing on the creek. Burt said it was the only crossing in a mile or two each way. Then he sent me off to the right to look for any cattle, but especially a heifer who should have calved. I looked until I found her and the calf about noon in a little grass area among the trees. She was actually leaning against a tree. In that small area the snow was all tramped out. It was like being in a snow-barrier corral.

I walked back and forth, making several new trails out into the snow, but she was confused and determined not to try again to get out. Finally I got them out and up onto a clear ridge toward camp, but the days were short and I could see we would never make camp, so I drove them down into a sheltered clump of trees, then went back to the ridge to get my bearings. I could easily see the mountain which rose just beyond the camp. I picked out several constellations of stars to help guide me to the camp, but I soon found that is little help if the trees are thick and tall and the constellations go down over the horizon. We came to a well-worn trail, and I felt quite secure, even with the mountain lions screaming in various directions. We came to a very large tree. The mare stopped and went to the right, leaving the trail. I circled around until we hit the trail, went to the same tree and turned off to the right again. We went back to the trail and repeated the same. I didn't know any better than she did, so I let her go. We soon came to the creek but not the crossing. I gave her her head, and she went down the creek and then up the creek a couple of times but no crossing. Then she stood a minute or two and with a big lunge we went into the creek and up the other bank. But after a step or two, her front hooves and then her rear were clawing a steep granite rock. Quick as I could I got my feet out of the stirrups and threw myself off onto the granite, then onto the narrow ground on the edge of the creek. I could see the big gray mare right behind me, her tail ending on the granite, her head over the creek bank. I shook myself and got her feet placed just where I wanted them, and also her head, when she gave a premature lunge and, with a big splash, she was in the creek. I could imagine a broken leg and a bad night, but I got down in the ice water. She got up okay, and I got her back up on the bank on foot. I crawled around until I found a trail at the edge of the granite. I led her up it and got back on, then she went like she knew where. That was good until we came to the main wagon road. Here I was a little concerned, for I wasn't sure, but we decided to go to the right and in a mile or two I saw a light. Burt had climbed up a tree and hung a lantern. It looked good to me. I pulled in at 11:30 p.m., the finest welcome I ever got anywhere. Burt was afraid he might have to look up a frozen, crippled, dumb college kid in the morning. We were equally happy to be home.

He had found a bunch of cattle, so next morning we took some hay out for them, got them back to the corral for a better feed, and the next morning set out for home. So far as Burt was concerned, this university kid was no longer a tenderfoot but was a part of the accepted brotherhood.

Earlier that fall I had taken four men up to the upper camp to build a log corral. Deer season had opened about a week before. We woke up the first morning to a light rain, good weather for buck hunting, so I told three of them to go get their bucks. They went off on foot, and within an hour one came back and wanted three horses saddled up to haul in three four-pointers. He had me interested, so I went out with him and here were three big fat four-pointers just as they were trotting along in line. We got them on the horses, and I asked one of the fellows to loan me his gun so I could look just around the hill. I hadn't gone a quarter-mile when here were four big fellows just laying there. I shot at one. The others got up and trotted off a little. Mine was still head up and still. I stepped to a tree nearby, rested the gun on it, and over he went. So I sent into camp for a horse. I bled the buck and that night we had four beauties hung up to freeze. Two days later, the corral finished, we loaded the four in the heavy spring wagon and drove down through the Wrights Lake area, which was filled with dogs and hunters, but only one buck was hung up for the week's work.

Down at the highway we loaded mine into the pickup and I set out for home, but stopped in Placerville for lunch. When I came out there was quite a crowd around the pickup saying they had seen lots of bucks come down the road, but this was the biggest they had ever seen. At the ranch we skinned him and severed his head, and he weighed 205 pounds dressed. He was a beautiful five-pointer, big and fat. He hadn't been barked at, he hadn't run a step. The venison was wonderful.

It was peculiar, but the country from 7,000 feet down was rugged with lots of brush or thick timber. It would be covered with hunters and dogs who would run the deer, especially the big bucks, up into the higher, more open granite and grass country, but very few hunters ever got up into the granite area. Of course, without a horse it would be difficult to get them to a car.

72

We got word that Dean Hunt of the College of Agriculture, who had gone up to the Barrett home place with me when we leased it, would be up for a two-day visit accompanied by Dr. Herring, the director of the Agricultural Experiment Station, both from Berkeley. We were delighted to see Dean Hunt again. Dr. Herring, located in Berkeley, was a veterinarian who had done some research work with a small dairy herd up the canyon above the campus. I knew him a little, but as director of the Experiment Station he had to approve any project before we could start, then our monthly reports on each project went to him for information and any suggestions he might have. After seeing some of the ranch and cattle, we went to my office in Phil's old house.

Dr. Herring handed me a project all written up and approved in Berkeley, but to be carried out on the ranch at Shingle Springs. Basically it would fence off a thirty-acre pasture, then cross-fence it so the first year one acre would be pastured and the rest retained in its natural state without grazing. The second year the one acre would still be grazed, plus one additional acre, until by the thirtieth year one acre would have been left natural for twenty-nine years and grazed only one year, and the other acres of course were all combinations in between.

The last paragraph warned the university that they must be prepared to build housing accommodations for the many visiting scientists who would be visiting from all over the world. This project was more fundamental than anything in Rothemstead, England, then the outstanding experiment station in the world. I guess I smiled a little as I read the final statement. Dr. Herring wanted to know what I was smiling at. I said I was wondering what good that was going to do the cattlemen. He told me that I would very quickly wipe that smile off my face if I were in Berkeley and understood "That anything that adds to the sum total of human knowledge is worthwhile."

After further discussion, I asked the natural question of who would be responsible for the management of the project. Would it be located on the ranch, but managed by the author of the project, or was it planned that I would be managing it? Dr. Herring observed that maybe it was about time we were discussing who would be managing the whole project up there. Dean Hunt felt it was time to prepare for supper with us. He and Dr. Herring would discuss the matter further in the evening, and he would answer my question in the morning. I had a good night's sleep. Dean Hunt said to me in the morning, "As long as you care to continue, you will be in complete charge of any and all activities on this ranch." My guess is Dean Hunt was laughing on the inside all the time.

I found Pat Kennedy had been the author of the project, so I took time to plan the minimum fencing required for the project. The nature of the project required that the protected plant growth also be protected from gophers, ground squirrels, rabbits, and deer, as well as cattle. There would be woven wire at least eight inches below the ground, as well as a good fence above and some cross-fencing. I designed the fence in detail, along with materials and costs, and took it all to Professor Kennedy. I believe my estimate was $500, ridiculous now but a good deal then. He was sure it wouldn't be that much. I showed him it would, so he buried the great project needing housing for worldwide visitors with the comment, "Oh, well, if it would cost that much, it isn't worth it." If Dean Hunt hadn't been present at our meeting at the ranch, I would probably have found the limits of academic freedom for one who smiles at the fantasies of another who is popular with the academic senate.

The winter of 1921-22 was severe; the grass was short and late, so we ran low on hay. I went to a neighbor to see if I could buy some. Our cattle were thin but his were thinner, in fact dying. He said I was just the fellow he wanted to see. His cattle had anthrax, and did I know what to do for them? He had lots of questions but no periods, so I didn't have to answer any of them. He said the university people didn't know what to do for anthrax. Did I know? I slid in a "What?" He said, "Feed 'em—feed 'em—feed 'em. That is what you do for anthrax." He may have had the wrong disease, but he sure had the right remedy. I bought some hay with mixed emotions, but I knew our cattle would get it.

I received a letter from Dr. Herring on official stationary, asking if I would write him a letter saying that we could move part of the cattle to the Berkeley hills above the campus and carry on a good range cattle experimental program there. If I would do so, I would not have to worry about an increase in rank and good horses to ride. I sometimes wished I had answered it and kept it, but all I did was burn it up.

The use of purebred bulls of high quality was bringing fantastic results. The weighing of individual animals as they left for the summer range, then at the upper camp before the drive home, and again at home, was giving very valuable data of interest to the cattlemen and the Forest Service. Our abortion studies, our project to determine pregnancy, and our many cost and time records were all going well.

I was offered the position of representing the Shorthorn Breeders Association in California, salary to be paid about two-thirds by national and one-third by California breeders. The salary was quite a little boost, which I needed for a while to get enough to start on my own. I sent in my resignation to the University of California, then got word that there had been a mistake, the national appropriation was to cover California, Oregon, and Washington, so I said that was fine. I would move to the Clarksburg land now, money or not.

We had the annual meeting of the El Dorado-Amador Cattlemen's Association in Placerville. George Wilson and someone else were nominated for president. I presumed it was George A. of White Rock, and George was elected. They all then said it was I they were electing. I told them I must decline as I was leaving soon. It was nice, however, to feel accepted by the group.

My thoughts were often on how I was going to produce a crop in Clarksburg. I had a chance to buy a team of horses for $230, and a chance to rent the team for $30 a month, payment in advance, so I collected the $30, went down to Van Voorhees-Phinney leather shop in Sacramento, bought a double harness for $30, and owned a team and harness and some furniture for the house on the ranch.

At this time, also, Bella and I were anxiously looking forward to the arrival of an addition to our family.

About April 15, 1922, my replacement, Al Lovejoy, came up with two or three of the folks from Davis. He opened his trunk. It was full of calfskin vests, guns, belts, all the trappings for a Hollywood cowboy. I was telling him what our program was. He had never heard of contagious abortion, so I suggested we get the horses and ride up on the hill where we could see more and be alone. I briefed him on contagious abortion and some other things he would need to know. We, of course, left, but I was told he wore one or two guns as a part of his uniform everywhere he went, occasionally using them rather menacingly. He apparently played the part of a cowboy as he

74

saw it. I was told that his father was a wealthy automobile man in Detroit who sent regular checks to keep him out here. How the university selected him I never heard.

Several years later the university comptroller came to me to say that Lovejoy rode off the ranch with five saddle horses. The university had written demanding their return, with no success, so they decided for some reason that I should go get them and return them to the ranch. Lovejoy's last letter to them said they could come get the horses if they wished, but they had better bring their shooting irons along and be ready to use them. I didn't go. Somewhat later he had a string of saddle horses for rent on the north shore of Lake Tahoe.

To wind all this up, I might add that at Picnic Day in Davis a year later I met Dr. Herring (maybe he hired Lovejoy). He greeted me with "Well, George, we now have a man at Shingle Springs who not only recognizes contagious abortion when he sees it, but he had the guts to tell us he has it in the herd." This reminded me of the little ditty which says, "When Peter tells a story about Paul, it often tells more about Peter than it does about Paul." I think I said earlier in this story that when Dr. Hayes, the vet at Davis, and I started the abortion projects, each project (Dr. Hayes and mine) carried Dr. Herring's signature of approval, and he had received monthly and annual reports on progress of each of the projects. His story told me he didn't read what he signed, or our reports. That is academic freedom.

Things happened rapidly. Bella went to the hospital April 14 with complications. The doctor was good, but on April 18 we had a stillborn son. The minister of the Methodist Church in Placerville came down, and we had a burial service with Mother Mack and a few friends at the little cemetery on the hill above the house on the ranch. The little service was a great assistance to me, with our immediate sorrow at our loss, but I had a deeper concern over the welfare of Bella who was still seriously ill. I got things packed up at the ranch while Mother Mack was with Bella at the hospital.

††† Move to Clarksburg

Near the last of April we got all the furniture packed on the high-wheel wagon with the high driver's seat and long brake arm. We hitched up the team with my horses in the lead, and the big old Percheron team on the wheel. We drove through K Street in Sacramento to the Cebrian Ranch in West Sacramento for the night, and on to the ranch the next day. We unloaded all and got the Percherons on their way back to Shingle Springs. Mother Mack came with me to help get our new house in order, as Bella was then out of danger but not released from the hospital until May 3, just 55 years to the day from the day I am writing this record.

The farm we were in the process of buying was 53¼ acres ours and 53¼ acres Harold Wadsworth's, in the middle of the Holland lands, three miles west of Clarksburg, between the Sacramento River and the Yolo Bypass. Clarksburg was small but relatively old, on the river front with Merritt Island to the south and Lisbon District up the river, north. The lands were below the Sacramento River at flood stage and our land below at any stage. The first levees built in California were on Merritt Island in 1852, built by Chinese laborers carrying dirt in baskets on their shoulders or by wheelbarrow. The Sacramento-San Joaquin rivers now have nearly one and one-half million acres behind levees. After the floods of 1961-62, mules and slip scrapers were used to cut deeper and build levees higher in the 1890s. Clam-shelled dredgers were used with booms of 60 feet, then 100, 200, and later 240 feet to reach far out for dirt. The Reclamation District 999 (Holland Land) was created in 1913 by a private company of Los Angeles and Bay Area investors, who bought the overflow land at $25 per acre.

The investors bought bonds for $100 each and got one share of stock with each bond. The Netherlands Company had financial problems and reorganized into the Holland Land Company. The bonds all paid off and the stock was worth over $100 at liquidation, so it was quite successful. The Netherlands Company had a competent, high-priced, nonresident engineering firm. The Holland Land Company employed Gus Olson, about three years out of college, as resident manager and engineer. No bonds against the land were sold. All was cash payment, and Gus Olson sold almost all the land with no commission cost. Over $2,000,000 were spent on 35 miles of levees, 150 miles of combination drainage and irrigation ditches, a pumping plant for drainage into Elk Slough and the river, and many miles of tree-lined roads. The land sold from $225 to $325 per acre, 10 percent down, 10 years to pay off. It was the cheapest and best of the several large farm land development projects of that day.

If I was able to devote a good deal of time to farm organization, church, and other activities, it was because of the reasonable price and the high quality of the land, and the counsel and encouragement of Gus Olson as friend and manager of the project.

The bypass is an area from one to three or more miles wide to relieve the Sacramento River. The high levees retain all the water that is safe within the river for navigation and for scouring the river so it doesn't fill with sediment. Then there are four weirs which permit the excess water to flow into the bypass area and on down to the bay. The bypass is cleared of obstacles, is nearly straight so water moves rapidly, and carries over four times the capacity of the river. This was the principal protection for Sacramento and the Delta against flooding. The levees bordering the Holland Lands were up to grade and cross sections, but many of the levees were not, and Gus Olson was always fearful a levee north of us would give way and spill over onto us.

Since then, levees have been raised and strengthened and Shasta, Oroville, and Folsom dams built, which give some protection, so the flood hazard is reduced but not eliminated. We used to often hear the Sacramento River mentioned as the most rapidly rising or falling river in the United States. As long as its high water is above the land level, it is a hazard.

Our house on the ranch was a comfortable but simple frame set on 2x12 redwood sills to be easily moved if need be. It was a 24 feet wide by 28 feet long. The living-dining room was 12x20 and the kitchen 12x8. The front bedroom 12x14, then a bath 12x6 and a small bedroom 12x8. Several years later we added a kitchen and a small office and enlarged the back bedroom, putting a dining room where the kitchen had been. Then we enlarged and screened in the front porch and added a workroom on the rear. When David and Erma moved in, we enlarged the front porch, so the house just kept growing.

There was an old willow tree south of the house, but no planted trees or shrubs. We had running water in the house, with a well and a gasoline-engine pump, and an elevated tank for storage. We cooked with a kerosene stove and had a kerosene water heater. We used kerosene lamps and room heater. There was no electricity or telephone, but we felt quite comfortable and had lots of good times in the old house.

We could go up Jefferson Boulevard to the I Street Bridge to Sacramento or west to Davis and Woodland, but in winter and most of the time we used the Clarksburg ferry and had a better road into Sacramento. The ferry ride was always interesting, sometimes exciting. It was not a cable ferry as most were. Each trip was a voyage usually smooth, but sometimes it got a little out of hand, and took several tries.

The company had planted over 4,000 black walnut trees along the roads, which added a pleasant touch to the level expanse. Many of the trees were grafted over to English walnuts. How they did it was due in part to the skill of the worker and partly to the hazard of killing frost. The row coming in Gaffney Road to our house is beautiful, and has kept us well supplied with nuts and often our friends. I find that they dry well spread out on the third floor of the house, and keep well for a full year or more if we put them in large grocery bags with a second bag upside down over the top of the first one. This method seems to prevent the spread of worms, and in the dark, cool back porch closet they are ready for shelling whenever I am. We nearly always take shelled walnuts and jars of honey from the sloughhouse ranch when we visit friends and relatives.

I think I said earlier that we had acquired a team of horses and new harness. As soon as we were settled in the house, I went to a ranch probably two miles above Knights Landing on the east side of the Sacramento River and bought a two-row bean planter, a high-wheeled two-row Planet Jr. cultivator, and a sled bean cutter, all for $70. So for $300 invested in horses and equipment, I was a farmer on 106 acres, half Wadsworth's and half ours.

††† Early Days on the Farm

I had Mr. Herbert Pollack plow our place. It was just three years from solid tules and full of humus, so it broke up beautifully. I then spent days going back and forth over that 100 acres on the cultivator to get the land ready to plant; I didn't own a disc or harrow. Then with a great deal of hope and wonder and advice from wherever I could get it, for I had but little row-crop experience, the team and I planted the pink beans on which we were staking our future.

There are many stories about farming and about how crooked rows are longer than straight rows so you get more crop from crooked rows than from straight. Straight rows are easier to cultivate (you get most of the weeds without cultivation blight), easier to irrigate, and to harvest. Driving a straight line is good training; pick two or more points ahead to keep in line with, sit erect, keep the eye in the middle, adjust the marker to mark accurately, then learn to compensate for the irregularities in the marker mark. This was one of the many places where army training was useful in civilian life. Thank goodness there were very few weeds at first, for I did all the hoeing and cultivating.

There was so much work to do the first year that we didn't spend much time socially. Some of the folks in the district when we first came were Herbert Pollack, whose family came from Indiana soon after we arrived; Lester and Sarah Holmes; Clarence and Norma Holmes; of course Gus and Mabel Olson; Guy and Agnes Fraser,

District Engineer who had been engineer on the Panama Canal; Irving and Lucille Smith, Holland Land Treasurer; Jim and Alma Leathers, Holland Land Company office; Howard and Helen Reamer; Al Parsons family; Bert and Jennett Swartz; Steve and Mabel Heringer; and John and Alta Herringer farmed in the Holland but lived up the river; Joe Silva. John Morgan and his partner, Clark. Ed Krull. Doc Case and Rena and Mrs. Darden, Norm and Erma Lawlor. On Merritt were Judge Colby's, John Krull's and Aunt Ida, Ray Heringer, Connor's, Bunnell's.

In August or September, the Clarksburg Farm Center met in the old wooden grammar school that stood up on stilts with big wide steps up the front. Judge Colby of Merritt Island had been chairman. Election was held, and I was back in Farm Bureau as chairman, and so on the county board of directors with Warren D. Norton, Farm Advisor.

Yolo County was the fourth county farm bureau organized with George Heche acting as the original farm advisor. While I was still a student at Davis, Niles P. Searles came, a very dedicated young fellow. I rode around the county several times with Niles while he was still organizing the center programs and getting under way. Warne came about 1920.

Extension then drew up, in consultation with the farm center's many projects to stimulate farm production, use of better seeds, accuracy of planting, irrigation, weed control, use of septic tanks, beautifying homes and school grounds, better roads, flood control—any and all projects to better farm production and farm life. Another of the continuing projects was finding and training for leadership many of the farm people. Warne was good at all, but marvellous at leadership training. This included many details such as being sure the meeting notices were out, the hall unlocked, wood or kerosene on hand for the stove, oil for the lights, and that someone was there early to have the fire going and the room warm and dry. I saw many Yolo County farmers grow in influence under Warne's prodding, encouragement, and suggestions.

Fall came and the beans ripened. The cutting sled was made of two 2x12s about six feet long as runners with boards across the top to hold them and to stand on. Then there were cutting blades on the inside of each runner bolted near the front and angling back so they were about three inches apart at the rear. You drove over each two rows, the blades cut the roots just below the ground level, and left just behind the three-inch opening a windrow of two rows of beans.

The beans are cut when the seed is mature but not dry so they do not shatter out of the pods. They dry a few days, then a man with pitchfork goes down each row to be sure all the roots are cut off, and all clods possible fall out as the beans are moved and placed into windrows of four, six, or eight original rows depending on the size of the vines and of the harvester.

This is where we were in the operation when I went to bed with fever and yellow jaundice for a week. It rained hard. All our year's work out in the rain, and I couldn't get out there. One of our neighbors dropped in and said not to worry, he would turn the beans over for me. I didn't, and he didn't, but I felt good about it until the morning I looked out and saw them flat as pancakes.

We had a few days of sun and wind. Gus Olson told Joe Silva to move in and harvest them for me. He didn't want to, for they were flat and not turned. Gus was a little insistant, so Joe moved in and got I believe 28 sacks per acre, one of our best crops. The next morning I got up to find someone to haul them. About dark that evening, I found Dutra in West Sacramento. He said he would gas up, eat a little, and be right down. He didn't show up. Guy Fraser was in his field just across Tule Canal. The truck had stopped. Guy asked if he was down to haul beans. He said he was, so Guy said pull right in and he did. There was my truck. We got Guy's out and into ours about midnight. Everyone was tired and the clouds were getting heavy, so we sure tore into it. They were the days of the old hard rubber tires on the truck, and my field was soft, so we had to pull every load out with the tractor. I had gotten an old Fordson, from C. Harold Hopkins in Davis, for $250, pay when I could. They went over to a landing on Elk Slough near Holland Land headquarters to go out by barge. It was daylight before we finished and came in for breakfast; soon after, the heavens opened up and down it came. I rushed over to the landing, but again Gus Olson had come to my rescue and had tarps spread over them.

It was a fair 24 hours of work for the first day out of bed, but the beans were in the sack and dry, and I felt fine and very thankful. By the middle of December, the beans were in the warehouse not sold, price low, and so was I. I didn't have a thing in cash to buy Bella a Christmas present. If I had $20 I would at least have bought a $10 present, but I didn't have it, so I went to town and shopped the windows waiting for an inspiration. I went by a music store. They had a new Steinway for $1,000. I told them I didn't have the price of a piano stool but I had beans and would give them a warehouse receipt for enough to cover the piano. It arrived in our little old house December 23. Bella wept with joy and thought the piano was great, but I must be out of tune. Youth was crazy then, too.

In early spring of 1923 we planted our first sugar beets for Alameda Sugar Company. This led to a broad expansion of acreage and finally the sugar factory in Clarksburg.

In May we decided we needed a new, approved concrete septic tank, so we set up a demonstration of how to build your own as a Farm Center project. We had all the forms, gravel, cement, mixer and all on hand, and had dug the hole. Warne had several from the farm engineering division in Davis as the demonstrators. Of course, the water table here is high, so there was water in the excavation.

All the technology of all the engineering professors could not get the pumps to drain the excavation, though they had plenty of advice from the sidelines. The tank went in some days later without fanfare or advice and is still good, but the day was well remembered on the Davis campus for many years.

The Fordson tractor deserves a word. We could plow, prepare seed bed, and plant with it, but cold days, wet days, almost every day it was used was a battle. I would crank, adjust coils, crank, heat up the carberator, cometimes build a fire under the crank case to heat the oil. Pour boiling water in the radiator, lay down on the ground and rest, then try again. It was not a delight or a contribution to composure, so in August before harvest I got a two-ton Holt weighing 3,600 pounds. It was a pleasure to drive and did an unbelievable amount of work.

In June, my brother Ralph married Racheal Kimball, the youngest school principal in the Los Angeles system. Ralph and Racheal came up in a very sporty looking Chandler. We decided we would go to the lake for a day or two. It was a Saturday, about time to start beet harvest, so we had a meeting all afternoon with Alameda Sugar Company officials. It went on and on until after 6 p.m. We decided we would go anyhow, but we had hardly any money. Lawlors was closed, so we couldn't get cash. We knew a fruit store in Sacramento, but it was closed. We had some food and dishes, so on we went, and got to Donnor Lake about 1:30 a.m. We got a tent, and Ralph and I went to a camp ground and cooked a meal and took it to the girls. Next morning we cooked breakfast along the Truckee River, wonderful, wonderful. We rented an outboard on Lake Tahoe and took a nice ride, but decided it would be fun to go on to Yosemite, so off we went again.

My older sister, Nellie, had married a Los Angeles architect, Arthur Lindley. We had no idea where they were, but we passed them by Emerald Bay, so we turned and met them. They were going to Tahoe, but they decided to join us so we went down to Mono Lake and up over the Leavinning Grade through Tioga Pass. The road was narrow and winding. As we got about to the summit, a little stream crossed the road. We were about stopped when a car came around the turn and stopped within a foot or two. It is no exaggeration to say their hats rose off their heads and their hair was straight up. They were scared stiff.

We were heading for Tuolumne Meadows Lodge. The lightning came, then thunder, then the downpour, and it kept up. The roads were pure dirt and slippery, so it was slow. We saw lights about 8 p.m., but it wasn't the Lodge. It was a summer tent camp, and the English couple in charge had closed up as they were leaving in the morning. They very kindly gave us a good warm supper, then they said there wasn't a dry blanket in the place, but we could try to fold them so we could get dry covers. The women were to sleep in one large tent, and the men in the other.

The thunder and lightning were trying to move right in with us, so the girls explained we were all one family and moved right in. At first we could spot cots under dry portions of the tent roof, but that soon changed, so we played musical cots all night trying to get out from under the waterfalls.

The sun came up bright and shining. It was beautiful, and we had hotcakes like they tell about. The air was bright and clear, the dust washed off all the greenery. It was beautiful on into Yosemite. We stayed in a dry tent in Camp Curry. Ralph and I climbed Half Dome and Clouds Rest. We saw the Fire Fall and all.

Next morning we decided we would like to stay another day or two, if we had some money, so we decided we would try out our new brother-in-law, whom we hadn't met before. As we met them, they enthused about the beauty of it all and how they would like to stay a few days longer if they had brought more money. We spent all of that day we dared to then, rationing out money to buy gas to roll us into the ranch, we spent all we had left for boxes of soda crackers and set out for Clarksburg, arriving that night, tired and hungry, but with rich memories of a great trip.

The old Dort which took us on our honeymoon and had been in and out of many mudholes was about to give up. So that fall we got a new Dodge for $1015, with extra-high-diameter wheels and tires to keep us higher in the ruts and the mud. It also had side curtains to button on to protect from rain and cold.

Gilbert Scott, my nephew, had been helping us and we were all going south for Christmas. We did not leave home until after dark, but we wanted to get a start so we could get to Los Angeles the next day. We headed for the Antioch Ferry where the bridge is now. We had blankets, but before arrival at the ferry slip, it was bitterly cold and we had to wait for the ferry, so we got out our side curtains, put them on, and it seemed like real luxury. A man came staggering up in the dark and wanted to be friendly. We were again thankful for the side curtains. He decided he wanted to die, and after staggering around awhile he went off the edge of the ferry slip in ice-cold water. Gilbert and I got him out, wrapped him in blankets, and got him in with us out of the cold wind. We let him out about two miles beyond the ferry. We were probably thankful for the side curtains more often than we are for air conditioning.

Our custom for years was to have Christmas eve and presents with my family in Los Angeles until about 11 o'clock, then drive to Banning and probably pick up Mary, Bella's sister, then on to Imperial by daylight to have Christmas morning and presents with Bella's family.

I found a note that before Thanksgiving I got a haircut, shave, and shine for 85 cents.

In December we purchased the Zubler and Duffey 20 acres just across the Tule Canal from our house. We had a new tractor, a new Dodge. The piano was paid for, and we had increased our land ownership by 40 percent. So we had much to be thankful for this year.

One of my friends in college was Bob Yelland. He was one of the outstanding men of the class of '15, and his lady friend was Zella Eddy, one of the outstanding women of the class of '14. Bob went to Shasta County as manager of the C. C. Moore ranch. C. C. Moore had drydocks and shipbuilding in San Francisco. Zella went up and taught school in Anderson, and soon after that they were married. I met Bob at a farm meeting in Davis in the spring of '23. The Anderson Cottonwood area was not doing too well, and Bob didn't see too bright a future there, so I insisted he come home with me that night and see our country. We crossed the river then on the I Street Bridge and came down through Freeport to the Clarksburg ferry. Bob didn't like the ferry. It looked like an ever-present hazard.

Next morning we went to see Gus Olson. Gus liked Bob and he was always more interested in selling to good neighbors than in just selling. Gus said, "Well, let's go pick out a piece of land." Bob said he had no money. Gus replied; "Let's pick the land and we will worry about money later." So we looked at several pieces and Bob went home quite happy. Shortly, he returned with Zella and Louise, Yvonne, and young Bob. They stayed with us a few days. They bought the land on Gaffney Road West. They built their home and were moved in before school started. The Yelland family, with three more children born in Clarksburg, were quite a factor in our lives and in the community and county. Bob had the voice and Bella accompanied him a good deal of the time. They were interested in the church, the school, Farm Bureau, and all the other activities of the community.

Many Clarksburg families were worthy of special mention, but the Yelland's were probably the friendliest. Bob was active in the Masons. I had been invited to join El Dorado Lodge No. 2 when we were in Shingle Springs, but felt I did not have the time then. In Clarksburg it seemed like almost all the men belonged to the Courtland Lodge, but I had quickly become involved in Farm Bureau, church, bean and beet groups, and felt I couldn't take time for another activity. Bella played for Bob at many of the Masonic meetings, so we often went to the dances and other public occasions.

We were getting along, but any time I saw a few days open, I did something to take in a few dollars cash. I made use of my engineering in college and in the army by running surveys as instrument man for the Holland Land Company and for the Great Western Power Company on their new line in the district, or using the tractor and equipment to do field work for other farmers in the area. The bean or sugar beet payments were great, but they almost all went to pay for land or equipment, so little cash incomes along the way were really welcome. Several times I collected several hundred dollars commission on land sales. I hadn't planned on it, but Gus Olson would send me a check after it was all over.

The winter of 1925 was wet. Bella visited in southern California in January. I went down the last week in January and returned February 1. There were hard rains in February, the river was above the piles at Clarksburg wharf, and 16' 2" in the bypass.

It was a great day in early March when we got electric lights, stove, heat, and water pump. It makes quite a change in living.

My older brother, Walter, and his wife, Emma, from Rhode Island, visited us for a week. We went to the mountains, but I remember best his fishing in Tule Canal; he pulled in mainly catfish.

I attended bean-grower meetings, and soon was going to Denver and later to Washington, D.C. for the bean growers. I note I went to the Farm Bureau board meeting in Woodland by driving to Sacramento, taking the railroad from Sacramento to Woodland and return. I also graduated to a Ford Roadster for $492.50.

We needed to sulphur the beans on the Spanggord place, so I used a sulphur duster with gas engine on the rear end of the wagon. I had made the turn near Jefferson Boulevard and was going back for the next pass when there was an explosion at the rear. I looked back and the sulphur was on fire with pungent fumes. The horses sure took off, and I was in the middle not sure if I should first put out the fire or stop the horses. As a result, I had quite a ride through and around the field and finally got back to put the fire out. The actors change with the years, but the problems are always with us.

We built the first 96-foot implement shed that spring for 35 cents per square foot, including $100 labor.

Father Mack passed away in March from one of his many attacks of asthma. Mother Mack came up in the summer and we took another trip to Yosemite Valley. We stayed a week or ten days at Camp Curry and it was delightful.

Baby lima beans were a new crop for us, and I planted 15 acres to try them. We got eighteen sacks at 12½ cents per pound, or $225 per acre. I tried for many years to beat it and never did, but it was surely encouraging.

That fall we got the telephone in. The monthly rate was low, but every local call was 10 cents. All calls were handled as long distance. You first call central and ask for your party. She knew not only the number, but just where he was and would be next. If we tried to give a number she would probably say, "Oh, he isn't there, he's at the store." If he wasn't there, she would probably tell you where he was going next and when he would get there.

Several years later I put in a call for Henry Wallace, Secretary of Agriculture in

Washington, D.C. Central there in the Department of Agriculture wanted to know what I wanted to talk about. Before I could answer, our Central said, "Look, when my party calls the Secretary of Agriculture, he knows he wants to talk to the Secretary and no one else." With a click, on came the Secretary. Our girls always got their man.

After harvest, I bought another 25 acres across the canal from Mrs. Alma Leathers.

The crowning event of the year, of our lives up to this time, was the arrival of an active baby boy on December 22, 1925. Bella had moved to an apartment in Sacramento a month or more before to be near the doctor and the hospital and enjoy a quiet rest. It worked beautifully and we were delighted.

††† 1926—A Big Year for Home, Farm, Farm Bureau, and Church

In 1926 the picklers were around wanting us to plant cucumbers for pickling. It sounded awfully good, and they grew well and got tonnage, but it cost an awful lot to pick them and too many were crooks and nubs. It sounded good, but we didn't grow any more.

Being a father with family responsibilities, I took out life insurance for $32,000. It seemed large then, but we needed more later.

In May we succumbed to our real wishes and bought a Buick.

With David six months old, we set out early in the morning for the regional Farm Bureau meeting in Susanville. We got to Nevada City and stopped to feed David, but had forgotten the nipples and other supplies, so we had to wait for a drugstore to open. The country was beautiful, but the road to Susanville was narrow and crooked. We were going around a turn on the outside as far as we dared when a power company car coming down climbed the bank as far as he dared to miss us, but tore off part of our fender on our new Buick. We looked; we couldn't have been further out on the road. There just wasn't room. We wired it up and went on for a great time as we always had in Susanville.

We had a new Harris bean harvester delivered for $2,850. It was a joy to run. It took four men—a tractor driver, separator man, and two sack sewers—but it was the best there was then.

This summer, we saw progress in organizing the church in Clarksburg.

Clarksburg was one of the early steamboat stops on the Sacramento River, the shipping and market center for Merritt Island and Lisbon districts. Then 26,000 new acres were reclaimed from the river and bypass flood waters, and many young families with little capital except reasonable education, willingness to work, and determination to build a good community for our families, moved in with full support from Gus Olson, company manager.

Soon several of the ladies organized and led a good Sunday School program. By 1926 the men decided we should have a church. Many denominations were represented by our people, but few had been affiliated with a church in the preceding ten years. We decided our church must have wide congregational determination; still we wanted denominational affiliation and support, especially for the minister.

We tried affiliation with congregationally oriented denominations without success. We then sought a denomination which had several federated and community churches. We held the organization meeting. The membership cards were passed out to be signed, but it developed the members of that denomination would be active members and all others associate members. An influential member said we hadn't separated the sheep from the goats in the community yet, and didn't plan to now, and the cards were never collected.

Next, the counsel of a Methodist District Superintendent was sought. He told us that Reverend Mark Dawber in charge of rural church work was coming soon. He spent three days with us. All was mutual admiration. He had been a prominent member of the English Labor Party and a close advisor to the first Labor Prime Minister, but after several years he decided government was not the answer to man's problems, and he came to Ohio and took a small rural church. His rural ministry was outstanding in building people and community betterment.

This was a time of exploring new methods of church organization to meet the needs of community churches. Reverend Dawber proposed that our local church be independent, but he would ask the Methodist Board of Bishops to agree to furnish us a fully accredited Methodist minister with the full rights and privileges of any Methodist minister so long as we requested it. We, of course, paid to the retirement fund, organizational expenses, etc., as well as salary.

We handled our own benevolences. Our first minister often had to explain this to his associates, but it soon developed that there is often need for unbudgeted funds, for mission work in the southern mountains, among California Indians, to save a failing church, for campgrounds, or some other cause. Our benevolences and often private funds were available to help these special needs. Our minister often took a week or more to help in a special drive in another church, so for 25 years the ministers and Bishop were highly pleased with the relationship, and it met our own needs quite well.

It was almost accepted that the minister of the Clarksburg Community Church would lead the rural church work for northern California and Nevada, both within his denomination and interdenominationally. He often played a prominent part in the national rural church work. We were active in establishing the Rural Church Research Project located at the University of the Pacific. We held a three-day rural church conference in Davis for many years. Several of our former ministers rose to positions of prominence nationally, as well as in the California Conference.

Then came a change in thinking that all churches should return to direct and full membership in a single denomination and several years after a new Bishop came to this conference our relationship was severed. We then turned to a minister with Congregational affiliation for seven years of productive work together. We rather drifted into the Congregational orbit with other ministers of that denomination, but without an agreement. We gradually felt more isolated and had a feeling of need to belong to a larger group where we might both contribute and partake and where our minister would feel full membership in his conference.

We had been happy with our Congregational or UCC minister. The UCC officials were very considerate of our wishes and needs. They did not pressure us. It seemed natural to seek UCC affiliation. We were highly pleased with our acceptance into the conference and services connected therewith. We believe it augurs well for the future.

Farm Bureau was growing rapidly in influence and power in the state. I was president of the Yolo County Farm Bureau and attended several state director's meetings.

Uncle Carter and Aunt Ethel Boggs from Medford, Oregon, visited us this summer. In August we all went up the Redwood Highway to Weymouth Inn. It was one of the nicest trips we have ever had. Each guest had a cabin with fireplace and wonderful food in the dining room.

In September, Bella's brother Bill, sister Eleanor and husband Dee, came up for a visit. Bill, Dee, and I went buck hunting up to the old cattle camp above Wright's Lake. I saw a buck on a flat above a small valley. I hit him, but he went right down into the thicket in the little valley. I slid down into the valley to try to find him, I was trotting along a trail on the valley floor when I came to a little stream and stopped to figure the best way across, when I heard a crackle and looked up. I didn't aim, just fired, and the buck fell in the stream right at my feet.

We had separated after pointing out the location of the camp, and Bill came in all right, but Dee didn't, so Bill and I spent that night, the next day, and next night looking for him. The third morning we were at Wright's Lake when Dee came riding in on a horse with his pockets full of food.

The first evening out he picked a place to sleep, and was about to lie down when he saw a bear track, so he kept going just a little way when he came to a cow camp. The door was unlocked as most were; there were bed, blankets, and food, so he did better than we did. The next night he came to a camp where a group up from Sacramento were having a party, so he did well there. His time was better spent than ours.

In December we got a new John Deere tractor. It burned stove oil, had two cylinders, was noisy and bumpy, but it really worked.

Farmers were not happy with a good deal of state legislation and big city control of the legislature. As I remember, San Francisco had four senators, Los Angeles County three, and Alameda two. Los Angeles was demanding representation in both houses on the base of population. Los Angeles was growing very rapidly and was much larger than San Francisco, probably larger than San Francisco and Alameda combined. The Farm Bureau, however, appointed a committee and drew up the federal plan of reapportionment for the state, with the eighty assembly districts being about equal in population, and each of the larger counties having one senator regardless of population in the county. This left eighteen of the smaller counties to be combined with a nearby larger county to form a senatorial district. This plan was drawn up as a constitution amendment to be on the ballot of November 1926.

All the farm organizations joined with Farm Bureau, and also many city chambers of commerce, in support of the measure. Many town and city people wanted the senate to be largely rural. The measure carried by a good margin in 57 of the 58 counties of California, and had a very large vote in Los Angeles County.

The California Farm Bureau meeting November 17-19 in Stockton was an occasion of celebration, and California was happy with the outcome. Governor Young then and Governor Earl Warren later often expressed approval of the arrangement, which continued successfully until Earl Warren as Chief Justice of the U.S. Supreme Court announced it as unconstitutional in favor of a one-man one-vote theory. And California has been the loser since. I never yet have seen how a practice in effect in Washington when the Constitution was adopted, and still in effect in

Washington, can be called unconstitutional in California. I consider the one-man, one-vote decision probably the most harmful judicial decision in my lifetime.

The address of Earle Houghton, President of CFBF, discussed some of the difficult problems facing agriculture in 1926 which continued until they brought on the depression of the thirties.

In July 1926, the USDA said from 1920-25 U.S. farming yielded exactly one-half of one percent on the investment. California probably did a little better, but not much. The years 1924-26 were called a period of great prosperity for industry.

The price of farm commodities August 1926 was 38 percent over the 1913 price. Other figures for August 1926 showing increases over the 1913 price were: Farm labor 74 percent; clothing 78 percent; fuel and lightint 108 percent; building material 77 percent; organized labor 122 percent.

Many banks in rural areas were closed or in distress. In one California county, agricultural lands declined in price from 1919 to 1924 census by 49 percent. Delinquent taxes increased in the same period 185 percent. Tax levees increased 1913-25 by 190 percent; in the same period county bonds increased from 0 to $4,156,000.

In another agricultural county, land value increased between 1919 and 1925 by 49 percent. Between 1912 and 1925, delinquent taxes increased 510 percent; assessed values increased by 92 percent; county taxes increased 207 percent; county bonds outstanding increased 1260 percent.

From 1920 to 1925 many county farms had value reduced 15-30 percent. USDA says farmers were paying 86 percent of net profit for taxes. All other industry averages were 34 percent of net for taxes. Farms pay 16.6 percent of gross for taxes; industry pays 11.9 percent of gross for taxes.

From 1913 to 1925, political subdivisions of California increased expenses 286 percent, bond indebtedness increased 197 percent, and assessed value increased 114 percent. Population increased 46 percent and new wealth 125 percent.

I include these income and tax figures, as it was these figures which caused the American FBF to develop the parity concept under which a pound of corn, beef, or cotton, etc., would buy the same amount of goods bought by farmers as it would have bought in 1909-1914 before World War I. Many people feel that it was this relatively low income for farmers which caused the depression for all in the thirties.

Another big issue in 1926 was the development of a water policy and plan in California. CFBF had taken the lead along with others, mostly in agriculture, in getting a state appropriation of $250,000 for a survey of the water resources. We got a new governor then who stopped the next appropriation to continue the study, so Farm Bureau got the banks to put up $100,000 as a loan to complete the study. The next legislature paid back the loan. Another big issue before the resolution committee was the passage of the Swing-Johnson bill to build Hoover Dam on the Colorado River, an act that has meant much for water and power in the southern California area and provided a better supply of water for Imperial Valley. The Johnson was Hiram Johnson, former governor of California, a very strong figure in the senate. Swing was the young attorney who arrived in Imperial Valley in time to convince the jury we had stolen the sows.

The resolution for the dam was good, but, as noted above, farm prices were very low and we were building surpluses, so I proposed that the dam be built but that the distribution system for irrigation water to new lands be built following approval by the secretaries of agriculture and interior.

The chief proponent of the farm resolution was Dick Blackburn, whom I didn't know. He was from Riverside County but also next president of the California FBF. About ten years later he was elected secretary of the American Farm Bureau Federal, and I was elected to fill his place on the AFBF board. I lost my amendment to the resolution, but from then on I was really immersed in Farm Bureau.

† 1927—High Water

This was one of the years when high water was lapping at the levees front and back. We all developed a healthy respect for the power and force of Old Man River, and we recognized his potential for destruction if a levee gave way and the water swept in. We all depended on the judgment of Gus Olson to warn us if danger was imminent. Our levees seemed high and strong, but we feared the levees above us filling Lisbon district and sweeping down on us. The river was high all along its banks. Some had already moved out to friends or hotels. Gus said it was time for us to move. We had no nearby relatives, and by now the Sacramento hotels were all full, so Gus and Mabel invited us into their home which we gladly accepted. In four to six days the danger was past and we moved back home. The Olson boys taught David to walk during that period.

Since then, Shasta, Folsom, Oroville, and smaller dams have been helpful in storing the excess flood water. The hazards of a levee giving way will always be with us, but we have not had a flood scare since.

Later, in the early thirties, when we were planning a new home, we debated whether we should build on the home ranch or buy a homesite near the river or Elk Slough, where the ground is higher and we could get the house above a probable flood level. We decided to live on the ranch but have a third floor, which is above the probable flood plane, where we might await rescue in case of flood.

The spring of '27 we decided we could enjoy the luxury of owning a Guernsey cow. She was a fine cow and gave lots of good cream-colored milk. We had lots of cream and made our own butter. Milking in the morning never bothered me much, but the evening milking was sometimes a problem both for me and the cow. If possible, I would get someone to milk for me, but sometimes it would be midnight before I got home, and then I would have to change clothes and go out and milk an unhappy cow.

We bought the Spanggord place, 47 acres, that fall.

Up to this time, after barley or bean harvest, all the straw was burned to get rid of it before plowing. I felt from the beginning that was wrong, especially in the case of bean straw, so before bean harvest I made a straw spreader driven by a V-belt to fit on the back of the harvester. It caught the straw as it was falling and spread it quite evenly on the ground so it disked or plowed in easily and added humus to the soil.

The spreader was a piece of heavy galvanized iron about 30 inches in diameter with four 2x3 pieces of wood about 30 inches long which were horizontal. It was a little more difficult to catch samples of the straw to see how many beans or kernels of grain were coming out over the rear end. Also, if you got too close, it taught you to keep your distance. This was the first spreader I had seen or heard of, but in a year or two they were installed at the factory and improved.

This was also an active year for me in Farm Bureau and farm legislation. Ralph Taylor was manager of the agricultural legislative committee this year. This was an organization of most of the farm cooperative marketing associations in California, with offices in Sacramento to work on projects of mutual interest to all the coops, but mainly the legislative interests in California and Washington, D.C. The Farm Bureau, State Grange, and State Chamber of Commerce cooperated closely with Ralph Taylor, so I had worked with him. Earlier he had taught agriculture at Imperial High School. He was a friend of Mary's and of the whole Mack family.

Ralph asked me to help him during the legislation session. My job was to help any way I could, but it was helping read all the bills which might affect agriculture or rural living, and analyzing them so our board of directors and members could determine what action if any we should take on each one. The legislature met then for four weeks in January, presenting bills, then recessed for four weeks so they and their constituents could study the bills. They then returned for the full session, which was then limited to 100 days in all.

We had a long list of bills we supported and opposed. We had to keep track of when each would be heard before committee, attend the committee meetings, testify as required, and keep track of all amendments or other action, and of the testimony of our friends and antagonists. Ralph then wrote a weekly letter to our members as to actions taken, or needed, and progress of the bills. The Capitol at night was a beehive of action, as most of the committees were meeting until 11 to 12 p.m. I would then drive home down Jefferson Boulevard, which was a misnomer as the mud and ruts were often so deep that the bottom of the car scraped much of the way. Little hassles with a mudhole didn't count, but I was never long delayed even on the wettest, darkest night when much of the driving was almost blind; still many times in broad daylight I was delayed and badly muddied on that same road. Frozen mud was much easier than liquid mud.

I guess I could be classed as one of the real first pioneers in radio broadcasting, as each Friday evening at 6 p.m. I would go to a little room upstairs in the Department of Agriculture Building, 9th to 10th and L to M in Sacramento, and broadcast a resume of the week's happenings. The building was vacated by then, and I usually was alone. First I had to heat up the tubes and make several tests to get the right power output, then shake the microphone to get the crystals in the right distribution, and try a few times to see if the signal was clear to the San Jose Station KQW, which was the first station licensed in the state. Then I would tap the mike a few times with a pencil until we got the right connection. Then came the test for voice volume, with the lines shooting up and down as the voice changed, and these had to be kept within a prescribed range to give a good signal on the air. At exactly 6 p.m. you started speaking for real, but you still had to watch all the gauges to keep a clear broadcast. Of course, Ralph Taylor handled the important testimony and contact with legislators and other farm representatives. I enjoyed the bill analysis, the broadcasts, and the attendance and testimony at committee meetings. I never ever learned to really enjoy the buttonholing of legislators to get assurance of their vote as we wanted it. It was a basic experience for three sessions, and was often helpful to me later in dealing with other farm organizations and with the legislative bodies in Sacramento and Washington, D.C.

Ralph Taylor was surely a living example of the fact that a lobbyist who is very meticulous in assuring that he is giving facts and an honest interpretation will get much further in the long run. Legislators will seek as well as take his advice. Lobbyists, like people, represent all shades of honesty and concern for the general welfare. Those who sell their services to advance single issues may appear to win the single victory by intrigue. Those who appear before the same legislative body year after year supporting or opposing many and varied bills will be effective in proportion to their ability to establish a solid reputation for honesty and sound judgment. This Ralph Taylor surely did.

Joe J. Deuel headed up the Law and Public Utility Department. Leon O. Whisell of the California Railroad Commission (now Public Utility) said, "As a member of the railroad commission, I desire to express my appreciation of the helpful cooperation of the Law and Utility Department of the CFBF. Of all the agencies organized for the consumer's benefit, this department under the able management of J. J. Deuel has offered more valuable suggestions and has been of greater aid to the commission than all others combined."

For the Farm Bureau, and also the Coop Council for whom I worked during the legislative session, one of our top bills was the pure-seed bill. It limited the number of noxious weed seeds that might be in seed, and if the label or advertisements claimed an "area or origin," then the seed must in fact be grown in that area. It went through the committees and passed the senate with very little opposition. The Agriculture Committee of the Assembly then went to finance, and here the seed companies really hit with all they had, presumably on orders and with money from their Eastern seed trade. They hired Samish, then the big wheel, wheeler dealer of the Assembly. The night before it was to be voted on for final passage on the floor, he threw a big dinner in the Senator Hotel. Samish explained the bill and why they should vote against it. Nobody, including him, knew what a noxious weed was or what it looked like, but he told them they only blossomed and showed up at night and he would take them over on the Capitol grounds and show them some, so well past midnight he had a group of august assemblymen crawling on their hands and knees looking for noxious weeds. The next morning, or later that morning, when the bill came up, everybody, it seemed, wanted to know what a noxious weed was and where to find them. Samish had the votes and we lost.

The annual California Farm Bureau's fall meeting was held in the Mission Inn in Riverside October 31 to November 2. Ed Bandy was the Yolo County delegate. Mrs. Eleanor Bandy was state head of Women's Department and I was alternate delegate.

Farm Bureau had taken over Radio Station KQW in San Jose, with Fred J. Hart still operating it for us. He also operated the County Farm Bureau Monthly and handled our Farm Bureau publicity. KQW was the first radio station licensed in California and the only agricultural radio station in the nation. It carried a full program of farm and Farm Bureau news each morning and evening, and was heard all over the West.

Von T. Ellsworth was selected as tax and research man for Farm Bureau. I mention it because he rendered great service to California farmers until the sixties. He was certainly one of the best, if not the top, tax authority in California, and recognized by industry, education, and the state as well as by farmers.

On the ranch, we were getting better established all the time. We planted the redwood trees north and west of the house and shrubs around the house as well as fruit trees and vines. The fruit trees later gave way to the garage and shop.

David by now was two years old and running around in great shape, but he needed company. Isabelle was feeling fine, but still conscious of our earlier losses, we celebrated New Year's Eve by moving Bella, David, and Mother Mack into an apartment about a block north of Sutter's Fort. I'm sure Mother Mack enjoyed David and liked to live with us and, of course, wanted to be with her daughter. Isabelle was in bed resting most of the time. It was quite rainy, but Mother Mack took David for a walk in Fort Sutter Park every day they possibly could.

† 1928

We started the New Year by painting the house inside and out to have it all clean to welcome a new baby. Richard M. (Dick) arrived in good shape on March 16, 1928, and we were all very happy, but they did not return home until about April 1, partly due to high water and mud. David had done a good job of training his parents, so Dick was much easier for both us and him.

The soil at Clarksburg was marvelous and forgiving of many of the mistakes I made. We had little surplus cash but still were doing well. I remember one day I was at the Spanggord place dreaming of the future and figured my next goal was to gross $50,000 in a year. I hadn't done it, but it seemed a realistic goal, and if I made it I would sure be on easy street. I felt things were going well. We had two sons, good health, and a good future.

The next incident in my life was one I seldom think of and practically never mention. I did not win, but I learned a good deal in a short time. I encourage others to do it, but it was not for me. Some men came to me and asked me to run for the assembly seat in the California legislature. They said that if I would run, Forrest Plant, a prominent young attorney in Davis, would act as my campaign manager. The district was Yolo, Sutter, and Yuba counties. I knew Fred Noyes, the incumbent from Yuba City. To me he seemed old, I do not know how old. He slept a good deal in session and committee meetings. He missed many of them. His only interest was his district.

I guess I was feeling a little confident. I felt the assembly should have more active and aggressive members interested in the general welfare. I never had been and am not now one who feels the state owes me or anyone else a college education, but I was quite conscious of the fact the state had given me an education, and I owed the state some service in return. My duty was to the people of the state, not the state as such, but this seemed a reasonable service, so I accepted.

On June 22, 1928, I filed nomination papers for the assembly and resigned as president of the Yolo County Farm Bureau so they would not be involved in the election. The primary election was to be held August 28, so there was about two months of campaigning which was quite simple compared to today. Then practically all candidates filed for both the Republican and Democratic nomination, so many elections were settled in the primaries.

All your votes were counted for you, but you must carry your own party to win. There was very little party politics in the legislative elections. I paid a courtesy call on the governor to tell him I was a candidate. He gave me his blessing all right, but warned me several times to remember that I was probably running against the most astute politician in the legislature who would be very difficult to unseat.

I appeared at political meetings, service clubs, farm, labor, and other meetings in the three counties, and was endorsed by most of the papers.

The morning after election day I woke up 300 ahead in the vote count, but knowing that a number of outlying precincts in Yuba and Sutter were still out, which would probably put Mr. Noyes over the top, which it did about noon. I sat in my chair and said, "What in the world would I have done if I had won?" The office then paid $100 per month salary. I could have still farmed, but I would have had to give up Farm Bureau, and I enjoyed Farm Bureau more and felt my influence in Farm Bureau was really far greater than it would be as one legislator.

I carried the Republican vote in every precinct in Yolo County except 1 out of 40, the Democratic vote in every precinct in Yolo County except two, but I lost heavily in Marysville and Yuba City. It was a great experience and turned out right for me. I went to Davis and thanked Forrest Plant and others, and came home much relieved. One does hate to feel you have let your supporters down, but that soon wears off.

The Yolo County Farm Bureau board had not met in July and August, so my resignation had not been acted on and in September it was not accepted, so I continued on.

My father had bought the 47 acres on which Darryl Merwin now lives and had leased it to Ralph to farm. In 1928 they built a nice new home on it. Mr. Lindley, Nellie's husband, was the architect.

While Isabelle and David were living in Sacramento, I built a nice large sandbox under the big willow tree south of the house. Dave, Dick, and Pat spent lots of good hours in that sand. Herbert Hoover was elected President of the U.S. in November.

The issue which created a good deal of interest was an official state trademark to be used on all fruit or vegetables leaving California. Simon Lubin, then of Weinstock-Lubin stores in Sacramento, was the chief spokesman for the project which needed legislative action.

Sun Maid, Sun Kist, Sun Sweet, Blue Anchor, Del Monte, almost all shippers had their private labels, and practically all farm groups opposed the plan. Simon Lubin was the son of David Lubin who had started the Sacramento store but was always interested in agriculture, local and worldwide. David finally set up the International Institute of Agriculture in Rome, Italy, with a grant from the King of Italy. Its chief duty was to collect agriculture production, consumption, travel, and other statistics from all countries of the world. He headed it up and gained broad respect for his services to agriculture. In 1949 his daughter insisted I visit his offices and sit in his old chair and inspect the files and records. It was in truth an inspiring afternoon. All his organization and records were the forerunner of FAO, Food and Agricultural Organization of the United Nations, also set up in Rome.

I was selected to speak at a good many meetings in opposition to the California Trade Mark project. The last I remember was in Marysville. There was a large turnout. Lubin was very insistent that I speak first and he last, so I spoke first. The crowd was with me. He was introduced, said he had come up expecting to speak first and get home early as he was very busy. It had now gotten late and he must leave, and he did. That was the end of the debates. It just faded away until the hearing before the legislature where the testimony was led by C. C. Teague who was to be appointed by President Herbert Hoover as a member of the Federal Farm Board. He was a man of a caliber to be president of the U.S. himself, and he, with A. C. Hardison and C. J. McFadden, formed a trio of men whose approval was almost vital to any important project in cooperative marketing or general farm policy in California.

† 1929

My father died on January 26, 1929. He would have been 76 on March 25 of that year. We had been at my home for ten days or so with the boys. My father was up and enjoyed the boys, but didn't seem quite up to normal. He complained some of stomach pains. I took him to the doctor one day, and the doctor thought it might be his heart, but my father said he was sure it wasn't. I urged my mother to call a good heart specialist as soon as we left for home early on the twenty-sixth.

We were on the ridge route when the highway patrol stopped us and said my father had died. We, of course, returned. The doctor had come and examined him, then had sat with him on the side of the bed. He said, "I'm pretty sure it is your heart, and you will have to take it easy." I am sure that is what my father heard, but when he heard it he just fell back dead.

I spent most of the spring and early summer in 1929 working with Ralph Taylor and the agricultural legislative committee. We started with a meeting of the Agriculture Legislative Committee, the Farm Bureau, and the Grange. The next two days the Farm Bureau board met to discuss position on legislation, and Ralph Taylor and I met with them. About this time the U.S. Secretary of Agriculture, Honorable William M. Jardine, said, "The farmers of California have a national strength far beyond their numbers, because they are well organized, and three organizations work in unison in the interest of their farm consitutents, and the results are surprising."

In spite of the heavy vote of the people of California in favor of the Federal Plan of Reapportionment, we had to oppose all through the session new efforts to pass and get on the ballot new constitutional amendments or a constitutional convention to give San Francisco, Los Angeles, and Alameda County five senators each and 25 for all the rest of the state.

One must go through a session to realize the complexity of all that goes on in the committee rooms, on the floor, and elsewhere.

The bills affecting agriculture include disease control, weeds, standardization of fruits, vegetables, and packages, land use, water transportation, trespass, dogs, coyotes, real estate, and on and on. Of the 150 bills on which agriculture took a position this year, 1929, success was achieved in all but four, and these were of minor importance.

In the spring of the year we planted asparagus across Tule Canal with pink beans interplanted, which gave us 17 sacks of beans per acre.

This year is best remembered in the U.S. as the year of the stockmarket crash, but for agriculture it was just another low-price year as we had during the twenties, to be followed by even lower years into the thirties; however, in the thirties, costs went down also.

† 1930

We started the 1930 crop year by cutting our first asparagus on February 28. It sold for 30¢ a pound, or $8.40 a crate, less 10 percent, or $7.56 for us. It seemed like lots of money. All the best "grass" was shipped East, early by express, then by refrigerated cars. Lower grades sold in San Francisco and Los Angeles. The total population of California in 1930 was 5,677,257; people were widely distributed, and many had their own fruit or a cheap supply nearby, so it was not much of an organized market as it is today.

We planted lettuce for seed, both New York and Boston. New York was the solid heads like Iceburg, so before the heads were grown we had to go through with a knife and slash the tops in two directions to release the pressure and let the seed stalks through. Boston lettuce has open heads, so the seed stalk comes through naturally. As the seed ripens it shatters easily, so we harvested early in the morning while the dew was on.

A man harvested two rows at a time. He used a burlap bag with a hoop in the top to keep it open and a rope to drag it between his legs. With a cycle-shaped blade, he pulled the seed stalks together above the sack opening and cut the heads off, shoving them into the sack with his left hand. The filled sacks were dumped into a nearby wagon, then the heads spread onto a 30' x 30' or 40' x 40' canvas to dry. After the stalks and leaves were dry, we rolled it in the dry part of the day, threw off the stalks, and piled the seed and chaff.

We had screens made of wire mesh about 3 feet by 7 feet with 1 x 6 boards on each side and end, with a handle and a man on each end. When the breeze was good, we shoveled the seed and chaff onto the screens, and a man on each end rocked it back and forth. The seed fell on the canvas, the fine dust and leaves blew away, and any coarse straw was dumped out. The seed was then sacked to be further cleaned by the seed company.

As we planted more lettuce, we got a swather and cut it while damp, loading it directly onto the wagon and then the sheet. I found I could pull a spray rig behind the tractor and each round spray with water the next 8' swath, if the weather was dry. The next round the spray would have soaked in enough so the seed shattered very little. It worked fine.

Later, during World War II, some tried threshing with the regular grain harvester. Lettuce has a sticky sap like milkweed, and we thought it would stick up everything in the harvester and not work. But it did work, so we sacked the seed on the harvester, then spread it out on sheets to dry for a day or two, then sent it to the seed company. Life and methods change constantly on the farm. In 1930 we had 100 walnut trees grafted to English walnuts, but we had a severe freeze that spring and lost most of the grafts.

I was president of the Yolo County Farm Bureau and attending many farm center meetings as well as statewide meetings on beans, beets, etc.

An important event of the year was Patty's birth on July 17, 1930.

† 1931

I spent the spring of 1931 with the Agriculture Legislative Committee again. During the February recess of the legislature we built the asparagus shed where we washed, trimmed, and packed the asparagus. Most of the larger "grass" was pressed into two-pound circular bunches and tied with ribbons to designate size or number of stalks per bunch. For other markets we packed loose-pack, ungraded for size, 28 pounds per crate.

For 80 acres of asparagus we used 10-12 cutters. They lived and ate together, usually owned a car together, and all rode in it, played lots, but worked hard and fast if need be, all on piece work, so they made good money but sometimes worked little and sometimes much. They did an excellent job.

President Hoover, who called Palo Alto home, knew the Coop leaders of California. We had some outstanding successes here, so he proposed the farm board of five men with $500 million to stabalize farm prices. Part of the plan was to buy up farm surpluses at low prices and store them until needed. They were also to encourage farmer coops for wheat, feed grains, cotton, livestock, fruits, etc., where the Coop would prepare the crop for market and sell the commodity. They also encouraged bargaining Coops such as the Beet Growers, Pear Growers, etc.

Sam Thompson, representing the Farm Board, came out this year and I believe stayed a week or two to help us organize the Central California Beet Growers Association. There was also a Southern California Beet Growers Association. Lester Holmes and I were elected directors from here, and Lester was elected president of the association. Gordon Lyons was then secretary and bookkeeper for Delta Farms Company which had an office in the Stockton Hotel where we met. Gordon was elected secretary, and I believe treasurer, of our new association. We didn't receive any money from the Farm Board, but they did give us a good deal of encouragement and also helped other beet growers in the same way, so we were able to meet with other state groups.

Pears along the river had been quite profitable. The Spanggord place of 47 acres was higher than most of the district and well drained, so I thought it might be good for pears. I was not sure I wanted to be a pear grower, so I decided to plant about two acres on the home place first to see if I liked it. They grew beautifully, but in a year or two the blight hit the whole pear crop on the river, and the succulent rapid growth got it the worst, so we cut and painted all the butts and bruises. Warren Norton, our Farm Advisor, wanted to see what he could do with it, and I was happy to have him. But time didn't seem to slow it down very rapidly, so after several years he decided he was done with it, and I was too, so we decided the pear orchard was the proper place for our proposed new house, and we pulled out the orchard.

† 1932

We celebrated New Year's Eve in Los Angeles. After considerable doubt about being on the highway on New Year's Day, we decided to try it. It was a pleasant surprise. We were the only ones on it. We stopped for lunch below Fresno. The service station boy next door had one customer that morning, and we were the only ones in the restaurant. Everyone going was already there and hadn't started home yet. We had always tried not to travel in holiday crowds, but we find Christmas and New Year's, at least early in the day, good days to travel.

On February 1 we had rain and snow.

Long-term cannery contracts had been 4 cents per pound, then 3½ and 3 cents. The Del Monte Company paid $100 per acre to buy up 4-cent contracts with several years more life. Then in the spring of '32 they came out with a 1¾-cent contracts, so Gus Olson, Bert Swartz, Babe Slater, and I decided to try to can our own grass in a rented cannery.

On March 8 we went to Farm Credit, Intermediate Credit Bank in Berkeley, to get a loan, but were refused. We went again March 14, 18, and 22, but to no avail. They just wouldn't loan. We tried several others. At first they would, then they wouldn't. Finally Gus went to Governor Anderson of Capital National Bank. He said he surely would if Zoller approved, so Zoller came down, looked at the other three ranches, then at Thornton Cannery, and said OK. All the other banks were afraid of the wrath of Cal Pac if they loaned to a Coop. We got 3¾ cents for our grass for the year. We canned also in 1933, then the price rose to a figure we felt we could accept.

After we decided to can our grass, Merwin Yelland and Pollack decided to try, so they made a deal with Tom Richards. Tom had the Burcutt Richard Cannery, but no money to pay help and run it, so he didn't plan on opening. Under their deal, Tom could contract some outside asparagus, and Herbert Pollock would deliver the money for the cannery payroll each Friday afternoon. Tom ran the cannery. They paid the same return we did.

Ray Morgan and his wife came to the ranch this spring looking for work, and I set them up in a small house by the oriental plane tree northwest of the shop. They were a great help to me, both here and in the bypass. She was a good cook and fed the men who boarded with them and was generally helpful. Ray was an excellent foreman. They came from Mendocino County and returned there after they left here. Frank Caldera ran the harvester for us this fall, and stayed on as mechanic until he opened his own shop on Clarksburg Road just off Jefferson Boulevard where Jim Cuped is now. Frank Caldera was the best harvester man I ever had and an excellent mechanic. He made, in 34-35, the cultivators to fit on the F12 tractors hanging between the front and rear wheels. As far as I know, this was the first tractor-mounted cultivator made anywhere. You had to raise and lower it by hand, but even so it was great. Before that we pulled two-, three-, four-row beet or bean cultivators (horse type) behind the F12, so it took a crew of three or four to cultivate and it was sometimes very dusty riding the cultivator. Later we used vacuum or hydraulic power to lift the home-made cultivators.

I had a Sunday School class of boys. We met in a concrete-walled room below the stage end of the grammar school auditorium. We sometimes took our lunches after church and went to the back levee or Winchester Lake or any open spot where we could have a fire and a little fun.

On May 1 we took the truck for a day in Coloma. June 10-12 we went for a snow trip to Camp Sacramento at the top of the Horsetail Falls grade above Placerville. At Camp Sacramento we had permission to stay and eat in the camp before the regular summer opening. We had good snow and lots of fun.

About the first of May in 1932, **President** Hoover had asked everyone to hire some help if they could, repair work, anything, as unemployment was really bad. I had my work at home pretty well caught up, and one day I was sitting in the beet field across the canal thinking what I should do next. I heard there was vacant land in the bypass. I figured out costs at 20 cents per hour for labor and all prices low. It seemed I couldn't lose money planting 200 acres of beets or beans out there, so I went in to see Gus Olson and leased 200 acres the first year.

There was a place for the Morgans to live and a camp for the men. There was an old barge on which we used to take tractors and equipment back and forth. We would drive down the levee bank to a landing place, then put 4-by-12 planks from the bank to the barge and drive on the planks to the barge. This was quite a delicate operation for getting the bean **harvester** over, but we did it.

For people, we used the rowboats. All the fuel came to the bypass by boat, and all the beets and beans at first went out by barge. Later years we fixed the barge so we could take the trucks and cars across as a ferry. The water supply was ideal even during the drought of the thirties.

At the north and higher end of the property was a reservoir built by dozing up a levee around the area. In the levee, by the borrowpit for the Holland Land Company levee, was a two-way gate. It opened for water to come in when the tide rose; and closed when the level was lower outside, as when the tide went out, so every high tide filled the reservoir and it was always fresh water that far up.

At the lower end of the project was a gate to open if we had too much water for any reason. We had a main irrigation canal down the center of the project and laterals every half-mile. To irrigate we had **spud ditches put in** every 100 feet. The endless chain digger mounted on a truck frame made a ditch 12 inches wide and 18-20 inches deep, spreading the dirt evenly on each side between the rows of beets or beans. One row was dug out with beets, none with beans, with 28 inch **centers**.

We continued to lease, 400 acres the following year, then on up till we had about 1600 the tenth year, when we gave the lease up as the land was sold. We always made money on the south end and broke even on the north, so on the whole it treated us well. In spite of the dry years, it flooded seven years out of ten. Only once did we lose any crop. It flooded so late we did not get to plant any of it in 1938.

Herbert Hoover was certainly one of the greatest men we have ever had for President. He had been elected in 1928 by a tremendous landslide. After four years he was the most abused. I saw him at the railroad station in Davis on his way home to Palo Alto to vote. He was exhausted, but he had the great comfort of knowing he had a history of service to his fellowman seldom equaled. In spite of absolutely unreasonable abuse for years after he left office, he never lost his dignity or his service to his fellowman. He and his wife were a great credit to the American people.

American agriculture had geared up during World War I to feed the American military and give much to our allies. President Wilson had said, "Food will win the war and write the peace." All of a sudden, in the fall of 1920, the bottom fell out of farm prices. I reported earlier that we were offered $3.25 for barley at harvest and fortunately sold at $2.25, but those who held on sold as low as 60 cents and it was a year later before it got back to $1.00 per cwt. Agriculture was in a depression from then on. World trade was at a standstill. Industry and labor were doing well with prices soaring, until the stock market crash in 1929 and the drastic unemployment by 1932.

All this time agriculture had been in trouble. The nation recognized it, but didn't know what to do. Hoover depended on the Federal Farm Board. Its chairman was Alexander Legge, former president of International Harvester Company, and members C. C. Teague of California; C. B. Denman, president of National Livestock Producers, former president of the American Farm Bureau Federation, and two other members, all strong for agriculture. They had done their best but couldn't hold back the tide.

The Farm Bureau was for the McNary Haugen Act to set tariff on some farm commodities, but principally to set up a board to encourage sale of surplus farm products at a price at which they would sell, and then assess an equalization fee on the domestically sold portion of the crop. The fee was to be used to raise the price to the grower for the portion exported. The farmers opposed any government subsidy; the equalization fee being collected from the domestic sales was to pay any losses on the export. Both Coolidge and Hoover had opposed this approach, and the farm depression had spread to a deep general depression.

† 1933

Franklin Delano Roosevelt took office on March 4, 1933. On the same day, Henry Aggard Wallace was sworn in as Secretary of Agriculture with Rex Tugwell, a Cornell University professor, as Undersecretary, and Jerome Frank as Attorney.

The Agricultural Adjustment Act was developed by Farm Bureau members, along with Chester Davis, director of agriculture in Montana, Clifford Gregory, editor of Prairie Farmer, M. L. Wilson of Montana State University, William I. Meyers or Cornell, later head of Farm Credit, and many others. It was quickly presented to Congress, passing the House in early April by a vote of 387 to 12, passing the Senate in May 53 to 28, and signed May 12 by the President. The National Recovery Act with its Blue Eagle was passed soon after, as well as a great deal of other novel experimentation in the field of government. Roosevelt and his associates expanded tremendously the sphere of action and the power of the federal government. We surely enjoyed his honeymoon with Congress, because most people were desperate for some economic relief and were willing and happy to try anything. He had won the election by a landslide, and many new congressmen had slid in on his coattails.

Maybe this is the place to tell the story of the congressman from Oakland, which he told me with variation several times. He was an attorney struggling along. The bar association had a meeting at the old Hearst home over the hills near Pleasanton, with a banquet and an evening of relaxation. He had talked of wanting to own a ranch, and sometime before daylight he had signed to buy a ranch in the Anderson-Cottonwood area of Shasta County. Very nice and valuable today, but then quite marginal.

He and his wife and family moved up and became real, honest farmers, raising mostly pigs on a little grain, grass, and acorns. He loved it, but his wife didn't. She was doing a good deal of the work. One day he passed the kitchen window with a pail in each hand. His wife called out the window, "Where are you going?" "Down to feed the pigs," he said. In a disgusted voice she said, "Well, look in your **buckets**." He said, "I did, and they were empty." She said she had had enough, and anyhow they were all out of money, so he got a job as assistant district attorney and put the ranch up for sale.

There were lots of lookers, some looking and boarding with them for several days, but no takers. Finally a Portuguese woman and her son came on a Monday. Friday his wife said, "Get them out, I won't feed them another day." But he felt they were serious and they had to stay another day. Saturday morning they announced that they liked the ranch, but didn't have quite enough money for the down payment. They would have to go home to get some more money. He asked how much they had, and that was just the minimum he had decided he would accept. So that was OK. He knew if they went to town, they would meet people who knew the ranch and the sale would be off, so he got all the papers signed up and had a big dinner that night. The next morning they all got up early for early mass, then back for a big celebration breakfast.

Joe, the new owner, was quite happy. His host asked why he had the big smile on his face. Joe replied, "Well, I was just thinking about how I had confessed to the priest how we beat you out on the down payment yesterday." My friend agreed that that was interesting, because that is what he confessed to the priest also.

They moved back to Oakland and hung out the old law shingle, and after a quiet day he came home to announce that he had decided to run for Congress. His wife told him he was crazy. He didn't know enough to run for Congress, and anyhow no one would vote for him. He replied she was right on the first part, but he was going to find out about the second part. He had figured out that the federal government was the only one who had any money, and he wanted to be close to the source.

I was in the House office building and saw his name on the door, so I dropped in for a little relaxation and a few words of wisdom. His wife was his secretary, and his son was on his staff. The voters of Oakland brought him back home about two elections later, but I am sure he provided sunshine and mirth to his colleagues and a vote for the President any time he needed it.

President Roosevelt used radio for his "fireside chats" with the American people. He told them what he had done and what he hoped to do, always with a spirit of optimism and friendliness and an assurance that if his plans didn't work out as he hoped, he would be the first to amend or drop them.

Roosevelt had a brain-trust of college professors, economists, and politicians. They were referred to as the group that met all hours of the day and night in the red brick building in Georgetown. Rex Tugwell and Jerome Frank, with several others, were in the Department of Agriculture, but they were in all the departments of government, devoting most of their time and energy to conceiving new ideas to extend the power and authority of government over the lives of people, and along with it ways to perpetuate the political power of the administration of which they were a part. It was a stimulating time in government when the administrative branch took precedence over the legislative, and tried to stack the Supreme Court so their new-found powers would not be challenged.

We had the land across the canal in asparagus. Many of us were growing a very fine quality of asparague (grass), so we decided to form the Holland District Asparagus Growers Association as a cooperative with William Lambert of Lambert Packing Company, our sales agency, with a wooden shoe as our trademark. The soil was rich and the plantings new, so the quality was high and we did very well. I was secretary, Crutcher Huntly was president, and Babe Slater was treasurer. Other members were: Guy Fraser, W. H. Caine, Steve and John Heringer and sons, Ralph Krull, Rueben Merwin, Robert Yelland, Gus Olson, Alfred Parsons, George and Herbert Pollock, Howard J. Reamer, Burt Swartz, Clarence Holmes. I plowed it out in April, 1942.

We moved to the bypass to start disking and planting on March 20. We raised beets for Holly Sugar Company. They went out on 400-ton barges, going directly by water to the Tracy refinery. We would get a barge a day, 200 tons for Cap Seaborn, and 200 tons for us, but we usually beat that. All the gas and oil came in on a Shell Oil barge. Of course, much of the beans, barley, onions, and hay left the Holland Land Company by barge.

I notice the taxes on the home place of 53 acres, the Spanggord place of 47 acres, and 20 acres across the canal, 120 acres in all, was $217.26. Government didn't do so much for us, or to us, or take so much from us.

J. C. Marshall (Jess) threshed peas for us. He was a great fellow. He had moved to the Woodland area from Arkansas. He was a great story teller, active in the church, Farm Bureau, 4-H Clubs, and any good cause. He moved to Clarksburg and bought a place on Willow Point Road.

Jess and Mrs. Marshall, Scud and Oneiva, all played an active part in the life of the community. They could always be counted on to help do good. We each packed our equipment in our Model T pickups and went camping above Nevada City one summer for a fine time.

Even though unemployment was terrible in 1933, we always seemed short on good crews for hoeing, etc. Working with the Berkeley U.C. YMCA, we set up a camp in the old camp building at the Silverdale railroad siding just off Central Avenue and had a group of about 50 students come up for the summer vacation. Farmers would pick them up and deliver them back at the camp. We supplied kitchen and dining equipment and army cots. They furnished their own cooks. It worked out very well for them and us. They came for several years. When they returned to Berkeley, some of them rented a large house where they continued their community living. That was the beginning of the cooperative houses, passing around the kitchen and household chores so they could live as well as they cared to, but cheaply. I believe they are still active.

We considered building a new house for ourselves this year, but the National Recovery Act set artificially high prices on all the materials, so we were advised by the lumber yard and others to delay as prices couldn't stay that high very long (all things are relative). So we put $4,883.00 into securities, figuring if lumber and wages went up, securities would also. But by next year costs were still going up, so we let the contract for our new house at $18,000 plus. By the time it was finished in May 1935, it was about $22,000.

I note that on August 31 of 1933 I sold 51 sacks of baby lima beans at $2.25 per sack. Pretty low.

This fall I bought the first F12 Farmall Tractor sold in Sacramento for $495.00. Ready to work, it cost $519.35. I got a Ford pickup for $323.88.

We also bought a Chrysler car. It was a very easy riding car, comfortable all around. It was what was called "free-wheeling." It was like shifting into neutral every time you took your foot off the pedal. It almost seemed to increase speed. We changed cars then every two years, as a rule. They had to be serviced every 1000 miles, valves ground every 10,000 to 12,000 miles, and engine overhauls were common, with new crankshaft bearings, new rings, and cylinders reground, new points, and occasionally a new carburetor. Accuracy of manufacture and assembly, better metals, and better oils and greases have all contributed to longer life. Gas with no tax was regular at 10 cents per gallon from a pump on the edge of the sidewalk into a 10- to 15-gallon tank, and we got 15-20 miles per gallon. Tires were the big expense. At first, 500 miles were good, and we often didn't get it. I have hit a small rock in the road and blown a tire on the first trip. We used to figure gasoline about ½-¾ cents per mile and tires 4 cents a mile or better; now it is just the reverse.

In the fall of 1933, Warren Norton got some of us together to set up the Woodland Production Credit Association under the new Farm Credit Act. I was elected president, Howard Reamer was elected head of the loan committee, and Jack Stevens was elected manager. We rented a little office upstairs on Main Street, Woodland. We each bought a share of stock at $5.00. The Association has grown far beyond our fondest hopes and has served the farmers well.

My first trip on a commercial airline was from Sacramento to San Francisco in a six-passenger twin-engine plane. My impression was that one wing tried to get ahead of the other all the way down, and the tail tried to follow them. It was rough, a little scary, but interesting. Of course, it was low enough to see everything.

My first plane trip to Washington, D.C. was in 1933 to a sugar beet meeting. The plane was a ten-passenger Boeing, 180 miles per hour most of the way at 3,000 to 5,000 feet elevation, but pretty close to the mountain passes. We stopped at Reno, Elko, Salt Lake, Rock Springs, Cheyenne, Grande Island, Omaha, Moline, Chicago, Cleveland, Pittsburgh, Washington; thirteen jumps and about 200 miles per jump. We left Sacramento at about 2 p.m. and landed in Washington about 11 a.m., 21 hours. It seemed a miracle. There were no limits on how fast a pilot could climb or descend, no radios much of the time, weather reports very vague. The pilot was on his own and you with him. Every trip was an experience.

†1934

I was quite active in asparagus affairs in 1934. The group of "grass" growers in the delta got together and decided to ask for a federal marketing agreement for asparagus. A committee was appointed—Peter Cook, Stew Brown, and several others, including myself.

Several years before this, the California Farm Bureau Federation developed a marketing agreement program which was being used in peaches, citrus, and several other specialty crops quite successfully. The growers would draw up a program suited to marketing their crop. It was then approved by the director of agriculture after

100

public hearings. Then an election was held by the director of agriculture. If two-thirds of the voters producing a majority of the crop approved the plan and elected a management board, the program was put into effect. They could require dropping some of the fruit soon after the size of the set was known, or set size or other grade standards to limit the volume marketed, or announce each week the volume of fruit which might be shipped the following week.

Alex Johnson, secretary of the California Farm Bureau Federal, had been on the AFBF committee in 1932 to draw up farm legislation. He got marketing agreements accepted in the farm bill being approved and lobbyed for it in Washington in 1933. I had watched the California programs pretty closely, and I had met the new U.S. Department of Agriculture administrators in connection with the sugar beet and bean programs. I saw that farmers did very well presenting their personal or organizational wishes.

Back to our asparagus committee. The first suggestion for drawing up a federal marketing agreement was that we would first have to get an attorney to represent us. I said, "Oh, no, we will do better representing ourselves," so of course I was delegated the job of drawing up the type of presentation and the type of agreement we should have. Pete Cook and Stew Brown were also on the committee. I worked a good deal with Harry Wellman, economist in the Giannini Foundation at U.C., later acting president of U.C.

The agreement applied only to cannery asparagus. Grass started production at different times in various parts of the state, but it was all shipped fresh until the increasing volume cut the fresh market price. At this point the canneries are open, and by the time enough grass is canned, probably in late June, the growers have harvested about the same proportion of their crop, so if canning was stopped, all would have been treated about equally. The proposal was drawn up and approved by the growers, so our committee with Peter Cook as chairman went to Washington to get approval. Peaches were a week or two ahead of us, but we were the second group to apply, so although it took some discussion we had the agreement in force that year.

Each cannery reported its daily and weekly pack. Professor Harry Wellman worked closely with us on cannery carryover, current output, and probable consumer demand. Stew Brown was agreement manager, keeping close contact with canneries to see that figures were accurately reported and on the same basis. Near the end of the season we watched very closely, and about a week ahead of time would meet and estimate the daily output, then pass a resolution that at 2:30 a.m., Friday June ——, all canning should stop.

The management committee was made up of canners as well as growers. I believe about seven were on the committee. It worked very well for several years. I believe it did increase the production of asparagus in the state of Washington and some other competing areas, as canners increased packs in uncontrolled areas.

We then switched to a State of California agreement under state law; under this agreement we set grades and other conditions. More green asparagus was being canned, so we watched that quite closely. At our meeting we would open a number of cans of different grades, dates of canning, etc., to see how our grades were working.

At a Western Regional Farm Bureau meeting in Salt Lake, several of the men who were also presidents of their production credit associations came to me. They said they had talked it over with associations having a majority of the vote, and had decided I should be the nominee for production credit's new director on the Farm Credit District Board including California, Arizona, Utah, and Nevada.

The new Farm Credit Act had passed early in 1933, setting up a new Farm Credit Administration, including the Federal Land Bank and Intermediate Credit Bank, along with the newly provided Production Credit and Bank for Cooperatives. At that time most of the capitalization was in the form of government bonds issued to the bank and farm credit bonds sold to the public. Three of the directors were selected, one each by the Land Bank Association, the Production Credit Association, and the Coop borrowers, each for a three-year term. Four others were then appointed by the President of the United States.

We all sat as a board for each of the banks. I was in the bank offices before the election on other business, when I was told Willard Ellis, the general agent, would like to see me before I left. I met him for the first time. He opened by, "I understand you are running as an opposition candidate but I want you to understand we take no part in the election and are happy to cooperate with you in any information you may wish." I told him that was the first time I had heard of any opposition candidate, and I wasn't mad at anybody. I was elected with few opposing votes. Willard Ellis held the top office in the district and also was chairman of the board. I soon found him a delightful person to work with, and we were usually on the same side of an issue. He did a great job of representing the interest of the individual borrower, not in being soft on anyone not trying, but on being sure we got the true picture of the borrower's problem. He was great at encouraging each bank president to do an effective job for his bank, but not at the expense of the borrower or another Farm Credit Bank president.

I was on that board for six years, by which time I was on the American Farm Bureau Board, the Sugar Beet Growers, and others, so I had to give up something.

The Mormons were well represented in Farm Credit. Willard Ellis' family were very prominent in the church, as was his wife's family. It was either Willard's father or his wife's father who was in charge of building the big organ in the Mormon tabernacle, and it was all built from scratch. The Farm Credit attorney was Richard Young. He was the oldest son of the oldest son of the oldest son of Brigham Young. He was quite an extrovert, loved to be with a crowd of people, and he was quite the hero in Utah—a great fellow.

They were a very live, clean-living group of people, but Mormons are supposed to be very abstemious, no stimulants, no tobacoo, no liquor. Dick Young always had a cigar, and a pocket full, but he also always carried a doctor's prescription saying he should smoke cigars for his health. They had a strict rule in the bank against any alcohol at lunch or before 5 p.m., but there was usually a nip after 5 p.m. and before dinner. They explained that there were two tenets in the church creed: (1) Thou shall not use any stimulants, and (2) Thou shall welcome your neighbor within your gates and bring him happiness, which means if he would like a drink you should be able to provide it, and to be truly hospitable you should drink with him.

There was much confusion in farm finances in those days. There were many problems in providing adequate and efficient services, building a staff in the Berkeley bank, training directors and loan committees in the local associations, and combining, where conditions warranted, the land bank and production credit offices for more economic and efficient service to borrowers.

When I went on the board, William "Bill" Meyers of Cornell University was head of Farm Credit in Washington, D.C. He was a great fellow, a top educator, and interested in the well-being of farmers, not in political use of farmers. But others in the Department of Agriculture, apparently with the blessing of Henry Wallace, wanted to build farm credit into a political arm of the Department of Agriculture, and all of us had to fight strongly against that objective. We would win a battle, but the politicians lived on. Farm Credit has lived through the infighting in Washington, and now all the government money has been repaid, so the local associations or borrowers elect the directors of the regional banks. It has been the practice for the President to appoint to the national board from nominees submitted by the district boards, but President Carter rejected the nominees and appointed a political choice, so "constant vigilance is the price of freedom."

The Sugar Act of 1933 had been set up separate from the General Farm Adjustment Act. Jack Daulton was head of the sugar section. He had been raised on the old Daulton Ranch across the Consumnes River in the Sloughhouse area. He had gone to Harvard and was Professor of Economics at Harvard, when Roosevelt selected him to head up the sugar section. The section had called a meeting in Chicago. Lester Holmes and I represented the growers there, and Earle Coke, then a farm advisor specializing in field crops, especially sugar, was also invited as a specialist.

The Mountain States Beet Growers didn't love us, because they felt we had taken some of their sugar acreage to northern California. While in the meeting, Daulton asked Earle, Lester, and me to go on to Washington with him to help draw up the contract, which was used that year between the Secretary of Agriculture and each individual beet grower. We knew the idea would not be popular with the Mountain States folks, but we went, and lo and behold several of them were sitting in the waiting room when we arrived in the sugar section offices. Pretty soon Jack called the three of us in, and we worked for several hours on the contract; it was generally drawn, so we were just filling in. Jack told us to come back about 4:30 p.m. and get a typed copy of what we had agreed on, look at it overnight, and be back at 10 a.m. with any further suggestions. Lester and Earle gave up fairly early that night, but it worried me and I stayed up all night trying to find the things I thought we had agreed on.

We were in the office at 10 o'clock. Jack asked if it was OK. I told him I had surely tried, but I couldn't find the things we had agreed on. He said he had expected that from me, but he would assure us that everything we had agreed on was in there, and if we would trust him we could be sure he would administer it just as we had agreed. This was my introduction to Harvard New Deal goobledegoop. I soon learned it was a studied art, known only to the elite, but still a communication media well understood by the initiated.

The department attorneys ruled that where the Sugar Act says the Secretary "shall" it means it is at his discretion. Where it says the Secretary "may," then it is obligatory on the Secretary. They ruled that where the Act says the Secretary *must* establish practices customary in the community in which the farm is located, it means he *can* set one set of practices for all areas in the United States.

We had a grower committee of five, I believe, to handle the sugar program in California, and I found I was chairman of that. It was mainly to see that each grower got a reasonably fair contract with the sugar company, and that workers were properly paid. It didn't take too much time and was quite effective. It was better than the later program of setting individual farm quotas out of Washington, D.C.

We had the California Farm Bureau Federation meeting in November, and I had been again elected as chairman of the Field Crops Department. As usual, I left early before the election of officers. I did see in a paper reporting the meeting that I was elected a delegate to the American meeting in Nashville, but I said "Darn these reporters. Why can't they get things right? I was field crops chairman." Just a few days before the Nashville meeting, I saw Ed Bundy, our CFBF board member, and he asked if I had my suitcase packed. I asked "for what?" He said Nashville. He convinced me he wasn't kidding, so I called Alex Johnson in Berkeley, and he said yes, I was supposed to be there, so I got two train tickets and Bella and I were on our way. I had no time for any preparation, but I figured Dick Blackburn, our CFBF president and AFBF board member, knew all we needed to know. We arrived Sunday morning and met Dick at the hotel. He opened with, "You are on the program three times and on the resolution committee on reciprocal trade agreements."

One was to discuss Farm Bureau-Extension Service relations in California. That was an easy five minutes. Number 2, Cordell Hull, the Secretary of State, would give the principal address of the convention on reciprocal trade agreements here in his home town, Nashville. One person from each of the four regions would speak for four minutes on reciprocal agreements. I told Dick I didn't know anything about reciprocal trade agreements and didn't believe California had a position. He said, "OK, you don't have to say much; anyhow, the proposed AFBF resolution is all written out."

The Farm Bureau-Extension statement was easy, but I listened to three people get up and tell how we had to support the reciprocal trade agreements and how essential they were to our farm export program, while wondering what to say. I was still wondering when my name was called. I knew our bean men depended on tariffs. Sugar did, lemons, almonds, and many products did, so I just got up and said really, I knew very little about reciprocal trade agreements. I knew Taft tried them, and they failed at that time, and we hadn't talked about or tried them since. I knew some of our folks still felt they needed a tariff and wouldn't want to give it up. Then it came to me to say maybe it would be all right if we had a provision that we would not support any tariff reduction if it would cause the price of the commodity to drop below parity.

I was just happy to sit down, but then I realized I was getting more applause than all the other three put together. Still, I was just glad to be done.

They had different resolution committees for each important subject. Our committee met in the hotel. Clifford Gregory, editor of *Prairie Farmer,* was chairman of our committee. A fine gentleman. He had been prominent in planning most of the farm legislation. I had never met him before. As soon as the committee met, probably seven members, there was weeping and gnashing of teeth. What will we do, we do not have an agreement. I hadn't seen Dick Blackburn, our president, so wasn't in a very good position to speak for California, so I sat tight. Cliff Gregory said to let him think it over, and we would meet for breakfast and maybe he would have an idea that would satisfy the committee. I do not know who, if anyone, he talked to, but he came down for breakfast and suggested we pass the resolution as written, but add at the end "provided we would oppose any cuts in tariff which would cause the price of the commodity to drop below parity."

I agreed that suited me. All were relieved and that was it.

I walked around, then took a seat on the convention floor, feeling all alone. Finally two 4-H Club boys came rushing up all out of breath. Was I George Wilson? Well, they were glad, they had been hunting all morning for me. Earle Smith wanted to see me on the stage. I hardly knew who Earle Smith was, except that he was on the AFBF Board and was pretty much the brain.

He was all excited and waved this resolution in my face. He said, I understand you added this final clause to this resolution. I said, no I didn't. I did approve, but I didn't add it. He said he understood I did, and that I was going to take it off and put the comma where it had been, and I figured I didn't put it on, I wouldn't take it off. He insisted I should, so I suggested he take it off when it comes up on the floor for action. I also suggested he had heard the applause yesterday, and might guess who would win. And I got my seat again. At resolution time, the reciprocal trade passed as written by the committee as suggested by Clifford Gregory.

They had a special resolution committee on sugar. Chester Grey, head of the Washington legislative staff, handled that resolution. It was what the National Beet Growers wanted, so it was all right with me. But I wasn't on the sugar committee, so didn't know what was going on. In the discussion on the floor, Chester Grey asked me to verify a statement he had made, which I did in just a word or two. Then there was a motion to table, and Ed O'Neil, with the dispatch he could use called for the vote and it was tabled.

Some of the folks from sugar states didn't like that a bit and demanded a vote to take it off the table. Ed ruled that out, and some got loud. Dick Blackburn then suggested that we proceed with the resolutions, then take up the sugar discussion at the end. All agreed. We finished the other resolutions. Ed O'Neil called down and said, "Now, George, you proceed with the sugar discussion." I wasn't on the committee or wanting to get into it, but he insisted, so I proceeded to present the situation as I saw it. There was a red light timer at the head table with a time keeper, and it flashed on me, but really I wasn't thinking of it and went on.

Charles Hearst, president of Iowa Farm Bureau and vice president of AFBF, jumped up and yelled, "Stop that man. He is overtime." Ed O'Neil turned to him and said, "Look, George Wilson didn't start this scrap, and if you knew him, you wouldn't try to stop him. Go ahead, George." I was done in a word or two. I really do not remember just what happened to the resolution, but I felt like I had quite a day for an introduction to AFBF.

The next summer, we had our Western regional meeting in the Rockies west of Denver. M. L. Wilson, Assistant Secretary of Agriculture, was there. I introduced myself, saying I had met him in Nashville. He said, "Oh yes. I was on the platform in Nashville." He was invited by President Roosevelt to attend the next cabinet meeting to report on the Nashville Farm Bureau meeting. He reported that if it hadn't been for the courtesy and skill of Ed O'Neil, the delegate body would have voted against the administration position on reciprocal trade and sugar. He was invited back to the next cabinet meeting to give more detail. Of course, the reciprocal trade resolution did have a tail on it that wagged the resolution in a way not planned on.

All this was quite a surprise to me, but more was yet to come. The next AFBF annual meeting was in Chicago. I was a delegate just trying to learn a little I sat near Earle Smith, president of Illinois Farm Bureau, during resolutions. On adjournment, I shook hands with many, including Earle. He said, "You have no idea what a relief that adjournment was to me. I have sat here all during resolutions watching you, and wondering if you and I were going to have another clash over a resolution. You know I spent two weeks in the Nashville hospital following the last meeting, because you challenged our trade agreement resolution." He reminded me of it several times through the years.

We came home from Nashville via New Orleans on the train, stopping two days. We stayed at the Montleone Hotel near the French Quarter. The first thing we knew, we were in Mr. Mannheim's antique store. It was tremendous and beautiful. Of course, everything seemed expensive to us, but we were building a new house and needed something for it. People walked through but bought little. It was the thirties. Mr. Mannheim said his last sale of any amount was to one of the Dodge brothers from Detroit several years ago. He took us out to lunch and to tea and invited us for dinner. The tea was interesting, on a side street in an old home. The lady who ran it waited on us. Everybody talked to everybody. The hostess served tea, sandwiches, cookies from table to table, each taking whatever they wished. She then announced she was going shopping, and from then on everybody went into the kitchen to replenish the plates and also passed them around to the tables. No money passed or any bills that I saw. It was a pleasant, homey experience. We bought a rug for the living room, a screen of gold leaf, an Aubusson, two firescreens, a wall hanging. We have been very happy with them, and still have all of them. The rug was very deep pile for those days. It was made in the Savanaria factory. Our children and grand-children have enjoyed playing on it. The wall hanging, also Aubusson, was cut from the panelling of the dining room of a French Chateau near Saumur, where I had been in 1918-19.

†1935

We had spent a good deal of time in 1933-34 planning the new house we wanted to build. It seemed like we didn't have much money to build a house, but I remembered well the beautiful home built by Mr. Paulin. The family had great times in it and enjoyed it to the full for two or three years. Then the children were gone most of the time, and in 1915 he passed away. None of the family had the money to maintain the home, or the need of such a home, and it was almost given away. I was sure I wanted the best home I could afford while the children were young and could enjoy it. It has served its purpose well.

We were fortunate in having Raymond Yelland, a brother of Bobs, as the architect. He was a natural artist and worked very hard to develop a place of comfort and beauty.

There was little building going on in 1935, so construction and building materials were plentiful. All the lumber which shows or is important was No. 1, and the

106

rest No. 2. Now there is no No. 1 available for building and little No. 2.

Reuben and Mable Merwin were building their new home, using the same architect and the same contractor.

We were 90 percent finished when the contractor collected all he could from each of us, homesteaded his own home in Oakland, paid up all his life insurance, took a vacation, and filed bankruptcy. Workers and subcontractors hadn't been paid, and some of the materials were installed but not paid for, so we had to finish our painting, lights, and many little details, and the bondsmen refused to pay the bills.

This was bad enough, but it was pouring down rain day after day. The bypass was about to flood. I was working night and day to try to protect it. On top of that, Dick was at home in bed with scarlet fever. We had a good nurse with him, Mary Wright, but even more important, Bella was expecting a new arrival shortly. Dorothy Anne was born May 17, 1935. We couldn't bring her back to the old house with scarlet fever present. So the deadline was set for us when we had to have the new house cleaned up, furnished, and ready to receive a mother and new daughter. With Mother Mack's great help, we got it all put together.

I was going to Oakland each month for the Farm Credit directors meetings. They recommended a top attorney in Oakland to try to get the bankruptcy set aside and collect from the bondsmen. After several months, the attorney advised me he could not handle it any longer and did not know of anyone who would. The entanglement and people involved would make it impossible to carry through. I went to the judge in bankruptcy court and told him this man was not bankrupt; the deal was crooked. He came right back that he knew that the minute he saw the names of the attorneys, but his job was to protect the bankrupt, no matter how crooked, so there was nothing he could do.

I paid the bills and was too busy to worry about it. Two years later I got a letter from an attorney in Oakland saying, "It will pay you to come see me." I got a second letter, so when in Oakland I called him and made an appointment for that afternoon. He was a fine-looking young fellow. His suit was expensive but dirty down the front, and the sleeves dirty and worn. He must have been of a prominent family, but a hophead or something like that. We went to the County Court House. Everybody spoke with considerable respect. He told me to come back to the courtroom the next morning at 10 a.m. He said I had contacted him just in time, as the case was about closed. I appeared. The judge said the case was reopened. The attorney for the contractor said, "This is most unusual, as the case was closed yesterday." The judge said, "The case is reopened," then asked if I had lost any money in this case. How much? Did I know Reuben Merwin? What did he lose? I guessed. The judge then said to me, "If I find in your favor, do I understand that this man is your attorney?" I guessed he was all right. The judge ruled that the homestead and bankruptcy was illegal, and his house would be security for his paying Reuben and me about $5,000 between us, and the case was closed.

I turned it over to Sumner Merring, my attorney in Sacramento, and he collected. The fee was very reasonable, either 15 or 20 percent. I am not sure, but I did wonder what would have happened if the case was closed finally the day before and I never knew of it.

I am still confused how I couldn't find an attorney several years earlier, and now it was so easy for a stranger. One must always remember that the courts and the law are fickle things of which one can never be sure.

We now had a fine family, two boys and two girls. The two boys, Dave and Dick, were in school and Pat would start the fall of '36. The boys were taking piano lessons from Mrs. Bayless. Pat played with the boys in about everything she could, climbing as high as anyone. We found her one day playing on top of the equipment shed roof.

One day I was surely scared when she was riding with me in the Ford truck. We turned left onto Willow Point Road, and as we did the cab door flew open and out she went. I grabbed and caught her skirt and held her on the running board until I could stop and get her back in and the door locked. It looked for a minute like disaster might have hit us, but it bothered me more than it did her and all was well.

Mrs. Sabina Gemini and her daughter, Mary, came to live with us and help in the housework. Mary was about 16 years old and went to school. Mrs. Gemini and Dorothy became great friends. Mary was very bright and did well in school, going through high school here and then on down to Berkeley where she was elected to Phi Beta Kappa in her junior year. We hated to see them leave. We still visit Mary every two or three years.

We bought a Ford V-8 coupe in 1935, in addition to the family car. It seemed pretty nice, $709 new.

For several years the Amalgamated Sugar Company of Utah had wanted to build a plant in Clarksburg. We had a number of dinner meetings with President Benning.

Canneries had earlier wanted to come into Clarksburg, but Gus Olson wouldn't sell them any land. He wanted to keep it rural residence, and we all agreed we didn't want the odor of sugar beet pulp in the community.

They agreed to barge all the pulp out of the area, and to pay a hauling allowance of 60 cents per ton for three miles plus five cents a mile up to 15 miles, and a few other small things. We agreed and building started. The whole building is on a single heavy slab of reinforced concrete so it would settle evenly. The factory was a big asset to us as growers, and has been one of the most profitable plants in the U.S. They started receiving beets in the fall of 1935. Lester Holmes was plant manager.

I was still attending Farm Credit board meetings each month and a few local and district Production Credit meetings.

The Sugar Beet Control Committee took a number of meetings at irregular times, and meetings in the state to hear any complaints, plus one trip to Washington. The Beet Growers Association held a number of meetings, plus a trip to Washington in September, and several to the National Beet Association in Colorado.

There were state and county Farm Bureau board meetings as well as center meetings, Rotary, church, and other meetings where I was invited to speak, so the days and evenings were pretty full. The AFBF meeting was early December in Chicago.

While the Clarksburg Community Church did not send benevolences directly to the Methodist conferences, we did contribute in many ways. The Methodist Church in Reno, Nevada, was having financial troubles, and the conference had been helping them, but they decided they must close. They then came to Clarksburg, seeking funds to reopen the church, collected several thousand dollars, and opened the doors. It has done well since.

Bella joined Zella Yelland as a golfer, took six lessons, bought a set of clubs, and found it a good relaxation.

On November 1 we still had lots of beets out yet in the bypass. I got all the trucks I could to help haul, and we were really moving them. The last day it started sprinkling, then raining, but we had 256 tons on the barge at 10:20 a.m. I paid 23 people for trucks rented that day. We only had to load, but it was all by hand.

November 27-28 we planted the lawn around the house and poured the concrete for the swimming pool. Private pools were a rather new idea then, but we thought the children should learn to swim and have the pleasure of the pool.

We had Patty stretch on her toes and measured from the ground to her lips. That was water level in the pool in the main swimming part, with a pipe handhold all around the edge. Then we roped off the shallow area for Dorothy. It was also high enough to drain into the drain ditch. Our family and the grandchildren have had lots of good times on the lawn and in the pool.

For several years Arnold Wayburn lived in our old house and ran sheep on the beet tops in the area.

† 1936

On January 6, 1936, the Supreme Court of the U.S. declared the Agricultural Act to be unconstitutional. It said control of agricultural production is a local matter, reserved to the states under Art. X of the Constitution, that the federal government could not enter into contracts to that end, and that processing taxes to regulate production was illegal.

Mr. Ed O'Neal, president of AFBF, called Farm Bureau and agricultural officials together. Chester Davis and Donald Kirkpatrick, Farm Bureau attorney, and others drew up a new soil conservation and domestic allotment act. It was drawn up to encourage soil conservation practices and production allotments under the general welfare clause of the Constitution rather than the commerce clause (Art. X). It was speeded through Congress and signed on November 1, 1936.

On April 12 I flew to Washington, D.C. for a sugar beet meeting to assess the effect of the Supreme Court decision on the sugar act, if any. Walking down a corridor of the Department of Agriculture, I met George Farrell, who was in charge of farm programs for the Western region of the U.S. He had just written me a letter saying I was to be chairman of the California committee to administer the new Soil Conservation and Domestic Allotment Act. I told him, No I wasn't. I already had too much, but he insisted that they all agreed that California would be the most difficult state to administer, and I was the only one they could agree on.

I told him I was a Republican. He said so was he and most of the people in the office, but they had agreed to do their best to make the act successful, and that was all they asked. I told him I was a farmer and was going to stay a farmer, not a government official. He said that was why they wanted me, and he agreed that it would probably take two days a month, but they would never ask more than three days a month. I told him I had a very definite policy, which was to represent farmers before other groups, never other groups to farmers. He said they knew that, and that was why they asked me. They really wanted to know what California farmers wanted, and it wouldn't work any other way.

I told him I would not tell California farmers it was a good act or make public speeches for it. He said they would never ask me to. Then I said, "Well, I am not at all sure that I am for the act." Then he said he wasn't sure he was, but was pledged to give it a fair chance, and that is all he asked. With those commitments definite, I accepted.

Bill Parker, later director of agriculture in California under Governor Olson, was a very dedicated and capable executive officer under the board. I continued on for about four years, the longest of any of the original state chairmen. George Farrell continued as director of the Western region and absolutely lived up to our agreement as long as he was in charge.

The officials in the U.S. Department of Agriculture were mostly inspired men and dedicated to trying to be helpful. A dedicated and effective few saw an opportunity to try to solve what they saw as social or economic weaknesses in our society, by means of federal government actions in ways never proven, or contemplated, or authorized in the Constitution as interpreted up to that time.

Then there were a dedicated and effective few who saw the chaos and economic suffering of the time, the feeling of helplessness and bewilderment, as an opportunity to build party and individual political power and to perpetuate that power. In some, all these drives were at work. Henry Wallace was often reported in the media as completely nonpolitical, and this opinion held for years, but during his first year in office, I asked him to be our banquet speaker at the California Farm Bureau convention. His response, after some thought, was "I believe it would be good politics for me to show up in California about that time (November)." Later I suggested the Sugar Act ruling was favoring Hawaii over continental beets. His response was, "What do you mean? The Hawaiians are Republicans. I would never favor them." These are trivial, but several times, and twice in public speeches, I have heard him say that the principal objective of the farm basic commodity program was to tie together the corn, hog, and wheat farmers of the North with the cotton, tobacco, rice, and peanut farmers of the South, then no one can defeat us. He then hoped it wouldn't be too hard on the farmers of the Northeast and West. He then went from Secretary of Agriculture to Secretary of Labor, to be sure that if he had the basic support of both farmers and labor, then for sure no one could beat him. His grandfather said that someday a Wallace would sit in the White House, and Henry was sure he was the one. I would never question his integrity or his good intentions.

The early farm acts of 1933-37 were not any great success, but also not so bad. They were of little effect during the World War II years, and since World War II they have gotten more political. They have become instruments to assure cheap food and to buy votes for incumbent congressmen, not to help farmers.

In the operation of the Soil Conservation and Domestic Allotment Act in California, we had many problems, as one would expect, but our greatest problem was that because cotton, sugar beets, and other crops were planted earlier in California than in other states, we were always late in getting the programs for the year. In 1940 they promised us this problem was overcome, and all rules would be out early.

On February 22 we were to have a large meeting in Sacramento with state and county committees and Coop and other farm leaders of California. Secretary Wallace would open the conference in the morning, and we would break up into commodity groups in the p.m.—cotton, beet, fruits and vegetables, rice, wheat, etc. The rules would all be in our Berkeley office ten days before, so our people could explain them. The big wooden boxes arrived in Sacramento the afternoon of the twenty-first, filled with paper just as it comes out of the mimeograph machine. Our staff stayed up all night sorting and stapling them. None of us had seen an advance copy or had any idea what was in them.

Dr. Howard Tolley had been head of the Gianinni Foundation, U.C. Berkeley, then had gone to the U.S. Department of Agriculture, Washington, as economist. He was now head of the farm program. He insisted I chair the sugar beet group, but I hadn't seen the rules, so I insisted he do it and he did.

The rules included requirements we had never heard suggested before. It put heavy emphasis on requiring an amount of alfalfa to qualify each acre of beets. The law was very clear that the conservation requirement to qualify beets should be "in line with the customary farming practices of the community in which the beets are located." In 1936 there was no alfalfa in our district heavy in beets.

Dr. Tolley considered our criticism overnight, and I went in for breakfast with him. He said right away, no need for discussion. This is not applicable. Let's sit down and write rules that are applicable. I told him I would not do that at all and be accused of writing rules to suit me, but I would get someone who would. I got Earle Coke, Agricultural Extension sugar beet specialist, and Dr. Robbins, head of Botany, U.S. Davis, who was also a sugar beet specialist.

They worked most of the day in the Berkeley office, while I had a board meeting in another room. When they finished, Dr. Tolley read the essentials to me. It seemed OK. He was the top man in the Department of Agriculture in charge of this farm program under Secretary Wallace. He told me to proceed on the basis of the new rewrite, and if we didn't have the new rules in two weeks, to let him know. We called at two weeks, three, four, and six; they were not ready. Then Swartz, Tolley's man for this region, told us we should have proceeded on the basis of the new writing, that he had seen the rewrite with six of the seven signatures needed, and it was sure final. We had then learned not to put out anything until it was official and final. Then they told us that Dr. Tolley's draft needed some minor amendments, and several weeks still later we got it. It was word-for-word identical to the original February 21 draft, except that one practice permitting application of two tons of manure per acre added the option of "the manure from two animal units." That was how much influence the administrator had in his own department. Politics and propaganda were coming in stronger. They thought I ought to be selling the program to chambers of commerce, etc.

I told Dr. Tolley I felt I should resign. He begged me not to. He had problems also. I agreed to stay if it would help him for awhile, but it was probably six months later I heard of a board meeting I hadn't gotten notice of. I believe Dr. Tolley had moved by then also.

They did tell me I was the last of the original chairmen to be replaced, and for some reason I had gotten $8.53 per day while all the rest of the chairmen got $5. per day, so I guess I was appreciated. This was too long a stay on this activity, but is OK if it shows why government controls of economic situations do not work. 111

Our old frigidaire needed work, so I bought a 15 cubic foot model, which was big for then. It was a real pleasure and we got lots of use out of it.

One of our Clarksburg institutions was a dinner on the first Monday of the month at the Elks Club in Sacramento. We set up a program committee for Farm Center meetings. We decided to meet in the Elks Club for dinner, and make sure the program for the center meeting in Clarksburg on the second Thursday was all in order. Of course, we planned for the following month's meeting.

We then started inviting a guest as speaker or discussion leader, then the programs were good enough, so we invited other members to join us. Then we made it a general meeting for the men. We discussed roads, schools, weeds, marketing laws in the legislature. Anything of interest. We never took a vote on anything, or took any action. That was reserved for the full Farm Center meeting. We had many outstanding speakers and programs.

I suppose the most controversial and maybe best-attended meeting was during a longshoremen's strike in San Francisco. We had lots of sacked onions just waiting for the strike to be over so we could ship them overseas. Lots of money was tied up. The Korean War was on. We had Harry Bridges and his right-hand man, Schmit. Bridges ate nothing, drank two quarts of milk, and talked until midnight, then drove back to San Francisco. Most of the time was spent answering questions. He would make your hair curl, but he answered every question, and you understood both what he said and what he meant.

Several months before this meeting, I had been invited to speak to the Vallejo Labor Council. They were on strike then, and first had quite a demonstration and training on how to picket, how to march and demonstrate, what to say or not say, etc. The members filled the room on the floor level, I was at a desk level about two feet higher. The officers sat at a table behind and two or three feet above my level, so they could see everything. Farm Bureau was opposing labor in important legislation in Washington at the time. I told them just why we opposed them and that we were going to win, and we did. I got a good deal of favorable response from the membership, but I felt like a laser beam was hitting me from the rear. I enjoyed the evening. We should have more like it with labor and other groups.

Russel McKowan and his wife, Cassandra, with their two girls, Suzanne and Jane, visited us in our new home. They were living in Yosemite Valley, where Russell was landscape architect. We had planned landscaping the grounds, but felt inadequate, so it was a great relief when he volunteered his services. I am sure he devoted a good deal of time to the plan. It was beautifully done. Then on April 25 a full truckload of shrubs and trees arrived from the California Nursery Company and were planted according to Russell's plan. We purchased a few from Sacramento nurseries to complete the plan, but the big order cost $143.27, and many of them were in one- and five-gallon cans and of excellent quality. This is just a measure of how valuable a dollar was in 1935-36, and how few people were buying trees and shrubs. Living to compare the value of a dollar in 1935 and in 1978 is an adjustment which I sometimes find difficult.

This is the year we planted an experimental plot of a few acres of soybeans. We threshed and delivered them to the university. I thought they did very well, but the price was low compared to pinks or baby limas, so we didn't plant any more. The university reports said the soybean plantings were a failure, and they were forgotten, but recently we have been hearing of interest in soybeans in California. They are a principal food native to China and all Asia. In 1914 they were being exhibited in the Midwest as a new experimental crop. Now they are a vital part of U.S. agriculture and a principal export.

I.H.C. came out with the F20 tractor for row crops larger than the F12. We thought them wonderful. About now, the first rubber tires came out for tractors. We feared they would leave furrows and also lack traction, but they soon proved they could do a better job than the V-shaped iron cleats.

This year we had 12 two- or three-day meetings of the Farm Credit Board; eight meetings of the Agriculture Adjustment Committee, plus trips; six meetings of the Asparagus Control Board; four meetings of the CFBF Board. There also were meetings of the California Beet Growers Association, plus two trips to Washington, D.C. and one to Denver for beets; ten Yolo County Farm Bureau director meetings; Clarksburg Farm Center meetings; Church Council meeting. It looks like jumping from meeting to meeting, but youth is wonderful and Ray Morgan, Frank Caldera, and others did a great job in keeping things going while I was away.

Bella went with me to Washington, D.C. in December. We stayed at the Capitol Park Hotel. Bella saw Washington with Mrs. Charles Kearney. He was president of the National Beet Growers.

In December we contributed $600 to the Clarksburg Community Church building fund. The architect for the church was Raymond Yelland, who had done our house, so we were working with him a good deal on the church building. Jess Rudkin was our minister.

† 1937

The year 1937 looks like a year of activity. On January 2, we went to Greeley, Colorado, for National Beet Growers Association. I was on the Executive Committee, and we had beet legislation in Congress.

February 2: Finished new implement shed 24' x 100'.

February 24: New sugar act was introduced to Congress.

March 1: UAL to Washington, beet growers.

May 28: Trip to Washington, farm credit.

June 17: Trip to Washington, sugar.

July 13: UAL to Washington, sugar.

September 2: American Trust Company deposit of $1000 on Pierson land, 368 acres.

September 10: The Farm Credit Board went by car to visit the district. Minden, Nevada on September 11; Twin Falls, Idaho, 12th; Salt Lake City, Utah, 15th; St. George, Utah, 16th; Lion Lodge, 17th; Apache Lodge, 18th.

October 7: UAL, Salt Lake, beets.

October 16: Community Church building, $600.

October 27: U.S. Senate agriculture hearing.

The Senate Agricultural Committee planned a trip and hearings through the West, including California, then they shortened it to make Oklahoma City the closest place. I did not plan to go there, but received a wire from Washington that they felt it very important that I go as chairman of the California AAA committee. The hearing was in a large auditorium and it was packed. The Oklahoma commissioner of agriculture chaired the meeting and ran it. Senator "Cotton" Ed Smith was committee chairman, but Senator Thomas of Oklahoma was on the hearing committee and up for reelection, so he handled it for the senators. All the early witnesses were from Oklahoma, and it could have been a record with Senator Thomas questioning: Your name? John Smith. Q. Just where do you live, John? Answer. Q. How many acres do you have, John? A. About 30, Senator. Q. I suppose about 10-12 acres cotton, John? A. Yes, sir, about 10-12. Q. What do you think it cost you to raise, John, about 25-26¢ per pound? A. Yes, sir, about 25¢ per pound. Q. And what did you get for it, John? About 18¢? A. Yes, sir, I think about 18¢. Q. And if you got about 32-35¢ a pound, that would be about right, wouldn't it, John? A. Yes, sir. I think 32-35¢ would be about right. Q. Don't you think we should adopt the principals of big business and join together to set our own price?

This was the routine until about noon, when a fellow Californian from around Bakersfield came up and asked to testify. I didn't know him and hadn't seen him before. He took the stand. Name, etc. Q. What is your farm acreage? A. 4,842. The tension rose. Q. How much cotton? A. 2,232. Q. What did it cost you to raise it? A. 12.146¢ per pound. Q. What did you sell it for? A. 18.47¢ per pound.

He was not very large or very tall, had a new suit, his hair was all shiny with some Philippino oil. If one person had yelled, they would have lynched him right there.

A fairly good group of us had lunch together. Cotton Ed Smith told some good Southern stories, and the tension was eased. The afternoon went on; I had registered my name but didn't care whether I spoke or not. About 4 p.m. the commissioner said the senators had to leave to get the train, so there would be no more witnesses. The Arizona chairman of AAA jumped up and said they wanted to hear another Californian testify. The chairman said, "He can if he wants to, but the senators will be gone and it will have to be short." The senators did not leave. I quoted the farm acreage in California, the number of farms, and the average acreage per farm, which was the same as for the U.S. I commented shortly on some of our problems and wants, and then said my observation was that, where any group adopted the principle of big business, the small man, the momma and papa store, or the shoe cobbler, some disappeared.

The chairman said, That's enough; your time is up. Old Cotton Ed Smith, who had had the newspaper up in front of his face all day to show his disdain, dropped his paper and said, "Go ahead, young fellow, as long as you want. It's the only common sense I have heard all day." So I had a little fun out of it and learned a little about such hearings.

November 7: Another beet meeting in Salt Lake.

November 17: Paid $1000 deposit on the Utter Ranch.

November 20: Closed the Pierson purchase.

November 16: California Farm Bureau annual meeting, Modesto.

November 18-22: Farm Credit board trip to Arizona—Phoenix and Tucson—and to Frank Boises' ranch for a barbecue.

November 27: UAL to Washington, beets.

December 10: SPRR to Chicago. AFBF annual meeting, Sherman Hotel.

Most of my travel was by plane at night to save time. But sometimes, due to weather or needing time to study up for a coming meeting, it was good to go by rail. They had the roomette, with a comfortable bed and toilet facilities. One could take his work, wake up early, and read, write, and study in or out of bed, then dress when you wished for breakfast, and go back for further work or study or to the observation car. And any time of the day you could have complete privacy to use as you wished. It was a little more expensive than the plane, quite a little slower, but good to get caught up on work, or to relax and meet people.

December 18: National Beet Growers annual meeting, Canfield Hotel, Greeley, Colorado.

My income for 1937 was as follows:

Farming	$71,696.79	Expenses	$50,424.57
Salary	1,154.82		
Dividends	1,521.11	Profit	$23,975.48
Miscellaneous	27.33		
	$74,400.05		

I remember saying that my objective was to gross $50,000 in a year. I do not know when I first did it, but I see I did do it this year.

The new sugar act was passed and signed in 1937. The Department of Agriculture drew up the bill after many meetings. It provided for the tax to be collected on all raw sugar. Roughly, the processor bore 35 percent, the growers 65 percent of the tax, and the growers got it all back, up to a limit of so many tons of sugar equal to production from 40-50 acres of beets. From then on, the payments were scaled down to where the payment was less than the tax. We felt we should get full payment for a larger acreage than 40-50. I did the work of figuring all the possibilities using different limits. It was a sort of computer job before the computer days.

The hearing was before the House agricultural committee. Our congressman, Frank Buck, was on the committee and was for us. I had given him all my figures. He sat next to a tall, slender, fine-looking member who would ask me several questions about my concern for the small farmer, then in the middle of my statement took off on quite a speech about his love of the small farmer. After my testimony, there was a recess. He came right down. He took my arm and said, "Let's go to the cloakroom." He told me he was for us, and the committee would report it as we wanted it. Every so often he had to make a speech for the small farmer for the record. His name was Bob Kleburg of Texas. Of course, his family owned the King Ranch in Texas, the largest in the U.S.

Charles Kearney, president of the National Beet Growers, was in Washington. He was a friend of Senator Norris, who was a Republican, but supported Roosevelt and the New Deal. Norris Dam in the Tennessee Valley Authority was named for him at Roosevelt's suggestion. He was quite a favorite of FDR and at the height of his power in the Senate.

The senator, his wife, daughters, and son-in-law had planned a Sunday lunch picnic in Rock Creek Park and invited Charley and me to join them. It rained pretty hard about time to set out, so they invited us up to the apartment to have a picnic lunch. It was a great privilege to hear many of the stories of the senator's long experience in the Senate and of political life in Washington. He was very alert; his speech was a little slower, but his laugh and the twinkle of his eye were still youthful.

Then his wife told of her experiences. The one I remember best was of their summer home on Lake Michigan, where they spent a good deal of time and had many guests. Then she said she had served notice on the senator that this year she was to get a new bathing suit. The senator had three, the old one he had always had, the one his brother left when he died, and the one a guest had left there. She didn't mind the fact that her suit was bloomers and skirt and long sleeves, but she was getting sick and tired of loaning it to her guests and then having to get into a wet, cold suit when she wanted to go swimming. I thought, my goodness, if only the relatively poor sales girls, who think they have to have a new bathing suit about every year, could just hear that story from the wife of one of the most powerful senators in Washington!

†1938

I see I started the year 1938 right by paying $10. for a life subscription to John Pickett's *Pacific Rural Press.* He was a great editor and father of Jack. That was 40 years ago, or 25¢ per year to date. Also on January 30, I bought a 1-H.C. Diesel 35 for $3500. It spent a long and useful life on the ranch.

At the CFBF meeting in Modesto, December 1937, Dick Blackburn had been reelected to another two-year term as president and Ray Wiser elected vice president. Dick had been spending a great deal of time on AFBF activities and worked very closely with President Ed O'Neal. President O'Neal asked Dick to come back to Chicago as secretary of the AFBF, so Ray Wiser became president of CFBF, and I was nominated by California as AFBF board member in Dick's place. The March AFBF meeting was to be held at Jackson Mills, West Virginia, so I bought a ticket from Clarksburg, California, to Clarksburg, West Virginia, to attend the meeting. I was elected by the AFBF board and took my seat on the board, to continue for 20 years.

Jackson Mills was General Stonewall Jackson's old farm, now owned by the state but administered by the university, I believe through the director of Agricultural Extension. The main part was a large green commons, or lawn, with a beautiful colonial central dining and meeting room at one end of the oval. All the way around the edge were convenient bungalows, mainly bedrooms, with a meeting room and fireplace. Nonprofit, public welfare groups kept the facility filled throughout the year. It was a most pleasant place to meet. We need more of them.

We usually had a January meeting in Washington, and March, June, and September meetings in Chicago at the Sherman Hotel House, on the roof. Of course there was an annual meeting each odd-numbered year in Chicago, and on even-numbered years in one of the four regions. Then regional meetings, commodity department meetings, president and secretary meetings, invitations to speak at state annual meetings, and after several years I was on the executive committee with its meetings.

I really didn't need more meetings, but the experience was certainly a major factor in my life. It meant meetings with many people prominent in American life, including presidents and cabinet members, as well as legislature, and three trips around the world. There were meetings of the International Federation of Agricultural Producers representing farm organizations of many countries where I met at least 25 to 30 chiefs of state throughout the world. At other meetings I met church leaders in the U.S., and the Pope in Rome.

David went to camp this summer.

Trinidad Sanchez came to us as labor camp contractor on the Pierson Ranch. Trin was a great fellow, he kept a clean camp, and served plenty of good food. He did have a temper, but men liked to work for him for he was honest and fair. He and his family lived right at the camp, so he always tried to run it as a part of his own home. He bought a place just north of the Pierson Ranch on the highway, probably 20 acres, with two nice houses and a camp on it, so he enlarged the operation and worked for others.

Trin organized the Charro group of Mexican horsemen, with their Charro costumes, fancy saddles and trappings. They were a feature of most parades in Sacramento or in State Fair events. He helped organize the Mexican Association in Sacramento. They helped needy countrymen, gave scholarships, held dinners and fiestas for the public. Mrs. Sanchez was a beautiful woman, and the whole family in costume was a thing of beauty.

They held a number of fiestas at the camp to raise money for the Red Cross, USO, Veterans hospital near Auburn, and other good causes. Lots of food, color, music, and dancing. They attracted large crowds from the river and Sacramento areas. He worked closely with the sheriff's office in many situations. He helped organize the Charros in Ensenada, Mexico, and was always quite the hero when he visited there. He was one of the well-known and respected citizens on the river. His son-in-law was head of Sears Roebuck's Insurance Company in Mexico City. On his daughter's return, he had a party in Walnut Grove. Lots of food, music, and song. It seemed like everybody on the river was there.

He loved his Cadillac, but about five years ago now he was going up Jefferson Boulevard on the first real foggy day of the season, and a Yolo County truck pulled out of a side road and cut him off.

The funeral was the largest I have ever attended. There was a whole squad of police at the church handling traffic. Cars were double-parked by the police for blocks. Sacramento County Sheriff Lowe and a number of his men attended also. Police Chief Kenney and his men were there, and many people, native American and Mexican, rich and poor. It was a great tribute to quite a man.

Bella and the children had a house at Lake Tahoe July 15-30. I was there a few days. The boys thought it was good but too crowded.

On September 3 I bought 154 head of 857 lb steers to feed off beet tops.

Bella and I went to New Orleans to the AFBF meeting. We stayed at the Roosevelt Hotel, and above the desk was a big sign, THIS IS THE THEODORE ROOSEVELT HOTEL. The AFBF commodity committees were provided for at this annual meeting, to get more consideration of nonbasic crops.

The bypass didn't flood during the winter and early spring in 1938, so we planted some grain which came up nicely. Then we had high water and a flood in April. We lost the grain and couldn't get the water off in time to plant, so worked no bypass crop in 1938. David had beets planted across the railroad tracks. I do not know just how many tons he raised, but his AAA payment was $50.66.

The CFBF meeting was in San Diego. On Sunday evening at 8 p.m. we had the California Farm Bureau chorus, with over 250 voices from seventeen counties. Frank Pierce was director. For a number of years we started the meeting off with the vespers service, and then had the chorus. I thought it was a marvelous way to start a conference.

Frank is a great fellow. He held many positions in the California Farm Bureau Federation, but always planned all our organizational meetings, led the singing, pepped them up in the morning, or as needed. He was assistant to the president in my days, and organized and managed the travel service. He was still, in January 1978, leading the singing, providing the entertainment, and organizing the AFBF meeting in Phoenix, Arizona.

† 1939

In 1939 we built a land plane in Frank Caldera's shop. This is of interest only because it was one of the first ever built, so far as I know. They are such a simple tool and still so useful in many ways all over the world. They are one of the steps toward modern efficient farm production. I do not think Frank had built five of them when he got requests to ship them to far distant lands. Marvin Land Plane Company started soon after in Woodland, and their export business was an important factor in their growth.

Emil Lang started with us as blacksmith. Emil was German, small but tough, all lean meat. He was a good blacksmith. All the welding was then done with hot iron. We got an electric welder soon after, and it was used on many jobs, but still the forge got lots of use, and we made our own harrows and drags and rubber-tired wagons. The forge was in the old implement shed where the office and hay barn now stand.

We built our shop (36' x 48') soon after this, in 1940. We used two electric welders and two men who could weld making all the frame and also the doors and windows. The iron bars, angles, and rods cost two to three cents per pound ordered from San Francisco. Total iron cost was $917.05.

Emil had been in World War I. He went down to San Francisco in World War II while he worked for us. He had a few beers, I expect, when he went to the enlistment office and signed up for the CB's construction outfit. They told him he would be going to Johnson Island in the South Pacific. He went to the harbor to see the ship he was to go on, then looked up the little speck in the ocean named Johnson Island, and came back home. They never heard from Emil again, nor did he hear from them. I guess the military is sometimes understanding.

I signed a contract for butane for 1¾¢ per gallon in Bakersfield and 1¾¢ per gallon trucking. We fitted the trucks, gasoline tractors, rain machine motors, and the stoves and water heaters with butane. We got quite a few tanks, but they were cheap then too. It saved lots of money on fuel and also on motor repairs as the motors ran so much cleaner and needed about one-third the repair work. The price stayed the same until 1942, when the war began, and it has been going up ever since.

During the war we had to report every truck, tractor, or car using petroleum products and tires, a long sheet of questions for each one. I filled out eighteen of those sheets and wrote in big letters across each one "THIS TRUCK OR TRACTOR USES BUTANE." I guess the help in Washington didn't know what butane was, so

118

when gas was rationed I got tickets for all of them. I didn't dare report it for fear I would lose all of them, so I would destroy most of them, just one of the many problems of rationing.

I joined the Commonwealth Club in San Francisco in 1939 and have belonged since. I have only attended a few lunches and section meetings, but I am glad to support the idea of the club and read many of the reports on the talks.

We had lots of room in the old dairy barn on the Utter place, and it seemed that, with the alfalfa and grain we had, we should do well marketing it as pork. So we put in the equipment and got about 60 good gilts. I had hired a good farm boy from Iowa, Ed Cavenaugh, and built a house for him (now Ken's house). Things went well for a while, then the pigs got sick. We got the Vet from the college at Davis. We posted a number of the pigs, and they had enteritis—inflamation of the intestines. There was no vaccine. Rice, bran, and molasses might help. We tried all the sanitation we could think of and rice, bran, and molasses with some improvement. Ed seemed very nice and knew his hogs, but he got to chasing around and was less attentive to his family and our pigs, so we closed out. It was a shame, but hog men were almost non-existent. The mild winters here probably encourage more disease to carry over, and in spite of the good weather and ample feed, hogs are a problem few have solved.

About this time, David got four ewes and lambs for his future farmer project. He also got a buck, which grew into a big fellow. He was the star performer at one of Bella's parties, where he decided to butt several of the lady guests and then put a foot through Bella's gown, so he lost popularity.

We had not been able to grow anything in the bypass in 1938, but we got a good start in 1939, both at home and in the bypass. We had just under 1000 acres of beets, and we produced 24,000 tons of beets, an excellent yield for those days with sugar about 18 percent. There were partnerships and corporations which produced more, but I had a list of the beet payments, and as far as I could see, I was the largest individual beet grower in the U.S. that year.

Bella flew to Chicago with me for the AFBF annual meeting. Our good friend, J. C. Marshall, was there, so Mother and J.C. went on up to Flint, Michigan, and drove back a new Buick. After the FB meeting, Bella and I drove down to visit our relatives in Urbana, then on to New Orleans and home.

I was then representing California beet growers in the National Association and in Washington. The evening of the AFBF banquet, I was going down the elevator to get Bella a corsage. Mr. David Pipes, who represented the domestic cane growers, said he had to see me. I insisted I had no time, I had to get flowers for my wife immediately. He insisted he had to see me, and he would get the corsage. When I got back to our room there was a beautiful corsage and a beautiful vase of roses for the room.

When we got to New Orleans, at the Monteleone Hotel, Mr. Farwell, president of the Cane Growers, met us. Mr. Farwell asked me what kind of a job I thought Mr. Pipes was doing. I thought very well. He said he sure ought to be, some of the expense accounts that were doming in, including flowers.

One day Mr. Farwell took me to the very prestigious Boston Club for lunch, and the next day Bella and I had lunch as their guests at home, an old Southern residence. The table was beautifully decorated and immaculate. The service by a colored girl was unostentatious but delightful. My wife commented on the beauty of the young lady, who was in her twenties, and her delightful manner. Mrs. Farwell suggested that her husband tell us the story of Mary.

As you might imagine, Mary's parents had served in the home of Mrs. Farwell much of their lives, and Mary had been brought up in the home as a friend and companion of Mrs. Farwell. The Farwells had been married not long after the close of World War I, and when they were ready to celebrate their tenth wedding anniversary, it meant that Mary had completed ten years of service in their home. They had decided something special should be done for Mary on that occasion, so they decided to tell her she would have a two-week vacation. They used that time to completely redo her room—new bed, mattress, wallpaper, carpet, curtains, all.

On Mary's return, with much gusto and pleasure, Mr. Farwell took Mary by the arm and escorted her up the stairway to her room. Throwing open the door, he said, "There it is, Mary, what do you think of it?" Rather overcome, she went over to feel the mattress, to determine her fear that it was new, then turned to Mr. Farwell and said, "What in the world have you done? What did you do with my old mattress? It had everything I ever earned in my whole life sewn up in it—$3,000." That was a lot of money about 1930.

Mr. Farwell was, of course, aghast, and told her the old mattress had been hauled off and burned. But just to make sure, they pell-melled downstairs and out into the backyard by the alleyway, and there was the old mattress. They ripped it open and, sure enough, there was the $3,000.

The tension was off for the moment, but Mr. Farwell told Mary that she must not do that again—there might be a fire in the home, and it would be burned, or people would hear of this and robbers might come. He told her he would not think of keeping money in the house like that, and she should let him put it in the bank for her. But Mary thought, "No, it was better in the mattress."

Several times later, Mr. Farwell raised the question with Mary, telling her of all the friends who came to their home whom she knew and respected so greatly, and all put their money in the bank for safekeeping. But still Mary thought it was better to keep the money in the mattress.

Mr. Farwell explained to Mary each time that he would get her a checkbook, and all she would have to do would be to write in the amount of money she wished to withdraw from the bank, then sign her name to the check, and she could get any part of it whenever she needed it. After a month or two, Mary said, "Mr. Farwell, you would feel a lot better and be happier if I would let you put the money in the bank, wouldn't you?" He agreed that was quite true, and so Mary gave him the $3,000.

A year or so later, Mr. Farwell became quite silent and not his usual happy self around the house, because all banks had been closed by federal decree.* He did not have cash for his own use, but what was even more disturbing was the loss of Mary's money. He could not figure how to reimburse her, or justify in her sight the action which he had induced her to take.

---

* In the winter of 1932-33, outgoing President Hoover, with the approval of incoming President Roosevelt, declared a bank holiday closing all the banks in the United States until confidence could be reestablished and banks examined.

He was still hoping for some easy way to explain this to Mary when she said to him, "Mr. Farwell, you don't feel very well, do you? Something is bothering you. Is there anything I can do to help you?" He said, "No, Mary, but I suppose I might as well tell you now what has happened. The banks are all closed, and I can't get any money. I can't borrow money from any of my friends, because they also can't get any out of the banks. I don't know how I am going to reimburse you for what you have lost through my fault."

Mary quietly replied, "Is that all that is worrying you, Mr. Farwell?" He said, "Mostly." She said, "Why didn't you tell me that sooner? Remember when you told me all I got to do is sign my name to a check? Well, I signed my name to a check and that $3,000 is up in the mattress, and if you need any money, I sure would be glad to help you!"

We drove west from New Orleans to Houma, the home of Mr. and Mrs. Pipes, cane growers. It was a typical Southern plantation community. Mrs. Pipes almost wept to think she had to welcome us into this little old cottage instead of the old plantation home. The "little old cottage" was built around an octagonal room in the center. On the walls were almost full-sized paintings of father, grandfathers, uncles, etc., in full dress uniform of the Civil War, the War of 1812, or War with Mexico, and all were still a part of the family life. Behind each wall was another room of a more personal nature, but we always must see the site of the old plantation home which had burned down. Finally we got to the old home site, the foundation still there, but a large tree at least 30 inches through growing up in the middle of it. Their little old cottage was really beautiful, refined, and comfortable. They were a most hospitable family, but we had just left Farwell's, a fine example of the New South, and Houma and the Pipes home still living deep in the Old. We came west across Texas, stopping in Imperial and Banning to see Bella's folks, and on home after a delightful trip to see the youngsters and Mrs. Gemini.

We had started the CFBF scholarship foundation and we gave $400. to help a good project. I note the good crops in the bypass and at home were kind to us, so we showed income $161,877.88, expenses $111,800, profit $49,670. It was a good year for us.

† 1940

It looks like 1940 was a busy year of travel and meetings for CFBF, AFBF, Beet Growers California and National, Farm Credit Association. Washington, Chicago, Denver, Salt Lake, Idaho, Wyoming, Yosemite, Berkeley, Los Angeles, Fresno, Susanville, Imperial Valley, Des Moines, Baltimore.

We dedicated the new Farm Credit building in Berkeley in January. Developing the floor plans and construction had taken four years. It was the finest office building in Berkeley, a delight to see and to work in.

Bought a saddle horse to use with cattle and for children. Bought a scout suit for Dick, so both of the boys were in scouts.

We bought 144 head of yearling steers in Bend, Oregon; ran them on pasture, then on beet tops. We had two milk cows, horses, and David's sheep, so we got plans from Davis for a Dutch, hip-roofed barn, animals below, hay above. We built the barn and inaugerated it with a barn dance, costumes, bridge, dancing, stunts, all.

We again rented a house at Lake Tahoe for several weeks. This house was across from the golf course as one leaves the north end of the lake on the road to Truckee. We spent a few days in Yosemite attending a meeting of Production Credit boards in the district.

Both David and Dick had beets, and David had some lettuce seed.

September 26 we bought 220 steers from Elmer Hill, for $8.60 per 100 lbs delivered, to run on beet tops.

November 13 the CFBF met in Stockton for the annual meeting. The National Beet Growers in Salt Lake December 5. The American FBFed met in Baltimore December 7.

The Land Bank had stopped all land loans in Imperial Valley because of the unreliability of water, as it came through the old system through Mexico. Now the All-American Canal was operating, and these conditions were largely corrected. Much of the land of the valley was being tile-drained. The district installed deep drains to remove the water, so it seemed the bank should again study the situation and consider land loans. The board met in the valley and saw the land, some very salty yet, some improving, and some well-drained with reliable good yields. We began making loans soon after.

The valley has had heavy losses recently (1977-78) from rain, floods, and winds, but for the most part in the last 7 or 8 years it has looked beautiful and produced well.

At the AFBF meeting in Baltimore, the World War II situation in Europe was on everyone's mind. Averill Harriman was one of the speakers, as was Chester Davis, then representing agriculture on the National Defense Advisory Committee. I was assigned as host to Chester Davis. He arrived about 8 a.m. He wanted to talk to Harriman who had just returned from Europe. He knew personally all the chiefs of state including Hitler and Mussolini, Chamberlain of England and Deladier of France, and had talked to all of them on this trip. Hitler had told him that he had briefed both Chamberlain and Deladier on the German intent to invade Poland, and that each had agreed they would not interfere or object. Harriman said he had checked the story with the Prime Ministers, and they had agreed it was true. But when Hitler did occupy Poland, the outcry of labor in both England and France was so great that the governments of the two countries felt they had to publicly denounce the action. It was after this that Hitler made the statement, "You can't trust a democracy." This, of course, does not justify Hitler's actions or the invasion. It does point out the folly of appeasement from weakness or any other cause, and also that things are not always as they seem to be.

†1941

The year 1941 started off with a National Beet Growers meeting January 21 in Cheyenne, Wyoming, February 11 in Ogden, and February 23 in Salt Lake. In some ways this was a great organization, full of politics and suspicion, but they were willing to work also. Charles Kearney from Nebraska was an especially able and dedicated president of the organization, very effective in Washington. Every year I was elected to the executive committee with the largest vote, I guess because I was willing to work without caring who else was who or what. The Colorado group was especially suspicious. When we were very busy in Washington, the top Colorado representative would come, then in a few days a second man would come to check up on the first, then in a week or so a third to check on the first two, and check-up was his duty. It was time-consuming, and hard on Charles Kearney planning the most efficient use of manpower. We always did very well, however, in eventually getting our objectives in law or in rulings.

I was on the AFBF rural credit committee, as well as on the farm credit board in Berkeley. The Farm Security Administration, set up to help those who could not get credit elsewhere, had gotten clear out of hand, long on employees, short on achievement, and highly political. The centralized government group in the Department of Agriculture were trying to control the Farm Credit system, so F. F. Hill, governor of Farm Credit, resigned, and the president put A. G. Black in as governor. Albert Goss, former master of the national Grange, now deputy governor of FCA, and head of the Land Bank, resigned. The Farm Credit Administration then got Marvin Jones, chairman of the agriculture committee, to introduce a highly central-ized bill designed to give government control of much of the farm land of America. This was an all-out fight through Farm Bureau and our FCA boards in Berkeley and elsewhere.

The Farm Credit bill spelled out how much the government loved the farmers and the family farm and wanted to preserve them and never again foreclose. It pro-vided that if the borrower failed to make payments for two or three years, the court would lease the farm back to the farmer for five years. During that time a committee would determine the true value of the land. (Presumably it was less than the loan.) Then a new 40-year loan would be drawn up. During the 40-year loan period, the land could not be sold or otherwise disposed of. The principal portion of each pay-ment to the Land Bank would be credited to the borrower, and, if he died, his estate would receive the principal so paid in. The land would go to the government.

It was all a fast play on the part of the small group in agriculture and interior, mostly those who wanted to get control of the land and water back into the hands of the government. They came into government in 1932 and are still there in 1982. For probably a year or more, Judge Marvin Jones from Texas and chairman of the House Agriculture Committee just would not believe we were right, but on his return for a new session he agreed that we were right and killed the bill.

We finally won out and later had set up an independent bipartisan board ap-pointed by the president to administer the FC system. Under this program, all the government money used to finance the Federal Land Bank, the Production Credit Bank, and the Bank for Cooperatives has been paid back, so the government has no money in the system. It is all farmer owned. The nine district boards are almost all farmer elected, and the national board members have been appointed by the president from persons nominated by the district boards until this year, 1977, when President Carter ignored the nominees and made a political appointment. Farmers should cry out so loud that that will not happen again. Eternal vigilance is the price of liberty.

The decision of Franklin D. Roosevelt to run for a third term in 1940, and the drive for centralization and political action in the Department of Agriculture, broke up the close cooperation between Farm Bureau, the White House, and the Secretary's office. I had been the only outspoken critic of the New Deal on the AFBF Board, so up to this time was not quite admitted to the inner circle.

Uncle George Putnam was the oldest man on the AFBF Board in age and years of service, but he was still young at heart and always loyal to Farm Bureau, so we held the September board meeting in Concord, New Hampshire. He was a direct descendant of Israel Putnam of White Mountain fame, and just as rugged. The country was beautiful. For many years after that we always ordered a case of maple sugar from there.

I went from there back down to Washington with Ed O'Neal, and we had a noon-hour appointment with ' The Little Flower," then Congressman La Guardia, a former mayor of New York City. He was plump but small. Ed and I had a sandwich or something from the dining room to eat in his office as he sat at his desk with nothing to eat, but the spirited discussion was interrupted several times to pour a full glass of whiskey, and bottoms up. He was surely a dynamo and helped out several times in getting city legislative help for Farm Bureau programs.

I gave several talks on the rural church, as I had for several years before this. Our Clarksburg ministers were real good men and soon came to be recognized, at least as California spokesmen for the rural church, and we had a good deal of activity. I note that in August we contributed $100. to the building fund for the Morris Chapel at UOP.

Demands from Europe and the war effort put lots of pressure on food production, and tomatoes were high on the list. At that time we planted the seed in hot beds, then set the plants in squares five feet each way, so we could cultivate both ways. The average production was seven tons per acre. Then we went to marking off the field, using planters, but planting closer in the row, and then went to direct seeding, hoping for 25-30 tons per acre. Tomatoes were quite a change from anything we had grown before. I remember saying many times that I thought it took more patriotism to grow tomatoes than it did to enlist. Finally, of course, it became routine, and they were good to us.

In the spring of 1941 or earlier, I had been asked to speak at the Rotary Club in Sacramento. With the war in Europe, we had lost a good deal of our fresh and canned fruit and vegetable export. We had very large packs of peaches which had not sold, and a large crop coming on, so the canners got together and set up an organization headed by an Oakland attorney. Each canner paid a large fee to join, which was held in a trust fund. If any sold below the minimum set price, then he was fined by deducting from his trust fund. The price set was above the effective demand price, so very little was sold. The carryover built up, and the growers had to bear the cost of this operation by dropping a larger percent of their crop. I said in the Rotray talk that I believed this was a combination in restraint of trade. The Federal District Attorney stayed and asked me more about it. Some months later I was called to San Francisco to testify before the federal grand jury. There was a witness waiting room. The manager of the Peach Grower's Association and several of the larger growers were there.

The canneries at that time would finance a grower or prospective grower to plant peach, pear, apricot, or other orchard, or asparagus, with a ten-year contract to deliver the fruit to the cannery. The loan was repaid out of amounts due the grower for fruit. This wasn't the case for all the growers, but involved many of them, so

124

many felt that what they had they owed largely to the canners. They surely didn't like the idea of having to testify either against their benefactors or against the facts or other growers.

The district attorney could have gotten plenty of evidence from the newspapers and a little checking, but I doubt if he got much from the growers. I expect the canners agreed to cease and desist, and the case was closed. I did learn that all farmers do not necessarily see things from the same vantage point.

I usually got up fairly early at home and went out around the ranch, then came in later for breakfast. One morning I came in and Dorothy was sitting at the table looking quite downcast. I asked the problem, and she said Dick had won three cents from her. I asked how come. Well, she bet Dick a penny that he couldn't bend her finger. He bent it, then she bet him he couldn't bend her wrist. He bent it. Then she bet him he couldn't bend her elbow. He bent it. She guessed she was just tired and worn out. Neither one of our girls ever felt weak or inadequate physically compared to the boys.

Ed O'Neal was a great leader of Farm Bureau. He proved his heritage as a very capable and polished Southern politician in the best sense of the word. This, with his Irish wit and his basic confidence in farmers and a desire to get recognition for them, proved most effective. His contacts with Franklin D. Roosevelt, Henry Wallace, and others in the early thirties, when they were filled with idealism and also needed his help, resulted in years of very close cooperation. The benefit was legislation and administration to help farmers enjoy some of the rewards of the industrial revolution and the rising standard of living in the U.S. California farmers did not agree with all the details of farm programs, but we did recognize the honest effort, and acceptance of some of them seemed the best compromise.

After the 1936 election, when the New Deal seemed accepted for granted, they became more self-confident. They felt they now had farmers of the South and Midwest almost solid, so now all they needed was labor to be unbeatable. The White House was less accessible and no longer a dependable ally in legislation. It was thought Henry Wallace could bring in the vote in 1940 for a third term, but reports to the White House questioned farm loyalty for a third term, and Wallace was sent to the AFBF in Chicago to get a pledge of support from Ed O'Neal and Earl Smith. They replied that they greatly appreciated the assistance they had received, but could not support breaking the two-term tradition, and farmers felt the same.

When the war began in Europe in 1939, the U.S. maintained neutrality, but shipped food and equipment to the allies. In February 1941 we passed the Lend Lease Act, under which the president was authorized to sell, lend, lease, or otherwise give food, equipment, and other needs to the countries designated by the president. We had large surplusses of storable food, so we shipped large amounts, and prices moved slowly up.

Top left, our first boy David & our first Buick;
right, our first home in Clarksburg, 1932

Below left – The ice was good for a week!
Below right, Dee, Bill and I with 4-pointer,
     above Wright's Lake

Below left, load of hay, 4-horse team, Shingle Springs
Below right, David Prescott Barrows, President UC Davis, on university mountain range,
     Shingle Springs

5
WORLD WAR II

Pearl Harbor

The AFBF annual meeting was in the Chicago Sherman Hotel during December 6 to 11. On Sunday morning, the seventh, came the shocking news of Pearl Harbor. First there was disbelief, then all sorts of emotions. The AFBF women had asked me to speak to them on Monday, the eighth. I was half-way through in good shape when the radio blared on. They announced, "The President of the United States," and FDR came on asking Congress to approve a Declaration of War. It was a dramatic moment. Anything I had to say from then on was of little moment, and all thought was, "How do we win quickly, how does it affect our families and friends, and what now comes first?"

At the banquet the next evening, Cordell Hull, Secretary of State, was to have been the speaker. Of course he couldn't come, so he sent Breckenridge Long, Assistant Secretary, in his place. The board of directors would have lunch with him in the house on the roof of the Sherman Hotel. I went up at 11:30 to greet the Assistant Secretary. No one else came until almost 12 o'clock. He seemed to need someone to talk to.

What had happened in Pearl Harbor?

Why wasn't the Navy prepared?

The State Department, he said, had known of the plan to attack for several weeks. They knew the date and hour for over three days. For almost three days they had known almost every detail.

Why didn't the Navy know and prepare for it?

Certainly someone would have to pay for this.

He repeated the events in detail. Later, as reports of the investigation were made public, they were almost exactly as he said. Admiral Short wanted to disperse the ships outside the harbor, but was ordered to keep them inside. There was plenty of time to send warning after the State Department was given the day and the hour to expect the attack. The President was alerted as soon as the State Department knew about it.

It was certainly an impressive twenty minutes for me, alone with a man close to the action, or inaction, bearing in part the heavy load of the tragedy, and feeling he must let some of it out.

††† Regent, UC and UOP

I had been on a trip somewhere, and on my return several people told me I was to be appointed a regent of the University of California by Governor Olson, a Democrat. I hadn't even thought of it, so it didn't sound reasonable, but I saw Bill Parker. Bill had been manager of the AAA office in Berkeley while I was chairman of the state committee, but he was now director of the State Department of Agriculture, and Bill had recommended me to the governor. He said we must go see the governor. I told Bill I was a Republican. Bill had told him I was a Republican, but that if I had been a Democrat everyone would call me a Communist. We went over to the governor's office. We talked a while. He asked if I was surely a farmer, because he was determined to appoint a farmer, and if I was a farmer I would be appointed. About two weeks later he appointed his son's law partner in Los Angeles. A few years later, Earl Warren appointed Gus Olson as a regent, and he did a great job. Olson Hall is on the Davis campus.

Of more real interest to me was that Dr. Tully Knoles came to the house one day in 1941 and asked me to be a trustee of the College of Pacific. I accepted, and have now grown into a regent of the University of Pacific. COP was the oldest chartered college in California. Its schools of music and education were well-known. Tully Knoles was highly respected, but the college was small, about 1300 students, struggling as were all private schools then. The faculty were underpaid and unpaid at the time. I have enjoyed the distinct pleasure of seeing it grow into the University of Pacific with a student body over 6000, larger than that of the University of California in my day as a student, and with prestige and respect along with the best.

The trustees of 1941 (only two of us are left, Mrs. Faith Davies and I), the Crummey family (Mrs. Davies'), the Covells, Jacoby, Morris, and others active at that time made very important contributions to the college. When we went out to raise money then, most gifts were below fifty dollars. A $100 gift was worthy of considerable recognition, and $500 was a major gift of which we received few.

Today we have thirty-six active regents and a good percentage highly successful alumni of the university. I feel sure the regents of the UOP would outrank the regents of UC, not only in dedication to the university and education in general, but also in prestige and accomplishment in their chosen fields of life. Foremost in credit for this progress have been President Tulley Knoles, President Robert Burns, and President Stanley McCaffrey, who have led the university for the last fifty-odd years. I do not believe any university in America has had as consistently high-quality leadership. It has been a great pleasure as well as honor for me to be associated with UOP.

††† 1942, Evacuation of Japanese

The evacuation of the Japanese was a matter of interest to this area. There were many more Japanese in the area between Sacramento and Rio Vista than there are are now. The Sakatas and a few other Japanese mingled some with the Caucasians, but they were more a separate group than now. Many of the adults did not speak English. California had land laws which prohibited Orientals from owning California

128

land. They did own some land through Oriental children born in the U.S., and by various means were finding ways to own and lease farm land.

When the State of California was setting up its land settlement projects in Durham and Delhi, one of the principal reasons cited for the need of the projects was that the demand for land by Japanese was so great that it was almost impossible for a young American to get started in farming without state aid. The reasons given then were just the same as the reasons for such state aid discussed by some today, but then it was competition of Oriental farmers, today it is competition of corporation farmers. I got started farming during those days. I didn't feel the Orientals were a threat then, and do not feel the corporations a threat today.

On Courtland Road the Japanese had a school where the children went every Saturday, or on other public school holidays, and also in the summertime. The teachers did not speak English; they were sent over from Japan and changed every two or three years, returning to Japan and new ones coming. They taught Japanese language, history, customs, etc. There was little if any criticism of the school in the community, but some questions after Pearl Harbor.

The Sakatas entertained prominent visitors from Japan, including the Crown Prince on his visit about 1939. Tom Sakata's son was an admiral in the Japanese Navy. The Sakatas and others drew most of their money out of the Japanese bank in Sacramento the week before Pearl Harbor, and Tom left San Francisco on the last ship leaving for Japan before December 7. There was no question that they knew of the plans of attack before we did.

There was of course concern but no hysteria in this area about the Japanese presence here during December and January. The FBI came down and met with a few of the farmers along the river to discuss the situation. The farmers said, leave them here. You assign two FBI men to the Sacramento-Rio Vista area, and we will watch for any problems and let you know the individuals who seem suspicious, and you can handle them individually. No such men were assigned to the river area. Rumors started. If we were on the road at 3-4 a.m., we would see groups of Japanese walking home or in cars, after listening to Japanese short-wave radio which came in best at 1-3 a.m.

There were, of course, many Chinese and Philippinos also in the area. The Chinese had windshield stickers, "I am Chinese." These were also put on Japanese cars. The Japanese military forces were in the Philippines, so we had some gang fights in the area. There were many stories of Japanese lookouts over the rugged hills facing protected areas on the Pacific, seeking or sending messages to Japanese submarines. Then some of the ruthless and talkative Japanese started talking about how they would soon own all of California and be telling us what to do. This talk got pretty common, so we were beginning to talk of setting up a home guard unit, to plan who the leaders would be and what we would do, in case of local disorder.

The government had not tried our suggestion of moving out one individual or family at a time as needed; they let conditions get so bad that the relocation order was about the only solution. There was quite a little time between the order to leave and the departure.

Many Japanese said, "Why are they doing this to us? We are good loyal Americans." What really convinced me that the move was necessary was the Japanese who probably honestly stated their loyalty to the U.S., but then would go on to say they could hardly believe what some of the other Japanese were doing. I was sure they knew far better than I did what some of the others were doing.

All this time we had a Japanese school girl, Kioko, living in the house and helping with housework. Mother asked her what she would do if some Japanese came and wanted her to commit some act of sabotage. She thought she would not do it. Then Mother asked her if he came the third or fourth time and said, "Now this is your last chance; the Mikado wants you to do it. Do you refuse his request?" She then said, "Well, I guess if he asked like that I would have to do it."

After the Armistice, the Japanese families were given their chance to relocate in the U.S. or to return to Japan. Kioko's family elected to return to Japan, as did many others. To me the miracle has been, not that some, or even many, remained pro-Japanese, but that so many both during the war and since have proved their loyalty to the U.S.

After the war, Weide Matsuda came to the house. He had been in a camp in Colorado. They hardly knew what to do when released, so a group selected him to come out and see what kind of a reception he got and then decide. I told him he could have a job if he came back, and soon after I gave him a lease. Not all, but a number returned.

They elected to not reopen the Japanese school. They have been far better integrated into the community than they were before. The farmers on the river recommended a different method of handling the situation, but saw no reason why any American should feel apologetic on account of the action taken.

The year 1942 was a year of activity. We all got involved in keeping lights low or out. We painted black over a good deal of the auto headlights. The tomato hot beds were a problem, as we kept lights under the cloth cover for heat in the beds. When almost all other lights were out, those beds would show up.

Everyone studied and learned the configuration of all war planes, ours and theirs, and stood watch at night looking for them and reporting all we saw. I was assigned to Howard Reamer's lookout but didn't stand watch very regularly, as I was away so much.

The March meeting of the AFBF Board was built around food production and the war effort. We had Ken Galbraith as our economist, and he had two noted economists with him. They had two long lists of food supplies and other factors, one list dated April 1917, the beginning of World War I, and the other December 1941, the beginning of World War II. The surpluses in 1917 were meager. In 1941 they seemed abundant to excessive, so the three of them were quite positive that there would be no increase in the price of farm commodities in World War II.

Galbraith had instructed at Davis some, then had been professor at Harvard before coming to AFBF. I told him I had taken Economics 1A and 1B at Cal thirty years ago and that was all, but I knew farm prices would go up during World War II. Since that time Galbraith went to the Office of Price Administration under FDR, was economic advisor to Truman and Kennedy, and ambassador to India. He has written in beautiful and often humorous language a number of books on economics, and has been a popular speaker. His economics has paid him very well, but it has

130

been very expensive for the U.S. He has a tremendous memory and a quick wit, but many plain farmers can beat his economics. I spend this much time on him because he represents a type of very clever, apparently brainy, intelligentsia.

In April 1942 I bought the Sloughhouse Ranch, 1500 acres, operating as a dairy but also some fattening steers on grass. I was interested in beef but kept the dairy cows, and they did very well for us throughout the war. We never fed any grain. We planted sudan to supplement the irrigated pasture, and we always had several cows among the top ten each month in the Cow Testing Association.

Mr. Saner had been rather prominent in the dairy group, but he had died and none of the boys wanted to take it on, so I bought it at a price equal to what the land bank had loaned on it in 1936. Land values then were lower than in 1936, which we often think of as the bottom of the Depression. I figures the land, $30,250; improvements $5,000; livestock $19,000; equipment $3,800; a total of $57,250.

The same month, April, I bought the lease and equipment of Gan Hitoni, one of the Japanese who was raising tomatoes in West Sacramento across the road from the Pheasant Club. I wasn't so anxious to go up there to farm, but the Japanese were leaving and those of us left had to keep the farming going. But the main interest was to get the farm equipment. All steel and manufacturing had been going to lend lease and the war effort for about two years, and it was almost impossible to buy any farm equipment.

AFBF had pledged all-out support to the U.S. war effort, and had supported price control if it was combined with wage control. The President proposed price, profit, and salary control, but wanted us to leave wages up to him. He finally got this from Congress and set up the Office of Price Administration under Leon Henderson. Wages soared, and, with military draft of much farm labor and high industrial labor rates, farmers found wages high and labor scarce. Since all the industrial production was for war, better or larger farm equipment was very scarce. The OPA set farm prices so low that expanded farm production was impossible.

We got a bill in Congress to provide that any price control on a farm commodity must have approval of the Secretary of Agriculture. The President sent a letter to the Senate Leader asking defeat of the amendment, but by all-out effort, Farm Bureau got Senate approval 48-37. This indicated the majority of the Senate was for us, but also a third-term president had lost some of his power even in a war atmosphere.

With increased demand at home and overseas, farm prices were inching up, and, then as always, this is not politically popular. The government tried to hold farm prices down by selling CCC-stored wheat at 61 percent and corn at 85 percent of parity. Though the President had neglected completely his promise to control wages, he went on the radio the evening of September 8, 1942, to stir the people up about so-called high farm prices. The city press then gave farmers a real beating about prices. The farm organizations fought back. Both Congress and the press saw our position and demanded that wages be controlled. Congress passed the Steagall amendment, providing that for those crops for which the Secretary of Agriculture asked additional production, the price should be supported at 90 percent of parity until two years after peace was declared. This was to avoid a repetition of the disastrous fall in farm prices after World War I.

131

Every county had one or more draft boards to handle draft calls and hearings for exemptions and to get the boy on the way to the recruitment centers. Many cases were routine, but some were especially needed in the farm operation, so we would appeal for an exemption or for a delay to finish some special operation. The boards were faced with many human crises and dramas. They all had a difficult job to do. The Courtland board sent their quotas, but they were kind and considerate with the boys and families, often present to see the boys off and wish them well. Another board I visited sent most of the people out crying, mad, disgusted. A little authority can bring out the best or the worst in people. In World War I we left home with street dances, flags waving, speeches, and parties. In World War II it was almost with secrecy and silence.

Labor was short, with the war demand for men for both the military and industry, so I bought a Siske beet loader. It was before the beet harvesters. We would dig the beets as usual, then top two rows and drag a V-shaped sled through to leave a smooth row with a ridge on each side, then top the beets by hand, six rows, and drop them in the smoothed row. The loader had discs in front to crowd the beets to the center and a potato chain to elevate the beets into the truck as it drove alongside. It was like most new equipment; it helped but wasn't perfect. But in several years we graduated to the Blockwelder digger and loader.

Dick graduated from high school this May. I had lots of speaking engagements this year. One I remember best was before the folks on the bleachers at the Imperial County Fair.

In September I got Alex McDonald, herdsman at Davis, to go with me and pick out six Hereford bulls for the SH ranch. Alex was then top herdsman in the U.S. and one of the very top judges of beef cattle in the U.S. We got the bulls from Howard Harter of Davis. He would go to the Midwest and buy a carload or two at a time and bring them out to sell to cattlemen. There were not so many purebred Hereford herds in California at that time. He got good young bulls and did very well. We also got a big Holstein bull from the State Mental Hospital at Napa. They had one of the best herds in the state.

The 1942 beet harvest was on us. Leon Henderson, head of the Office of Price Administration (OPA) and almost Czar in Washington, had given wide publicity to a ruling that no company could use increased wages as a reason for getting increased price for their production, if the wages had been raised without his permission.

Spreckles Sugar Company had started harvest in the Marysville area and were slow on deliveries for lack of harvest labor—toppers and loaders in those days. Carl Maroney, president of Spreckles, sent word for all his growers to pay 15 cents more per ton of beets to harvest labor, and if that wasn't enough he would raise it, and the company would reimburse the growers for the extra cost.

That was okay for beets, but the growers had the same or similar men working in beans, alfalfa, and other crops with no reimbursement. The growers called me. I told them I wasn't a Spreckels grower and so Maroney wouldn't listen to me, but they insisted I try, so I agreed. We had been trying to get the ceiling price on sugar raised, so I decided maybe I should call Leon Henderson and get him to tell Carl Maroney he couldn't do it without OPA approval. Then I read in the paper that the governor of the State of Washington had tried for a week to call Henderson on the phone and hadn't gotten through yet. So I decided to call the AFBF offices in Washington and have them tell him I was going to call, and for him to please accept the call. Then I called Charles Kearney of the National Beet Growers Association. Then I decided my real trump card would be Senator O. Mahoney of Wyoming.

Leon Henderson had been selected as top staff man for the Joint Economic Committee of the House-Senate, of which O. Mahoney was chairman, and had helped bring Henderson to prominence in Washington. The senator was out in the state campaigning when I got him. He asked, had I called the secretary of agriculture? Why not? Because Maroney was a tough Irishman and Henderson was the only one to handle him. So he said he would try. I saw Bill Parker, director of agriculture for California, and told him my problem. That was fine, for the governor of California had an appointment to talk to Henderson at 9:30 a.m. on Monday morning. Parker would be on the line, and they would tell Mr. Henderson it was important that he talk to me when I called. Parker would call me as soon as they hung up.

I waited until 11 a.m. and called Parker. He and the governor were still waiting for the call. I felt a little depressed, but said now or never, and gave Henderson's office a ring. His secretary said, "Is this the Mr. Wilson, a friend of Senator O. Mahoney, the Farm Bureau, the Beet Growers, etc?" I said yes. Well, the Chief of OPA has just stepped out of his office. Can you hold the phone a minute while I look him up, as he is anxious to talk to you. He came. Well, this is the most ridiculous request I have had yet. Have you called the Secretary of Agriculture? No. He is the one to talk to; why did you call me? Because Carl Maroney is an awful tough Irishman, and you are the only one who can handle him. Finally, "Well, this is the craziest yet, but I will see what I can do."

I had just rested a minute to recover when Seattle called. This is Seattle office, OPA. They understood I had a problem. What could they do? In several more minutes it was Los Angeles OPA. They would have their Oakland office call, and I told them all I knew. He would look into it and probably call a hearing in Oakland. He would like me to attend.

About a week later I got a call from Oakland OPA to come to a hearing there a week later. I got there and found Carl Maroney and Earl Coke, then vice president of Spreckels. The Oakland officer was a fine, quiet, but tough administrator, a retired businessman.

At first Carl Maroney was just put out at the whole intrusion into his business, then when he saw it was a serious hearing, he decided it was all out of order for me to raise the issues as I wasn't a Spreckles grower and didn't represent anyone but myself. Earl suggested they better not press that point any further, as I was probably a proper spokesman. The officer figures Carl meant well and was normally a man of real good judgment, but he really made a mistake and Carl came back with, "Well, we wouldn't have done it if we could have gotten men, but now we have to use mainly women and children for this heavy work, so we felt we should pay more to make up." I asked Carl, "Where are these women and children?" Earl said, "That is what I was wondering." The officer than gave a very well- thought-out admonition to "sin no more." There were no more raises ordered by processors. Wages were going up fast enough, so they soon caught up anyhow.

I had a good deal of admiration for the way OPA handled the situation. The growers were happy and Carl Maroney and I were good friends until his retirement.

Now, in 1978, we have a vocal farm group demanding 100 percent support for farm prices in protest of the high costs and low income of farmers, especially grain farmers. It is of note that the AFL-CIO has gone on record in support of this demand, for they know government control of farm prices means low prices to farmers and cheaper food. Now, for the first time, more of the food dollar goes to labor after harvest than goes to the farmer. High wartime labor costs and shortages speeded up many labor-saving innovations. Hay was a good example, for there had been few changes in thousands of years. Steel replaced the wooden fork. Over 100 years ago the mowing machine replaced the scythe, the wagon replaced the oxcart.

In 1942 at the Sloughhouse we used horse-drawn mowing machines, raked with a horse-drawn dump rake, driven crosswise to the mowing. It collected the hay, then the driver tripped it to dump the hay in a windrow where it dried a day or two, then, driving lengthwise over the windrow, it was collected and dumped at regular intervals in shocks. Then, for a better quality hay, a man with hand fork would gather any stragglings, shape the shock more solidly and uniformly so the wind would blow it less and the rain penetrate it less. The hay cured in the shock. Then came the hay wagon with a high seat in front. You used one to four men to pitch the hay onto the wagon. It was easier and more efficient if men worked in teams of two. If each put his fork properly into the shock, the two men could lift the whole shock clean onto the wagon, you could place it better on the load, and it was more dense so it rode better. Anybody could load hay, but a good job required a good deal of skill and co-ordination. So it was a one- to six-man job. We then drove to the barn and unloaded with a "Jackson" fork, a hardwood triangle with the pulley in one corner and four curved tines on the opposite side. The tines, about 2 feet long, are pressed into the hay. A rope goes from a carriage on a track in top of the barn down to the Jackson fork, back up to the carriage, through the barn, and down to a horse or team to lift the fork into the carriage and pull it through the barn. A small rope is tied in a latch on the Jackson fork, so when the load is where you want it to drop in the barn, this rope is pulled to drop the load and pull the fork back. A good operator can unload quite rapidly. If you are using two wagons, the loading crew stays in the field loading the second wagon while the first is unloading, but in any case it is hard work and often hot and dusty.

We grew our last asparagus in 1942. By February after the war began, Kaiser was advertising for labor in the shipyards. The Philippino boss came to agree on wages at so much per 100 pounds for cutting grass. They lived across the canal. He was back in a day or two. "Boys no like, need more money," so we agreed on higher pay. This was repeated several times, then I told him this was the final figure. If they didn't like it I would plow it out, but he came again. I said no, and put the plow in that day. It was good for a year or two more, but I felt asparagus was not really an essential wartime crop and maybe it should be in a more needed crop anyhow.

The cutters all went to Richmond to the shipyards for the big money, but in about three months they were back wanting a job. I thought they were making big money, but they showed me their paychecks. The wage seemed good per hour, but after all the deductions, it was less than we were paying for a 10-hour day of hoeing, and much less than piecework.

134

†††1943

In 1943 we bought a hayloader. This is hooked to the rear of the wagon or truck. You do not shock the hay. It has spring tines on a cylinder about five feet long to straddle the windrow, and an elevator 5 feet wide to elevate the hay to the load. This takes a truck driver and two men on the load to distribute and pack the hay. As the load gets higher, the footing gets pretty unstable, and the danger of a man and fork falling off, or stabbing his partner, really bothered me. This lasted two years, then they wanted a third man on the load, for it was hard work. You couldn't decide when you wanted a little rest for that flow of hay kept coming. Two men with forks and loose footing was bad enough, never three, so we changed the system. We were mowing with F-12s or a small A.C. tractor. We raked with a side delivery rack directly into windrows, then bunched into larger shocks with a buck rake on an old car chassis. Then we used an old truck chassis, mounted an old differential on it, and built a big buck rake with teeth ten feet long on the rear of the truck. We bucked the hay into large shocks, then after curing collected several of these on our big buck rake, about 1½ tons per load, and headed for the barn at 25 miles an hour. We dropped the load to the ground in front of the barn and pulled out for another load, to be back at the barn about the time the Jackson fork crew had the last load in the barn. This way with three men working hay and a boy with the Jackson fork team or pickup, we found the cheapest haying we ever had.

After several years of buck rakes, we went to bales, as they were easier to feed out. After we sold the dairy most of the hay was fed out on the range.

For the oat and vetch hay to be fed in the haybarn near the big reservoir, we raked it into windrows, then picked it up with a hay chopper, blowing it directly into the self-unloading wagon. Then we put the tractor on it and went to the barn, dumping it into the blower in the barn. We have continued that up to 1978, and it is the cheapest way of all.

For a cattle ranch, a pitchfork is still in active use, but we do not buy several at a time like we used to. Maybe one on the hay press is all we use up to winter feeding.

The iron wheels on the old F-12 tractor were rough and slow. I wanted rubber tires to almost double the speed of mowing and raking. Montgomery Wards and Sears and others were advertising tractor tire sales, as there was a surplus. They would look like pretty small tractor tires today. I applied for permission to buy a pair from the ASCS committee. I was turned down. I appealed to the state committee and was refused, saying it was their job to conserve rubber. I later told the IHC dealer I needed tires but couldn't get them. He said he could get them, and the next day I had them— at a higher price, of course. The dealer could get them; the farmer couldn't. But in spite of shortages, we produced one-third more crop this year than farmers had prewar.

We needed rubber boots for bypass farming, and ours were all worn out. Different workers would be using them, and boots need to fit, so I needed several pairs to fit various people, or one pair would do with lace boots, which give a good deal of adjustment for size. I went to Sacramento Rubber Company. At that time you had to find just what you wanted in the store, get the correct description and the assurance it was available, then go to the war board office and get a permit, if possible. Then, with the permit, you could buy the article.

The store said I couldn't buy lace boots; they were only for miners; farmers could only get plain ones. I told him all I wanted him to do was say they have the lace type for sale. I would worry about the permission, so he gave it to me. I took it to the war board office, and the girl asked if I was a miner; she said I couldn't have them. I insisted on going to the supervisor for determination. The supervisor came to the desk and said, "Oh, Mr. Wilson." She lived in West Sacramento. I really didn't place her, but she knew me and took the slip back to her desk. She called for the girl to come get it and deliver it to me. The girl mumbled, with a sour look, "It sure ain't what you know but who you know that counts around here." So I guess the moral is, you win some and lose some. The one pair of lace boots took less rubber than two or three pairs of regular.

The big farm problem was shortages—labor, equipment, supplies, etc.—so we got the legislature to pass the California Farm Production Council Act, with the approval of Governor Earl Warren and an appropriation of $1,600,000, as I remember it, and seven members appointed April 9 and 10, 1943. Frank Shay, manager of the Prune and Apricot Association of San Jose, was chairman; I was vice chairman; A. J. McFadden, a citrus-walnut grower of Orange County, and probably top Coop man in the state, was on the Executive Committee. We got Professor R. L. Adams, an outstanding farm management professor and organizer, as manager. Other members were Loren Bammert, later president of National Cattlemen's Association; Joe Hart, very prominent dairyman; Camille Garnier, fruit and vegetables from Los Angeles County; and W. L. Smith of the state grange.

The U.S. government set up a farm labor procurement group in each state under the direction of the Director of Agricultural Extension Service, headed by B. H. Crocheron in California. There was a labor office in each county separate from the Extension office, with separate staff, but directed by the Farm Advisor. The state office was downtown Berkeley under Warren Schoonover. We agreed Professor Crocheron should be advisory to the production council, and the council advisory to Professor Crocheron's labor activities, so we would cooperate closely.

Col. Jay Taylor of Texas and later General Bruton of the Army Engineers represented the U.S. in handling the Bracero program, which brought workers in from Mexico. When the first sugar act was passed in the early thirties, U.S. sugar production was low, farms were small, and beet acreages quite small, so often in the mountain states the farm family or neighbor women and children did the thinning, hoeing, etc. Then acreage expanded and laws limited use of children. Full trainloads of beet workers would go out of Sacramento for the mountain state beet areas. We were all short of labor for beets. We got a law through Congress to allow selected Mexican workers to get nine-month visas to work in the U.S. in beet cultivation and harvest. The first year we got them, but our embassy did little to screen them, so most were cab drivers, bootblacks, etc. from Mexico City. Some came in large numbers from a small farm area of Mexico, and raised fears in Mexican farmers that too many would leave, creating a shortage and high wages for them to pay.

At the end of the first season some of our beet growers went down to Mexico and met with the Association National de Cosecheros, their farm organization, and

136

with Mexican and American officials, to develop a mutually beneficial program. After several days we drew up a 10-point program on which we agreed.

Tom Robertson, Alberto Salinas Ramos, president of the Cosecheros, and I took it to the foreign minister and got his approval. His office was on the third floor. We went out for lunch, but the elevator was not working so he suggested we walk down, saying, "I have found that it is much easier to go down than up either in life or in politics." The beet growers had used the Mexicans several years when the World War II came, and the program was greatly expanded for all crops in other geographical areas.

With the big increase in numbers of workers and many Americans newly involved in the program, we repeated many of the problems and had many hang-ups and delays. Farmers were frantic for labor and had lots of promises but no men, so Tom Robertson was asked by Colonel Jay Taylor to go to Mexico to see what the problem was. The U.S. Embassy said they had sent all they had orders for. Tom got lots of wires direct from grower groups to the Embassy and stayed until he got things moving.

Tom's father had gone with an American colonization group to Los Mosches, Mexico. Tom was born and raised speaking English but more Spanish, and also had learned several of the Indian dialects, which he could speak fluently. About 1911, the revolution had started and he was due to start high school, so he came back up to Ventura County. He finished school, got married to a great girl, Dorothy Utt. They farmed and raised a good family. Tom became active in Farm Bureau and was chairman of the Vegetable Growers Committee. He worked till he wore himself out, so had to spend a long period of rest and recuperation.

Dorothy's father loved fishing and camping in Baja, California, and knew it well. Tom and Dorothy decided to move to a ranch in Baja where they could enjoy some work, some siestas, write some, and enjoy life as it came. They both like people and have a great dedication to helpfulness, so Tom soon found himself dedicated to building better relations between the U.S. and Mexico, the governments, the people or individuals of the two countries. They later left the ranch, which was about 75 miles south of Ensenada, and moved up to Ensenada. They built a home and a trailor village called San Miguel Village about six miles north of Ensenada, right on the coast with a good deal of property in the adjacent hills where they subdivided and developed water and electricity now servicing many beautiful homes.

The California Farm Production Council was appointed April 9-10, 1943. Our first report to the governor was September 1, 1943; a little over four months later we had provided housing, kitchens, and other equipment for 30,000 farm workers. Ten thousand were in camps privately owned by farmers. Twenty thousand were in 75 camps, under the jurisdiction of the council and the state or county, located in 29 counties in the state. We also had child-care centers at canneries or shipping sheds.

We had busses for transporting workers from cities to farms or canneries. We dispatched many trucks to transport crops. Most of the labor camps were old Civilian Conservation Corps camps built in the thirties to employ young people in state or national forests or parks. The "CCC" was very active for a few years and then closed, as civilian employment and army enlistment or draft cleared them out.

A number of canneries had furnished a good many small houses for labor, and for some reason they were now idle. Some state militia or national guard camps were surplus. We would determine what and where we needed camps, then buy the best we could and sell them at a price mark-up of 10-15 percent to labor associations of farmers, or private farms or others willing to house farm labor.

We had appropriated $100,000 to hire teachers or others to supervise student groups. We set up nursery schools for children of working mothers. Mother paid 50 cents per day, we paid up to 30 cents. Where protein livestock feeds or fertilizers were short, we procured them where we could and made them available to farmers, buying if we had to and selling at a mark-up to cover costs. We could sometimes get galvanized iron sheets from a government or other agency.

We got some additional state appropriations. After VJ day, we bought all the surplus military or shipyard buildings and materials we could and sold them at a mark-up to farmers, as they were needed on the farms. Then, as soon as we felt our duty fulfilled, we closed out all operation and returned about $2 million to the state.

It was lots of hard work, but we enjoyed it, partly as a wartime duty and also because we could make the most of our own rules and adjust quickly to the needs for full production. We bought quite a few buildings at the shipyards in Richmond, put them on a barge, and brought them up the back cut. We had a drag line to help get them off the barge and up the levee. The oil house, the insecticide house, and the roof north of the shop are some of them. Bob Yelland's house was made of four or five of them as the base structure. They were almost all built to pick up with a drag-line and move as needed, and made of the best lumber.

On February 24, 1943, we had a meeting in Washington of the Farm Organization, Farm Bureau, Grange, Cooperative Council, and Farmers Union, the last more token than real. We met during the war as conditions dictated. It was very helpful in meeting agricultural needs during the war and in laying the groundwork for a better transition from war to peace. We set the framework for cooperation in the New International Federation of Agricultural Producers (IFAP). This was an organization of free and independent farm organizations of the free countries. "Free and independent" farm organization is a relative expression of intent running from the American concept to the Yugoslavian idea of freedom, with many of the European groups about midway between, but that came later. About this time I had completed my six years on the Farm Credit Board of Berkeley—one of the most pleasant and productive assignments I had.

In the spring we plowed out about 40 acres of irrigated pasture at the Slough-house and releveled it. I notice in the notes that Emil Lang and several other of our men were buying quite a few war bonds on a monthly basis.

Airline travel was rationed. There were four levels of rank: No. 1 could always fly; No. 2 if all the seats weren't taken by 1s; No. 3 next, and so on. Theoretically, if you were in flight but stopping at an airport, and a 1 or 2 wanted on, you would have to wait for the next plane, but I never had that problem. My classification always got me on, except for the 5 p.m. plane out of Washington. It was all generals or equal, so I waited for the next departure. I was happy with the classification I had, and of course if you had one you were pretty sure you could fly; otherwise it was very difficult. I still rode the train on a good many trips as it gave time for study.

Remembering the chaos after World War I about this time, amid all the rush and confusion, a group of national civilian leaders organized the Committee for Economic

138

Development to anticipate and lay plans for the postwar adjustments. Top people were on it. They stimulated many people of all sorts to plan for their own adjustment. They were a vital factor in minimizing the problem. The CED is still in existence today, but less visible. Along with others, I spent quite a little time developing a proposed "Guide to Post War Planning" which was approved at the September 1943 AFBF Board meeting.

David graduated from high school in June this year. His eighteenth birthday would be December 22, 1943, so he of course registered. It hardly seemed worthwhile to start college, so he worked on the farm.

The U.S. Air Force was building up, but there was still little activity in getting the Army organized. Most enlistees were still just doing guard duty around airfields. The only real action visible to us was the Merchant Marine, and they were really active. I suggested that to David. After a few days he decided he would like to sign up. I asked the manpower office in Sacramento. A woman in there said they needed sailors all right, but as he was a high school graduate, why didn't he try the California Maritime Academy in Vallejo? He could take two years training there and graduate as a second mate Merchant Marine or as Ensign, U.S. Navy. He considered that, but without enthusiasm. He decided he would like to go to San Francisco and sign up on a ship and be on his way. Going down we saw the Maritime Academy sign and decided to drop in and see what it seemed like. The Commanding Officer and David seemed to get along real well, and David signed up to take the entrance examinations, which were still a month or two off. Several hundred were signed up for the 100 to be accepted, so we came back home and farmed. The exams came, he passed in good shape, and had another wait until he went down to be sworn in July 10, 1944.

†1944

By spring 1944, the war was bitter in Europe and the Orient, but the worst was over in Europe and we were doing better in Asia. In addition to farming and attending Farm Bureau and Farm Production Council meetings, we were starting postwar planning meetings with the county farm bureaus and the extension service. These later became helpful in making the adjustments. We sold 100 calves at 610 lbs, 11 ¢/lb. This was up fromprewar, but low compared to today, even at recent low prices.

The CFBF annual meeting was held at the Municipal Auditorium in Sacramento. Governor Earl Warren was dinner speaker. Prof. B. H. Cocheron ended his talk to the CFBF meeting with the statement,"It is hoped the Farm Bureau will continue to stand firm for the independence of farm life." The AFBF annual meeting emphasized international cooperation supporting the suggested United Nations, the International Monetary Fund, the International Bank for Reconstruction and Development, but also emphasized that these were no substitute for sound domestic fiscal policy. The AFBF favored international trade on a sound basis and supported the new International Food and Agriculture Organization (FAO).

Allan Kline, then vice president of Iowa Farm Bureau, was sent to England by the Office of War Information to meet the people on the street or farm, on up to the Prime Minister, to study feelings and needs. He was there during much of the London air raids, and formed many friendships.

We built the cattle corrals at the Sloughhouse Ranch and built up the levee along Deer Creek.

I note that on February 5 we got electricity into the Sloughhouse Ranch. PG&E later sold to SMUD.

Some high spots noted for the spring of this year were:

Feb. 16: Yolo County Farm Bureau bean dinner. This was quite a dinner, as we had given up the bean dinners during the war, but could now begin to see the end, so we celebrated.

Apr. 13: President Roosevelt died in Warm Springs, Georgia. Harry Truman took office as President.

May 8: Germany surrendered. Italy already had.

A prisoner of war camp was set up on Clarksburg Road. We paid to set it up, then the sugar company paid the government for the labor, and we paid the sugar company the same rate as we would have for civilian labor. I needed them to thin beets in the Pierson district. The beets there were planted late, so I was the last grower to need them. They told me that all the men were already assigned and there were none for me. They then said they had a group of twenty or so sergeants, all part of the Rommel Africal Corps. They had been prisoners over two years and never had done a lick of work, so they might not want to start now. The U.S. Army would not make them work as they were not sure sergeants should work.

I loaded them into the truck, went to the job, lined them up, told them I had been in France in World War I. I knew they were tough, but I could be too. We could cooperate and get along fine. It was up to them. It was getting hot, and thinning beets is hard work to break in on. One man passed out in the field from exhaustion and was in the hospital in Sacramento for several weeks. I worked pretty closely with them, so we soon got adjusted and did very well. I found that they were not getting any solid meat to eat, only the entrails and other inside organs that we never eat, and little of that.

I told the U.S. officer in charge to remember they may be prisoners, but we were paying the same rate for their work that we paid other workers, and we insisted they be well fed with real meat as long as they worked for us. They were better fed and did the work better.

Each gang would have so many feet of row to hoe or thin, or pick or load, each day, and when that was done they could quit, sometimes early, sometimes a little late. Occasionally I would have to get them out of the truck to finish up their allotment of work, but really we got along very well.

They wanted to put on a show for their entertainment, so Bob Yelland and I agreed to get clothes and other props for them, and they invited us to see the show. We took our wives and also Dr. W. W. Robbins of Davis and his wife. We visited with them after the show, which was very unpopular with the U.S. officer.

Several years later Bob and Zella Yelland were seeing Europe in a rented car. They came to the German border and checked in, but their papers were not right and the guard told them they couldn't enter. Then, "Yes, you can, Mr. Yelland." It was one of the former prisoners who had worked for Bob.

On May 15 I went to San Francisco to attend the United Nations organizational meeting for ten days or two weeks. Had lunch with Ambassador Pearson of Canada, McDougal of Australia, Albert Goss, Master of National Grange, Allan Kline, AFBF, Ray Ogg, Washington office FB, David Brinkley of Coop Council. Signed in as consultant and got pass signed by Alger Hiss as general secretary, later tried and convicted of giving information to Russia.

Our group included representatives of almost all the national organizations, business, labor, professions, women, political, etc. We would meet each morning with our own group, then usually Secretary of State Statineous or Senator Connally, Harold Stassen or another U.S. delegate, a delegate from Canada, or some other person of prominence would speak to us of the progress as he or she saw it. Then we could make any suggestions we saw fit. We saw the possibility of the U.S. having one vote in 150, but assumed it would be further out in time than has developed.

As I saw it, we planned an organization of those who sought peace and were willing to join a group organized for that purpose, and others could join as they met the requirements. As the conference developed, the objective changed to getting all nations and especially Russia into the organization. She was given three votes, besides all her satellites, to our one, and many other concessions were made to get Russia to agree and sign the charter, so it has never been the strong organization originally designed. The formation of the economic and social committee was felt by many to be the principal accomplishment of the conference. We asked at our meeting how the human relation clause would be carried out. The answer was, "We are trying to make an international omelet without breaking a shell." Parts seem rather visionary, parts prophetic, but it represents feeling as it was during the war looking toward peace.

This September board meeting was held at the Edgewater Beach Hotel north of Chicago. The atmosphere was so relaxed, and short opportunities for walks on the beach with other board members was so pleasant and conducive of better acquaintance, that I wished we might meet there often. One of my first actions after becoming president of the CFBF was to plan the Asilomar leadership conference each springf to build our volunteer leadership and let leaders and staff become better acquainted.

†1945

Action in the Pacific was moving rapidly. On August 6 the bomb was dropped on Hiroshima with devastating effect, after Japan had been offered peace in return for surrender and refused. On August 9 Nagasaki was bombed, and Japan realized the destructive power available to us, so on August 14, 1945, Japan surrendered. President Harry Truman of Missouri had the battleship Missouri steam into Tokyo Bay, and the official surrender was signed on September 2, 1945. General Douglas MacArthur took over the administration of the government of Japan, and rebuilding and reorganization of the nation was started.

In October I went to Guelph, Canada, with Allan Kline, Mrs. Sayre, Mrs. Sewell, Ray Ogg, Hassel Schench, and Wilson Heaps. The Grange, Farmers Union, and the National Conference of Farmers Cooperatives also represented the U.S. Others included were independent farm organizations from free countries of Europe and India. This organization meeting was to set up the International Federation of Agriculture Producers. This was part of the great interest in international organization, increased trade between nations, and special emphasis on dealing directly between citizens of the free countries through organizations not controlled by government. It was very interesting to meet the farmers from the various countries and hear how they hoped to solve their problems.

Jim Turner of England, later Sir James Turner and then Lord Netherthorpe, stood out as the European leader, and Allan Kline as the American. They were good friends from Allan's visits to England during the war. The European view was far more favorable to government controls than the Farm Bureau position. Allan Kline was elected president of IFAP about 1953, but Farm Bureau was gettin disenchanted with IFAP because they wanted to solve all problems through government laws and regulations rather than free enterprise, economics, and trade. I felt it best to stay in the organization, though I didn't like many of the actions, but as soon as I retired from the AFBF board, the AFBF dropped their membership and have just recently renewed their participation.

We were still picking tomatoes on October 20, by hand of course, which was pretty late. We finished beets on November 11.

Above left, Dave and Dick in their sandpile; center, Now there are three, including Pat; top right, Topping beets in Clarksburg

Below left, Bacci ball on our lawn; right, Mother in garden, southeast corner of home

6
RURAL CHURCH ACTIVITIES

We were very active in rural church work during the forties. I covered earlier the organization of the Clarksburg Community Church. I have enjoyed my efforts to expand the influence of the church, because I believe it is so vital either to the life of our nation or community or to the life of the individual.

Rural churches are mostly small, but there were lots more of them and they had a far more vital influence on people than the city churches. Furthermore, in the thirties and forties, over half of the children born in the U.S. were born in rural areas and got their Sunday School training in rural churches, so the rural church has a great influence on the whole nation.

In 1938, at my suggestion, the California Farm Bureau Federation had invited by personal invitation all the rural church ministers and many from city churches to attend our annual meeting in Sacramento. The Sacramento churches cooperated by inviting many of them to stay in homes to lower the expense. Many of the ministers rode in with Farm Bureau members. They had some meetings of their own, but attended much of our meeting to better understand the problems and thinking of farmers. We set up a rural church committee in CFBF, and for many years had a breakfast or lunch in connection with the annual meeting. These were usually very well attended.

About 1939, seeing the amount of social and class legislation being proposed by FDR and passed by Congress, the AFBF board asked President Roosevelt to call a national conference of leaders of business, labor, and agriculture to hold a series of meetings to discuss the social and economic problems facing us to see if we couldn't solve some of these problems better by negotiation and agreement than by compulsion through legislation. He always said he would do it, but he didn't get to it, then the war came on in Europe and he was too busy. I felt these meetings were still desirable and finally decided that the group who could and should do it was the leaders of the Catholic, Protestant, and Jewish churches.

I contacted my friends of the social action groups, the Methodist, Presbyterian, Congregational, and other groups, thinking this would be right down their alleys, but not a one gave any encouragement. They said you couldn't get the three groups to agree. They felt the groups to be invited weren't interested in what the church thought. I would tell them to let me do the worrying about those things. All I wanted was for them to support the idea, but not a single social action leader would give support. I went to my friend, Bishop Baker, and he gave some encouragement. He discussed it with Bishop G. Bromley Oxnam on the Executive Committee of the Federal Council of Churches. Then the federal council organized a preaching mission of outstanding ministers and laymen to visit several cities for several-day meetings. Oakland was on the list. Bishop Oxnam, E. Stanley Jones, then famous for his work in India, Harper Sibley from Indiana who was president of the U.S. Chamber of Commerce were speakers. Bishop Baker arranged for us to meet at the hotel after the evening meeting. They were quite favorable to the idea and said they would support it. At the next meeting of the AFBF board, they approved sending a request to each of the three groups to call such a meeting, and I was asked to see Father Ryan of the Catholics to get their support. He was at Georgetown University. His welcome was minimal and austere, but as soon as I explained my visit, he blossomed out into a most pleasant expression and he assured me full cooperation—but I must not leave until I had met three of his young men. They were devoting their lives to a study of how the Catholic Church could win rural America. Two were there; they were interesting and dedicated young men. The idea of the church setting up a research project to help direct their growth was new to me, but seemed just as logical if you want results as is research in any other field. Religion should be a growth industry interested in research and development.

In due course the first meeting was called for Washington, D.C. I wired to the Farm Bureau right away to try to get it changed to some small college town away from Washington, where it would be restful and quiet, no phone calls to distrub it, or political distractions. This was done, and the reports were very hopeful. Two more two-day meetings were held and a proposed 10-point agreement was drawn up for presentation to the various associations.

After the end of fighting in Japan, another meeting was called in Washington. The churches announced that they would have top-level resource men present for the two-day meeting. We convened with a fine group from labor, business, agriculture, and staff people from the church. The resource men were Leon Keiselring, who believed any problem could be solved with plenty of government control, staff, and cash, and an economist in the Department of Agriculture, whose main qualification was his reputation for accuracy in predicting the outcome of federal elections.

We had hoped that with church leadership, the guide would be to right, justice, equity, common good.

The second afternoon, the secretary of the Council of Churches came in. He said he came to see if we wanted to hold more meetings, and if so, when. The answer was yes, and the labor men said they considered these meetings the most important they attended, so set the date and they would be there. Business and agriculture concurred. That was the last meeting called.

The churches accepted the challenge to bring the groups together, hopefully to discuss our mutual relations under the inspiration of the Sermon on the Mount, rather than in a materialistic political atmosphers of Washington, D.C., but the social action (materialistic political action) group in the church were in control, and they saw little

144

value in seeking answers on a higher plane. I probably hoped for more than was attainable with these conferences under church sponsorship, but I did feel the church lost a great opportunity.

Of course, the National Association of Manufacturers and others did set up the Conference of National Organizations including the same groups to bring close cooperation and understanding between all these organizations.

I was a delegate to several of their conferences and a programmed speaker at one of their meetings. So far as I know, I was the first to use the idea of the Third World. Wilkie had written the book *One World*. Then came the "Cold War" and "Two Worlds," the idea that everyone worthy of note was aligned with either the U.S. or Russia.

I have just looked up and read my talk of February 5, 1951, where I actually discussed four worlds:

1. The U.S. with the concept of equality, and dignity of man, and the state created to serve him.
2. The Totalitarian World where man is clay.
3. Established countries of Europe and elsewhere who protect citizens in considerable freedom but have not fully declared for either totalinarianism or freedom.
4. The hundreds of millions who have recently gained freedom but have not yet determined their place in the society of nations.

It is interesting in 1978 to read that talk of 1951, for while many of the established free countries of the world were then largely dependent on the U.S. for economic aid to live and rebuild, still many of their leaders were saying that Russia and the U.S. were both wrong, and they should not get squeezed between the two, but that they should pull the undecided new nations into their orbit and then be strong enough to cast Russia off on one side and the U.S. off on the other, and thus regain world leadership.

NATO has held us together through necessity. We have weakened our dependence on individual freedom and the idea that the state is made to serve the citizen.

The Conference of National Organizations met about twice a year, business, agriculture, and labor. AFL attended regularly. CIO would drop in, and other labor groups attended. Positions were stated in speeches and discussions, but no votes or actions were taken. I thought it was very helpful and would like to see it again at both the national and state level. It was very helpful just to meet the leaders, then as you heard of their actions later it was much easier to understand the real meaning.

In the CFBF we had a Rural Church Committee. At each annual meeting of CFBF we had a breakfast or a lunch for the committee and any who were interested. These were well attended. We discussed rural church problems and the Rural Church Conference held in Davis, usually in April, and also setting up of the Rural Church Research Project. The committee recommended, and the CFBF board approved, Farm Bureau support of these activities, and of Frank Pierce and the field staff devoting time to encourage attendance and support of the conferences and the research project. Frank was a big help.

In 1941 I gave an address at the Annual Methodist Conference in San Jose, *The Challenge of the Rural Church*. By a motion from the floor, the talk was mimeographed and sent out to all churches and conference delegates. The Bishop said that would be the first time any talk at conference had been so distributed. I spoke at the Napa Church in October, the Placerville Church, and again on November 12 at the Mission Inn at Riverside at a conference of leaders in business, labor, and agriculture, called by Bishop Baker. This was an all-day Saturday to Sunday noon conference. I was also asked to give the closing five-minute talk.

In 1944 the Federal Council of the Churches of Christ in America had the First International Religion-Labor Conference, including 225 delegates from AFL and CIO, also YWCA and two representatives from industry, none from agriculture, but they approved an 8-point rural program for religion and agriculture. This and similar actions of the Council of Churches, where they did not show the courtesy of inviting two farmers out of 225 when they were to discuss and pass fundamental statements in relation to agriculture, branded them as a social-political group rather than religious.

The First Rural Church Conference was held in Davis, April 4-5, 1945. Elliot Fisher, minister of the Clarksburg Community Church, was the chairman; Jess Rudkin, formerly of CC Church, and I were on the Rural Life Commission of the Northern California Council of Churches. We had seven speakers of national repute in the rural church field, and locally Knowles Ryerson, Dean of College of Agriculture; B. H. Crocheron, Director of Agriculture Extension in California; Walter Dexter, State Superintendent of Schools; Ray Wiser, President CFBF; George Schelmeyer, State Grange.

Murray Benedict, of the Gianinni Foundation, and I took up the most of the first morning. He had told the world how badly treated tenants were in California and how bad the whole social situation was. They asked me to speak on *A Survey of California Farming.* I said I would, if it could be solely a compilation of information from the most recent farm census, which was interesting. I do not remember all the figures, but the owner made a little more, not much, than the tenant. He was about six years older; he had a little better house. The tenant had been on the same land four years against the owner's six. The tenant had a newer tractor, a newer automobile, and more total investment in equipment. It was difficult to say which was the better off. Dr. Benedict then came on and told how tenants moved every year, seldom could stay long on one piece of land, and all that.

After lunch they said our talks had differed so much, they wanted both of us on the platform to answer questions. I told them I had not entered a single idea or interpretation of my own. I had only copied directly from the census. And Professor Benedict certainly had access to the census and had studied it. I knew Murray Benedict, and how radical he was, and asked why they invited him to speak. I was told they had never had a meeting of the Rural Life Commission without inviting him as resource man. It is really a shame when a group of that kind cannot have full confidence in the truth of statements by college professors. He was never invited again.

Bureau of Agriculture's economics figures show that 1941-44, in Imperial County, 12 percent of farm property was purchased by tenants or laborers. In Tulare County 1941-44, 18 percent of farm property was purchased by tenants or laborers.

At the SEcond Rural Church Conference at Davis, April 23-25, 1946, we had Mark Dawber, D.D. from New York. He helped organize the Clarksburg Community Church and got us going well. We also had C. M. McConnell, Ph.D., Professor Rural

Sociology, Boston University; A. A. Brock, California State Director of Agriculture; Ralph Taylor, Agriculture Council, Sacramento, with whom I worked in the twenties in the legislature; B. H. Crocheron, Director of Extension, California; Knowles Ryerson, Dean of the College of Agriculture.

While sociology and economics of agriculture got into this program some, there was more concern for the rural church, what it means to a member, and the best method of providing an active ministry. I was for that.

The 1947 meeting was April 7-11. This year was Monday dinner, 6 p.m., through Friday noon. The new leaders for this year were Bishop Baker; Tully C. Knoles, President UOP, one of the most popular speakers in California; True D. Morse, President Doane Agriculture Service, St. Louis, Missouri, later Deputy Secretary of Agriculture with Ezra Benson under President Eisenhower; David Lindstrom, Professor of Rural Sociology, University of Illinois; and Bishop Walters, Episcopal Church.

Ministers and laymen from all denominations came to the conferences and seemed to get a good deal out of them. I was especially interested in the Episcopalians. There were several from California and several from rural mission churches in Nevada. They were a very dedicated and hard-working group. We had more on church architecture (function), aids, finances, church organizations, recreation needs of rural church, church in action.

The 1948 meeting March 29-April 1, one day shorter. The first evening started with dinner and music by the Clarksburg Community Church choir. The evening speaker was John Wilkins, his topic, *The Christian Church in Rural China.* John was our first minister. This year's program was developed by the ministers and was again more sociology and economics and less building the rural church.

The rural church or town and country movement had now advanced to a point where the Board of Bishops of the Methodist Church decided to call a National Methodist Rural Life Conference in Lincoln, Nebraska, July 23-31, 1947. It was headed up by Bishop Baker, whom we had helped train here, and all information on the conference should be sought from Elliot Fisher, our former minister and friend.

Money was scarce, but we wanted our rural church people to be there. I had a new Buick, so I volunteered to fill it up with young ministers who couldn't otherwise go, so they would have no transportation expense. I was about to wind up with three district superintendants, but I told them if I was going I had to have at least one young minister.

The young minister was a fine-looking and cultured fellow. He had graduated from Yale in chemistry, and was doing well in the rubber tire industry, when he decided to devote his life to the ministry and went back to Yale Divinity School. He was on his first charge in California. He sat in the front seat with me. Probably in Nevada, he asked what farm organization I belonged to. I told him, Farm Bureau. If we had still been in California, he would have walked back home. He was for the farmers union, who represented small farmers. The Farm Bureau represented big farmers who had "no interest in their hired labor or the land." Some of the Farm Bureau board members had hundreds of thousands of acres of land and lived in a penthouse in New York. I had heard all that before, and it was a no-win discussion, so it faded quickly.

On Sunday afternoon we were driving across Wyoming, several hours ahead of our schedule, when I saw a sign to King Brothers Ranch ahead. I asked if they would like to drive in and see Burt King. Rev. Christianson had been in the Wyoming Conference and had known Burt, so he was delighted with the idea.

Burt was up on the summer range five to ten miles back in. As a young man, Burt had been a sheepherder in a purebred flock in England. A Wyoming rancher bought several hundred head, and they sent Burt to care for the sheep on shipboard and on the train ride to Wyoming. Burt decided to stay on, then got sheep and land of his own, and by now I believe he had the largest purebred flock in the world and shipped breeding stock to all parts of the world. He was then sixty years old or more.

We came over a little saddle of land, and below us was this low house which looked like it had grown into the landscape. Burt came out waving his full-length white apron to us. "Come on in." His cook had left that morning; his wife was out hunting rocks with the president of the university, and Burt was just peeling potatoes and starting supper for the men.

The district superintendents and I sat in the living room while my young Yale graduate stayed in the kitchen to help Burt. Soon they came in and we all sat around. My young friend said, "Mr. King, how many acres of land do you have here?" Burt said, "What do you mean, under fence, or all together?" He wasn't sure what he meant, so Burt guessed about 138,000 acres under fence. Gradually the young man realized that he had just finished peeling potatoes with the Farm Bureau board member who lived in a penthouse in New York and had no interest in his help or the land.

When we climbed into the car and bid Burt goodbye, my young friend turned to me and said, "I guess I have got to change my ideas about some things."

All the Methodist bishops were at the rural church conference and on the program, but the shining light was Dr. Hugh H. Bennett, chief of the Soil Conservation Service, USDA, author of a book on soil conservation. The book was for sale everywhere. Pictures of soil-conserving practices were on every wall. That was the center theme. Bennett deserves credit for dramatizing a problem, but he also politicized a problem in a way which may have left either a plus or a minus for the whole operation.

Most of the daytime was taken up with work in eight study groups, and I am sure those were of some continuing value to the rural church. One of the issues was that over 51 percent of the children born in the U.S. are born in rural areas and help set the future course in America. By far the greatest number of churches were in rural areas.

On a per-capita basis, the contribution per member was far higher for ministerial salary in rural churches than was true in even the largest, richest city churches. Still, it was almsot unheard of to send either a rural minister or layman to the General Conference of the Church.

Each morning, 8:30 to 9 o'clock, they had inspiration worship, and I enjoyed it. I liked to sit in the gallery where I could easily see the stage and the gathering. This Vermont minister told the old story about the old farmer: The soil conservation man came to tell him how to plow and farm his land. The old farmer isn't interested and tells the visitor he doesn't need any help, he has already worn out three good farms. That story is okay the first time to make a point, but told over and over to get a laugh to me isn't funny or respectful, so I turned to the fellow next to me and whispered I'd like to see all the preachers who have worn out three good congrega-

148

tions stand up. It was just an innocent whisper, but I guess everyone in the house heard it. I didn't mean for anyone to hear it, but I know some got the point.

Driving home, we got to the big open-pit copper mine, out of Salt Lake. There was a Mormon Stake House, and it was about time for evening services. Rev. Christianson said, "Let's go to the services and we can give them a good sermon. They probably haven't had one for some time." We went and introduced ourselves. He was called on for a prayer, but it was probably the best service we had attended for some time. They did not need a bit of help.

For several years we had talked of the need for a full-time man on research work for the church. The Northern California Council of Churches, of which I was a director and at one time vice chairman, the Davis Conferences, and the Rural Church Committee of Farm Bureau, all discussed the idea quite completely. We studied past experiences in appointing such men. They had all been appointed to help city churches estimate future growth and advise on best location of new churches, and maybe collect statistics, but were soon organizaing meetings or doing other leg work for the person or agency employing them. Probably they were using a man for whom they had no other assignment at the moment. We farmers wanted a man trained for research, with full time for research, and as much freedom in use of his time and talents as a man in the College of Agriculture or General Electric Research Department.

We farmers decided we should call it the Rural Church Research Project. Our city friends told us farmers would not support that because farmers didn't understand research. The College of Pacific agreed to furnish us rooms, office furniture, equipment, and a secretary. We had collected some money to get started, about $8,000, but it took $9,000 per year. The 1947 CFBF resolutions included rural churches and support of the projects. The board authorized Frank Pierce to help the project, so Frank, Jesse Rudkin, then assistant to the president of UOP, and I held many meetings in support of the project and keeping up the finances. We set up a committee of thirty, fifteen farmers and fifteen from various church groups.

We selected Dr. Richard Myers, a man raised in a small Kansas town. He was a Kansas rural minister, then entered WWII as chaplain. He went to Illif in Colorado on his GI educational grant to take work in economics, sociology, and statistics to train for church research work. He started off in high gear and kept it up. He started out estimating California and county growth curves. He then sought a method of determining probable individual church growth, the number of new members on confession of faith. Church membership was no indication, church attendance was closer, but still low relationship, Sunday School membership and then attendance were closer, but Sunday School attendance of the previous year was a reliable indicator. We then studied membership campaigns to increase Sunday School attendance. We found if a Sunday School gained twenty members in a campaign, then added about three classes or groups, they would retain the total members as of the campaign end, but if they sat back and didn't add more classes, they would a year later have as many attending as they had at the beginning of the campaign. Twenty would drop out. It takes about one leader for each ten members in any church, Sunday School, or similar group, depending on membership participation. This means that a church building needs plenty of small classrooms, so each person can participate somehow in each meeting, and of course it may mean more teachers.

We studied church finances and how to get adequate salary and recognition for rural ministers. Rural churches average a good deal more per capita for salaries than even the rich large city churches. Sixty percent of small church income goes to salaries, against 19 percent of the budget for churches with over one thousand members. This leaves a small church with 40 percent for current expenses and benevolences, whereas the large church had 81 percent for those items. This study did bring a shift in how denominations assessed their churches for denomination and benevolent expenses.

There was widespread criticism of the large number of competing churches; it was felt many should consolidate to save expenses, so we studied this quite closely. We found that competition was just as desirable and stimulating for churches as in other areas. The more churches there were in a town, the larger and stronger each church was; if the Methodists painted their church on one corner, the Baptists painted across the street. If the Presbyterians had a picnic, so did the Congregationalists. I was speaking a good deal at Rotary and other clubs. I made a practice of saying I turned at the Methodist Church, or any other reference to church; if it was a church town there would be further references to church. If it was not a church town, the subject didn't develop.

The Comity Committee of the Council of Churches was a standing committee whose purpose had been to discourage new churches until this need had been proved. After this study, the position changed to trying to see that no growing community was churchless. We got good donations from Charles Geothe, Lowall Berry, Sears Roebuck, Cal Pac, General Petroleum, and others, but most of the contributions were in small amounts from farmers, and hard to find.

Everybody was enthusiastic about the work and nothing of the kind was being done elsewhere. I had been involved full time as president of the CFBF for a year when Dr. Dick Meyers got an offer from the Greater Chicago Council of Churches to be on their staff to help locate best locations for new churches and help analyze the problems of some of the churches, and he decided to accept it. I was sorry to see him go. He was doing a great job here, and it was new research into church problems and how to solve them. The church leadership liked and made use of his work, but they never really saw the need of independent research and never tried really to find a replacement.

Looking back on the last 25 years (1952-1978), we see a generation of materialism and judgment of others, with wages per hour, poverty, financial wealth, or housing as the only measures of well-being, solving the problems of race, minorities, etc., through confrontation, violence, and governmental compulsion. During this period the church has lost membership and respect and has not asked forgiveness of its own shortcomings.

The church has done little to assure all ministers a reasonable salary. It is still the bastion of radical discrimination. It has shown little concern for its own growth. Of course, there are exceptions, and the fundamental or evangelical churches have enjoyed rapid growth. I believe and hope that we are on the verge of a real revival in personal acceptance of Christian faith as an answer to our social problems. Maybe our rural church research was a generation too soon and it will be revived.

Maybe I should close this church discussion by bringing the Clarksburg Community Church up to date. We had John Wilkins for eight years, then he went on to a prominent position in the Methodist Church. Then Jesse Rudkin. Jesse participated in all the activities of the community. He visited a great deal. He was a leader in the rural church movement. He enjoyed our state as well as local farm bureau meetings. We built the church building under his leadership. He enjoyed raising money for the church and helped many other rural churches in their campaigns. He was with us eight years. He later became assistant to the president of UOP.

I should mention Bishop Baker here. He got his early recognition as head of the John Wesley House at the University of Illinois. He believed in academic and ministerial freedom of speech and supported some far left ministers, but he was very kindly, honest, and sincere and a good friend of ours. He was very favorable to our Community Church as an answer to the rural church problem.

We next had Elliot Fisher, another worker and great in his visiting. His calls were short, but he visited everyone and invited them to church. He headed up the Town and Country Church Commission for the Methodists and also for the Council of Churches. They brought the Fisher kids to the community, and he later became our daughter Pat's father-in-law. The Bishop needed Elliot for a district superintendent if we would release him, and he went on to positions of leadership in the Methodist Church in New York and Evanston, Illinois.

We then had a young minister, Eugene Brackney, for two or three years. Eugene Brackney headed rural church work in California, but he was not rural minded. We then had Howard Daulton, who had been active in the rural church movement both in California and nationally, and Clarksburg Community Church was known all over the U.S. as being very active with rural church work. Bishop Baker moved again to southern California, and Bishop Tippet replaced him.

We heard rumors that Bishop Tippet was not pleased about our relationship with the church, but we couldn't believe it. Bishop Baker had been so pleased with us. Our former ministers were now prominent in the conference, and the whole conference seemed friendly. Our ministers of the CCC or its members had probably done more to help other churches in case of need than had any regular Methodist church, and that seemed to be recognized, but we heard more rumors of the Bishop's feelings, so we invited him up to speak at Sunday service, then to our house for lunch and a meeting with our council after lunch in our home. He didn't care how much money we gave to Methodist churches or causes. If it didn't come through church channels, it didn't mean a thing to him. Conference was coming soon, and we had several days to decide to get completely in or completely out. I reminded him our agreement was with the Board of Bishops, but that was not material. I told him an ultimatum of that kind gave our folks no option but to get out. If we had a year or two to counsel among ourselves, we quite probably could agree, but he insisted on a decision in days. This sort of autocratic unilateral decision was exactly the reason there is a diverse group of many denominations. No one had decided we didn't want to be Methodist in the beginning. We had done so well for 25 years that we had forgotten that, but here it was.

We found Dr. A. R. Boone, an older man, very quaint and gentle, a natural teacher. He was Congregational, and the young people went to the summer camp at Casadera. Then we had Martin Recio and then George Westerfeldt.

During our first 25 years our ministers were so active and connected with outside activities that we never felt alone or isolated, but our recent ministers were not associated with outside groups, and some felt we were not welcome to join other women's, men's, youth, or other Christian groups. I felt we would be welcome in about any group we wished to join, maybe Presbyterian Youth group, Baptist women's group, Lutheran men's group, but the congregation felt we should join a denomination. After a study, the United Church of Christ was selected and we joined. We have little if any more outside contact. It has done little harm and about the same amount of good. Our minister for the past year has been Jim Meadows, a nice young fellow, product of the generation which I am afraid I do not always understand.

I have spent a good deal of time on the church and affiliated work. At various times I have felt that, if I were to be remembered for anything, it would be for work in the rural church field. I am listed, how I do not know, in the 1952 copy of Who's Who in Methodism. The older, maybe more sophisticated denominations have left me cold, with what seems to me lack of religion and lack of concern for their withering. The people have demonstrated that it is not the church, but the denominations, which they are leaving and going to the gospel groups whose growth records have not been so well recorded. Many of the young people seem to sidetrack the church and go directly to the Bible for guidance. The Bible and the church are both essential to Christian growth, and the fact that that growth is evident today convinces me even more that this world is ruled and directed by God, not man.

Governor C. C. Young (seated with pen). At left is Ralph Taylor, 2nd from left George Wilson; right rear, Ed Snabble, Atty for Farm Bureau Federation. Seated right is Alex Johnson, Secretary CFBF

7

POST-WAR YEARS

†1946

The war was over. There was lots to finish up for the Farm Production Council, and lots of planning for the future in Farm Bureau at both the state and national level. And, of course, the big question was, how could we avert a disaster in farm prices as we experienced after World War I? It meant adjustments on the farm and in the home, and many meetings. Ranch equipment was about worn out, and there was a great scramble for tractors, new or used, including war surplus.

I got a railroad round trip ticket to Chicago. They had Pullman cars with roomettes; the beds were crosswise to the car and on an upper level. The road beds had gotten very heavy use, with a minimum of upkeep during the war, and the big rubber pads under the cars which acted as shock absorbers were about pounded out. The cars swayed so that I felt I was about on my feet one minute and on my head the next. At lunch in the diner we hit a bad sway, and at the table near me all four chairs fell on their sides and the couples flat in the aisle. The railroad office called me in Chicago to say the train back had been cancelled. I told them I wasn't even interested, as I already had my air ticket back. The planes were jammed also, but I had flown enough so that I could first call the head office and they would send the ticket to the hotel.

We built the pole barn at the Sloughhouse and bought the Fox hay chopper to chop the oats and vetch hay and blow it into the barn. It was used every year for 32 years with almost no upkeep or repair. This year (1978) is the first year it hasn't worked.

In June I went to Washington, D.C. to the AFBF board meeting, then was appointed to represent Farm Bureau at a meeting of the National Educational Association in Atlantic City, and especially to meet and have dinner with the school superintendents of cities of over 100,000. This was a very prestigious group.

I took the train from Washington to Atlantic City. The coach was wooden construction. The lights in it were old gas lamps, and they had never been remodeled to electricity. Every board in that old car shook all the way to Atlantic City. I have never ridden anywhere when I was so uncertain as to ever reaching my destination.

The NEA convention is a great show. Several told me that the superintendents of cities of 100,000 really controlled policy within NEA. They had two Cornell professors compare the states over a period of years, with special concern for the quality of education and the dollars per ADA in the various states, with the idea of raising the quality of education and what might be done to help equalize educational opportunity, in the USA.

I was surprised. The dinner discussion was limited to gambling and night life in general. Maybe this was just a form of bragging, but it was all I heard; then the Cornell professors presented their findings. It showed Mississippi, Louisiana, Georgia, and others improving their position, but still far behind, and great variation between and within states. They suggested the need for more equalization.

They then went around the table calling on each superintendent. Two were mildly favorable to the report. All the rest were very sure that they had no intention of letting anyone else get any of their money. Inviting us to the dinner was a public relations effort, but really it didn't improve my respect for the school leaders.

David graduated in June as an ensign in the Navy or a second mate in the Merchant Marines, but the war was over so he came home. Dick graduated from high school in June.

In the fall we contributed to Jess Rudkin to help the Methodist Church buy a campground at the north end of Lake Tahoe. They had done their best, but hadn't been able to raise enough to buy the land, so it would fall through unless Clarksburg would raise several thousand dollars to close the deal. We raised the money. They sold the land just recently for several hundred thousand dollars.

We had a truck strike during harvest. They tried to stop farmers delivering in their own trucks, but farmers were determined also, and we got our crops delivered.

The California Farm Bureau annual meeting was in Santa Cruz. We had Bob Sproul, president of U.C., as banquet speaker, Alexander Heron, past controller of the State of California and now of Crown Zellerbach, Asa V. Call, president of the California State Chamber of Commerce, and Allan B. Kline, vice president of the AFBF. The talks by Edson Able, assistant director of utilities department on "The U.S. Reclamation Service and Irrigated Agriculture," and by Von T. Ellsworth, director of research, were excellent.

The big Farm Bureau event was the AFBF annual meeting in San Francisco. It was the first meeting after travel restrictions were raised. People wanted a trip, and so many sons had camped or embarked in California that many wanted to see California. There were sixteen special trains from the Midwest and Northeast. Nine thousand people came by train, 14,000 attended in all. The headquarters was Fairmont Hotel, and the meetings were in the civic center buildings.

The big event of the meeting was the rodeo and big steak barbeque at the Cow Palace. With thousands of steaks to cook, some were a little raw, but we had all the beans, salad, rolls we wanted, and the smoke of a good barbeque. As an unscheduled event of the rodeo, a Brahman bull jumped over the high gate of the starting chute, ran all the way across the arena, up ten or more rows in the stands among people going in all directions, and then retraced his route exactly back over the tall gate into the starting chute. It was a great evening.

We had a very good couple who milked and cared for the dairy all during the war, but soon after they left, then it was a steady string of milkers.

During the war they needed all the milk they could get, so grade A or B made little difference, but afterward you had to be grade A to get a price. That meant tile walls and many other things in the barn and milkhouse, at least $10,000, which was lots of money then. With all the changes of milkers, we had gotten some mastitis in the herd. I went up one day and found Godfrey milking as he yelled, "If all these milkers can quit, I can too.' All this made it easy to decide that now was the time to switch from milk to beef only. So we sold the dairy cows and adjusted to beef about 1948.

†1947

This was a busy year, with adjustments from the problems of war to those of peace. In February the AFBF had twenty-seven states represented in appearing before the Senate Agriculture Committee and the next day before the House Agriculture Committee to present AFBF, international trade, aid, and other policies. Secretary of State Marshall was there to lend support. It was quite a show.

It seemed quite a little of my farm equipment was out of date, or for crops no longer grown, so we held an auction sale in February and sold $11,500 worth of equipment. It seemed like lots of money then, and it cleaned up the place. An auction sale is a good idea just for good housekeeping. We bought both a Ford sedan and a Buick. We bought both David and Dick a NW Mutual Life Insurance policy.

David and Erma were married August 17 in the Lutheran Church in Sacramento by Rev. Robert Romcis. David went on to college in Davis and Erma worked.

The Davis alumni decided to raise money for a student union building on the campus. We gave $500 at that time.

I had been chairman of the Soil and Water Committee of the AFBF. Romey Short of Arkansas, Charles Shuman of Illinois, and Herb Voorhies of New Jersey were the other members, all top men in AFBF. We held a three-day conference in Omaha, Nebraska, in October with presidents or others from twenty states. The committee had been very active for years but generally considered a Western regional interest, but by now it was getting to be of broad general interest to all except the Northeast. We worked hard, including evening sessions, and I was tired, but my plane didn't leave until about midnight, so I went to a movie and slept all through it, then went to the airport. We started our take-off, then came back. The stewardess said all off for a while, Denver Airport is closed, so we must wait for it to clear. I told her to just forget me. I would be in my seat all buckled in when they wanted to take off. So I was soon asleep. I woke up east of Denver. It was really soup, could hardly see the wing tip. It was smooth but ominous. One could feel the tension in the air. The stewardess came and got my name, address, nearest relatives, the works. I looked around and everyone was stiff with fear. We made a quick pass over Denver, then on up to North Platte, and landed. Four other DC 3s had recently landed there. The passengers said it was terrifying, we had done everything except roll completely over.

Of the five planes there, all had lost their antennas, four had been hit by lightning, and crews and passengers were the most forlorn, beat-looking folks I had ever seen. But I was fresh as a daisy. As each plane came in, they went to town for more sandwiches. All the crews had used up their eight hours, so we waited for a planeload of crews to fly up from Denver. They lost their antenna on the way up. We finally got sorted out and on our way again. I suppose that was the roughest trip I ever flew, and I missed all of it.

I went to New Mexico Farm Bureau annual meeting November 6-8, as speaker and to attend sessions for AFBF. Mr. Albert Lee had one of the old Spanish grants in northern New Mexico with sheep and cattle. His riders were mostly Indians born and raised on the ranch.

One young rider was drafted for service. He could not read or write. They sent him to San Diego for Navy training, then off for action on a destroyer and kept going west day after day on water. They shot at people they didn't see. Finally a **Kamikasi** he didn't see bombed his ship, it exploded, and he went overboard with a broken hip. They rescued him and got him on a hospital ship and back to San Diego, and after some time, discharged him to go home. He wanted to break horses again, but Mr. Lee told him he better rest up with his family. He finally let his sailor ride, but he found it too painful so he went to stay with his folks. In two weeks he was back. He told Mr. Lee he must help him. His folks thought he was crazy. They just sat and looked at him all day and said he is crazy. He said his boat would sail all day and go into the setting sun but never fall off. It goes to the other side of the world but doesn't fall off. They fight and kill lots of people, but never see them. He insisted Mr. Lee go see his folks and explain to them that he isn't crazy and why the ship doesn't fall off. Mr. Lee was still looking for someone to explain to him how to explain it to them.

The Tennessee Valley Authority (TVA) had become a very controversial and political issue. Farm Bureau, especially in the South, was very positive in support of TVA, but almost equally sure we didn't want any more of the same.

A commission of three headed by David Lilienthal had directed all its activities in a very dedicated, nonpolitical fashion. Their headquarters were in the TVA area, not in Washington, D.C. Ed O'Neal, president of AFBF, wanted some of the AFBF board to see it in operation, so about eight went down after the March board meeting. Lilienthal was just leaving to go to the Atomic Energy Commission, which was just authorized.

We had dinner and spent the evening with him and the other board members for an overall viewpoint, then we spent the week traveling over the valley seeing and discussing all the activities. There were many activities, but power development and distribution and fertilizer manufacture and distribution were the most important and controversial. Then there were roads, schools, recreation, etc. Charlie Shuman, president of Illinois Farm Bureau and later president of AFBF, was one of the group. Farm prices and demand were still pretty good, as we were still shipping cotton, wheat, corn, rice, etc. overseas.

About every noon and evening there would be a lunch and dinner for us, attended by local farmers and officials, and after the meal we would have talks and questions. Charlie or I would say, "Now farming is pertty good. Do you think we really need these farm programs out of Washington?" The reaction was always about the same. Some farmer would say, "Well, sir, we hadn't thought much about it but no, sir. I don't really believe we need them now. We can do all right." Maybe another farmer the same, and then the Agricultural Commissioner or Director of Extension or other official would get up and say, "Now, whoa. Let's back up here a little. Our boys down here don't understand the language you boys up North use. They didn't get the question. We can't get along without the money, can we, boys? We've got to have those payments, don't we, boys?" The answer was always, "Oh, yes, sir, yes, sir. We got to have them." We got our answers rather clearly.

The TVA Authority gave free fertilizer for demonstration plots in the area, then they gave a good deal of fertilizer free in the area to expand its use. We asked how they justified giving this free fertilizer. The answer was, "Well, the water falls on their land before it gets to the generators, so we feel we should give them the fertilizer to help pay for the water which falls on their land." It was a new and interesting theory, but might get terribly complicated if broadly applied. If there is a will there is a way. I had heard so much about their cheap power that I took PG&E rate charts back with me for this trip and asked about some of their rates and practices. Right away they told me many of their electrical engineers were former PG&E people and they knew PG&E. They would compare with any Eastern power company, but didn't try to with PG&E. TVA did a great job of getting reasonably cheap power to many farms which would not otherwise have had electricity for a long while. Even with TVA lines going down a farm road, some did not subscribe for power at all, some for only two or three small lights, few had many household appliances and few motors over ½hp, and none of the heavy uses for irrigation and other uses now common on Western farms.

On June 15, 1947, SMUD took over from PG&E at Sloughhouse Ranch.

The Chicago AFBF meeting was held in December. Ed O'Neal had carried AFBF through the Depression and the farm legislation of 34-36-37; he had pretty well unified the Farm Bureau into a truly national group. The AFBF membership had reached 1,275,180, almost exactly one million more than the 276,053 in 1931 when Ed O'Neal took office. He was 72 years old with health failing, so he announced retirement, and Allan Kline and Romey Short were elected as president and vice president. This was a move to more dependence on economics, less on government. These were two of the best brains I have known, dedicated men who worked well together. Before long, Allan brought in Roger Fleming as secretary-treasurer, a real doer. They made a great team.

I had spoken at the Sacramento Rotary Club several times, and Gus Olson had invited me to join, but I always felt I was too busy. Now I decided if I was ever going to get acquainted with the people in Sacramento and start to taper off a little on work, I better start, so on 12-29-47 I joined with Gus as sponsor.

†1948

In 1948 I rented the Dutra Ranch on Dillard Road. We raised beets, beans, and oats, apparently paid $6,000 rent. I kept it about three years, then gave it up.

Went to Washington, D.C. latter part of January (Allan Kline now president) to work out Farm Bureau legislative approach.

February 20: AFBF Committee Washington and Conference of National Organization in Atlantic City.

March 15-20: Commodity and board meeting, Chicago.

March 24: Western regional meeting in Phoenix.

There were so many meetings of county, state, and American Farm Bureau, and beet growers, rural church, etc., that there seemed little time left for farming. College of Pacific and Northern California Council of Churches took some time, plus talks at Farm Center and county meetings as well as Chamber of Commerce, Rotary, Lions, etc.

June 3: Pat graduated from high school.

June 14: The AFBF board meeting in Chicago, then from 21-24 I was one of Farm Bureau's representatives at the Republican Convention in Chicago. We met with the Platform Committee.

Our family had been together at Lake Tahoe for vacations and had visited relatives in southern California, but we had not taken a real vacation together.

David was now married, so we decided that with Dick, Pat, and Dorothy we should take the boat trip to Alaska before we were all split up. Several years earlier we had a boy from a dairy farm in New York stay with us for six months or so for the experience of seeing what life in California was like. I always felt a boy should see some of the world away from home while he was footloose. David had his cruise down the west coast of South America as part of the CMA training, stopping off for a look at several of the major ports.

We thought Dick might return the visit to the farm family in New York. He fixed up an old Ford coupe and went back near our relatives in Urbana, Illinois, and got a job for a farmer there for several months. Then he went on to New Jersey, visited the Elliot Fisher family, and got a job there.

On Sunday, September 12, Dick came in from New Jersey. We saw some of Washington and then took the river boat down to Mt. Vernon. It was a beautiful day, and it was good to see Dick looking and feeling well after five months of work and travel. He decided to trade the Ford for a motorcycle to come home on. It was winter in Wyoming, and the rain and sleet froze solid on his pants. I expect the coupe looked good from there, but he got on through all right and overall had an interesting experience.

I had purchased five tickets for Alaska, hoping Dick would get back in time for the trip so we could have a vacation together. We saw he couldn't make it, so we invited Isabelle's sister, Mary Hill, to go with us. She is always a good addition to any group and we, and I think she, enjoyed the trip, but it was later than we thought so far as our little family getting together for a trip. We drove up to Vancouver, went over to Vancouver Island where we stayed at a chalet, spent several days seeing Victoria, Buchart Gardens, and points of interest, then back to Vancouver, boarding the *Prince George,* a brand-new ship starting its third voyage, at 9 p.m., July 31, 1948. The ship was new, the food excellent. Our first stop was Ocean Falls, a lumber and paper town. It was beautiful, up a narrow channel like a Norwegian Fjord. The streets were clean, and the tuberous begonias in hanging baskets and yards were beautiful. I thought I knew of no U.S. town so clean, neat and beautiful, it must be Canada. I asked back on the ship and found it was a company town, Crown Zeller-bach, U.S. owned.

We stopped at Prince Rupert, Ketchikan. Here we had the show by the cancan girls. The show delayed a little, waiting for the arrival of a baby sitter for one of the girls. We stopped at Juneau and Skagway, then took the railway up to Carcross, then got on the steamer for a ride down Taku Arms Lake headed for Ben My Chree. It was a beautiful clear night, so light until quite late, then we pulled up to the shore and put lines on a couple of trees. Then the quiet was absolute. We all slept a short night, then on to Ben My Chree, luxurious in flowers, vegetables, grasses, growth of any kind.

We came back to beautiful Mendenhall Glacier and cruised all through Glacier Bay. On our return we went up one of the channels so narrow it almost seemed like one could reach out and touch the upright mountains on each side. Water falls were fine, feathery but almost anywhere you looked. It was one of the finest parts of the trip. We drove home from Vancouver in two pretty full days. It was a delightful trip.

Mother and I took much the same trip twenty-six years later, this time in early July. This time we could not take the railway to Carcross, as the railroad bridge had been burned out by a fire. Probably the greatest surprise in the recent trip was the several miles that the glaciers had receded in the twenty-six years elapsed. This last trip, Buchart Gardens were enlarged a good deal and delightful. We then took the ferry from Victoria to Port Angeles, Washington, then west on 101 through the virgin timber and on down the coast. It was inspiring and beautiful. I recommend it.

I should say a word about the CFBF regional meetings. The state was divided into regions, from several to 8 to 10 counties to a region. There was usually a summer and winter meeting, the latter in the valley, the summer in the hills—often Susanville for us. County boards attended, but all members were invited. For many this was the principal outing of the year. State officers and staff attended as invited, but the agenda and entertainment were all arranged by the region. Any issue of general interest could be discussed and often a solution agreed on. They were strictly the member's meetings.

For the summer meeting, the whole family came often, staying over a few days to camp, fish, hike, swim, or whatever. They were great occasions for getting acquainted. Some meetings were one day, but some were afternoon meetings, continuing after dinner in the evening, then Saturday to 3 p.m. It would be great if they could be revived.

The AFBF also had regional meetings lasting three days which many members attended. As the AFBF's programs and problems became more complex, it was necessary to have the meetings more organized and efficiently working, so they were streamlined to president, secretary, and boards; very necessary, but I wish we could still work in an old-type regional meeting every two or three years.

On September 8 we met in Washington with the Grange and Coop council, coordinating our approach to national farm and legislative problems.

November 9, 10, and 11 we had the National Town and Country Conference in San Jose, California. Elliot Fisher had a very prominent part in the meeting. They had asked me to discuss the 160-acre limitation in a debate with Dr. Paul Taylor, head of Department of Economics of UC, Berkeley. I objected that I thought there were more important issues facing the rural church, but they insisted, so I agreed. He claimed the 160-acre limit went back to the old philosophers of ancient history. It had been law through the life of the USA and made almost sacred by Abraham Lincoln.

Lincoln provided gifts of 160 acres to all Civil War veterans. They could have bought unlimited acreage for $1.25 per acre.

Dr. Taylor had been introduced as "The" source of information on this subject. The crowd was with him. I think it is fair to say they were with me at the end, especially the question period when he denied and then admitted he had been on a retainer from the Department of Reclamation at $50 a day, equal to at least $250 a day now.

After the evening session they had planned a meeting of the committee on Farm Labor Housing of which Dr. Paul Taylor was national chairman. A friend of mine who was on the national committee insisted I come to the meeting, which I had not planned to attend. I had been vice chairman of the California Farm Production Council, which had more experience in actually providing farm labor housing than anyone else in the U.S. Our office was in Berkeley where Dr. Taylor lived. He had never visited us, offered suggestions to us, nor to Professor B. H. Crocheron, also of the University of California, who was in charge of farm labor procurement in California. Still, Dr. Taylor was chairman of the national committee and presumed to be an authority on the subject.

We entered the room a little late. The meeting was just started, but as soon as he saw me walk in, he asked to be excused for a minute to move his car as he had it parked where it must be moved. He would be right back. He never returned.

The annual CFBF meeting was held in Sacramento. Dr. Robert Burns, President of UOP, was the Sunday evening speaker. Also present were Goodwin Knight, Lt. Governor of California; Mrs. Raymond Sayre of Iowa, chairman of Associated Women of AFBF and president of Associated Country Women of the World; Roger Fleming, secretary AFBF; B. H. Crocheron; William Knowland, U.S. Senator from California; and Mrs. Isabelle Wilson, vice chairman of the CFBF Home Department and chairman of the Resolution Committee and the Education Committee.

I attended the Nevada, Idaho, and Utah annual meetings, the California State Chamber of Commerce, and the New Mexico Farm Bureau annual before going to Atlantic City for the AFBF board and annual meetings.

†1949

On February 14 we bought 3 polled Hereford bulls from Helen Reamer and 6 purebred cows from George Pollock at $550 each. We leveled the field at Sloughhouse Ranch for irrigated pasture, and paid J. C. Marshall rent for Wilson Brothers and Goodwin.

Tilly Lewis had trouble paying for the 1948 tomatoes, and it was still very difficult to buy new equipment, so we accepted a relatively new TD-14 tractor 1 H.C. track layer in lieu of the amount still due.

Cobb, a chemistry professor, and others at UOP organized a Death Valley trip for seven days at Easter time. Pat, Dorothy, Mother, and I went. They had a bus, but most people drove their own cars. It was a delightful trip. We took our bedding and camped out. We had a cook crew, all the participants did KP and other chores. The flowers were in full bloom and beautiful. One night we went out alone on the sand dunes to be there before sunrise, and we got some beautiful pictures of the sunlight and shadows in the early light on the dunes. It was also very interesting to follow the tracks of the bugs in the sand, sometimes climbing up the steep sand banks then sliding down and trying again. We took a side trip over to Hoover Dam and Lake Mead. We visited the lowest spot in the continental United States, about 300 feet below sea level, and could see from there Mount Whitney, the highest spot, 14,495 feet. The weather was delightful, but the last night we had a campfire in Alahama Hills, very large smooth boulders said to be the oldest formation in the world. It was cloudy, so we found a cave to sleep in, but others were outside and it poured down rain. The rest were soaked, so we all spent the rest of the night on the high school gymnasium floor.

I was at the lunch table one day in April when the phone rang. It was George Denney of the most popular program on radio, "Town Hall of the Air." He wanted me to go with a group of about thirty on a world trip. It was a surprise request. I was busy and felt I couldn't get away for that long. As I was telling him no, I suddenly remembered the statement of Henry Ford that I had read years before, "All a person gets out of life is experience," and maybe I should get this experience, so I said, "Call me back in two days and I will tell you." I called Allan Kline, and he said to go and represent Farm Bureau. David and Dick were home then. Many people had gone around the world on ships. It was still an exciting idea to go all the way around by air. I found after our return that I was the ninety-sixth person to fly around the world on any commercial flight of any airline.

Federal Agricultural Producers organization meeting, Guelph, Canada

Above, harvesting lettuce seed at home place
At left, Bella and me

Below, in the Trade Office at Rotterdam

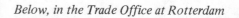

8
FLYING FARMER

The idea of the "Town Hall" trip was to increase knowledge, understanding, and friendliness among the peoples of the world on a people-to-people basis. The Flying Seminar represented organizations whose combined membership represented thirty million Americans:

American Association of UN
American Association of University
    Women
American Bar Association
American Civil Liberties Union
American Farm Bureau Federation
AFL
American Legion
American Library Association
American Municipal Association
Association of American Colleges
Association of Better Business Bureaus
Columbus, Ohio Town Meeting
CIO
Foreign Policy Association

Fraternal Order of Eagles
General Federation of Womens Clubs
Independent Business Men
Junior Town Meeting
League of Women Voters
Lions International
National Association for the Advance-
    ment of Colored People
National Council of Negro Women
National Educational Association
New York Stock Exchange
Town Hall, Inc.
U.S. Conference of Mayors
U.S. National Student Association

We covered 33,000 miles. We saw London, Paris, Brussels, Frankfort, Berlin, Vienna, Rome, Istanbul, Ankara, Nicosias, Tel Aviv, Cairo, Beirut, Damascus, Karachi, New Delhi, Calcutta, Hong Kong, Manila, Tokyo, Honolulu. While the project was nongovernmental, we had the full cooperation of the State Department, the military, and Economic Cooperation Administration. We had to get eleven visas and three military permits (Berlin, Vienna, and Tokyo), fill out twenty-eight life histories and thirty-eight passport pictures, besides extras for emergencies.

We all met in New York on June 24 for State Department and other briefing, for meeting and getting a little acquainted, and for a big dinner and send-off with Madam Pandit, sister of Nehru, Prime Minister of India, as speaker.

The next morning we went to the airport, and here was the brand-new Pan Am

Strata Cruiser, a big double-decker, with a large bunting-draped platform from which we had a nationwide broadcast inauguerating our odyssey and the new plane. I waved them off and got a plane back to Chicago for our AFBF directors meeting, then went to London. Air travel to Europe was still new. The New York waiting room was pandemonium, crowded with travelers and well-wishers. I rode in the cockpit with the pilots from Boston to Gander. It was beautiful, and watching all the moves of the pilots, navigator, and engineer were very interesting.

† England

We arrived in London June 30. We stayed at the Harrington Hall Hotel. It had no elevator, and the room was so small I couldn't get far enough away to take a picture. But we were lucky to have any room, as much of London had not recovered from the bombing. It was a sad sight.

Of personal interest was the reception given by Col. Stewart Roddie at his home. The front of the house was bombed out, so we went in the alley. The stables along the alley were all crowded with people living in them. It was hot downstairs, so we all went to a room on the second floor up a narrow stairway, through a low passageway to a large room with skylights all still painted black but now open to let air in. We were received by Princess Marie Louise, granddaughter of Queen Victoria. Her hair was grey, but she was the liveliest one there. Most cried about the loss of country estates. It was the first party after the war attended by royalty. They had strawberries and cream. I asked an American woman why she was there, and she replied, "Oh, I inadvertently married an Englishman." It was an honor and pleasure to be guests at the reception. The gay mood and appreciation of strawberries and cream gave a little idea of the years of austerity even after the end of bombing, but it was also evidently the end of an era.

England is slowly reconstructing the physical damage of war. She is also reconstructing from colonial capitalism to socialism. Her colonial capitalism was based on cheap raw materials and manpower in her colonies and at home. She also had the idea she could prosper by eliminating competition in her colonial markets and by discouraging industrial development in her colonies and elsewhere. These practices, capped by the ravage of war, have left English industry inefficient and antiquated— entirely unprepared to compete with the modern industrial production of the world.

Today's plight seems to come from widespread use of the franchise by the labor group, dissatisfaction with working conditions, and inability of the older ruling group to bring modern efficiency to the physical and social machines of England.

I believe 85 percent of the laboring people questioned said they opposed the labor government program, though they supported many individual phases of it. The conservatives talked of loss of summer and winter homes and financial accumulations, but their whole position seemed best summed up by Sir Robert Boothby, Scottish member of Parliament, when he said, "It was a great show while it lasted, but it is all over and we all know it." Colonial capitalism, as practiced in England, has been found wanting. That must not be taken as a condemnation of democratic capitalism based on free enterprise, equality of bargaining power between industry, labor, producers of raw materials, and the consumer which I hope we are still striving for in our country.

In spite of the present unrest, England has a great heritage of stability among all classes of her people. She may go lower before she develops new leadership, charts her course, and again takes her place in the family of nations with a balanced, expanding economy, but I am sure she will find a way to prosper on production rather than austerity.

† Paris, France

In Paris we found life color-work-hope and optimism. France can exhibit life in her darkest days, still there seemed to be a new quality to France. With a 48-hour week, labor unions are teaching increased production in schools. Government is work-at it. They are gambling on increased production. If they lose, the austerity will be terrible—I believe they are going to win.

I saw on farms good use of some of the most modern devices. Then I saw pick-up harvesters covered with men. I saw rubber-tired steel wagons built to last a century with no thought of efficiency of operation. I saw men and women harnessed to spray rigs while new rubber-tired row-crop tractors sat idle in the sheds. I do not emphasize these things to be critical or superior, but to point out that United States farm equipment is built mainly to save expensive and scarce labor. Europe and the near and far East even more needs equipment to produce and save more.

France is still short of dollars, but she has achieved a high degree of recovery, most prices are reducing, currency is stabilized, taxes are meeting budgets, and exports increasing. Rent control in effect since World War I has so discouraged new building that housing is now the big problem. The French appreciate United States aid and feel the need of a European trade union, and free convertability of currency at the earliest date possible. France has many problems, but I believe she will be a stronger nation in the generation ahead than in the past.

† Berlin

We stopped at the beautiful airport in Brussels on our way to Frankfort and Berlin. Here, we thrilled with the precision of "Operation Victuals" still carrying 8,500 tons of essentials to beleaguered Berlin daily. At the top it was 12,000 tons. Every three minutes, day and night, the planes went over. Looking down on the farms I called Captain Meyers' attention to the poorer upkeep and farming compared to what we had been seeing. He said we had just crossed into the Russian Zone. I only have his word for the reason, but the difference was readily apparent.

In Berlin the desolation was unbelievable, the past all horror and the future a blank. Berlin is terribly bombed physically and as badly bombed mentally. Somber faces are seldom lifted to see above your shoetops as you pass. (One wonders how secure is social security, which Germany had more than any other country before the war.) Streets are cleared of rubble and now most sidewalks, but building reconstruction is still very limited, mostly to private homes by family labor. We were told over 50 percent of the children were underweight and 50 percent of those had TB.

The seminars here, each with 40-70 German leaders of government, education, agriculture, professions, labor and all walks of life were sobering. They were very hopeful of the Frei University where, for the first time, students are admitted on the basis of ability, not class or economic status. They told how the Russians solved a good deal of the Nazi problem by taking 22,000 Nazis out of 100,000 people in the better part of Berlin, how the Russians lost the elections and then put on the Blockade. On questioning from Irving Brown, AFL, as to German plans for the future—a planned or free economy—the reply was, "The state was deeply involved in public expenditures at the end of the Bismark period, so planned economy by the state is old in Germany." Planned economy takes time to reap its harvest.

We were also told, "Germany can become economically sound, but we cannot have a democracy in this generation. The young people are frustrated and do not know where to turn politically. The older people have tried the Kaiser, the Republic, and Hitler and failed in all. They are disillusioned."

Some warned against building Germany as a new military force against the East. "That would only elevate the militarists who were largely responsible for dictatorship," they said. "We want no more swaggering officers," said one. These German seminar members with whom we met were all serious and sad-faced and, as we learned more of them, we found that practically all had spent months to years in Hitler's concentration camps because they had elected to defy totalitarianism, and when they talked of democracy, it was more than leisure armchair discussion. It carried meaning and considered determinations. They again decided on the side of the democracies when the blockade was placed, though the future was uncertain and they knew of the 4500 names in the City Hall of Berliners who have been taken by the Russians since peace was supposed to have come.

Oh, yes, Mayor Reuter and his aides are working us for all they can get, playing both ends, but fundamentally we are all in the same boat together and we must not sacrifice them. I am not trying to interpret all of the people of Berlin, and I understand there are all shades of feeling in the Western Zone, considerable Nazi, but we still have a partnership with the anti-Nazi, anti-Communistic leadership in Berlin.

We were housed in the dormitory of the Frei University, which I thought meant the tuition was free, but no, it meant that the farmers and mechanics children were free (allowed) to enter along with the elite.

Mayor Reuter of Berlin, and Frau Loder, former mayor and 14 years a member of the Reichstag, showed courage and determination standing up against the Russians that few are called on to prove.

We went to the opera in East Berlin to see "The Enchantress." It was well done. As we got our tickets, we got a copy of the opera in English. The house was packed. The costumes looked like they had been in the trunk for a long while. The ladies in the audience did all possible to dress for this first opera since the war, but they were all cotton dresses. The bouquets of flowers were thrown onto the stage with great glee and accepted graciously, but they were wild or simple garden flowers tied with a string.

I got the officer to take me and the Decker's out to see some farms. The Russians had, in 1945, stripped the farms of livestock and machinery, but of course some had been hidden and saved. Food was so scarce the farms were producing to the limit. Greenhouses were full of vegetable plants. We stopped at the old airport. It had been the Kaiser's military parade grounds, then the airport, then with the blockade the US military flew in sprinkler pipe and planted all the land to vegetables. They used the big nozzles like in Hawaii and got great production. A few hours on the

166

farms were a great tonic. They were all busy working hard, not thinking much of either the past or the future.

Several of us went to the Intourist Russian Restaurant in East Berlin. It was considered the best food in either East or West Berlin. You went into an office with a lot of Russian military, checked in, then several of them led you upstairs and through several tunnel passageways into a large dining room. At times you wondered if it was really a good idea, but the meal was good and the bill in dollars only. In West Berlin, dollars, marks, and US military script were used.

In West Berlin, lots of people were repairing the roofs or other parts of their homes, and where public buildings were useable, the rubble was cleaned up, but so far very little repair work was under way which needed new materials or equipment.

The situation across the Brandenburg Gate was very noticeably different. There was more dirt, less rubble cleaned up, less activity, less hope. The Russian military was sullen, the German people were sullen.

In our meetings with the West Berliners, they were anxious to talk to us. They found it a little difficult to understand how we had people from all groups. Education, finance, agriculture, labor, were all traveling together, all differing in our thinking where we cared to, still all agreeing on many things. While the raids were much less common, still the Russians were coming across the boundary at night and returning with some victim, hoping to break the will of West Germans to resist. The meetings were solemn, but they gave us all a little insight into man's fight for freedom of thought both against Hitler and Stalin, and I hope they strengthened each of us a little.

In each country we visited we were received at a formal reception by the Prime Minister and several of his cabinet. Also by the U.S. ambassador and his staff at a briefing and a dinner, or by the military government in Berlin, Vienna, and Tokyo. We had the large public Town Hall of the Air meeting with two local and two American speakers on each side of a current issue in the country. Also, we had several seminars with appropriate selected persons interested in the issue discussed, as well as all of our group. These were arranged beforehand but presided over by Chester Williams. Then several of our group would tape a broadcast to America arranged by Brooks Emery from each Capital we visited.

At no place was there any plan for seeing any of the farming. After having considerable difficulty arranging a farm visit in France, I made up my mind I would somehow see farms in each country.

† Vienna

While Berlin was divided into four separate sectors, Vienna was a unit with all four nations in control as a unit. The four powers governed Vienna, but outside the city was Russian and a permit was required by the Russians. This was a sore point with the Austrian government. The U.S. military government wouldn't even ask for a pass. My friend, Ed Dodd, formerly USDA, now head of Food and Agriculture (FAO), an affiliate of the United Nations, had a U.N. passport which allowed travel at any time in any nation. He had requested a green card weeks before, but it wasn't ready, so he waited a week in Vienna, much to the disgust of Chancellor Figl and Foreign Minister Karl Gruber.

The Chancellor was holding a lively state reception for us. He had told me he graduated with a degree in agriculture. I asked a U.S engineering major who was feeling good if he couldn't get me out to see farms. He told me it would take at least six months to get me released if they caught me, so I told him I knew someone who would get me out and I walked over to the Chancellor. He was delighted, called his Minister of Agriculture, and told him to arrange it. The next day three cars showed up, so I quickly found Anna Lord Strauss, Leage of Women Voters, and John Barnhart, American Legion, and we set out.

A few miles down a beautiful shaded road came a load of hay drawn by a pair of long-horned oxen. I asked if our driver could slow down a little. The deputy minister insisted on stopping our car and getting out to stop the oxen, and then on my getting out to take the pictures, the best of the whole trip. He then asked if I wanted to go back a mile and take pictures of the Russian airport, but I wasn't interested.

The wheat was beautiful, then being harvested with a scythe and shocked by hand. The bunkhouses were brick, stone, or concrete with implement sheds downstairs and sleeping, dining, etc. upstairs. Large storerooms had shelves on the wall covered with large round loaves of heavy dark bread, and plenty of potatoes, apples, roots, melons, etc.

With all the hard labor, there was little thought of labor saving. The trucks were big heavy deisels with high beds on trucks and trailers. The crops were beautiful, neat and clean. Americans out in the Russian area were a curiosity. We got the VIP treatment; after seeing the farm we would go to the house, talk a little, then the wife and girls would go to the basement and bring up the best of the fruits, cheeses, wines, etc. Then we drew around the table, the farmer reigning from his high chair, and the women darting into the kitchen or cellar for an extra goodie. They would never sit down with us.

In all that area they had songs and stories to tell you. Water alone was not fit to drink, nor was wine alone, but wine and water half and half was perfect. Miss Anna Lord Strauss seemed quite prim and proper, but she was vitally interested in everything, could swing a scythe in the wheat harvest like a veteran. This was not only a memorable day for me, but what farm trips we could crowd in became very popular with the entire group.

The crops of Austria are the best in many decades. Much of the music, life, gaiety, and food of Vienna is returning. They are thinking much of renewing the culture which really seems to be a vital influence in the lives of most of the people of Austria. Their love of St. Stephen's Cathedral and the popular subscription to quickly erase the damage to the Cathedral seemed a mixture of pride, religion, and love of things beautiful, but was very real.

There was a very urgent demand to terminate the occupation, an insistence that we all leave, but that the Americans should not go too far—only retire to Germany, for the Russians would still be very close. Austria was a Republic, then occupied by Germany, now by four powers. "We will sign a state treaty, not a peace treaty as we were not at war," the Austrians say. "We want complete freedom before the older men who once knew freedom have all passed on."

Our last evening in Austria, we went over the mountain roads to Kahlenberg Inn for dinner, looking down on Vienna ten miles away. On the return trip we stopped at Gruzing and joined the local people in song and dance, a delightful farewell.

† Rome

General Clay's plane took us on to Rome. This was another world...the Colosseium the Forum, the Appian Way, St. Peters, lots of people. Berlin had been ruins, a confusion of buildings and people. Vienna had some war damage but not dominant; they had determination and hope. Rome had ruins, but now the ruins were the pride of Rome. A military government, as in Berlin and Vienna, is austere at best. In Rome it was the Embassy again.

Ambassador and Mrs. Dunne gave us a marvellous reception at their home and gardens. They attended every meeting we had in Rome. They represent the best of the foreign service. They were ably assisted by Mr. Zellerbach, head of Economic Cooperation Administration in Italy and head of Zellerbach Paper Company of San Francisco. It was my pleasure to renew acquaintance with Mr. McClelland, Agriculture Advisor of ECA, former head of California Lands at Bank of America in San Francisco.

The people of Italy know the United States the best of any people we met. They understand us, like us, and are happy to express appreciation of ECA and other aid from the United States. The cooperation here between the Embassy, ECA, and the Italian officials in the constructive use of ECA and counterpart funds was very fine.

The depressing factors seemed to be poverty and overpopulation. It seemed to me much like the overproduction of the thirties which was underproduction in the forties. The real need is stimulated industrial production to bring new income, new use of raw materials, and to help relieve the pressure of population on the land. Counterpart funds are being used to develop 1,500,000 new irrigated acres, to improve 5,000,000 acres of land for increased production, to take schools and drinking water to farm villages which have never known them. Italy is making rapid progress, has a new alertness to her problems, and a desire to solve them. She has not known a satisfactory economy in modern times, so she must do better than meet old figures.

Italy is most desirous of a European Union and feels it essential to her progress. She also realized she must encourage a large middle class of people to preserve democracy. They say they had a victory over Fascists, but it will not be real until they solve the problems which bring Fascism and Communism. While still short of dollars, Italy is the only country having favorable trade balances in all the European countries.

All one day the whole party went toward the coast to see farm development. Ten thousand acres of the Pontine Marshes had been drained and reclaimed for farming. The houses were good, all the same, livestock below, living quarters above, with electricity and running water. We had lunch on the beach and most went swimming to relax and cool off.

McClelland was doing an excellent job, and his enthusiasm was infectious. His greatest personal pride was in introducing sweet corn as a human food in Italy. Corn on the cob was at all embassy parties. Another very interesting Californian was Miss Lubin of Sacramento, daughter of Simon Lubin, originator of Weinstock-Lubin stores in Sacramento, also of the Institute of Agriculture. He had felt there should be an International Institute of Agriculture to record international statistics and progress in agriculture. He finally got the King of Italy to put up the money, so they located the building in a large park in the center of Rome. He was the administrator, and his daughter was his secretary and loyal admirer. The activity had been absorbed by the new Food and Agriculture Organization, also of Rome, but Miss Laura Lubin showed me all three of the original buildings and insisted I sit in her father's old chair at his desk.

Her sister, Countess Evangelina Lubin Silenzi, had married an Italian Count and lived in a villa by the river surrounded by a high brick wall. He had been in the Italian military during the war, and she lived alone in the large villa. The gate was locked, so we pulled a cord that went up through a pulley to a tomato can half-full of rocks by her house door. She came out and welcomed us in. The house was beautifully furnished, but not really lived in, until we got back to the kitchen area where she had a wood stove for heat and cooking. During the American occupation and after, U.S. soldiers had kept her supplied with wood crating for her stove.

They were fine women, both happy to see someone who knew something of Sacramento. But visiting the villa reminded one of how hollow title, money, and fame can be.

We went to a displaced persons camp on the edge of Rome. There were 170 thousand DPs in thirty-one of these camps in Italy. They were from all parts of war-torn Europe. They were hoping to get to Brazil and were learning shoe and furniture making, cooking, tailoring, weaving, and other trades, and Portuguese. We ate lunch with them, simple, plain, but Okay. It was the best of the thirty-one in Italy, but very good compared to the desolation and hopelessness left behind them.

Rome was full of life and traffic. It was the only place where people would wave flour sacks with the American aid insignia on the sack to express appreciation of the gifts of food.

We had a late dinner in the old Ulpia Restaurant, two flights below the street in the old market place of ancient Rome, finishing up in time for the 2 a.m. departure of our Turkish Air Lines plane for Istanbul. We had a beautiful sunrise view of Athens as we flew low over the Acropolis and the U.S. Mediterranean fleet in the harbor.

† Turkey

Istanbul was strikingly like San Francisco—hills, water on three sides, white buildings, much new construction and very modern, the people a little different, but all full of vitality, ambition, and pride. As one viewed the great mosques with the round domes and the slender minarets piercing the sky, then watched the great throngs come in and wash their feet and then enter to pray, it was for a while a different world.

From Istanbul to Ankara I sat in the rear seat and got lots of pictures; we were again on the well-operated Turkish Airways. The Turkish stewardess came back and said in a very soft voice, "You like my Turkey, don't you?" Then, "You would not be taking so many pictures if you didn't like us." As we approached Ankara, she went up to see the pilot, and he did a couple of figure eights over the city so I could get more good pictures. As we got into the airport waiting room, big signs were on all walls. Absolutely no cameras allowed on airplanes or in the airport.

The old town of ten thousand was perched on top of the hill around the Citadel in biblical times. The new city just 25 years old with 250,000 people, was built on the plain three thousand feet above sea level. The city is truly modern, broad streets, beautiful parks, schools, colleges, hospitals. Hotels not exceptional as yet, but the essentials are there. The pride of the people is almost boundless. And well it may be, for I doubt if there was ever a 25-year period in our history when we progressed more rapidly.

Attaturk had for twenty-five years been a benevolent dictator. New alphabet, education, votes and equality for women. He had recently died a great national hero. The women almost worshiped him. Literacy has risen from 10 to 50 percent and will approach 100 percent in a few more years. This was done by adopting the Roman alphabet in place of the difficult Arabic. Women have been raised from servitude to absolute equality with men. They are not only permitted to work as hard as the men in the fields, but are judges, legislators, officials, doctors, and lawyers, on a basis of equality. This is made more simple by the family custom of the young married people living with the in-laws, so as children and household duties develop, they may be cared for by the other women while the mother carries on her work or profession.

The seminars were many, well planned, and enlightening. The one on the role of Turkish women was outstanding. Women came from all parts of Turkey, some had walked forty or more miles to get there. The military statues in the center of the city include women as carriers of the heavy artillery shells over rugged mountain trails.

Turkey is a very productive land of great climatic variation; many of our crops originated in Turkey. They have lots of untapped resources. They are not overpopulated. Roads were one of the greatest needs in Turkey.

Their budget for education is second only to military, and the teachers have a missionary zeal, but they need more education, roads, and industry. Eighty percent of the population are farmers living in forty thousand villages, over twenty thousand having schools. The American colleges there have a great influence, and there are over six hundred Turkish college students now in the United States.

They had set up a sort of agricultural extension service. They decided only rural boys and girls were qualified to work with farm people. At the end of the fourth grade in school, they picked the best pupils for four years training as school teachers or as farm advisors, the latter then attended one of the twenty-one rural institutes. These were set up on vacant land. The teachers and children built the buildings from the ground up and added to them as needed. They built the play equipment, the simple farm tools, everything. You have seen the plastic models of horses, men, etc. which we can buy, with all the internal organs accurately formed and colored so each can be removed and studied. In one of these schoolrooms we saw these whittled out of wood with pocket knives, with each organ amazingly well formed.

They felt Americans could do no wrong. I was invited to dinner in the home of the dean of the College of Agriculture. As I was leaving, his wife asked if I would like a remembrance of Turkey. She came back with a glass replica of Will Rogers spinning his rope.

One evening we went out 2½ hours to a village to see a mobile unit show a crop production film to folks who had never seen a movie before. It was a rare privilege.

George Denny asked ten of us to go make a courtesy call on President Ismet Inonu before the morning seminar. He was very gracious, showed us the public rooms of the beautiful palace, then went into the library, arranged us in a circle, then sat on the edge of the table and said, "Now let's have a town hall meeting here." The questions and answers went on and on, most friendly, interesting, and enjoyable. He had the finest cherry soft drink I ever tasted. I asked what he would think of trading a group of California farmers for a group of Turkish. He said nothing could delight him more. After return home, he sent me a request to come back with a group of California farmers to spend three months with his farmers. I surely regretted that by then I was so busy I couldn't take another three months or even three weeks off.

All the conversation was through interpreter, but it went very well. As we were about to leave, he said we must go up to his private library upstairs. It was a large room, simple but beautiful with a grand view out over the city. Many of the books were American in English, both popular and scientific in nature. He showed pictures of all his family. It was a delightful visit, it seemed like between old friends. The morning was past, but we were all inspired.

The last evening, dinner was in the garden at Karpies under the trees near the old wooden hotel.   On July 27 we left Ankara for Nicosia, Cyprus.

†Cyprus

There was no regular air service from Ankara to Tel Aviv, so we went to Cyprus where the U.S. Ambassador's plane was waiting. It could not take all of us on one trip, so half of us had a delightful trip to the top of the mountains and around Cyprus until the ambassador's plane returned to take us to Tel Aviv. The English governor of Cyprus gave us a delightful trip to historic and interesting points on the Island, then to a dinner on the sea while half of our party went on to Israel in our ambassador's plane.

The ambassador's plane sounds pretty fancy, but it was an old, battered, dull brown, rusty U.S. Army DC-3 cargo, bucket seats folded up on each wall, small portholes and air vents, about 2 inches in diameter. Our baggage was all piled up in the front of the cabin. We found we could cool the cabin down a little by rolling up sheets of Time magazine and pushing them out through the small air vents to form cups to direct the fresh air into the cabin. We arrived after dark. The city reminded me more of Miami than any other place I know; lights, people everywhere, and our hotel, the Yarkon, was right on the sea.

† Tel Aviv, Israel

Tel Aviv, again a new city of 250,000. The first impressions were of a modern city full of people, children and activity.

The schedule here planned traveling seminars with a Jewish leader or two in each car to discuss with us the problems and what we were seeing. My counterpart was one of the early migrants to Israel 35 years earlier. He was a farmer, mainly citrus. His father had been chief justice of the Supreme Court in Israel. He was also commander of the Jewish forces during the siege of Jerusalem. The commander of the Arabs attacking force was a close schoolboy friend of his, and they were still good friends.

He felt he and his Jewish friends who had migrated in the early 1900s were about as unpopular with the new Jewish arrivals as were the Arabs. Most of the abandoned orange orchards had belonged to the Arabs and had been well-cared-for by them. The new Jewish government had run the Arabs out, if they weren't killed in the fighting. The government had not paid the Arabs for the orchards and other lands, so no one was farming them and they were dying. They are still not paid for in 1982. There were some Arabs who remained in Israel; even several of the members of Kismet (Congress) were Arabs.

We met often with Mr. Ben Gurion, Prime Minister, and other leaders. They had a tremendous job to do in a short time. There was little time for the leaders to be concerned with the welfare of the new arrivals. In sixteen months of existence this State had the problem of its own organization and the immigration of 265,000 new people speaking 30 to 40 different languages and with as many different backgrounds. It is truly a melting pot.

We met with many of them in the debarkation camps; some had been there many months. The people rushed about us to try to tell of their hopes and their difficulties. It was a Tower of Babel. There are 70,000 in such camps, which physically are not as good as the DP camps they had left, but still they had unbounded hope for the future. With all their disappointments, they were still hopeful that it would mean freedom and opportunity for their children.

We visited and ate lunch in the communal dining hall with the members of the communal farm at Gevat. Here 150 families dry farm, carry on dairying, have vineyards and orchards, and raise food for their own needs. The government is by a committee which directs all activity. Husband and wife have one room, the 315 children under 18 were all taken from the mothers at birth and reared and schooled in separate quarters in the village. The parents can have the children an hour or so in the evening. Couples were recently granted tea for a cup together in their own rooms twice a week. No money is used. No outside labor employed. All are granted equal clothing or other conveniences of life. All work 48 hours a week and have a two-week vacation a year with $28. allowance for the vacation. You can leave any time, but with nothing. Three-hundred of the 400 farm communities are of this type. Some of the others are as independent as our farms, though they nearly all sell cooperatively. The others represent variations between the extremes.

The Israelis felt superior to the Arabs militarily and every other way, but still they realized the possibility of a new attack at almost any time, so their first thoughts were on security. The many kabbutz were to get as many as possible quickly located and producing food, but most were located at military strong points or strategic areas, and were militarily organized to provide quickly a maximum number of people on the ground for defense in case of attack.

There were Jews from every country and every race. While we were there, a shipload of black Jews arrived. They were a problem for many people said, "What are we going to do? We thought we had been scattered around the world, but now we are coming back to the homeland to enjoy a pure race of people. We often asked each other, Where are the Jews, for few look like the New York or other Jews with whom we are familiar."

We visited Nazareth, a city of 18,000 Arabs, of which 4000 are refugees. About 12,000 are Christian Arabs, the rest Moslem. We visited Mary's well and the old home and carpenter shop, each covered by a church. The Sea of Galilee was calm, quiet and beautiful with the highly colored fishing boats slowly moving about on it. We had a fish dinner aboard one of the boats as we rode down the sea at sunset and into the Jordan River where many of us had an impromptu swim. We visited the Weisman Institute, a research Institute, organized by President Weisman, an outstanding scientist. They are doing much fundamental and practical work on use of products of Israel. We could well exchange ideas on uses of citrus products. Maintenance of high wages and costs for the Near East along with many barriers to trade has made it very difficult for citrus producers, until today many of the groves are abandoned and I would think almost half of the groves are now beyond rehabilitation. The hills around Nazareth and Jerusalem are rocky, but much of the valley land is very good and much of it not now farmed. The hills would support much more livestock. The Jewish settlers of 30 to 35 years ago have developed into good farmers, with a love of land and ability to farm equal to any race. The newer arrivals are about 5 percent farmers, so today only 16 percent of the population are farmers producing 50 percent of the food needs. The goal is 25 percent of the population farming, which will give sufficiency in all crops except wheat.

The immediate problem of Israel is the absorption of the new population and a stable, productive economy in which goods can be produced at a price for which they can be sold at a profit. The state is a labor state. Wages are very high without yet getting comparable output, so production costs are excessive. The appreciation of education is great, but they are maintaining four separate but parallel school systems with separate administrations and budgets all at public expense. This seems divisive among a people so in need of cohesion. The problem overshadowing all else is security, for they know a small determined band defeated the Arab forces. But the Arabs are still on the borders and the 900,000 displaced Arabs all want their lands, homes, and businesses back, and new outbreaks are possible at any time.

This is one of the real tests of the power of the United Nations—can the UN set a course and pursue it to the end, to bring agreement and peace between such nations where real conflicts exist? The whole world will be more secure if this is settled soon.

In Israel the admiration for Ralph Bunce, colored American diplomat, was very high. When we visited the Arab countries we found an equally high regard for him. He has been a great emissary of good will for the United States in the Near and Far East.

I was asked by Brooks Emery to be on his program, making a tape in each country for return to the US for broadcast. It was to be done in the large air-conditioned Habimate Theatre, using the equipment set up for the Town Hall Meeting the same evening. I had tried to write a fair analysis of what we had seen in Israel, but Brooks read it and thought it might be considered as critical, so said he would not dare put it on. I saw the American Ambassador, Mr. McDonald, sitting near the back of the hall, so I went back to visit with him. He was a very plain man, not Jewish but very popular with the people of Israel. He asked why I wasn't broadcasting. I showed him the script. He said he certainly could not see anything wrong with it. He then told me many of the problems they were facing. It was reassuring to me, as I was also on the regular Town Hall of the Air meeting that evening for a short statement of what we were seeing in Israel.

In the stress of all the assimilation of new people, there was little time for

174

explaining to the people how and why. The Jewish speakers knew of the Town Hall question period and were almost in a lather. I was flanked on the platform by Mr. Horowitz, Minister of Finance, and Mayor Rokach. They kept asking, "What will they ask?" The four speakers spoke, the questions were requested, and it seemed like the whole audience rose with hand in air. The Jewish speakers were soaking wet with perspiration flowing, but at the end they each said, "We made it. We made it." It was their first exposure to questioning.

All the next morning was spent with Foreign Minister Sherret in his offices. We returned to the Beach Cafe for lunch with the Mayor and Mrs. Rokach, and half the party flew back to Nicosia. I walked around Tel Aviv and came to what they called the old Arab quarter of two- or three-story buildings, several blocks long and several blocks wide, every building dynamited to complete destruction. They said it had been done after all active hostilities were over, so the Arabs would have nothing to come back to. Probably the thing which impressed me most was that almost every Jew with whom I talked felt he must impress upon me that he was not interested in Judaism as a religion, but solely as a state.

I am always appalled as I read the Old Testament; the Jewish people started in slavery, then the entire group wandered in the desert for forty years, then massacred everyone to occupy their promised lands, then slew themselves and others by the hundreds of thousands until David and Solomon unified them again. They built Jerusalem as the crown city of the world, then it was happiness and grandeur, followed by more slavery and more wandering. Cyrus sent them back to rebuild Jerusalem, then slavery, wandering, and now back again in Jerusalem. They prospered as a nation only when their trust was in God.

It was a great privilege to visit the holy places of Christianity. I was delighted to see the land so much more productive than I had pictured. One could not help but absorb some of the thrill of the enthusiasm and hope of people from the four corners of the world throwing themselves into making a better freer world for their children if not for themselves.

We again rode the bucket seats to Cyprus to enjoy another pleasant visit at the beautiful but uneasy island, then we got an Arabian American Oil Company (Aramco) plane; they had volunteered to fly us into Cairo and from Cairo to Beirut.

While in Paris, we had gotten word that maybe we shouldn't try to go to Cairo as Egypt would not accept any travelers from Israel. We held a little caucus and wired back that we had our visas and would be arriving in Cairo on schedule. The reception and program, of course, would be up to them.

We arranged for the Israelis to not stamp our passports in or out of Israel. The embarkation point of our flight was Nicosia, and we arrived and left on an Aramco plane, so all were happy.

† Cairo

We arrived in Cairo as it was getting dark. The airport was empty except for a guard or two and the customs and immigration officers. The flight over the delta of the Nile had been a thing of beauty, a farmer's dream—tremendous, productive, all it is supposed to be. We saw and heard the jackals and a number of hyenas as we drove across the desert into Cairo.

We were rushed directly to a late tea on the roof garden of the Press Syndicate Club, a most beautiful and ultra-modern building. I doubt if there is a press club in the US equal to it even today. Here we had a roof garden party buffet, with welcomes and the history of Egypt, then rushed to the Semiramis Hotel right on the Nile. There, in a large flower-and-fruit-filled room overlooking the Nile and the Pyramids, they told us that this was to be our headquarters. There would always be someone to answer the telephone, and if we had any want or wish, no matter how large or small, just pick up a telephone wherever we might be and call "Operation Bridge." We would get that room and our wishes would be met. They said, "We are calling it 'Operation Bridge' because we believe you people are the ones who can bridge the gap which has arisen between the Arab and American people over the Israel trouble, and we are anxious to see that gap bridged again." I believe that was a sincere wish, for our Egyptian hosts gave us every opportunity to better know and understand them. There were calling cards for each of us, English on one side, Arabic on the other, programs, maps. They had Tourist Police to assist us.

We were shown our rooms, then rushed to a beautifully dedorated spot on the bank of the Nile, where we boarded a newly painted sternwheeler much like the old Capitol City Sacramento to San Francisco. The levee bank was covered with potted plants. To the music of the military band and with full moon above, we slowly glided up the Nile to the Barrage or diversion dam.

There were several hosts for each of us, and food, food, food on the deck, a roast fish three feet long, pig, lamb, beef, everything. We could dance, eat, or sit around on deck in little clusters learning of Egypt, its people, its problems, from our host committee and prominent guests. We were meeting the people, and floating on the Nile River which for three thousand years has been the lifeblood of the world's oldest civilization.

We arrived at the dam about midnight and got off to see the irrigation museum with all the devices for lifting or regulating the flow of water. From the very beginning of time, man's ingenuity has been amazing. The river traffic, mostly powered by sails on this full-moon night, was enchanting right up to our return at 3 a.m.

One could write quite a chapter on our visit to Egypt. They doubted if our coming was a good idea, then decided to go all out for us and surely did. It was like the Arabian Nights. All the meals were fantastic. They opened up a beautiful old home for us to see, harem rooms and all, and served an old-time lunch as in the harem days. You ate from a low coffee table, propped up with a group of pillows, or you could eat prone on a couch with a low table before you, just as the old pictures. It seemed a little foolish, but after all the rich food provided and consumed, you understood the reason in these arrangements.

Cairo is the site of the University of Mohammed with its 7000 students, which in 1971 will celebrate its one-thousandth anniversary, and also the University of Cairo, with buildings for 500 students and teaching 4000.

Here our seminars developed clearly the struggle between classic education of the few for culture and a narrow range of professions, and the great growing demand for teacher-training for primary schools, basic literacy for the people as a whole, including women, and vocational training for production as a way to a higher living standard for all.

176

This country of twenty million people is dependent on five million acres of farm land. It has increased its population 50 percent since 1900, while farm land was only increased 2 percent. The investment of wealth was limited largely to jewels and land, so prices have risen to as high as $2500 to $3000 per acre for bare land. The pressure of population has driven cash rentals from $40 to $250 per acre per year. Lack of education, tropical diseases, malnutrition, inescapable debt, and social stratification limit incentive and production per acre.

Since only one-thirtieth of the water of the Nile is being used, and as land, minerals, oil, and electric power are available, it would seem that the possibility for development is great.

A year ago Egypt appropriated $5 million to survey the natural resources, but found she did not have men to run survey gangs and had to give up. It seemed to strike like a bomb. For one thousand years she has schooled for culture only. Now she wants to develop her resources for a better life on earth for all her people. Culture alone has failed her. She must start at the bottom to educate many for production. She wants a better life for her people and a little dynamic leadership could quickly put her on the road to rapid development.

We saw farms with gravity flow of water from the Nile. We saw men sitting by a ditch with a wooden tube probably 10 inches in diameter and 8 feet long, with a wooden carved spiral in the tube and a handle on top for the man to turn. He would raise the water a foot or two to a higher elevation. In a few cases there was just a shallow well from which water was raised in a three-gallon pail and poured by hand into the irrigating ditch. Most of the farming was good; almost all ground raised two crops a year and some three crops. At the rents paid it had to be productive.

We saw one of the social villages, of which there are many. If a village of five to ten thousand farm people puts up $7500 and 2½ acres of land, the government will put in schools, farm advisor, vocational training for boys and girls, child clinic, hospital beds and nurses, and one doctor to several villages. It was a great sight to see men in red fezzes and long cotton nightshirts playing volley ball, and the pride of the girls is their needlework. They have many problems, but some day these will again be a great people.

On our last day, we climbed the pyramids at 5:30 in the morning, and managed to stay on the go all day. The Town Hall meeting was to be on our last evening, followed by a farewell dinner at the Mena House near the pyramids. We had all brought Tuxedos and evening clothes, but this was the first stop where it seemed appropriate to wear them, so it was decided to dress for dinner. We had orders to have our luggage in the lobby of the hotel at 5:30 the following morning for our flight to Beirut. So at 10:30 p.m. we suggested we should leave to pack and get a little sleep. But when we got out on the front porch, there was a group of white horses and forty camels all lined up. We were to take our pick for a moonlight ride around the pyramids.

We all mounted camels, men in tuxes and women in evening dresses, for our ride. We got over by the Sphynx, and here was a group of Bedouins by their tents playing and singing in the full moonlight. It was perfect, so we sat on the camels for a desert concert for about an hour. There was another round of goodbyes—but no, they had special busses there and we must take a moonlight bus ride across the desert. We were tired, but too exhilerated to say no, so, as on the first night after the boat ride on the Nile, we again got back to the hotel at 3 a.m. to have the bags in the lobby at 5:30. We left Cairo exhausted!

I think it was due largely to the Egyptian's preparation and effort that we did our basic job of helping people understand people as well as we did at any point. Our Ambassador Patterson and his staff gave us lots of time for good briefings, and a marvelous garden reception and dinner, but they were sure they were in a hardship post. They had little confidence in the Egyptian people, and really I am sorry to say were doing little to get acquainted.

One of our host committee was Saba Haboshy Pasha, Minister of Finance. I thought he was one of the best minds we met on the trip, and now I am told he has for some years been one of the most highly respected lawyers in New York City.

† Beirut

Aboard the plane I propped my eyes open long enough to see the Suez Canal, then slept soundly into Beirut. The American University people were our hosts here. The plan was to stop at Beirut for two days rest, but every minute was taken up.

First was lunch at the American University, then a briefing on the refugee problem and a trip at our request down the coast to Sidon to two refugee camps. The camps were terribly crowded into 10 x 10 tents. There was a little schooling in the open. Food was running short, and no organization responsible for caring for them. They were all Arabs, but both Christian and Muslim. They wanted to go back to their homes, shops, and farms where their families had lived for many generations. There were nomads who followed the flocks, but they were a small minority.

We stayed at Hotel Tanios in Aley on the hills above Beirut. It reminded me of a Hollywood set, all facade. I was on the fourth floor, no elevator working, no bedding until finally I got one sheet, and then the band with dancing and gambling all night long. We had a seminar dinner at the hotel that evening.

The next morning we made an 80-mile drive inland to Baalbeck to the ruins of the seat of Baal worship, later temples of Greeks and Romans, and still later a refuge for early Christians. We had lunch at Zelch in the mountains above Beirut, given by the Foreign Minister and Lebanese leaders, then to the summer home of the President of Lebanon where we had another seminar on technical possibilities for Arab countries. They saw considerable possibilities of irrigation, drainage, power development in Syria, Lebanon, and other Arab countries, but they had little money for development and were not sure they wanted to develop these resources for refugees rather than their own people.

It was late when we got back to the hotel, and later when we were able to eat. The band was still blaring, so several of us decided it would be well to get a taxi and drive in the moonlight to Damascus, have the morning there, and get the plane for Karachi. It was a beautiful ride. We were in Damascus a little after daylight. I bought some beautiful hand-woven silks in Damascus. We were on the street called Straight, the place where Paul was let down over the wall in a basket, and saw many other sights. Damascus is presumed to be the oldest continuously occupied city in the world, controlled by many states and religions. It became the center of the Moslem world about 700 A.D. and has been Moslem ever since.

As we came down in Basra, Iraq, for gas, we flew over the large date gardens.

It was our only view of large corporate farming. It was orderly and beautiful, and, as we saw the broad Tigris and Euphrates rivers with their waters and the wide expanse of land, it seemed here again a vast area was calling to be made productive.

The people of Iraq were there to tell us of what American oil development meant to them and how the struggle with Israel had cut production in half, as the refinery was in Haifa, Israel, and they would not permit the oil to go there. They say they produce 85 percent of the world's dates and have oil which looks like refined motor oil.

In addition to the Tigris and Euphrates, there were several other live rivers running across the great stretches of desert. I thought of the tremendous opportunity for development, but little did I realize that twenty years later I would be there on foot selecting 25 thousand acres for development and getting a good start on that project in the Khuzestan Desert of Iran.

†Karachi, Pakistan

We arrived in Karachi after dark and were divided between the Palace and the Beach Luxury hotels; really the names were not descriptive.

Pakistan is located on the northwest and northeast corners of the old subcontinent of India and is primarily Moslem. East Pakistan has 42 million people. West Pakistan, where we were, is a little larger than Texas and has 38 million people. The two areas are over a thousand miles apart by plane or over two thousand by boat. Many feel partition a mistake, but what is done is difficult to undo.

Half of Karachi's pre-partition population of 300,000 crossed the border to India and over 600,000 Moslems fled back into the city which now harbors one million people. With DP's and population rapidly increasing, the poverty and actual starvation is a very real thing. The poverty, filth, and sadness were indescribable.

It is difficult for an American to properly orient himself in a country whose government is barely two years old—and most of that two years war of the bloodiest type. Two years ago the Governor General and Prime Minister had to take pens, pencils, and paper from home to start governing 80 million widely separated peoples, and today the Foreign Minister points out his need of books about countries and statistics to help him meet his duties.

England had built up quite an active civil service in Colonial days, but the civil servants, teachers, and commercial people were almost all Hindu. The Moslems were not only farmers, but engineers, railroad engineering and maintenance. Very few were prepared for government, business, commerce, education, or the many tasks of a new society, many in a new land with untried government at almost all levels.

Eighty-five percent of the people are on farms; the cities are filled with people and yet more people. Ninety percent are illiterate. Still, West Pakistan, the size of Texas, has more irrigated land than the United States. The last project finished i brought in 6 million acres, the next few years will bring 5 million more. The desert land, waiting for water, seems unlimited. The water of the Indus has hardly been tapped. The problem now is need of drainage as the cheap irrigation water is bringing rising water tables.

We had full briefings, receptions, and seminars, and a packed Town Hall meeting. The men missed the afternoon meeting at the Prime Ministers home. Begum Liaquit

Ali Khan, of the All Pakistani Women's Association, was hostess. The women of Pakistan were very active in nursing and other hospital work, and in the Women's National Guard, where they drilled and also rendered any worthy service.

As the sick, wounded, hungry and homeless came in great hordes to their new lands, the women of wealth seemed for the first time to realize a social responsibility to these poor people, and they fed, clothed, and otherwise cared for many of them.

Edith Sampson, a colored attorney from Chicago, was one of the best minds in our group. The Begum asked Edith a good many questions about how she happened to come on the trip and who financed her expenses. She financed her own. The Begum was gone for a few minutes and came back, told Edith how appreciative they were of Edith joining the others to come see them, and handed her a check for $10,000, saying the All Pakistani Women's Association wanted the pleasure of contributing to her expenses. Edith, with all her great dignity, replied that she understood that it was the custom in the Orient to accept gifts in the friendly spirit in which they were offered, and she most gratefully accepted it. She had also seen the marvellous work the women of Pakistan were doing in the hospitals and in caring for the refugees, and nothing could please her more than to have this opportunity of presenting this check to help carry on the work of the Pakistani women. I am sure the women of our group had seen many dramatic moments, but they all said they had never seen one equal to this.

The women's clubs still carry on these social services. I presume the number of people affected is small, still it is a new attitude which may develop into real progress for the masses. The apparent desire of the leadership to face and conquer the problems and the potentials of the country for development made one feel hopeful that great advances will develop.

† Delhi

We flew Karachi to Delhi at night, arriving at 3 a.m. Still-homeless refugees slept about in the road, dominating the scene into the Maiden's Hotel in Old Delhi. It was a spacious old wooden building, two-story with a wide veranda, sitting in a parklike compound. We had about an hour of sleep when our boy came in with tea and toast. Each guest had a man assigned to him for his stay. He carried the baggage, took care of the room, brought in the tea and toast each morning, prepared the bath, turned down bedding, ran errands, but most important, each room had two or three large paddles hanging from the high ceiling. They were connected to a long arm outside the room, and when you were in the room day or night, he spent most of his time pushing that arm back and forth to stir the air in the room. It was a much-appreciated service.

Both transportation and gasoline were scarce, so we were permitted to rent a car for our stay for each four people with a daily limit of 50 miles. Our driver was Ned, a modern man. He had hit two horses as he drove across the road in front of them. He backed the car up, and I thought sure he would hit a man. I asked if he wasn't afraid he would hit someone. He seemed quite surprised at the question, and he said, "No, why should I be afraid? He should look out. We have too many anyhow."

Every stop we made was important in getting better acquainted with the people of the world. But India seemed a little special. Mahatma Gandhi, shot 18 months ago, was probably the most influential man in the world. Nehru, inheriting the mantle of Gandhi, possessed of a brilliant mind and ability to write, was a world figure. The impact of the tremendous population made India a rather special area of world influence.

We were entertained in the garden of Prime Minister Nehru our first evening, with many prominent guests. Then he gathered our group in a small circle in the garden, and for two hours he explained his plans and hopes for India.

He said he had promised his people economic independence within ten years after independence. He knew he couldn't do it, so he would never mention it again or they would throw him out when they saw him fail. He was going to become known as the leader of the Orient, then named off all the other countries who could not challenge him. Then he hesitated and said, "Now China has gone Communist, we will not hear from them for the next 20 years." He said it was wrong for a state to be set up on religious lines, so he felt one of his top goals was to see that Pakistan failed because it was conceived as a religious state and that *must* fail. He told us how a recent survey had shown that from 25-45 percent of the food produced in India was eaten by birds or animals after harvest and much before harvest.

Monday, August 15, was independence day for India. We spent the morning seeing the city, then went early to the program and the Prime Minister's speech at the Red Fort. We had seats near the front, but the mass of over one million people stood all through the park with loudspeakers hanging in the trees. I sat in the aisle seat in the front row to get good pictures. We were early, so I looked around a little for any better vantage point. An officer asked what I was looking for, so he told me to go over with the press corps of photographers, but stay with them. Nehru came out to inspect the guard, so I got right up front with the press and got good pictures. He and his party went inside Red Fort, and I was looking for a way to get back to our party. I saw a security guard coming toward me, so I looked the other way and saw the press photographers going toward the Red Fort. I ran over and joined them, and got more pictures of the Prime Minister and his party until they climbed the steps to the top of the Fort, then I followed right along. Aside from the English Ambassador and his party of two or three, I was the only Westerner up there. Looking out over a sea of one million faces, all men dressed in white and ladies in many-colored saris, was an inspiring sight I probably will never see again. It is hard to visualize such a mass of crowded humanity.

That evening we were invited to Government House, former home of the British Viceroy, now the home of the Indian Governor General. It had 340 rooms and a mile and a half of corridors fabulously decorated. There were three thousand guests, but Governor General Rajagopalachari welcomed our group and talked a while. His duties were largely cermonial. That such wealth and show could live so closely integrated with such poverty of body, mind, and soul is difficult to realize.

It would be a shame for anyone to go to Delhi and not drive the 120 miles to Agra to see the Taj Mahal. I have been there on each of three trips to India, and it was worth it each time. The Red Fort in sight of the Taj Mahal is always worthy of a visit. It was the fort and palace of Shah Jahan, not the spectacular beauty of the Taj but large, diversified, interesting, beautiful, and a record of life. A few miles before Agra is another tomb built by King Akbar for himself and his Christian wife. It would be a great attraction, but it is not quite equal to the Taj Mahal, so is seldom heard of.

We were kept busy with seminars. At one the editor of the principal paper was telling us of the complete freedom of the press, even greater than in the United States. One of us asked how come he had just been released from jail. He replied, "Oh, well, I just committed an indiscretion."

Our Town Hall meeting was packed and jammed. Maybe I should first say that every day while we were there, there were two or three items in the daily paper of lynchings in the United States, and the issue was raised daily. There were also many stories of caste, tribal or family disputes in India where one to twenty-five people would be murdered, but none of those were due to prejudice. They were just spontaneous anger, and that was human; you couldn't blame people for that. The color line in India was a little different than in the U.S., but still it was desirable to be light complexioned and undesirable to be dark.

Edith Sampson, our representative of colored women, was one of the principal speakers at the Town Hall meeting. She told of discrimination in the U.S. which must be eliminated. Still, she also told of progress made by the blacks in science, art, poetry, music, sports, diplomacy, and so forth.

During the question period, everyone wanted to ask Edith about discrimination in the U.S. Finally she said, "Now I told you things are not right, but getting better, and here I am. I was born poor, raised poor, but I went to school and worked to get an education. I am licensed to practice law before the Supreme Court of Illinois and the Supreme Court of the United States. Now who have you got? Who have you got?" She took the house by storm.

Some months after our return, Nehru visited the U.S., and they had a large reception for him in the Waldorf Astoria, New York. I was invited but didn't go. Eleanor Roosevelt and all the bigwigs of government, business, and society were there. At the door, as Nehru entered, he passed them all and walked across the big hall to Edith, talked to her a few minutes, then went back and met the dignitaries.

We flew on from Delhi to Calcutta. I had often heard of the Hell Hole of Calcutta. It was terrible, filled with refugees from East Pakistan, and dying on the street was literal.

We had waited at the Delhi Airport until 4 a.m. for a late plane arriving Calcutta at 7 a.m. We made our way to the Great Eastern Hotel, as lavish as ever. We saw some of the city, had an Embassy briefing, then went to a Chinese restaurant for lunch. I will never forget that meal. The food even looked clean—what a welcome relief.

We ate dinner at the hotel at tables for four with eight waiters per table, each with high red cloth headpieces studded with jewels, long red coats, sword belts and all, held over from the days of English colonial splendor.

About India one can say almost anything and it will be true. To paint a descriptive picture with a few strokes of the brush is difficult. The country, its people, its habits seem almost as old as time, but we participated in the second anniversary of Independence. Here were people, 380 million of them, 75 percent of them underfed, and we were told 40 million a year are dying of starvation. Hunger here was not something you wondered about. It was real, it was there staring at you on every turn. We heard much about the United States. In every country every act of the United States Senate which might in any way affect foreign policy is front-page news, more

182

so than at home. Here in India we heard that Americans are adolescent and immature in their thinking. We have no culture. Our workers are robots with no time for love of home or family. We are leading to war by over-preparedness and too much armament. We make too many speeches which flame up fear. We turn down every Russian proposal so she may get discouraged and be forced to war. We are trying to preserve economic status which is not deserved. We weaken the position of all dark people by the use of our machinery, and the Marshall plan is white aid to whites and belittling of all dark people.

Mr. Gandhi, son of the Mahatma, said, "We do like Americans because they break new ground and follow methods free from snobeery." It was notable that the Indian leaders who had been in the United States were far more favorable. Mr. Nehru spent considerable time with us. It was interesting to see the improved relations and understanding which developed among all the folks with whom we met in the few short days. I have had two letters telling of the tremendous influence of Mr. Nehru's visit to the United States on his understanding and appreciation of American people and policy. The feeling on American capital was mixed. They prefer it to any other outside capital, but fear political control will follow capital. They are more fearful of private capital than of government loans to government. Many people there do not oppose Communism, only the way it is being administered. They do oppose that. They feel capitalism and Democracy are opposites which cannot be brought together so they must oppose both Communism and capitalism and lead the other nations of the world into a third world force which will cast off the leadership of both the United States and the USSR. England is giving a good deal of support to that thinking in India. We may find ourselves isolated instead of isolationists if their program prevails. The Russian influence in India against the United States was considerable. It was based mainly on capitalism, our support of nations holding colonies, and discrimination against colored people.

The English influence in India against the United States was probably more effective and was against American capitalism and American racial discrimination. The English newspapers carried almost daily front-page stories of racial discriminations in the United States, distorted and exaggerated. A prominent English spokesman on world food problems was there ahead of us to warn the people against any use of Point Four assistance from the United States. India has at least three billion dollars of private wealth in gold, silver, and jewels, but confidence and know-how for industrial investment is lacking, so it will not soon be used. Here again new land to be farmed and the possibility of improving presently farmed lands seemed almost unlimited right where hunger was the most real. The conditions, however, under which the masses work are so discouraging that there is little incentive, hence low production per man and per acre. I was told that in places around Bombay animals and birds consume 50 percent of the production.

We heard much in India of culture versus materialism and of racial discrimination. Their understanding of us and our understanding of them leaves much room for improvement. They can be and want to be a great force in the world. We have many common interests and should be pulling together. It is tremendously important that we understand each other better.

Our flight from India to Manila was memorable. We stopped for gas in Bangkok just as day was breaking, the view from the air of the beautiful city below, and the miles of water-covered rice paddies just whetted our desire to return and meet an Oriental people who have known independence, and see how they have used it.

The trip over the islands "sliding down the hill" into the airport at Hong Kong is an inspiring and exciting experience. What the future holds for Hong Kong is clouded, but then it was an international port doing a tremendous business in dealing in goods from the four corners of the world. The beauty of Hong Kong Harbor lingers in every traveler's mind. Beauty, interest, excitement are all blended in.

On the long flight Calcutta to Hong Kong, on to Manila, we were using a DC4 with long spacing between seats. It had practically bed-length extension to the reclining seats, and Pullman-car-like draw curtains to keep out light or distractions at night. This permitted relaxed privacy and contributed to comfort and sleep. Seated together were Roger Kvam, our 18-year-old, and Althea Hottel, Dean of Women at Penn State, when the steward lowered the lights and closed the curtains. Roger bounced out, denouncing such an arrangement as nonsense and didn't think it a bit funny. Of course, everyone else thought it the funniest thing so far. I guess it just proves you can't please everyone.

† Manila

Our arrival in Manila was the most dramatic, for it was 9 p.m. and pouring rain. Here at the airport was the band, banners of welcome to individuals in the party, banners of welcome to all, and many hundreds of highly adorned and enthusiastic men and women leaders of Manila to overwhelm us with their reception. This was only a forerunner of the whole stay in Manila.

The city was badly damaged, largely by artillery and by fire as the Americans drove the Japanese out. It is now being rebuilt rather rapidly. The city was full of life and action—lots of newly gained wealth—and it seemed like everyone was looking for a new way to make another dollar. I felt it must have been somewhat the spirit of Sacramento, California, in the early days. The rural area is beautiful with green, verdant growth everywhere. The farm people live in fairly good houses, not well-to-do by city standards, but still we saw no signs of malnutrition, disease, or effects of consuming poverty.

The seminars centered largely around how to get American capital and know-how for industrial production, but even more around trade relations with the United States which would help the Islands export their sugar, hemp, tobacco, copra, rice, and fruit, and especially help them develop their many crops and industries. Their farm organizations now are commodity groups only. I had several conferences and a delightful dinner with their farm leaders, discussing setting up an over-all farm organization for which there was a good deal of support. The interesting incident came with the discussion of how to finance it and, as we left, the plan was to have the government give them 12,500 acres of new land on the Island of Mindanao. They would equip and farm it and finance the organization on the profits from the farm.

I had hardly caught my breath when the meeting adjourned, but who was I to know a better way in that far land anyway. Then, too, I know they are better financiers than we, for with over sixty thousand college students in Manila alone and most of them in private colleges, we found colleges are highly profitable private enterprises.

184

I visited a college of agriculture with the owner, Mr. Araneta. It had its livestock, poultry, horticulture, agronomy, and all the other departments along with research. It was only eight years old and not quite paying yet, but would before long. The natural resources of the islands are abundant. The population is 20 million. It could reasonably grow to 50 million. Taxes equal about 7 percent of the income and the budget is balanced. Money made on the islands is largely reinvested there as the people have confidence. There is a great desire for education, but the schools are very inadequate in the rural areas and teachers difficult to find. Rural schools average four years, equal to about two here. Schools are used for two or three shifts a day, so average only 2½ hours per day per child.

American influence is very apparent in the islands. They are our friends in an area where so many of the world's people live. I hope our influence has helped them and will help them more in demonstrating to their friends of the Orient that it is possible to raise the living standard of great masses of people, and that the American way of education and incentive will help do it.

Manila was certainly a city of activity, business everywhere, the streets overflowing. Highly colored, flower-bedecked, rebuilt jeeps were honking and dodging everywhere. People rode in and hung on this principal mode of transportation.

My counterparts were the Aranta brothers. One was Minister of Agriculture and owned the College of Agriculture, managed largely by his wife. Another brother was head of farm credit. His other interests were a clothing and tailor shop, farm equipment agency, an optometrist, and a dairy which was his greatest personal interest. The cattle looked fine, and the growth of legumenous feed was fantastic, but the dairy was plagued by sterility problems. He claimed he had solved it by feeding dried seaweed imported from California. All other milk was buffalo. The third brother was head of customs service. They had lots of one-man conglomerates.

We had several seminars, as well as a town hall meeting, embassy briefings, visits in the city and country. There was lots of war damage, but also enthusiasm, life, and hope everywhere we went.

Several of us went to visit the opposition candidate for president, Dr. Jose Laurel. He had the support of the Huks. He had been chief justice of the Supreme Court of the Philippines. He stayed in Manila to help care for the people when the others left before the Japanese occupation. We said we would like to meet the Huk leader. Our host said he would have a car and driver at the Manila Hotel at 5 a.m. to take us up into the mountains for the meeting, as it was a long trip for one day. During the night someone called from the U.S. Embassy saying we should not go, and they would make it very difficult for any Philippino who cooperated in the trip.

We left Manila amid the cheers of many of our host group, who had also been there to welcome us.

As we were waiting to board the plane for Tokyo, we were told the plane had to take a full load of gas, so they could only take part of us. They then agreed they could take all of us if we left our heavy bags, so we just dug out shaving equipment, etc., and left our baggage behind us. In the air they told us the Chinese Communists were flying the area between Hong Kong and Okinawa and might be trigger happy, so we flew a wide circle to get to Okinawa about midnight for more fuel and a checkup, then on to Tokyo.

†Tokyo

We were housed in the Ga-Jo-En Hotel, a former naval barracks on a hilltop above the city. Our briefing from the military was thorough and efficient. Then we went to the American Embassy, built shortly preceding 1941 Pearl Harbor.

Mrs. MacArthur showed us around the house, including the family silverware. They had left the Philippines in a PT boat at night, but in the past three years almost every piece of their silver had been returned to them by people who found it scattered all over the country. The General entered through the kitchen and the air was electrified. His presence could be felt the moment he entered. A few people seem to permeate the air with electric waves, and he was one of them.

During and after the meal we discussed many issues. Here and elsewhere on the trip I realized the great privilege of having so many peoples of broad interests who could ask the right questions to get answers to vital questions.

General Marshall and General MacArthur were our ranking generals, distinctly different in type and often of differing viewpoints. One of our group asked our host what he thought of General Marshall. He replied, "Certainly no one could be critical of a great gentleman like General Marshall. The only one you could question was the man who didn't know any better than to send a Puritan to China." This was in response to President Truman having earlier sent General Marshall to China to report on the situation, and he reported that Chiang Kai-Shek's government was corrupt and weak, and that the Communists were reformers.

The job of eliminating Japan as a potential aggressor is largely done for the immediate future at least. The forms of democracy have been pretty well set up and the people seem to be pleased and happy with them. The condition in China may influence our position in Japan. It is relatively easy to occupy a defeated nation to enslave it, but occupation to liberate and develop democracy means people must have food and a feeling of security and hope. This is costing the American people about 500 million dollars per year. The problem of economic self-sufficiency is complicated by a population, already burdensome, still rising at the rate one million per year, and by the loss of Japan's trade in the Orient and elsewhere.

The schools have made great strides in democratization and extension to girls as well as boys. Still, they told us that in Japan where the grandparent and parents spend so much time training children during the first six years of life, it is slow for schools to change thinking. It was also pointed out that the individual has so long been told by government that it is now a slow process to build individual initiative into the thinking of the mass of people.

In 1721 the population of Japan was 21 million. In 1846 it was nearly 27 million. In 1949 it was 81 million. Until 1846, abortions and disposal of surplus babies was freely practiced. Partly under foreign influence and partly because the Japanese military leaders wanted more population, these practices were stopped. Population has risen over 300 percent while food has increased a little over 200 percent. For the next 20 years a 25 percent increase in population is considered sure, while a maximum food increase could not exceed about 8 percent. Abortion has again been legalized in Japan for economic as well as health reasons. The problem is real with them.

I went to Tokyo to see the city and buy some gifts. During the day a typhoon

186

landed on us—pouring rain, terrific wind gusts. All traffic stopped; no taxis back to the hotel, so I sought refuge in a downtown hotel lobby taken over as an American officer's lounge. They had just invested $2500 in new drapes for the big windows facing the street. We could easily feel the difference in air pressure as the gusts of wind came by. Then Wham! The big plate glass windows shattered, cut the new drapes to sheds, and a sea of water poured onto the floor. One of the officers invited me to spend the night on a spare cot in his room, about tenth floor on the protected side of the building. We could stand in the window and see many sheets of galvanized iron flying through the air, hitting windows and shattering more glass.

The next morning an officer took me to see the farming and to assess the damage. The typhoon was passed, people were all over their roofs repairing the damage. Many buildings, palms, and other trees were down, but the rice just bent with the wind and then stood upright. The farming was beautiful, small plots all hand worked, but the yields of about 6000 pounds per acre were the same as our mechanized yields in California.

We went to a farm cooperative hall meeting for lunch. September 1 is a normal time for such storms. The normal format was to assess the damage in the early morning, then go to the hall and compare notes and estimate the community damage, enjoy a good meal, pray it won't be so bad next year, and then have enough sake to forget the damage. This was unusually heavy damage, so they started forgetting it before noon, we ate a little, and left.

Japan had many farmer's cooperatives before the war, but they got very political during the war. General MacArthur disbanded them and was now setting up new ones. Under land reform, almost all land is now held by the farmers. The farms average 2 acres and the maximum size is 7½ acres or 5 acres of good land. The work is all hand work. Farmers have had the benefit of inflation though it is now against them. The farms look thrifty and reasonably prosperous. While the Japanese like the government under which they are now living and the $5 million United States aid, 70 percent in food, still they agree that time only will tell whether they can and will themselves carry on and advance the present conditions. Willingness of their former enemies to accept their manufactured goods and sell to them raw materials will be an important factor in the outcome.

We had a very large and active Town Hall meeting in Ernie Pyle Theatre. We left Japan with a high appreciation of the job being done by the U.S. military in rebuilding all aspects of life in Japan. The Japanese were industrious and ambitious to succeed, but they were still confident that their great asset was cheap, loyal labor, and that they could price us or anyone else out of the lower quality market. This was their objective. It was some time before they recognized they should build for quality as well as price.

We left Tokyo at midnight. Our main trip and objectives were behind us. We landed on four-square-mile Wake Island in the glaring sun, on Midway at 10 p.m. for two hours, then on to Honolulu, arriving about dawn, 4 a.m. We enjoyed the Halekulani Hotel right on the beach with its many small guest houses hidden in the trees and flowers.

The Hawaiian stop September 2-8 was filled with seminars, dinners, lunches, luaus. Harold Wadsworth, Dean of the College of Agriculture in Honolulu, had been called to a South Pacific Conference on agriculture, so I had the pleasure of escorting his wife, Dorothy, to the College of Agriculture luau. Among the trees and flowers it was surely a thing of beauty. It emphasized the cosmopolitan social mix of Americans, Hawaiians, Japanese, and the Oriental races all working equally to prepare and enjoy the evening. I took plenty of pictures to help remember the beauty of the evening. Our Town Hall dinner was impressive as was our **Town Hall** evening session under the trees on the beach to exchange our final impressions of the trip and make plans for our final meetings in Washington, D.C., October 14-19. We visited the island, Pearl Harbor, the cemetary, the sugarcane and pineapple fields. It was a full program, but in a quiet, restful setting. Today it is difficult to realize that Honolulu could have been so quiet and restful in 1949.

The flight to Los Angeles was mostly sleep. The welcome home at the Sacramento airport was now my goal.

It is hard to believe that any globe-circling trip any time in history could have given an equal opportunity to meet people, high and low, of so many different races and nations, under conditions so favorable for understanding **and** expansion of good will.

††† Overview

We saw many well-operated farms on the trip making a major contribution to a free world. First I will describe practices retarding farm contribution, then point to the favorable factors we saw, followed by a few suggestions of ways America might aid.

In Europe, many still know hunger and malnutrition, but as we got well East we saw thousands of human beings knowing all degrees of malnutrition, up to starvation itself. These were people similar to us intellectually and in their desire for education, good home life, and opportunity. The farm resources of these countries are more than ample to maintain a high standard of living for all the people.

There is growing recognition among the leaders of the necessity for eliminating the restraints to production and substituting incentives to production. Still, we found millions of farmers paying excessive rentals and 50 to 75 percent interest on cash advances.

There are practically no schools for farm youth. Debt was inherited and passed from generation to generation. One is born into a caste or stratum, never to change. The result is low production per man and per acre. Education in these countries has been for culture, not production. Investable cash goes to real estate and jewels. Progress demands some education and capital investment for production.

The oppressive practices are time-honored, complicated, and difficult to overcome. Still, in twenty-five years, we have seen the women of Turkey rise from servitude to equality. I doubt if any country in the world has ever advanced as rapidly in its history as has this country of Turkey.

We saw the social welfare villages of Egypt. We were inspired by the rise in social consciousness of the Oriental women with their new-found freedoms. In Japan we saw land reform almost completed in two years. The new city buildings in the Orient are ultramodern.

188

Most rapid reforms follow violent upheavals. But I've great hope that the people can enjoy rapidly rising living standards in our generation and in peace.

We surely learned that great natural resources do not make education, homes, hospitals, recreation, and other good things of life. These things are byproducts of a society and government which provide incentive to production. The producer must have the opportunity to educate himself for production, to choose his field of production, and to get the benefits of his production.

America can contribute to a free world by practicing all the ideals of democracy in America. We can aid in development abroad of effective agricultural research and extension services, including work among youth. We can encourage training of farm youth for off-farm work, to speed industrial development and relieve the pressure of population on the land. International exchange of students, farmers, and other groups seeking knowledge and understanding will help.

I favor strengthening the office of Foreign Agricultural Relations and United States Information Service to provide needed information and assistance in meeting international problems. We should work for elimination of the irritating inefficiencies, continuously changing practices, and other needless barriers to trade. We can encourage industrialization of undeveloped areas and aid in the development of equipment adapted to the special needs of the various people. I believe that by pooling our ideas with others, when and if requested, we can contribute to a free world.

I see very little benefit in wholesale feeding or financing until the basic restraints to local production are met. I do believe we can do some selective feeding through schools preparing youth for production, or for workers on productive works.

We need a positive approach to those underdeveloped countries which seek our aid, not just a passive good will to maintain a friendship which some day may be needed. We need to render aid quickly and in many little ways so that many scattered individuals will receive a new hope and demonstrate that production will bring a better life and opportunity. Those experiences can spread to bring hope and incentive to many people.

We must recognize, too, that our lives and lands are safer if the people of the world have a better life and, further, that it is in our selfish interest to aid others because our economy does not do well on the decline or when static. Our economy does very well on expanding demand from mass markets able to buy our production. These markets will come to us if the people of the world have so expanded their production as to have some surplus with which to buy the things which will make life more attractive for them.

Many thanks are due to the Farm Bureau members who made it possible for me to participate in this endeavor, also to the Department of State, its embassies, the host committees, the officials, and the folks on the highways and byways who helped us in our understanding of the other people of the world. We admire every country more for having shared a few days in its struggles and its successes. People must better understand people.

Above left, Nehru in garden answering questions for Town Hall members. At right, Nehru inspecting inspecting troops on 2nd anniversary of independence in India. Below, cargo boats on the Nile.

Bottom left, Barnhout of American Legion and I hearing "instant translation" of local speakers. At right, Edith Sampson and I at Town Hall meeting.

Above, National broadcast at departure of Town Hall meeting of the Air, World Tour At left, the world's best salesmen—in the Philippine countryside. Below, Farm Commodity leaders of the Philippines (I am in middle)

*At left, Isabelle and Saroya,
Queen of Iran, at World
Affairs banquet in
San Francisco. Above,
Appian Way in Rome.
Below, CFBF banquet in
Long Beach, 1954*

Above, American Farm Bureau Federation board in oval office with President Eisenhower
Below, Farm Bureau meeting in Napa County, 1952

At left, hand-made wooden screw to elevate water from main ditch to lateral in Egypt. Below, suited up to fly jet.

Below the plane I flew at 600 mph.

Bottom, parachute jump of 800 men, an impressive sight.

9
HOME AGAIN 1949-1954

Home and the family really looked good, and so did Clarksburg and the farm. I had taken over 1300 pictures on the trip. I had about 400 slides duplicated for gifts to members of the party. This required returning a good many of them several times, as the art of duplication was still young. Each time, as they used new chemical formulas, some would be better and some worse. I have recently shown the originals with slight deterioration, but the color in some duplicates that I showed were pretty well washed out.

Isabelle went back to Washington with me in October. We enjoyed a reunion dinner given by Miss Strauss and the Givers in the Givers' home. It was a most pleasant evening; they were truly a great group of people, each of broad experience before we left, and each far more seasoned and experienced on our return.

The trip was not financed in any way by the State Department or Government, but they and the Department of Defense gave us a great deal of assistance in each country visited. They asked us to report on our return as to what we had seen.

On Monday we met all day with State Department people and they had a dinner for us that evening. The Secretary of the Treasury, who had met and followed us in Europe, was most commendatory of the good we had done. Tuesday afternoon we met with Secretary Johnson of Defense in his office. Tuesday morning I had met with the Secretary of Agriculture and his foreign service staff. The last meeting was the Town Hall of the Air public meeting and our report to them and the nationwide radio audience.

I was one of the four speakers on this occasion. We had each prepared our four-minute statement and shown it to George Denny. He had made two or three minor suggested changes in my statement. I thought they were minor and of little importance, but if George wanted them I would accept them. But the more I went over the statement, the more I realized how helpful a few simple word changes could be. I have never forgotten that, and it has helped me many times since.

Mr. and Mrs. Denny had invited Edith Sampson and the Wilsons to have dinner with them before the broadcast in Constitution Hall. The dinner was to be in the prestigious Carlton Hotel, across from the Statler, in Washington. George had a table reserved, but, as we approached, the head waiter stepped in front of us with arms outstretched to forbid entrance to any colored person. George tried to plead with him but to no avail. George and his wife, Jeanne, were furious. We entered the Statler a little hesitant, but we were seated without question. George talked all through the meal of changing the subject for the evening to give national publicity to the problem of race discrimination. Edith was cool and unperturbed during the whole incident, saying that was old stuff to her. She had met it often and it was accepted as a fact of life.

Constitution Hall was packed, and we were still not sure what George would do. He told of the incident and how terrible it was, then the program proceeded.

George Denny and his wife, Jeanne, who was his production assistant, were great Americans. They brought public discussion of national issues to the American people. Their show had top rating in the U.S. They made a great contribution to serious analysis of public issues. We need them today.

The CFBF annual meeting was in Long Beach.

The big event of the fall was the wedding of our Pat and Wesley Fisher at the First Methodist Church in Sacramento on November 12, 1949. Dr. Elliot Fisher and Howard Daulton performed the ceremony. There was a large crowd, with the reception in the church.

† 1950

In January I was in Washington, D.C. and called the Pakistani Embassy about some colored slides I was sending for the Prime Minister. They said it wasn't announced yet, but he was coming to the U.S. in May. I asked if there was anything I could do. They said he would like to see some California farms.

The Pakistani Consulate in San Francisco called and gave date, people, etc., and offered to help in any way they could. Several weeks later they called to express regrets that U.S. State Department didn't approve. They called a week or so later to ask if I would still plan the day, as it was back on the schedule; then it was maybe, so my next trip to Washington I called on the protocol officer in the State Department. He had all sorts of fears, not interesting, late return; finally he said all right, pick him up at the hotel in San Francisco at 9:30 a.m. and have him back at 3:30 p.m.—and I don't care what happens in between.

On May 16 I spent the day with the Prime Minister's party at several events in Sacramento. We were challenged all day by Baluchestani pickets carrying placards. The Prime Minister handled it very well.

On the 17th we had the cars lined up at 9 o'clock and were all ready to leave at 9:30, except the Pakistani Ambassador to the U.S. kept us waiting ten minutes, very much to the disgust of the Prime Minister, so the ride to Orloff Dairy Farms at

192

Pleasanton was very quiet. The walk around the dairy loosened things up, but still the P.M. was quite somber. "Their Red Sindi cattle would out-produce these." The Red Sindis produce 7 to 8 percent butterfat like the buffaloes. We then went over to Jose Rose's ranch in Contra Costa County. The Prime Minister was short and a little rotund; Joe was a big, tall Italian. Soon after they met Joe walked up to the Prime Minister, shook his finger in front of him to get attention, and said to Liaquat Ali Khan, "Now, your Highness, let me tell you about farming in the United States. It's pretty good, pretty good. There are just two things wrong with it. Glass-eyed bankers and high government taxes." I thought the Prime Minister would explode. His ambassador was a banker, so he could laugh at him. The day was made from then on.

They had crop dusters alerted to fly right in before us on the tomatoes with dust, then a second with a fertilizer application. Then we moved back from the road and a plane dropped rice seed so the seed pattern could be easily seen on the road. This really impressed them. We then went with quite an entourage to the old Bishop Ranch, where they still used the old bunkhouses and the ranch cookhouse for feeding. It was 11:45 a.m., so the dining table was set up with a piece of apple pie and a slice of cheese on it before each plate. As we went through, the Prime Minister reached over and got a slice of cheese. I was sure then that the day was going well.

We then went to Mr. and Mrs. Howard Wiediman's home to see a typical ranch home with a newly remodeled kitchen. There was lots of canned fruit, and a deep freeze on the porch. The questions flowed out. Who did the cooking, who canned the fruit and vegetables? He was amazed to hear that Mrs. Wiediman did it all. Then the deep freeze full of meat and vegetables—he told his Minister of Defense who was with us to order a deep freeze for him to keep his ducks in.

We then went to the old Community Hall at Cowell for lunch. This was an old frame building with wide front steps leading up to the porch and entrance. The local women prepared the meal and the 4-H Club boys and girls served it.

The Prime Minister was delighted as the 4-Hers gathered around him on those steps. I was worried for fear they might not hold all that weight. The 1x12 boards for the table tops were set up on wooden sawhorses with butcher paper on top for a tablecloth. By now we had quite a crowd for lunch. The meal was very plain, but three times the Prime Minister turned to me and said, "This is the best meal I have had in the U.S." There was no formality. The 4-Hers delighted him. He was completely at ease and felt among friends. The 4-Hers put on their demonstrations.

The only request made by the Consulate was that I have a helicopter demonstration if possible, so I contacted Hiller in San Jose. They had three copters on hand for us and had been demonstrating them to the military aides. Right after lunch they put on quite a show for all of us. The Pakistanis bought all three of them. Eleven years later I met Hiller's foreign sales manager. He said he had just been in Karachi. One of these helicopters was still in active use, one had cracked up and was being used for spares, and one had been flown out of the country and never returned. I thought they did well to still have one flying after 11 years.

I told the Prime Minister that there was a schoolhouse nearby, of a type of architecture which would be appropriate in the hot Pakistani areas. I had contacted the school people ahead. We opened the door to a classroom, and he got the whole picture, white youngsters, black, Chinese, Japanese, Portuguese, Italian, all mixed in together, all getting the same instruction. I didn't say a word about it, nor did he, but he got it all. We then went to the Walnut Growers Association packing shed in Walnut Creek and got the story of farmers Coops statewide. We were back at the Mark Hopkins at 3:30 p.m.

The protocol officer had gone with us. At the hotel he said "You win."

Within a year or two of his return, Liaquat Ali Khan was assassinated, a real loss to Pakistan. Several years later we were invited to dinner by Chester Davis, then a regents professor at Berkeley. He told us that he had visited the Prime Minister in Karachi after his trip to the U.S., and he said his day on the farms in California was by far the best day he had in the U.S.

Later I was talking to Ted Schultze, Agricultural Economist of the University of Chicago, a friend of Mr. Nehru of India. When Nehru was planning a trip to the U.S., the only request he made was that Ted Schultze take a day to show him an American farm. It was arranged, but called off through the State Department, who set up so many limiting requirements that Ted said he couldn't meet all of them. Then Madam Pandit, Indian Ambassador to the U.S. and Nehru's sister, called on Ted. He told her the story. She exhibited her famous temper in the State Department, and it was on again. Nehru called it one of his best days on the trip. Our State Department seems to feel they must overwhelm these visitors with our automobiles, airplanes, plants, and stuffy dinners and cocktail parties.

In our big industrial plants, they may be awed, but they see no points of common interest. In elegant dinners they excel, so they leave bewildered, having seen little of common grounds on which we can expand our mutual interest. It is only on the farms that they find this mutual understanding.

I have just seen a note that we paid Mary Borden $21. for 14 lunches for the Prime Minister and his party. I am sure it was not only the best meal but also the cheapest he had in the U.S.

It would be useless to list them, even if I could, but I gave a tremendous number of talks throughout the year to service clubs, Farm Bureau, church, and other groups on the trip around the world—many talks and many colored slide and moving picture shows. One of the more interesting meetings was the Senator William E. Borah Conference on the causes of war and conditions of peace held at the University of Idaho in Moscow, Idaho, held in April this year. These conferences were held for at least five years. They seemed to be an honest effort to encourage peaceful solutions to international problems. My observation here again was that State Department people seem to say, give us a big enough military and we will maintain peace. The military seemed to say, if we can learn to understand people and their problems, we can maintain peace in the world.

Another very interesting meeting was the National Preparedness Orientation Conference in later November, 1950, in the Pentagon.

In December I bought 55 replacement heifers, 679 pounds at 22¢ for Sloughhouse from Drummond, Montana.

194

† 1951

The war was going on actively in Korea and the Department of Defense felt it desirable to invite leaders in agriculture, industry, and labor to come in for briefing and open discussion of issues involved. There were 33 from agriculture, 49 from industry, and 28 from labor. It was a real privilege to see in action so many of the leaders of industry and labor. Most from agriculture I had met before.

The meeting was opened by General George Marshall, formerly Chief of Staff during World War II, now Secretary of State. He thought that General MacArthur's Inchon landing would go down in history as the greatest military operation of all time. And he did it with very little help from Washington. Then he went on to say that General MacArthur had integrated 30,000 Koreans into our army on three weeks' training and had organized a new Korean division every four weeks. We took two years to prepare a division for Europe. The military organization in Korea was probably the best in history.

The U.S. had known peace and war. We must now develop a plan for partial mobilization from which we can move very rapidly. We have 27 divisions and 22 combat teams, many special units in the State Militia, and a tremendous number of reserve officers, but our laws are not adapted to partial mobilization. To start in Korea we had 4 divisions in Japan, 3 in the U.S., all very incomplete.

We must not build to a high peak, then slide off, but build an enduring system. The problem is, "What is an enduring system that the public will support?"

We need materiel now, but we also need a basis for a rapid system of production which will permit an increase of 200-400-600 percent in our stride. As part of a United Nations operation, we must have a solid front with 50 nations. It was bad enough with only two in the last war.

Lt. General Gruenther, Deputy Chief of Staff, later Chief of NATO, was next. His message was that the military was calm but concerned. We do not want war with anyone, especially Chinese Communists. You do not win, and it is in the wrong place.

Russian steel production is 25 million tons. They have 175 divisions, can quickly get 320 divisions Their oil is fairly vulnerable; they have 40 thousand tanks and are making six thousand per year. The situation is explosive. The area of decision is Europe. (Sounds like now, in 1981.)

Anna Rosenberg then spoke of manpower. Leon Keyserling, Economic Advisor to the President, said, "The free nations of the world must be able to *maximize production quickly. The strength of a country is in its flow of goods and services.* How can we strike balance between freedom and restraint?" He believes in the force of reward to bring production in peace. In national defense we need to think of what we can give as well as what we can get. *We need balance between government controls and voluntary controls.* The problem is not *basically military or economic, but political.* We must find a way to work together in this new situation.

Deputy Secretary of Defense Lovett's message was, "We need wide understanding of the problems. We can get your confidence only by performance."

Stewart Symington stated the need for people to help in government jobs and for people to help public opinion. He also said that the concept of the UN was that the world wanted peace. Russia does not seek peace, so after five year's effort there is no UN police force.

After discussion from the floor, William Greene, President AFL, spoke. "How can we prevent inflation?... Must produce more...cannot reduce civilian needs too much or too long. Government must give facts. Inflation is the result of policies of government, industry, labor, and all. We must pay as we go. Higher taxes for everybody. Jim Carey, Secretary-Treasurer CIO was concerned about contracts to electrical plants in Eastern Europe using Communist labor. There were many comments by leaders of agriculture and industry.

I have included considerable detail to give a little feel of the thinking at that time and that similar meetings of leadership in government with leaders in private life might be very helpful today. Maybe we have so many meetings of government people with minorities, oppressed, weak, forgotten people that there is little time left to meet with the average public or leaders of the groups of producers in 1980.

We had the regular AFBF board meeting in January, and afterward we went to the Conference of National Organizations in Atlantic City.

I had been invited to give one of the principal presentations on the subject, "The Role of the U.S. in the World." I presume this meeting contained more top leaders in business, agriculture, labor, and other fields than any I have spoken to before or since. It was a rather thrilling experience—a large auditorium filled with top leaders. Interestingly, I was followed by another Mr. Wilson of Clarksburg, West Virginia, Past National Commander of the American Legion.

We gave one-quarter interest in the Utter Ranch to David, Dick, and Pat, now all married, and reserved one-quarter interest for Dorothy, then 16 years old. Dorothy was given her quarter in 1959.

We borrowed $50,000 from the FLB on the property, partly to have the money, partly to cut the size of the gift taxes. The county-assessed value on the ranch was then $25,288 for the land and $4,180 for improvements, $29,468 total. For the three-quarters given in 1951 the gift tax was $7.50. For Dorothy's quarter in 1959 the gift tax was $250, so taxes were going up pretty fast then. We are sure the Utter Ranch has been, and I hope for a long while will be, of value to the children.

The boys were back home and I felt that, with the alfalfa and grain in the Holland District, it would be well to put a feed yard for cattle at the Utter place. I was devoting a good deal of time to design and locating material and equipment for the project.

The rural church work was active. Jess Rudkin, Frank Pierce, and I spent a great deal of time on the conferences and research project. We contributed $100. to the new church building in Courtland.

David, Dick Wesley, and Roger were all on the payroll at $250. per month. On November 17 I paid Glen Rose, David, Dick, and Wes $800. each as their share on the tomatoes.

Ray Wiser, president of the CFBF, had been in the hospital for a long siege, running the CFBF largely through Frank Pierce who visited Ray often in the hospital, and Louis Rozzoni, the vice president. On Ray's recovery, he was very active in the California Heart Association, the California Highway Transportation Group, and the Commonwealth Club, so he had not over three days a week for CFBF.

My place in CFBF was representative on the AFBF Board, and I paid little attention to the politics or office management of CFBF, but I heard a little of administrative problems. Then one day several of the older board members came to the ranch and said Ray was going to resign, and I was the only one they could agree on to fill out the term. I had never thought of it. I did not want a full-time job, but when they returned I agreed to take it for a $12,000 a year salary, instead of the $15,000 it had been paying, provided I was expected to devote only four days a week to the job. This was more time than the president had been spending. I felt with the boys home my being there three days a week would be enough, and things would work out all right.

I attended the next board meeting. Ray's resignation was now officially accepted in a regular board meeting. I was elected to fill the position and also be president of the insurance and other companies. Of course, Ray occupied the corner office for the rest of that day. I went in to see him. He said he was confused. He hadn't intended to resign, only to make the offer. I had never had any problems in dealing with Ray, and didn't have any during the turnover. Ray had had a long sickness and nervous disorder. He had submitted a formal, legally prepared resignation. Louis Razzoni was first vice president. He had been spending full time in his office running the Cal Farm Supply Company and the approved seed programs. I asked him to continue those activities, which he did as long as I was president.

The first thing I found out was that it was not a four-day-a-week job. About the second week, I came home for the weekend. The boys were waiting to ask about some farming problems. I told them to wait a minute. I went into the office and wrote out a simple lease and asked them to sign it. They couldn't make any mistake worse than waiting for me to get home. They wouldn't make as many as I did in getting started. That let me devote all my thought to FB and was best for the boys in the long run. I do not believe I have ever interfered with their farming since that day.

November 11-14, 1951, was the CFBF annual meeting in San Diego on the old World's Fair grounds, a beautiful setting. Governor Goodwin Knight of California spoke Monday evening on "Let's Not Forget Our Heritage." Hassil E. Schenck, President of Indiana Farm Bureau Federation, was a principal speaker. Our banquet featured Mexican senoritas to sing and dance and Nazarea Cruz Garga, Secretary of Agriculture of Mexico, and also Mrs. Raymond Sayre, chairman of "Women of AFBF," a great mind and leader. I was here elected president of the California FBF by the membership. All my farm bureau stationary during my term carried the heading "Freedom is the Issue."

On November 21 I spoke to the Arkansas Farm Bureau general meeting in Little Rock, Arkansas. It was of special interest, as there were two simultaneous meetings, but one program. Each speaker spoke first to the AFB meeting (White), then was rushed over to the Arkansas Baptist College to speak to the Negro Farm Burear Convention. I followed Governor Sid McMath both places. The music was wonderful. I told the Negro group of our "49" trip with Edith Sampson, and how she got the white folks to love her people by first getting them to love Edith. They really enjoyed it. The Negro Convention was well attended and they were a fine-looking group of folks. It was a privilege to speak to them.

†1952

I left for Mexico January 6 for the three-day Farm Labor Conference at the Del Prado Hotel. These meetings were with the government officials and representatives of the "Asociacion Nacional de Cosecheros." The problems seemed minor but some were important to them, and they seemed to need assurances and understanding directly with our growers. At that time Mexico City streets and sidewalks were a constant hazard with broken surfaces and holes in the streets; you moved at your own risk. The city was old, beautiful, and interesting, but the poverty and rubbish were in full view. The people were always friendly, the flowers and parks spectacular. As I write this in 1979 I must note the changes. The improvements and building of the last 25-30 years have been a miracle. Mexico has made spectacular progress. They have done it on their own with the tremendous stimulus of the Bracero program.

I had spoken to the annual meeting of the California Warehousemen's Association. So Mr. Lyons, also national president, invited me to speak to the National Association Meeting in Palm Beach, Florida, all expenses paid for Bella and me at the Biltmore Hotel. It was a fine group to speak to, and we were royally entertained. Mr. and Mrs. Ford, secretary of the Farm Bureau, showed us Florida for two days, including the citrus and vegetable country. We saw the Cypress Gardens for the Aquacade, and visited with Air Force Colonel David Paulin, Commander of the Air Base there, a son of Hal's.

We then went on up to the AFBF Executive Committee in Washington D.C. I met with California State Chamber of Commerce folks in the morning, and spoke to the San Francisco Rotary Club Number 2 at a joint meeting with Oakland Club Number 3, at the request of O. D. Jacoby, chairman of the board at UOP.

February 7 through 10 we held the Volunteer Leaders & Staff Statewide Meeting at Asilomar to let the F.B. staff and leaders get better acquainted, to swap ideas on local and state problems, and set programs for the year.

March 25 Don McColley and I went over our Farm Bureau program with Governor Earl Warren. The Governor later visited the board at our meeting in Berkeley. He told them he was in almost full agreement with Farm Bureau policy. Our relations with the Governor were excellent all through the four years of office.

I refused an invitation to go to Geneva, Switzerland, to the ILO meeting (International Labor Organization), as I was too busy in California.

Some years before this there had been a general strike in San Francisco with all business tied up. Finally a group of farmers armed with pitchforks paraded in San Francisco. This helped end the strike. Before that all farm business from Bakersfield north was with San Francisco, but the farmers cut San Francisco off and nearly all business went to Los Angeles—no farmer convention in San Francisco, no farm contact if possible. San Francisco employed a public relations officer to try to get the farmers back into San Francisco, so in April we had a little good will as the city presented and planted two rhododendron plants at our building entrance.

We organized a good will trip to Mexico from April 26 to May 4 for twenty-eight California Farm Bureau people. We rented a DC3 for the trip. We were royally received, and we visited with President Alleman in his office and presented gifts of California fruits.

The American Ambassador in Mexico was William O'Dwyer, former mayor of New York City who had recently married Sloan Simpson, a celebrated model and beauty. He invited us to meet at the Embassy residence, first in the basement theatre where we had talks by the political, economic, cultural, and agricultural attachés giving very fine analyses of the situation in Mexico. After each presentation, O'Dwyer would jump up and say the seats are too hard, we must go upstairs and have a drink. After all the presentations and questions were finished, we went upstairs, met his wife, and had drinks. They each carried around a Coke.

We had a dinner that evening in the banquet room of the Del Prado Hotel. The Bracero program was up for renewal at that time, and all the media publicity was that Mexico would not agree to renewal. The U.S. Department of Labor had four men who had been in Mexico City for over a month negotiating with no progress, and they told us we would never get renewal. We invited these men to the dinner. We had invited President and Mrs. Alleman and the Mexican Secretary of Foreign Affairs and his wife, as well as others from the U.S. Embassy and Mexican friends and officials.

President Alleman sent word he could not attend. This meant the protocol officer from the Embassy had to change all the place cards to see that rank was properly recognized. It took at least a half-hour to figure out and change them. Ambassador O'Dwyer told us to be sure not to announce the dinner until he gave the signal. He and the Mexican Foreign Minister got in a huddle in the far corner of the room. Our Labor Department men were quite irritated by the delay in dinner, and reminded us we would never get the Bracero program extended.

Soon after the protocol officer finished the place cards, the Ambassador gave the signal. We were all seated, and he and the Foreign Minister jointly announced that all was agreed and the Bracero program would be continued. Isabelle was seated next to Ambassador O'Dwyer on one side of the long table, and I next to his wife on the other side. They were both excellent conversationalists.

I had been in Mexico City about 1940 to get the original program set up to bring Mexicans into the U.S. to help in sugar beet production. Then, as the program was enlarged to cover all crops and other areas of the U.S., we spent several days with the Mexican farmers as well as government people working out a program to be helpful to us in the war food program and not harmful to Mexican farmers. I was also involved in meetings in Mexico City after this 1952 trip to get renewal of the bracero agreement after official negotiations had broken down.

It was a shame that the program was terminated by action of Congress at the urging of church, labor, and other groups, when it was not only a great aid to the U.S. but by far the most successful of all our foreign aid programs in helping to build a developing country at a negligible cost to the U.S.

We had a summer picnic May 15 in the Berkeley hills for all Farm Bureau employees, including affiliates. It was lots of fun and helped get all the employees acquainted. Then in July we had the board meeting at Camp Radford in the San Bernardino Mountains Sunday through Wednesday, and the staff from Thursday through Saturday. They brought their families and we had fun, but also good solid classes on Farm Bureau objectives and how to reach them.

Going through the 1952 date book, there were so many interesting meetings and people that it is difficult to pick a few examples, especially as the occasions are so diverse, but I should mention the Pan American Airlines dinner on Friday, June 6, for Around the World Club members. We took Louis Rozzoni with us.

The dinner was the idea of the owner of the Cliff House (then San Francisco's most popular and historic restaurant), of Mr. Hiller owner of Hiller Helicopters, and Mr. Kent of Skipper Kent's Restaurant where the dinner was served. All the food was specially flown in from places served by Pan Am. Even the ice was flown in from Mendenhall Glacier in Alaska. The Ming salad, squab, chicken, spices and herbs were from Peking. The prawns were from Mexico, the numaki from Hawaii. We had Celestial Chicken from Canton and Sub Gum from Hong Kong. The pea pod Chow Yuk was from Shanghai, the Patna rice from India. The pineapple was selected the day before in Hawaii, the coconut from Panama, the mango preserve from Malaya, and guava from the West Indies. The wine Alsace was French, and the coffee came from Congo Africa.

It was a great evening with many great stories. On my left was Mrs. McLaren, wife of the architect of Golden Gate Park. About 1940, while Pan Am was still using the flying boats, they commissioned Mr. McLaren to landscape all the airports on all the Pan Am routes, so she flew with him. They had great experiences, and she had the brains to tell it right. People came from Seattle, Denver, Chicago, Los Angeles, of course, and every other point. It was an historic evening with lots of good will and humor.

We had a meeting of the AFBF Soil and Water Committee of which I was chairman, followed by the AFBF board in Chicago. We met with the Republican Agricultural Plank Committee and stayed for the Republican Convention and for meetings with their agricultural and other committees. Sunday July 6 I went to the railroad station to meet the California delegation, all pledged to Earl Warren as the favorite son candidate, but they were a sorry-looking crowd; they had a hard trip, with lots of dissention still boiling over.

For the convention we occupied a box assigned to the AFBF in the front row of the balcony, the best in the house at the Chicago stockyards. We were surrounded by America's first families and leaders in business. General Douglas McArthur gave one of the more dramatic speeches. The meetings had been lasting until midnight or after, so the last day I packed my bag and took it with me to the Convention, which was not far from the old Chicago airport where my plane left about 1:30 a.m.

About 5:30 Eisenhower and Nixon had spoken, and the meeting adjourned rapidly. It is somehow a terribly hollow, lonesome feeling to find yourself alone, when for days before it had been a crushing jam of humanity.

I decided I might find some of the newspaper and radio reporters in the bar and get a few different views of the Convention. I looked up the bar, but it was about empty, too, so I took a stool and asked for a limeade. I had to verify the order a time or two, then the bartender called down the row, "Mike, Mike, get the cookbook, the man says he wants a limeade." About the time I got it, some of my reporter friends came in and invited me over to their table. We killed an hour or so discussing various aspects of the convention. The bar is the place to go afterward, for I saw through their eyes many things I had missed before, and of course each of them saw a different show.

General Eisenhower had been approached by both the Democrats and the Republicans to be their presidential nominee. He refused the former and barely accepted the latter. After the convention, he took time to plan and get some rest for the campaign. He spent time at his mother-in-law's in Denver.

He invited farmers and livestock men to meet with him for a day. I was elected as spokesman and chairman for the farm group, so I sat at the head table with Eisenhower on one side and Sherman Adams on the other. This was about his first such group meeting. He was not really sure whether the whole thing was a good idea or not.

Governor Warren appointed me to the State Civil Defense Counsil on food and nutrition. I attended a few meetings in San Francisco and Sacramento and got a vision of the inefficienty and the unreality of thinking by the civil defense staff. I cannot be sure whether it pointed up the great need of civil defense planning, or the uselessness of such planning.

August 29 was Farm Bureau Day at the State Fair. It started off with a talk to the 4-H clubs in convention at Davis at 9 a.m. Next was a talk with Roy Rogers over KFBK at 11:45, then on to lunch with the Fair Board and other guests and our Farm Bureau members; also awarding of the trophy to the winner of the Farm Bureau race in front of the grandstand.

The next morning at 7 a.m. was the Sacramento Host Breakfast at the Senator Hotel. The host breakfast was given by a group of Sacramento businessmen to honor the State Fair Board and the Board of the State Chamber of Commerce; they invited citizens from all over the state; by 1981 this meant 1000 people. I have been invited and gone every year since, if I have been in the country. The Governor has always been the principal speaker, except 1975 when Jerry Brown refused to confirm his acceptance, so President Ford was invited and became the principal speaker. Jerry Brown came, and he has confirmed acceptance early since then. Everyone likes to get there early and meet friends whom you seldom see elsewhere during the year.

The California Teachers Association had gotten on the ballot a constitutional amendment, No. 2, materially raising the state appropriation for schools. It would go in the constitution and supersede any and all other state appropriations. Thus the school appropriation would be sacred, regardless of any financial crisis the State treasury might face. A few years earlier the California Farm Bureau Federation had initiated and gotten approval of the first state appropriation for schools, so this we favored, but we opposed placing it in the constitution above all other state obligations. The teachers had really worked on this. They had labor, the media, and, it seemed, almost everyone lined up for it.

I asked our board what we should do. I was told there was nothing we could do; they had the vote all lined up and there was no possibility of defeating it. I told them my only interest was, what did our resolutions say about putting such things in the constitution? They all agreed the resolutions opposed such use of the constitution, so that set our position. We might not win, but we would try. This became the big issue of the year. It took a great deal of time and many meetings.

One of the early ones was in Sacramento with a large turnout of influential people. I was in the minority, with little vocal support, but after the meeting many came up to express support for our position. At the end was a little lady, Mrs. P. D. Bevil, who said, "Oh, Mr. Wilson, we pray for you every night and we surely hope you will win. We are almost all for you, but our hands are tied. We can't do a thing. We have refused to support No. 2 so far, but we will have to before long." Then she said, "I am the president of the California Parent-Teachers Association. The teachers run our association, so we will have to give in, but we are just as strongly opposed as you are." She was a great supporter of Farm Bureau all during my time in office. I learned then, and often saw later, that if you believe you are in the right, you will receive help from some of the most unexpected places.

One of our Farm Bureau men was scheduled to debate the issue with a proponent of No. 2 at a meeting of the Parent-Teachers Association in Ventura County. It was given wide publicity, and there was a large turnout including several of the press. On arrival, our man was told that it was planned that the proponent would speak first, then he would be called on to reply. This was OK, but as soon as the proponent finished, the chairman announced the meeting adjourned. There was protest, but the chairman said the PTA by-laws said no opponent should be allowed to speak at any PTA meeting in opposition to the PTA position. The newspaper protest against the action was quite positive and resulted in repeal of that provision in PTA by-laws.

We did not defeat No. 2, but we did get vote enough to convince everyone in the educational field that Farm Bureau was a force to be reckoned with. Our committee on education was invited to attend and was listened to in school meetings.

This year General Dwight D. Eisenhower was elected President of the U.S.

On October 12, a group of about thirty-six Mexican farmers and wives came as our guests to San Francisco. They returned by bus, going through central California and down the valley to Los Angeles and the border. The County Farm Bureaus had lunches and dinners all the way, so they saw a great deal, and many of our members had an opportunity to meet them. They were at Clarksburg for lunch. Tom Robertson was with them, and many prominent Mexicans were in the group. We had several trips each way after this and made many friends. It was also the start of the California Farm Travel Service.

The 1952 annual meeting of CFBF was held in Fresno November 9-13. Vespers and the County Presidents Dinner were held on Sunday evening. The California Rural Church Research Project Luncheon was held Monday and was well attended. On Tuesday there was a dinner banquet; we had Dr. J. Whitcomb Brougher, Glendale Baptist Church, a great speaker and humorist. On Wednesday was an organization breakfast with Roger Fleming as speaker, always the best. Bob Kirkwood spoke on "Your Public Schools, What Next?"; Roger Fleming on "Organizing to Succeed in Farm Bureau"; Joe Duell, "What Caused the Change?" (water); Hon. Cullan Oakley Hunter, M.C., "Water Problems." Oakley is now the highest-paid federal employee except the president. The 1952 membership was 64,559, an increase of 3,200 members.

In November, I went to New England and spoke at the Vermont, New Hampshire, Connecticut, and Massachusetts annual Farm Bureau meetings.

The AFBF annual meetring was in Seattle; resolutions December 3-7, annual 7-12. The Land & Water Committee met on the eighth, with the Assistant Secretary of Interior as speaker for the proposal to set up a Columbia River and a Missouri River commission, patterned after the Tennessee Valley Authority. The Central Valley of California Commission was on the drawing board to be pushed next. Our members were out to kill it. They were there in force and determined. They killed it that day, and it was buried soon after. As chairman, my job was to protect the speaker and hold the crowd in reasonable restraint.

The Alsop Brothers syndicated column covered the story in detail, saying it was the most complete defeat they had ever known a federal official taking. If they had won there, our position on the CVP would have been even worse than it is today.

†1953

On January 8, I met with Governor Warren to go over the California and AFBF programs with much of the discussion on water.

On February 2, I gave the keynote talk to the California Agricultural Extension Conference in Davis, on Responsibility of the Farm Family in the World Community.

February 10, Allen Kline, with the American Farm Bureau board, and I met with President Eisenhower in the oval office. Getting onto the grounds and into the oval office is quite formal. The meeting was relaxed with many questions back and forth.

That morning, our Land & Water Committee met with Mr. McKay, Secretary of the Interior. Then several of us met with the Secretary of State, and also several of us visited with Secretary Ezra Taft Benson of agriculture. I got back to the hotel feeling it had been quite a day of visits for a country boy. In my box was a note from Vice President Richard Nixon saying he had heard I was in town; please drop by and see him. So the next morning I did, for quite a discussion of water and cotton. He urged me to drop in often to keep him in touch in relation to water, as it was a problem the President was personally very much interested in, and I believe he honestly was. Also his Secretary of the Interior seemed to be, but the determined desire of the little group in the Department of the Interior went relentlessly on for greater power and control over land and water. Power of the U.S. presidents, vice presidents, and secretaries come and go, but small determined groups seeking power seem to go on forever.

The number and diversity of speeches I find in the date book month after month is amazing. On April 27 it was Reno Rotary and the Nevada Farm Bureau board of directors. I attended all the Nevada annual meetings, and Florence Bovett attended ours.

The Rural Church Research Project took a good deal of time; in May we gave $1,000 for its support. Dick Myers, our project manager, was doing a great job.

I was awarded the State Farm Award by FFA.

We held the summer delegates meeting in Berkeley May 25-26. All county and other officers and volunteer workers were invited to attend those meetings. The atmosphere was informal. We reported on what actions had been taken on annual meeting resolutions or other actions of interest. We discussed how we could do a better job for Farm Bureau members, but it was not a resolution passing meeting unless for a very exceptional situation. Much was done for the good of Farm Bureau in these meetings.

I was appointed one of several Farm Bureau representatives to the IFAP (International Federation of Agricultural Producers) meeting in Rome. Bella went with me. We arrived Milan on May 29, spent several days. We occupied the fourth balcony at La Scala Opera, and also visited Lake Como. Allen had to go to Rome for a IFAP board meeting, but Gladys traveled with us on a tour bus, leaving Milan May 31, stopping at Florence, Perugia, and other stops along the way. The farm land was all used; sometimes a crop of alfalfa or grain or row crops grew between rows of grapes, with fruit trees interplanted, so they had three-layer farming.

The roads were the same, travelers on foot, bicycles, motor scooters, horses, oxen, cars, and busses, several levels of speeds dodging and weaving, and horns blowing continuously.

I am no real student of art, but the shops and museums of Florenzia were beautiful as is the city itself. We also went to Venice, and the glass factory on the island. It was all beautiful.

The IFAP is a federation of national farm organizations. The first requirement for membership was that they be free, independent, and farmer controlled, not controlled by or associated with government. It was set up largely by the English and European farm groups, though Allen Kline had participated in the organization, and this year Allen was president. It was run by an executive committee under policies set in the by-laws and by the membership meetings. Yogoslavia had applied for membership. A committee chaired by Allen had visited Yugoslavia and determined that their organization was not free and independent, but was controlled by government so not eligible for membership. But at an executive committee meeting which Allen could not attend, they were ruled eligible and admitted to membership, even though the bylaws said a new member could be admitted only at a full-membership meeting.

Allen felt we must abide by our bylaws, so he appointed me to the bylaw-constitution committee whose responsibility it was to recommend approval or disapproval of applications for membership. We knew we could not win, but we held it up until the last minute and got recognition of our position.

We had heard of the beautiful mountain village of Bled in northern Yugoslavia, its summer Capital, so we got reservations June 14 by train to Trieste, a beautiful city at the head of the Adriatic Sea. Our travel plan called for going to Trieste, then north into Bled, so at the junction we took off our bags to go north, but porters put them back on the train and said we were going to Lubiana. We took them off, and they put them back. Some of the Yugoslavians who had been at the IFAP meeting said we better go to Lubiana, and they would have one of their group get off with us to be sure we got a hotel there, etc. Some did.

We took the train to Bled the next morning. It was beautiful in the mountains. The summer Capital of the Yugoslavian government was on a little lake. We checked in the hotel, took a little walk, and returned. The manager was so glad to see us, as two officials had come to see us. We wondered "What now?", but it was the president of the Veterinary College in Lubiana, and a professor, who had come to see that we were well received. We were the only Americans in the area. They had a small car, and they got the local Vet, who was something like a farm advisor. We visited a number of the farms in the area. It was an unexpected treat. Most were small dairies, all neat, the work done with scythe and oxen in the old style, but beautiful and delightful. The college president said he had had a year at Ames, Iowa, Vet School, and they had entertained him so much that when he heard there were some Americans at Bled, he decided to drive up and get his revenge. They were delightful hosts, named Provstick and Popitch. We wanted to see some of Vienna, but were told there was only one U.S. gateway to Vienna and it would take two days to get in that way. The direct rail trip from Bled to Vienna went through the Russian check point, and we could never get through there.

The train was packed with vacationers. The fares were very low. By the time we got to the Russian check point, it was dark, and we could see a big party up the hill at the hotel. We just made ourselves as invisible as possible. A Russian soldier walked through the train, but no checking, and we were on our way. Vienna was delightful.

In Vienna, the opera across the street from the Bristol Hotel, where I stayed in 1949, was still under reconstruction, but the Schoenbrun Palace was beautiful. We saw the summer opera and heard great music in the park. We then flew into Paris to meet Dorothy and the UOP tour group led by Eleanor and Alonzo Baker. I left for the AFBF board meeting on June 26, while Mother joined the tour with Dorothy and saw much of Europe and the British Isles.

We started the Asilomar Conferences, and they proved popular for over twenty years. The purpose was to spend several days together each spring when the volunteer leadership officers and the staff leadership could get together, get better acquainted, and discuss our common goals and how best to achieve them. They served their purpose very well.

July 14: Lunch with Jesse Tapp, Chairman of the Board, and Mr. Lundberg, President of Bank of America.

July 16: Breakfast in Los Angeles on Boy Scouting, a lunch in Fresno with Ezra Taft Benson, Secretary of Agriculture, where he left the political leaders of the San Joaquin Valley to come in and have lunch with our Farm Bureau group.

August 13: Spoke to the students and faculty of Mills College on "What is Ahead for Agriculture."

August 26: Dinner with Governor Knight in Palace Hotel.

September 2: Spoke to Montana Annual Meeting.

September 5: Host breakfast, Sacramento Senator Hotel.

September 25: New Mexico Farm Bureau Annual Meeting, Los Cruces.

September 28–October 3: AFBF Chicago Board.

October 11-12: Meeting Western Region presidents, Salt Lake City.

October 15-19: Represented the AFBF at the annual meeting of the Mexican Asociacion de Agriculturos & de Cosecheros. I was given a medal and elected to life membership.

October 23: State school administrators annual meeting in Hotel St. Claire, San Jose. They had asked me and three professors from the School of Education in Berkeley to be there for a 1 p.m. panel discussion. This was Friday; I met in the appointed hall at 1 p.m. with the three professors. Finally a staff man showed up to report that all the administrators had left after lunch, as they were not going to get home late for any meeting. We had been invited by their officers. It was a sad commentary on moral duty and common courtesy.

Sunday, November 8, the CFBF 1953 annual meeting started at San Jose. We had a fine, well-attended Vespers service at 5 p.m. Sunday evening. Monday was all the commodity meetings and Tuesday the other departments. Wednesday we had the president and secretary's reports. At lunch we had Hon. Thomas H. Kuchel, U.S. Senator, who had handled our cotton legislation. In the p.m., State Senator George Hatfield and Frank Wooley of AFBF. Frank was always a great fellow with a great talk. Dinner, Charles Schuman, president Illinois Ag. Association, was principal speaker. He was later the president of AFBF. He was a good AFBF director, a good economist, a very good spokesman for American agriculture. **At the annual banquet** we had three past presidents: A. C. Hardison, Richard W. Blackburn, and Ray Wiser. We sat 1500 people and had the tables decorated with 4000 begonias.

We gave the first Distinguished Service Award to Alex Johnson, secretary-treasurer of CFBF, 1921-1941. We started thirty-year pins to people who had served thirty years either in Agriculture Extension Service or as high-school vocational agriculture teachers.

We also had at the convention Ken Ketch of Cal Poly, SLO, and his class in journalism. They attended every session, commodity sessions as well as general meetings, wrote up news releases on each, and helped get all the data right for the regular news service reporters. They picked their top man, and we sent him to the AFBF to report. It was a great program for us and for the boys.

†1954

January 6: Portland Oregon to kick off Oregon membership drive.

January 8: Sacramento Department of Agriculture 8:30. Governor Knight at 10:45 and Ed Voorhies in the evening.

January 11: Met with group setting up Farmers and World Affairs in Washington D.C. Visited Roscoe Cattell, head of the Bureau of Mines. He was a student with us at Berkeley in the YMCA, then in the Hilgard Club. He was the smartest of our group. He was head of the Texas Oklahoma District of Bureau of Mines in the oil rush period just before World War I. Then he enlisted in the Army Engineers and sailed for France, still in civilian clothes. Was loaned to the British to help find oil in Algeria, Morocco, etc., then returned to Bureau of Mines to be in charge of Louisiana–Mississippi area where all the large gas discoveries were coming in both on land and under the Gulf waters. He then headed up the research and manufacture of helium gas at Amarillo, Texas, as a safe gas for the dirigibles used to hunt down German U-boats **during** World War II. For the several years before my visit with him on this trip, he had been in charge of the research and development of oil from oil shales at Rifle, Colorado. He then figured that they had the processes well enough worked out so that, whenever gasoline got to 35¢ per gallon, it would be economical to use oil shales. Whether the problem today is still the economy of production or the high cost of ecological restraints, I do not know.

Roscoe represented the finest of the old school of public servants; able, honest, dedicated, proud of his agency and its accomplishments. He certainly had made a great record of aid to the development of the gas and oil industry in the U.S. I visited in his office several times. He knew just where to find every map or record. I never saw a pencil, pen, or pad of paper out of place on his desk top. I guess we were friends partly because we were different, especially the desk top.

January 12: This attracts my attention, as 25 years ago I was **at Mendocino City** for the annual meeting and dinner of Mendocino County Farm Bureau. That is just two miles north of Little River Inn in this beautiful coast country where we are spending a few days in May 1979, wracking my brain and my records to write up for our grandchildren a few of the activities and thoughts of life during my generation.

January 14: I had always wanted a boat where we could get out on the water, river, lake, or ocean and enjoy the fun or the relaxation and quiet. I seriously considered a 30-foot cruiser where we could stay for days of solitude, but then I thought of the hours of servicing, cleaning, and repairing the boat and I gave up, thinking I would be taking care of the boat instead of it caring for us. I compromised and ordered a 15-foot Fiberglass Wizard built in southern California. So David and Mother drove down and picked up the boat and trailer, picked me up in San Diego, and we drove 60 miles below the border to see our friends, Tom and Dorothy Robertson in Ensenada. There we christened our new boat in the Bay. One day we took the Robertsons and went 12 miles out to the Todo Santos Islands. Near the islands we met lobster fishermen collecting fresh lobsters from their traps. It was about noon, so they suggested we take a walk on the island; they would land and have the lobsters all cooked and lunch ready for us on our return. It was wonderful. No lobster which has been in a market for days or even hours can compare with one which jumps about directly from salt water into the pot, then is devoured quickly by hungry campers. We used the boat some on the river, but used it less and less and finally sold it.

January 20: AFBF Western Regional Conference in Salt Lake. These were great meetings of the officers of the eleven Western states where national, regional, and state problems were fully and frankly discussed to the benefit of all.

February 5: I went up to the Pacific Lumber Company at Scotia in Humboldt County. This was an interesting assignment. You are a guest of the company, and you are shown all through the mill and the yards right in the Redwood country with mostly redwood lumber. Then a big dinner, and you are the speaker of the evening with time for questions. You spend a delightful night in the guest house and leave on a hearty breakfast.

Scotia is rather isolated from any large city and it is a single-interest operation. So the company felt its middle management staff should have a broader contact with the world and its happenings. They maintain a good library and several courses of study, but each month they have an outside speaker on any subject of interest. They were far better informed on the many activities of the world than most big city dwellers. I was surprised to receive a check for $150. for an evening; I felt it was quite worthwhile.

February 25: I was invited by the Dean to speak to the senior class in economics at Stanford University. This was a class of 40 to 50 students, five or six professors, and the Dean.

I discussed what I saw as the economics of the farm program, some of which we in California approved, and some we did not, and said why; then we had questions. The first set the pattern of their interest. "We know the AFBF has a powerful lobby in Washington. We know the lobbyists use dirty tricks; what we want to know is what are the dirty tricks you use?" I tried to explain that a lobbyist interested in one bill might deceive and win, but lobbyists who work with Congress year after year on many bills must work constantly for a reputation of being trustworthy, knowledgeable, and honest, for in the long run they succeed only as Congressmen trust them. Of course, all through life we meet a few people who are good story-tellers, and we like them even though we know they are not true, but that is the exception.

The class let me know they believed the Farmers Union was smarter and represented the small farmer more than the Farm Bureau did. I pointed out that the Farmers Union had practically no membership in California, and was quite small nationally, while the Farm Bureau had as paying members about two-thirds of all farmers, either California or U.S., so we had to represent family farms. But I felt maybe they were telling me more about what they were learning than I was telling them.

After class, the young professors and a number of the students followed me into the Dean's office. It was long and narrow, with the Dean's desk near the window, and I sat with this group near the entrance. They raised many questions. I was delighted to have a chance to answer. But they persisted in saying they had a right to an adequate supply of cheap food, and anyone knows that a man will work more efficiently working for himself than he will working for another, so they had a right to demand food be produced on small farms at reasonable prices to consumers. I told them I knew the man who built the first utility trailers in his garage on an alley in Phoenix, Arizona. He was working for himself and did a good job. Did they then feel that I had a right to demand that all trailers be built in alley garages by individuals? "Oh, of course not, that is different."

Then, without thought, out slipped my question. Who teaches you all this stuff? Every eye went over my shoulder to the Dean, and back came a voice I had forgotten was there, saying, "Not me, not me, I don't teach that."

I am sure I have said earlier that, when the U.S. government asked farmers to plant fence-to-fenceline for full production to feed the troops and our allies in World War II, we as farmers replied that we would be glad to, but we must have some assurance that we would not be left with huge supplies of food and fiber for which there was little export demand, as happened after World War I. So Senator Steagall proposed the Steagall amendment, which said that any crops for which the Secretary asked all-out production would have support at 90 percent of parity for two years after the termination of hostilities.

Officially there was no date when hostilities terminated in World War II, so no two years after date, but demand dropped off and large supplies of so-called basic commodities and dairy products accumulated in government storage, and prices in the marketplace fell. Farmers could see the futility of this, and Farm Bureau spent most of its time after 1948 trying to have supports dropped from 90 percent to 65 or 70 percent, which would have halted the volune in storage and encourage sale in the marketplace at home and in export.

Some of the finest statements made against high price supports in agriculture were made by Truman during what seemed to many to be his futile campaign for reelection. But somehow *Brannan*, recommended *by* Agricultural Secretary Clint Anderson to fill in the remaining several months of a fading administration, saw fit to convince Truman that the farmers under Brannan leadership had cast the deciding vote for Truman. The farm program became a party political issue, which it had not been before. So government agricultural commodity holdings continued to accumulate. There is little incentive to buy any product which is held in surplus today and probably will be in greater surplus tomorrow

President Eisenhower was elected in 1952. The surpluses must be moved, about $10 billion of wheat and corn. They were depressing prices. They were costing $1 million per day to hold, some were deteriorating in quality. Something must be done. So the Eisenhower Agricultural Trade Missions were set up, one to northern Europe, one to southern Europe and Africa, one to Latin America, and one to Asia. In the President's message of January 11, 1954 to Congress, he proposed that "several trade missions be sent over the world to explore the immediate possibilities of expanding international trade in food and fiber."

I was appointed for the Asian Mission. We arrived in Washington on April 7 for four days of briefing conferences, shots, etc. We were to study marketing and trade practices, removal of road blocks to U.S. export, currency problems, ways of increasing consumer preferences and improving quality, packaging, and handling of U.S agricultural products. We were briefed by all the embassies of countries we were to visit. President Eisenhower, in his office, said our mission was to seek ways and means of increasing international trade under conditions that will favorably affect the prosperity of both the buyer and seller; what products of ours they can use, and how do we make them our customers? Second, what do they have which we can use and develop plans for mutually beneficial trade? We then had pictures on the lawn with the President.

World Trade Mission delegates, 1954. In center front row are Clifford Hope, Chairman of Agricultural Commission; Ezra Taft Benson, Secretary of Agriculture, Homer Brinkley, Chairman of group

A. J. McFadden, Bella, Earl Coke, George Wilson, Mrs. Coke at California annual meeting.

ASIAN MISSION

Another World Trip

Our party consisted of: Chairman, Homer L. Brinkley, Executive Vice President of the National Council of Farmers Cooperatives; our Executive Secretary was Tim O. Engebretson, Foreign Agricultural Services, Department of Agriculture; Gordon Boals, Director of Export Programs for the Millers. National Federation, wheat and flour; Fred A. Hobart, Board of Directors National Cattlemen's Association, Pampa, Texas, cattle and animal byproducts; T. O. Kluge, Manager California Plum & Apricot Growers Association, San Jose, California, fruit and vegetables; E. M. Norton, Executive Director National Milk Products Assoc., Washington D.C.; F. Stuart Russell, Farm Editor of Des Moines, Iowa *Register & Tribune* (we often roomed and traveled together—he was well-known and respected as a farm editor and a fine person); R. C Travis, Tobacco Consultant of the Burley Tobacco Growers Association, Lexington, Kentucky; George Wilson, President California Farm Bureau, Clarksburg, California; Mr. and Mrs. Earl E Hanway, Casper, Wyoming, *Wyoming Press*.

We stopped in Pakistan, India, Thailand, Indonesia, Singapore, Philippines, Hongkong, and Japan. Left Washington, D.C. Sunday, April 11 at 2 p.m. and New York at 4 p.m. for Shannon via Pan Am Stratocruiser, arriving at 4:30 a.m.

It was evening when we were met in Rome by members of the U.S. Embassy staff. Francis Flood, Agricultural Attache, was our helper and host at a dinner in the airport. Left Rome 10:15 p.m for a six and one-half-hour flight to Cairo at dawn. The eight-hour flight over the Sahara Desert got us into Karachi in the early afternoon. We spent four and one-half days in Karachi. Horace A. Hildreth was U S. Ambassador.

King Saud of Arabia visited with 100 personal escort who came in their private planes for a state visit, including several of the princes. There was a garden party and lunch for the visitors and guests; 2,000 were invited, including us. Two square city blocks in the park were cleared off and covered solid with Oriental rugs. A bandstand-type building was erected in the center where the official party lunched and could be easily seen. The 2,000 were seated at small tables for 6 or 8 all over the area and served lunch—a very spectacular scene. It was all prepared days before. Saud and party stayed at the house of the Governor General, about four blocks from the park. The official guests came in carriages, four horses and outriders To prepare the way, the trucks had dumped piles of sand all along the official way. Men would shovel the sand into fiber baskets, which they helped the women lift onto their heads The women carried the sand to the proper place on the street, and, balancing everything just right, the sand would fall from the basket like a waterfall and hit the palm of one hand, which spread the sand out evenly over the street so the horses would not slip and fall.

King Saud was followed by his body guards, 20-40 in number, little black men in wide flowing white robes with scimatars schowing in each fold of the gown along with a few small machine guns and other objects of offense or defense. They were silent and moved like cats, smoothly and gracefully. They looked like greased lightning. The next day all the Oriental rugs were piled up in front of every rug merchant's establishment, borrowed for a day.

Pakistan had experienced a drought in 1952, so they appealed to the U.S. for help with food; we gave them 700,000 tons of wheat free. They must give it to the poor, or sell any surplus to others and use the money for agriculture or water development. They took us out to the airfield (military) where they had long tiers of wheat in 100 Kg bags (220 lbs). The Pakistani farmers were like the French. As soon as the U.S. wheat showed up, they found there was far more wheat in Pakistan than they had supposed. They told the U.S they didn't need any more, but it kept coming. They wanted us to help stop it They said what we saw on the runway and other supplies was enough for a future drought. The Agricultural Attache was Harry W. Speelman. They had a party for us. Mr. and Mrs. Wills, economic advisor to the Embassy had a buffet dinner for us. Mr. Norton got sick and left the party to return home from Karachi. I filled in as best I could for dairy products.

April 16 we left for Bombay; spent ten days in India, about one-half the size of the U.S. with 360 million population; Bombay 3½ million people.

We stayed at the Taj Mahal Hotel. It was Easter, and I went to a Protestant, I think Methodist, church nearby After the sermon they had communion service, and the people came forward to the Chancel. Next to me was a Hindu woman in Sari. The wine was prune juice, and before she drank it she crossed herself as in a Catholic church. It seemed a little unusual. Mr. and Mrs. Shearer of the U.S. Consulate Office entertained us, and here we met D. N. Khurody, milk commissioner of Bombay, who took us to the Milk Colony. Fifteen thousand water buffalo are hand milked at the Colony Project—good buildings, good milk manufacturing facilities owned by the state, but animals owned by individual farmers We attended Rotary in Bombay. Homer Brinkley was the speaker. You could choose either a vegetarian or a meat meal.

We flew 800 miles to Delhi into 112-115 degree heat. George V. Allen was the Ambassador, quite new in Delhi following Chester Bowles. He had a party for us at the Embassy. Dr. C. C. Taylor was Agricultural Attache; he stayed with us all the time as well as having us for dinner.

We met Dr. Panyabro Deshmukk, Minister of Agriculture, who was also President of the Farmers Forum of India, and the one who invited us to come back in 1956 to aid in Farmers Forum organization. He had a delightful dinner for us at the Delhi Gymkhara Club.

India has 260 million acres under cultivation farmed by 40 million families, or 6½ acres per family. Forty million acres are double-cropped and the irrigated acreage exceeds 50 million, which is far in excess of U.S. irrigated acres.

New Delhi was 25 to 30 years old in 1954 and belonged to the new era, while Old Delhi was definitely the old.

We had many meetings both with government officials and with traders and business leaders, with visits to the warehouse and shipping areas. There was a great shortage of good storage space, and the Kapra beetles seemed to eat much of the grain in storage so the losses were very heavy.

We took a Sunday to go to Agra to see the Taj Mahal and other sites of interest. The Taj is certainly one of the seven wonders of the world because of its size, symmetry, and beauty. We stayed overnight at the Hotel Lauries to get the benefit of seeing the Taj by moonlight. It was built by Shah Jahan about 300 years ago, entirely of white marble, hauled 120 miles on carts, as a tomb for his wife. It took twenty thousand laborers and artisans seventeen years to complete. I have beautiful pictures, still a delight to see. Up the river a short distance is the old Red Fort, not as spectacular, but to me very beautiful and interesting and worthy of the time to see it at leisure. Also near Agra is the Pillar of Asoka, part of a temple built 1,600 years ago. The pillar shows no signs of rust. It may have been carved from a meteorite, using flint tools.

In Bangkok, Stuart Russell and I stayed in a very nice home of a friend of his situated on one of the busy klongs. Our bedroom on the second floor faced the canal with all its life and color. We were awakened each morning by a houseboy bringing coffee and toast and a wrap-around robe. By the time we were up and shaved, our breakfast would be set out on the porch overlooking the canal, where still in pajamas and robes we could look directly on all the activity below us. Some boat people were selling drinking water, some vegetables, some clothing, anything we go to the store to buy. We could have spent the whole morning there and loved it all.

We met one day with school people and doctors in relation to use of dry skim milk in school lunches. They assured us that they were not interested, as they had adequate school lunches. That evening, however, the Minister of Education came to our room to talk. He said they were using a milk made from powdered soya beans. The children drank it, and it added needed protein, but he knew the animal protein in cow's milk was better, so what could they do to get it? He had samples of the soya bean milk with him. It really wasn't bad, especially if they added some chocolate. A simple practice like milk for children has its problems. When they gave children allowances of milk powder to take home for use, they found that in many cases the parents saved it, put it back into empty packages, and sold it to the shopkeepers for resale. Where they mixed the dry milk at the school and gave it to the children, they had other problems. Even the teachers had little idea of sanitation or cleanliness,

213

and diseases spread. What seemed to be quite simple innovations can prove to be quite complex and have quite unexpected and unwanted results. Graham L. Quate was Agricultural Attache, and he was a great help to us.

Rice is the staple and principal crop of Thailand. The average farm was about ten acres. Most of the Thai officials spoke to us in English. The Premier, who was also Secretary of State, gave a luncheon for us in his beautiful palace, a fantastic meal with many toasts and much good will. Each of us was given a sterling silver cigarette case with our names, and also our hosts name, engraved on the back.

The Minister of Agriculture had a lunch for us on the official yacht on the broad Me Nam River. It was alive with commerce of all sorts, strings of barges loaded to the gunwales with a tiny little launch towing the whole string.

On the ship everything seemed shipshape and immaculate, surgically clean, but I moved to the rear of the ship to get a picture, and over the stern at water level was a platform on which was a waiter dunking the glasses in the river to wash them, and in the river was everything. There was a luncheon by the Minister of Foreign Affairs; a dinner and Thai Classical Play as guests of the Under Secretary of Agriculture; a luncheon by Lewis Davis, Manager Bangkok Branch of the Bank of America; a dinner by Graham Quate; and a luncheon by the Bangkok Chamber of Commerce. It sounds like Thailand was more social than business, but it was a most enjoyable stop with a great group of people. Foremost Dairy Company put in a modern plant to reconstitute dry skim milk soon after we were there. We visited it on our trip in 1956. We left at 8:30 a.m. on May 4 for Djakarta.

Djakarta, 10 degrees south of the equator, is the capital of Indonesia. Formerly Dutch, it had grown from 250 thousand people before the war to 2 million in 1954. As we flew over the dense jungle country, we looked down and saw this neat city of red tile roofs, which certainly had a Dutch look to it even from the air. The city was well laid out, with a large open canal running through the middle of the main street. It was all purposeful. The women washed clothes in it, the children played in it, the people bathed in it. It was also the convenient sewer system for the city, but each day it was completely flushed out.

We were housed at the Transaera Hotel, a Royal Dutch airline hotel, but quite modest. The U.S. Ambassador was Hugh S. Cumming. The Agricultural Attache was Dr. Horace V. Geib.

On May 7 we were driven 40 miles east of Djakarta into beautiful lush green country, good farm country. We stopped at a rubber plantation and got a good look at the harvesting of latex for rubber. We saw lots of rice, coconut and papaya trees, casava roots, nutmeg, cloves, cocoa, coffee, remia grass, and jute.

We visited the government experimental farm at Bogar. Rubber was Indonesia's most important export, but the price was exceedingly low. We could have done well by buying rubber at the very low price and helping them during a difficult period of their development. Rubber, copra, tea, pepper, palm oil, and tobacco were their most important exports, and rice and wheat flour the most important imports.

We had an appointment to visit President Sukarno in the afternoon. The Djakarta Chamber of Commerce invited us to have lunch with them. Their primary interest in us was not what they could buy or sell from the U.S., but could we intercede with President Sukarno to get him to free up the channels of trade? The Dutch traders had profited by restrictions, the new operators got even more restrictions enacted to their benefit. But for the businessmen of Djakarta, it made trade very difficult, and they could easily see it was seriously restricting development of the new country.

We learned a great deal in Djakarta of the crops and problems of the tropics and of a newly emerging nation. We didn't increase our purchases or sales as much as we would have liked. After four days at Djakarta we checked out for Singapore. We flew over many heavily wooded islands, almost all with rivers that stood out as the reddish brown water flowed into the ocean, building new deltas where there was no other sign of modern man.

Singapore is a few degrees north of the equator. We were entertained at a dinner given by Mr. and Mrs. Jack R. Johnston, the U.S. Consul, in their home over-looking the city. Many prominent British Chinese and Malayans were included, so we got a cross-section of the problems and hopes of Singapore, and a good night in the Old Raffles Hotel before going on to Manila via Saigon.

We stopped for refueling at Saigon, but it was the day after Dien Bien Phu had fallen and the French were pulling out in great confusion, so they would not let us outside the airport waiting room. After a 12-hour flight, we arrived in Manila at 9:15 in the evening. The Embassy folks took us to the new Bayview Hotel. We woke up rested on May 9, which was Sunday and Mother's Day. We had a trip that after-noon through the farm country. Admiral Raymond A. Spruance was our Ambassador.

The trip from Manila to Hong Kong took 3½ hours. Hong Kong includes 392 square miles, and has 2 million population—9,500 British, 13,000 non-Chinese, and the rest Chinese. It is one of the busiest, most beautiful, and most colorful ports in the world. We stayed in the Miramar Hotel in Kowloon.

The movement of Chinese into Hong Kong was a real problem, as they came in by the thousands. This meant much hand work normally done in China was started up in Hong Kong, but also it was a great problem to house and feed the new popu-lation. One of the established bankers, I believe Armenian, took an interest in these newcomers. He set up a program where he had a committee to pick what they felt were worthy recipients, then he would furnish the land, modern pigpen facilities, and several sows to set them up in business. Early mornings and Sundays he would personally visit these places to see how they were doing. He helped many, and I recently saw where he was Knighted by the Queen for his social services in Hong Kong. Ann Cutting and her sister knew him well.

Tremendous numbers of eggs came in from Red China for production of both chickens and ducks for food in Hong Kong. We looked across at a hill, and it looked like bed sheets hanging on lines to dry, but when we got there it was vermicelli made from soya beans; they were crushed, then forced through strainers in long strings, and dried on clotheslines. When packaged, the strands are tough but good food. The refuse is fed to hogs. Sunday evening we had a three-hour motorboat trip around Hong Kong Island. The boat belonged to General Chenault. It was a converted PT boat on which we had a delightful supper.

While Hong Kong's actual importation of food or other products for domestic consumption is relatively small, still its position as importer for distribution all over Asia makes her market very important. I bought hand-embroidered tableclothes and napkins in Hong Kong as well as a suit, ivory and other gifts. It was a 6½-hour flight to Tokyo over Okinawa and Formosa.

Japan is about the size of California with, in 1954, a population of 87 million people. The average farm was 2½ acres. Land reform was initiated under General MacArthur. The General directed the Japanese government to take measures to insure that those who till the soil of Japan shall have a more equal opportunity to enjoy the fruits of their labor; prewar tenancy was widespread with high rents. John M. Allison was Ambassador. He had us to lunch in the Embassy where we had lunched with General MacArthur five years earlier. We stayed at the Imperial Hotel designed by Frank Lloyd Wright, with a caterpillar exhibit in the front area. Japan must import 20 percent of its food supply, plus lots of cotton and wool.

One of our nicest occasions was a Japanese dinner in a beautiful tea house hosted by Dr. Nasu, Professor Emeritus from Tokyo University. He headed up the Japanese young farmers program in cooperation with the California Farm Bureau. He has visited in our home several times. He was later Japanese Ambassador to India and made trips to Washington D.C. as an elder statesman.

I noticed that if I ordered toast for breakfast, I got one slice of white bread. If I ordered raisin bread toast I got one-half slice. They looked on raisins as a delicacy or confection. Raisins in California were cheap and of high food value, so it seemed to me there should be a good market in Japan. I made my report to the raisin growers of California. The raisin crop of 1954 was not large, and the price had risen, so I couldn't convince enough growers to get action at that time, but now that export market is a vital factor for California raisins.

In Japan especially we get a good deal of complaint about our quality of cotton. The problem was that we had a very wet winter. It had been the habit to store the baled cotton standing on end in the bale yards, but the winter was so wet water stood on the ground and in time soaked an inch or so into the bales. The losses had been arbitrated and the buyers very adequately paid for loss, but still they talked a great deal about it. Since then bales held over winter in California are under roof or otherwise protected.

The cotton South had switched a good deal of their cotton acreage to pasture, soya beans, corn, and other crops, so they were not using all their allotted cotton acreage. In the irrigated areas of California, Arizona, and New Mexico, we were short on the acreage we could and should be using for cotton. Many of the acres we should be planting to cotton were going into alfalfa, sugar beets, and vegetables, which we were already producing in surplus and thus further depressing the prices of these crops. The cotton growers asked for a law to increase materially our allowable cotton acreage, but it was really of much interest to all our farmers. Senator Kuchel presented the bill, but it caused consternation in the South just to think of anyone outside the South presenting a cotton bill.

The California cotton growers and Coop leaders came to me and said they wanted to work with us, but they would just have to handle the lobbying through the Western Growers. However, they would look to me to call the shots. I attended most of the principal meetings, and they had several people on the job in Washington all the time. We did very well, and when the Christmas vacation was near, the Southern folks said we had put up a fine fight, and they would give us half of what we were asking for. If we did not agree, and it carried over to the new year, we would not get anything. Most of our growers thought we should accept as soon as they heard of it. I called Senator Kuchel and told him not to compromise a bit; to come home empty handed was OK, we would win later, but no compromise. Senator Bob Taft had just died, and Kuchel said he had resolved to live like Bob Taft and fight all the way through for what he believed was right, so if I said no compromise, he would be very much pleased.

We had quite a meeting in Fresno with Kuchel and Congressman Oakley Hunter and the growers. Some growers were fearful, but Kuchel just talked on what we needed to win, and we did win quickly after the Session started.

Cotton acreage for California under the old law was 697.866 acres. We got Congress to increase that by 238.194 acres to a total of 936,000 acres. Getting 238,194 more cotton acres for California and taking 238,194 out of competition with other California crops was probably the most effective action during my four years in CFBF. It came from understanding and cooperation among all California interests involved.

The Japanese also complained of grade on wheat. I went with them to inspect the wheat from a cargo then unloading. The grade was OK, but still we felt there was justification for complaint on wheat and corn grade quality. Under Farm Bureau prodding, grain grades have been improved and also the grading service. Grade stories are often exaggerated, but still it is exceedingly important that export shipments be up to specified grade or better.

On our trade mission, we let the world know what we had. We found out something of what the world needed and what they had to trade for what they want. We found out a good deal about the types of credit or financing available in the world, and what is needed to make sales fit the needs of various countries. We certainly found that selling in the world markets is not a one-shot program, but needs continuous contacts with potential buyers and their wishes. The place of agricultural sales in our whole economy and balance of payment position indicates a need for active programs for export sales of farm products, carried on through grower groups or private trading companies with government encouragement of policies which will stimulate our export sales. This means constant and agressive cooperation between our farm group and our U.S. State Department.

At left, Stewart Russell and I in Thailand. Russell was an outstanding Agricultural Editor for the Des Moines Register. Above, print on all shipments to Pakistan following WWII., and a demonstration of thanks in Italy—the sack had held American wheat.

Below, top left, preparing rice levees in South India. Workers were paid 7¢/day and only got to work 3-4 days/week to spread the work to more people. At right, women hoeing in France, with hoe handles handmade by each lady. Bottom left, planting rice in the Philippines. Bottom right, the vegetable market in Tokyo.

11 BUSY FARM BUREAU YEARS

At the summer meeting of May 24-25, 1954, we decided to seek transfer of the Central Valley Water Project from the U.S. Department of Reclamation to the State of California, to be financed by revenue bonds. We secured organization of a State Study Council composed of most of the statewide organizations concerned with school problems, with Van T. Elsworth, Director of Farm Bureau Tax Department, on the program committee.

June 8-12, Washington D.C. for AFBF board meeting.

June 14, reported to the National Cotton Council on Trade Mission findings in relation to cotton in Asia.

June 20, talked at Cal Poly S.L.O.

June 21, CFBF staff picnic at Turtle Rock Ranch. This was a fine day of barbeque and games to consolidate staff.

July 12-13, board meeting Camp Radford in San Bernardino mountains.

July 14-15-16-17, Staff conferences, CFBF Staff, inspiration-education; know Farm Bureau program and how to carry it out.

July 21, KPO broadcast on export trade.

August 9, Don McColley resigned as Secretary to manage Wine Institute. Don had done a fine job, but this was more pay and less travel. Dick Owen employed as Secretary-Treasurer of Farm Bureau.

August 4, Bella and I were invited to Pakistan House for dinner.

August 18 20, spoke and attended AFBF Staff Institute at Univ. of Illinois, Urbana.

September 2, spoke Sacramento Rotary Club on trade mission.

September 7, lunch at Palace Hotel, Senators Knowland and Kuchel.

September 9-10, conference on monetary and fiscal policy, Washington D.C. This was one of the annual conferences called by Allan Kline including Under-Secretary of Treasury, Martin, Dir. Federal Reserve Board, fiscal policy man from White House. Top consultants from Princeton, Harvard, Cal, Chicago , Ted Shultz, Harry Wellman, etc. This was when these men met to discuss fiscal and monetary policy for the U.S. They always said it was the only time they all got together to talk freely on policy, no special bill or action. They couldn't talk to bankers, financiers, or manufacturers without the press and public statements. Here no one expected a newsworthy action, so they could meet with Farm Bureau and discuss freely. It was a privilege to be included and listen.

September 13, lunch at the Union League Club of San Francisco. I was guest of the shipowners. California had temporary legislation exempting from property tax the ships in any California harbor on tax date in March. They wanted the new law to be permanent. They stated their cases. I told them we would consider it, but what were they going to do to modernize their ships or get the rates down so we could afford to use them in foreign trade? Captain Fay of the River Lines sat next to me, and he said, "Look, I have been in this business for 50 years. In that time we have substituted electric motors for gas engines on the hoists. We have changed the size of a sling load from ¾ of a ton to ½ a ton." One of the first acts of the original session of Congress was to establish a subsidy for the merchant marine. They have had fantastic subsidies for over 200 years, so they have no need to increase efficiency.

September 16, spoke to Rotary Club Oakland, and next day to the League of Women Voters of Berkeley on world trade outlook.

October 8, U.C. College of Ag. Advisory Council. I was chairman and worked with Harry Wellman in selection of the committee, but by this time the University Academic Senate had little use for Agricultural Extension and little use for Agricultural Research except as it might be pure or fundamental research under the idea that anything that adds to the sum total of human knowledge is worthwhile. President Bob Sproul, Harry Wellman, and others with whom we dealt on the committee were all right, but they were not calling the shots. The main interest at this time was to get the farmers on the advisory committee to recommend closing out the 2 year non-degree work at Davis as beneath the dignity of a great university. The substantial old timers at Davis opposed closing it out. Our advisory council refused to approve closing it out, but it was closed.

October 18, spoke at Univ. of Nevada general meeting in the gymnasium.

October 19, the folks in Oregon insisted I come up to a rural church conference in Corvallis, Oregon State, where Shirley Greene of the Congregational Church was to give the keynote speech and final windup. He was one of the original social gospel group. I was late for his talk. They broke up into workshops, and I went to the one he was heading. The farm fellows told me what he had said and asked me to respond to it in this session, so I did. When I finished, Shirley said he agreed with everything I had said so we had little chance to really debate the issues, but that was typical of almost all that group. They wanted to love the poor, the weak, etc., but they were never sure how except to have government use taxes to do it.

October 30, had lunch with Secretary Ezra Taft Benson at Pomona College. We discussed sugar beets. He asked me to sure follow up with Under Secretary Wayne Morse, who directly handled the sugar program, but to let him know if there was any problem as he was personally interested.

This was when I wrote the letter to Morse and addressed it "Personal" to be sure he would get it. I told Earle Coke that I wrote the Under Secretary a personal letter. He said "Good, how did you do that?" Earle was right. I got a reply back, but I am sure Morse did not write it though his name was signed to it. I very seriously doubt that he ever saw my original letter. I wrote back and got another reply that I am more certain Secretary Morse never saw By this time the issue was moot.

As I go through my date books, I am amazed at the number of lunches and dinners I had with the Secretary of Agriculture, especially Benson.

November 4, meeting with Dr. Nasu and Mr. Koda in relation to the Japanese young farmers program.

November 6-11, California Farm Bureau Federation Annual Meeting, Long Beach. We had a farm equipment show with this meeting.

Sunday Nov. 7, Vespers Service at 4:30 p.m. and dinner for County Farm Bureau President.

November 8, Commodity and Home Department group and commodity dinner, with Allan B. Kline, President AFBF speaker.

November 9, Young Peoples Breakfast, Farm Center Officers Conference, Young Peoples Dept., Water Problems, Wild Game & Public Lands, Tax Sect., Rural Health Dept., Safety, Cal Farm Insurance. We had the Lawrence Welk Show 8-9 p.m. and his dance orchestra 9-12 p.m. in the Municipal Auditorium.

Wednesday, November 10, 7 a.m., organization breakfast. This was a peppy, humorous meeting, well attended. All county membership committee and other reports on membership to date and goals for new year. At 9 we began meeting with Long Beach Municipal Band, Diamond All-Star Girl, All-Star 4H Boy, President California Future Farmers, Farm Bureau Rural Leadership Trophy to senior in the College of Agriculture showing outstanding leadership qualities, reports of General Secretary Frank Pierce, and Secretary Treasurer Richard W. Owens, report of the President. At 1:30 Earle Coke, Assistant Secretary of Agriculture. Grover Turnbow, Foremost Dairies. Grover had designed and built forty reconstituting plants to make milk out of powdered skim milk or combinations with whole milk. These were placed throughout the world, some for our World Hunger Program, some for the industry, some for the armed services, and some for Foremost Dairies. At 6:30 was the annual banquet, speaker Edith Sampson, colored woman attorney in Chicago, member of our Town Hall World Tour in 1949, U.S. Representative to the United Nations. She took Mrs. Eleanor Roosevelt's place in the United Nations and did a far more effective job. I spent a day with her at the U.N. on two occasions. Everyone loved her. She was most effective.

She came out from Chicago just for our meeting and was in attendance at our whole meeting to be sure she got the feel of it. She usually spoke extemporaneously, but she felt this talk was so important to her she must write and read it. During the meal she was concerned, and finally called a building attendant and asked him to get a stronger light for the podium, as she could not see to read her talk. I told him and her No, we didn't bring her out here to read a talk, we wanted her to just talk to us. Remember this was 1954. In about all of my talks after our trip of 1949 I had emphasized the importance of our breaking down the color barrier, but it was not a popular issue. Farm Bureau had many members who had come to California from the South, some generations ago, and many recently. I thought we might see a few vacant chairs at the banquet and possibly more during the talk. During the speech she just talked to us. Discrimination was openly discussed, but in a friendly way. The applause was tremendous with a standing ovation. It seemed like most of the people came through the line to congratulate her, and a number of people said to me, George, if bringing this talk to them was the only thing I did in Farm Bureau, it would still be worthwhile.

At this annual meeting Rich Rominger was elected chairman of the young people's department. As I write this he is Director of Agriculture in California.

December 29–January 3, I reported to the board that Dr. Nasu of Japan would like, in addition to the current program, for several hundred young Japanese farmers to live on California farms for about a year, and then return to expand the program to include 1,000 workers, similar to the Mexican farm labor program. I felt there would be merit in having them stay 8 or 18 months to cover either one or two heavy labor periods. This program was approved by the military and manpower officials in Washington, but then died. I had worked pretty hard on it, but I guess it was too soon after the war.

We received a check from the State compensation insurance program for $95,953.74, this was in addition to the regular refund based on losses. This was savings from funds set aside for future losses or costs, and the cases are now closed. It was our desire to refund it to members, but this was about impossible to figure, so we allocated it:

Reserve for workmen's compensation	$12,203.74
Promotion for workmen's compsensation	17,000.00
Employees retirement trust fund	18,000.00
Complete payment on unsecured loan fund (CFBF building)	8,750.00
Reserve for commercial losses	40,000.00
	$94,953.74

A good deal of determination was required to see that all such windfall payments were used for the purposes indicated above, and not for current operation of Farm Bureau. This policy had the building obligations paid off when Farm Bureau wanted to build the new building on Telegraph Avenue.

Again I attended a group of state annual meetings: November 16, Lincoln, Nebraska; 17, Pocatello, Idaho; and 18, Medford, Oregon.

December 6, Louis Rozzoni and I flew to San Antonio, Texas and joined the California Farm Bureau Special, an all Farm Bureau train headed for the AFBF meeting in New York. We rode across Texas with them.

Ken Goy was travel man for the railroad assigned to this train. He asked if I would like to go up to the cab of the locomotive. Of course I did. To my surprise, after a little while, the engineer asked if I would like to drive it, which, of course, I did. He gave me a few instructions, then handed me the sheaf of travel orders. I was in control for 20-30 minutes. Of course the engineer was available, but I was surprised at his ease and confidence in me. The sheaf of orders was an order on each sheet. Road bed soft here, cut speed to 50 mph, pass this point at 10:22, CAUTION, object sticking out of passing freight car; slow to 40 mph for bridge. There were a number of trestles across various gulches. It was unbelievable. From the height of the cab the timbers and ties looked like matchsticks. I couldn't see how such frail timbers could possibly hold this big outfit up. I still have that sheaf of orders in the office. Driving that locomotive and flying the army jet certainly were my most exciting modes of travel, and I believe the locomotive comes first. We had to leave the train after a few hours and fly into New York to attend the AFBF board meeting and resolution meetings ahead of the Convention.

Allan Kline, in my opinion, was one of the greatest Americans of his day. He had had a heart problem, so he had not been able to get life insurance except at a heavy premium. His doctor had warned him many times that he had only weeks or months to plan on. He had had fainting spells several times under stress, so he went to his doctor again and was told that, unless he gave up the stress and strain of his office, it was now only hours he could hope for. So at the opening session of the meeting he announced that he planned to offer his resignation at the close of this meeting. It was not election year. He did not intend to resign until he knew who his successor would be, and the successor could be selected during the meeting.

We had made great progress in establishing the position that farmers were best off to look for their incomes from the marketplace and not from government, that low support prices might be accepted if they were low enough to not build government-held surpluses, but high supports were not helpful to farmers.

There was, of course, a lingering support on the part of a few for high supports, and Allan would stay on rather than see that group win leadership. Charles Shuman of Illinois, a sound leader, well schooled in economics, was the undisputed nominee. In recognition of his outstanding service, the meeting awarded Allan and Gladys a Carribean cruise for rest and relaxation.

† 1955

The year started off with a three-day staff meeting. There was a dinner and an evening with Mexican officials in San Diego regarding labor. Returning on Saturday, I had a few hours with Mother and Bernice, and then spoke at a noon luncheon of the Los Angeles University Women's Club.

Isabelle and I went to rice and labor meeting in Dallas, Texas. Rice growers have done well most of the years since 1955, so it is difficult to suggest that a different course might have been better, but we in California were always looking for ways to depend less on government. The production and demand for rice in the world was very nearly in balance, so I asked the rice men if they didn't feel it might be well to drop the government program and depend on the free market. They felt that might be a good idea, then someone asked if that meant rice would no longer be classed as a basic commodity. There was no sure answer to that question, so almost all decided they would rather keep the government program than to lose the classification as a basic commodity. I then saw how difficult it is for people to give up a benefit or privilege, whether the need is current or not, and the longer it is enjoyed the more difficult it is to give it up.

We flew on to Washington for sugar meetings Saturday and Sunday afternoon. Monday, January 17, the AFBF Executive Committee spent the morning with Secretary Ezra Taft Benson on agricultural trade and other issues. At 1:30 we met with Secretary of State Dulles, his Assistant for Economic Affairs Mr. Waugh, and others. Monday evening we attended a dinner where Mrs. Smith of Nebraska and her committee of Farm Bureau women did a beautiful job of presenting the Farm Bureau program to a number of Senators and Congressmen who were their guests.

Tuesday afternoon the Executive Committee went to the White House, where we had a very pleasant and I believe profitable half-hour with President Eisenhower. Our new AFBF President Charles Shuman of Illinois did a very nice job of presenting our program. Such White House visits give one renewed confidence in our basic stability. Tuesday evening was the American Reinsurance Board meeting and Wednesday evening the committee on Farm Bureau publicity.

Wednesday afternoon I visited with Vice President Richard Nixon. He will surely be known as the busiest vice president to date. He is doing a great job, and he has not lost touch with the man on the street. We then had a fine conference with Mr. Rankin, Assistant Attorney General, on "Who owns the water of California rivers and streams." Our objectives appear to be so similar, "absolute protection to beneficial users of water," that we should be able to get together. (*Note added in 1979:* I do not doubt Mr. Rankin's honesty or sincerity, but his views have not prevailed, the scheming bureaucrats with the Department of Interior and the Attorney General's office have consistently driven for public ownership of water, power, and land.) We met Friday morning on expanding foreign sales. The afternoon was spent with social security and internal revenue people on the new social security problems. Next was Capitol Hill, and it was after 6 p.m. when a discussion of issues with Senator Kuchel closed the week.

After seventeen years on the AFBF Board, each meeting brings new thrills and a deeper appreciation of the great organization to which we all belong. We are moving our surpluses into trade, but the more we succeed the stronger the forces against us seem to grow. The national welfare, as well as farm welfare, dictates that the State Department must get in tune with Main Street and the farms and villages of America.

We in Farm Bureau had been working hard to get the ownership and control of the Central Valley Project transferred from the Reclamation Service to the State of California. We wanted all future projects to be designed, built, and controlled by the State of California. The Berryessa storage and distribution project was being planned by both the state and the reclamation service to provide water to both agriculture and industry in the Bay Area. The state felt they had developed a plan to finance the construction of the project and pay off the cost. The state engineer told me that reclamation officials had told him "You just try to build the Berryessa Project and see what happens to you."

I had Joe Duell prepare a file of all the material we had on the pros and cons of the U.S. versus California construction and control. As soon as I arrived in Washington, I called the secretary's office for an appointment on Saturday morning. Most federal offices were still open Saturday morning. His secretary said the Secretary—Fred Seaton—had an appointment in Chicago for Saturday, and would have to leave Friday evening. On my return to the hotel Friday afternoon, however, there was a note from the Secretary himself saying his plans were changed. His staff all thought he was leaving, so he had told them that they did not need to come to the office on Saturday. If I came over he would let me in and we could have all the time we needed without interference. I stated my case and had the file of reports with me. He asked if I would furnish him with a set; he said he was very much interested and wanted to study them personally. He unlocked a drawer in his desk, locked the file in the drawer, and said he would get at them the first thing Monday morning. About three months later, a young man came to the Berkeley office. Secretary Seaton had opened the drawer on Monday morning, and all the files were gone. He searched everywhere but no one knew where it was. He did not dare write or phone me, for if I sent a new file, it would disappear before he got it, so he waited until a trusted aide was coming to California to get it for him. I comment on this particularly because it was in Eisenhower's time long before recent discussions about wiretapping and all that kind of thing. But this was happening at that time, and I'm sure there was a good deal of it going on then and before that. I'm sure I have reported before that Earl Coke, Assistant Secretary of Agriculture, had told me on several occasions to never phone him at the office, nor write there, but to call at his residence at night or address the letter to his residence, as that was the only way I could be sure that he would get it. This is a terrible indictment of the way things are handled, but I mention it as my only direct experience with a thing of that kind. Nevertheless, it was my experience.

Following a busy week in Washington D C., we flew to Miami, Florida, met Allan and Gladys Kline at the airport, and went aboard the good ship Evangeline. Sailing was smooth and very pleasant. We stopped at Port au Prince, Haiti, beautiful in its way, but poverty was dominant. The third morning we came into Ciudad Trujillo, which they say is the spot where Columbus first set foot on American soil, and where he is now buried. The city was old, but the streets and markets were clean and the police well-dressed and snappy. They had been led for 25 years by Dictator Trujillo. If he had retired then, he would have been a hero. People were saying that he had done a great deal for the people and the country, and they still greatly admired him, but his brothers and friends were robbing the country. A few years later he was in disgrace.

We found Jamaica beautiful. We took a trip into the mountains and had a raft ride down the rapids of the Rio Grande. The rapids were a little oversold but it was a fun trip.

We were invited as delegates to the National Cotton Council meeting in Houston, Texas January 31–February 1. The council is supported by growers and the cotton trade. They do a great deal of work to support and expand use of cotton at home and abroad. I admired their business-like way of operating. Having won the legislation that transferred a large acreage of cotton to the irrigated West, I had been appointed to a cotton advisory group to the Department of Agriculture and urged to be a regular delegate to the Cotton Council, but I never became very active in either.

We then went to Mexico City for February 2-3. The AFBF asked us to go to represent the AFB at the annual meeting of the Cosecheros. We spent a night in Havana, Cuba. It was very crowded, but we finally got an expensive room on the top floor of a large but run-down hotel. We expected to stay two days, but took a tour of Havana and decided to leave.

We stayed at the Geneva Hotel in Mexico run by the Swiss. There was good food, and many Americans stayed there. We attended the Cosechero meetings and saw the new museum at Chipultepec. The Mexicans were pleased at AFBF recognition and we enjoyed it.

February 9 and 10 were spent in Salt Lake at the Western Regional Conference, where Farm Bureau officers and interested members came in from the eleven Western states to discuss problems of interest to our region—water, use of public and private lands, and crops of interest.

We stayed through the 12th for the Western Region Presidents and Secretaries Conference. We, of course, discussed Western regional problems, but these meetings were more to discuss how to best organize to carry out the AFBF programs, including membership.

February 15, I spoke at a large meeting in Salinas called jointly by World Affairs Council, League of Women Voters, and Farm Bureau. This was on world trade.

February 18-19 was spent at the seventeenth National Farm Institute at Des Moines, Iowa, on "The Farmer and the Free Society." I was scheduled, and gave the following statement in a panel discussion.

For Panel Discussion of **"Farm Policy for the Cold War"**
National Farm Institute, February 18, 1955

George H. Wilson, President California Farm Bureau Federation
and Director American Farm Bureau Federation

One of the first essentials of a successful farm policy for the Cold War is an expanding economy at home with relatively full employment and well-distributed income. This assures a good domestic demand for farm production. Since 1940 agriculture has increased its production per acre by better than 40 percent and its production per man by 80 percent. It is still, however, necessary to further cut costs of production in order to maintain a satisfactory net income. Expanding foreign sales of American agricultural commodities is a second essential. This requires establishment of private free enterprise for American traders throughout the world. They are our best ambassadors. We can expand trade materially under present conditions by reduction of barriers; some our own but particularly those set up by foreign countries.
We must develop a continuing trade beneficial to both the buyer and seller.
Give-away programs with very few exceptions are not helpful. They are only a

226

temporary relief to hunger with no fundamental and lasting benefits. If, however, we trade our surpluses for rubber, tin, bauxite, or any other material produced in a foreign country, then they not only get their food from the United States but they also get employment, governmental stability, confidence and a feeling of mutual interest and friendship. The first shipment of this type is apt to be followed by additional trades which eventually bring stabilized economies and governments in countries where we are so desirous of maintaining governmental stability as part of the struggle in the Cold War.

Trade can be a most powerful weapon in any political struggle among nations. It, however, can be a dangerous instrument. The stringent restrictions now placed on American importers in vital spots such as Hong Kong if long continued will eliminate the American trader in these spots where we need them most. If we are to win the Cold War, we must recognize that it is incidentally a material struggle for production, but more fundamentally a struggle between concepts of social and economic well-being. Tractors, airplanes, and bath tubs have not made America great. These are the byproducts of a revolutionary society, economy and political life first pronounced in this country in 1776 when our forefathers declared "all men are created equal and they receive from their Creator certain unalienable rights." It was this recognition that the rights of individuals are granted by our Creator and not subject to withdrawal by government which is the basis of our productive capacity. Under this concept, we have in large measure given to individuals the benefit of their production. This philosophy is nearly as revolutionary in the world today as it was in 1776. This represents the goal sought by the world's people regardless of their religion and the political philosophy of government under which they live. We will win the cold war when we learn how to extend to other people those basic concepts of the rights of individuals and an understanding of the fact production and economic stability come largely through incentives which give to each individual the benefit of his production.

The outstanding characteristic of the United States is our ability to take children of humble origin and make of them producers of great works. Most of the people of the world are born of humble origin. Most die humbly, in poverty and ignorance. Almost all people of the world long to see their children become producers of great works and many of them look to us to help them find the answer.

🖎

The final banquet was Saturday evening, with U.S. Attorney General Herbert Brownell, Jr. as principal speaker. But the weather was terrible, and he was tied down in Detroit. After I arrived, J. S. Russell, who was presiding at the dinner, told me the problem. He said I would sit at the head table, and he would call on me to fill in for the Attorney General. I, of course, had nothing prepared but the conference reporter got a statement.

Four years later on our trade mission to Asia, J.S. Russell, Farm Editor of the *Des Moines Register and Tribune*, was one of our party, and we roomed together a good deal of the time. He was a very fine and highly respected farm editor.

Young People's Leadership Conference at Asilomar, Friday, February 17 to 20, with Rich Rominger presiding. February 25-27 Farm Bureau Leadership Conference at Asilomar, 200 present, well attended.

March 3, Agricultural Council meeting Sacramento all day.

March 4-10, Los Angeles Chamber of Commerce, Ag. Committee,

March 15, 1:30, State Chamber of Commerce San Francisco, Central Valley Project.

March 26, Cattlemen's field day at Sloughhouse. I talked at lunch on what farm bureau is doing. Governor Goodwin Knight was there as the guest of honor.

April 6, looked over soil conservation service projects in San Bernardino County had dinner with the SCS Board and Mary Hill.

April 7, met with the Kern County Board.

April 8, met at noon with Fresno County Board and dinner with Stanislaus.

April 9, met with San Joaquin Board, lunch at FB building. April 10-20 was spent meeting with county boards at lunches, dinners, all occasions throughout the state.

April 22-23, Washington D.C. for meetings on cotton.

April 25, spoke to Conference of Western Hospitals in San Francisco Auditorium on "A Forecast for America." It was a large group and they welcomed a viewpoint from a farmer.

Friday, April 29, we met with the Coop Council in the College of Agriculture to go over the College of Agriculture and U.C. budget. We did this for each U.C. budget presented to the legislature. We made suggestions, some of which were accepted. Of course we were still free to sponsor special bills for changes or additions we wanted, and we did, but we knew the University budget and actively supported it in the legislature where needed. So the University never needed to appear directly to actively defend their budget.

May 3, Washington D.C. Met with Jimmie Utt of Ventura County, Chairman of the House of Representatives Agricultural Committee. He was a brother of Dorothy Robertson of San Miguel Village, Ensenada, Baja California.

Early in March I had received an invitation from Charles E. Wilson, Secretary of Defense, formerly President of General Motors, to participate in the joint Civilian Orientation Conference May 5-13. I contacted all the board and they all felt I should accept the invitation. It was quite a week. Seventy men from business, industry, education, newsmedia, and agriculture accepted the invitation. We met in Washington, Thursday May 5, at the Mayflower Hotel. We had an official breakfast at 7:15, followed by a morning of talks, then luncheon at the Pentagon and more talks until 4 p.m., when we were assigned to red, white, blue, and gold flights. I had known Dean Frank J. Welch of the University of Kentucky. We roomed together when we were doubled up. Bill Henry, the news commentator, was in the group, as was Jay Taylor, President of the National Cattlemen's Association; Earle Nuzz of Quaker Oats, whom I had met before; Robert Johnson, Vice President of United Air Lines, whom I saw a good deal of.

Friday, arrived at Quantico, U.S. Marine Headquarters and school; attended an afternoon reception by the Base Commander and dinner in the evening. Father Hesburgh, then and now President of Notre Dame University, was called on to give the invocation. He announced that he had just received special dispensation from the Pope for all of us to eat steak, and it soon appeared. It was well received.

Early Saturday we were out for flag raising, then were bussed to a battle area.

A plane flew over and dropped a simulated atomic bomb, mushroom cloud, noise, and all. In a few minutes the operation leaders parachuted down, then a whole flight of helicopters came over the horizon dropping jeeps, artillery, and supplies. More helicopters came low over the horizon, disgorged their live cargo, and quickly the jeeps were rushing to their missions. There was much artillery firing as needed. The men wore masks for protection. The idea of the exercise was to decimate and confuse the enemy with a small atomic bomb, then rush in quickly and secure the area. We were not as schooled to fear nuclear activity then as we are today. I expect halfway between is nearer to right.

We then climbed into helicopters for a ride across the 55,000-acre reservation to a lake where amphibious tanks crossed the lake and climbed the far shoreline to reduce concrete pillboxes and other structures. With perfect timing, the marine fighters and bombers bombed and strafed. Then came waves of helicopters from a simulated carrier deck to reinforce the amphibious landing party with fresh men, flame throwers, and added fire power. The flame throwers were devastating, throwing a solid flame 50 yards ahead, withering everything in its path.

We boarded two Convair planes, which accompanied us the rest of the trip, to fly over Williamsburg, Yorktown, and Jamestown to the Norfolk naval base, where we boarded the famed aircraft carrier *Intrepid*. She had seen much hard duty in World War II. She pulled right out, followed by other crafts from battleships to submarines.

It seemed every type of aircraft the navy owns flew by through the rays of the setting sun. Then a helicopter put on a sub-search demonstration, and after dark we witnessed a night attack on a sub.

Next morning, all the types of planes carried on the ship were going and coming after demonstrations of bombing, strafing, and other activities assigned for that flight. Standing on the bridge one could look down on the flight deck and see all the action. It looked like utter confusion, each deck hand in a bright-colored sweat shirt, each color designating the man's duties so a trained crew could quickly spot a man's job.

The planes were all parked below the flight deck, with wings folded up to save space. In proper order they were placed on the large freight elevator which raised them to the flight deck, then they rolled to take-off position about mid-ship. Propeller planes were held for warm-up and pilot check, then released, and off they went with a roar, losing elevation as they left the front apron, then heading up and away. They landed from the rear, with only the rear half of the ship available to them, coming in with tail low. A big hook under the tail would grab one of the steel cables spread across the deck with springs at each end, allowing the cable to give some but still the deceleration was abrupt.

There were cables and nets in front, in case the hook didn't catch or hold. There were also men on the rear of the ship with big flags watching the approach closely to see that the pilot was coming in on a safe pattern, and also being sure that the planes landed ahead of him were off the landing deck. If all wasn't clear, they waved wildly for the pilot to get back into pattern for another try. Landing at 200-250 mph, they often came to a full stop within 60-80 feet. For jet take-off, they were trying a new American-made steam catapult of higher power so the jets reached a speed of 250 knots per hour in several hundred feet.

The *Intrepid* carried 85 planes. They all carried live ammunition, I believe about 12 bombs apiece. Over the target they are released by the pilot as wanted, but sometimes they do not release, so the plane lands with one or several bombs. When the plane is so quickly stopped, the bombs fly on to the deck and slide in all directions. Why no one was hit I do not know.

One flight of about a dozen planes came on a strafeing run right alongside the ship. It didn't seem 100 feet. As they leveled out, maybe 50 feet above the water, the bullets were hitting the small waves and ricocheting off. As the planes came up, the sound was terrible for they were picking up their own bullets into the engines and ripping the fins right off the jet engines. They all landed all right, but we went below deck later to see them and the fins were all broken off. It was a mess.

At night, using 3 million candle-power searchlights, they put on an anti-sub search and destroy. The battleship U.S.S. *Wisconsin* was 10 miles to our port side when she cut loose with her 16-inch guns with live ammo. We heard the order to fire, and 40 seconds later towers of water where the shells landed were kicked up right in our wake 1,000 yards astern. Helicoptors landed and took off, lighter-than-air blimps were on and off.

One could go on, it was all so interesting and fantastic, but after a full day and two nights we were back in Norfolk ready to board our Convairs for the flight to Eglin Air Forse Base in Florida. Eglin is the testing ground for all air force purchases—napkins to B-52s. In fact, the day we arrived we welcomed the first B-52 purchased by the Air Force. It had left **Seattle** 2,200 miles away and flown nonstop, arriving on time at Eglin. This eight-jet monster could leave with a load of bombs, fly nonstop to Moscow at over 600 miles per hour, and return. Twenty-four years later, as I write, it is still our main dependence.

Out before us a B-17 flew by and dropped its full load of twelve 500-lb. bombs, as it had done in World War II ten years earlier. Then came the B-36 intercontinental bomber with over one hundred 500-lb. bombs, leaving a chain of devastation over one and one-half miles long.

At Eglin we had bleachers for 5,000 people and they were filled: civilians, enlisted men, ROTC officers, Congressmen, Senators, at least seven Governors, and directly in front of us was the Prime Minister of Thailand, his wife, and staff. I also saw Prime Minister Sukarno of Indonesia and staff. We had met both prime ministers on our Trade Mission trip in 1954.

We went to the training jet hanger, and in the briefing room they gave us the ten instructions for bailing out of a jet. In the next room they told us to disrobe, and we were measured for a jet flying suit and helmet with oxygen mask. Major Cecil B. Richardson got me strapped in with mask on and gave me final instructions. He fired up the T-33 trainer, and off we went as smooth as silk. At 11,000 feet and 400 mph we checked out our communication, and he asked if I wanted to fly it. "Sure." He revved it up to 570 mph and turned it over. He warned me that it likes to climb, so hold a little pressure in the stick to keep it about level. The stick seemed exceedingly sensitive, almost only a thought and it would go right or left up or down, but it was quiet and smooth and responded just as you expected it to. I could see why executive jets were popular. I probably flew it for twenty minutes, and he said to bring it down. He said it was all mine, but at about 10,000 feet I could feel him take over the stick and we slid in for a nice landing. One of the major thrills of my life.

We boarded our Convairs again for Fort Benning, Georgia Infantry School. On Wednesday, May 11, we went over the grounds of the army paratroopers where the training is really rigorous. Benning is also the training grounds for the Rangers, who are ready to fight in jungles, swamps, or the frozen north. They said all army lieutenants must now take either airborne or ranger training.

There were towers for parachute training and various contraptions to simulate jumps. Many of us went up the 250-foot tower and jumped off in a "parachute" designed to give the feel of the fall and still land safely.

They put on a full-scale battalion parachute jump. First from nowhere came six planes, from which jumped the advance guard of the battalion. Then a flight of cargo planes which dropped jeeps, artillery, and supplies. Then the sky seemed full of planes and out jumped 800 men. One never forgets the sight of 800 inflated parachutes. With so many, some had to collide, a few tangled, but all finally got free. The ambulances were there, but two sprained ankles were the extent of the casualties, less than an average Saturday afternoon with 800 football players involved.

Next day we saw the latest in new equipment, including the 280 MM (11") gun and the "honest john" 762 MM (30") surface-to-surface rocket, which screamed off its rather simple launcher and reached supersonic speeds in 4½ seconds. It almost disappeared as soon as you saw it, headed for a target six miles away which is its minimum range.

We saw television in use so commanders in the rear can see the action at the front. Jeeps move into position to see the front lines, set their cameras, and the picture comes on the screen at the command post, or reconnaissance planes overhead shoot the pictures for the TV screen at command headquarters.

Machine guns and hand guns of all sorts were set up on a firing range in front of us, and we could try all we wanted with live ammunition and plenty of tracers so we could see how we were doing. These were up to 37½ MM (1½"); the large ones were on tripods but still had quite a kick.

Here at Benning, as a finale, we saw a simulated battle by the Army Air Corp and Marines, starting at daylight and going on into the night. The flame from the rockets and from the hideous flame throwers, with all the bombs bursting, was unbelievable, unreal, but the tracer bullets added a sort of beauty to the awesome scene. It all wound up with a concentrated mad minute where every weapon in support of the infantry fired all it had in a two-mile-long front.

The week of May 23 started off with the midyear delegates meeting in Berkeley on Monday and Tuesday. I always enjoyed this. It was our report to the membership from all the counties on how we were carrying out the resolutions and other Farm Bureau activities, and how we could improve our service to farmers.

Wednesday and Thursday were CFBF board meetings, and Friday and Saturday Cal Farm Insurance, Supply, Service, and other company boards.

June 8-9-10 was the Western Regional Meeting in Estes Park, Colorado, a beautiful mountain setting. Many of our people made these their regular summer vacations and came every year. We mixed business and fun. The Forest Service folks entertained us one evening with a fresh trout dinner in one of the mountain camps along the trout stream. We had a good evening of entertainment.

At these regional meetings we thrashed out our regional problems—land, water, transportation, many others—and the national leadership met with the state and local leaders. Thus they understand far better our needs and our wishes. Every day was crowded with meetings, talks, etc. As I look at my date book I wonder when we got the office work done. We had a delightful dinner and evening at the home of Mr. Katsumo, the Japanese Consul General in San Francisco, in appreciation of the work with the Japanese young farmers.

I spoke to a large and enthusiastic group of Kiwanians at their district meeting in Reno on "Building International Loyalty Through Trade."

We sponsored a young Korean, Yun Du Yung. He went to Sacramento City College; he did very well and was no trouble for us at all.

One of the most interesting incidents of the summer of 1955 was the visit to California of the Russian farmers. I had been asked by the State Department and by one of the farm writers for Country Gentleman and other national magazines to plan and handle their week in California.

They were to arrive in San Francisco, visit the College of Agriculture, Davis, have lunch in our patio for the thirteen Russians and about fifty others. I had invited some from Davis, from California state government in Sacramento, and neighbors and farm leaders. But as publicity got out about the tour, I was amazed at the requests we received from people wishing to attend. Of course, there was quite a list of pressmen traveling with them. They had been visiting farms in the Midwest with wide press coverage.

About three days before they were due in San Francisco, I called the leader in the Midwest. He told me that they had just served notice on him that they did not want to see any more small farms, that they were big farmers, and unless we showed them big farms in California they were not interested. We had been having a great deal of political and press criticism of the big farms of California. We had big farms for them to see, as well as small ones, but I was not going to put the spotlight of publicity solely on big farms. So I told him I had been asked to show them California farms. We had selected a cross-section of California farms and farmers for them to see and meet. He said they seemed positive, so I told him to get someone else to handle it. They got the University, and we had all the publicity about the San Joaquin farmers using Cadillacs and Lincolns for ranch cars, and not one but several being parked around the private swimming pool while they enjoyed a drink and a swim. The publicity was not a service to California agriculture. I would have been happy to show them or any other farmers California farms and farmers as they are, but not just to help spread Russian or local antifarm propaganda.

I met all day with the California Cattlemen's Association Board in San Francisco. As I looked the men over, I thought, Boy, what we could do if we had such a powerhouse as this on our board. There were many outstanding individuals. The main issue was legislation in which we were both interested. However, when they went around the table to get individual opinion, some were very unclear as to what the legislation

232

would do or was intending to do. Practically all gave an off-hand personal appraisal of what CCA position or action should be. No more than two or at most three had a meeting of their local cattlemen to take a position. It was a very impressive demonstration to me of the value of Farm Bureau with its county and center meetings to help develop and determine policy. Today the CCA is doing things very well.

August 25-29 the Forest Service took Ralph Nissen and me on an air trip to see seeding, burning, and other improvements on Forest Service grazing lands. We covered the area from Sacramento north. Some of the seedings and improvements were very spectacular, but still the area improvement is so small in relation to the area now going bad and needing improvement. The trip gave us a chance to get better acquainted and enjoy a pleasant outing. The fact is that about 50 percent of the land in California is owned by the federal government, and it is deteriorating every year in its contribution to production of either grass or timber, while there are hundreds of thousands of acres of similar land in private ownership which has increased dramatically its contribution to production of grass and timber.

Septermber 16 was an important day to me. This was the day I bought a new Mercury for the family, getting ready for retirement from Farm Bureau. The Merc cost $2,589.96. I had announced in early summer that I would not be a candidate for reelection. I had enjoyed the office very much and believe we had strengthened FB, but I believed a change was in order both for Farm Bureau and for me.

We had a meeting of the IFAP group USA and Mexico at Guayman, Playa Del Cortez Hotel. Also with us were Earle Coke and Jess Topp of Bank of America. Charles Schuman, President of AFBF H Alp, head of commodity work and especially poultry, and Jim McConnell and A. J. McFadden of the Coop Council, were delegates. Very unfortunately, Charles picked up a bug which stayed with him for some time, and he lost all interest in Latin American travel and meetings.

After the **IFAP** meeting in Guaymas, Tom Robertson, Jess Tapp, Chairman of the Board of Bank of America, Earle Coke, Vice President of Bank of America for agriculture and Mexican loans, went down to Culiacan and met Dr. Rigoberto Aguilar Pico, Governor of the State of Sinaloa, Mexico, who was a very fine gentleman, a medical doctor. He had developed the State of Sinaloa a great deal and built a dam for irrigation water for the area around Culiacan. Jess Topp and Earle looked the country over well and agreed to loan money to the government of Mexico to complete the dam and water distribution system. We flew over to La Paz for an evening and on up to Tijuana.

October 31 was Farm Bureau night at the Cow Palace Livestock Show. They always gave Farm Bureau quite a little favorable publicity on Farm Bureau Day.

November 2 I gave the following testimony before the U.S. Senate Committee on Agriculture and Forestry in Fresno.

My name is George H. Wilson, President of the California Farm Bureau Federation, farmer in California since 1916. My principal crops include sugar beets, tomatoes, seed crops, beans, hay, grain and cattle. The California Farm Bureau Federation consists of over 60,000 farm families in all of the agricultural counties of California. In addition to our general activities, we have Commodity Services, including ten commodity departments well represented throughout the State.

It is difficult to make an accurate statement as to the position of California farmers in November, 1955. Certainly net farm income has dropped materially in recent years—in fact, in every year since 1947 excepting only 1951. While this is due in part to the fall in farm prices it is as much influenced by the increase in farm cost of production. Farmers are being pinched. Our California population has increased rapidly but both number of farms and number of farmers has remained about stable.

The other factor which is effective is somewhat psychological in that while farmers are feeling the squeeze, they are seeing wages and profits rise quite rapidly for those who were already better compensated than we were. This hurts—particularly where these raises are brought about by governmental action such as the recent increase in minimum wages which has tended to raise farm costs further, ability of labor to practice secondary boycotts of our products, high transportation costs by rail or water, and other restrictions to trade.

Since 1920, except for the war years, farmers have been continually faced with surpluses. We have tried throughout this time to raise farm prices through government action without at the same time adding to the surpluses. This we have not accomplished. You may remember that after Pearl Harbor and even after we were actively in the War, we still had acreage restrictions on the production of wheat and sugar, because of the heavy surpluses then on hand.

Most farmers have come to the conclusion that it is just as impossible for farmers to get a fair price for their commodity in the marketplace while our warehouses are bulging as it is for the producers of radios, television sets, Fords or Chevrolets to get a fair market price for their commodity when everyone knows their warehouses are bulging.

It would seem then that our first objective must be to reduce the total farm surpluses to a point where they are not a depressing factor in the market. We have done a good deal with the active support of the Congress in developing legislation and programs which have encouraged increased exports of the surpluses. We hope the actions already taken will result in more exports in the year or two ahead. This may require some changes in State Department policy. Commodity Credit Corporation should trade more unneeded perishable farm surpluses for valuable and easily storable strategic materials. We also need agricultural representation in the economic section of the Department of State.

A realistic appraisal, however, would indicate that even with stepped-up foreign and domestic sales we will not reduce our surpluses effectively if we continue to add to the supply in the warehouses as fast as we now are. In 1954-55 we sold and gave away 2.1 billion dollars worth of our surpluses but added 3.2 billion dollars worth. This, of course, is a net loss to us. We, therefore, must develop an efficient means of actually reducing the overall production of farm commodities for which there is no active demand today.

During this period immediately ahead of us much could be done by the Department, colleges and others in assisting farmers in cutting the cost of production for the purpose of increasing net farm income. With a little ingenuity, imagination and research, a number of methods can be developed which will cut farm costs and at the same time result in reduced production. This would help both net income and price if the reduction in costs exceeds the reduction in gross income. We support further increase in appropriations for research and extension. We will insist that more emphasis be placed on cutting cost of production, increasing markets and efficiency of marketing.

I must call to the attention of this Senate Committee that taxes are one of the farm costs which have increased materially and about which something can be done. For example, I would refer particularly to the gasoline tax and the transportation tax. These taxes were war measures which fall particularly heavy on farmers. This was acceptable during the period of war and relatively high farm income even though it may not have been entirely equitable. Today, however, the gasoline tax has been, to all practical purposes, changed from a general tax for the support of government to a highway tax. In this case simple justice indicates that gas used for nonhighway purposes should be exampt from this tax. Even as a general tax I would call attention to the fact that farms use more horsepower than all of the factories of the United States combined. In our factories this is largely electric power and a special tax on electricity was taken off several years ago. The farms use gasoline as a source of producing horsepower to a far greater extent than any other group of primary producers in America. Consequently this tax falls particularly heavily on agriculture at a time of materially reduced net income.

One of the other heavy costs placed upon agriculture is that of transportation. The tax now placed on the transportation of farm and other commodities becomes very oppressive at a time when we should not be called upon to bear this special tax. The elimination of these costs could be brought about shortly by the Congress and could make an immediate and direct contribution to the net income of farmers.

We oppose 90 percent price supports in peacetime. A return to 90 percent fixed supports would be economic suicide. The Act of 1954 is not flexible enough. Flexible supports alone will not solve the problem—they may give us time to solve our problems. Any program of cash payments to a 90 percent or other level above the market price is ultimately disastrous for both producers and consumers. All crops should have the opportunity to use marketing agreements.

I realize that water is not directly within the jurisdiction of the Senate Committee on Agriculture & Forestry, but we know of your interest in this area and believe we should comment upon the necessity of the Congress quickly and clearly restating legislation which recognizes fully the ownership of the water by the states and not the federal government. This has been the oft-repeated position of the Congress and the courts for over 150 years but has been recently challenged by those who would take rights from individuals and centralize these rights and power in centralized government.

Under state water law, water is assigned to individual pieces of property where farmers have continued rights to their share of the water available so long as it is beneficially used. This is a primary human right directly comparable to the right of the workman to the continued possession of his tools, or of the doctor to his medical instruments, or of the attorney to his law library. Water in an irrigated area is one of the essential tools of production and livelihood for the farmer. If the federal government can now by any means, as they are now trying to do, deprive a farmer of water, his principal tool of production, then it is only a step to deprive the working man, doctor, lawyer, or other citizens of their tools of production and their human rights.

This struggle between state and federal ownership of water is a struggle between highly centralized government and human rights of individuals.

We thank you sincerely for this opportunity to appear before you and particularly for your courteous and impartial approach to this difficult problem.

I officially announced to the Board of Directors that I would not be a candidate for reelection at the annual meeting. I had then (1955) worked with Agricultural Extension and Farm Bureaus for 42 years, and had held an office from Farm Center Secretary to President of the State Farm Bureau, and membership on the American Board and its Executive Committee from 1916 through 1955—39 years. Today, August 24, 1979, I write this as a member of the House of Delegates, which adds up to 69 years, including 63 years holding an office.

We all worked hard to get Farm Bureau in the best possible shape to turn over to the new president, but mixed in with it were many good wishes and farewells. The Insurance Company had a good party and presented me with a nice globe of the world illuminated inside.   At Farm Bureau staff party we were presented a Retina II camera with extra lenses. The office staff presented me with a diamond-studded Farm Bureau pin. I still have all these and have enjoyed them greatly.

The annual meeting was November 6-10 in San Francisco at the old Whitcomb Hotel. The ladies started the program with a delightful tea at 2 p.m. in Polk Hall of the Civic Center. At 4 p.m. a beautiful Vespers service was held in the same hall with dignity and sentiment, a most fitting opening for a convention. At 6:30 was the dinner for the county presidents, the board, and the officers. This was a happy way to start the convention, but also the place for anyone to ask any questions or make any statement for the welfare or smooth operation of Farm Bureau.

Monday was a beehive of activity with the commodity and women's meetings, and that evening the big commodity dinner in the Civic Auditorium with Allan Kline as speaker. Tuesday started at 7 a.m. with the young people's breakfast in the Crystal Ballroom of the hotel. These breakfasts were an inspiration. At 11 I spoke to the Farm Center Directors in Larkin Hall of the Civic Center, a big turnout of fine young and old leaders of Farm Bureau grass roots. The dinner and dance Tuesday was in the Civic Auditorium.

Wednesday started at 7 a.m. with the organization breakfast of all county membership chairmen and wheelhorse workers. There were awards for "most new members to date," and setting of goals for the year. The general session was in Polk Hall; at noon, a luncheon for principal speakers; evening, a banquet in the auditorium.

Thursday was business, resolutions, and the election of Louis Rozzoni as California Farm Bureau President. Nobody ever deserved recognition of loyalty and years of hard work and unselfish service to Farm Bureau more than Louis Rozzoni. I was happy to see him get it. I had hoped a little in my own mind that Allan Grant, a younger member of the board, might be elected, as I felt sure he would eventually be President of the American FBF, as he now is. Maybe it is best this way.

Monday, November 19, I flew to Green Bay, Wisconsin. Attended their meeting Tuesday and spoke at their banquet that evening on "Selling Agricultural Products Around the World."

All day I had seen many posters of the "big fish boil" that night. I just couldn't imagine a really good boiled fish, so when time came I watched the process carefully. They caught these fine-looking whitefish in Green Bay that day. In a park by the auditorium were large, and I mean large, copper kettles full of water and a roaring fire underneath. The ritual starts. The volume and temperature of the water must be exactly right, then each minor ingredient goes in at just the right time and temperature. Then the potatoes, and eventually the fish. You have to be an old-timer before you know exactly when the fish go in. I was a convert, for properly executed boiled fish is delightful.

December 1, I spoke to the Washington State Farm Bureau at a banquet in Yakima. Ralph Gillespie was President.

December 4 I went to Washington D.C. to a Watershed Conference for two days, then back to Chicago for the AFBF Board and the annual meeting.

I was of course no longer president of the CFBF, but I was still a member of the American Board. The AFBF resolutions committee is all the state presidents, so that was Louis Rozzoni, and I was free.

I should mention the large number of letters I received very kindly referring to the years of work with Farm Bureau and wishing me well for the future. They were good years. They brought me a broad experience and education. Sometimes what I thought was a good idea didn't even get off the ground. Sometimes I failed to do what I should have. Occasionally others disappointed me, but on the whole the cooperation was marvelous both with staff and with the volunteer leaders. The volunteer leaders and workers are, of course, the power and strength of Farm Bureau.

† 1956

The old year ended with extra time at home for Christmas, but by January 2, I was starting the new year in Washington at the Executive Committee meeting; I had been reelected for another two-year term on the Board of the American Farm Bureau Federation. The executive committee met in Washington to go over our general legislative program for the coming year. Then I was asked to be principal speaker at both the Utah and Idaho annual meetings January 10-12, and immediately after went to Asilomar for the CFBF board meetings. January 16 it was back to Washington for the AFBF Board, so I didn't spend much time at home. On the 25th I was on the Ed Murrow television show, the top talk show of that day, to discuss the farm situation. On the 26th and 27th the Western Regional policy committee met in Salt Lake. This was for the purpose of discussing the policies of the Western region, but also of discussing how the Western region could best cooperate in carrying out the overall policies of the American Farm Bureau Federation in the Western region.

This was the year of the floods at Yuba City when the levees washed out—homes, orchards, everything destroyed in a large part of that area. Many people lost their homes, there was some loss of life. I went up to see it. As long as I was farming in the bypass and lived down here below the waters, I wanted to know a little about how it looked under those conditions. It is really distressing to be on the levee and see trees, houses, doors, windows, floating down the river in a manner that is very, very sobering. It is a fearsome sight in fact. Men from here spent a good many days helping to clean up the debris and make it easier for the people to move back into the area, even when they had lost part or all of their homes. I wasn't able to participate in that personally because I was away so much, but it was an effort that everybody in the country participated in to help the folks up there get reorganized again.

The International Cooperation Administration asked me to go to India to study the farm organization of India. We had already signed up for a semester at the American Institute of Foreign Trade at Glendale, Arizona, so I agreed we would go to India after the semester. The importance of foreign sales had become very prominent in Farm Bureau and other activities, and I felt I would like to know more about it. I had decided to go to the American Institute of Foreign Trade in Glendale (near Phoenix), Arizona, which was highly recommended by a number of people. We loaded up the Buick and set out to be students again on February 1.

About 1939 a group decided to build an airfield for training civilian pilots—or military pilots for that matter, although it was a civilian activity. They built the runways, the hangars, and so forth, and had started with some students when the war broke out in 1941. Of course, this was a great opportunity for the Air Force to take this facility over, and they used it during the war to train a great many young men for the air corps. They built up the residence area, the dining hall, the classrooms, as well as the actual flying area. So a group of American businessmen got together and decided they would set up a school in foreign trade. They signed a contract with the government for this facility. They put very heavy emphasis on language, Spanish, French, and Portuguese. Words were spoken by instructors and repeated by the students, repeating and repeating until the pronunciation and the vocabulary were correct. Grammar was taught in very much the same way. In fact, we did not have any books until just a few days before we left near the end of the semester. The teachers were rotated every two weeks, so that the students would get the benefit of the Mexican, Cuban, Spanish, and Argentinian or other accents and idioms. It was a most interesting experience, and I think there is no question but that it is the best way to learn a language if you want to actually learn to speak, read and write it effectively.

I also took foreign trade, marketing, Latin-American country studies, and Far Eastern country studies. Bella took the languages and the Latin-American country studies so that she got most of that phase of the work. Part of the faculty were permanent professionals, and part were retired corporation executives with years of overseas experience. This was very valuable instruction, coming from both standpoints and therefore more effective. Most of the students had their bachelor degrees, a few had several years of overseas experience. Some were sent by their employers for further study. They were the hardest working, most dedicated group of students I had ever encountered. They knew why they were there. They knew this was their last opportunity to get an education before they actually went out into the field and had to compete for a job and then get the job done properly.

We were encouraged to attend Mexican movies where all the shows were in Spanish. We had dances often, with Latin American music and instruction in South American and other foreign dances. Liquor was served at 25¢ a drink until 10 p.m., then it was 50¢ a drink. This was to discourage extended private parties in the rooms ahead of the dances and get the people to come early to the dances, and it was also to watch the actions of the students; any excess use of liquor was noted on the student's record. It was felt that excessive use of liquor should be noted before overseas assignment. As in most cases, the graduates from there spent a year or more with the company getting better acquainted with the particular company and all of their programs and operations. Then they were sent overseas. Of course, with the great variation in habits and customs and being far away from home.

If one tended toward excessive use of alcohol, it was a lot better if they were able to determine it before a person left his schooling and entered into business.

One of the interesting factors was that I paid a tuition fee to go there, and I had to pay $25. for Bella. This was required in all cases that the wife pay $25 and take eleven units of study, including language and the studies of the countries. This was an effort to try to familiarize the wife with the language, customs, and atmosphere that she was apt to meet when she arrived in a foreign country, instead of just going in cold and being completely overcome by some of the poverty, sometimes filth, and always different customs and habits on the part of the people.

I took several days off for commodity meetings in Washington on February 14-15, followed by more meetings in Chicago for land and water and a board of directors meeting. When I returned from those meetings, I had trouble sleeping at night, an upset stomach, I felt nervous, and felt I just had to do something, so I went to a doctor and asked him if he could give me something to settle my stomach a little and make me feel better. He gave me a couple of pills, and I commented "I guess this is reason enough to see why a couple of old duffers like us shouldn't try to go to a school like this and compete with younger people." He said, "All the rest of those kids came in here two months ago to get these pills and they've been on them ever since."

The February 14-15 meeting in Washington was the culmination of considerable prior effort toward a market-expansion program. The National Wool Growers had an active program requiring a small assessment on each sale of wool. The money was used for research, advertising, and promotion of lamb and wool. The AFBF refused to support that program, as we felt it should provide that any wool grower not wishing to support the program could be exempt from making the payment, or have an easy method of having his payment refunded to him, and that it should be easier for sheep men to terminate the program if they wished to. Also there was a background feeling that a specialty fruit like oranges might profitably advertise to increase demand, but if basic foods got into big promotion campaigns we would only add the advertising costs without increasing the total use of foods. Neither the California Farm Bureau Federation nor I personally had any strong feelings on the matter, but I did feel that the AFBF should either work agressively to reach agreement with a commodity group, or offer a substitute which would fill the need. In this spirit I worked in my room for a couple of days on a program to help stimulate demand for all farm products, for food and fiber in both domestic and export markets.

To explain the overall idea, I wrote up quite a detailed project and how it might be carried out, and sent it into the Resolutions Committee for consideration. They sent it back saying I knew they couldn't adopt anything as long and detailed as I had sent in, but they liked it and if I would scale it down into a statement of principles, they would be glad to pass it. One of my friends volunteered to do that, and so the "Food Comes First Campaign" was authorized.

It had taken time to get the program launched, but this Washington meeting was the big moment. We were agreeably surprised at the turnout. Representatives not only of State Farm Bureau but principal farm cooperatives were present, plus excellent representation from the national meat packers, grain dealers, General Foods, Quaker Oats, and similar groups. We met all morning with Charles Schuman, President of AFBF, as Chairman. We broke up into two committees, one to expand domestic use of foods and fibers, the other to expand foreign outlets. We met that evening and decided to appoint a committee to report back the next morning, which was done.

The export committee proposed the setting up of an export office, probably in Rotterdam, as a joint promotion and sales office for U.S. foods. All readily agreed to pay their share of the costs, but asked the AFBF to employ personnel and administer the activity. I thought that was fine, but by now Farm Bureau was so enthused that they said AFBF would set up the office and bear all the costs. We set up the office with a good man, George Deitz, in charge. He had been Agricultural Attache to the Netherlands before he came with AFBF. The U.S. Coops and private companies were friendly, but they didn't really use the office, for they didn't quite feel free to use it if they weren't paying their share. The cost should have been divided. Bella and I visited the office; it was fine but not what it should have been.

We decided the President of Farm Bureau should appoint a committee to provide an appropriate platform to kick off a real effort to expand the use of foods and fibers at home and in export.

The general program was called "Food Comes First." It was used in food advertising all over the U.S. Most of the State fairs in the U.S. and many County fairs had "Food Comes First" booths. These were sponsored by nutrition groups, home demonstration medical, and other groups. There were prizes awarded in many high schools all over the U.S. for the best essays by students on the value or use of foods. In California, for at least ten years, county winners of these contests attended a conference on food at Asilomar and spoke throughout the county. It was surely an idea that didn't want to die. It may be time to try something like it again, but let it be adequately funded by the sellers as well as Farm Bureau.

On April 5 I enjoyed speaking to the **Glendale Ariz. Rotary Club. We had a number** of social engagements which helped make it more interesting down there.

On April 19-20 I went to Purdue University for the National Institute for Animal Agriculture. This was a most outstanding two days of talks on the area of the use of meat in the 20s and 30s, pointing out how if we had just eaten a little more meat in the 20s and 30s, it would have used up the surplus of grain which we had, and would have gone a long ways in solving the agriculture problem we went through all those years when we piled up grain year after year.

We got word about this time from Washington to go out to Luke Airforce Base and get our shots for our trip to India. This was not far from Glendale so we went over to the Airforce hospital. Of course the country down there is dusty, and we weren't at all surprised when we saw the floors and tables covered with dust. But they took us back to the room where we were to get the shots, and everything in there was covered with dust. There wasn't even a sheet on the cot, and the mattress was covered with old bloodstains and just looked terrible. An aide gave me a shot, then he asked Bella to get up on the cot and lay down there while he gave her a shot. When he finished giving her a shot, he looked up and yelled down the hall, "Say, what was it I gave this woman? Horse or monkey?" Well, somehow or other, that kind of settled you down. We thought we'd seen about enough of Luke Airforce Base. We, of course, had our shots for the moment. We were told to come back for more, but we didn't go back. I sometimes wonder.

We left Thunderbird on May 18 to drive back home, stopping in Banning to see the folks there. We had an interesting dinner on May 23 at the University of Pacific where the board of regents entertained the faculty that evening before the board meeting the next day. It was a most enjoyable occasion. I think we ought to repeat it.

I had a lot to do, getting visas for India, making final arrangements for our trip. Another complication came up, in that Ralph Tutor, formerly of the Department of the Interior, a prominent engineer in San Francisco, asked Earl Coke to head a party to Afghanistan to make a study of the Hellman Valley Project there which had been built by Americans but somehow or other hadn't worked out very well. They wanted an analysis as to just why it hadn't, and how it could work. Earl Coke told him he would go and head the party provided I'd go, and so Mr. Tutor had us down for lunch one day in San Francisco and urged very strongly that we go first to Afghanistan and make that study, then continue from there on over to India for our program there. Of course I hesitated a little about that because we already had put our trip to India off for quite a while, and I didn't like to ask those folks to wait any longer. However, Mr. Tutor asked me to meet with his man Ralph Wadsworth in Washington. Wadsworth would have been the manager and handler of the program. I knew Ralph rather well as a water engineer here in California, and being the brother of Harold

Wadsworth, a very close friend of ours and with whom I bought the first land in Clarksburg in 1920. Ralph asked me a number of questions about my ability and qualifications for being on such a group, and then he asked me if I felt that I would be capable of helping to write up the report. The report was a very important part of any such study, of course. Well, I told him I presumed I could, but didn't have any particular experience in that area. He asked me two or three times, and finally I said I wasn't sure whether I could or not, because it seemed to me that he was kind of fishing for some other answer. Then he said, Well, George, I think I'd probably better get a University man to fill that position, so I can have him to help write up the report at the end and make sure I've got a man of experience. I told him I guessed I couldn't make it.

I did of course go on to India, I did write a report of our program in India, and this report was printed. They tell me that it is the only report of its kind that had been printed and they tell me that it was sent to all the United States embassies around the world as an example of the kind of report they liked to see as a result of these many projects we had of sending folks out to make studies I don't mean that as bragging; I do mean to refer to it as just one more example of how somehow or other prople just fundamentally believe that a farmer can't do anything except farm, that it's unreasonable to expect a farmer to write a report or anything of the kind.

On our several trips to Mexico where we would meet Tom Robertson and Alberto Salinas Ramos, the president of the Mexican farm organization, they would encourage me to participate with them in a project of developing farm land in the Viscaino Desert right in the center of Baja, California, about 550 miles below the border of the United States I gave it some thought, because I had always had a very keen appreciation of what Gus Olson had done for us in helping us get started here in the Clarksburg area, and I had always hoped that maybe somehow I could do something to help develop an area somewhere that we could help young farmers who didn't have very much to get started. I couldn t see any opportunity of doing that in the United States, and it looked like here there was a possibility of doing it in Mexico by going down there to the desert, developing the water, studying the methods of irrigation, the crops that could be grown, the time of year that was best to handle them, and all that sort of thing, and then sell the land at a reasonable price to young farmers and have somebody stay there to help them along the way and make sure they made out successfully in the operation This had been pretty much a dream, but in June they asked us to come down for a few days and look the situation over.

David and I went down with Hollis Roberts from Bakersfield who had a two-motor plane belonging to the oil company that his brother headed. We went down there and flew around the desert country and got a pretty good look at it. We saw a big salt flat and landed on that. This big salt flat was just as level and as hard as any concrete landing field would be, and had plenty of size to make it easy for take-off and landing at any time Of course it made this a rather attractive place to use as a starting point and to make camp. We did make camp there. Alberto Ramos came in with a jeep, and we spent three days traveling around the country, looking it all over, trying to figure out whether it was a reasonable project and if it was, how did we go about it?

242

Finally, on June 24, on a Sunday morning, we left Sacramento at 7 a.m for San Francisco. Dorothy had gone down the day before to San Jose to stay with Pat and Wes. She would later be going on to the University of Pacific. We arrived in San Francisco about 8. Pat, Wes, and Dorothy came up from San Jose to spend an hour with us and see to it that we got a good, appropriate send-off, which we appreciated very much.

We arrived in Chicago and spent the next day in land and water conference, then the board meeting lasted until Friday afternoon. That afternoon we went out to the home of Allan and Gladys Kline, had a beautiful dinner there, spent the night, and the next day they took us to the airport, which at that time was fairly close to their home in the western part of Chicago.

Our first evening in Washington we had dinner with Mr. and Mrs. Dana Reynolds at their home, and learned a good deal more about the origin and activity leading up to our assignment to India. He was one of these fellows who was mixed up in everything. He had not done a great deal, but was fairly prominent in Vermont, a kind of gentleman farmer, and then he became assistant to Senator Aiken of Vermont. He then became involved in many activities in relation to agriculture in Washington, and just seemed somehow or other to be involved in about everything that was going on without really being officially responsible for any of these things.

We took it easy Sunday, took some pictures, spent a little time around the Lincoln Monument in the evening. Monday and Tuesday we got orders, visas, final yellow fever shots interviews, and so forth. Bought a wash-and-dry suit, which came in very handy in India. We had an excellent discussion with Gwin Garnett, the Farm Bureau Advisor in International Affairs. He himself had been in India and made an excellent report, which I had an opportunity to read over, of the agriculture of India. We had a conference and lunch with M. L. Wilson, Assistant Secretary of Agriculture on Tuesday morning. All details cleaned up, we went to New York on Tuesday evening.

That afternoon we went to a show with our cousin Elizabeth and had dinner with her that evening. We met Hilton Richardson again at 9 p.m. and went down to the New York market with him until about 11 p.m. on the Pennsylvania piers. We saw the oranges, lemons, grapes, mostly from California. It was a very good experience. The fruit was handled quite orderly, although some was in rather bad shape, especially coming in from areas other than California. We didn't see much bad coming in from California.

We packed up and rushed around on Thursday morning to get Lebanon, Syria, and Spanish visas, and got to New York air terminal at 11:30 to take off at 1 p.m. There was still lots of confusion at Idlewild, but nowhere near as much as when the group started off on the Town Hall of the Air trip in 1949.

At left, early Farm Bureau leaders, l-r: Allan Kline, next president of Farm Bureau, in my opinion one of the great Americans of this century; George Wilson; Ed O'Neil of Alabama, who unified Farm Bureau as its '31-'47 President.
Center: Cattlemen's Bar-B-Q at Snyder Ranch at Michigan Bar (beyond Sloughhouse, Calif.).
Bottom: Our Food-Comes-First breakfast. President Eisenhower, principal speaker, is at far right.

12
FARMERS FORUM OF INDIA

We landed in Santa Maria, the Azores, about midnight. The approach to Lisbon was beautiful. We arrived at 7:30 a.m., went to the Tivoli Hotel. We took a taxi ride out into the country and saw some of the farming, castles, and spent most of the day. The trip was beautiful. The country looked far cleaner and more prosperous than I expected. Much of the grain was irrigated with furrows several feet apart.

Saturday, July 7, 1:30 p.m., we left for Madrid, where we stayed at the Palace Hotel, and had a very fancy bathroom, telephone and all. We took the bus trip to Toledo and the city tour with Mr. and Mrs. John Conrad of Davis. Both Portugal and Spain looked well-kept, and invited one to spend some time driving through them.

We got to Rome late Monday, July 9, and went to the Flora Hotel, two blocks from the Excelsior where we had stopped at other times. We saw Ray Ogg on Tuesday. Ray had been secretary of the American Farm Bureau Federation, and then went with the Department of Agriculture as the Agricultural Attache in Italy. Tuesday morning we went to his home for lunch, then went to cattle feeders and met with the Italian farmers in the afternoon. They would like more transfers of Italians to the United States and of American farmers to Italy, and of students back and forth in order to help learn a little more of how we handle California agriculture. Ray Ogg took us to the airport and saw us off in the afternoon for Istanbul, stopping en route at Athens.

We stayed at the Park Hotel at Istanbul, overlooking the Bosporus. We had a fine ride around the city including the mosques, the bazaars, and so forth. We saw some beautiful copper, cheap, but we couldn't buy it because of the difficulty of exchange and shipping.

On July 12 we had a beautiful ride up the Bosporus and the Black Sea. We came back over the hills to the city We left Istanbul on the flight to Ankara. The big change there was the great increase in the roads between the cities and the villages. Ankara had a large, new airport and had grown very rapidly We got settled into the hotel fairly early in the afternoon, so I decided I would go down to the Pan Am office, see the girl down there, and see if she would go out to dinner with us and show us a little of the city that evening. She was quite hesitant, and finally she mentioned her husband and I told her we would be more than pleased to have her husband come along. She called him and they agreed to come. His name was Emol-Rasin Demir. He had been educated in the U.S., was the chief protocol officer in the Army of Turkey, and had been in charge when President Eisenhower, then head of NATO, came to visit them in Turkey. So he gave us the same tour that he had given President Eisenhower, and it certainly made a delightful and enjoyable afternoon and evening. We went to Attaturk s tomb on the top of the hill. The growth of Ankara had certainly been phenomenal from the time we were there in 1949.

Friday morning July 13, we got up at 5:30 a.m. and went to the top of the hill in the old city. They had certainly cleaned it up. We shopped a little, but saw little to buy. We rested about an hour over some tea in the youth park. I went to Rotary and was asked to be the speaker. I presented a Rotary emblem from Sacramento We left Ankara at 7:40 p.m. for a two-hour flight to Beirut and the Bristol Hotel. It was nice; the food and orchestra excellent. We rented a car to see Beirut.

Tom Robertson had introduced me to a Lebanese who had left home as a youth, moved to Mexico and settled in Ensenada where he had done very well as owner of a furniture store, but he had not written back to his mother or his brothers at any time since he had left home in Lebanon. He had asked me if I was going to Lebanon to look up his brother and his family. His brother was engineer in charge of the waterworks for the city and area around Beirut. We got a car and driver and picked up the brother and drove to Baalbek, often called "The temple of the sun," which is called by some the most imposing Roman ruins in existence. Some of the columns are 7½ feet in diameter and 62 feet tall. This was the home of the worshippers of Baal, often referred to in the Bible Then we went to lunch at a beautiful restaurant which was built across a mountain stream, with vines overhead. We went further up the stream to the mother's home and the sisters of our Ensenada friend. They were completely overcome to think that they were touching someone who had brought word of their son and brother. We really couldn't tell them much, but he was alive and well and prospering, and that seemed to be enough. They would hardly let us leave; the mother just hung on and hung on, delighted to think she was looking at somebody who had actually seen her son and could bring her word that he was doing well.

We drove over to Damascus where they had air conditioning in the hotel and about froze us out. We saw antiques, the Damascus cloth they were weaving so beautifully, the "Street called Straight," and many other items of Bible times. I believe Damasucs is considered the oldest continuous city in the world. We bought

246

gifts and a little cloth, brass, and other items, and shipped them home from there.

We left Damascus at 11 a.m., stopped at Basrah for fuel, and again looked down on the Khuzestan area of Iran, never dreaming that we would be back there about 13 years later looking at farmland and starting a farm operation in that area. We got into Kurachi about midnight. The city is much improved, certainly from '49 to '54, but still it has a long way to go. The hotel was all right, but certainly not outstanding. It was still crowded, struggling to build a new nation. It is a shame that the Aga Aly Khan had been assassinated and the Begum, his wife, assigned to Denmark as the ambassador. They could have made a tremendous contribution to the development of Pakistan.

On July 20 we flew to Lahore; there we were received by Dost Mahammed Khan, Mr. Karem Jan, and Mr. Ahaad, all of whom we had met in California and entertained here in our home. They lived in Peshour, still higher up in the mountains above Lahore, and we had planned on going up there to visit them. But they had terrible storms at the time, roads were washed out, airlines were not flying, so they came down and met us and spent several days with us in Lahore. Lahore is a beautiful city, old, still much as it was when the English left it. We were invited to have lunch with the Governor General of the state in the beautiful old English home that he now occupies which sets in a large park all its own. The trees there are particularly outstanding and attractive, and there are a great number of birds. We had a very interesting visit to the church there. Bella had gotten quite well-acquainted with the wife of the Minister on our trip from Karachi over to Lahore, and we visited them again on Sunday after church.

We also met the Jenner family. He was coordinator for ICA in that area. They were very fine folks, and we were really a little surprised when they reminded us that they had visited us in our home. They were outstanding in the fine way they entertained us, introduced us to a number of the people and gave us a better idea of that part of Pakistan. One of the interesting incidents there was that they had tried milk in the schools, dried skim milk reconstituted, but it had been a failure because of lack of cleanliness in the utensils they were using, so the children got sick. They decided, however, that they would make a wafer out of the dry skim milk, which they did with the aid of a candy company in the area, and gave two of these wafers each day to the youngsters. They were very attractive from the standpoint of the youngsters, and seemed to fill the need of a glass of milk. There were several advantages, one, their folks could not take them away from the children and sell them to somebody else, they were clean, and they served the purpose.

We arrived in Delhi a little after dark and were received by a delegation from the embassy, many garlands and beautiful flowers of course. The garlands of India impressed me more than the leis of Hawaii, partly because they are larger, they are more varied, and they are an important part of every reception and activity. They took us to our hotel at 55 Golf Links Road. This was a rather modest place, used as a location for transients and people as they arrived and left Delhi. The next day, of course, we met many of the American delegation, the people we were going to work with and under, and many of the Indians. In fact, we spent the next two days in meetings of that kind and getting acquainted with the office of the farmers forum India under Dr. Deshmuk, minister of agriculture, who was president of the organization. Of course he didn't spend much time in the office; the office was under Mr. Sharma who handled everything under Dr. Deshmuk's direction. I had a rather simple desk in a simple setting, but I was very pleased to have my headquarters in the headquarters of the Farmers Forum, rather than having it in the headquarters of the Technical Cooperation Mission which was the American activity in New Delhi.

For several days we attended in New Delhi the conference of all the technical cooperation mission people who came in from all over India for this conference and reorientation. Of course I was just new; but we met many of the folks whom we met later in our travels around India, and got better acquainted with what the United States was trying to do over there. The agricultural end of it was under the direction of Mr. Parker, a marvelous fellow. He had his office in the American building where the technical cooperation mission was, but he also had a regular office, secretary and all, in the office of the Ministry of Agriculture of India, so that he worked very closely with the people of India and certainly made our time over there much easier and much simpler in regard to travel and that kind of thing.

It was rather interesting and maybe worthy of comment that I went into one of the meetings rather late. They had already started with a movie. There seemed to be a vacant seat not too far from the door, and I went in and occupied it. When the lights came on I looked up, and on one side of me was Bill Hermes who had been Assistant Farm Advisor in Yolo County, a very fine fellow who I knew very well. He had taken a year off to travel and get better acquainted with the work in the foreign field. On the other side of me was Davis of the Agronomy Department at U.C. Davis for the Agricultural Extension Service. He was a friend of many years.

We got our first week's travel arrangements scheduled, and on the morning of August 5 we started out in an International carry-all with seats for about eight people and the baggage. You might say that even though we had a party of four or five, we always had all the seats occupied, as there was always somebody who was very anxious to get on to the next stop. Sometimes we wondered if they cared much which direction we were going as long as they had a chance to ride. Nevertheless, there was a great shortage of transportation and it was a great convenience if they could get a chance to ride with us instead of having to walk or find some other means of going. That was one of the things that interested us all the time—the number of people who wanted to join the party.

We had Satwat Singh, who had laid out the plan for the week, and we were going to be stopping at his home. We picked up M. S. Randharra, the second man in the Ministry of Food and Agriculture to go along with us for the trip. Of course we went to his home, and that required having tea for a little while. We looked over his artwork and some other things, which is an interesting part of most every stop.

We then went a little west and north, about 120 miles, to Ambala, and then about 25 miles from there to Mr. Singh's 300-acre farm, four miles east of Patiala. We stopped at a new town made up almost exclusively of refugees from Pakistan. They were sikhs who had moved in there and were hoping to start farming, but in the meanwhile they were carrying on what they called cottage industries of making cloth, paper, weaving, and many other things which could be done by hand and done cooperatively. This of course was one of Ghandi's things to try to get all the people to actively be doing something which he called cottage industries, making something useful either for themselves or for sale. It was really quite a factor in helping hold India together during those times, and was far superior to being idle.

Mr. Singh had a very fine cotton experiment going on not very far from his house. The crops were really beautiful, showing the benefits of fertilization and other methods of farming. He had in his operation two Ferguson tractors and five yoke of oxen. As one went about India, very often there was a small tractor, Ford or Ferguson or something of the kind, out in front of the house. Primarily it was a status symbol, and when I asked about it, they said, Oh my goodness, you can't afford to use it. It costs so much for gasoline, you can only use it for a few things. They used it for plowing mainly, but they felt it was not for cultivating or anything of that kind. In reality, that is where they really needed them the most. By using power, they could pull 3-4-5-row planters at a time and get straight rows, which would make it fairly easy for them to come through again with the tractor and cultivate the straight rows to get rid of weeds. But the way it was handled, there were a great many rains, which brought the weeds, and the weeds would keep coming and they couldn't keep up with them by hand. They would then plow the whole thing up and replant. Many times we saw fields that had been planted three times. Well, that certainly is not the way to produce a crop. The only real reason why it had to be planted several times was because the weeds got ahead of them and took the crop, and the weeds got ahead of them because the rows were so crooked that all hoeing had to be done by hand. They just couldn't keep up with that rapid growth. That is just one of the things; equipment itself doesn't solve the problem unless along with it you learn how to adapt the equipment to your particular circumstances.

Next morning (August 6) we went out to view the Maharajah's farm. This was a 640-acre square farm with a beautiful home right in the very center of it. It was a two-story home with beautiful furniture. It had the most beautiful rugs that I've seen anywhere. You went up a stairs outside to a deck on top where you could be either in the sun or shade, and they served meals and teas up there. From that vantage point you got an excellent view of the orchard. The orchard consisted of oranges, lemons, limes, loquats, grapefruits, and other citrus fruits. The Maharajah said that he got all his information about the production of these fruits from Robert Hodgson, Farm Advisor in Los Angeles County, who specializes in citrus fruits and kept in touch with the Maharajah afterward, sending him bulletins and otherwise advising him on how to plant and care for his trees.

Next morning we went to the government offices, as is done so much there, to meet with the development minister and development comissioner and a few farmers.

Of course, on such occasions you again have a good deal of tea. Then at ten o'clock we went to a beautiful library building there in Patiala. We met with a hundred farmers, members of the farmer's forum, about ten percent of whom spoke English so that we had to use an interpreter. There was a fine-looking group of men, almost all sikhs. At least one signed up as a life member of the farmer's forum. There were about 80 life members in that particular area.

Most people seemed to live on the farms they are operating. We visited the old fort and museum, and the home of the Maharajah. The fort and museum of course was a part of the Maharajah's establishment. It was just unbelievable the amount of military equipment they had there. They had cannon that they mounted on elephants; they had spears, rifles, sabers, everything in the world in the way of military equipment, and a tremendous amount of it. Of course each one of those Maharajahs was the governor of practically a small nation, and as such each had their own military.

After lunch we went to the guest house to see Mr. Wahi. I had met Mr. Wahi several times at international federation of agricultural producer's meetings. He was a member of the parliament there in India. As was so common, he had organized quite an organization of farmers of his area which he said in the IFAP meetings was a farm organization the same as other organizations, farm bureau and the kind, but there is no question that in fact it was a political organization to keep him in office. But many of the members of the government maintained such political organizations to keep themselves in office; only a variation in the kind of organizations kept.

We went out into the farming area and saw a bunch of 4-H club boys. Their uniforms were practically the same as the 4-H Club in this country. Some had calves, several had citrus, and other fruit and vegetables. It was certainly inspiring to see them and to see the pride with which they wore the uniforms, and see the tremendous growth they had on some of those trees in a relatively short time and some of the fine calves they were raising. When you saw that, you just couldn't help but see the tremendous possibilities of rapid improvement in a country like India if you could just get the young folks organized into a worthwhile project which would give them real confidence in themselves and assurance to go ahead and become producers.

We then visited a nursery where they had mango, citrus fruit, and many other trees being prepared for plantings. While there were some plantings all the time, this was a relatively new operation. We then visited the grain coop in Nebla. There were about 139 individual members in the coop; about 20 belonged to the coop credit society. They could get money through that to help in their operations. Although in checking into the credit, I found that India has a farm credit law based on the American farm credit law and very much like it. I think they loan money at 15 percent, which sounds a little high and sounded higher then than it does now, but that was relatively cheap compared to the 50, 75, and 100 percent that was being charged for money, a tremendous cost for borrowing money. Still, with that difference, only about 5 percent of the farmers of India use the farm credit system of India. It just either wasn't going to compete very much with the money lenders, or it wasn't very efficiently handled; I never could get the real complete answer on that, but it is an indication of the necessity of really doing a job of getting your money out and taking care of people as well as having the legislation to do it, which is often talked about but amounts to very little.

250

Many of the Singhs are very prominent in the military, including generals. We arrived for tea at a beautiful home with an outstanding display of swords, guns, skins, tigers, rhinoceros, and many other types of game. This is a very distinguished looking family, and a fairly large family. While they called it tea, they had far more than just tea for us, but when they came out with a big platter we saw on it some hors d oeuvres that looked very much like a good old American hot dog or sausage. We grabbed it and took a big bite out of it. It was good, but rich; my goodness, I don't think we had every tasted anything quite as rich as that was. It was made out of a number of different things, all put together with honey that was somehow half-way solidified. We got those other places afterward. We were a little more knowing after that, but our first introduction to them was quite a surprise.

Then we went to the Rotary Club where they had called a special meeting on a separate night just for me to speak to them. I did, of course, and got a very fine response and some fine letters afterward expressing appreciation. We considered it one of the most privileged and pleasant evenings that we had.

Tuesday, August 7 we again stopped at one of the villages with lots of refugees where they had a definite plan of courses for training the people in the cottage industries, making cloth, paper, pottery, and many other products. They employed them here and paid them so much an hour or day. They also made equipment to speed up the spinning and some of the other work, and trained the workers in the use of this equipment. By using that they could increase their production per day by about 3-4 times, so they not only were making this equipment by hand, but if they wished to leave there, they could go out and operate this equipment efficiently enough so they could make a reasonable days wages out of it. They were employing about a thousand workers at the time we were there, paying them about 5 rupees a day.

We stopped at a village where they were instructing the women in sewing both for themselves and others so they might make a living at it. At the time they had about 15 women sewing and being instructed. We hadn't been there very long however until quite a few more women gradually came in, I'm sure that morning they were really more interested in seeing what an American woman looked like than just what the sewing class was. The village had also put a brick drain down their main street; the street was wider than a path, all right, but not wide enough for two automobiles to pass. Nevertheless the main street in the village had a drain down each side of it. It was very much cleaner and looked much better and was a big improvement for that village. They also had on the main street a school where quite a lot of youngsters of all ages attended; most were sikhs and it looked like an interesting group of youngsters.

Chandigar is a new city which will be the capitol of the new state of Punjab, made up of three of the old states. They couldn't agree on which of the old state capitols they would use so they decided to build an entirely new capital. This of course was built primarily with money furnished by the government of India, but the states had contracted to pay it back. Although one of the governers had us for dinner one evening just before we left India, and I asked him what the chances were of paying the government back, he said that was something so far in the distance that they didn't think of it. It was a beautiful layout. The city covered 156 square miles, and they provided that there could not be any heavy industry in the city, nor could there be any heavy industry within 5 miles of the city limits. This was to be the capital and homes of people working in the capital, practically a tremendous park with beautiful living conditions. What the final result is, I am not sure. It is a good deal like and in fact is a forerunner of Brazilia down in Brazil, where they went way out in the forest to build a capital city. The streets in parts were pretty well in; they certainly were expensive. There were some beautiful large homes in large yards. The government buildings are very modern looking and were somewhat occupied at that time.

We had tea at Mr. Johnson's house. He was one of the technical staff from the United States, a specialist in the breeding of hybrid corn. He later got his seed developed. They had quite a large assembly there of Indian and American folks to celebrate the production of this hybrid corn seed, then at the end of it they said, "But how are we going to get the farmers to buy it and use it?" Johnson said, "We're going to sell it to them." All the folks, both Indian and American, said "What do you mean, sell it to them? They haven't got any money to buy it; we've got to give it to them. We may have to pay them to get them to use it!" He says, "That seed cost 6¢ a pound to produce and there's not one pound of it going to leave this building unless we get 6¢ on the barrelhead before we give it to anybody." They said, "Well, who is going to sell it for you?" And he says, "We're going to sell it, our own people here that produced it, if we can't get somebody else to." He did; he went out, and they sold it in no time at 6¢ a pound cash, paid for, which most had thought was impossible. It should have been one of the lessons. In spite of all you hear about the poverty, there still is plenty of money in India in the hands of the farm people to pay for good seed, fertilizer, or anything else that they think they need to help in their operations, if they just are assured that they can be adequately paid for their production.

I was interested that after we got back home I got a letter from Mr. Johnson wanting to know if I knew where he could get a job—this was about a year later. He wanted to know if we had a job for him. He had stayed another year and then left; I don't know why he left, but I am sure that his taking the initiative of going out and selling that seed himself didn't help his standing with many of the folks over there.

Wednesday, we set out to see the Bakra Dam. We drove much of the way along canal bank; the canal is very large. I think they said 12,000 cubic feet capacity and it was full, bricklined. There were two power plants on the canal, one used to furnish power in Delhi, the other used to furnish power to build the big dam at Bakrah up the river further. The canal diverts water from the river at a diversion dam which is a series of gates in the river. Several large canals take off from the river below the dam. They hope to irrigate 6 million acres of land with this water, 400,000 kwh power development. They claim to be the world's best irrigators and a very high duty of water, but I don't know.

We stayed at the canal resthouse, and some of the officials, including Mr. Herringer, assistant to Mr. Slocum, the over-all manager who was in the States at that time, spent the evening with us discussing the whole canal project and its construction and possibilities. It was well along in time and seemed to be doing very well, but the next morning Mr. Herringer had breakfast with us and had quite a story about all the

252

restraints to production and the delays which were caused Apparently it was just determination that kept moving the dam along. It was about like the Hoover Dam, about the same height and width, and I think a very well constructed project. The total cost was $20 per acre foot with 8¢ per acre annual maintenance cost. The cost to the farmers was about $2 per acre cash crop harvested plus cost. If they didn't harvest it, they didn't pay.

I read and wrote notes for most of the morning until time to leave about 11 a.m. for Jullundur. We stopped on the edge of town and looked at Singh's pear orchard farmed by Moslems. The trees appeared to never have been pruned and some were badly rotten at the base. Some were about 24' in spread, but most were about 12' and went high in the air. He is getting two sikhs from the States to prune the orchard this winter. We forded streams and got stuck on one bank, arriving at the Honeymoon rest cottage in the hills about 1 p.m. for lunch. Several men came in for lunch; the rest house was very nice, but has since been burned out. We got to Jullundur about 4 p.m., a town of refugee farmers but highly organized in cooperatives: credit, farming, sales, tubewells, machinery coops, and a sugar refinery coop being built.

Satwart Singh's family first stopped here. The people are well educated, with many pen pals around the world. Many who emigrated to the U.S., Canada, and other countries went from here. Each refugee got 20 acres of land with the provision that he plant 75 percent of it to fruit, citrus, mango, etc. The government supervises the whole procedure. The plantings are moving along fairly well. Citrus planted two years ago had full rows of cotton interplanted and almost hiding the trees. Singh and brother have 60-plus acres of beautiful, sandy loam soil. The crops looked good, cotton, sugar cane, etc.

We went four miles West to see a Tubewell Coop. There are 29 members farming 400 acres using six wells. They employ a technician to handle the pumps, and also a member secretary at 45R per month. We went to Kharan and met farmers of Khara, Gordon Colony, in the library building. That was a very good group. We had translaters and discussed Farm Forum. They seemed ready to organize right away with the aid of the BDD; at his suggestion Niranjan Singh formed Ad Hoc Committee.

On Friday, August 10, Omar Singh came to lunch with some fine-looking young folks from California. We came back from the Tubewell Coop and went to a meeting of farmers in Amritsar at 5 p.m. This was a fine group of 35 or 40 sikh farmers. Many questions, then tea with rich sweets. The leader was Ram Singh Randhiwari. There are about 100 life members in the Punjab and 81 in Pepsu. We went to the park in Amritsar where Gen. O'Dwyer massacred up to 2000 sikhs, muslims and hindis, without notice because they were holding a mass meeting protesting the Rowlat Act, making illegal assembly of more than 5. This was in 1919 and fired the demand for independence. We then went to the Golden Temple of the sikhs. This is apparently an artificial lake with a golden temple in the center. The walks are of marble and the outside of the lake is surrounded by temples and various buildings of importance to the religion. Every sikh temple has a free hostel and place where any sikh can rest and eat for a few days at no cost. The chants and music in the golden temple were very impressive and interesting. At one time sikh law superseded civil law. There were a good many sikh volunteers who wear a semi-military costume and

253

go heavily armed with daggers, swords, spears, etc. They are a select group who agree to volunteer for any sikh service.

We spent a week in New Delhi resting, writing up notes on our trip, and getting ready for the next one.

Sunday, August 19. We left New Delhi at 8 p.m. on a two-hour flight southeast to Luchnow. We were met by B. P. Singh, a fine-looking young farmer. He took us to the Carlton Hotel to an air-conditioned room. The weather was hot and humid most of the time we were there, and air conditioning was a great idea but often clammy and not very comfortable. Many of the hotels had high ceilings with large electric fans, sometimes with variable speeds which we found preferable to refrigeration.

Monday morning early we went shopping and got two saris, then went to a sugar cane experiment station. There are other regional stations for the various sugar growing regions. There are 4 million acres of cane in India supplying 136 sugar mills. India produces 1.8 million tons of refined sugar, 3 million tons of Gur (a concentrated and dried sugar cane juice used mostly in villages). Consumption of white sugar is 10 lbs per capita, Gur consumption is 18 lbs per capita; 20 percent of cane goes to white sugar, 60 percent to Gur, and 20 percent to molasses and open pan sugar. India cane averages 13.5 tons per acre, with top production 40 tons per acre. This is 12 months in cane, ratoon 8-10 months, giving about 2/3 of planted = 20T to 60T in 22 months. Price is set by government, R1/7 per mound. Some bonus is paid for high-sugar percent varieties. Price is FOB factory with uniform deduction for all sugar hauled by rail or truck. If factory shows profit above certain percentage, it must share profits with growers. Average sugar percent for India = 9.93 percent.

We met Dr. Parker and Mrs. Patel, who has an agricultural institute near Baroda, Bombay. They raise tobacco, pay each student a stipend, run the college, and make a profit. They raise tobacco and tobacco seed, sell at auction, and after 25 percent down get full pay in 15 days. Other farmers may be two years getting payment. Mrs. Patel's farmers pay 25 percent cash rent and are very happy.

Then came Mr. S. B. Singh, State Minister of Agriculture and father of B.P. We discussed farms, and government with him, as we went 25 miles north and saw 40 ton sugar cane 10-11 percent sugar variety and several types of cover crops.

We visited a village 35 miles north, saw a cattle bazaar where they sell 400-500 head twice a week. There was a dense crowd milling around with cattle in all directions. A prospective buyer and seller would sit cross-legged and put a roll of bills on the ground between them and put more down or pick some up as the crowd around cheered them on. Finally they agreed on a price and the procedure is repeated.

We visited a training center where they train about 150 village level workers and others for 1 year or 18 months. They are in three classes, train at the school for four months, then take a half-day in school and a half-day in villages getting on-the-job training under instructors. They have farmed enough to try out improved practices, and train the boys in the practices. They have developed a smokeless stove for the homes, also are trying out many house and barn plans, latrines, wells, storage bins, and other village or home improvements.

I spoke in the hall at the school to 75 farmers; they were real villagers. All was well interpreted. They listened well and the leader announced that they wanted to start a Forum right away.

We then went to a village to see Japanese rice culture and cover crop use, then to a village to see a young farmer's club; these were boys 10 years and up. One of the farmers gave the club land to farm; they had small plots, about 20x30, of corn, rice, peanuts, cover crop, and other things. They were very proud, sang us some songs, and did very well. They say there are 5,000 members in U.P. These seem apparently new, but this one was doing well.

Along the way we had tea with a landowner with 160 acres in sugar cane, mangoes, cover crops, seed, etc. The cattle market is his. The land here is a sandy loam, most of it farmed. It rained most of the time.

The Singhs are opposed to ceilings, coop farming, and all government controls.

B. P. Singh, Bishan Mansinghad, R. P. Singh had dinner with us, and then we went to a show with them, the Rajah's son, sister-in-law, and other relatives.

On our return trip Tuesday morning, we were traveling a beautiful tree-shaded road, when we saw at the side of the road ahead a woman bent over all set to spring ahead as we got by, but she was a little anxious and sprang ahead at a run, head down. She ran right into the rear-view mirror. We were doing 35-40 miles per hour. She was knocked flat out on the road. The father driving made no move to slow down. I could see her on the road and people gathering around. I insisted we go back and see if we could help her. The driver thought it quite unnecessary, but finally stopped and backed up while his son ran back to see. Her family were there and they were sure she was all right. I am sure they were very kind and considerate people, but this indicated the low value of human life. I have seen that demonstrated in several countries.

On our return at noon I put on my coat and we went to see the Governor. We had a very nice discussion on India in general. He was more anti-English than most. He did not share the confidence in the future progress of India, much concerned about increased population. We discussed forum some, but it was hard to keep on the subject. As usual, the place was spacious and the gardens very beautiful. We were invited to an at-home with the Governor and the agricultural education folks at 5:30 p.m. It was a very nice tea with all seated and a good deal to eat. Bella was the only woman there.

Mr. Myers was in Luchnow during the war and got interested in India. He got private capitol in New York and set up the first village development project in India. He has several soil conservation projects which are working quite well. He also is selling farm tools and equipment to farmers in villages. Mr. Myers believed they might try some pilot projects in farm forum activities. He thought forum was desirable, but only at local level. We may get him to sponsor a project.

In the afternoon we went to the U.P. Industries store and got 3 small plates. As usual, the service was poor and the goods fair, although the store was large and the things well displayed.

For dinner, we went to a restaurant where we and Mr. Wilkey were guests of the Singhs and their families.

On Wednesday, August 22, we left from the airport at 10 a.m. for Patna via Banares. A good deal of the country was covered with water from the rains, but this seems to be normal. We arrived at 12:20 and were met by the Director of Agriculture.

We had lunch at the Flier's Club in the airport building and then left for Ranchi in a Beachcraft Queen at 2 p.m. It was a beautiful trip flying low over the country, but when we got to the hills after many tries we couldn't get through on account of the low clouds, so turned back, arriving at Patna at 3:30 p.m. The pilot called the car and we were off again at 4 p.m. for a dinner for us at Ranchi at 8 p.m. They said we could make it all right, 150 miles. We arrived at 11:30 p.m., 209 miles. It was a beautiful trip up. We stayed at the SE Railroad Hotel, with excellent accomodations and a beautiful yard. We of course missed our dinner; the Law Minister spoke in my place.

Thursday morning we were met by Dr. H. P. Srivastave, Director of Extension. He took us to the training school for BDOs. We discussed the Forum with the officer group and then spoke to the student body for about 1½ hours. At 11 we met with Mr. Narajai Sinha, Minister of Cooperation, Mr. B. C. Patel, Deputy Minister of Agriculture, Mr. B. P. Klandal, Minister of Law, Mr. B. Mandai, Project Executive Officer, and one or two others. We had excellent discussions and a dinner. They favor close cooperation between Forum and Extension, oppose Coop farming and ceilings.

At 2:20 p.m. we took the car and a jeep with several officers under Fr. H. P. Srivatava and went 25 miles south of Ranchi to see the country, and especially the Irish and sweet potatoes and a few peanuts being planted in place of rice. Rice gives about 2 maunds at 20 rupees per maund, or 40 rupees per acre. Young Irish potatoes bring 20-30R per maund on the farm and they get 10 maunds and sometimes 20 or R200 to R500 per acre.

The added cost is seed (fertilizer about 400 lbs). The sweet potatoes do not do as well, but still much above rice. The potato plantings are widespread, so it is beyond the experimental stage and doing well.

We visited a 13-acre farm very well run by a dedicated Indian as a demonstration of farming and cottage industry. It is only a year old on land not farmed before. He raises rice, bananas, honey, papaya, oil seed crops, etc. He has at least 3 oil seed presses of advanced design, powered by one bullock each. They sell the oil and use the cake for fertilizer or cattle feed. There were several looms making raw silk cloth. They were run by boys whom he pays by the yard. Three blind boys make bamboo and rattan furniture and other things. Others card, spin, etc. He has several buildings and is building more. He has an excellent dug well 42' deep x 16' to 30'. He expects to get electricity soon and put in a pump.

We then visited the cauliflower and other vegetable gardens right on the edge of Ranchi. They do very well and almost all have wells with long poles and stone on the short end and a bucket on the long end. A bucket holds maybe 2 US gallons, and in dry season it is 30 feet to water. They will irrigate 2 acres. These wells were pushed by extension. There are many of them in the country too. Out from Patna with level country we saw many pumps which would raise the water up to 4 feet.

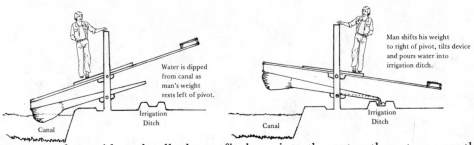

Water is dipped from canal as man's weight rests left of pivot.

Canal

Irrigation Ditch

Man shifts his weight to right of pivot, tilts device and pours water into irrigation ditch.

Canal

Irrigation Ditch

The man stands outside and pulls the outfit down into the water, then steps over the weight and lifts the outfit, dropping the water in the ditch. They said one dip raised 18 gallons of water and you could raise 1800 gallons an hour. This seems high, but the thing looks good. We had a very nice dinner this evening at the SER Hotel.

On Thursday, Mr. H. P. Srivatava came at 9 a.m. and we went six miles north to the Agricultural College just getting started. We met with a group of farmers and others, about 30 people, more than expected. I spoke; it was interpreted and we had a good many questions. They seemed quite favorable to forming the Forum. I had agreed to speak at 2 p.m. at the Ranchi College for the Law Minister, but the Minister of Agriculture was quite insistent that we have an easy trip back to Patna and leave at least by 2, so he called it off. Two boys came from the college, however, to escort me over. Srivatava was still insistent I not go.

The left front spring of the car arrived Wednesday p.m. and it was just repaired by a little after 2, and we were on our way to Patna at 2:30. We were guests of the State at the Hotel in Patna. I had to slow the driver down, as we were doing mountain road curves on two wheels in the rain, then the battery went dead as the connection came loose. We fixed that up in the rain. Then the battery bounced over into the fan. It seemed like the whole car had fallen apart. I tied the battery back with the string to his pajama pants. Next the motor started missing on one cylinder, and then on two. I cleaned up the distributor and it helped awhile, but not long. Finally, nearly dark, he got one renewed spark plug and it helped one cylinder a little, but not long. He insisted on overloading the engine at low engine speed. Of course we stopped several times for tea.

About an hour out of Patna we got a flat tire and finally got to the circuit house Patna at 11:10 p.m. I told our driver not to come in the morning. The Information officer had waited from 5 to 9 for us. The dinner was still waiting, so we had it and then bed.

By Saturday, after breakfast, our trusty driver and Pontiac were still on four cylinders out of six, so we told him to take us to the airlines office and we would go out on the bus. We got there without incident. Got on the airport bus. It was also short of cylinders, but went half-way out and ran out of gas, so they commandeered bicycle rickshaws, and we rode in glory to the airport—in pouring rain. There was our Pontiac and driver and the Information Officer. He was very nice but full of apologies.

We are now a few miles out of Delhi on IAC on time on a good flight. I figure on this trip we have driven within 40 feet of 4 million people and missed all but one. It has been an enjoyable and interesting trip and I believe a profitable one.

The ministers certainly seem to appreciate candid answers to candid questions, especially if your reasons are logical. Many of their problems are old to us. They know where they stand, but not why, in words. Our stating why seems to be very helpful to them.

We were met at the Willington Airport by a TCM car, saying to go directly to Wilkeys for tea, but we went to 55 Golf Links and got settled. Got some things at Miss Clouse's and then went to the copper shop. Had to pay R45 for packing and mailing coffee trays which cost R85.

Went to Wilkeys. We rode with them to the reception given for us and the 16 Indian farmers going to Australia. The reception was at 6 p.m. at the Chelmsford Club across from the Ministry of Food and Agriculture. Clifford Wilson, Parkers, Wilkeys, Englebretsen's, and others for TEM, the 16 farmers going to Australia, 12 or more members of Parliament, the Deshmuks, and the Forum group and Ministry officers. It was a very nice affair.

On Sunday we went to church with the Wilkies. Satwat Singh and his friend came over after lunch. Mr. Neswi, Member of Parliament who had been at the tea, came over and later the Sharmas. We had tea in the room, then they took us all through the Birla Temple and then to Mr. Neswis for tea. Soon after getting home Satwat Singh's sister and daughter came, so with packing we had a full day, leaving the hotel at 10 p.m. with Mr. Wilkie for Palan Airport and Nagpur. The plane was a DE4, 5 seats across. It got off on time and was full.

We arrived on Monday in Nagpur at 1:45 a.m. We were met by Indian Ministry folks with a car, also by Dr. Deshmuk's man in a Buick, and Sol Resnick's driver was there with a car also. We went to the Mount Hotel, Nagpur, not too good. We were met at 9 a.m. and went to see Dr. V. G. Vardya, Director of Agricultural Research and Education. Had a good talk, then went to Mr. B. G. Ghati, Director of Agriculture, and Mr. S. P. Muchram, Development Commissioner. There was a good discussion. The Development Minister definitely got behind the Forum. Had lunch at Dr. Earl Moore's, poultry specialist. At 3 p.m. went to a Coop headquarters where a number of Coops meet and met several directors. That evening Sol Reznik took the Moores and Wilkeys and us to his club for dinner.

On Tuesday, after breakfast in the hotel, we were met at ten by Dr. Deshmuk and Mr. Clifford Wilson in a big Buick and started on our trip to Amraati (some call it Amrarati). Wilkey followed with Sol in the jeep. We stopped several times, first at a school with a public address system. Three girls sang for us and Dr. Deshmuk and I addressed the group, a large one, of adults and children all sitting on the ground with legs folded under. Seems to be so easy for them and they sit so for hours. Inspected the school, then went to the next stop, a rest house where we had tea and omelet. At the next school we walked between two lines of boys who snapped into a salute as we passed. We removed our shoes and entered their temple. Inspected the garden plots, then once again they sat (in the sun) on the ground, more than 100 of them, and listened to Dr. Deshmuk and me talk. Then we drove on to Amraati, where we were established in a rest house and had our lunch. At the last school they put garlands on us. We were garlanded everywhere. Dr. Deshmuk and I talked to the students, then they rushed up to get autographs. From there we inspected the girl's home.

Dr. Deshmuk is President of the Shri Shivaji Education Society, which we visited from 3 to 3:45 p.m. This is semi-private and semi-public. Dr. Deshmuk main-

258

tains 60-odd institutions, colleges, high schools, institutes and other educational activities. From 4:45 to 5:15 we visited Ganchi Gramodyog Mandir, a cottage industry group where they spin, make soap and furniture, etc. From 5:15 to 7 we visited the Home Economics Center where they are training girls as village level workers in home economics. The facilities were simple, the gardens and vegetable and fruits were very nice. We had tea and musical entertainment, all nice, with more garlands.

From 8 to 9 p.m. was dinner, followed by entertainment at the college by the students, boys and girls. The songs were to old folk song tunes, but words about increasing farm production, cooperating with VLW, and Gran Panchayat, less drinking, more work for India, etc.

Wednesday morning, we went out about six miles to see an orphanage. This is another of Dr. Deshmuk's interests. It was private, but now government puts up half and private funds half, and Dr. Deshmuk has control of the government's half. They have improved it a good deal. Mothers have babies there, stay about 10 days, and leave them. The girls stay until they are married, the boys stay until they go to high school or get work. A public elementary school was next door.

We visited a farm operated by the society for farm boys. They have studies and also learn by doing. They have separate projects as well as work on experimental plots, a dairy, etc. They were all shined up and everyone working hard, demonstrating every phase of the operation. There seemed to be several hundred students. It was amazing the effort they had gone to to clean the place up, decorate the entrance, etc. We next went out to Reosa Village, about six miles out. It is the village of the Mahollys. The father is head man of the village, and with his son he farms 300 acres. They have electric lights, about 12 motors (small), 6 electric pumps, about 12 lights in shops, and 10 homes in the village had lights. The young Mahollys and Mrs. Deshmuk had visited us in Clarksburg several months earlier.

All statistics on farming cattle, people, lights, pumps, wells, etc. is kept very much in detail, in many villages. Tea of course.

We rode further out the same road and saw some good farming and good crops for that fair soil. These were several hundred acre farms on the best of the soil. They all belonged to money lenders who had bought them up very cheap in the 30s. Lunch.

From 3:45 to 6 p.m., meeting with Young Farmers in the college hall. It was again packed to overflowing. Farmers, some old, on seats, and the students covered the floor and a wide aisle down the middle. The President of the Young Farmers, a lawyer I believe, read quite a speech including their program. Deshmuk spoke and all was interpreted, then we had questions.

From 6:30 to 7 p.m. we watched a soccer game put on for our benefit, then had a nice dinner of 15 or so. Clifford Wilson left for Nagpur and a 3 a.m plane to Delhi.

Thursday we were up early for a 6 a.m. breakfast, then were off for Nagpur with Sol Resnick. Dr. Deshmuk and Satwat Singh went to some meetings together. Mrs. Deshmuk was off for Bombay to sell savings bonds.

We arrived in Nagpur at 9, and left at 10:35 for Hydrabad in a DC3. The landscape for 150 miles north of Hydrabad is covered with small reservoirs. These have been there larger or smaller since the Mogul days.

Arrived at 12:15 and were met in rain by Schisman Reddy, Vice President of Farm Union, and others. Taken to the Ritz Hotel and given the room of the Princess, the wife of the youngest son of the Nizam of Hydrabad, said to be the richest man in the world. The hotel formerly was the son's palace; the prince now lives in a much more modest home. The hotel is on top of a hill in town and is very nice, indeed, a palace. Our bedroom was very large and also the bathroom. The tub and floor all tile with a tile drain to catch the water overflow, though the only means of filling it was three buckets for bringing in hot water. No scales were really needed as there was a large mirror in the right front and rear corners so you could easily see how you were doing. The Nizam lives in a big palace on a hill 1½ miles from here. He is still Governor of Hydrabad State until October 1, when Hydrabad State will disappear.

Went out about 20 miles to see some fertilizer and cover crop work. When the reservoirs are dry, people collect the silt deposit of heavy black clay soil and spread it like fertilizer. Reddy, Vice President of Union, went with us. He is an able fellow, farms several hundred acres. The Union has 6000 members, R5 per year dues, try to have 20 members from each village. Reddy sells subscriptions to a monthly magazine put out by them for R5 and that is about all of the program. He feels the planning comissions should consciously plan higher production per man instead of higher production per acre.

Went to the Schumans for dinner, played games until 9 p.m., then ate and was shown some excellent pictures of work with fertilizer, etc.

Friday, August 31, we met in lobby and discussed organization with Mr. Ragbotham Reddy. Went out to Training Center and then to the Research Station and spoke from 11:20 to 12:20 to room full of research men and faculty from other institutes nearby. Talked and wrote in p.m. At 7 p.m. went to Reddy's house. He had a fine group of 35 or so farmers and others leaders in. We discussed Farm Bureau and farm organization for 1½ hours, then had an excellent Indian meal, after which we talked in small groups until 10:30 p.m. and came home.

Saturday was a fine morning. We went out to visit seven villages with the BDO and some of his men. First was Uppal Village, where the villagers were building a new school for the first seven grades. They had a lot of children there to meet us and they seemed very enthusiastic. One of the leaders swore he would not shave until the school was finished They also had a group of 12 new houses in the village, the block put up R300 each and the people the rest for each house. They had a good Panchayat meeting place, a radio etc; batteries dead, but getting new one. The spirit was excellent, garlands, songs, dances, and all.

One of the villages doing well with new houses was Pardi Colony. The people listed as ex-criminals seemed to be doing very well. In Kushaiguda Hamlet of Khapra they had a meeting place and veterinary center. They delivered milk into Hydrabad; this was mostly range land. Fifty boys and thirty girls were in school. The VLWs and all were doing well. Farmers were favorable to organization. The women mix a paste of cowdung and sand and then spread it over the floor of the front porch and the rooms in the house. This makes a hard smooth floor easy to clean and they say sanitary. After the house is cleaned up they draw a design on the ground in front of the house with a white lime or something. This signifies the house is clean and ready for visitors. For special reasons they paint figures or designs on the front walls.

Sunday, September 2, the Shumans took us to the airport and we got off at 12:50 for Madras, arriving at 2:50. We were met by Mr. William Walker, commercial consultant, Mr. S. K. Swami, who lives 400 miles south of Madras and is secretary for the Farmer's Forum there. Stayed at the Ritz Hotel, very nice, suite on 2nd floor overlooking Bay of Bengal. We checked in and took a walk through a fishing village to the beach. It was dirty, but the beach fine and lined with picturesque fish-boats. Followed by many kids. Walker and Swami took us to the government house to meet a group of farmers and agricultural folks and the Minister of Agriculture. I spoke to the group and had some questions but there were too many officials with group for good discussion. After a little ride around Madras, which was very nice and relatively clean, we went to dinner with the three home economics women, Miss Armstrong, Miss Logan, and Dr. Gassett. All were helping organize the home economics work in five colleges in Madras. They were all part of the Tennessee University team. It was very nice.

Monday, we had breakfast in the room and left at 7 a.m. for Chunampet, about 70 miles south of Madras. This was a beautifully developed large landholding, apparently two brothers owned it. One is operating the farm. Their names were C. Rama Swami and Muthukumara Swami. Most of the land had been turned over to the tenants and workers. That was not too well farmed. He was developing a beautiful 20-acre garden, trees, etc. with the center nicely laid out. The rice was Japanese method and he expected about two tons per acre with fertilizer and all. He used green manure compost pits. He hired lots of his old workers for 7 hours a day at 9 annas for men = 11½¢ for 7 hours; 7 annas for women = 9¢; 4 annas for children = 5¢. He could not hire all who wanted to work. There is more unemployment he says now than two years ago.

We had lunch in the village home of the Swamis. They had quite a dairy by the house, Red Sindis and Buffalo mostly. This is where we first drank milk directly out of a cocoanut.

On the way back we stopped at village Vallipuram, saw some green manuring, and a Arawheel at work on a Fordson in a rice paddy. On arrival in Madras we went to Fort St. George, an old English base on the waterfront, and met with Shri M.E.S. Raghava Chari, Additional Development Commissioner Rural Education and Training. Mr. Dasican, a farmer south of Madras, who was at the IFAP in Mexico City, came in. He is also on the Farm Forum Council. He invited us to dinner at the Cosmopolitan Club. We went but should have eaten at the Ritz. We drove about the city a little before dinner and thought it looked very nice. On returning to the hotel we met Miss Alta F. Thomas, Home Economics Advisor, Madras. She seemed very capable.

Tuesday, we left for Bangalore. The country below us got rougher with some hills and the land not the best. There were still lots of tanks but most of them dry, as the rains were very short. Nearer Bangalore the villages were more orderly, the streets straight, the houses better. This was apparent also after we got on the ground. We were met at the airport by quite a group with immense garlands. They were tube roses with three oranges in each, very heavy, and perfumed the room all the time we were there in the West End Hotel.

Our principal Indian host was Mr. B. Dasappa, Deputy Director of Agriculture, former president of the college and other government positions. We stayed at the West End Hotel, apparently an old English hotel, large, sprawling, with good meals.

Mr. and Mrs. Gilbert R. Muhr, the soil testing advisor, spent a good deal of time with us in addition to having tea for us Monday evening; they are fine people who came recently. Mr S. V. Haredas, Secretary of Mysore Agricultural Experiment Union, accompanied us and was very nice but did not take the lead. We drove out to the Agricultural College at Hibbal where I spoke to the students and faculty.

The city is 3000 feet elevation, the widest streets and cleanest of any we have seen. A delightful climate and place to live. We saw some of the city and visited the College and other places. At 2 we met the Minister of Agriculture and the members of the Mysore Agriculture and Experimental Union. This group is 35 years old, set up by Dr. Coleman, a Canadian and head of the college, made up of college folks and farmers. They seem to be doing a fine job, the best in India so far as I know. They have 4500 members in Mysore. Discussion after talk was good about 25 farmers there. Went to Muhrs for tea with 25-30 people.

Wednesday we left at 8 a.m. in two cars going south. Stopped at a good agricultural experiment farm on the way. Breeding better silk worms, etc. At 10:30 a.m. arrived at Mandya and training center for village level workers. Made several stops. Had lunch at the Sugar Company Rest House Mandya; it was a very fine rest house. In p.m. drove on to the Ryots Multipurpose Cooperative Society, Ltd. Mandya. They had a fine new building for farm supply, a good board room, a big quonset warehouse for fertilizer storage and sale, and a long brick building of individual go-downs for the members to store grain or other products to hold for a better price. The Coop sells it but in individual lots. Had a good meeting here with the members.

We went on to Mysore, a beautiful city. On the way we passed through a large irrigated area. Soil of a sort of red, not too fancy looking, but the sugar cane was the best we have seen and other crops very good lots of rice well farmed, 4000 lbs/acre.

In Mysore we met the Farmers Agriculture and Experiment Union and had a good discussion. They will join Forum. We then went to the reservoir, lake, and dam and the gardens below it. We waited for 7:30 for them to turn on the lights in the gardens and got home about 11:30. The lights were beautiful in the garden.

On Thursday we went out about 6 miles to visit the farm of B. K. Narayana Rao, an IFYE who was in the States in '53. The farm was 60 acres. A very nice house on the place. His mother lived with him, unmarried. He had citrus groves, mango, bananas, cocoanut, beetlenut, hybrid corn, coffee, rice, sugarcane, Pan leaves, and several other crops. The place was farmed little if any when he took it, some was swampy. He had three wells. He was dressed in a plaid shirt, blue jeans, and U.S. work shoes. We had a very delightful tea with excellent sweets, etc. He was a fine young man anxious to help farming and farmers.

We then visited a couple of government farms; the orchards were poor. Mr. and Mrs. Muhr took us to the public market and the gardens and then we all went out to the college at Hibbal where I spoke to the student body and faculty. This was a pleasant occasion. We got back just in time to go to tea and dinner with Mr. Anahonca Behr. We went first to the home of Mrs. Kitchell, wife of the head of the Massey-Ferguson Harris Co. for tea and then to the Bangalore Club for dinner. The

Club and dinner were both nice. Mr. and Mrs. Cox of the company were also present. They are having a great deal of trouble training mechanics even though they maintain a school and farm. One dealer has all of north India and they have south India.

They pay R350 per month for good salesmen prospects, but they claim they have never gotten but one good one. The salesmen will not crank a tractor or do any work on it—that is a helpers job. Salesmen do not perspire or get dirty. They say if anything happens to Nehru or the country goes far to the left, the Army is ready to take over.

We left Bangalore at 7 a.m. on Friday, stopped at Hydrabad, Nagpur for lunch, and arrived New Delhi at 3 p.m.

On Saturday, September 8, Mr. Sharma picked me up and we went to the Delhi State FF meeting It was out by the tall minaret outside Delhi. They had quite an exhibit of equipment, seeds, sanitation, cottage industries, etc. The meeting was in a large tent with at least 300 present.

Along with all the rest on the platform, I sat on the floor on bolsters. Guests sat on chairs on each side of the platform. The women all sat on the ground to the left front, the delegates on the ground to the right front, and all the rest filled the tent sitting. There was a tent in which they ate. It was a two-day meeting, speeches in the morning, group meetings in the afternoon, entertainment at night, and groups and resolutions the second day. I only stayed the first morning Dr. Deshmuk and I gave the talks aside from welcome etc., then two others spoke at some length.

On Sunday we went with Dr. Deshmuk to the governing body meeting of the Forum. The discussion was very general and very free. After discussion Lal Singh or someone would say "This is the way it should be," and if the Chair agreed they went to the next subject. No vote was taken during the several days of the conference. Mrs. Shah MP was present, also Maharani of Patiala. She was present as a farmer and a sponsor and heavy contributor to YP department.

Monday the Forum met in plenary session. Dr. Deshmuk spoke, Mr. Vains message was read. The Minister of Defense spoke, then I did. It was well-received. We went to the picture show in the evening in the post-grad dormitory of Pusa Institute.

On Tuesday the Forum met in sections. The discussions were very good but no votes. I attended all the sessions. Had lunch in the tent on copper trays, native food OK but hot. Attended the Y.P. sessions and spoke in PM. Very good meeting. We went to 5 o'clock tea at the Claridge Hotel with the former Chief Minister of PEPSU, his family and a few friends. I asked who was going to pay for the new capitol city of PEPSU, the new capitol of the state. They borrowed the money from the government of India, but no one ever expected to pay it back.

On Wednesday the Farm Forum Council finished about 1 p.m. I looked over machinery exhibit and Central Tractor Agency until 3:15 p.m., then went to TEM and got Davis to go to Dr. Deshmuk's office at 4 p.m. He wanted a good deal of financial help for Forum.

On Thursday and Friday I cleaned up some mail, went over expense accounts, travel orders, arranged for next trip, went to Forum and started on report. Wrote suggested schedule for 20 farm leaders in U.S. Visited Dr Deshmuk with Dr. Parker in relation to aid to Forum. Went to Anderson's Agricultural Attache's for dinner for 10 IFYEs from U.S. and Gloria Ward from California, Los Angeles County. The IFYEs sang and made a very good showing. Several Indian IFYEs were present.

Saturday, September 15. I took purchases to the Chinaman's to be packed and sent home, packed up rest of things to go to Miss Clouse. Spent the p.m. in the Forum office going over trip and future of Forum.

Sunday we went to church with the Davises. Most of the IFYEs were there, getting on well. Dr. Parker came over to discuss letter from Washington re aid to Forum. In the evening went to a very nice dinner given by Dr. Deshmuk at the Chelmsford Club for us, Dr. Parker, S. K. Dey, Dr. Roy. We were entertained by a very clever magician after dinner.

We left Delhi airport at 8:40 a.m., Monday, with Mr. and Mrs. Sharma there to see us off. Arrived Jaipur at 9:40. We were met by V. N. Kak and Ram Singh, Secretary of Rajasthan Farmers Forum. They took us to the New Hotel out on the edge of town. As we approached, there was a group of women sitting on the ground in the street near the hotel entrance. They had heavy hammers breaking big rocks into little ones for the roadbed.

We thought the food there was excellent, so I asked the man waiter who did the cooking in the kitchen. He came right back, "Why, men, of course. Women can't do hard work like that." We wondered.

Most of the household help is men. Men as cooks, houseboys. Once a houseboy, always a houseboy. Women do much of the washing, laundry, hoeing, cultivating, harvest, all that.

We were sent with a guide to see the city palace of the Maharaja in the morning. He took us all though it and it was very wonderful. A tremendous armory, very beautiful . The rug room was filled with old rugs on the floor, hung on the wall, and a great many piled on a central table. This was where they held the banquet for Bulganan of USSR. It was about 80 x 120 feet in size. The outside audience hall was also quite beautiful, the old pictures were interesting. The gates to the old city are quite beautifully painted and the buildings of the main streets at least are all pink. They call it the Paris of Asia. We took several pictures in the palace and in town. We also visited the astronomical garden outside the city palace, sun dials, instruments to determine longitude, latitude, and many other astronomical problems.

In the afternoon Ram Singh took us to a village to see the block printing on homespun cotton. Here you actually saw what had been a large, beautifully constructed town, prosperous on production of hand-blocked homespun cotton yardage and hand-made paper sold around the world. Then with the coming of the industrial age the industrial weavers were put out of business. Many of the people now work at these things. It was like looking at history before your eyes to see people again trying to compete and revive an old industry. We purchased several pieces. We also saw the paper making, both smooth and blotter. We went to the cottage industry emporium in Jaipur and got some toys and shoes for the children.

On Tuesday Mr. Ram Singh took us out at 8 a.m. to see villages west of Jaipur on the Bombay Road. We stopped at a very poor one, took a picture of the oxcart, well, etc. We then met a VLW who wanted us to see a good village in his district, so we went west again a little way and then had to walk a half-mile or so south over

264

a new stone road the villagers were building. We first came to the new well they were just finishing up. They seemed quite pleased with it. Then we went to the shrine and met the home economics village-level worker. She started an Ember Charkha, spinning wheel. Then other women started theirs and then the kids until ten or so were going. There were several boys, one boy was especially good. The VLW woman then started a sewing machine and the children sang songs for us. We of course had tea. Then the children danced and sang some more.

The village level worker knew everyone by name and introduced us to each of them as we met. One man brought out his organ. I expect about 10" deep 14" wide and 24" long, the kind made famous by missionaries. He played for the dances and songs. It was hot and humid and two men stood behind Bella with palm-leaf fans to cool her off. Here the untouchables were more prominent because they stood on the outside edge and enjoyed the party, but they would not really enter in. A man came by with his camel and Bella mounted for a ride. I am sure it was not all as planned, but those 100 or so people had the best laugh in years, including me. The young man and lady, village level workers in that village, treated all the people as equals and the effect was dramatic.

We went to the shrine and were given a leaf like an alfalfa leaf off the altar. It was blessed and then we ate the leaves. We visited the larger shrine and by this time they had a bullock cart all ready to take us back to the car. The bullocks were watered at the well which had a good concrete cattle water trough, and then on our way. We surely felt honored and privileged to have had the pleasure of those hours. The village level worker was Chiter Mal Sharma, CD Block, Sangance, village Mahapura. At 2 p.m. the block officer came and took me (Bella stayed home) to see the village work east of Jaipur. We saw new roads, a village of 24 houses which had been flooded out and the houses destroyed. It was moved 100 yards or so onto a hill and a new village planned, new well, school, playgrounds, and they were all to build new houses, all with a good deal of government aid. This was surely too much government and the relations between officers and people was not good. I was introduced to the head man of the village but no one else.

We saw several new schools, wells, latrines, and other works and had tea. At one school of two men teachers, the spirit was good and the teachers very enthusiastic. They put on calisthenics drill with two short sticks connected by chains carrying metal discs which made quite a bit of noise.

There was lots of work on the part of officials but little real cooperation with people and I felt much of it would not soon be used. Many villages had pumps, latrines, and other improvements finished. We also went to a cattle-breeding farm. There was too much building for the cattle and not used. There was artificial insemination station and castrating equipment, but little use of either. We also went to a government grass farm. It was too new to judge. On return Ram Singh was ready for a ride around the city and a walk in the parkway, and then dinner and bed.

On Wednesday, September 19, a guide arrived at 8 a.m. to take us sightseeing to the old fort and castle at Amer 8 miles north of Jaipur. The trip out was interesting, passing many of the old houses, temples, and burning ghats of the Maharaja and the Zamandars, including the water palace in the lake from which the Maharaja shot ducks. We walked up the hill to the palace and in the courtyard we rode the elephant.

There is quite a temple in the palace and they offer up a goat every day, killing it in the courtyard and on special occasions a bullock. People offered food. It was blessed on the altar, some left on the altar and some returned. An orange spot was then placed on each forehead.

This palace was the one used before the city palace was built. It had some very fine marble carving and the rooms with the walls and ceilings covered with small convex mirrors were very interesting and fine. They say there are many tigers in the hills about the palace now.

We then went back to Jaipur and as we got to the edge of town went to the tombs built for the Maharajas. As we approached the place a lot of vultures swooped down on a donkey laying by the roadside. As we entered the gate we heard a shot on the hill. The guide said it was the people scaring off the tiger which had just killed the donkey. He claimed they often found tigers asleep in recesses around the edge of the enclosure when they came in in the morning. It is illegal to kill them. If one is reported as bad, it is the responsibility of the Maharaja to send his sons or friends or relatives out to shoot it.

We then went to the museum in town and saw that. At 4 p.m. Ram Singh came and we went to see the Director of Agriculture Samarth Raj and all his assistants. Had an excellent discussion of Forum, etc. Then we went to the V.N. Kak farm. He had quite a group there. Saw his dogs, chickens, cows, all kinds of fruits, etc. All appeared to be playthings.

Back at the hotel, the Minister of Development and Agriculture Ram Miwas Mirdna came and we discussed irrigation changes and Forum for over an hour, until 9:30, then had dinner. Jaipur was full of color. The streets are wide, the people looked pretty good.

Thursday, Ram Singh and his wife came at 7:15 a.m. She went off to college at 7:30. We picked up Kak, stopped at a cattle breeding farm started by a disciple of Ghandis, and on to the airport, where Ram Singh saw us off. Singh is an attorney about 33 years old but was raised in a village and seems to have a very sincere interest in the welfare of village people. He gets on very well with them. Believe he might well go to U.S.

Left Jaipur at 10 a.m. Stopped at Jodphur about 175 miles south of west. This is dry land farming but most of the land appears to be planted. It is old Mogul country with castles and forts on the hills. Was the world center of polo at one time and produced jodphurs. Then flew west of south about 220 miles to Ahmedabad, flying over Mt. Abu. I was surprised at the number of flowing rivers. We then flew 135 miles south of west to Rajkot.

We were met at the airport by Mr. Shah, Director of Agriculture, and B. J. Trivedi, an IFYE, who was in the U.S. in 1954. They took us to the guest house which was the former home of the Nabob and we had his old room assigned to us as guests. The bedroom was 20' x 40' with dressing rooms 12 x 12 and 12 x 20, and bathrooms 12 x 16 off each dressing room. There were 17 chairs, 2 davenports, 4 ceiling fans and 1 floor fan.

We went 60 or 70 miles south to Junagadh, about 50 miles from the Arabian Sea. The principal crop was groundnuts and they were beautiful, some irrigated, most dry-farmed, but we thought the best farming we have seen anywhere unless Mysore.

We talked to the students, boys and girls, at this training center which was an old Raja's house. Had tea and then went to the experimental farm. This was recently forest. It is headed by Dr. Z. H. Patel, a very active gentleman of about retirement age. He has cleared 1200 acres and planted 800 acres, getting ready to work. Has good reservoirs and pumps. Looks like a well-handled layout. Getting dark, so we set out for Rajkot arriving at 9:30 p.m.

Friday we left at 7:30 for Jamnagan 60 miles northwest, six miles from the Gulf of Kutch. Arrived at 9:20 a.m., assigned a room in rest house, old Raja's place. Met J. L. Jobanputra, the Collector of Jamnagan, had another breakfast and set out for a subsidized farm out several miles.

This is a sanitarium and farm set up by a religious sect of Hindus by the present leaders grandfather. They get a subsidy from government to do research and demonstration planting. It seems to be very well run. We looked over the place, rice, peanuts, gowar, corn, millet, etc., and then returned to the building porch to talk to 60 farmers gathered there for the occasion. It went well and on completion they presented me with a Buddha and Bella with a stole, very nice. I should say on our arrival they were all lined up in two columns. A lady stepped out and put garlands on us and then a spot of red paint and then threw rose petals all over us. They say this is getting the works.

After the discussion we went to the dining room, all sat against the wall. We had big brass trays in front of us with three brass bowls on each and a bath towel to put over our knees and use as a napkin. This was a game. Waiters came by with a large bowl of food and slap a handful on your plate, followed by another waiter doing the same. Finally we refused more food, so they would act like they were looking the other way, get about two steps past you, then slap another handful onto your plate before you could resist. Most of the folks eat on banana leaves with a bowl only for soup and no utensils.

They brought on at least a dozen foods, most of it good, some too hot of course. They ate everything including the soup with their fingers, or they say hands. This is several days later and we are still OK.

At about 1 p.m. the Collector took us to see the Maharaja, His Highness' farm, Saheb of Nawanagar in Jamnagar. He is now equivalent to governor of the state. He was in World Wars I and II. He and the HH of Patiola were on the British War Council. He was Indian delegate to U.S. in 49-50. Looked about my age but fat. Seemed to know all details of our trip and a great deal about farming. Said he wanted us to see ordinary faming as it is, not just show places. Showed us his art, etc., accumulations. I told him that we had observed that people looked better, seemed more confident and roads and phones were better in the old princely states than in the English-ruled areas. He said, Well we had the English breathing down our necks all the time and we had to show them we could do it better.

Left at 2:30 on the road back to Rajkot, but turned off to right to visit the farm of Trivedi, the IFYE. It is an excellent farm 22 acres and they have another of 30 acres. They had fine rice, millet, sugarcane, and citrus trees and groundnuts. Tea here of course and toasted green peanuts. They were good.

We then went to a new agricultural general college out in the country at Alia-bada. Dr. D. R. Mankad was president. We met a high-school girl from Massachusetts there. She was barefoot and working with the other women. She said it was a great experience for her, and I believe it was. We went to the farm and had another discussion and tea and left for Rajkot about 6:30 p.m.

The area north of Rajkot was not as good as south in soil or rainfall, but the farms are larger, about 40-50 acres. HH said they have lots of stock. The people look very alert and confident. The men's costumes are like Bulgarians, very colorful. Some men had three earrings in each ear.

Saturday, September 22, met at 7:30 by Dr. C. C. Shah, Joint Director of Agriculture for Rajkot, and Trevedi, to be taken to airport. Dr. B. S. Kadam, Director of Agriculture for Rajkot, also came over and went with us. We certainly enjoyed that Rajkot visit very much.

We flew back to Ahmedabad, met by Emil Jhaveri, Secretary Gujarat, and Kishah Somay, a progressive farmer associated with the Forum. He was also an IFYE. We went to Jhaveri's 80-acre farm. It is his uncle's, plus father, self, and brother. They have been housing and feeding dairy cattle for about 30 years. There are 250 buffaloes and 250 cows. Jhaveris furnish space, fodder, and concentrate, then take the milk to their plant in Ahmedabad, put it in smaller milk cans and have boys deliver on bicycles around town at 10 annas per quart (12½¢). The 38 families own the cattle and are paid on a cooperative basis. There are 80 families on the place. They of course have lots of manure and the crops show the influence of it. They were excellent.

Most manure is used for cooking, heating or building walls. The uncle cooks on a gas burner in a kitchen run by gas developed in an outside tank from putting in about 25 pounds of manure a day. They say it is practically trouble-free.

We went to I. B. Model Farm about 1200 acres owned by a Bombay businessman. It is very well run. He uses 40 pair of bullocks and 3 tractors. His citrus was the best I have seen.

At 2:30 we went to the office of Krishak Samaj on Panhor Napa, second floor in city. It was a spacious office with about 10 desks set around. They are sloping and about 10 inches off the floor. A lawyer comes in weekly to advise members. About six pressmen were there for a press conference, went well.

Left at 3:45 for Dehgam Community development center in the jeep. They said it would take 20 minutes, but we arrived at Printia just at 5 p.m. and it has just started to pour rain. I was soaked. A crowd was still there huddled wherever possible. They said 200 women, 300 men, and lots of children were there from 4 p.m. in the rain. They had dances, talks, songs, quite a program lined up, but we got on a porch, received many garlands, said a few words, and got on our way, still pouring and roads full of water.

Passed up B. F. Model Farm where they had a cattle show and program and 500 people for us, also passed up Chandrala where they had a crowd and program.

Arrived at Dabhoda Village about 6:15. They have a very nice hall, but there were few people there on account of the rain. The women had a very nice handiwork show. We visited it and the veterinary center. Neat and nice. The castrator was the main equipment, but not used. It was about 7 p.m. before our other cars got in and the crowd showed up. Eight girls about 16-18 came in for a dance. Then a group of 15 children with a picture of Nehru and sang a song of his love of children and the country. This was the only time when Nehru was featured. Next a group of 16 girls, 8 in village women costume and 8 in village men, put on quite a dance. Some sang, followed by a speech by the BDO, then Jhaviri, then mine, interpreted. This of course all started with many fine garlands and bouquets and tea.

We got off about 8 p.m., rain pouring, roads full of water, stuck several times and got to the rest house about 9:20 p.m. Bella did not go, fortunately. They said that in 1954-5 the Bombay State was top state in development work and this block judged the best in the state. Several people came up with several roses as individual gifts. At the end they presented me with a design of birds made by one of the women from cardamom seed.

Sunday Jhaveri picked me up at 9 a.m. It had rained all night but cleared in the a.m. His car had skidded coming in and knocked in the left rear fender. We went to his friends house and got his car and the friend, his wife, and sister. Jhaveri, Bella and I went sight-seeing to the university, then back to their house for tea and saw her saris, part of the wedding dowry, many of them very beautiful. We went to Harijan Ashram; across the river on the bank is the home of Gandhi. It is simple with the home offices, guest houses, cow barns, cottage industry, etc. Here the resistance movement was planned.

Jhaveri lived on the grounds for 6-8 months with his family as his father was a follower of Ghandi and spent some time in jail. His uncle had been in charge of the cattle there. Ghandi raised the cattle only for bullocks, but now they raise them for milk too, but will have nothing to do with buffalo. The place, maybe 10 acres, is well kept up and lived on by his followers.

We then went to the Gomtipur Tower which is a mosque minaret. If you climb to the top and shake it you can feel it shake. It is noticeable and remarkable, but not enough to be easily measurable. Got back to circuit house about 1 p.m., had soup and dessert, and I went out with the group to a Krishak Samaj seminar and farm at Vatwa. There was a fine group of 75 or so farmers there, one woman. They put on the most garlands and bouquets I have ever had. They were above my ears and eyes. The garlands filled a bushel basket besides the big bouquets. They were beautiful; they handed me a list of questions about U.S. agriculture to answer.

Ahmedabad is a cotton mill town of about 900,000 people. The women at Dabhoda were the most alert and like U.S. girls of any we have seen. The farmers seminar at Vatwa was one of the best groups of farmers, the I. B. Model Farm was excellent, as was Jhaveri's, but still I did not feel the whole area was up either in farming or looks of the people. It may have been me who was off. Jhaveri did a fine job of caring for us. We caught the 5:05 p.m. train for Anand. At the guest house we met Mr. Patel and others. We had tea, dinner, and went to bed.

Monday, September 24, we left the guest house at 6 a.m. with the manager of the dairy Coop to visit two villages and see the women bring in the milk to the collection centers. They bring it in in brass bowls, pour it into a 1-pint or ½-pint brass measure sitting on a larger pan with a spout going to the 5-gallon cans. The receiver puts two fingers down in the cup of milk to see if he thinks it is watered; if so he takes a sample for test.

Each one brings a record book which the bookkeeper fills in and the paymaster pays each one 3 annas (3¾¢) per pint for the milk. At the end of the year they get a bonus on any savings of the Coop. It is then picked up by truck or by a tractor and trailer and hauled to the central plant. The Coop has 84 pick-up stations.

They have a fine new modern plant where they pasturize, cool, make butter, Ghee, and dry skim milk. The fresh milk is sent to the Arrey plant in Bombay by rail twice a day to be bottled and sold. The Coop sells to Arrey at about 4 annas a pound or 10¢ a quart. It is pasteurized again in Bombay.

In the p.m. we visited the Institute dairy and then the main agricultural building. This all well done. For dinner we had company, two Patels and Mr. and Mrs. Chillson and son. He is Kansas Dairy Specialist. We talked Farm Forum and India until 10 p.m.

On Tuesday, Bella went out with Mrs. Chillson. I visited the fields and outside departments of the Institute with Dr. Patel. He went to the U.S. in 1920 as a student, stayed 6 or 8 years I believe, knows most of the U.S. and gets a great kick out of it. He is an excellent host and this has been the most restful and easiest stop so far.

Dr. M. D. Patel, Director of the Institute, is in Rome, Italy, at a World Dairy Conference. I understand we have his cook and the meals are excellent, as well as the whole management.

Tobacco is the big money crop here, though I have seen the best sugar cane here I have seen anywhere, but it is mostly sold as candy or to make juice in town.

The Institute here is private, started with donations and gets a specific grant from Bombay State for the college work and some other grants, but it is run by a board of trustees independent of government and each of ten departments have their own land, about 100 acres each. They farm it, carry on research, and demonstrations, but are also expected to show a profit to run the Institute and build any new buildings they may want. All the departments show good profits.

At 3 p.m. we left for Chakalashi Village 9 miles northwest of here and arrived at 4 p.m. They had a big crowd, a welcome sign, and an arch put up for the occasion, etc. The buildings were excellent. They are starting a new 28-room school building. The milk Coop society has a two-story receiving station with the board room upstairs. They have a potato Coop and are considering a cold storage plant. They have a kindergarten and library building with an assembly hall and a 4-5 storey clock tower. Water is piped to a series of stations where women gather to fill their jugs. They hope to pipe water to the houses as soon as they can build a sewer system.

Dairy and tobacco seem to furnish the money. We gathered in the hall and had songs and dances. Welcome. I spoke, etc. Garlands. The woman worker was an outstanding looking young woman. The girls were at least equal to the best we have seen. The woman had a good handwork exhibit. We had tea.

This village is surely ready for a Forum. Got back about 7 and had dinner at Patels. Daisy Patel, Chillisons, and Mrs. Patel, wife of the director, were there. It was a regular Indian dinner.

Wednesday, September 26, at 8:30 a.m. we went to a private college of 3000 students, counting grades. It was started about 1947 by an engineer. They got farmers and other land owners to give them 800 acres of land. The people gave land and for every acre given they gave back a lot in the town site, the lot worth more than the acre, and the college is going. They have fine buildings, laboratories, hostels, etc.

They also have good foundries and machine shop. They make all their own sewer and waterpipe, brass faucets, locks, hinges, furniture, terrazza tile flooring, bricks, concrete work and all. They sell large orders of concrete pipe, sewer pipe, tile, etc., and just have a large order for 30-foot prestressed concrete power poles. The going price was R150; they bid R89. They plan and are building part of a 40-acre concrete plant. They expect to profit first on the concrete pole contract, and then at concrete RR ties and other items so they can employ a large group and make a profit. They have fine labor housing and all get free education for their families through college.

The professors are mostly retired from private industry and draw little salary. The tuition including hostel is about R1500 per year or R4500 for three years. We had lunch here at this college and a discussion after. This is the best thing I have seen in India, no government aid of any sort. Went back to the Girand Agricultural Institute and spoke to the student body and then to a faculty tea with more discussion. A group then came over for dinner at the guest house and we got off for Bombay at 11 p.m. in an air-conditioned sleeper for two. Upper and lower, one bed roll with extra sheet and pillow.

Thursday, arrived Bombay at 7:30 a.m. We were met by Reserve Bank officer and car and Anil Jhaveri. Stayed at Ambassador Hotel. Did a little sightseeing in Bombay, then went to lunch at the Reserve Bank with S. C. Ryan, Prof. D. G. Karvi, and Roy Sillers, Agricultural Officer with U.S. Consulate. Had a good discussion. Karvi particularly thinks things are going well. Ryan more realistic.

Went to consulate and visited with Turner, U.S. Consul. Then a meeting at 4 p.m. with B. S. Hirey, Minister of Agriculture. The Director was for the forum but the minister feared it politically. Director took us to Captain Mohite, Development Commissioner. He is virile; has sent a very good directive out to all workers to aid the Forum. He was at the Delhi meeting. Went to Roy Sellers, Agric. Officer, for dinner. Mr. B. L. Sethi who visited us in California is now Secretary of the Central Cotton Control Committee; he was present as was Jhaveri, Director of Mill Cotton Research Institute, several others. Good evening.

Friday at 8 a.m. went to Arrey Dairy Colony with Sellers and Jhaveri. Milking 400 buffalo per unit and 30 odd units over 12,000 head, 23,000 plus head counting dry stuff. Tone (lowfat) milk now 3%. Went to see village industry school where they make hides and shoes, soap, matches, furniture, spun and woven goods. At Jhaveri's home for tea, they gave me birds and Bella a handbag; fine folks.

We went to dinner with B. B. Patel, brother-in-law of Dinesh Patel of Davis, at the home of his mother, a nice apartment on Malibar Hill next to a large clubhouse. Dinesh's father had been to Africa on a trip. He has cotton gins and business there. He was still in Karachi on his way home.

Saturday, Sepatmber 29, we got up at 3:20 to get the 6 a.m. plane for Belgaum. We were met by Shri T. R. Neswi, member of parliament, S. G. Futani, deputy director of agriculture, and Dharwar, division secretary of the Farmers Forum.

In late morning we went to Gungargatti, Taluka Dharivar Community Plantation, and grassland and tank improvement. This was open community pasture on a hillside. The government assigned it to a group of farmers, who planted it to mangoes, forest trees, and grass, and were building a tank to get water for the trees. They all came around and I talked Forum for a while. They keep a watchman on the place to keep stock out, and cut the grass by hand, a good project. We then saw the Agricultural College at Dharwar, with very good buildings and a fine plant. The Principal asked me to encourage boys to stay on the farm. The farm is making money; he is a hard worker.

A "sentimental voyage" and a lunch stop in India.

We had lunch at Dharwar Gymakhana Club as guests of Mr. and Mrs. Sathi, Collector of Charwar District. This couple was, I believe, the best civil servants we met in their interest in the welfare of farm people. Under Indian civil service one advances in grade but you may be assigned to any type of work. They were assigned to leave soon for Bombay clerical work. It is the English idea for a civil servant to be trained in all lines of work rather than to enter a specialized line of work and rise in rank within that specialty. Very few civil servants ever develop a close relationship with rural problems and needs. Sathi is a real live wire, and his wife is also very active in social village work.

From 2:30-3 we visited the agricultural museum in Dharwar. Sathi is President of this farm group who operate a museum. It was an old building used in the war. It has been rehabilitated with good gardens and an excellent agricultural exhibit. Farmers can then buy in the warehouse behind the museum, fertilizer, good seed, sprays and spray equipment, etc. They can get credit also if needed. They expect to build a hostel and meeting place for farmers next to it and clear out a big square in front of the building.

We also visited the agricultural research station and poultry farm at Charwar; well run. The cotton work here looked good.

It is difficult to really understand another religion. In India some people wear gauze cloth over their mouth so they will not inhale and kill a gnat or other insect. Most will not eat beef, some will eat mutton, more will eat poultry. Many will not eat eggs as it will take a life. At every poultry station we visited they told how people would watch for days to see if the hens and roosters ran together, then they would usually leave satisfied that it was all right to eat eggs.

In '49 the cattle had free run and there were may cattle on the city streets. Traffic moved around them and drivers were more protective of the cattle than of people. There were, I thought, fewer cattle in '54 and '56. Hindu police would not disturb them, but Moslem and Sikh police would remove some of them at night.

From 4-5 p.m. visited Navalur Community Development Block. They had a fine

272

handwork and cattle exhibit here. We bought and have the blankets from the big pair of bullocks. Spoke here to a large gathering of farmers and then Sathi took us in the jeep to see the development in the village, school, Panchalat building, children's playground, and many other improvements to include moving the village to other side of improvements as new houses are built. We then looked at some gowar planted Japanese cultivation style. They claimed four times the yield. It looked fine.

Stopped at Rayapur afforestation demonstration on a hillside. They dug trenches and planted forest trees. These were staggered on the hillside x x x x x / x x x x x and seemed to be doing well. Livestock are kept out by a cactus fence and a watchman.

From 6 to 6:20 we visited the Hubli agricultural produce market committee. They have warehouses, offices, cattle sheds, etc. The committee is set up by law covering the district. They started handling cotton and now include grains and about all products. Growers in the district must sell through them. On the committee are growers, government, brokers, etc. It is fairly old and seems to be quite successful. We went to Neswi's house in Hubli, then to Taluka Hubli to inaugurate the Karnatah Farmers Forum and have dinner. This was a fabulous affair with village decorations, cattle show, big tent with 1500-2000 men, women, and children. It was quite a sight with lots of ceremony, holy water, incense, paint, flower petals, and all. The harmonium was foot-pedaled, drums, songs. We were welcomed and sped on our way with the big horns. About 60 men who had been to the Delhi meeting started the organization. I was not sure of the accuracy of interpretation. It sounded political to me. After the meeting we drove to a large temple for the dinner, banana leaves and fingers, until 11 p.m. Then we went to Hubli and on to Haveri for the night, arriving about 12:30, tired.

On Sunday, September 30, we were up at 6:45 but didn't get breakfast and away until about 9 a.m. Went to Sangoa Community tree plantation. Mangoes were 1-2-3 years old, doing well and grasses planted. We each planted a mango with burning sacred fire, holy water, flower petals, paint, feeding plant a cocoanut and all before we put it in. I hope they grow. We visited a fine agricultural school two years for boys to go back on the farm and be a village level worker. Good livestock here. Spoke to students and the Livestock Improvement Association members. We visited several villages not on the program. We were getting very late, 2½ hours, and planned on passing up Tavar-Mallal villages, but they were waiting on the main road and insisted on our going in about a mile. We went in in the jeep as the road was bad. The main street of the village was decorated, etc. whole length with the palm leaves. We saw this palm only in this area, a sort of ragged leaf. They then had a covered area and here we met and spoke briefly. The reception was tremendous. It made one feel bad to see such humility. They ran along side of the car and about mobbed us as we went out. Everyone wanted to touch your hand. I took the pictures here of the big carriage on which they carry the idols. The cardamom garlands here as elsewhere were beautiful.

We stopped at the cattle feeding farm at Bankapar, dairy cattle. A farmer here brought in some angora goats from USA. He was crossing with native goat and very happy with the cross.

We stopped at H. A. Patel's garden at Shiggaon, betel leaf and bananas, looked fine. Say, there are lots of cobras in there. Crossed the road and saw a fine layout 160-acre farm, lots of oxcarts, wooden plows and other equipment. They were enlarging a well in solid granite, carrying the rocks up on their heads from 40-50 feet down. Tea again; in fact, tea at every stop and garlands. Got to Hubli and T. R. Neswi's home at 1:20. He had a group of 10-12 men in. We had a fast lunch on trays and got on our way about 2 p.m.

We arrived in Bombay at 7:15. Sellers were waiting for us. We rushed into other clothes and went to a very nice Indian dinner at Sethis, with plates, silverware and all. It was a nice group of about 12 folks. We were late to bed and up early for Gwalior.

In picking a candidate for parliament or other elective position, the local congress party governing board present their candidates to the district, a regional body, and two observers from the center. The proponents present the case for each candidate and the district governing body then pick their nominees for each office. These nominees are submitted to the Center governing body which finally select the Congress party candidates. An MP has about 800,000 people in his district. An MP or other government official does not select the position he would like to run for next. The party tells you what you run for next.

Monday, October 1, we got to airport and saw young Mr. Pandit. He had come to the hotel in Bombay wanting help in setting up a dairy Coop about 40 miles out of Bombay, something like Anand. They have some members and some money and are shipping milk in and distributing it. Need cooling and pasteurizing equipment. I recommended he get Chilson down now before he gets too busy. Landed in Aurangabad in a Heron, an English four-motor plane with about 12 passengers, without incident. Caves are out of there and a tomb for a queen is similar to the Taj Mahal. This is in the city.

Went out at 9:30 to take off and got stuck in the mud. We tried to get it out but they would never give it a real chance, so gave up about 10:15, sent for a DC3 and got away about 2:30 p.m. We were the only passengers.

The country northeast of Bombay is quite rugged and surely has some good dam sites. Then the country gets open. All cultivated but few villages and small, looks like large holdings. Forests in mountains.

Going to Indore is somewhat rough and forests, more villages, but still not too many, good water in streams. I like some of the country around Indore and there are bigger fields around Bhopal (15 acres average I understand). Villages are small and neater. Many tigers here.

India is slowly but steadily reducing the number of unproductive cattle. They told the people they were setting up beautiful parks for the cattle outside the city. These were like beautiful American cemeterys where the cattle could be protected in a life of ease. In fact the parks were forest areas enclosed by barbed wire fences where the cattle had shade and rest but very little grass so they did not last long.

Soon before we left India we were invited to the inauguration of a tannery beside one of the parks where they tanned the hides. This was a government project. Before the people gathered the dry bones for bone meal but never used the meat or hides. The value of the hides was a rather large item with the millions of cattle and buffalo in India. The story often told by Hindus was that in the early days in case of hunger from famine or flood, the people ran out of food and would eat the draft animals, then when the rains came they would not have oxen to plow the land so it became a part of the religion to not eat the animals even in dire need. I feel quite sure that soon India will produce far less cattle to eat their food and also more Hindus will gradually eat more meat including cattle.

Our travel to the villages and farms of India was complete. It had been a great privilege and experience. At Embassy gatherings we were always introduced as the couple who had been in more Indian villages than any other Americans. We still had to analyze what we had seen and heard and what would be helpful in expanding the usefulness of the Farmers Forum of India.

On October 11 I was asked to speak to the TOM staff, on the 15th to the Agricultural staff of the Embassy, on the 16th to the Embassy staff with lunches and dinners. Dr. Parker was a great deal of assistance to me in writing up the report which was finished by October 16. It still had to be typed, so Wednesday morning, October 17, we took the plane for Srinagar in the Vale of Kashmir, one of the world's real spots of beauty.

Kashmir is adjacent to Pakistan and mostly Moslem, but was and is held by India, claimed by Pakistan. We stayed at the Nedous Hotel, an old, wooden, spacious hotel in town. Many stayed in the houseboats on the Jhelum River. We especially liked the fireplace in the bedroom and plenty of wood.

Sri Datan Singh, Minister of Agriculture for Kashmir, was notified of our visit and certainly made it most enjoyable and productive for us. We went one day to Gulmarg, part way by bus then horseback; it was beautiful. There was rice on terraced lands above 7,000 feet. The farmers trim the new growth of branches and leaves on the trees and press them into the tree crotch 9' above ground so horses and oxen can get food during deep snow.

Timber was cut in 4' lengths, branded and put in a mountain stream to float down to the mill. The logs are short to get around the bends in the stream. Many sink but are still good pulled out years later. One of my best pictures ever is a rural road lined with poplar trees.

From the top you look across the mountains all snow-covered, 24,000 to 26,000 feet high.

Another day we went to Sonemarg and saw corn and rice growing over 8,000 feet. Along the road we saw a sawmill with large logs propped up at a good angle so one man stood on top of the log, the other man on the ground, and they sawed boards ¾" to 1" thick. We saw a small stack of rice moving in the road toward us. As it got close it was a man carrying I imagine 500 lbs. from the field to the threshing floor. He sat on a culvert head to rest. I asked him to let me try it. Two straps came over the shoulders to help carry it. It was just all I could do to rise with it on me and then walk a few hundred feet. Some of them went at a running walk. The soil in the valley was a yellow clay, but every twig or leaf was mixed back into it until they had a foot or so of made soil to grow saffron and other crops. They gather the stems of pollen from the blossoms of the plant. They go onto the lake in a scow, reach to the bottom with a fork, and pull up the vegetation and

275

all the mud they can until the scow is full, then spread it on the shore to build up very rich soil for vegetable growing.

Sri Datan Singh took us to see the old Mogul Gardens planted in the Mogul days. They were beautiful. It was a rare pleasure as several of the places were available only to royal and other famous visitors.

We took a shikara boat ride on the lake at sundown. The lights and reflections were fantastic. The stores here were fantastic also, beautiful cloth for dresses, rug weaving and old rugs. We bought quite a bit and all was good. We flew back Monday October 22. Only five days, but they were full and memorable.

On our return the report was typed and printed into pamphlet form. On October 25 I took a copy to Mr. V. T. Krishnamachari, head of the commission for the economic development of India. The government election campaign was at its height with Mr. Nehru, Prime Minister, out campaigning. Mr. Krishnamachera said, as I was about to leave, "Now we have some people running around this country talking about equality—equality, equality. It does not mean a thing. Now you people talk about equality of opportunity, that means something. And the English, they don't care one way or the other." Prime Minister Nehru was president of the Commission for the economic development of India but had never attended a meeting.

We enjoyed a farewell party about every evening.

We left Delhi October 26 for Calcutta. Spent the day sightseeing and left October 27 for Dacca, East Pakistan. We were met by Mr. Richardson, TCM, and Bernice Montgomery, a village worker from Mississippi I believe. She took us for quite a trip to several villages. It was all the delta of the Ganges and at late flood stage.

We went to see a young farm leader. His land was in rice, a long-stem variety which ripened during river floods so they went out in rowboats, used the sickle to gather the heads. They cut them off, put them in the boat, then rowed ashore and spread them out to dry. This year the floods were worse and lasted longer, so they were using long-tined rakes to rake the heads off the bottom, bring them up, cut off the heads and load them in the boats. Life was difficult.

We went to a little island a little larger than his house. He was very proud to show us his "CARE" package of a shovel, hoe and rake, brand new and clean. I asked him if he ever used them. He said "Oh no, they are too pretty to use. They are to look at." I hope they are well-used by now.

Dacca was jammed with people and traffic of all sorts. Most interesting were many little buggies which looked like toy stagecoaches with latticed windows so the women could see out but not be seen. We arrived on Saturday, went to the hotel. I paid with money I had left over from West Pakistan. This was the same money they had used as a Colony of England, but while we were in India they had called it in and now it was illegal to have any in your possession. The U.S. consulate had new money and could redeem it but they were closed on Saturday and Sunday. Finally the consul by phone from his home told the clerk to give me new currency for what I had and he would redeem it Monday, so we were relieved.

The plane left early Monday morning far out of Dacca. We arrived at the airport early but near plane time the police told us we couldn't leave without police clearance. I said I didn't need it as I had a special passport. They said that is why you need it. In Delhi Bella on a regular passport had to get clearance but I didn't. There was no time to return to Dacca so I argued. The plane arrived, but the police were determined. The pilot tried to fix it up, but couldn't, so he came by on the run, grabbed Bella on one arm and me on the other. The motors were revved up and the plane steps came up right behind us, and we were on our way to Burma.

We saw the Shwedagon (Golden) temple with all the golden domes, golden buddha shrines. It is fantastic and must be seen to be believed. They also had built a large pavillion out on an open plain which they hoped would become the world headquarters for buddhism.

Tuesday October 30, we went on to Bangkok, Thailand, for five days. We took the boat trip through the markets and saw everything bought, sold and delivered on the water's edge or over the water. The system of Kongs or canals is much like a system of streets. That is where the people live.

One day we got up early and went 100 miles north to the old capital city of Thailand. The road parallels the Yom River. In the 100 miles we crossed a small rise planted to corn, all the rest was solid rice on both sides of the road. Over 75 percent of the crop land of Thailand is in rice.

They were holding a conference in the school for the 4H clubs of the region. We were honored guests. As the program started, we were amazed to see Mrs. Sayre of Iowa. She was president of the Associated Women of the American Farm Bureau Federation and also of the Country Women of the World. It was great to see her.

The program, the songs, the demonstrations, were exactly the same as a similar conference would be in California. The uniforms were the same and they were all in uniform. They held hands and swayed back and forth as they sang the same songs.

We visited the Foremost milk reconstituting plant which was doing well.

We flew straight south along and across the Malay Peninsula to the Island of Penang. This was a delightful spot with a large white open hotel used by the English for holidays and vacations. Off the west coast of Malaysia, verdent and tropical, we saw lots of monkeys, shrines, all quiet and restful. We recommend it for weary travellers.

1957

I was really amazed to see the number of talks I gave this year on India. They were given to Farm Bureaus, Rotary, Lions, Kiwanis, church, school, Chambers of Commerce, World Affairs Councils, League of Women Voters, University Women. Most were talks? some were slide shows. They were well received and I hope added to our interest in and knowledge of East Indians and similar people.

On January 13 I went to the executive committee and AFBF board meeting in Washington D.C.

On the 19th, Yolo County Farm Bureau had their Bean Feed. I mention it because the farmers donated the beans, onions, prunes, olives, and so forth. It was all prepared by Eleanor and Ed Bandy. Ed was former President of Yolo County Farm Bureau and then for many years a member of the board of directors of CFB. Eleanor was former chairman of the Home Department and then Superintendant of Schools in Yolo County. They were a great couple.

On the 14th of March, I spoke for LowellBarry at the Lake Merritt Breakfast

Club, which represents much of the leadership in the Oakland area. This was quite a group who had breakfast once a month, with an outside speaker. That night we had a meeting on world affairs at the Claremont Hotel with a very nice dinner. A good many Bay Area people were present and it turned out to be a very interesting discussion.

On the 16th we went to Jesse Rudkin's for dinner. Jesse had been our minister here at Clarksburg. He then was with the University of the Pacific as Development Officer. He did a great job for a good many years and played a very active part in being very helpful to Bob Burns and the whole administration of the college.

March 28-30 I attended a meeting on the Stanford Campus on "U.S. Representation Abroad." This was one of a series of regional meetings with speakers and round-table discussions. The 75 participants represented business, the military, education, medical, legal, and foreign policy organizations, state department, labor, State of California, and the press. There were civic leaders and one farmer—me. There was a reception by Dr. Sterling, President of Stanford University, and a marvelous bar-b-que dinner at the bome of Bob Kirkwood, Controller of the State of California who lived at Saratoga. There I saw, for the first time, steaks ordered out of Chicago especially selected for quality and, boy, were they marvelous.

Eleven hours were devoted to the discussion, then there was a three-hour plenary session to discuss the final report of the session, which was well organized. The conference was worthwhile and I am sure many new viewpoints were reported back to Washington, but all reports were as planned by the permanent staff of the State Department. One of our participants was an attorney for Standard Oil Company of California, and I felt sure we would get the benefit of his experience in seeking aid for the oil company operations abroad, but in fact he was most conscious of favors he would be asking so he was most aggressive in seeking State Department good will.

On the 31st we had dinner with Alonzo Bakers at Elliot Taylors. He is in charge of admissions at UOP. This was a delightful evening and certainly made a good birthday party for Bella.

Beginning April 5, we spent eleven days in the Viscaino Desert in Baja California and other parts of Baja with Tom and Dorothy Robertson. We went down in pickups, camped out, and cooked our meals along the way. We cooked breakfast and dinner, but lunch was made up after breakfast so it did not delay us much. Tom and Dorothy had their jeep with a 12' boat and motor on top.

One of the delightful stops was on Manuella Lagoon north of Guerrero Negro. Tom and I used the boat with a lantern and tin pan reflector in front. One rowed while the other stood up in front and speared fish or crabs. We threw the crabs onto the embers of the campfire. They were delicious. We camped one evening on a little spit of land going out into Concepcion Bay. We set up camp and got the fire going, then while the girls were getting dinner Tom and I took the flashlight and spear and just walked along the edge of the water. One would lead the fish close to the edge with the flashlight while the other handled the spear. We got two nice fish.

Concepcion Bay is surely one of nature's beauty spots. The wild flowers were beautiful. There were the many types of cactus. The big cordons, much like the

278

saguaros of Arizona, have ribs much like wood. They are used for roofs in the houses, for fence stakes and many other uses. The ocotillo or spider cactus has bright red blooms; the cholla is most valuable for fire wood. The pin cushions, barrel, old man, pipe organ, beaver tail, fishhook, prickly pear, torch cereus candeleria—these grow tall and slender with a white spray of flowers at the top, making them look like giant candles.

We stopped at Bajia de Los Angeles, went fishing and got six yellow tail in a short time. One of them we took with us and that evening wrapped it in foil and laid it in the embers to cook. It was delicious for a couple of days.

The roads of course were terrible—ruts, sand, rocks—just plain bad. One hundred miles was the limit for a long day. In its way, it was beautiful and all interesting and exciting—at the same time restful.

At that time you could get coffee at a number of different ranches, if you asked for it, but that was about all. The only gasoline was what you might get out of a barrel that the rancho might or might not have. We made many trips down there later on, and learned that if you took along some onions or some walnuts or something else they particularly liked—especially eggs—you could first ask for coffee, and they'd give you some, but then if you brought in some potatoes, onions, nuts, eggs or things of that kind, the first thing you knew you would have a delightful meal on the table for you. They certainly were happy to receive extras of the kind they couldn't buy locally.

May 14 to 19 we attended the pre-International Federation of Agricultural Producers tour. We started in Chicago and visited the International Harvester Co., particularly the foreign sales department and factory production. Then the Quaker Oats experimental farm was exceedingly interesting. They raise chickens, sheep, cattle, hogs of all kinds, feeding them various quaker oats products to get their observations and the basis for improvement of their products. Then we took in the Dekalb Seed Company, which was one of the originators of hybrid seed and also of improved seeds of all kinds.

The IFAP meeting ran from the 20th to 27th on the campus of Indiana University at Purdue. Farm leaders from India were there. When they arrived in San Francisco on June 8 they were entertained by the Indian Consulate General in his home for tea. This was Dorothy's graduation day at UOP, so we went there and I was privileged to place the hood on her as she received her diploma.

On June 10 the Indian leaders were guests of Louis Razoni, President of the CFBF. They saw the farm bureau in the morning, then were guests of Harry Wellman, Vice President of the University of California, for lunch at the faculty club.

On the 11th they were guests of Earl Coke, now Vice President of the Bank of America (formerly Director of Extension in California and assistant secretary of agriculture in Washington D.C.) He discussed banking in relation to agriculture, he being in charge of all agricultural loans for the bank, and also all their loans to Mexico which were largely agricultural. Then we left for Davis, stopping in Winters to visit the Cal Fruit Exchange packing sheds. We had dinner that evening at the Memorial Union on the Davis campus, where we discussed the functions of the University of California in relation to agriculture and farmers.

On the 12th was a tour and demonstrations on the Davis campus. That evening we served a barbeque at our home, and they stayed in local farm homes overnight.

On the 13th we visited the Department of Agriculture in Sacramento, had lunch as guests of Rotary Club, then tea at the Kartar Singh Ranch in Yuba City. Next we went to a dinner and farm center meeting at Tierra Bella School where Bachans Teja, a Hindu, was center chairman. A large group of Indians were farming around Yuba City, mostly from Punjab. Many are married to American women, and I thought them a fine group of typical women.

On the 14th we toured the Marysville-Colusa area and dinner was served by the India Society of Yuba and Sutter counties, whose president was Mr. Balwant Sidhu. After dinner, Mr. Neswi, a member of the Indian Parliament, told me that he had decided to withdraw a bill he had presented in parliament to limit the size of Indian farms to 10 hectors or 25 acres. The group was surely impressed by the prosperity and the standing of the Indian farmers they had met.

The 15th was spent in the Stockton area, and the 17th in Stanislaus County, where we were luncheon guests of the Modesto Irrigation District, then on to Fresno for dinner with the Farm Bureau directors.

The 18th we visited cotton, walnut and grape farms and had luncheon served by the Indian farmers of Fresno County. Dinner in the evening was at the Kern County Farm Bureau's annual meeting. The 19th we toured the Bakersfield area and arrived in Hollywood. I had to leave for the AFBF committee meeting in Chicago. The Indians spent a couple of days in the Los Angeles area as they wished.

On the 27th I arrived in El Paso, registered in the hotel, and found none of the Indians had arrived. I checked with registration, room service, and the head waiter to be sure they knew my party were Indians and not U.S. blacks, for I feared I might have a real problem on my hands, but it all went well.

On Sunday, June 23, we left El Paso for Juarez and Torreon, arriving at 6:17 p.m. to a regular home-coming reception. The Indians were quite impressed by the warmth of the reception with many embrazos and so on. We visited the Torreon irrigated lands and talked with the various farm people there.

The 26th and 27th were spent in Monterey, which is quite an industrial city, with International Harvester Company and many other U.S. plants located there. The Indians were amazed at the good will, thinking that the Mexicans would be fearful and resentful of the U.S. so close on the north. The Indians had been trained to fear U.S. economic colonialism as worse than political colonialism. I was a little concerned that at a dinner in our honor they showed a picture of the landing of the U.S. Marines in Vera Cruz many years ago. The Mexicans were very apologetic. The Indians didn't understand what it was all about.

On June 28 we went to Saltillo, the state capital and the home of the College of Agriculture. There was great fanfare of trumpets and flags as it was also graduation day for the senior class. They presented me with an honorary certificate of graduation as an "engineer of agriculture" and builder of international friendship.

June 29 we left Monterey for San Antonio, Texas. As we came through inspection, I did not have a health certificate with me, but the guard never hesitated. I was at the rear of the Indian group and he first said, "Are you with that group?" I said "Yes." He says, "You got problems enough. Don't let me hold you up." We had hurried but very sincere good wishes on parting, as they were going in twos and threes to various agricultural colleges to finish up some matters of special interest. I was tired but well-pleased with our look at California and Mexico. In their reports almost all said California and Mexico was the highlight of their American experience. I left San Antonio for Chicago and Columbus, Ohio, where the AFBF board was meeting.

We spent early July at the Sloughhouse and a good deal of the time on estate planning.

On July 22 the CFBF board met at San Louis Obispo Poly Tech, followed by the staff institute on the 25th.

On Saturday, July 27, Dorothy Anne married Roger Abley at 4 p.m. in our yard. A semicircular hedge about 8 feet high was the background. Behind the minister was a white wooden lattice arch. Patricia and Camillas were two of the bridesmaids. David, Dick, and Roger's brother were ushers. Nancy and Cynthia were flower girls, and Kenneth was ring bearer. The ministers were Dr. Boone of the Clarksburg Church and Dr. Elliot Fisher, Patricia's father-in-law. Chairs were on the lawn, and a white runner extended from the sun room door to the arch. There was a large crowd of friends for the service and the reception north of the house. They now have three fine children, Helen, John, and Lauren.

On the 29th I spoke to Walnut Grove Rotary, and to Sacramento Rotary on August 1. On August 6 we had dinner at the Japanese Consulate in San Francisco with our friend, Dr. Nasau, being guest of honor for the evening.

August 10 was Alonzo Stagg's 95th birthday in Anderson Hall dining room on UOP campus. He still had a fine build, but he was quite stooped and his hands shook a good deal. I had not seen him for several years, and I hoped they would not call on him to speak, as I did not want to see him weak. He was called on to speak, however, he walked up pretty shaky, but his voice boomed out "What do you mean, 97 yards return, it was 100 yards return." He was on his way in all his glory and a pleasure to hear.

On August 31 was host breakfast. September 2 was the Paktunistan dinner. Dr. Khan, a Sacramento dentist, used to talk a good deal about getting freedom for Paktunistan, an undeveloped mountainous area northwest of Pakistan. He gave a very nice dinner for a number of years, urging freedom for Paktunistan. I am sure few of his guests knew where it was or what the real conditions were, but he was a gentleman and we attended until one day a man walked into his office and shot him.

The 15th was the State Fair Farm Bureau dinner. These were quite important occasions with large delegations of farmers who attended the fair on that day, and of course directors of the fair. The Governor nearly always came and other prominent individuals and representatives of other farm organizations.

September 23-28 was the commodity and board meeting in Chicago.

October 7-10 the AFB executive committee met. On the 11th I spoke to the annual meeting of Idaho Farm Bureau at Pocatello. On the 12th I spoke to the L.A. and Imperial counties annual meetings. November 10-14 was the CFB annual meeting in Fresno. On the 17th, I was speaker at the Mile City Montana annual meeting. On the 25-26th was the Colorado Farm Bureau meeting, at which I was dinner speaker.

Frank Kemp, former president of GW Sugar Company, also spoke. He was a dynamic figure in sugar.

December 3, the AFBF board and meeting in Chicago. On December 26-28 we went to Mexico as representatives of the AFBF to meet with the Associacion Nacional de Cosecheros in Mexico.

1958

On January 7 I spoke at the Sutterville PTA at the request of Mr. and Mrs. Rudy Volz. On the 19th we spoke at the Sunday morning service in Courtland church on the subject of higher education.

February 4 was spent at a Sierra College meeting on India. On the tenth was a Northwest Farmers Forum in Spokane, Washington, where we had good discussion for two days, principally on wheat and other crops in the Northwest. Several farm groups from Canada were represented.

Our Food Comes First breakfast was held February 24 at the Statler Hotel in Washington D.C. in the presidential ballroom. The program started with breakfast at 8 a.m. Fifty-six representatives of the press sent in reservations and were there. We were a little disappointed that Vice President Nixon was representing President Eisenhower, but when the White House Staff saw the size of the affair, they decided they had goofed and rushed word to Ike to get there as soon as possible, so we soon had both as our guests for breakfast. We had three outstanding presentations on food from the U.S. Chamber of Commerce, the American Medical Association, and the President of Iowa State College during the morning. An excellent lunch was addressed by Ezra Taft Benson, Secretary of Agriculture, then a full afternoon until 5 p.m. with top speakers, and a committee meeting that evening. It was a success beyond our fondest dreams.

On April 29 we had a California Food Conference from 10 a.m. in Sacramento addressed by Governor Goodwin Knight and many outstanding leaders. Practically all the states held state-wide meetings on "Food Comes First."

On June 8-13, the Western Regional meeting was held in Zion Park. We took Carmel and Charlie Hamilton with us to a fine meeting in Zion Park, but also did quite a little traveling around and visiting the Southwest.

I let Helen Reamer talk me into attending the meeting of the Republican State Central Committee in Los Angeles on September 6-7. It was interesting but not enough so that I would want to spend much time at it.

On the 13th we left Sacramento with Burnell at 8:14 a.m., stopping at Ensenada, and on to Viscaino and La Paz at 5 that evening. We left La Paz at 8:10 a.m. and arrived in Mexico City at 1:54.

On the 18th we saw Worthington pump people regarding pumps and many other items that we had to check up on in Mexico. The 19th we visited the

Rockefeller Foundation people with Dr. E. G. Williamson and discussed many of their activities including the World Poultry Congress which was to be held very shortly. The 20th we left Mexico at 7 a.m. with the weather clear, arriving in Mazatlan at 10:35, Guaymus at 12:45, and Ensenada at 3:55. The next day we arrived at Tijuana at 11:35, San Diego at 12:15, leaving at 12:25 and arriving at Sacramento at 3:55. This detail shows what can be done with an airplane getting around the country when you don't have to worry about the roads.

The San Francisco State College had a summer course for foreign teachers teaching English as a second language. They made some weekend trips out of the Bay Area. On September 26, 14 men and 11 women came to spend the day in Sacramento with the State Department of Education in the morning, lunching with Governor Knight at the Salvation Army Camp. They toured the Capital and Libby Cannery, then visited Fort Sutter, where we met them and brought them to Clarksburg. Fifteen of our farm families hosted them for the night, then showed them our community and the sugar factory in the morning After lunch they returned to the school for a 2 p.m. return to San Francisco. All the farm people appreciated the opportunity to meet these folks from various countries and spend time with them.

I flew to Washington on October 8 and was met by Tom Beal Jr., Top economist of the State Department. We had briefings, got passports, met with Meyers of Foreign Agricultural Trade, Mr. A. Richards, Dr. Felice, specialist in agricultural trade, Earl Fox and Gus Bergermeister, top men in many activities including trade in the Department of Agriculture.

On the 14th we left New York for Geneva. The U.S. made a practice of sending four citizens to sit in on the GATT, General Agreement on Tariff and Trade Conference, held each year. We were there October 16 to November 4. Our group included the U.S. Chamber of Commerce president-elect Richard Wagner, the AFL-CIO attorney Stanley Ruthenburg of Washington D.C. The U.S. citizen representing consumer interests was Mrs. Enid Robinson of Hampton, Iowa, and agriculture, George H. Wilson of Clarksburg, California. The main purpose of the conference was to study the Haberle Report, a study in trends in International Trade related to trade with underdeveloped countries. It was very apparent that its writer had little understanding of the poverty or lack of incentive to produce in many areas. I read the report in detail, was quite critical of it, and told the U.S. delegation that in my opinion it was a very poor report and nonfactual. They were flabbergasted that I should question the authority of a person like Haberle of Harvard. He was supposed to be one of the top economists of the U.S., although in fact I had not heard of him up to that time. A couple of days after we arrived, Dr. Bell came as White House Staff Economist. He came to my room and we went over the report in detail. He said he had never thought of questioning the report, but that I had pointed out the errors to him so he could see them easily.

The U.S. had an office in Geneva for the delegation. The GATT offices and the working sessions of the conference were held in the Leage of Nations building located in a large park like area overlooking the river. Practically every morning started with a delegation session in the office at 8 a.m Here the official delegates reported on what they had done yesterday and what the plan was for today. There was ample opportunity for questions and discussion. Then we would discuss the U.S. position in relation to issues raised. Additional officials came in for several days to observe or to bring new issues for discussion.

On most days, there were committee meetings discussing various issues. We attended several of these as observers. We had some free time to look up watches or other gifts or just to see Geneva, but most of the days were filled with meetings or study of special issues.

I was very fortunate in that Tom Beal, head of this delegation, had been a principal speaker at one of our annual CFBF meetings. He had arrived early and attended several of our commodity and other meetings. He had no idea that such meetings were being held by any group in the U.S. He was so impressed that he stayed over the next day to see more. His wife, a very efficient and attractive lady, was now with him in Geneva in a rented apartment. They invited me over several evenings for a delightful dinner and very free discussions.

The only commodity issue the State Department had on their agenda was how to export more U.S. coal to Europe. I asked Tom how they became interested in that issue; he said it was simple. The coal people were the only ones who came to them with their problem and then furnished data to support their request.

The order of precedence was very clear. First state, then commerce, then labor, then, if time was left, agriculture. Felice was the Agricultural Department representative. He was well prepared, but the basic work should have been done by farm organizations and the Department of Agriculture working with the Department of State in Washington before the GATT Conference.

We had several plenary sessions of the contracting parties which we all attended. I especially remember one on the European Common Market. The French led off with their very tight trade policy, with minimum room for negotiation. It amazed us all, including the other European partners, who seemed as surprised as we were.

I attended two luncheons at Geneva Rotary. Under the Marshall Plan we had been helping the European countries rebuild their industrial complex while we were getting on with the old. The Swiss were jubilant at the size and number of orders they were getting from U.S. corporations for Swiss-made machine tools and similar equipment.

After a number of receptions by various delegations, on the last evening Windom White had us at his home for dinner. He was then leader of the General Agreement on Tariff and Trade, and has held that office until quite recently (1982). It was quite apparent from the discussion that he was very dependent on the U.S. for the leadership to make effective the General Agreement on Tariff and Trade.

Allan Kline, President of AFBF, had represented agriculture the previous year. Ruttenburg, representative of AFL CIO, had tried to include in the GATT program a provision that we would include a program whereby if another country would pass labor legislation with minimum wage, 40-hour week, and so forth, we would give that country compensating trade concessions. As a part of regular GATT conferences, the countries would have to report on what labor legislation they had passed.

Back in New York on November 4, we all went our way, but with the agreement to meet in Washington on Wednesday, December 10, for a reception at the home of Tom Beal. Bella had arrived in New York ahead of me.

Richard Nixon, then Vice President of the U.S., and his wife had made a trip around South America designed to be a good will trip, but Communistic activities were at their height and he was very badly treated as a representative of the U.S. George Denny felt this was a very bad situation for the U.S. and our Good Neighbor program, so he organized a citizen-to-citizen trip around South America, the same trip Nixon had taken. We had the same type people as on the 1949 trip around the world, including some of the same people.

The trip was planned with a University or other recognized local group as our hosts to plan the conferences and the big Town Hall public meeting in each capitol city visited. We each had a counterpart person to receive us, to see that we met the local people interested, in my case in agriculture, and to generally act as personal host in that country. We left New York on November 6 and arrived back on December 6, an average of just under four days per stop.

I was asked by the AFBF to represent them on this trip. The members of the seminar included: Mr. George Denny, Jr., Mrs. Jeanne Denny, Dr. Minnie Miller, Mr. and Mrs. George Wilson, Mr. Alfred P. Shaw, Dr. F. S. Crockett, Mr. Serafino Romauldi and Mr. Seymour Brandwein, Mr. Paul K. Reed, Mr. John Barnhart, Mrs. Edith Sampson, Mrs. Homer Frye, Mr. John D. Hoffman, Miss Toni Nirenberg, Mr. and Mrs. Phil Bigley, Mrs. Charles U. Culmer, Mrs. Oscar M. Ruebhausen, Mr. George G. Hagedorn, Mr. Jaime Foneca, Mrs. James C. Parker, Miss Dorothy Height, Dr. Walter W. Eshelman, Mr. Jack Teac, Mr. Robert Boomer, Mr. Robert Salisbury, Rev. Arthur C. Kiernan.

At left, typical garlands received in India (here in Bangalore).
Right, I'm under this load of rice going to the threshing floor—all I could handle, but a typical load for an Indian carrier.

Top left, 4-H boys; right, home-made grain &
seed planter. Ctr left, an ox-cart load of hay,
right, a lumber mill in Kashmir. Belowleft, plowing for rice; right, women
threshing wheat—note silver anklets. All in India.

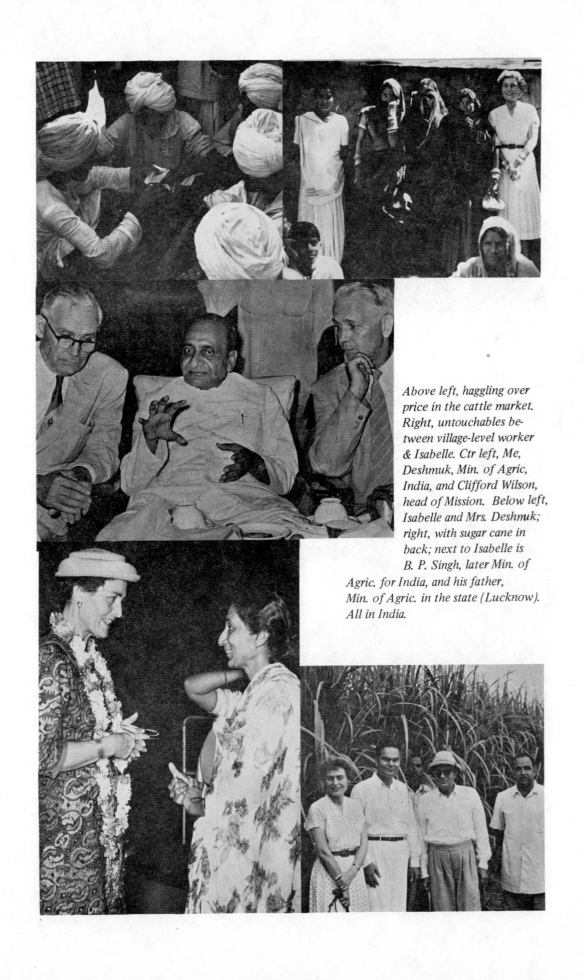

Above left, haggling over price in the cattle market. Right, untouchables between village-level worker & Isabelle. Ctr left, Me, Deshmuk, Min. of Agric, India, and Clifford Wilson, head of Mission. Below left, Isabelle and Mrs. Deshmuk; right, with sugar cane in back; next to Isabelle is B. P. Singh, later Min. of Agric. for India, and his father, Min. of Agric. in the state (Lucknow). All in India.

Above left, most holy shiek's temple in Amritsar; right, walking the "straight path" between poplar trees in Kashmir.

VENEZUELA

Below left, buffalo grass with Him Fulmer, 6'4" tall, standing in front. They grow two crops per year! Right, forest leveler used in Venezuela. Bottom left — Yes, we have bananas! Right, coffee seedlings grown for Venezuelan coffee association members.

13

SOUTH AMERICA

† † † 1958, continued

Venzuela

Venezuela is closer to the U.S. than any other South American nation. It extends 1750 miles along the Carribean and Atlantic oceans, about as large as Texas and Oklahoma combined. Population is 6 million, or 17 per square mile. The population is "mestizo," native-Spanish cross 65 percent, white 20 percent, negro 8 percent, and Indian 7 percent.

A provisional government was in control in 1958, a 5-man junta with legislation by decree. The president of the junta is Chief of State Rear Admiral Wolfgang Larrazabol. A free election was promised and held late in 1958.

U.S private investment in Venezuela is about 3 billion dollars, greater than in any other country except Canada. Venezuela was our leading foreign supplier of petroleum, and second of iron ore. Venezuela is closer to the eastern U.S. than the Gulf of Mexico ports. Petroleum represents 62 to 65 percent of government income Ninety-five percent of their oil is exported, 65 percent to the U S. (1957).

Language was of course a limiting factor, but most of the folks spoke some English and IBM supplied us with portable simultaneous translation equipment and an operator was used in larger meetings.

The complaints were mostly from students, and included "The U.S. takes Latin Americans for granted. ' They felt we don't recognize differences in different countries of South America that the U.S. favors dictators, favors Europe and Asia with economic aid, favors U.S. private investors in oil, etc. and takes excessive profits.

287

They felt we flood local markets at the expense of local industry and encourage segregation.

The South American universities are mostly national and are provided for in the Constitution. They are financed by the constitution allocating a percentage of the gross national income to the universities, which are autonomous bodies. They are self-administering. The president, staff, and faculty are chosen by faculty and students. The university grounds are sanctuaries against political law. Students have actually sat in their dormitories in Caracus and shot rifle and pistol bullets at policemen on the street or in passing cars and the police couldn't enter the grounds to seek the assailant or stop the acts of violence. Many students and faculty publicly announced that they were Communists or Communist sympathizers.

My counterpart was Eduardo Mendoza They were a very prominent and highly respected family. He had been Secretary of Agriculture, and had managed a good deal of farmland. His grain elevators were more modern than any I had seen in the U.S. They were more automated, almost completely dust free, and one man could control everything from a control station. Dr. Mendoza imports all kinds of agricultural commodities. We still get Christmas cards from the Mendoza family each year.

The Dictator was still very much a part of most conversations. They all said he had built the two high-rise buildings in the center of Caracus and the big Humbolt Hotel on top of the Rock with the cable car going up to it. They were for show and for him to brag about. They all claimed he had done nothing for the poor and nothing to help farmers or farming. The U.S. State Department had awarded him some kind of an honor, so we were accused of being for dictators.

Our meetings were occasionally confused by Communists, but for the most part we had fine people really speaking friendship and cooperation.

The statement was often made that oil had brought wealth to many in Venezuela, but had widened the gap between rich and poor. That may be, for many of the poor seemed to be in a different world little affected by the added national wealth. Where a new school was located in a poverty area, many of the youngsters were not either working or going to school. I felt that generally speaking there was a good deal of the oil money trickling down to the poor.

The government set up a commission to study agricultural reforms for congressional action. Some of their findings were: Farmers net income is over 800B per year. They consume little and produce little. They need long-term capital. The men land, and market are good. Rockefeller has helped in rice production by developing virus-resistant varieties; the Rockefeller activities are well accepted.

Venezuela does not desire groups (such as banks, advertising and insurance com panies) who do not bring in capital but only take it out. Foreign capital is more welcome if it joins with local capital.

There are now new people in government and many adjustments are taking place Many business people now in government are trying to develop the underdeveloped part of the country. They believe in better prices for farm products, and feel the U S. must allow reasonable credit. Venezuela has never failed to pay their debts; they are now one billion dollars in debt. Venezuela has good labor relations and a will to succeed, with a growing middle class.

Our labor people, AFL-CIO, Mining and National Education Association, in their statements, "loved all the people of South America and were so sorry that our State Department was so unfriendly to the South American countries."

We drove around with Eduardo Mendoza, then went to his home for coffee and met his wife and daughters. At 6 p.m. we went to visit Admiral Wolfgang Larrazabol, President of the junta.

†Bogota

On the flight to Bogota I sat by Mrs. Kane, National President of PTA, and told her I did not like some of the statements of Walter Eshelman of the National Education Association, and if it would not embarass her I was going to make a statement if he continued some of his criticism of the U.S. She said, "Oh, she wished she could herself, but they just could not challenge the teachers."

We arrived in Bogota in the evening, a beautiful flight and a most hearty reception. Bogota was less industrial, modern in some ways, but still more colonial.

At an Embassy briefing, we learned that they feel we do not know enough about them, that we try to force coffee prices down, we have an extensive Point 4 and P.L. 480 program. Ten percent of the people get some food from the U.S. They have the strongest church-state relations in all of South America. The government closed protestant churches and schools. The attacks on Nixon were deliberately organized by the Communists. Violence against protesters started ten years ago. Ten percent of the budget is for education; 40 percent of the people are illiterate, 50 percent of the population lacks schools.

In 1949, there were 100,000 people killed in guerilla warfare. In 1953, Rojas came in to restore order. He was very popular then, but he became a dictator and soon became very unpopular. He was overthrown last year. They are now under a junta and all important offices were divided 50-50 between two leading parties. The new President took office August 7, 1958.

There is a definite program to increase production in agriculture and industry. Colombia offers foreign capital the same treatment as domestic capital. An independent corporation is developing this valley. Communication, electric power, irrigation education, technical education, will be expanded throughout Colombia. Production of cotton, oil, soya beans and livestock is increasing; the soil and climate are excellent.

They had a fine lunch for us with our host committee, our counterparts, members of the government, and so on. What was very much in their minds was their recent dictatorship—they began with a President and ended with a dictator. They again referred to the U.S. supporting the dictator.

Again, the Labor men were saying how sorry they were that "our State Department was so unreasonable...Labor was against dictators, etc." I said I was just a plain U.S. citizen, not associated with any branch of U.S. government, but still proud of my government. I said I would like to ask a few questions.

I am told, I said, the man you call the dictator was elected in free elections to be President by the largest vote any President had ever received in Colombia. Yes, that was right. He was popular for some years and then he called off the coming election and he became a Dictator. You do not want the U.S. to interfere in your domestic problems. One day your man became a dictator. What if we had decided a day before you did that he was a dictator? What would you have done to us? So it seems to me the question is, just what day did he become a dictator? They jumped up, threw their napkins in the air, and yelled, "That is the question—just what day did he become a Dictator?" I heard that anywhere I went after that lunch. They knew they had been pushing us to see how much we would stand for, and when we answered them in fun as they were putting it out, they loved it and it broke the ice for all of us.

We saw their schools and health-care centers, their Colombian American Association, their salt mines with all the sculptures. We heard much of the valley of the Magdalena River where they had controlled mosquitoes and malaria with DDT, and now this fantastically rich area was awaiting settlers to reclaim it into productive farm and cattle-grazing land. They were proud of their history and education. They were very anxious to become the cultural center for South America.

In Caracas, here in Bogota, and at all the other stops we held meetings with our counterparts and other groups in which we were interested. We had preplanned seminars with leaders, civilian and government on subjects of mutual interest. Here we got into free discussions on many issues. Then we had one open Town Meeting in the largest hall in the city where two representing the U.S. and two the local country took 5 minutes each to discuss an issue, then they could ask each other questions. The audience then asked questions of any speaker. These were always interesting, sometimes lively, often the only chance they had to question their own leaders in government or business life.

One can't begin to cover all the private receptions, sight-seeing trips, visits to schools, hospitals and other activities, but we were busy every minute, gathering more information and, I believe understanding, and I am sure they were analyzing and dissecting us every minute of the day.

†Peru

Peru has a coastal desert 25-40 miles wide where the seaports and Lima, the capitol, are located. Lima is a city of charm, gaiety, and tradition. The climate is similar to San Francisco.

The backbone of the Sierra, up to 22,000 feet above the sea, is where most of the people live and where the mineral wealth is found. East of these hills are vast, uncharted hill and forest lands, the tropical lowlands and the headwaters of the Amazon. This part equals 60 percent of the area.

When Pizarro arrived in 1531 this was the nucleus of the highly developed Inca Empire. The viceroy founded in Lima in 1542 extended from Panama and included all Spanish territory in South America except Venezuela. Peruvian independence was proclaimed July 25, 1821, when Lima was the most aristocratic colonial capitol in America.

Following the revolution of 1948, Peru had two presidents elected for six-year terms, then in June 1965 Dr. Prado was elected and Peru was sound politically. There are no signs of revolution now. The present government is free, but has little experience in democracy.

The Ambassador said Peru was the most friendly to the U.S. of any post he has held in 27 years. Peruvian press coverage of U.S. news is very good. There are many

290

Peruvian students in the U.S.A., and they were all surprised by the anti-Nixon demonstrations. We were swamped with regrets.

The U.S. provides 20 percent of the national budget for education; fifty percent is allocated for Indians. The ambassador has $50,000 to translate English professional books into Spanish for the university.

Local people are willing to furnish labor and material for 80 percent of school building costs. Government cannot furnish the 20 percent and teachers to all counties wishing schools.

There is a 1200-bed hospital in Lima for white-collar workers—it is closed to others. Employees pay 3 percent, the employer 3 percent, and government 1 percent of wages. The government built the hospital for the military and now extends it to the middle class.

Peru wants more investment and technical cooperation to be used for education, public health, and agriculture.

There is a U.S. tax advisor in the government; 12,000 income tax returns were filed with 8000 paying tax; of these, 112 paid 80 percent of the taxes. There are land, personal property, and transportation taxes.

The U.S. had donated 100,000 tons of foodstuff to help relieve a drouth. Loans made during the drouth have been fully repaid by the Indians. The economy is fairly free with few controls on export/import. Edith Sampson said, "As a result of confidence, money flows."

Peru regards restrictive trade proposals in the U.S. with resentment in view of its efforts to stimulate private enterprise as we suggest and because it buys more from the U.S. than it sells to us. The exports are raw materials. Prices have declined, cutting government income and bringing inflation and unemployment. We see short-term difficulty but the long term looks good. Few miners are employed because of quotas, but prices are now up 15-20 percent.

Peru, Chile, and Equador claim 200-mile limits in the sea to conserve fish. The I.C.A. (International Cooperation Administration) is helping build roads into the jungles.

Clarence E. Pike, Agricultural Attache, gave us a good trip to see some of the agriculture, old and new. Sixty percent of the population are farmers. I was interested in the irrigation ditches on rough, steep mountain sides. They were built, they said, by the Incas four-hundred fifty years ago. The grades seemed perfect and their ability to evenly spread water on those steep hills was almost unbelievable.

Mr. and Mrs. Achilles, the Ambassador, had a delightful reception for our group to meet our U.S. staff and many local people on November 13.

The topic at our Public Town Hall meeting was "Pan-Americanism: Myth or Reality?" I felt some of the remarks of Raul Ferrero in the Town Hall meeting were pertinent and typical of South American feelings. "The U.S. should help in our economic development with technical know-how and capital to render fruitful their natural resources and manpower which are enormous." The aid would be to complement their own efforts.

Their population growth absorbs one-half of their production increase, so they need our help. They realize they must increase their work effort, increase yields, and improve their economic system to better distribute the national income among the masses, while we, the U.S. should eliminate discrimination that affects their products, through quotas, tariffs, and dumping.

They want to feel they are partners of the U.S. on a free and honorable basis; a two-way traffic, to give and to receive. They wish to make the Pan-American ideal a concrete fact. Only thus, peacefully—slowly—will it be possible that an idea which belonged to the elite will spread throughout our nations, for continental solidarity.

The Western Hemisphere requires preferential treatment from the U.S. now preoccupied with distant countries, disregarding their vital flank—Latin America. (We were reminded everywhere in South America that they are near to us, and Europe is far.)

Life is now a challenge to do away with poverty and to achieve the common good both for individuals and for nations. It is the duty of the underdeveloped countries to extend democracy from the political to the economic level. Our Town Meeting in Peru lasted for four and one-half hours and was covered by press, radio and T.V.

In each city we had two organized seminars—one on economic problems and one on social and cultural problems. These were attended by our counterparts and specialists in the various fields. From all reports, the press coverage was tremendous. I imagine it was the most free exchange of opinions they had heard between citizens and foreign visitors.

Lunch time and the afternoon were free. We visited the city and some of the countryside. Some farming is almost vertical.

At 8 p.m. we attended a buffet at the Embassy hosted by Mr. and Mrs. Walter Howe. It was a delightful evening.·

†Chile

We arrived in Santiago, Chile, at 4 p.m. At 6:30 we had a press conference at our Hotel Carrera, followed by a reception around the swimming pool on the top floor.

On Monday, November 17, we had a briefing and motion picture by the Ambassador, Hon. Walter Howe. Chile, on the southwest coast of South America, is more than 2,650 miles long—no wider than 250 miles at any point—and is larger than Texas. Chile has a northern desert, the central agricultural area where 85 percent of the people live, and the southern forests. Chile is divided into 60 percent desert and mountains, with 10 percent arable land The people are mostly of Spanish Caucasian descent with American-Indian influence. There are many German immigrants. Chile is 70 percent literate.

Chile is the second coffee producer of the world. They also produce iodine for the world's need. Fifty percent of their imports are from the U.S. and forty percent of their exports go to the U.S. Chile is now importing where she used to export.

Agricultural production goes up 1.6 percent per year; population goes up 1.7 percent per year. Twenty percent of the population receives food from the U.S

Along with Argentina and Bolivia, inflation is worst with world cost of living increases at 61 percent in 1953, 71 percent in 1954, 84 percent in 1955, 38 percent in 1956, 17 percent in 1957, and 27 percent in 1958. There has been a 700 percent increase in money supply in 7 years.

292

Chile reinvests 7-8 percent of GNP in development, as compared to the U.S. who reinvests 15 percent. Most of the industrial production was uneconomic. The copper company was taxed 90 percent of their profit, so they did not reinvest. U.S. companies provide best wages and housing of any.

The Communist party has been in Chile since 1921 and is most effective in Latin America.

On November 18 we received a briefing by President Allesandre, who had been in office only two weeks. He talked of the middle class in Chile and the 15 or so parties. He has support of two strong parties, but not a majority. The power of the President in Chile is very broad. He can veto parts of bills, he appoints all governors. There are no legislative bodies in the state, but they are in the towns.

Chile has a long and proud tradition of democratic government. Since 1900, presidents were all elected honestly and held office for the term. They had a dictator about thirty years ago.

Agriculture is the main economy. Minerals are the principal exports. Ninety percent of the copper is U.S. owned and is their main revenue since 1932

We saw some countryside and farms as we rode in taxis out to Vina Undurrago at Santa Cara, one of the principal wine industries of Chile. It was set in a beautiful park with attractive buildings. Horsemen in native costume performed and we got a super welcome.

Their advertising money went for shows instead of printed advertising They did it nicely. The Chilian Air Corps flew in two helicopters and took some of the party for a sight-seeing trip. There were lots of native dances in which we all participated a little. Some of the musical instruments were interesting and new to us. This was a great day and a great show

At 7 p.m. we attended our Town Hall meeting in the conference hall of the University of Chile. It was well attended, and I was one of the speakers. An American woman had married the son of the former President She was now a widow and wanted me to come down to manage her extensive landholdings for her.

I am including here my talk at this meeting The opening talks were really to get the subject before the people—they then asked further questions of the speakers.

Talk in Chile, November 18, 1958

A myth is a beautiful story usually told to illustrate a great truth. One could easily develop such a story of the origin and destiny of the Americas. Your history and ours has been similar. We have our O'Higgins, San Martin, Bolivar, Hidalgo, Washington, Lincoln, and others who belong to all of us.

Maybe it is symbolic that the two great continents, north and south, are held together by a narrow cord, but this cord is a strong one and far deeper and broader under the surface than it is on top. Our inheritance came largely from Europe; ours more from northern Europe, yours more from the Latin countries.

But, we have not read enough of the history, culture and development of our respective countries Histories at best, tell us what was, and fail in giving the feeling of the present day, either in material or in spiritual progress. We need to accelerate our expanding study of Spanish and hope we can simplify our spelling of English so both you and we can learn it more easily. Panamericanism will never be the reality it should until we know each other and communicate freely. Today s jet age demands that the North-South trail be made wide with much two-way travel.

As the industrial nations have developed, they have learned the techniques of using capital, science and mechanical power to increase production per man and thus earn increased income per man.

We, the producers of the raw materials of the world, have not learned as well how to use capital, science, and horsepower to increase our production. This is not because we who produce raw materials are less able, but because the problem is more difficult.

I have used the words *we, the producers of raw materials,* because we, the farmers of the United States, have a gap between our income and that of industrial America, just as we see the gap between the raw material nations and the industrial nations of the world This situation does not exist because people want it to. Our government, supported by our people, has spent very large sums of money to help raise the income of our farmers. Unfortunately, good intentions and generosity are not enough, and success has been limited. We as farmers, however, have learned some things from the experience. Little, if any, success has come from efforts of government to set prices, control production or otherwise interfere with the proper functioning of the market place. What success we have had in raising the income of our farmers has come from research, education, cooperative marketing and improving availability of capital to farmers thus increasing the production per farmer.

Most of this was made possible through development of farmer owned and controlled organizations based primarily on study of our own problems, on the farm and in the villages and then use of our combined efforts to attain our objectives.

A generation or two ago many people felt industrialization of other countries was competitive and should be discouraged. On the contrary, the record shows that our exports, both industrial and agricultural, are far greater to the industrially developed countries because of their greater spendable income. The North American people have the same interest in a high well-distributed income among the raw material producers of the world In spite of the best intentions, we are undoubtedly making some mistakes in our Latin American cooperation. We did in our farm program at home.

We have learned, however, that real and lasting progress comes through research, education, availability of credit on a sound basis, the application of sciences to increase production per worker and above all, a real study by the people involved to find the solution to the problems, and an organization to make these solutions effective.

The Creator of the Universe joined us together.

Our histories are similar; our hopes and dreams of the future are similar. We have fought for our freedom and we know it is our most precious possession. To maintain this freedom demands eternal vigilance in our generation. We have several times joined our forces in this fight for freedom for all mankind.

Panamericanism is not yet perfected but we are the same kind of folks—under-

294

standing, helped by language learning, the jet plane and above all, people-to-people contacts will soon change Panamericanism from a myth to a reality.

We received a great send-off from the Chileans and headed over the Andes to Buenos Aires.

†Argentina

The flight from Santiago to Buenos Aires is one of the great sights of the world. The climb is steep to get above the marvelously beautiful snow-covered Andes. The view was breathtaking, and then you drop down over the fruit and vegetable area of the Argentine with its great plains of fertile land.

Argentina is about the size of the U.S. east of the Mississippi—2300 miles north to south, 900 miles east to west. It is also much like the U.S. in diversity. The origen of the people is Spanish, Italian, German, Anglo Saxon and slavic; Caucasian is 96 percent and literacy is at 85 percent.

Argentina enjoys the highest standard of living in South America Agriculture is the chief source of wealth and provides 90-95 percent of exports.

Buenos Aires is a beautiful city with wide drives and roads, beautiful parks and public buildings. One of the highlights was a boatride upriver through the city. The banks were covered with green vegetation and flowers of all kinds and colors. Also, many highly colored birds added their beauty. It seemed a delightful place to live.

On Sunday, our last day, we took a ride out beyond the edge of the city. The native grass was beautiful and made fantastic livestock feed. We arrived at an English-looking country home which was the country weekend home of our hosts. The ranch had been a large one owned by the hostess's father, beautifully landscaped with many planted trees and shrubs. Peron had confiscated most of the homestead for a public park

They took us to see the family home built of marble, all the steps, porches and downstairs floors were of marble. The reception hall was large with many silver trophys won for best cattle in the shows. At each end was a solid silver trophy at least five feet tall for "grand prize bull" and, of course, many smaller trophies around the room The family were of English extraction The brother now resides in the house and manages the remaining property; he came dressed in Levis and boots. His operation is raising a great many ducks in man-made pools and shipping them, frozen, mainly to Germany

They all wore diamonds like rocks. They would love to visit the U.S. but couldn't get permission to buy dollars or take enough pesos out of the country to make the trip.

They asked me to send them literature about 4-H clubs, which I did.

They had barbecued lamb for dinner, prepared by the cowboys. They set in the ground a forked stick about two feet from the fire, then cut proper sized chunks of meat and put them on a sharpened stick which rested on the forked sticks at just the height and distance from the fire that they liked. The real delicacy, however, was the intestines, well cleaned, and roasted over the fire and cooked until crisp. They are really quite good, properly done.

The Farm Organization people wanted me to have dinner with them in their building and spend the evening, but it was the night for the big town meeting so they came with me to the meeting, then I stayed with them in several meetings until midnight The building was a beehive of activity when I left.

†Uruguay

We found Uruguay a beautiful country with Montevideo a truly beautiful city. Uruguay is the smallest of the South American countries, sitting between the two giants—Brazil and Argentina.   Montevideo lies about 20 miles   south of Buenos Aires diagonally across the river.

Since 1952,   Uruguay has been ruled by a nine-man executive council elected by the people and the council rotates the presidency with terms of one year. The Colorado party was in power 90 years. The opposition is the Blanco party. The winning party has 6 of 9 in governing junta with the minority having 3. The majority in Congress may not be the same as in the junta.

The Communists operate more freely here than any other South American country. Of 1,420,000 registered voters, 900,000 cast votes; of these, 19,500 were Communists. The Communists have a teachers union.

The people love liberty. There is a high degree of individual education.   Free public education is provided from kindergarten through university so that boy or girl, Uruguayian or foreign, may become a doctor, lawyer, or engineer without spending a cent. Elementary school is six years and then they take an examination; some go on to secondary school for culture and some to technical schools. Most high-school teachers are professionals who spend part time teaching, to bring a better balance between facts and culture. About one-fourth of students go to private schools. Private education accentuates culture and science.

Uruguay is the first South American country to legalize divorce, to adopt woman's suffrage, adopt the eight-hour day, and to effect the separation of church and state. Uruguay has the least class distinction, the most religious freedom, most honest voting, longest history of civil rights. There are 240 U.S. missionaries out of 700.

The government took over the insurance business in 1918, leaving 20 percent to private companies. The government operates railroads, refineries, electric power, telephone and telegraph, alcohol, fertilizer, cement, although Lone Star Cement is the largest foreign investment in the country.

Freedom from income tax stimulates private development. There is no individual or corporate income tax, but excess profit starts at 12 percent, going up to 30 percent.

Labor favors production for use rather than profit. There are 250,000 in organized labor, 75,000 in Communist unions, and 25,000 in Socialist unions.

Wood constitutes 40 percent of total export and meat 20 percent, followed by other agricultural exports.

I remember Uruguay as a delightful holiday land with an easy-going holiday spirit.

† Brazil

We left Montevideo at 5 p.m., November 26, and arrived in Sao Paulo at 8:15 p.m. The next day we started with a most interesting talk by Dr. Joaquin Muller Carioba of the Uniao Cultural Brasil Estados Unidos. His "Survey of Brazil" is so excellent that I will give it here.

It is my intention to give you a bird's eye view of our history and of the agricultural and economic development of our country.

This country was discovered on the 21st of April 1500, eight years after Columbus set foot on Guanahani. It did not happen by mere accident. The Portuguese admiral Pedro Alvares Cabral, sailing from Lisbon to the Indies, had orders to follow a course that would take him substantially to the West in order to find out if there was any land there.

The impression received by the discoverers was such that the secretary of the fleet, Pero Vaz Caminha, wrote a most enthusiastic letter to his King, praising the beauty and fertility of the land. He said anything would grow if you just planted it. The first name given to the colony was "Santa Cruz," later changed to "Vera Cruz," and finally to "Brazil." The first settlement was officially established in 1532 in Sao Vicente, right next door to Santos, the main port of our State and of this country.

Soon immense alluvial gold deposits were discovered, as well as diamonds and semiprecious stones in great abundance. The expeditions that went hunting for these treasures, and all of which were led by paulistas, were called bandeiras. Their members are the bandeirantes. The hardships they endured and the distances covered in their roamings are well-nigh incredible. They have their counterpart in the American pioneer. After the gold was exhausted, not many lasting towns remained.

The political changes that took place in Portugal during the 16th and 17th centuries little affected the life of the colony. These changes, however, were in a sense the consequence of the fabulous wealth that flowed from here, and evidently also from other colonies to the metropolis. The riches undermined the morale of the Portuguese people to such an extent that King Phillip II of Spain had little difficulty in conquering that country in 1580. Naturally, the colonies came also under Spanish reign. When Phillip II's son reopened the war against the General States, Prince Maurice of Nassau attacked and conquered the northern part of Brazil, where he stayed from 1630 to 1661. He started extensive developments.

The first time European politics really brought about a change here was in 1807. King John VI of Portugal decided to transfer his whole court to the colony in view of the imminent danger of invasion of the metropolis by the Napoleonic forces under Junot. Soon after he raised the colony to the status of a kingdom and established a government that was independent from Portugal. He also opened all Brazilian ports to international trade, a very important event in our history.

On September 7, 1822, while in Sao Paulo, Pedro received orders from Portugal cancelling his autonomous reign. Right then and there he declared the independence, although without any intention of paying allegiance to his father.

It did not take long to establish an organized government. The same year he was crowned Emperor of the new nation. The first foreign government, incidentally, to recognize the sovereignty of the country was the United States of America under President James Monroe. After a few years Pedro I abdicated in favor of his young son Pedro II, who was a grandson of Empress Maria Thereza of Austria.

Pedro II eventually transferred the reign to his daughter Isabel. Upon the proclamation of the republic on November 15, 1889, the whole family left for Europe in exile. Isabel's last important act was the abolition of slavery in 1888.

The political organization adopted at that time closely resembled that of the United States. It was a federate republic under a presidential regime. There were 20 autonomous states.

During the following 42 years there was quite a bit of political unrest. The republic seemed unable to get on an even keel. One of the reasons was the deteriorating economic situation, based practically on only one product: coffee. What once had been a great asset had, little by little, become the source of much worry and headache. There seemed to be too much coffee. When the great crash came in 1929 the country was ready for a change of regime.

Through a completely bloodless revolution Getulio Vargas became dictator in 1930. Following the example of Mussolini and Hitler and other dictators throughout the world, Vargas based his power on the labor classes. He introduced a very advanced labor code. Although nobody will deny the necessity of protection for the workers, there is no doubt in my mind that these laws are to a large extent responsible for the extremely low productivity and high cost in our industries.

The peculiar irresponsibility of Vargas' administration caused a most alarming lowering of the ethical and moral standards in our politics. In 1947 the dictator was forced by the army to resign. Soon afterwards, when normal elections were held, he became a Senator and later was again elected President of the republic for 7 years.

Our very first export product was a valuable reddish hardwood, called pau Brazil. It's color reminds one of embers, in Portuguese, *braza,* hence pau Brazil, or Brazil wood. Soon sugar, an expensive product at that time, became an important item of our overseas trade. Later, in the 17th and 18th centuries gold and semiprecious stones overshadowed everything else.

Naturally, this being a colony, the wealth produced was transferred to the metropolis. During the last century there were only two products of any importance as economic factors: coffee and rubber.

The latter was produced from trees scattered in a native state throughout the area of the headwaters of the Amazon River. You can, even today, tell what the rubber boom meant, by observing the ruins that are left. Among them is the magnificent theatre in Manaus, capital of the State of Amazonas. There was a time when the most important theatrical companies from Europe would perform in Manaus, without deigning to come to Rio or Sao Paulo. Luxurious passenger boats plied the route from England directly to Manaus, 900 miles up the Amazon. People went to school or vacations in Europe without ever having seen the rest of Brazil.

All this glory came to an abrupt end when about 50 years ago an Englishman concealed some rubber tree seeds in his walking cane and took them to the East Indies. The latex produced there on orderly and well-organized plantations was so much cheaper than ours. Efforts have been made to again increase production.

The other product that became prominent during the last century is coffee. People have called it "General coffee" because all our economic battles are either won or lost through its influence.

In 1925 this country contributed 72 percent to world consumption. The figure has shrunk to 39 percent. As I see it, this decline is due to the controls instituted by the government.

When the surplus became larger and larger toward the end of the 'twenties, over 80 million bags were destroyed. If you realize that even today the total world consumption is but 43 million bags, you can see what this means.

Webster's definition of "valorization" is the "act or process of attempting to give an arbitrary market value or price to a commodity by governmental interference . . . used chiefly . . . by Brazil." Some people contend that this policy of valorization is the umbrella provided by Brazil under which other countries, especially Africa, have been increasing their crops very considerably.

I've told you this only in an attempt to explain some facts that, in my own opinion, have a bearing on our present economic situation.

The U.C.B.E.U. has a tremendous program, over 6,000 regular students a year in language courses. They were then building a twenty-storey building on land given by the City of Sao Paulo. A listing of their activities covers four pages, single-spaced. Similar organizations were in all the cities we visited, but Sao Paulo was the most active.

Sao Paulo is the industrial and coffee city of Brazil. My counterpart there was an attorney and owner of a large coffee, sugar cane, and wheat ranch northwest of Sao Paulo. We went by train and were met by his foreman in a 1938 Chevrolet car. We stayed overnight in his home.

The coffee was on hill land but planted in regular rows. The shrubs were large and seemed quite productive. The coffee was washed in running water, then spread to dry on a large cement floor. There was a village of wooden houses for the help. He also had a mill to make flour from the wheat. The sugar cane was on lower, more level land, and he had his own sugar cane mill which he had bought in France and had it erected in 1954. He processed the cane for several of his neighbors, making raw sugar.

I imagine the ranch was family-owned. He did not appear, act or talk like a man of wealth. He had two bookkeepers, full-time, in the office. He had to keep two books for every employee, one for himself and the other for the employee who bought sugar, coffee, and wheat or flour from him as well as being paid. The employee's book must also have a copy of the employment contract and of the social security payments which amounted to 38 percent of the salary.

Social security had nice big hospitals in Sao Paulo and Rio, but his employees had little chance of ever getting there, so they got little for the 38 percent.

He had a two-ton "cat" on the edge of a field. It hadn't moved for some time. The tracks were badly worn, but new tracks would cost more than the new tractor.

The grower gets 50 cruceros for each dollar value of coffee exported, 98 for sugar, 140 for other crops exported, but pays 250 cruceros for each dollar value of imports. There were additional fees collected, so it took $5. worth of coffee money to buy $1. worth of tractor tracks, plus freight, duties, and so forth. It was a "mission impossible."

We drove to Santos and saw coffee in all directions. It was a lively port. All our group were guests at Sao Paulo Rotary Club at the automobile club. On the 29th we attended a reception at the home of Ralph L. Burton, U.S. Consulate, a very pleasant evening with Brazilian friends, before the Town Hall meeting.

†Rio de Janiero

My counterpart here was Dr. Alberto Martins Torres, Agricultural Technical Officer.

On Monday, December 1, we were briefed by Ambassador Briggs at the U.S. Embassy. He reminded us that Brazil covers half of South America and has half the population. Brazil needs development. The U.S. is advising on this and will give some aid. A large part of the money of the rich is invested in real estate.

Primary education is compulsory, provided by State and Federal governments. Most secondary schools are private with little state help; they are mostly professional, industrial, or commercial. The federal constitution provides 10 percent of federal income for education and 20 percent of state, but not implemented yet. Primary schools are still inadequate. All parents want schools for their children. Workers cannot afford private education. Point 4 is giving scholarships, but should give more. There is much red tape and tax on importation of books into Brazil.

There are boy and girl scouts in Brazil. Boys must have a certificate of having finished school before they can get work. In north Brazil, boys marry at 17-19. In the cities it is 25.

We enjoyed a delightful lunch as guests of American-Brazilian institute on the terrace on the 12th floor of their building, followed by seminar on economy. There was much criticism of the Washington coffee agreement; it was made to sound like it was our fault. Finally I asked if it wasn't the Washington agreement because the meeting was held in Washington. They answered "yes." Wasn't it true that the U.S. had no proposal but supported the proposal of Brazil and Colombia? Again, yes. Then they all laughed and guessed it was the Brazil proposal which the U.S. supported.

Later we were discussing wages and I had been out to the coffee plantation, so I asked which would the workers prefer—social security or higher wages? The answer was, "Oh, wages, of course...." Well, would they prefer the money be spent for social security or education for the children? Answer, "Oh, education, of course...." Then they said, "But you do not understand politics. You have to be for social security."

The next day we attended a second seminar on politics and had a typical Brazilian luncheon. On the third we had an interview with President Kubitschek, held the Town meeting at 3 p.m., then another meeting that evening.

On the 4th we went sightseeing to Sugar Loaf and up to the Christ of the Andes. Very inspirational. Some of our party flew over to the New Capital City of Brazilia and came back with very great admiration for the architectural design and beauty. A reception with Ambassador Ellis O. Briggs of U.S. wound up an interesting trip.

†††Reflections on South America

Following our too-short trip to South America, where we met very fine people in each country and saw all our eyes could absorb, we could not help reflecting on the difference between North and South. It seemed the early migrants came to the North American colonies to settle and establish their families. Those who chose South America went for adventure or to mine, sending the wealth back to Europe. Few went there as permanent settlers at first, and the old beginning carries over to a remarkable degree.

On the other hand, one can see the great similarity of the goals and objectives of the citizens of today. The differences are in degree and in point of time.

Our labor representative talked a good deal about how terrible the low wages were—$2, $3, $4 a day. I sometimes remarked, "How terrible? I have worked many days at 1-2-3 dollare per day, and I wasn't mad at anyone and no one was mad at me." Truly we wanted to see all people, city workers, farmers, all of us get our fair share of the benefit of their production, but the difference is a matter of time. They will probably raise wages more in the next twenty-five years than we did in the last twenty-five.

It was a marvelous opportunity to meet people of all degrees of power and influence in South America and increase our understanding of them, but it is also a great experience to spend five weeks of high pleasure—as well as some disappointment and almost mental and physical exhaustion—getting better acquainted with such a broadly knowledgeable group of U.S. citizens, each outstanding in his or her field of endeavor.

Each of us was better prepared to meet new challenges at home. I believe we were somewhat of an inspiration to the people with whom we met and gave some assurance of our interest in them. And I am sure they were analyzing and dissecting us every minute of the day.

In each country visited, we had a dinner at the U.S. Embassy with some embassy staff and we received considerable aid and briefing from the Agricultural attache and others. We also visited with the President or Chief Executive officer. In most cases we discussed with the President the setting up of an Inter-American Farm Organization of the present farm organizations of Latin America, the U.S. and Canada. The reaction was almost universally favorable; they felt such a farm organization would be their best defense against Communism. Practically all the countries had old and respected farm organizations. Most of the organizations were single enterprise such as cattle, dairy, cotton, tobacco, sugar, etc.

The larger countries had large buildings with Association offices, committee rooms, and bed and dining rooms for the members coming to Association meetings or personal business in the capitol city for a few days. Some had very complete farm supply stores in the basement. Most were organized before they had a National Department of Agriculture, and the organization started keeping crop and livestock production, weather, and other records. Some did work on disease control and were still active in those fields.

We had a beautiful flight from Rio to New York, stopping at San Juan Puerto Rico on the way.

On December 7 we were in Boston for my last AFBF annual meeting as a member of the Board of Directors. I was awarded a beautifully worded plaque by the directors of the eleven Western states for years of service to Farm Bureau. We did a little sight-seeing, as one always can in Boston, and then back to Washington, D.C.

December 10-12 we were with our GATT observer group for a dinner at the home of W. Tom Beale, then drew up the report to the President and reported at the White House to Secretary of State Strauss and Under-Secretary Dillon.

On December 12 we met for lunch with Charles P. Taft, son of President William Howard Taft, and brother of Senator Bob—Charles Taft was in our section at the Old French Cavalry School in Saumur, France. I attended the Earle lectures in Berkeley when Taft addressed three sessions. He did a marvelous job, largely in support of private enterprise at the time when the Social Action groups were becoming quite active in the churches. After that he became very active in the National Council of Churches and was president of that group at or about this time.

He was dressed in almost work clothes and an old sweater, being one of the crowd. After lunch, he asked each of the four of us how we stood on the Reciprocal Trade Agreement legislation then before Congress. I told him we were for it, as we always had been, but it needed some amendment prior to passage. He called on Ruttenburg and AFL-CIO was all for it and would support it. Taft then took off on how wonderful labor was and you never could depend on the farmers.

The facts were that Cordell Hull, Secretary of State and original sponsor of the Reciprocal Trade Agreement, said publicly many times that he never could have gotten it through Congress originally if it hadn't been for the aid of the AFBF. I wasn't active in it, but the AFBF had always been the principal factor in continuing its support. Labor never really worked for it.

Taft's statement was typical of Council of Churches attitude. Labor was always right, farmers were not worth counselling with!

We arrived in Clarksburg after a long absence to get ready for Christmas and the New Year.

†1959

Since about 1940 I, or we, have made quite a few trips to Mexico, first to work out a program for Mexican workers to come up to the Western U.S. to harvest sugar beets, then to meet with Alberto Salinas Ramos, President of Associacion Nacional de Cosecheros (Harvesters) and Mexican farmers and government officials to work out problems created for them and for us. I remember the 10-point agreement which we then took to the Mexican Foreign Secretary for his approval. Then we had the Bracero Program for all crops and I went down several times to get that extended, once at the IFAP meeting in Mexico when Bella and Dorothy were with me.

We had three goodwill trips to Mexico while I was President of the Farm Bureau and a group of about thirty Mexican farmers and wives toured California as our guests. During these trips, Tom Robertson and Alberto Salinos Ramos told me of the Viscaino Desert in Baja California. They had set up a company to colonize and develop a large acreage of desert land.

302

14
VENTURE AND ADVENTURE IN MEXICO

In the early fifties, I was asked to join in the Mexican project. The general plan was to buy from the government 50,000 hechtars—125,000 acres— of desert land to be developed with deep wells, roads, a town, harbor, etc. We would sell the land to young Mexican farmers at a profit but still a reasonable price to be paid in full in ten to twenty years. We then might retain part of the townsite and farm equipment, chemical and petroleum sales as we might wish.

Water was, of course, the vital question. On the southern border of the land was a large dry salt bed, smooth and hard as concrete, a perfect landing field for a DC3 or even larger plane. Alberto had a well drilled near the salt flat, but the water was salty. He had a second one drilled near the middle of the east boundary, but then he moved near Beunos Aires. Near the southeast corner, they got water all right but the land was rough with scattered small plots of good soil.

The natural rainfall was 1-2 inches per year average with the rain falling on scattered areas so the grass came in scattered areas and the cattlemen would move the cattle accordingly so needed wells for water. Tom and I looked up many of these hand dug wells, measured the depth to water as well as depth of water, the thickness and types of soil. The standing water level was about level, rising some as one went toward the ocean until it got almost ground level in places. There were high, steep, barren mountain slopes to the east, and the geologic service said an underground rock ridge near the coastline helped hold water in the basin.

There is quite a farm development west of La Paz—about 100 miles—called the Valley of Santo Domingo, with the town of Constitution near Magdalena Bay. They had 600 wells there in 1959, but some of the farms were abandoned. The Mexican geologic service associated with oil exploration says there is water in Santo Domingo for 20,000 ha (50,000 acres) for irrigation while in the Vizcaino not less than 50,000 (125,000 acres) can be dedicated to agriculture. We generally figured that would permit irrigation of 25,000 acres for our project, with grazing for cattle or goats on the open land.

As I've said, I bought the first 53 acres of land in 1920 on a shoestring. We received much aid and encouragement from Gus Olson, manager of Holland Land Company, which was a great aid to us. I have always hoped that it might be possible to return the aid to some young farmers. I couldn't see any possibility of doing this in the U.S. with such high costs and our limited resources. So this project in Baja, California, seemed just what I had hoped for, so I agreed to lease 1,000 ha for twenty years. Later, Bernell Harlan, who had entered the program at Tom Robertson's request, agreed to join me in buying one-third interest in the whole project, Bernell taking one-third of the one-third and I took two-thirds of the one-third interest. This really meant that we financed the project from there on.

We cut brechas (openings) on the edge of each 10,000 ha lot so the surveyor could run his "lines " We studied all the area to see if we could see any relation between the growth of plants and type of soil. There was a good deal of variation in the growth but we could not relate it to soils or value for farming.

We picked a 100-ha plot of land and staked out the well site. We found Angel Sanchez who had a rig up near San Quentin. He brought the rig down on a six-wheel truck. After delays getting the right drill equipment and then tubing, he got the well down about 200 feet. The water stood at 90-95 feet and when we got the pump and GMC 671 diesel engine hooked up we pumped 2,000 gals per minute at 1800 rpm speed with only a five foot draw down of the water level. (We visited the old place last year, 1982, and the same well, pump and GMC are doing a good job on about 300 acres.)

Bill Talbert and a group of his friends made a payment on land for citrus trees. Before we could properly tell Mexican farmers that the land and markets were good, we needed to try farming and get some idea of crops, markets planting and harvest dates and, of course, good crops and varieties, so I volunteered to move down and determine the uses and value of the land.

All this was part of what we worked on as we made many trips to Mexico. We built a camper, home-made but pretty good, on back of the pickup, put extra tanks for gas and water, loaded it down with camping equipment, food etc., and, on February 4 at 4:45 p.m. we said good-bye to our home. We reached the Fowler Motel that night, stopped at Ralph's for breakfast and at Mother Mack's at 4:30 p.m. for the night. We arrived at Tom's in Ensenada at 12:30 noon on the 6th.

We left Ensenada at 5 p.m. the next day for the desert, stopping at Colonia Guerrara. We started again at 5:30 a.m on the 8th, arriving south of Catavina rancho in pouring rain and a gale. We went through Punta Prieta at 1 p.m. on the 9th, and arrived at Rancho Yachata on the 10th, where we stripped the reverse gear and broke the crank case. We sent the gear to Ensenada, then settled down to wait. We were like two lost souls in the wilderness, but we had a beautiful camp and a rest. Bernell flew over on the 19th, landed and got us, then got parts and fixed the pickup. Ramon drove the car on to camp. We took off with Bernell at 10 a.m. to Ciudad Obregon. We visited the Rockefeller Experiment Station in the afternoon.

The station here was part Rockefeller and part Mexican. Most of the workers were Mexican, trained at the College of Agriculture with Rockefeller's help, and were now involved in wheat and corn breeding. At this time the only characteristic they were interested in was yield per acre. They had no problems of machine harvest or appearance. For them white corn was human food and yellow corn for cattle and hogs. This was quite a problem when we shipped yellow corn to them as point-four aid. They felt it was not human food. Their corn was hand-picked so irregular height was of little concern. We pulled and measured some stalks at the ranch—they were fifteen feet tall. We planted hybrid seed from several of our States as well as that raised in Mexico.

On February 21 we went to Santa Rosalia where we found a pump and flew into camp about 5 p.m We got right to work, moving all we had from Piloto Camp to Rancho Margarita. We were using a railroad rail to drag down the shrubs and then used a cable and tractor to fell the dataillos and cordones That was a thrill. We had to be sure the cable was high enough on the palm or cordon so the top wouldnot hit you or the tractor when it fell, for when a cordon hit the ground it was so heavy that everything shook. A year after they were uprooted and hauled to the edge of the 200-acre field, the dataillos put out a full bloom in the spring.

We had frost on February 24 and 25. We cleared land, burned brush, and surveyed boundaries—we kept busy. On March 5 three truck loads of supplies came in including palm for the roofs. We set up the Eversman to start leveling land and built a two-wheeled dump flat-bed to haul off remains of burned piles, making it much faster and easier. We started a cook house with plywood sides and thatched roof.

On the 14th Bernell flew in, Next we started a shop with plywood and palm roof. By the 20th we got the irrigation pump going in a fine flow of clear and soft water. On the 22nd we flew with Bernell to Guerrero Negro and Ensenada to see A. J. and Mrs. McFadden at Tom's. We had a barbecue at Tom's and the next day—the 26th, my birthday—we were awakened by a Mariacha orchestra—an old Mexican custom. We left that day for San Diego to get pitchforks and meet the sprinkler man.

On the 28th we took a cargo plane to Guerrero Negro. Aero Carga flew bombers a little larger than a DC3. There were rings in the floor and walls for tying the cargo down. The passengers came aboard to fold up a seat on the side wall if there was room, or sit on top. The return cargo was lobster, turtle, or anything going. We later shipped pigs down in crates on "Aerocarga."

The salt company had an airstrip in Guerrero Negro used for private planes, but the large dry salt lake was much larger and smoother when dry, so Aero Carga landed there. We took a taxi to the ranch. After we left Guerrero Negro, the taxi driver did not want to go. We stopped for dinner. He wanted to go back. To get into the ranch we then had to go south on Highway 1, almost to Los Angeles, then come back up a new brecha to the camp. We got to Rancho Tablon, but he didn't want to go further. He asked Urbana Arcc if it was possible. Urbana asked who he had in the cab He said "George Wilson." Urbana said, "Well, if he says it can be done, it can be done, so go on." We did and made it at 11 p.m.

By April 1 I was working hard getting the land cleared and other things. We had a crew of twelve. I needed a haircut by now very badly. They told me one of the men clearing land was a barber. He said he could cut it if I had a razor. I told him all I had was a safety razor. That was O.K. I sat on a box while he cut the hair, then he asked for a razor which I got. He lathered me up around the neck and took the razor, unscrewed it, took out the blade and held it in his fingers while he shaved me. I sure sat quiet!

The roads in Baja are the world's worst. Sand, sharp rocks, ruts, many to choose from. The ruts got deep and rough, then would come an occasional rain, ruining some roads and making them impassable, but on others, the sand would run down the ruts and fill them up so for a while they were like floating on a cloud. Local men might get a shovel, pick and wheelbarrow and go out and fill in the ruts or otherwise improve the road. Passers in cars or trucks would give the volunteer workers 5-20 pesos (1 peso = eight cents). That was the only upkeep the roads got. On April 2 we dragged the new road to Tablon.

On the 15th Burnell and Adolph flew in. Three men were paid off; the ten left were plenty now. About a week later Art Starbuck and Phil Graham came down and set up rain pipe, putting couplers on pipe, etc. We bought the machine for setting up pipe and used it a great deal. We ran pipe to sprinkle the air strip. If one sprinkled the sandy surface and used Eversman plane on it while damp for a few passes it would pack down in fine shape. The same was true for the roads after a light rain.

Cipriano, our foreman, married Francesca, the cook.

On May 15 we started working nights, levelling land, etc. On the 27th we went to Guerrero Negro for parts, and stayed for dinner and spent the night with Winters. Back at the ranch, we put up a water tank to have water in the houses.

On another trip to Guerrero Negro on June 20, we got stuck at Cantina. We got a ride to Lagunitas and stayed there all night. Ramon Aguilar took us to the jeep, which we fixed and came home to find Bernell, Tom and Alberto there.

Dick and Camillis arrived at 6 p.m. on the 23rd, and Bernell and Tom left on the 24th. We now had the best air strip in Baja.

On the 27th we started planting corn, and on the 30th it rained. Planting and rain alternated. By July 8 we still had 65 acres to plant. Bernell and Tom came back and by the 11th Bernell had finished the planting. On July 13 we planted pasture, then Bernell, Bella and I left for home.

On the 20th we got a tourist card in Sacramento, then flew with Bernell and Hattie. We had lunch in Tijuana on the 21st and spent the night in Tepic. We started to take off in the rain on the morning of the 22nd, but the rain closed in so we waited for it to open up. The sky was filled with beautiful, billowy clouds. We flew higher, but so did the mountains. It was beautiful, but we decided maybe we should look for an open spot to land when, all of a sudden, there was a clear spot. We looked down and saw thousands of diamonds—Mexico City. We dove for it, landed nicely, then slid off the runway. We cared for our business and flew on home.

We returned to the ranch in early August and came back to Clarksburg on August 29. I recall that the temperature on the ranch on August 24 at 2 p.m. was 92 degrees.

On September 21 we were in San Francisco at the Palace Hotel for a dinner sponsored by the World Affair Council and the Commonwealth Club, both of which we belong to. The speaker was Nikita S. Khruschev of the U.S.S.R. His statement that he would "bury us" was much in people's minds. He spoke with lots of punch

306

and bravado—no holds barred. The dinner was attended by Mayor Christopher, Governor Edmond G. Brown, a representative of the President, Henry Cabot Lodge, and the president of the Commonwealth Club, Gardner Johnson. All of them spoke, so it was quite an evening.

On October 9 we started our house in Baja, 16' x 32' and 8' to the roof. The wall studs were 2' x 3' with 3/8" plywood on the outside and inside with rolls of fiberglass insulation in between. The roof was 2 x 4 with plywood top and underneath and 4" of insulation in between. We used aluminum windows and doors. We had washbowl, toilet and shower in the bathroom, with a solar heater outside for hot water, sometimes steam, a gasoline stove to cook on and kerosene house heater. There were shelves 8' high between the bedroom and the dining area and bookshelves about 5' high between the kitchen and living room. There was a sink in the kitchen.

The floors were sand or dirt with several woven reed mats spread around. Bella deserves a "Purple Heart" or something for keeping house as she did before. It was quite warm in winter and cool in summer, relatively speaking; certainly a luxury compared to what we had before. Our homemade camper on the back of the pickup was augmented with a canvas about 10' x 16' out from the east side with a 4' high wall of plywood to enclose somewhat on three sides a dining/living area with a stone camp fireplace for cooking if desired, or heating water for washing. We cooked on a gasoline stove. Bella slept in the camper and I had an army cot by the south wall.

One of the compensations was the clear nights with sky and stars all clean and shiny. One could read a newspaper outside on a clear moonlit night. One night I woke up and thought I saw something moving on the plywood wall by my bed. I moved and it moved. I raised my arm and it moved too; it was clearly a shadow. I looked out and it was the morning star and another close by causing light enough to throw a distinct shadow.

About this time, bringing in many things for the ranch and our new house, I had the camper completely filled with all manner of things, about solid to the roof. I stopped at Barbara Todd's to get papers showing what I was importing into Mexico. She said to drive into her office yard. She opened the door, took a quick look, and said "get out of here and luck to you." We rolled right through without a question. We usually got papers but they seldom asked for them.

We bought a Minneapolis Moline corn sheller and a rubber-tire trailer, then left for home in Clarksburg in late October. On October 27 I attended a UOP Regents meeting, then left for CFBF Convention in Los Angeles on November 1; the convention was held at the Statler Hotel. On November 3 I was awarded the California Distinguished Service to Agriculture award which, of course, was greatly appreciated but likewise CFBF had done a great deal for me and many others.

We left Los Angeles for Ensenada on the 5th, leaving again on the 8th for the desert. We arrived in camp at 6 p.m. on the 10th.

The 13th was spent working on the corn sheller. There have been many surprises and delays as well as breakdowns to delay us, but I suppose the biggest has been the yield of corn. Our corn was all imported seed or from the Experiment Station at Ciudad, Obregon. No acreage of corn had been planted within one-hundred miles. We felt we should not be bothered by ear worms or other pests the first year, but they showed up by the millions. It took quite a bit of time to get dust to spray them. We were promised planes to spray, but they were always delayed and finally we decided it was impossible. We got hand pump dusters to do it, but by then it was too late to do much good. I never would have believed so many worms could show so quickly from nowhere.

We were not sure the rain machine would work for corn, but it was O.K. We left a blank row about every fifty feet and used high risers set in the middle of the twenty-five-foot pipe. The irrigator held it above his head and carried it by the riser to the open row. When the corn got high the water whipped the leaves a little but not bad. We laid the 6" headline straight north and ran three sprinkler lines east and two west so two men moved all the five lines each morning and evening. Our 1960 crop was far more diversified and we had the dusters so we had little trouble from worms.

The corn was white corn all picked by hand the first year and shelled by hand until we got the sheller. Most of it was sold on the ranch to people who walked in, came in cars, trucks or on burros. It was interesting meeting them. The large flow of water was, of course, the real sight and experience for most of them.

As soon as we got the house, Bella planted flowers and they were always of interest. The biggest thrill was to see the women who came in from many miles around. They loved to take the hose, turn on the faucet and see the water run out on the ground. All the water they had ever used they pulled up out of a well and carried it, often quite far, to their camp and then used it sparingly. Here each house had running water and flowers the year around.

Bill Tolbert and his group from Ventura County sent down a lot of tangerine, orange, and lemon seed to be planted in a lathed seedbed to grow seedlings to see how citrus would do here.

On December 11 we started for home in the pickup, arriving at El Arco, Punta Prieta, the Sky Ranch, Ensenada, and San Diego on successive days, and finally reaching home on the 18th.

†1960

On February 19, 107 sacks of Urea arrived at the ranch in Mexico. Starting on the 24th, we planted melons, cantaloupes, cucumbers, squash, tomatoes, peppers, cabbage, corn. On the 28th we castrated pigs. On March 2 we planted onions, carrots, radishes, beets. We noted that fifty percent of the watermelons had sprouted.

On the 3rd Frank and Mrs. Lyons flew in, along with six others. They left for the beach at Scammon Lagoon to do some beachcombing; it was good to see them.

The temperature was 44 degrees at 7 a.m. and 85 at noon, the hottest yet. We killed the first of the pigs, a big fat stag. The Mexicans like them fat. We delivered two hogs to Pemex on the 4th, rendered lard, and nailed and painted bee hives. We built mounds for the hog lots, and by the 7th we saw that most of the vegetables were coming through.

In mid-March we flew home to Clarksburg by UAL, and returned April 2, flying in high winds from Ensenada to the ranch. On arrival we saw some small plants covered by sand. I covered the skylight over the living room roof and the temperature dropped immediately.

On the 11th we put out the bees, which did very well. On the 14th we planted potatoes. On the 20th we went to Sta. Rosalia. The post office had sent the corn seed back to Rockefeller in Mexico City. We attended Rotary at the old French Hotel. On the 21st we left Sta. Rosalia at 2:30 p.m. and arrived home at midnight.

We finished the rain pipe cart, which worked O.K., thinned vegetables and planted corn. On April 26 we picked the first zuchini and crooked-neck squash.

On May 3 we had a busy day in San Diego. We bought wholesale groceries for the ranch, signed up at Poultry Producers to get feed for the pigs, and from 11 a.m. to 4:10 p.m. searched for citrus trees and barely got back across the border before closing at 4:30. We then got bean seed and hog feed via Aerocarga truck for Ensenada.

On the 4th it rained all day. We went to Ensenada airport and the plane was not in yet from San Domingo with a load of chili. We went to Tijuana and got my immigration papers fixed up, then to Dr. Berlanger, the Vet, and found we needed a Mexican permit to get the pigs across.

We landed in Guerrero Negro at 11:50 the next day, to find Jesus was there with 16 boxes of vegetables. We sold ten in Guerrero Negro and sent six on to Tortugas.

Marshall Dickenson had flown in, and we spent the 6th with Marshall laying out and planting 36 citrus trees just south of our buildings. (When we stopped at the ranch in 1982 they looked real good and were told they were producing well.) We found some worms in the pasture, corn and radishes, but not like the previous year.

The next day we picked and packed vegetables and started building a packing shed. The next day we sorted hogs for size and planted seven acres of pink beans.

On the 14th Cipriano went to San Ignacio with a load of squash, but could not sell much. Of course, one of our reasons for being there was to find out what we could sell. People ate a few vegetables out of their own gardens, but had never bought them before. We killed a pig for Pemex and also sold vegetables the next day. On the 18th we found the new purebred gilts had arrived at the U.S. border.

We left Guerrero Negro, fifty miles from the ranch, at 1:50 p.m., got stuck twice in the sand, once for twenty minutes, once for 1½ hours. The roads were terrible! We finally arrived home at 9:30 p.m.

The Mexicans were experts at driving in sand and more so at getting out again. The simplest way was to kick sand up on the sides of the tires, then rock the car from side to side. As the tires on one side were raised a little the sand would flow under the tire and the rocking would pack it a bit. Then you start the engine at a low speed, probably putting it in second gear, and start slowly and smoothly so the tires did not spin. If they broke a spring they would cut a datailla to a short length and put it between the upper and lower spring and go many miles quite comfortably. "Necessity was the Mother of invention."

The purebred gilts had been in San Ysidro on the U.S. side of the border for days awaiting papers. They were finally crated up for the flight down and Jesus and his family left for Guerrero Negro on the 20th to get the pigs. He arrived back at camp on Monday, the 23rd, but no pigs—they were still awaiting papers.

Burnell and Hattie arrived about 5 p.m. on the 23rd, and on the 25th they flew with Bella and me to Sky Ranch near San Quentin to buy an AC harvester and side delivery rake for $1,000. We went on to Ensenada to see Tom and Dorothy. The pigs were still in San Ysidro at Barbara Todd's place. They needed a permit from National Economy as well as Agriculture. We arrived back at camp 7 p.m., two hours and 13 minutes from Ensenada.

The next day Bernell, Cypriano and I went to Guerrero Negro to meet the District head of Pemex. He wanted vegetables. We went on to Tortugas Bay, then to Santa Rosalia where we arranged to ship the vegetables by Aerocargo. There appeared to be good gravel in arroyo back of Tablon.

Bernell and Hattie left for home on the 28th.

The "topos" or gophers were everywhere eating roots. You could see where the runs were in most cases. I made a probe for poisoning them. It was a sharp pointed piece of 3/8" iron pipe. You could easily feel when you hit a run. Poison tablets were dropped down the hole. We also fertilized the corn, two sacks of urea per acre, and 1½ sacks per acre for the sweet potatoes.

On June 1 we started irrigating all night. On the 4th we put supers on the bee hives. On the 5th the Delegado—like head of County—and Villavacencio came to take a census. There was more corn, vegetables, hogs, etc. here than in almost all the area combined, so the "Jefes" came to record it.

The bees were very valuable for the vegetables and alfalfa seed, but they took lots of attention. We finished pens and water piping for the new pigs. Cipriano and I took vegetables and meat to Pemex Camp, 21 miles in 1 hour 50 minutes, to Comacho, 17 miles in 1 hour and 30 minutes. Lagunitas was 13 miles, 1 hour 10 minutes; San Francesqueto was 9 miles, or 40 minutes. All of these were on the best roads!

Marshall Dickerson arrived on the 22nd about 7 p.m. with a full load of laths, seed, insecticide, etc. to build the lath house, 20' x 30'. We needed this to plant citrus seed for future trees on 200 acres, as well as windbreak seed.

On the 23rd we dusted corn, made a lathhouse, and planted one pound (2200 seeds) of Troyer for rootstocks. In spite of the hot afternoon we had many visitors. On the 24th we took a number of soil samples, picked watermelon, cantaloupe, cabbage and pumpkins. The watermelon was superb. I didn't believe they were as good as everyone said until we got home to Clarksburg and ate a watermelon. It was definitely inferior in taste to what we had on the desert. Those desert melons were sweet and marvelous; all our visitors said so. The temperature was 94 degrees.

On June 27 Ibarra of El Arco store bought 482 pesos (a peso is eight U.S. cents) of corn, watermelon, etc. for his store. Sales were fine but it took many of them to pay 482 pesos ($38.59).

The next day Raul Villavicencio of Pozo Aleman came for melons. In the late afternoon his father came for one watermelon, sat and ate it, then kept putting more into his pickup until he had 211 pesos' worth—only about $17. in U.S. but it was lots of pounds of melon.

On June 29 it was 104° F in the afternoon. We set up and started the refrigeration in the house— a most welcome addition!

Sometimes the pictures of our trucks and visitor's trucks, pickups, cars, mules and other things, should have been recorded for history. Many buyers came in on foot and ate all they could before leaving with all they could carry.

One thing I could never understand—our truck tires seemed to blow out almost without reason but many Mexican trucks came in with the tube actually showing in the tire and they were not a bit concerned.

July 2 we picked a truckload of watermelon in the morning for Villavicencio and another in the afternoon for Guerrero Negro.

About 4:30 p.m. Bernell, Hattie, Dr. Michilbacker and our Patty flew in; it was a glorious sight when we saw Bernell's Bananza or any other plane fly over and know we were to have company for a while.

The next day we collected insects with Dr. Michilbacker, then went to Guerrero Negro at 11 a.m. to receive the nineteen purebred pigs we had been waiting for. They were a little peaked, but in good shape. On the 4th we went to El Arco, Guerrero Negro, and Lagunitos looking for pigs, We and the pigs arrived at the Ranch about 11 a.m. They were home at last, and in time produced some fine specimens and fine pork and "chicharrones."

Dr. Michilbacker put parathion on the squash bugs. We scraped a dirt mound for some warehouses, and on the 7th we picked good striped watermelons and put them in the warehouse.

On the 8th Guillermo Hale arrived with feed and insecticide. Cipriano had been telling me of him for so long I felt I should know him. Cipriano called him Hell, which I felt was wrong. Some years ago the grandfather of the man who owned Hales Department Stores went to Baja and got a concession to develop a portion of the peninsula. An English company had the concession for the area around San Quentin. This Sr. Hale was a grandson of the original Mr. Hale.

We thinned the last of the melon plantings. We sold over a ton of watermelon plus cantaloupes, string beans and other vegetables to Sr. Hale of Assension.

The Power family who was camped southwest of us came in for lunch and dinner and we had a good visit.

Bernell arrived about 3 p.m. on the 16th, and Bella left with him on the 18th. They left about 10:30 a.m., and we spent the afternoon hauling rock and poisoning rabbits and gophers. These "topos" were about to eat us out of house and home. We put a hog fence around the alfalfa, but still the rabbits were everywhere, so we dug holes along the fence line and put a wooden box with a cover on top fixed so any weight on the top would open the lid and let the rabbits slide in. We got seventy rabbits in one of those the first night. The alfalfa land was also full of gophers, so we flood-irrigated it. That would force the gophers out of the runs to the surface. The dogs were there to get the gophers and, just a little further off, two or three coyotes would wait to rush in for a nice morsel. The dogs and coyotes kept a reasonable distance, but they did not seem inclined to try to run the other out. The coyotes would follow the irrigator just like the dogs did.

We also learned that coyotes love watermelon. They would jump on the melon and crack it open, then claw it in two parts and eat every bit of the red part right into the rind. There were two Mexican women on the ranch who would go out in the morning with a couple of sacks. One would put a sack over the end of the rain pipe and the other would lift it up at a good angle so the rabbit which had slept in the pipe would slide down into the sack, and they had a meal.

On August 2 we started pulling onions. On the 3rd we set a generator on the pump motor and had electricity. Bernell, Bella, and Dick and Camillas arrived about 5 p.m. on the 5th.

The Pemex mechanic came over and helped us overhaul the GMC motor for the pump. They got water from us, so came over to help us out.

Jesus made lard and crackling (chicharrones). The Mexicans loved the cracklings, and so did I.

On the 8th Bernell, Dick and Camillas left again, and our A.C. harvester arrived. It was surely a help for the wheat, alfalfa seed, milo, etc.

On the 12th the truck left for Guerrero Negro at 1 a.m. with two dressed hogs and a load of vegetables; they returned with twenty barrels of diesel. Keeping enough diesel on hand was always a problem.

On the 15th we levelled the road to arroyo crossing and put corn cobs in the road where the sand was worst. This helped a great deal in packing the sand.

On the 19th Cipriano brought 3800 palm leaves to thatch the warehouse roof. This made a very neat and efficient roof. Twin 671 GMC motors also arrived, so we had spare motors and parts as needed. This was a great help in keeping a regular supply of water. We also helped by putting one or two heat exchangers on, in place of the radiator. In the same shipment was an elevator for handling corn and bean cutters. We had already gotten a corn sheller and a one-row corn picker.

Roman Aguilar says about September 1 is a good time to plant corn to get less stalk and more corn. On September 4 and 5 it rained 2½". On the 6th we hand-picked corn, which yielded 5500 lbs per acre. On the 12th Cipriano and two helpers went to the hills to cut fence posts.

On the 14th David got Patterson to fly him down to get me; I was needed in Clarksburg. The Trinidad Sanchez labor camp at Courtland was being inspected by both State and Federal inspectors. The federal inspector was out to get Trin. The State inspector said the camp was OK, but the federal inspector said "no." He then asked to see Trin's books, remarking "We will get him somehow...." Trin's temper exploded. Dick and one or two other growers had to hold Trin back or he would have floored the inspector. The camp was closed by the federal government, so all the growers were short on labor right at harvest time. I saw the U.S. office, and they told me this particular inspector was seldom sent out, but he got them into trouble every time. But the camp was closed, and harvest time was passing.

David was cared for by men from other camps where he was also getting men, but Dick depended on Trin's camp only and he was not able to get men from other camps until too late. He lost about $10,000 income, which was pretty serious and also discouraging.

Back at the ranch in Baja on the 19th, we were having one of our usually

312

clear nights when we heard Cipriano outside calling Satelite–Satelite. We rushed out and could see the first U.S. satelite, just as plain as could be, moving across the sky.

Bernell arrived about 3:30 p.m. on the 30th, leaving again October 5. We harvested milo on that day, with Bella sewing sacks, finishing on the 6th. Milo was better than three tons per acre.

On the 13th we were up at 5:15 to start for home in Clarksburg. We flew on Aerocarga to Tijuana. I had been appointed as a member of the Permanent Agricultural Committee of the International Labor Office for a three-year term. They were to meet in Geneva, Switzerland, from October 24 to November 4, 1960. We thought it would be a good idea to have a change of scenery and a new experience, so we accepted.

We arrived home on the 14th; it always looked awfully good. We had passports to get, many social activities, and our family to see—so it was all a great rush—and we got a plane on October 20 for Baltimore airport. We took a bus into Washington D.C. to get final instructions.

We flew Washington to New York, then on to Rotterdam. We spent the day with George Deitz of the AFBF and the foreign trade office located there. We had lunch in the high revolving restaurant, then a boat ride to see the harbor, the biggest in the world. It was tremendous, with all sorts of specialized loading and unloading equipment for various classes of freight.

We took the train to Amsterdam on the 22nd, where we were tourist sightseers on the streets and canals, then went on down to Geneva.

The ILO session started on the 24th. The meeting was opened by Assistant Director General of ILO. He said their endeavor was to promote social progress in the rural sector, which had stemmed from its special responsibility to insure that workers of all categories, hired, semi-independent and independent, would benefit in an equitable fashion from economic and social progress. Then we heard from a representative of the U.N. food and agriculture organization, and the WHO (World Health Organization).

I had in my pocket a letter from Dr. Frank Parker who was in charge of U.S. mutual assistance in agriculture in Delhi when we were there and was now Assistant Director of FAO. The letter told me of the lack of cooperation between ILO and FAO and expressed hope that I might help improve the cooperation. But now when the representative of FAO reported, he told only of the great assistance ILO had been to FAO and how much the fine cooperation was appreciated.

The first item on the agenda was welfare facilities in agriculture; these were all listed and supported. The second item was the application and supervision of social legislation in agriculture. All sorts of government inspectors and laws including encouragement of organization of trade unions in agriculture were named. The third item was the contribution of the ILO to the raising of income and living conditions in rural communities. This was to create demand for ILO to become more deeply involved in the rural sector. ILO wanted authority to cover all areas of improvement now covered by FAO, WHO, etc. It also wants supervision of application of social legislation in agriculture. Where it would not be practical to establish a special system of supervision of social legislation in agriculture, steps should be taken to specialize a sufficient number of officials in this type of work.

Many of those present had been delegates year after year. They loved it and supported the ILO line all the way, so it wasn't really very invigorating or interesting. I remember the Russian report. He sat about two desks from me and kept his eyes on me all the time. His report was given in Russian but interpreted so I got most of it, which was how wonderfully Russian rural labor is treated and how terrible it is in the West. After his speech, he came to my desk and said in good English, "Well, what did you think of it?" I had a sheet of paper on the desk on which I had written, "That ain't the way I heard it." I handed him the sheet and said, "that is what I thought of it." He said, "You are right, absolutely right." We talked several times, and he seemed very anxious to know about the U.S.A., but his interpreter followed him most of the time and then he stayed with the line.

The English representative of the farm labor union told how terribly farm labor was treated, and for a real clincher he stated that he knew places where labor had only dirt floors in their houses. Of course, that set me up, so I asked if I might ask a question. "Please tell us just what is wrong with living in a house with dirt floors. My wife and I have been doing this for some time and we kind of like it." In such an environment there was really very little opportunity to make a constructive suggestion for improvement or to hold a real discussion for the benefit of farmers or farm labor.

Bella got to see a good deal of Geneva and it is beautiful and interesting. We rented a car and had a beautiful trip to Chamonix, France, and rode the cable car to the top of the mountain. Another day we took a bus ride around the lake. We left Geneva for London on November 4, then took a train to Liverpool. There we boarded the Cunard Liner for New York.

We soon met a very interesting couple. He was head of the Unitarian Church in the Washington, D.C. area. We spent a good deal of time with them. At least one day was quite stormy, the waves breaking over the foredeck of the ship. We had costume parties and all the other recreation activities on shipboard.

We saw the Statue of Liberty on November 13—still a thrill to me. The next day we took a plane to Chicago and then a train to Champaign, Illinois, where we spent the day on the family farm. The renter and manager were drying corn, his wife was driving truck.

†1961

After Christmas in Clarksburg, we left January 2 to drive to Ensenada.

We saw Leo De la Rosa. He called canneries for us, but they do not can vegetables. He talked to a Guadalajara produce dealer, but they have a surplus until March. We next called Ruffo, but he could not can; he said a cannery at Colonia Guerro could can. We called all the Ensenada stores; they said they used a little and it had to be cheap. We took our freight to Aerocarga.

On the 5th Cipriano took the GMC truck to San Ignacio with two tons of white corn and three sacks of yellow, three sacks of beans and three of sweet potatoes. Jesus went to San Ignacio with his family; the baby was sick. On the 6th I made bins for pipe fittings, bolts, etc. in the shop.

314

The crop of sweet potatoes was fantastic. The books say four tons per acre is good and 7 tons tops, but we got 14 tons per acre of beautiful tubers. The local people loved them, but there were not enough people to eat them all. We sent some to Ensenada and Tijuana, but we couldn't sell them there as the sweets of a grade too low to ship east from California were dumped in Baja at a price we could not even truck them up there for.

I had gone to the College of Agriculture folks to see where to buy the seed or plants. They said there were only two certified seed growers in California that they could recommend, so I got plants from one of them near Colton. Our sweets were grown far from any others which might be infected; they were probably the best disease-free seed available. I thought maybe we could get a special permit from the U.S. Secretary of Agriculture to sell them for seed, so I checked with the plant quarantine folks in Sacramento and they could not be brought into the U.S. even with a special permit from the Secretary of Agriculture in Washington; neither could we ship them across the U.S. to Canada, so many of our very special sweet potatoes were fed to the hogs and sold for cattle feed.

We had clouds of crows in the pig pens over the fields eating the corn, beans and other sprouts as they came through the ground, sometimes going down the rows picking out the corn, milo and other seeds. I missed too many with the 22, and shotgun shells were expensive and inadequate, so I got several Zon guns. They had a supply of carbide in a tank and a supply of water which dropped into the carbide to form a gas. When there was enough pressure they blew off like a gun, really quite loud, to scare the crows. This worked fine for a few days, then the birds would pay no attention. It worked fairly well if we shot a few crows with a shotgun, then the gas gun would scare them for a day or two. Sometimes it seemed like **man**, weather, birds, broken equipment, and bad roads were all working against us.

On the 22nd we made eight farrowing pens for gilts and set up the grinder for grinding milo for the pigs.

We gradually got equipment for doing better farming and also for the house. We bought some things from two Americans who lived south of us for a while. The electric clothes washer was a big help. Bella had been using a washboard by hand.

One family moved down in a house trailer pulled behind a pickup. Coming south they had two small dogs locked in the trailer, but at one point they saw the dogs running alongside the pickup. They checked and found the trailer floor had dropped down from the side walls, either dragged where ruts were deep or hit a tock or some obstacle. They roped it up and came on. It was OK for stationary living, so we bought it minus the wheels for, I think, $25. U.S., and set it up near our house. It was fine for a guest house.

On the 23rd we made hot frame beds for planting tomato seeds to raise plants, and on the 25th planted the seeds in the hot bed. They would be moved to a cold frame and then to the field. One gilt farrowed that day and more on the 27th.

A truckload of supplies arrived on the 29th, and he bought 111 cartons of sweet potatoes to sell along the road north.

Bernell and David flew in the afternoon of February 6. David shot four rabbits.

We built more hog houses on the 10th and on the 25th put cement floors in all the hog houses and pens. By March 18 we had a total of 84 small pigs on hand.

We were doing lots of planting, all kinds of crops, at this time.

I attended a two-day board meeting at UOP on the 27-28th. I left on April 7 to drive to Los Angeles.

We got to Banning for church and had dinner for all the family at the Banning Inn. We went to Palm Springs and on to Indio to the U.S. Date Palm Experiment Station to see about buying date shoots to plant in Rancho Margarita, but they were sold out for the year.

We went to Indio to see the Farm Advisor and Roy Nixon at the USDA Date Experiment Station. We arranged with Don Mitchell to get shoots. They ship mainly to the Middle East. We crossed Kane Springs Julian Highway 80 to San Diego. We agreed that though we thought part of Baja was pretty dry and barren, we did not remember any place as dry and barren as parts of that road.

Over 40 people were there to get on the plane with lots of cargo, so we could take only a few essentials. We again stayed at Caseta house and left Guerrero Negro at 11 a.m. in a Ford taxi with very weak springs. We got to El Arco about 6:30 and left at 7 p.m. We put a hole in the gas tank and lost all the gas, plugged the hole with soap and had a half-can of gas to put in, so got to the ranch at midnight.

Monday, April 17, was our 40th wedding anniversary.

We found the corn in the northwest corner of the field was all gone—taken by the crows and rats. We dug two rows of comotes (sweet potatoes) for Urbana Arce; we sold him twenty tons for cattle feed for 3,000 pesos—$240. On the 19th we set up the corn sheller and shelled four tons. We earmarked and nose-ringed the weaner pigs.

On May 12 Bernell, David, Kenny and Dr. Bill Gibson, Associated Seed Co. of Ciudad, Obregon, flew in at 5:30 p.m. The seed company was anxious to have us grow lettuce seed for them as the area is so isolated from other lettuce and hopefully diseases and insects.

On June 3 we planted lime, tangerine, and Mexican lime trees. On the 10th it was 65° outside at 1 p.m., the first cool weather for a month.

On the 16th we hauled an aluminum building from the Pemex camp to our camp. We also bought several houses and a toilet or two. They had been built to house Pemex crews, were well-insulated and comfortable. We also bought—cheap— at least one-hundred barrels of diesel from Pemex, which we hauled to our camp.

We left for Clarksburg on the 23rd, being met by David, and spent Sunday, Monday, and Tuesday at home. We sold Sloughhouse steers at 20¢ a lb., 910 lbs net.

We left Sacramento on Wednesday, June 28, arriving back at the ranch on the 29th. Everything looked OK. The U.C. Davis wanted us to plant some Jajoba seed for shrubs that produce beans for very high heat resistant oil with several good quali- ties. We planted them, irrigated and hoed, but no one from Davis ever came to see them or asked about them. They grew very slowly even with irrigation and cultivation. They are a great new idea—about every generation—that lasts for a while.

On July 10 we planted the date palms from Indio along the drive into the house. They were still moist around the roots except where the paper was worn through. We put bean cutters on A.C. and cut beans on the 13th. The vegetables were coming on strong. Cut and piled beans and hauled alfalfa. We were getting our desert roads in better shape in all directions from the ranch, but still folks got stuck on other roads and we would help them get going again.

On the 20th we went to Guerrero Negro with twenty-one dozen sweet corn, twenty-five watermelons, eight cartons of squash (small) for Juan Ibarra's store. The corn was all gone within two hours. On July 21 we threshed beans.

Douglas Rodeck, Chief Engineer on the dredge, arrived during the night on the 22nd and worked on the GMC all next day and until noon on Monday the 24th, which was the day we finished the bean harvest.

On the 28th we picked 200 lbs of tomatoes.

When we went down the Minneapolis Moline tractor was pretty old and the tires about to give out. When we ordered new ones I hoped to get a size larger in circumference to get more traction in the sand, but we could not get them so I decided I would put the old tires on over the new ones. This gave more surface on the ground and worked perfectly. If the pull got a little heavy, the new tires would spin a little inside the old tire so it did not dig into the sand and we could usually get moving.

August 27th we built concrete foundations for wire mesh corn silos, with an elevator over the top to fill them. Then we started corn picking, storing it in the wire silos then using the elevator to take it out of the silos and shelling it as we were ready to sell it.

It may be well to comment here on the cattle and cattle camps. The cattle had been living in that area for many years with little change in type. A cattleman would usually have three or four camps scattered in the area. They were usually thatched walls and roofs surrounded by a fence built of cordon ribs or other native wood, probably a small garden inside the fence but not a great deal. A hand-dug well, probably about one-hundred yards from the house, often with only a bucket and rope to draw water, maybe a winch to be turned by a handle to raise the bucket of water, all by the women. A camp might set idle for a year or more, but having three or four they could move to the location where the feed was best. The rains may be very spotted and one area not have much rain over one or two years, while others not far off did much better. The area around the camp is usually barren of any green as the cattle roam quite far in the night, but as the day heats up they come to the well for water, usually in a trough, then stand or lay around the well and camp in the afternoon. They are often milked once a day when they are fresh so they are gentle and used to people handling them. Most of the year they move slowly, seldom more than a slow walk, but if a good storm brings green feed, especially if they get two or three well-spaced rains, then it is miraculous how the green grass and shrubs grow and the cows kick up their heels, run and play and swiftly put on fat so they look like real beef cattle. I do not believe our beef cattle put on weight at any time as fast as those cattle do.

When the cows are ready for market, they carry six to eight head to a truckload. Maybe I should say they did. They drive until they see good food, drive off the road and dig holes to back the truck into, putting the dirt in mounds at the rear of the bed, then back the truck into the holes and let the cattle off to feed during the night. Early in the morning they load them back in and are on their way. They know each animal and if one is a little difficult to load they may tie a rope around its horns before they turn it loose, then it is easier to lead it into the truck. The meat as you order it is apt to be tough, but it does have character and flavor to it.

On September 8 we ran beans over the bean cleaner to prepare for sale, and on the 10th irrigated palms and grapes. We finished the milo on October 7.

Sr. Palacio, territorial secretary of agriculture, and Sr. Olechea, territorial secretary of ganados (cattle) were here on the 13th, along with their pilot. Palacio said he would send up an agronomist to put in field trial plots.

Below: Our farm truck on the "freeway to Baja," and our home in Baja. With Isabelle is Ernie Jacobson.

It began raining at 4 a.m. on December 7. We bought a deep freezer from a neighbor, put it in the warehouse, hooked it up and it worked OK. Cipriano returned after dark, then went back to San Ignacio to go on the truck to get wheat in La Paz.

By Tuesday, December 12, Cipriano had not yet returned from La Paz. Bernell arrived about 4 p.m. Bernell and I left at 8 a.m. on Friday for La Paz. We stopped at San Ignacio but had no word of Cipriano. Stopped at Villa Constitution, still no word of Cipriano and the wheat. We flew to La Paz and saw Chito who said Cipriano left Tuesday, December 12, to pick up wheat in Santo Domingo. We could not see any truck on the highway up to twenty miles north of Purissama where we ran into low fog and had to drop down and follow the coast line where even in the fog we could follow the white line of the breakers. We followed up the San Ignacio river to San Ignacio. The pickup was still in the same place. We arrived at the ranch at 5 p.m.

Cipriano drove in on Saturday, December 16, about 6:30 p.m., thirteen days after he left in a hurry. This was just part of life in the desert. You always wondered, you never knew. If the truck was between the ranch and Ensenada, I would often think it should be back and wonder why it wasn't or where it was. I would ask Cipriano and he would say, "Oh, it will be back tonight or tomorrow. He had a flat tire and is tied up in Punta Prieta." It seemed magic, but the underground telegraph line works for the folks tied into it. Every passerby gives all the items of interest on the road. I do not now remember just what held up Cipriano on his trip to La Paz for wheat seed, but it makes little difference. It may have been tires, fuel pump, spark plugs or a friend needed help. The reasons changed but the delays were ever with you. One of the things that interested me about life down in Baja was its similarity to the stories and the pictures of the West in the 1800's, and I often commented that it was a great way to get acquainted with your wife.

Vegetables, grains, and all went out in small volumes but the result of the years work was about as follows: By October 16 harvest was about complete with some sweet potatoes and watermelon still in the warehouse. The corn did a little over a ton per acre in spite of insects and some water shortages. The milo was 160 tons on 70 acres, or 2.3 tons per acre. Our plans for the Fall call for five acres sweet potatoes, ten acres of alfalfa, and 80 acres of wheat. For 1962 we plan 60 acres corn, alfalfa or pasture, milo 62, potatoes 6, beans 10, vegetables 6 acres—total 160 acres.

Flowers in Baja

The several years we lived in Baja, California, we were pretty well tied down to the details of farming and living. It was a large rugged area pretty much in its natural state. Some people saw it as barren, uninteresting, with little to see. All the cactus had a few characteristics in common. Still, the sizes, the shapes and characteristics were so varied that we found them very interesting and some of the flowers are among the most beautiful of all flowers. If you compare them with orchids, which are so well-known and admired, the cactus flowers equal the orchid in variety and beauty. The cactus flowers do not survive as well after separating from the plant.

The flowers that spring up after a rain are varied, colorful and beautiful. One reasonably good rain will bring some, but two or three well-spaced rains will make a fantastically beautiful carpet, covering wide areas of land. The spring flowers come every year, but the absolutely gorgeous sights come after a year of good temperature and well-spaced rains.

One day near the end of one of these fantastic floral years, I was out in the pickup and decided I should take home a few of the desert flowers. The desert Verbena, a rather delicate flowered plant, was still flowering so I was going to pick a handful. They have long runners, so I just followed to the main stem and roots. I pulled it up and put it in the pickup bed. Our house wall was eight feet high. I took the Verbena plant in and tacked the root at the ceiling in the living room corner. The spray spread eight feet out on the floor. To our amazement the flowers stayed fresh for nine days. In places the mallow, topped by its yellow flowers, would grow higher than the pickup top.

†1962

We spent most of January in 1962 near home. The National Co-op Council held their annual meeting in San Francisco and asked me to attend. It was a pleasure to meet many friends from all parts of the country. I was able to clear up some misunderstandings between Co-op's and FarmBureau. We had few differences, always short-lived. We also enjoyed the Yolo County Farm Bureau annual meeting in Woodland and the State meeting of the California Beet Growers Association in San Francisco.

The family saw us off again on January 30 for the desert, arriving at Bernice's in Los Angeles about 8:15 p.m. We arrived at Tom's on Wednesday the 31st. Munnos had no room on the plane, so we drove down to the Sky Ranch and saw the country around San Quentin on February 4.

On Thursday, February 8, we went to the Tijuana Airport and took off with Munoz in the rain. We stopped at Bahia de Los Angeles where we met Bob Baughton, helicopter pilot for Erle Stanley Gardner. He said the current prime minister of Pakistan was aide to Liaquat Ali Kahn on our trip to see California farms in 1957. We arrived on our air strip about noon. The weather was beautiful. Everyone was there plus Bruno Mayoral, cattleman and land owner from Santa Rosalia and La Paz.

Cipriano and I went to Guerrero Negro the next day to send a wire to Tom and get supplies. Sandy Cutting was the new head of the salt works. His wife had a Chinese mother and Scotch father. She was surely full of life and he was a real mining engineer and great administrator. He later managed mines in Nevada where he died, and she is in Mesa, Arizona. We still correspond.

On the 14th we built a hotbed 48 feet long for tomato seed. We planted watermelon seed on the 16th, hooked up electricity to the wash house, toilets, guest house and trailer. We also shelled all the corn that was left and made a form for a concrete foundation for a new almacen (warehouse).

On the 20th we poured the cement for the almacen and a cement pad for the airstrip. The cement pad was under the propeller at warm-up so the wind from the propeller would not suck up sand or gravel and possibly injure a propeller or break a windshield. This was a real hazard. John Glenn went around the world three times in four hours, fifty minutes on this day.

The 21st we planted tomato seed and mowed alfalfa, and the next day set up the grain cleaner and cleaned two and one-half tons of corn. On the 24th we showed movies in the evening.

We left on the 26th, ate on the road, and arrived in Santa Rosalia at 4 p.m.— pretty good time–8½ hours. We left Santa Rosalia at 12 noon, ate on the road, and arrived home at 1:30 a.m., 13½ hours.

On the 28th Jefe of Colonization, representatives of McFadden Cotton Buyers and Bank of Agriculture Credit, and about twenty farmers from San Domingo came up. I agreed to try planting five acres of cotton. (Note: there was lots of cotton planted and a gin being erected near the ranch when we were there last year, 1982.)

We were told of several government people being at the ranch while we were away for Christmas and in January, also of land buyers looking around. Maybe I should have started more agressively, protecting Bernell's and our interest, but I figured that was up to Alberto or Tom. Maybe I had the fox protecting the chicken coop in Alberto.

I guess I have not said we were paying our help 30 pesos per day, some better. The general farm wage was 15 pesos, so we never had any problem there.

On March 5 we put in sewage pipe and cesspools for the toilets. Bernell and Tom arrived about noon. The next day Bernell, Tom and I went to Santa Rosalia and got contracts for all our labor to sign. All the men signed them and Bernell and Tom returned.

On the 9th, Ing. Victor Perez Novelle, "Jefe" of Hydraulic Resources, Guellermo Arranbody, a Jefe of Weather Division Hydraulic Resources, and Captain Gilberto Millan Calles, a pilot for Hydraulic Resources, came to get information for a report on how many wells to allow. They stayed for lunch.

On the 10th we made a map of crops and what to plant. On the 16th Sandy Cutting, Bremmer and Mike the pilot flew in for a visit. They were very much impressed and never forgot it. By the 17th half the ranch was planted.

On the 19th Colonization and bank men from La Paz spent the afternoon here. On the 20th Munoz flew in and said Erle Stanley Gardner wanted to camp here next week. We were pleased and decided to stay for at least part of it. On the 26th Munoz came in with Erle Stanley Gardner and crew about 2:30 p.m. Pickups arrived about 5:45 p.m. with Tote Goats.

On the 27th we visited the Gardner group, rode motorcycles, etc. The helicopters did not arrive. Cipriano returned from Santa Rosalia; the boat came but no diesel. On the 28th Bella and I rode the "burritos" of Erle Stanley Gardner. The helicopters arrived about 2:30 p.m. and made three trips to the mountains moving almost all to the mountain camp. As I said, the helicopters were two days late getting in.

Mr. Gardner is a very active man, interested in many things. He had with him as helpers some folks who were very active doers. I had expected there might be some delay, so I made plans to get hunting guides, horses or mules needed for a deer or other hunt. I suggested that as long as they were delayed they should spend a day hunting in the mountains. His crew boss said they would love to, but he didn't believe the old man would go for it. They were right. Gardner said, without hesitation, "This is a business trip and you can't mix business and hunting..." so it was quickly decided. But we did have fun riding the burritos and just talking. The trip was to get the material for a new book "The Hidden Heart of Baja." He sent us a copy of the book with an inscription:

To Mr. and Mrs. George Wilson
with many thanks for all the things
you did to make this expedition a success.

Yours, Erle Stanley Gardner

On all his trips Gardner has his regular crew to do all that is necessary for success, but he also takes a friend with no duties except to help him relax and just talk. This trip he had Col. Jose Guttierez of Calexico where he had a riding stable. On a previous Baja trip he had a Chinese friend. Gardner commented to his friend when they got well below the border "Well, we have left civilization behind us now." His friend replied, "No, Erle, you have not left civilization behind, you have just left urbanization behind." Seldom does a whole book say so much so clearly.

Gardner stopped in to visit us here at our home once and then he and his secretary, Jean Bethel, visited most of one afternoon. He is a quiet man, I believe one would say a simple man, that is why he is able to write in a plain, simple way that satisfies his readers.

On the 29th we went to Tijuana with pilot Francisco Munoz, and the next day Tom and Pepeta took us to Tom's in the morning and then we drove to Banning for a birthday dinner for Bella, driving home to Clarksburg on the 31st.

On April 3 we sold cattle from Sloughhouse, and on the 7th attended Picnic Day at Davis. We saw lots of our friends, which was a treat after being away so much. After a beet growers meeting in Stockton we were at the Los Angeles airport for lunch on the 11th before going to Tijuana and Mexico City to get papers fixed up properly for purchase of the Baja land. We were assured all papers were in order. We left Mexico City on the 16th, returned home briefly, saw Bernice, went to a Rotary meeting in Los Angeles, saw Disneyland, visited Tom again, and were back at the ranch on Baja on the 29th.

We finished planting the tomatoes, and were visited by Alberto Ramos, Caesar and Margarita on May 4. Alberto told me he had come to Santa Rosalia to file papers for his share of the lots. Said he had picked up a man on the street and paid him a few pesos to swear to Alberto's identity and integrity to get the papers. On May 6 Cipriano and Alberto and family left for San Ignacio.

On May 18 we started harvesting wheat. On Saturday evening, May 19, Ernie Jacobson of Selma Trailer Co. came in with his house trailer. He welded and braced up his trailer. Ernie Jacobson was the man who, ten or twelve years earlier, working for National Geographic, got a similar house trailer, drove it to the Arctic Circle, then south to the Antarctic, and returned to Panama where he sold it. He decided now to drive to the south point of Baja, California. He says no question about it, that is the worst road in the world. He never saw anything as bad on his earlier trip. This was his third stop to weld his trailer back together; we had the only welder in the area. He was a very interesting visitor.

Luis Hajes Badillo and another man from Colonization, Vidal E. Cesina Ibarra, head of Ganaderos of San Ignacio, Dr. Raul Pineda Penalira of S.I., Romiso Rivos, head of Colonization of La Paz, and Ing. Jose Lopez Martinez from Hydraulicos in Mexico came in for a visit.

On the 22nd we stood up the wheat sacks. On the 25th the Johnson family from Davis came, had dinner and stayed all night with us. The following day Bella and I went to Guerrero Negro and voted.

On the 30th Cipriano and I left for San Domingo in the Commando, which was larger than the Jeep. We arrived the next day, ordered sacks and twine, and got to La Paz at midnight. We saw Alberto and heard his tirade against Tom. We got supplies, saw Olechea of Immigration and then U.S. Consul in Tijuana, and left La Paz at 2 p.m. on June 7. At Constitution we got sacks, twine, and dinner.

By June the corn and alfalfa had grown a great deal. Farming was continuous but routine. On the 19th Alberto Salinas Ramos flew in with a pilot and a man from Tourism, staying only an hour.

June 22 was the first hot day of the season. On the 23rd we went to Guerrero Negro with pork, tomatoes, vegetables and shop work. We spent a very pleasant and interesting night and day with the Cuttings. Left about 5:30 p.m. and arrived at the ranch at 9:15 p.m.—I believe that was a record run, only 3 hours and 45 minutes for 50 miles.

Munoz had left parts and a letter for the Chevrolet truck caravan. On the 25th we went out to Highway 1 to deliver the parts and letter.

The Chevrolet Truck division of General Motors decided to base their advertising program on a run down the full length of the peninsula of Baja, California, about 1100 miles south from the U.S. border. Studebaker and several other U.S. companies had tried it with passenger cars, as well as several foreign cars, and all had failed. Few had gotten half-way down. Such a drive was a three-way test—car, tires, and driver. Some would have succeeded if they had employed Mexican drivers and oversized air cleaners with plenty of tires. This Chevy truck caravan had at least ten trucks, one refrigerated, full of food. One big dump truck was full of tires. One pickup had a high platform, a tripod for cameras to get pictures overlooking the caravan. The president of the truck division was with them. They were really fitted out. We invited them to stop in for a hot shower on the way back, which they enjoyed.

Several men from La Paz made a business of going to San Diego and Los Angeles, buying several used cars and driving them to La Paz for sale. They would get three cars and drive down the road together. It reminded me of the Western movies as they would come into any village wide open, slam on the brakes in a cloud of dust, get a coke or two, and then leave wide open in a cloud of dust until they got out of sight where they slowed down to a car-saving speed.

One day two old men, I believe one was 80 years old, drove down in a Volkswagen van. They had a good deal of clearance, but they made it down in good shape and I presume back.

Two men came down who were interested in plant life. They went to the area between us and Guerrero Negro, left the car, presumably to explore, and they were never heard of again. People looked all over for them but no success. One day Sandy Cutting was flying from the south back into Guerrero Negro when a bright light reflected from the windshield. He got the location well identified and went back with help in a jeep. The car had plenty of gas, oil and water; nothing had been disturbed. They stepped on the starter and everything was "go." The men had apparently lost their way and never got back. Healthy young men can still get lost. The indigenous people do quite well, 'though they occasionally get confused and lost, but the country tries the stamina and endurance of the newcomer.

In reviewing our progress to date, we realized that our farming had taught us many things, but had been more expensive than we planned. The extra costs were due to transportation problems, which were even more difficult than expected with both excessive costs and time lost in equipment repairs.

Ranch income was drastically reduced by lack of market, equipment break-down, and insect losses which resulted in lower yields. Also, yields were reduced through unsatisfactory planting dates and other reasons connected with experimentation. We felt justified in this investment in farming partly because we felt it was necessary to learn as much as possible to aid farmers as they started to farm in the area and partly to show the prospective farmer-buyer of the lands. Further, it was generally understood by all persons involved that we had signed and paid for the lease agreement and that the lands being farmed would be part of the land covered by the agreement.

I raised the question several times with Alberto Salinas Ramos as to whether we were justified in proceeding with the farming without recorded title from the Mexican government and without certificates of inaffectability. I was always assured that was taken care of and certain and that it was all right to proceed. He became concerned about these same matters, but that was a year or more late. Among the things Alberto Salinas Ramos was to do in Mexico D.F. was to get investors, immigrant or whatever class of visa papers appropriate and legal for me to carry out the farming program on the Vizcaino desert. These papers were promised but never received, and I do not know of his having taken any steps to get them. He still has my U.S. passport and vacination certificates.

The farming on Rancho Margarita, "the 80-hectar experimental project," proceeded in 1959-60-61. In 1961, even though we had proven the land and water, the enthusiasm for carrying through the colonization program seemed to have cooled. I suggested then that it would be best for us to step out and to encourage the government to study the project. We decided to plant a little less in 1962 and possibly plant very little in 1963, as we had proven our principal points.

During 1961 and early 1962 we were told by Alberto Salinas Ramos that the Agrarian Department of Government had raised the land prices and cut the amount we could have to 10,000 hectars in 500-hectare lots, and it would be necessary to submit new names to apply for these lots, twenty people in all. The names were prepared by Alberto Salinas Ramos and Tomas A. Robertson. We were also told by Alberto that the government was interested in buying our interest in Rancho Margarita or all of our interests on the desert.

In April 1962 we received an urgent call from Alberto to come immediately to Mexico D.F. or we would lose all. Tomas Robertson and I arrived in Mexico D.F. on April 11, 1962. Alberto said the titles had been signed by the President of the Republic and sent to Sta. Rosalia for recording and then withdrawn by the Agrarian Department and were being held there, and he had announced he was going on a hunger strike at the base of Juarez Monument starting about April 14 if he did not get the titles before. At this same time he told me of the great resentment against North Americans, of how the government believed there were twenty-five North American families on the ranch, and many other ridiculous tales. He said he had met the night before with Lic. Miguel Aleman, President of Mexico, and Gen. Olachea, minister of defense and former governor of Baja, California, and that Gen. Olachea had told him the only solution was for me to sign a letter saying I wanted to leave. I felt then, and far more strongly now, that ninety percent of this was in Alberto Salinas Ramos' mind and he was the one who, for some reason, wanted to

324

get rid of me. I felt this because many of the representatives of government had visited us on the ranch and, while of course they were courteous, I felt sure their expressions of friendship went far beyond the area of courtesy. They knew what went on at the ranch and I am quite sure reported it here in Mexico D.F. These folks included Pemex, who were at the ranch often during their exploration and drilling in the area. They got their drinking water and meat, vegetables, etc., from us. Also, Colonization, Hydraulic Resources, Agricultural Credit Bank, and the representatives of the governor's office visited with us. We always tried to be helpful in every way we could, and they seemed grateful. While I had wondered about some of Alberto Salinas Ramos' statements and actions before, it was at the April meeting I became concerned, but not to a point of any proof of intent to defraud. I asked him to arrange for sale of the wheat and to get the sacks for wheat to me before May 15 as we must start harvest by then.

On May 30 I got a wire from him saying the sacks would have to come from La Paz, B.C. By then we needed the sacks so much that I got in the pickup and drove to Villa Constitution and arranged to get the sacks and sell the wheat. I went on to La Paz that night. The next morning I met with Alberto in the hotel room. He told me I must sell the wheat in his name and his name only and that I must not appear in the sale. He then, for the first time, started in on a long tirade against Tomas Robertson, which was so different than it had been in the past that I said nothing. I saw Sr. Leopoldo Olachea at lunch that day and told him I still did not have the proper papers. He had checked in Mexico D.F. and found Alberto had done nothing toward getting them. Alberto came up as we were talking and again promised to get my correct papers right away. I was told by La Paz friends that Alberto was also doing all he could to discredit me there, and that he came to steal the wheat.

Alberto came to the ranch by plane, possibly two weeks later, with a pilot from La Paz and two other men. He was pleasant but methodical and seemed to be interested in showing the men the equipment, pigs and crops on hand, and then took off saying he had an appointment in Sta. Rosalia with tourism folks.

The next I heard, he came to the ranch June 28, 1962, about noon with a man, Daniel Romero of San Ignacio. They were in a new, yellow landrover painted with "Rancho Margarita" on the door, followed by "Alberto Salinas Ramos, Prop." There was no embrazo or other welcome of any kind. He just said, "This is Sr. Romero, he is taking charge of the ranch as of now and the men will follow his orders...." I finally had to admit to myself that this was robbery and he planned on stealing the ranch and everything on it.

Always in the past I had given into him if he was determined that his way was right, or at least I hadn't opposed him. Now, however, I replied that this man was not taking charge of the ranch now, nor tomorrow or next week, and neither was Alberto taking it over now or tomorrow or next week. If he wanted to propose a settlement of any reasonable nature he should write it out and send each of us a copy, then we would meet and discuss it. He then pulled out a telegram which was supposed to be from Mexico D.F. saying the government was accusing me of spying, running contraband, and other ridiculous things, but through his intervention on my behalf the government was giving me eight days to get out of Mexico for good. I felt sure he had written the wire, for the words were his words which I had heard before.

He got quite excited, so to attract his attention I tapped him on the front of the shoulder with the ends of my fingers and said, "Now, Alberto, you listen to me for a while, I have listened to you too long already." A minute or two after this he said, "Oh, you hit me and hurt me," and then several minutes later he said, "I came very near pulling my gun and shooting you when you hit me." The discussion was direct but not heated. He said he might as well leave. I again suggested he draw up and submit a plan for settlement. I asked him whose money bought the new car and he said it was a government car. He then left.

I had an appointment coming up with an associate from Hawaii on July 10, so I went north on July 3. I had some delay in getting a new U.S. passport as Alberto Salinas Ramos still had my old one. I got a Mexican visa which I thought was all right to settle up my affairs and returned to the ranch July 17. I felt I should not ship the wheat to La Paz without knowing how it was to be paid for, so on July 24 I went to La Paz. I dropped in to see Sr. Leopoldo Olachea to make sure my papers were all right. He told me it was fortunate as he had to make out another report on me and my activities, which was done.

While in La Paz I got wires from Tom Robertson of the fantastic activities of Alberto Salinas Ramos against Tom mainly, and me some, so I flew to Tijuana. We discussed the things and it appeared we must be alert, but friends in Mexico D.F. could handle the situation at the moment. I returned to Rancho Margarita July 31 agreeing I would be ready to return if necessary to stop the blackmail against Tom. On Saturday, August 4, Bella and I went to Guerrero Negro to see if there was any word. There was none from Tom, but the immigration officer showed me a wire from Sr. Leopoldo Olachea, Immigration officer in La Paz, saying I should see him as soon as possible. The only practical way to get to La Paz was to fly first to Ensenada then down from Tijuana to La Paz. I wired Sr. Olachea I would arrive as soon as possible, not knowing what for.

On seeing Tom Robertson in Ensenada, I was told the immigration officers had an order for me to leave Mexico, but I could report as reasonably convenient and leave in three days with no bad record against me so I could get appropriate papers and return as soon as I cared to. It was then Saturday evening so I planned to report Monday and go right out. A scurrilous article appeared in the Sunday paper in Mexico D.F. with headlines linking Tomas Robertson and me in land fraud in Mexico. This headline took the top six inches all across the Sunday morning paper in Mexico D.F. We were accused of espionage, running contraband, spying, having a secret wireless telephone, selling large acreages of land near the coast to foreigners. It sounded terrible. In fact, the government had a file at least eight inches thick on me and the operation, all favorable to us. They needed me to prove no government officials were involved in any such activities or permitting such activities. I was picked up at Tom's house about 9 p.m. Sunday evening and told I would have to go into Ensenada for a few minutes.

The "Jefe" was called in. They called Tijuana and said I was to be sent to Tijuana in custody of Rudolfo Valladolid Jefe de immigration. I was in old clothes, no hat, no suitcase, and the car key in my pocket, but they would not stop at Tom's

326

for me to get my things. We surely burned up the road to Tijuana. I was taken to two or three immigration offices and always told I would be taken to Rudolfo, but at midnight I landed in a cell in the Tijuana jail. There were six of us in a cell with an army cot but no springs, mattress, or blanket. It was a noisy but interesting night. They got the clean-up and kitchen gang up at 4 a.m. They really swabbed the floors and walls. I took a bun for breakfast; the gruel and coffee did not appeal. At 9 a.m. I was called out and taken to Rudolfo Valladolid and told I must leave for Mexico City on the first plane at 11:30 a.m. Commandant Robles came in and said he would be sure my bags got to me and the car keys got to Bella.

I enjoyed a pleasant trip to Mexico D.F. with my young officer friend. When we landed at 9:05 p.m., feeling quite rested and relaxed, the Stewardess in a very commanding voice said "All passengers, and I mean ALL passengers, will remain seated and no one rise until Mr. Wilson has deplaned." I suddenly realized that was me, and was impressed. My companion rose as I did and we got off and met my escort of three officers who delivered me to the immigration offices. There I met Lic Rafael Hernandex Ochoa, sub-director general of Poblacion, and Lic Jorge Saracho, director general Juridicos. We talked until 11:30 p.m.

After trying several hotels, they made a reservation at the Guillow Hotel and took me there at 12 p.m., telling me to return at 10 a.m. to meet the same two men. They wrote up a statement which I signed. They then said Mr. Shapiro at the Embassy wanted to see me and that I would need an informal request from him to get proper papers.

Bernell and Tom came in that day, Monday, August 6. I was also told by Lic Ochoa that I was free to do as I saw fit in Mexico, but I could not leave either the city or the country and that I would be called by the "Procurodaria"—attorney general—in a few days.

Mr. Shapiro saw Lic. Ochoa Tuesday morning. I should say that Alberto had written a letter to the Embassy telling what a terrible fellow I was. They had discussed and assigned Mr. Shapiro and Mrs. Anna Gomez to get the data and follow the case. Anna Gomez was a top attache and had accompanied us on our California Farm Bureau Federation good-will trips to Mexico.

On Friday, Mr. Shapiro took me to see the ambassador Horace Mann and we discussed the case and the University of the Pacific spanish language college. On August 6 or 7 Paul Posz, former U.S. immigration officer in charge of U.S.–Mexican border, arrived and we went to see Col. Carlos I. Serrano at his house and office Fundicious 183. The Colonel said he would take over the case and furnish the attorney for us. He was aid to President Aleman and lived in an adjoining home. His office reminded me of an Indian Majarajah's office. He turned us over to Lic. Luis Roa on his staff. He analyzed the situation and reported to the Colonel, who then called in Lic. Juan Pablo Alcocer, whose father is a good friend of the Colonel and Vice President of the National Bank of Mexico.

Bernell left Thursday and Paul Posz on Friday. While in Paul's room in The Regis expecting to go next to Col. Serrano's, I was called by phone and told a man would call to see me in 45 minutes. He was from the attorney general's office, and after a coffee we went before Lic. Raul Lozaro Martinez and an interpreter. We made some changes in the statement written in the office of Lic. Ochoa. We then went into a question and answer period running from 10:30 a.m. to 4:30 p.m. without stopping. He would dictate the answers in Spanish. He found the case quite complex and difficult to understand, and when the statement was read back to me there were many errors in it, so I refused to sign it. I agreed to sign a statement that there were errors which we would correct the following day, but he would not permit that, so we started to reread and correct until 5:30 p.m., and we were not done, so we left without signing to return at 9:30 a.m., Saturday, August 11. Much time was spent demanding that I produce cancelled checks which of course I could not at that time. Paul Posz had left, and I went direct to Col. Serrano. He invited me to meet him at 7 a.m. and he, Ron and others and I would go to his ranch for breakfast. We went. The ranch layout was beautiful. I would have liked to stay longer. At 10 a.m. we started correcting testimony; the atmosphere was better. I added a few more things and signed it.

We went to 5 Palma St. to see Lic. Raul Cervantes Ahumada. He was a friend of Tom's from Sinaloa, candidate for governor of Sinaloa, professor of law at University of Mexico, poet, author of law books and codes, and many other things. Tom retained him as his attorney. Time Magazine's Spanish edition featured him on its cover picture. We went to his house in Mexico for lunch on Saturday, August 11, as soon as we finished in the attorney general's office. He and his wife took me to their weekend ranch house about ten miles beyond Cueranavaca. It was a beautiful place with large swimming pools, shallow and deep, with plenty of fresh spring water running through all the time at just the right temperature. He also had ducks, geese, monkeys, wild boar, and other animals and birds as well as horses, cows, pigs, etc. There were many other guests there, always two tables in the dining room and sometimes three. We spent much of the time going over the case, the papers, and all. It rained so hard Sunday night that we left at 5 a.m. Monday, for he had a 7 a.m. class at the university. We came on to the hotel and then to the Attorney General Lic. Rosas office.

Rosas said he was President of Centro Ganadera Cualitenoec, and they had not received a cent from us. Tom said he had made out one check directly to them for $8,000. Rosas said he had not received it, then disappeared.

On Tuesday, August 14, we met before Lic. Raul Lazaros Martinez, with Alberto, Tom, and our attorneys. Alberto agreed to the first signature of his on papers or contracts and denied the others. Some time later he was not sure, but doubted it. He said he had spent 450,000 pesos on Rancho Margarita and that his boys had done much of the work.

I doubt if the actual hearing lasted an hour, then we were told that if we did not hear from them by the weekend we would be free to go. I believe it was Wednesday p.m., the 15th, that Lic. Cervantes Ahmada met with Alberto Salinas Ramos and his sister Henrigueta Salinas in his office and discussed a liquidation of the Impulsura Agricultural Ganadera SAM with him and Henrigueta as liquidators. Lic. Cervantes Ahmada dictated an agreement of liquidation and arbitration to be signed by Tom, Alberto, and me. It was of course in Spanish. I agreed to it in principal subject to approval by Col. Serrano. It seemed to me quite weak. I gave my copy to Lic. Alcocer and he discussed it in Col. Serrano's office.

About 9:30 a.m. Saturday, August 18, we left the hotel with Lic. Cervantes

A. and left about noon for another weekend at Cuerranavaca. This time he also had two men from Morelia on business and we really did little business except to drive into Cuernavaca for groceries etc. and then to see Sr. Eduardo Guttierez who was very friendly. He had put out 25,000 pesos to Alberto early and lost it, and he was anxious to help any way he could. He and his wife and two beautiful children drove over to Lic. Cervantes A. and discussed the matter and had lunch and then returned.

I should say that Gen. Alfredo Breceda was most cooperative all along, met with us many times, came out to Lic. Cervantes A's ranch on Sunday, August 12, talked to Gen Olchoa and told him he was a friend of ours. He knew of the case, and said to use his name wherever needed in government to explain the case. Gen. Breseda also invested early and pulled out.

Sr. Calderon, who represents the Torreon group in Mexico and has for 30 years, came and had a meal with us. He was an early loser. He is now quite elderly and had a bad cold. I think he was not able to do much, but was interested for us. Chito Jeffroy was at the hotel all the time with his wife and Bueno. He was helpful.

Monday morning at 9:30 a.m. Lic. Alcocer and I met with Col. Serrano. He talked on the phone with both Lic. Cervantes A. and Tom. Col. Serrano's activities and counsel were outstanding. He made valuable contacts for us. Lic. Cervantes A. was to leave early Monday for Obregon, but he stayed until after a late lunch hoping to contact Salinas, which he did not. Tom signed a power of attorney to Lic. Cervante A. and left early Wednesday, August 22.

We started actively to get my papers to leave. The attorney general's office cleared me Wednesday and Lic. Ochoa gave clearance Thursday, but Lic. Alcocer's uncle died Thursday and the funeral was Friday—one of the largest ever in Mexico D.F. On Friday evening at 7 p.m. Lic. Alcocer and I met Lic. Ochoa in his office and I signed the request for papers.

Alberto filed an embargo to prevent our selling anything from the ranch. The embargo was a mercantile embargo granted in the third district court of Mexico City for 450,000 pesos. There was no record of its having been filed in Sta. Rosalia. I insisted on knowing my right to sell perishables under an embargo. Lic. Cervantes A. said to pay no attention to it, but gave me no real assurance.

Tom called and said Alberto had made a good deal of trouble for him up there. He also said there was a letter from Remiro Mendoza in La Paz saying an embargo had been placed on the wheat so he could not collect for it.

I had been there almost three weeks and it was difficult to see why so long. However, all the folks with whom I dealt were most courteous and friendly, apparently wishing to be helpful.

I left Mexico D.F. on August 28 for Tijuana. Tom and Bella met me. Bernell arrived at Ensenada the next day, and we flew to Guerrero Negro. The wheat was still there. On the 30th we were on the ranch picking corn, dressing two pigs, and picking vegetables for Guerrero Negro.

On September 6 I was back in the U.S. and attended a Rotary State Fair dinner, followed by the host breakfast next morning. On Sunday September 16 Covell College, UOP, was presented with a fine collection of books in Spanish by the government of Mexico. We had dinner in the evening and spent the night at

Rudkin's, driving to Tom's next day and taking Aerocarga the next to Guerrero Negro. We had lunch with the Cuttings and he flew us to Rancho Margarita.

On the 19th Cipriano and I had to go to Sta. Rosalia. Wednesday evening was Rotary dinner, so I decided to put lots of hay in the pickup and then fill it up with watermelon for a special feed for Rotary. We arrived at Santa Rosalia at 9:45 p.m., a little late but not too late for a watermelon feed in Mexico. We got to the French Hotel and the Rotary day was changed, so we went to bed..The road had been rough and we were in a hurry, so when we got out the next morning the melons were broken and spoiled.

Jesus had a lawyer from El Arco sue us for overtime, no holidays or earned vacation, and all sorts of things. The hearing was in Santa Rosalia at 1 p.m. on the 20th. Cipriano went in to find out where and when it would be, while I waited outside. After a while I decided to look him up. He was really going to it with Jesus and the judge. During my stay in Mexico D.F. I had looked up the labor law. It was quite detailed and severe for industrial labor, but for agricultural labor there was, I believe, a fifteen day notice required and if you furnished a house the employee had a right to stay in the house until he got another job, or a maximum of thirty days. They were suing for everything.

The discussion was, of course, all in Spanish and I missed some of it, but the judge would tell me I had to pay and I would say, "No, the law says I do not have to pay." The judge would say, "You are right, you do not have to pay." Then Jesus' lawyer would get all excited and after more talk, the judge would tell me again that I had to pay. I told the judge I had promised to pay 1,000 pesos severance pay but he didn't seem to pay any attention to that. A big fellow, big stomach, shirt open, all hanging out, walked in and sat down at the end of the judge's desk. He would keep me posted in English. The routine went on. I had to pay! I didn't have to pay! Finally the judge said, "Did you promise him 1,000 pesos?" I told him "Yes." That was wonderful, what was the argument all about? If I would pay 1,000 pesos that would close the case. Our visitor at the end of the table said, "If you agree and the judge signs it then the case is closed and can't be reopened. If you do not agree now you are right, the law does not require you to pay but Jesus can keep on bringing the case up...." I wrote the check for $80. U.S. and left. We saw Jesus and his attorney on the street, very forlorn. They could not get the check cashed. I walked into an office and got the 1,000 pesos for them. They then thought I was a miracle and were very happy.

A legal officer said Alberto had been in to embargo the ranch, but the office had refused to accept or file the embargo so we were free to sell anything we wanted to. There were "chabasco" warnings (hurricane), so we left Sta. Rosalia at 6 p.m. and got to S.I. at 10 p.m. and got a room at Dona Maria's.

The wheat was still on the wharf waiting shipment south, so we decided we better get to Guerrero Negro and get it protected. Arrived 5:30 p.m., got two more trucks and two more men and moved 490 sacks, 220 lbs each, to the pump warehouse by 4 a.m. and it poured down rain. I slept on a boat at the wharf and got well rocked to sleep. We covered the rest of the wheat a little better. We worked in the rain to protect all we could. We left in the truck at 1:45 p.m., got stuck twice and got to the arroyo about fifteen minutes from home when Cipriano yelled

"Agua" and slammed on the brakes. The front tires were inches from the water rolling down the Arroyo Seco. We knew the truck could not make it that night, so we decided to walk across and on to the camp. Water was flowing by in big waves with plenty of bushes, some with spines, to tangle you up. We got a rope, tied it around our waists and set out, but half-way across we knew the next half was deeper and we never could make it, so we got back to the truck, backed out and went to the Cow Camp at Rancho Nuevo. Cipriano went in and they said for us to come in. They rousted two young fellows out of bed to use sleeping bags on the floor. We took off our soaked clothes and rolled in for a good sleep.

About daylight the Senora woke the young men up, and they dressed and got out. Then she came with a cup of hot coffee for each of the others. In five to ten minutes, all was quiet and I was sitting on he edge of the bed getting nerve to pull up the soaking wet and cold pants when the door opened and there was a cup of coffee for me. It was welcome. I got out and stood by the fire a little to warm up, when the Senora suggested I go in and talk to the Senor. He surely looked old, shriveled and cold. I didn't suppose he planned on getting up, but at the appropriate moment he arrived, was served his breakfast and the others in order, and we were ready for a new day. Mid-morning we set out again. The water was lower and not much brush and debris in it, so we roped up and walked across and into camp at 1:30 p.m. At Rancho Nuevo the bed was a blanket over a piece of plywood which was fine for me. I could have slept on spikes, but when I woke up in the morning, right by me, leaning against the wall, was a mattress and springs for the bed.

Monday, September 24, we sold nine pigs and watermelon. There was only a little water in the arroyo by evening. We were selling lots of pigs, corn, vegetables and were busy harvesting and selling. After selling a good many pigs we still had 128 head. Some photographers flew in on October 27 to take pictures.

††† Comment on Crime in Baja

Much is heard of crime and violence in Mexico. We heard or saw little of it outside of Alberto Salinas Ramos. When we first went down there was a good deal of talk about a man found dead in the dry mountains out of El Arco. Everybody seemed to know all the characters involved. He had been taken for a walk. No one knew by whom. Early one morning I was in the shop. A touring car drove in. Soldiers and rifles and ammunition belts kept emerging. They had a new lead. Someone had been around with a couple of 500-peso bills. The military officers asked if we had seen anyone around the camp with a 500-peso bill. We had not. We filled the soldiers with watermelon and then put melon in all the vacant spaces in the car. I was relieved to know that was all they wanted.

We were driving out the road to Tablon one day and saw a man walking on the desert. He seemed about starved and his feet very sore. He worked about a week and then quit. He wanted us to give him a ride four miles to the highway. One of Tom's grandsons and another boy had come down to visit for a few days. They agreed to take him. We advised them to be very careful. One sat in the back seat with a rifle. When they got to the main road he wanted them to take him north toward El Arco. He got out at El Arco and they were coming home when they met the local police who were looking for someone who had recently committed a robbery. The police told the boys they had contributed to the escape of a criminal, so the boys would have to help find him or they would be subject to arrest.

The boys led out, followed by the law. They saw him ahead on the road, so they stopped him without incident. The police came up and took over. When they frisked him he had a coke bottle hidden in his sleeve. He had hoped to have only one driver in the car, then he could come down with his left arm and the bottle on the driver's head, throw him out and be on his way with the jeep. With two boys, he didn't get the chance.

Francisca, our first cook, had a daughter, Maria, about four years old. She was a doll. Cipriano fell in love with her so he married the mother. She was still our cook for the crew when we had one. She came from San Ignacio. Often at 9 or 10 p.m. Cipriano would rap on our door and say Francisca was sick and had to go to the doctor in San Ignacio. Francisca felt that being the wife of the "patrone" of the largest ranch in the area, she really should have a cook, instead of being one. She came home one day feeling fine. She had a new doctor who understood her problem. She had been getting her stomach too hot—she shouldn't spend so much time close to the stove!

There was a great shortage of doctors in the rural areas, so young doctors who had received government aid in getting their education agreed to serve rural communities for two years; some stayed on.

No one in three or four years can learn everything about how another group of people live, but I worked with the men in all the jobs on the farm. We bought our needs in their stores and mixed with them daily. We found their objectives in life, their joys and sorrows, were similar to ours. Maybe one should say, similar to ours of fifty to a hundred years ago, but they are modernizing very rapidly.

In November I was supposed to receive papers so I could leave and reenter Mexico without any problem. They didn't arrive, but neither did we have any problem at the border.

Dorothy watches the digging of our well.

Top left, a typical Baja ranch home; right, a church on the Ejido Viscaino adjacent to the land we farmed in the Viscaino Desert. Ctr left, our watermelons after a visit by coyotes; right, Bella and Earle Stanley Gardner. Below, Bella on one of Mr. Gardner's Tote Goats.

Top left, in the ditch — a frequent event when traveling in Baja; right, one of our best products — Cipriano is in center. Ctr, our wheat harvest. Below, sunrise and sunset on Baja — they were spectacular.

Top left, meeting President Aleman of Mexico, right, receiving AFBF Distinguished Service Award from Charlie Shuman, Pres. AFBF, in Colorado Springs, 1960. Ctr, a typical fence in Baja. Below, the worst of Baja — I made the papers!

LA PRENSA $1.50

el periódico que dice lo que otros callan

Registrado como Artículo de la Clase en 2a Administración de Correos de México el 30 de agosto de 1925 | MEXICO, D. F., DOMINGO 5 DE AGOSTO DE 1962 | AÑO XXXIV | NUMERO 12.608

ILEGAL NEGOCIO CON TERRENOS

The text on the sign in the image reads:

RUFFO BROTHERS FISHING
BOATS
HOTEL "Los Arcos"
LA PAZ, B.C.
DATE March 29 58
ANGLER WILLSON
FISH Marlin
WEIGHT 165 167 TIME 10 20
TACKLE Med.
BOAT Delfin
CAPT Lucero.

The Best of Baja — Bella and I had a spare day in La Paz, so we went fishing. We rented a boat from Ruffo Brothers; Bella got hers within 5 minutes of casting, but it took 35 minutes to land. I got mine on the line within 10 minutes. We soon had our limit, so we quit for the day. Bella's weighed 167 lbs, mine 165.

15
HOME AGAIN 1963-1968

We went to the California Farm Bureau Federation meeting in San Diego November 11-15. In December Bella and I were at the AFBF meeting in Atlanta, Georgia.

†1963

We went home to Clarksburg in January, and on the 29th we spent a day with Jess Rudkin in Nevada City for UOP. People loved to see Jess even though they knew he was raising money. On the 30th Spreckles Sugar Company had a nice party for the beet growers at the Bohemian Club the evening before the Beet Growers annual meeting.

I spent a good deal of time on church work. In early February I was asked to be Chairman of the Northern California Council of Churches, but discussed it with Lowell Berry who had presided, and decided not to.

We decided to put Johns Manville shingles over the wooden exterior of the old Saner home on the Slough House ranch. The ceilings are very high in the house, so it was a long way up to the roof. I tried several contractors but none would take the job as the men would not climb so high to install them. I finally just went to Sears and ordered the material installed and Sears had one of their contractors do it. We had the same thing done on our house at home, but they left without doing the dormer windows on the third floor, so I had to get up there and do it myself.

I was invited to participate in the National Security Seminar at Asilomar. These let you know what many people were thinking.

On March 13 Ezra Taft Benson, Secretary of Agriculture under President Hoover and later President of the Mormon Church, gave a fine talk at American River College. It was good to see him again. On the 14th there was a farm center meeting in Clarksburg.

The regular World Affairs Council of No. California held their conference May 3-5 with national and international speakers. There were many groups; the meetings are always stimulating.

We attended a fine dinner for Dr. Nasu, a good friend, elder statesman of Japan, at the Claremont Hotel. In the latter part of August we attended a foreign policy conference at the Palace Hotel in San Francisco. On the 27th we went to Lovelock, Nevada, to check our cattle on feed there. They were getting a good start.

On September 22-25 the mayor of Koblenz, one of Germany's large cities on the Rhine, stayed with us. He was very able and gave us a fine view of how Germany is doing. He spoke at the Chamber of Commerce lunch at the Sacramento Inn. He was especially interested in Sacramento as an inland port.

September 25 was Bracero Day in Woodland. There was a parade, lunch, and speeches of appreciation of braceros as good workers and good citizens in the community.

We left for Mexico on the 29th, and left Ensenada to return October 2. We brought Cipriano and Francisca up with us for a few days. I thought David might hire him, but he didn't. Probably was for the best as maybe Francisca wouldn't be happy so far from San Ignacio.

November 13 the Clarksburg community entertained overnight a group of Egyptian farmers. We had two fine people. The 18th Sacramento had a farm-city banquet in the Governor's Hall at the Fairgrounds. It was well attended and the decorations were exceptionally well done.

On the 25th we left for Hereford, Texas, to see Pat, Wes and girls.

I was elected President of the Sacramento World Affairs Council. We had monthly luncheons for the directors of the Council, a monthly meeting at Mrs. Robbin's home at which someone speaks and often shows slides on foreign travel. I had shown pictures four or five times. We had public dinner meetings with a talk by someone from the State Department, or a foreign speaker, on his home country.

†1964

I was keenly interested in the World Affairs Council and wanted to do more. The Sacramento–Yolo port was new, doing well, but needed more publicity and actual trade, so I decided to use some I had learned at "Thunderbird," but use experienced people in Sacramento and San Francisco to develop a good six-week evening program on how one gets started in foreign trade. I set up a committee of local men interested in the program. Chas. J. O'Connor, of the Sacramento Chamber of Commerce, helped with planning, writing letters, programs, etc. We also got considerable help from Mr. Phillip Creighton of the U.S. Dept. of Commerce, Wilson of the University of San Francisco, and Mr. Bill Muriale of the Bank of America Foreign Trade Department. Much of my time January through May was devoted to the course on World Trade. There were many trips to San Francisco to see people. There were weekly 7:30 a.m. breakfasts with our Sacramento Planning Committee, etc. We held our meetings at California State University, Sacramento, getting dinner at the cafeteria, then going into a room assigned to us to eat together. This was followed by two speakers who were active in foreign trade. Each spoke on a selected subject followed by questions. We set a limit of twenty students in our plan, the tuition to be $35. for six dinners and classes, then a day as guests of the San Francisco Foreign Trade Club being shown the activities on the wharf and in the offices, then as guests at their regular lunch with their speakers. We found we had twenty-eight students before we could cut off registration, but twenty-eight was good and there was hardly a single absence.

We planned a graduation dinner in the El Rancho in West Sacramento. The place was decorated beautifully by the travel agencies organized by Dick Patterson. There were folk dances, a Japanese tea ceremony, color guard, singers from three colleges, two bands, and a host committee to welcome all. Enthusiasm was high all through the dinner. There were graduation certificates for the 28 students. The address on world trade by J. A. Correra Sr., Vice President International Banking Division of the Bank of America, was excellent. I read it over again in 1984, and it is still excellent. We had a larger group of Sacramento business people at this dinner than we had expected. Our group met occasionally for the next two or three years.

The world affairs council had the pleasure of a large luncheon at the Senator Hotel with the Chilean Ambassador to the United States, Sr. Guttierez. There had been some criticism of the handling of the U.S. Aid program with some of the Latin American countries, so the State Department asked some of the states to set up programs with some of the countries. California was paired with Chile. It was a disaster as it was just a pleasant haven for political appointees of the governor.

I was to introduce the Ambassador, so I asked the secretary of the California leader of the project to give me the resume. She didn't get it to me until the morning of the luncheon, then it was three pages long, telling how wonderful the California leader of the project was. As she gave it to me she said, "Now I want you to use it just as it is because I stayed up until 3 a.m. writing it." I read over half of the first page and saw it was of no use to me. Earl Warren Jr. was then put in charge of the project, but he told me it was too political for him, and then our friend, James P. Wilson, tried but it was soon terminated.

Sr. Javier Irarrazaval, a young man twenty-eight years old, is brother-in-law of the Ambassador, and he stayed with us several days to see more of California. I would love to spend several days with him now as I thought he was a coming leader.

On January 12, 1964, Helen and John Abley were baptized.

On March 8 we dedicated Burns Tower and attended a dinner for faculty and regents at UOP, followed by a regent's meeting the next day.

On the 14th was the camellia parade. My job was to assist princesses and other guests from the parade conveyance to the reviewing stand and provide coffee.

The Asilomar world conference was held May 1, and on May 9 we had a one-day conference in Sacramento on "A world without war" chaired by Henry Teichert. The first speaker was Alan Cranston, candidate for U.S. Senate. His talk soon deteriorated into a straight campaign speech. I got up after one of his heated statements against his opponent and broke in with a statement that as president of the world affairs council and a co-sponsor of the conference, I insisted his subject was "A world without war" and that he stay with that or sit down.

On May 15 we had a Congo student at our home overnight.

We attended a UOP regents meeting on June 13 followed by dinner. On July 13 we attended the GOP convention in San Francisco. They nominated Barry Goldwater. On July 16 I introduced Allan Kline at Rotary Club.

Pepita Bitterlin was herself quite a person. Her father was Sr. Gefroy, a French engineer, who came to Baja, California, as manager of the French Copper Mining Co. which built a large mill in Santa Rosalia and mined the copper in the surrounding area using a narrow-guage railroad to haul men and material. He married a Mexican senorita who was reputed to be the best shot on the peninsula. She was a fine-looking lady but taller than he, strong of body and of mind. They went to France for both business and pleasure. The children were schooled in France so spoke the language fluently.

Pepita graduated at the "Cordon Bleu" school of cooking and that was her life. She had the El Rey Sol restaurant in Ensenada as well as other investments. If it had been in Los Angeles or San Francisco it would have been one of the very best. Her parents were in France when World War II broke out and France was occupied. They moved to Vichy, the temporary capitol of France. She became the head of the French resistance group and she lived and worked out of a home next door to the German high command in France. She felt that was the safest place to be and to watch. She wore two pistols all the time and slept with them under her pillow at night. One of her principal jobs was locating French and American pilots who went down and get them on the underground railroad out of reach of the Germans. She was really head of the family. Pepita was an excellent business woman and mother, a fine citizen in any country.

In September, David and I looked over the Hart Ranch on Consumnes River below Elk Grove. We understood that the agent for the Hart family was very gruff and tough, hard to do business with. We hardly knew how to approach him so I suggested to David that in our course of foreign trade which he had attended we had heard that one of the bank's services should be to introduce you to a prospective business associate, so I suggested to David that he ask the bank to do that. The bank wrote a very nice letter introducing us as a preferred account. The date was set and we were welcomed as friends of the bank and it was very easy to work out a lease. We should have offered to buy the property at that first visit, but it has been an important part of David's operation. The ranch was available for sale, but we did not know that. David Belcher of the Spreckles Sugar family offered to buy the ranch if he had a good tenant, so on November 2 we had lunch in San Francisco with Mr. Belcher. He bought the ranch and Wilson Farms has farmed it since.

Fall Colors

We left home on September 12, 1964, to see the U.S., Eastern Canada, the colors of historic New England, Williamsburg, the Smokies, the South, and Pat, Wes and the girls. The speed limit then was 70 miles per hour, so Nevada, Utah, and Wyoming passed under us fairly rapidly. We spent the first night in Rawlins, Wyoming, the second in Nebraska, and the third in Iowa. We went south from Chicago to see the folks in Urbana, then to Paris, Illinois, to see my cousin Byrle, then on to Detroit and Dearborn Village—this was near Ford's home where he had built a village made up of replicas of famous homes and buildings. We stayed in the home of one of the revolutionary leaders. There were antiques of all sorts.

We then went across to Windsor, Canada, and on up the north side of Lake Ontario to Montreal. We were already getting good color and some beautiful views. Montreal was a large modern city full of life and business. We followed the St. Lawrence River to Quebec. This was a walled city on the hill, French speaking, old, antique. It was interesting as a museum but quite a contrast to Montreal.

We were now on the south side of the river and north of the Gaspe peninsula. There was lots of fishing, a little farming. The expanse of water was wide looking north to Labrador and northeast to Newfoundland. This was late September and the chill of winter was already in the air.

Gaspe was a town of probably 10,000 people, mostly fishing. We followed south and west around the peninsula to Campbellton and crossed into New Brunswick. Some of the colors we saw here were among the finest on the trip.

We crossed back into the U.S. at Van Buren, Maine. We crossed Aroostook County. This was one of the areas I really wanted to see because of its fame as a potato county, both commercial potatoes and seed, and it was often referred to as one of the richest counties in the U.S.

The soil was stony, the stones small and smooth but many of them. Potato harvest was in full swing. I only saw one modern digger which was pulled down the row and loaded directly into the trucks alongside. Most were dug by the old horse-drawn potato diggers which elevate them on a potato chain, shaking out most of the dirt and rocks and leaving the potatoes on the ground. Canadians, mostly women and children, picked the potatoes up in baskets and placed them in barrels which were then loaded onto flat bed trucks by a crane on the flat bed.

The workers were very similar to our Mexican workers who came in for temporary work. The crop was not good and the only houses which looked well-kept were those which had signs welcoming the hunters and fishermen. They were painted and the yards had nice flowers.

Some group was using government money to build a sugar beet factory there, but the local people said it would never work as they couldn't raise good beets there. The local people were right. That day was a real shock to me, as I had hoped to see a very prosperous farming area.

Southern Maine looked much better. The leaves were in their glory. The houses were better kept. We crossed New Hampshire into North Windom, Vermont, then up to Montpelier east to Fanconia Notch and south through New Hampshire. It was all beautiful. The leaves, the mountains, and the many streams and lakes— the whole country is clean, rugged, and hospitable. Many homes said "bed and breakfast." Many farm homes had maple syrup in all its forms, fruit candies and antiques, many home-made dolls. The people, like the country, were rugged and also beautiful.

We came into historic and beautiful Lexington and Concord, Boston, Plymouth Rock, and we went to the end of Cape Cod, all orderly, well-kept and impressive. We stopped at Sturbridge Village, a replica of the old colonial days. All the people dressed on Colonial costume doing the cooking, blacksmithing, wheat

337

grinding, harness making and all just as in the Colonial days. The old water-driven mill was grinding wheat and corn. We took a carriage ride. It was inspiring, but were impressed by the number of small farms and homes showing the old Colonial life. All seemed well done and well patronized. These all seemed to be free enterprise, not State or Federal.

It has been my hope for years that someone might buy the old Hamel ranch across I80 from Davis and use the old house and barns to set up such an exhibit and then the Antique Farm Machinery Club of U.C. Davis could furnish the old equipment and operate it for profit for the club and income for the students. I feel sure many tour buses would soon add it as an attraction to their tours of California.

We went to Riverside on Narragansett Bay where we had a summer home when I was a boy. When we lived there it was in the woods with lots of wild grapevines all through the trees. Now it is all built up.

In Hartford, Connecticut, we visited my nephew, Gilbert Scott, and his wife Wilma. We were impressed by the beauty of the Yale campus.

In New York we visited George and Jeanne Denny in their apartment overlooking Central Park. We had dinner and went to a show with Chester and Mrs. Williams. He was a leader in my world trip in 1949. Then we went to Philadelphia where we saw the area with Althea and Mr. Hottel, who gave us a delightful day seeing Philadelphia. We visited Gettysburg, beautiful and impressive.

We drove through Washington and on to Richmond, Virginia, for the night of October 6, then early to Williamsburg. Every American should spend a little time in Williamsburg. It is beautiful, interesting and surely inspiring. It lets one live the early, important and inspiring days of our national history.

Next we drove the Smoky Mountains Trail. There were many beautiful rhododendrons, and they say earlier many azaleas. They were beautiful in with the deep green foliage of all kinds. We visited the Hermitage, home of President Andrew Jackson near Nashville, Tennessee.

Our next objective was Eleanore and D. Anderson, Isabelle's sister living in northwest Arkansas. Beautiful mountain area garden and stream. We went one day to see the large Rockefeller Windrock Farms where they raised fine Sta. Gertrudis cattle. They had them. Then we went over to Siloam Springs right on the Oklahoma border to see J. C. Marshalls. He had been one of the farm bureau leaders of Yolo County who moved to Clarksburg, still a leader, a great doer and a great story teller. We surely missed him when they moved back east.

It was another 500 miles through Oklahoma and into Texas to see Pat, Wes and the girls. We spent the week of October 12-19 there. The folks in Hereford and that area are very active. As I write this in 1984 Wes is Mayor of Hereford, a Republican with a world of friends in both parties.

We saw all of Bella's folks in the Banning area and Bernice and Ethel in Los Angeles, then stopped at Madera to see some cattle we had to feed there.

Then on October 20 it was Home Sweet Home. Thirty-eight days and 9,271 miles.

On October 27 the UOP regents and their wives met at the Stockton Country Club for dinner.

On the 28th I saw Sam Mosher of Signal Oil Company at his Los Angeles office. Sam Mosher was one of the leaders in the fraternity house in Berkeley. He had a short leg, so operated a walnut orchard in Los Angeles County during WWI. Bob Berring was in naval aviation. After the war, Bob got a "tea kettle" which was affixed to an oil or gas well and produced high-test gasoline mixed with regular to produce "quick starting winter gasoline" when we cranked cars by hand. Sam borrowed $3,000 and they set up a partnership, spent $2500 on office furniture, and sold their product to Standard Oil Co. and others. After three years Sam paid Bob five million dollars for his half of the business. Sam set up Signal Oil Company. He and Natomas Co. bought U.S. President Lines SS Company. Sam was chairman of the board of Flying Tigers, and the largest orchid grower in California. I asked Sam one day if he had taken a good trip or cruise on the President Lines ships. He had planned on it several times but was always too busy to go when the time came. He was also a regent of the University of California. He was too busy to relax.

In November I went to see the UOP land in Sutter Basin with Bob Winterburg and Bob McMaster given to UOP by Mr. and Mrs. Walter Raymond of Knights Landing. There was the home and land in Sutter Basin and also a large acreage in the bypass. It was all rented out to about six tenants who had leased it from Mr. Raymond. The bypass was subject to flooding. I did a great deal of work getting better acquainted with the land, its flooding history, the crop rental and upkeep costs to the University, then handled the sale of the land to Jack Anderson who had a beet contract on land north of Woodland to help put him through college at Davis. He then bought, leased, and farmed more and more land until he was worth millions, all on farming and the increase in value of land.

†1965

Jim Fulmer, a long time friend, flew with me to Washington D.C. on January 9 for briefings from the U.S. Department of State and Agriculture and from the Venezuela Embassy to prepare us for a six-week's trip provided by "Farmers and World Affairs," seeing the farms and farmers of Venezuela. I had participated earlier in setting up the organization in the belief that world peace and human welfare would be advanced if farm folks of the nations of the world were personally better acquainted. Jim was U.C. '14, a dairy man from Dixon.

Venezuela has no book publisher, so schools use few books. Their books came from Madrid, Mexico, and Cuba. President Bettencourt, the first elected president since the dictator, has built the schools about 75 percent in five years.

Venezuela was one big cattle ranch until World War I. It was one of the poorest countries in the world until 1950, now oil provides the government one billion dollars per year. The Land Bank furnishes most of farm credit, the small loans at 3 percent interest up to 6 percent as loans get larger.

Eight years ago Venezuela imported almost all its hens and eggs. Now exports eggs and imports some feed. It has 6½ million head of cattle. On the plains it takes 10 acres per head to feed cattle on natural grass. Production per head is low, but in Caracas and Lake Maracaibo area the cattle are crossed with fine Brown Swiss, Holsteins and Santa Gertrudes and other fine registered cattle, and in those areas the grass is beautiful and plentiful.

Venezuela has a 5V program similar to our 4H.

On January 18 we went west to Maracay with 200,000 people. There are about 600 agricultural extension workers in Venezuela. They are trained in a practical school of agriculture, 60 percent farm boys and 40 percent town. Of these, 80 percent go into extension. There are two other schools with 250-287 students. Three similar schools are under Department of Education and one is private. There are 1000 applicants for 150 freshmen.

The woods were beautiful mahogany, cedar, araguanay and others. This is cotton country.

There is tobacco farming and a very modern 50 percent Phillip Morris cigarette factory that hires 1300 people, 600 in the factory. They contract with 170 farmers on three-year contracts. Virginia and Burley tobacco. They spend more for insecticide than for fertilizer. Net profit is about $250. per acre. The price to the farmer is about the same as in the United States. The factory has six technical men advising farmers on production. The company pays 7½ to 8½ percent interest. Farmers pay 9 percent. They make 2,000 cigarettes per minute with filters, 3,000 without or 2,500 packs per hour.

We went to the cane sugar mill in El Palmar; they process 4,600 tons per day of cane. They burn the baggasse in the boilers to run the mill. They get 7 to 12 percent sugar in the cane, have a 12 month growing season.

The Maracay Experiment Station works in close cooperation with the University Experiment Station.

We saw the Heinz cannery. They can papaya, lime, guava and other local fruit juices. They also can tomatoes, solid or paste. A sample of every batch canned went to the home office in the U.S.A. Quality was kept up to U.S. standards except Venezuela was a little sweeter. We visited a large irrigated farms project, staying with farm families overnight. There were 100,000 hectares irrigated with 125 miles of canals. This year they will farm 160,000 hectares.

Corn is $80 per ton. You can buy farms for 10 percent down with 15 years to pay out. Interest is 3-6 percent.

We had dinner at 9 p.m. as guests of Banco Agricola, then went to the Association which was like a country club. Arrived at the farm of J. Sanz at 12 p.m. and was entertained by the birds, roosters, and dogs from 4 a.m. on. The hospitality was genuine.

We went out to a large cattle ranch owned by a German. He had Charlais and Brahma bulls. We saw monkeys in the trees and also parrots and other highly colored birds as well as wild hogs, and alligators in the sloughs.

We saw a school and an experiment station full of good equipment and good buildings, but only one researcher and assistant. A research man from Davis had been there four years.

We visited the city council of Calahosa and had lunch at the Association. We visited the campasino farms. They were fair but the houses were bad and dirty. There was no electricity or running water or any gardens. The houses were in

340

groups of six per 100 has (40 acres each). The school was adequate but dirty and it did not seem that the parents were much interested in the children going to school. It seemed to me that parents seeking a government allotment of land should be required to send their children to school.

At Acarigua on January 25 we went to the experiment station working on cotton and oil seeds, sesame, safflower, etc. One young man we met said "One of our greatest needs is old people. We have to do the work of both the young and the old...."

The government owns much of the land and rents it to the farmers. The soil looks good. Water level is 60M = 200'. Rain is 60" per year. Portuguesa 110,000 Has in production, with 10,000 more planned next year.

The farm of Cristobal Gomez and two others is 800 Has or 1,760 acres. They use two pumps to raise the water 10 feet from the river. It cost about $125. per acre to clear the land. Hardwood trees will pay almost all if you can sell them. They expect to get title to the land in ten years (free). There are 600,000 acres of similar land in the area near rivers. They pay no taxes, rent, principal or interest on the land. They had nine large-wheel tractors lined up at the camp we saw. Cotton and rice were the principal crops.

On the cattle ranches in the good feed area the heifer calves spend five days with the cow and then go into the calf barn where they are on open pole floors 4' high to be off the ground. Bull calves go for meat at an early age unless they are good enough for breeding. The fresh cows are milked once a day and the calves nurse them through the night. The cows then go out to pasture. They have 9-10 Ha pastures which they irrigate each eight days, pasture two days then it grows— 31 days.

Merida is south of Lake Maracaibo about 30 miles. The Andes are rich in forests, soils and minerals. I was amazed at the quality of the roads. Also at the quality of the soils in those steep valleys and steep hillsides. Minerals are coal, copper, phosphate and marble. Many bananas go to the U.S.

They have an excellent forest products lab. They stress management of natural forests and plantation of forests. The University of the Andes organized in 1811 has 4,000 students. We had lunch with the University of the Andes faculty. It was nearly 5 p.m. when we finished and left Merida. We drove about 40 miles southwest and met a group of coffee growers about 50 miles east of the Colombian border.

The coffee growers have a 45 cent tax on each sack of coffee exported to finance a co-op. They now have over $10,000 in the fund. The coffee seedling is 3 months in the nursery in plastic bags; there were 200,000 in the nursery we visited. It is then 3-4 years to harvest.

The seed is germinated 48 days, then planted here in a plastic bag for 7-8 months until it has several branches, then is taken to the Fincas at 7¢ each. There are 90 co-op members, 1300 growers in the area. Elevation here is about 3,500 feet. The best coffee grows at 2,000 to 4,000 feet. Coffee grows best in 30-40 percent shade. The higher the caffeine content the better the flavor and aroma.

Their plan is to have co-op officers meet weekly and members monthly to train for co-op activity. There are two 5V clubs for boys, four 5V clubs for girls, plus four home ec. clubs for girls. The farmers and their wives are club leaders.

We got to our dinner at 8:30 p.m. Our hosts had already eaten, but we had a good evening.

One of the better land reform projects is the dairy area in Coloncito. There are still many trees but wonderful grass. These allotments were 150 Has (370 acres) but the law says anyone can enter vacant land and start farming and even where a man is farming part or most of his allotment, the government will not protect your right to the land if a part is not farmed. No farmer in the area still had all his 150 Has of land.

I slept on a cot with mosquito net covering. With children, parents and grand-parents, the house was full. They were very nice people, hard-working and interested in community development. A refrigerated truck picked up the milk.

The government provides a laboratory and two vets for the region. They travel over the district and care for and artificially inseminate the cattle free.

They use pandola, elephant and guinea grasses. They can pasture 2.3 cows per Ha (one cow per acre). They have about eliminated T.B. by killing all infected cows. Most farmers milk 40-60 cows.

The 5 p.m. meeting of ganaderos started at 6:15 p.m. They had five complete slates for officers. The third ballot was a tie. The fourth ballot had 44 votes for 41 present. The next vote, No. 2 slate, won 26-17.

Here we saw the electric tree crusher. About four were built by LaTourneau, who had been a top "cat" man and then left to build larger tractors, trucks, and other equipment. Two came to Venezuela at $1 million each to clear forests. They had drums 8½' in diameter and 20' long front and rear with 50' wheel base. The drums each had two 50 hp electric motors to drive them. There was a large super-structure above on which were located twin 6-cylinder Cummings diesel motors to generate the electricity. The cab would seat five. Out in front at a height of 15-20 feet was a 6-inch heavy iron pipe to push the trees over. The big drums on the ground had many grousers like we used on iron wheeled tractors before rubber tires. Along with it was a large four-wheeled crane to pick up trees and haul them into piles or windrows or to work on the crushers. They say it cleared 22 acres per day. They were very successful in clearing land, but the company failed.

We arrived at Carora on February 9, east of Lake Maracaiba. This was a fine area of very strong independent people.

The cattle were exceptional. They used principally fine purebred brown Swiss bulls on native cows. Calves at 8-9 months weigh 500 lbs. They kill the steers at 2½ years at 1050 lbs.

Most meat in Venezuela, as in other similar countries, is killed in the morning and sold by night. With refrigeration in Caracas and supermarkets, the better herds contract with the supermarket for the year and steers that weigh 1050 at 2½ years go to the supermarket and lighter steers are sold locally.

We had a wonderful lunch in the afternoon, then visited a sugar mill.

The next day at Hacienda Santa Rosa we saw a brown Swiss steer weighing 2,300 lbs, another 7-year-old brown Swiss steer at 5,000 lbs. Four steers at 18 months weighed 1,540 lbs. Both men and cattle here were outstanding.

Carlos Herrera Zubellaga had 150 cattle trophies in his home, which was large and quite elegant. We left there at 7 to get to the hotel and dress for the fare-well dinner set for 9:30 p.m. We talked, laughed and drank until 11:30, when they said they thought we ate at the hotel. We soon left. They stayed until 2 a.m. They had failed to tell the club we wanted dinner. It was a great group of men and we all had an interesting night.

On the 11th we went to a sugar factory. It went broke under private manage-ment, so the government took over. It was owned 75 percent by government and 25 percent by growers; now it is 72 percent–28 percent. There are three government directors, two growers. Sixty growers own stock in the company. They were pay-ing growers $9.35 U.S. per ton of 9 percent cane. The sugar experiment station was quite complete and worked closely with growers on all aspects of growing cane.

A beautiful cattle ranch that was privately owned was taken by the govern-ment for land reform. It was planted to corn one year then was idle for thirty years, so government gave the university money to buy 100 purebred heifers in Texas and Florida for $800. each. The cattle are now poor. The students will not do one day's work on the farm. Another ranch was bought by a private owner seven years ago. He sells crossbred bulls at $110. each at weaning and registered bulls at 750 to 1,000 dollars each.

I spent a day and night on the Hacienda of Antonia Dugue Herrera. A beauti-ful layout, home and ranch. The largest beef producer, they said, in Venezuela. He had gotten Cebu cattle from the large ranch in Brazil. There was still an embargo against bringing any cattle in from Brazil on account of foot and mouth disease. He had selected a large group of bulls and had them transported close to the border so in a few days the embargo would be lifted for a day.

He also had a cattle ranch in Spain which he visited quite often. After break-fast he got up and put on his two pistols and belt. His wife said, "Isn't that awful, I have to see that every morning and wonder how he will be coming back. Squatters are around all the time. The government will not do a thing to help protect your landholdings, so he and some of his men have to be ready at all times to protect it...."

On the 13th, a Saturday, we went to a fantastic ranch, with marvellous grass, plenty of trees for shade and beauty, large old ranch house with spacious lawns. The owner, maybe 60 years old, had developed the ranch himself. He had 10,000 head of cattle. All were milked once a day when fresh. He had large milking barns with the milk piped directly to the refrigerated tanks for daily delivery in refrig-erated trucks. The beef was sold for the year at 35¢ per lb. We had a delightful barbeque here. He said the meat check came every week no matter where he might be in the world. They kill up to 30 head every other day.

They run a 250kw electric generator, employ 150 men steady, have two schools for 300 students and six teachers for six grades. Population on the ranch was 600, all Venezuelans.

We went to a dairy farm with the finest dairy equipment I have ever seen. A De Lavalle salesman must have come and sold everything they make. It was a 660-acre ranch new in 1954. They had recently imported $200,000 worth of pure-bred brown Swiss from the U.S. He lost most of them with foot and mouth disease. He had just bought another 138 head in the U.S. to arrive soon. He will keep them in stanchions for six months, then turn them out nights. He hopes to not lose over 5 percent to foot and mouth. He believes importation of cattle will soon be stopped; those with purebreds will make a killing. There are now 100-150 purebreds coming to Venezuela daily.

They get seven cuttings a year of elephant grass six feet tall each cutting.

They pay labor $2.60 per day with house, lights, water, milk, bananas and meat. Top men get $6.60 per day. To maintain the pastures they use an iron tank roller like we do, but it has three or four road-grader blades, sharp, welded on at an angle to cut any weeds or bunch grass not eaten.

We visited a beautiful valley with hills on each side. The workers worked and lived in the valley. The malaria death rate was tragic. If two or three children survived in a family of ten to twelve, that was good. The bosses and owners lived in homes up in the hills and were little affected. The government came in with DDT and practically eliminated the mosquitos and malaria, so the population exploded with no schools or jobs available for all. It seemed I could see the problem there as I had never seen it before.

The Association President was rather depressed as he had just received from the government a letter saying they were coming to see him about expropriating his ranch for distribution to camposinos.

On Friday, February 19, we drove from Valencia back into Caracas. We again met the American Embassy people to discuss what we had seen and then we met with the Venezuela secretaries of agriculture, cooperation, interior. They asked our opinion of their land reform program. It was better than most countries because of the oil money the government had to spend on it, but we noted especially their good roads and how every time they built a new road into a new area the people moved in, set up a small camp, started clearing the land and farming at no expense to the government. The response was, "Yes, that is true, but if you are in politics here you have to be for land reform...."

I fear we as a nation have encouraged land reform as an idea with very little study as to how to accomplish it, so as a concept all over the world it has failed with the possible exception of Japan where it was quickly and effectively done by General McArthur and the army.

The hotels we stayed in were outstanding, fitted out like vacation hotels. Our tour directors, Ruth and Von Peacock, did a beautiful job of designing and carrying out the tour. I sincerely hope that each of the six participants have been able to use our experience to help build understanding and friendships.

Governments vary greatly throughout the world, but people, their native abilities and their hopes, vary far less than most of us think.

The Saturday night we were in Caracas Jim and I were just going to bed when we heard several shots on the highway nearby. I remarked, "These technical police who were all over the city are too trigger happy and are going to kill someone...." The morning paper told of four peace corp boys just arriving in Caracas for a conference who did not see a police check point and passed it. The police followed and shot a tire out. The boys got out, hands in the air, and the police shot two of them. One in the heart. Joseph R. Ripley, twenty-four, of Orinda, California. His father was Joseph W. Ripley, treasurer of Safeway and a Regent of the University of the Pacific whom, of course, I knew.

344

††† Clarksburg

We borrowed $190,000 from the FLB to pay off the boys' loans from American Trust Company and finance the year's farming, at 5%, later 5½%. We settled down to routine life—UOP, world affairs, world trade, Slough House improvements, and a trip to Hereford, Texas, to see Pat, Wes and the girls.

On June 14 the Venezuelan farmers arrived to return our visit. Jim Fulmer and I, with the help of the agricultural extension men, had planned a trip for them in the Clarksburg, Davis area. A day in Sacramento visiting co-ops, the legislature, etc., a day in Marysville. Peaches and other fruits, rice, grain and livestock, then a day in San Francisco. The Venezuelans stayed with host families while they were here. The farm bureaus of Sutter and Yuba counties provided a fine lunch in Marysville.

The group arrived in Washington D.C., then flew to El Campo, Texas; Los Cruces, New Mexico; Los Angeles to Disneyland then Visalia; Sacramento; from here to Denver, Colorado; Indianapolis, Indiana; Washington D.C.; then New York City to see the World Fair, and home. Von Peacock was with them all the time. A great leader.

On July 9 I spoke to a group of Peace Corp folks going to India.

Elliott Fisher, father of Wes, died of a heart attack in New York City airport. The Memorial service was at UOP. Six Methodist bishops spoke.

I was still on the Yolo County Economic Opportunities Commission. By October our administrator had resigned, so we had to select a new one. We had two women members from Davis who were always critical of us because we did not have enough recipients of aid on the commission, and we did not give adequate consideration to the poor.

There were three applicants for the administrator position. There was a young man from Davis listed as a book publisher, but he had never published a book or had any other job worthy of comment. There was a retired naval admiral, and a Mexican then in the Department of Employment for the State.

I was for the admiral. He had spent his life on shore in housing and he seemed to welcome the challenge to do a good job, but a military man was just unthinkable to the group. The Mexican had been editor of his high school and Humbolt College year books. He edited the paper for the Department of Employment, and his job was to induce the large employers like the PG&E and Telephone companies to employ more minority group people.

The Davis women couldn't think of employing a Mexican for such a position. "How would he ever write up a project or report?" We selected the Mexican but the ladies wanted to be registered as voting "no." I pointed out that I hardly believed they wanted him to read that they had voted "no" every time he read the minutes of that meeting, so they withdrew the request. He did a good job, then went to a higher job for the State. He was a member of Sacramento Rotary Club for a while until he moved away. My experience is that those who weep most for the poor and foreign seldom have faith and confidence in them.

In early November the TWAD Co. Transworld Agricultural Development Company meeting was held in Lafayette. John Stanley was President.

On the 19th we went with Bob and Zella Yelland to our U.C. Berkeley class of 1915 Fiftieth anniversary banquet. People came from far and wide and it was a great evening. Bob Sproul, 1917 and past president of U.C., was there against doctor's orders but he gave a short but inspiring talk, as he always did. He was great.

On November 28 the California Farm Bureau Federation met at the Claremont Inn, Berkeley. On December 7 we flew to Hereford to see Pat and family and on to the AFBF meeting in Chicago.

This year we gave UOP $3,000 to encourage excellence in teaching, and we gave our children $5,000 each for Christmas.

†1966

January 21 I attended the T.W.A.D. Company meeting in Lafayette Inn. The T.W.A.D. Company started as an idea of John Stanley, who had been in the commodities department of CFBF, and Fred Hotes, President of Uniconsult, an international consulting firm in the agricultural engineering field. Each stockholder would pay in $10,000 as capital in the company to do consulting, advising or actual farming any place which seemed best in the world. The $10,000 limit was set so no one would be hurt too badly if it was lost.

Our hope was that we might make a profit and expand the operation rather widely in the world and inspire other to do likewise. We had 27 members from Imperial Valley to Richvale, Glenn County. We were advised to incorporate in Nevada and flew to Reno on February 8 and signed the incorporation papers.

In April I spoke to the Rotary clubs of Grass Valley, Placerville, and Lodi.

June 9 and 10 we entertained in our home at Clarksburg a group of Egyptian farmers on a tour by Farmers and World Affairs. They were outstanding and very interesting men.

September 6 I spoke to the Sirs Club in Sacramento. Sirs is Seniors in Retirement. That is the only meeting of retirees I have attended.

I spent a good deal of time analyzing possible projects for T.W.A.D. Company. John Stanley had proposed projects in Iran, Lebanon, Ethiopia, Australia that I particularly remember. I studied his cropping plans, equipment need, cash flows, and found they looked attractive but did not fit into place in cases. The more I studied it the more I saw the complexity of operation so far away. How to assure equipment, fertilizers, and pesticides and other chemicals became quite complex.

Out of these studies I decided that we at least know California farming, but we also needed a partner to assure the supply of farm equipment, and one to assure chemicals of all kinds, and one to handle the financial and local political problems of the nation we were operating in.

†1967

We attended Ronald Reagan's governor's inauguration in the County building at the old fairgrounds. A gala event.

On March 11 we enjoyed a very pleasant international friendship lunch at the Confucius temple—all sorts of Oriental dishes.

On March 16 I spoke to the Oakland Rotary Club.

April 6 we had the Clarksburg church dinner celebrating affiliation in United Christian Church.

On my 75th birthday I was unanimously elected president of TWAD Co. (Trans World Agricultural Development). We had gotten slowed down. Some members wanted to get out and we permitted any who wished, to do so.

Occidental Oil Company had bid for a concession in Libya in which Oxy agreed to spend 5% of the net for the agricultural development of Libya. We might get the job of consultant to draw up the plans for best use of the 5%.

About mid-April I met Leo Anderson who had been employed by Development and Resources Company to supervise the development of the irrigation project in the Khuzistan area of Iran. D & R Company was organized by David Lillenthal whom I had met as Chairman of the Board of the Tennessee Valley Authority. He went from there to head of the Atomic Energy Commission and then to the privately owned D & R to research and develop projects, public or private, anywhere in the world.

They had been retained by the Shah of Iran to develop the Khuzistan desert area of Iran, build a dam on the Dez River, prepare the distribution system, roads and all, produce sugar from cane, and prepare for general agricultural production. This task was about completed, so Leo returned hoping to set up his own consulting firm. He felt he would need a group like TWAD Co. to help plan farming projects, so he worked with us.

We met Armond Hammer, president of Oxy, and his men, and after several meetings we agreed to look Libya over and draw up a proposal. We also employed Warren Schoonover who studied Egyptian soils after he retired from agricultural extension as top soils man. On May 6 Warren, Jerry Fielder, Leo Anderson and myself were at the Los Angeles airport looking for a blue bomber refitted with new rotary engines to give it speed like the commercial airliners. We had pilot, copilot and navigator across the Atlantic.

We were airborne for Chicago at 7:50 a.m., arriving at 2 p.m., then over Detroit, Montreal and Quebec, arriving at Goose Bay, Labrador at 1:05 a.m. where we had a quick night's sleep at an airport barracks. We then decided to fly down to Gander to have a little motor work done. We had lunch and took off for Shannon, Ireland. We could see lots of icebergs and floating ice, then one could easily see the line where the warm gulf stream came in and the ice was no more. We arrived Shannon at 2 a.m., had dinner and bed. At breakfast I ordered stewed prunes and got a bowl of 48 prunes. Jerry ordered a glass of milk and got a big glass and a full pitcher of milk. The pilot said they needed to change exhaust pipes so we would be late leaving and arriving, so we decided to stay over for an early start the next day. We rented a car and went to the Lakes of Killarney and then drove via the coast back to Shannon, a beautiful trip.

We left Shannon at 6 a.m. on May 9 for an interesting day across France, Sardinia and on across the Mediterranean to Tripoli. The white buildings and blue sky pierced by the many minarets was quite dramatic. We were also impressed by the amount of land in olives, almonds, citrus and alfalfa.

We checked in the Vaddan Hotel and then went to the Oxy offices.

On the 10th we saw M. S. Jallala, director of agricultural extension service. He was very friendly and agreed to give us letters to his men in the oases asking them to provide us with landrovers and help see the country and meet the people.

We met several men from NASA (National Agricultural Settlement Administration). Mussolini had sent many Italians to colonize the coast of Libya. They had planted orchards, vines and grown many crops, but most left when Libya got its independence by United Nation action in 1950. The Libyans seemed to want us to first develop the oasis at Kufra as that was where King Idris was born and his father is buried there. Then they wanted us to see if we could develop the agriculture of the area which had been colonized by Italians. This was a large area, with roads, fences, and houses, but would require better irrigation and farming and management practices to make it an attractive farming area.

We then spent considerable time in the U.S. Embassy. The Ambassador was David Newsome, whom I had met earlier in Karachi and Manilla. He had just returned from a jeep trip to Kufra. This was considered quite a rugged trip for an ambassador to take. The Libyans were quite proud of his daring.

We studied many reports on agriculture, water, economics on file in the Embassy, then went to see the Libyan minister of agriculture who was very helpful.

King Idris seemed to be very popular and the people in government office seemed anxious to build a better Libya and to seek American help. There was no hint of the trouble to come to Libya fairly soon.

By the time we got the bedrolls, cots, food and all on board and then got permission to fly, it was 4:45 p.m. We set out to find the Oxy concession where we would spend the night. I sat at a window and kept a log every several minutes of the crops, type of land, topography and roads crossed, wells seen, pipelines, etc. At 6:30 we were over oil wells. We flew over many oil wells but couldn't locate Oxy, so at 7:15 we set out northwest to Benghazi where we spent what night was left in the Palace Hotel, entertained by the band in the casino. I think the bedrolls didn't appeal to the pilot.

We got out at 4:30 on Friday, May 12, to a then quiet hotel and went to the airport for breakfast, but the cafe was closed. We took off at 6:23 from Benghazi. The first ten minutes were lots of grain, but the land looked good for the first 30 minutes, then oil wells and several oases. There was 22 minutes of outcropping of rock in rough country, then more open desert.

We went too far south so turned north and then west and there it was—the oasis of Kufra with all the palms and the village standing out. It was Friday, the Moslem sabbath, but they all came out to meet us on foot, by mule, bycycle, and even a car or two.

They took us to the government farm run by a representative of the Minister of Agriculture. Also present was the Director of Farm Credit and a veternarian. A little of the water was artesian, but most came from hand-dug wells about 6½ feet in diameter, most of them 12 feet deep with a maximum of 22 feet. Most had I think about a 4 hp diesel motor on a 2" pump and suction pipe which pumped into a concrete tank about 16' x 16' and from that a valve and pipe to regulate the flow into the irrigation ditch.

It was always colorful and interesting to see those men dressed in what looked like nightgowns cranking those 1 cylinder diesel engines, but they all did it.

Water accumulated in the well and in the reservoir if they had one. They would pump three to ten hours then shut off the engine and let it accumulate

348

and start irrigating again. Most ran 3-5 hours and most crops were irrigated every day until they got started, then 2-7 days. Farm Credit would loan on the pump-engine for three years. Wells loan up to $1,000. Summer temperature in Kufra was seldom over 96° with top 105°. Sounds usual for Sacramento.

The houses were walls around an open courtyard with one room roofed over for sleeping in bad weather. There were other courtyards for animals, storage, etc. The walls were built of naturally formed blocks which were mostly rock salt which collect 6-8 inches under the ground surface. It was present as salt blocks or as sand stone in all the oases and towns we saw. Where it is rock salt the crystals sparkle in the sun as referred to in the bible.

Kufra is a series of oases with palms in the lower land. Some dates cure dry and some sticky and are eaten like bread.

There seems opportunity to improve water yield of shallow wells, the distribution of water, the use of land and control of salt accumulation. Surface deposits of soil are found and hauled to mix in the sand for increased productivity. In places the crops of vegetables and alfalfa look good. There are often two or three crops intermixed in the same little pads. Much of the wheat and barley land could be double-cropped with Sudan grass for animals or beans for people.

While we saw around the government farm our hosts went to the mosque to pray. We were invited to a very abundant and pleasant lunch on a large porch. We of course removed our shoes. There were rugs on the floor and pillows to sit on. There were about 20 men present. We were all given soap and towel to wash before eating as water was poured from a tea kettle. We washed again the same way at the end. The food was varied, abundant and tasted good. There was soup, two meat courses, plenty of bread and vegetables.

At the end an elderly gentleman came in who was a friend of the king and his father in Kufra. He was much revered by all. He was a Samesie teacher and leader.

We left at 5 p.m. and landed at Oasis Oil Company strip and camp at 6:40. They gave us a most hearty welcome, dinner and bed. They had good water from a well 400 feet deep; water stands at 100 feet with little drawdown. It is desalted for drinking but is used direct on trees and plants with no ill effects so far.

We flew over to the Oxy camp and then drove to Aguila Oasis. This is a very good community and the people quite progressive. They have a fine school. All the crops here look very good. The farms are on the slopes above the floor of the oasis. Irrigation was watering for 3 hours with ½ hour recovery with 2½ inch pipe.

Children go to school from 5 to 16, six years elementary, five years high school. There is a nurse here and a doctor for this area. Teachers are trained in Beirut, Egypt and Madrid.

We went to Gialo Oasis east of Oxy camp. We passed lots of ammunition dumps of 2½ inch artillery shells left over from the war. There were also skeletons of military planes from WWII. There were two new windmills not yet used.

On the 13th we landed at Sebha where the Yugoslavs were building an airport. The Controller of agriculture supplied us with a landrover and driver. He said the roads were bad but the driver was good. I understood that better when we returned safely from the trip. We used the roads some but going across the open desert was better, much smoother. There was some green brush and grass almost everywhere, not much but some. We could do 35-40 miles per hour over the desert very nicely, but the roads were terrible. There were many tracks in the desert, some I am sure were years old. Very confusing. Many camel tracks and also many of small animals. Some areas looked good for farming.

We stopped at Bint Beya. It has 800 people and many children in school.

The Yugoslavs were drilling a deep well using all U.S. equipment. They said 60 miles south of Sebha they drilled eleven wells and got lots of good water.

On the 15th we went from Sebha to Broch. There were many artesian wells. They are drilled, then flow artesian. One is used by 100 farmers as they wish to use it, but the valve is shut off at night. Some day many acres of the Sahara will be very productive farm land.

Our landing fee for the plane in Sebha was $155. U.S.

Back in Tripoli we went to work on our reports. We saw the minister of agriculture and his assistant. The minister was very encouraging. The undersecretary then said they wanted to see Kufra a beautiful model oasis which would be a tourist center like Palm Springs.

Tuesday evening we were guests at a delightful home dinner of Mr. Al Gangeni outside Tripoli. Our host was eighty years old, is young in spirit, a great sense of humor and knowledge of the Arab world. The dinner was a state affair.

Wednesday afternoon we drove 35 miles west of Tripoli to see the farming and the ancient Roman city at Sabratha. We were amazed at the quality of the pears and apples produced on the Mediterranean.

Thursday morning we got out early and visited the Gargani farms at Garabuli 63K east of Tripoli. Lots of olives being crushed for oil. Then we saw the Roman ruins at Horns-Leptis Magna, a large city and beautiful.

We left Tripoli at 5:30 p.m. on Thursday, flew over Tunisia, Sardinia and into Nice at 8:45 and went to the hotel in Monaco. Friday we saw the Riviera, including Grasse and the Gorge de Loup, then went to Rotary in Nice that evening. Many Rotary officials were present as the R.I. meeting started the next day.

Saturday the 20th we arrived at the Hotel George V in Paris about noon. Mr. Cochran, president of Oxy, met us and Dick Vaughan came in later. We went over our report. They seemed to like it, then went to dinner at 9 p.m.

On Sunday we had breakfast with the Oxy group, including Dr Hammer. Dr. Hammer approved and asked me to return to Libya with him about Wednesday. That met with the approval of our group, so I saw them off for home later that morning. Dr. Hammer was interested in our report, but his mind was elsewhere. Two weeks earlier he had the idea of buying Kern County Land & Cattle Company.

He offered to buy so many shares at a price well above market. Then Tenneco jumped in with a higher bid. He had a problem. He could fight the new offer and maybe win, or he could sell the shares he had just bought and without a fight have $18,000,000 clear profit. That is what he did.

The Oxy group met with Bechtels and authorized Bechtel to engineer plans for a pipe line which they hoped to have in in 8 months so they could sell oil. They believe the 5% for the first year could exceed one million dollars and grow rapidly.

Libya looked good then. I worked on studying material and writing reports.

350

I went to a Paris boat show and to Rotary in the Pavillon Dolphine in the Bois de Bologne.

I flew to Tripoli again with Dr. and Mrs. Hammer. On Friday we went out to see the new oil well producing 83,000 barrels per day 30 miles west of Aguila. The soil here was very good and the water OK to drink or for irrigation. The gas from the well was blowing off like two tremendous blow torches. The heat and noise was tremendous. It was certainly impressive.

We were ready to return to Tripoli. Dr. Hammer was already on the floor for a sleep. I was in the navigator's seat. The pilot was revving up the motors getting ready for take-off. There was a sound like a shot. The props had picked up a rock and it hit the windshiels which broke into 1,000 parts. The pilot slipped quickly into the co-pilot's seat and had it rolling soon without Dr. Hammer knowing of the incident.

We went out over the sea so Dr. Hammer could look for a good harbor site for loading oil.

Friday evening we went to an Oxy dinner party at Jim Blom's. Eighty people were there. The Geophysical Company head says there is lots of soil in the sand in some places. The Bechtel folks say when digging a trench 6 feet deep for a pipe line, the wall will hold for two days without sluffing.

The chief of the Geophysical party which surveyed concession 103 where the 83,000 barrel well came in said he had also surveyed that property with the same crew for Mobile about three years earlier and even when he got out the old charts and looked at them they were fair but not good. I asked what the difference was. He said only the equipment. They would now have to do the whole world over again. That was 1967, seventeen years ago; now as I write this I am sure they have improved in this period.

Before 1950 Libya had very few schools and hardly any university graduates. I have never seen such an active desire for education as one saw there. Whether in Tripoli or out in the village the minute a school was built it was filled. Students and parents wanted education and really worked at it.

I left Tripoli airport at 10 a.m. on Tuesday, May 30, and arrived home Wednesday at 8 p.m.

In the Tripoli office Dr. Hammer told the Oxy controller to make $250,000 available to us and all seemed ready to go. After our return home we had a meeting with Dr. Hammer and his group. It developed that we were the fourth group to make a study and report on the project and ours was far superior to any of the others, and they were ready to go ahead on the basis of our report.

In the meantime he had talked to David Lilienthal, who told him that Leo Anderson was the Rolls Royce of the consulting and development business. We had planned that Leo would head the project for us, but we had not made a final deal with Leo. He had been a big help to us and I wanted to give him $10,000 in stock in the company so he would have the same as the rest of us, but several objected and I did not fight it through. I should have been more insistent.

Pat and Wes and the girls planned a vacation at Winter Park Colorado Idlewild Lodge, so we decided to join them for a week. We left home June 23 and drove to

Anne and Sandy Cuttings the first evening. He was then president of Goldfield Mining Company. It was a large open pit operation. Lots of dust, no paint. The house was fine inside, but pretty rough out, but as usual the hospitality was unbeatable.

We were welcomed by the Fishers June 25, three days from home, and had a wonderful time with them. The flowers were beautiful. The girls rode the horses. We just relaxed and enjoyed the landscape and the company. In the hotel I looked at the library and here was a book "Kufra the Jewel of the Desert." I was probably the only one there who had ever heard of Kufra, so I read the book and they told me to keep it.

July 2 as we went out to pack the car there was ice on the windshield. The day's drive was trees, rivers, streams, flowers—a beautiful trip. We stopped in Banning and on to Bernice's and early to bed and home July 5.

Mealer Home Service built for $12,000 what was to be the office and hay or equipment storage. David recently (1983) had walls and three large doors installed to make it the shop for handling larger equipment.

I spent a good deal of time at TWAD Co. planning our future, studying over projects in Lebanon, Ethiopia, Australia which John Stanley had proposed for our consideration.

An indication of the times was Lowell Berry had sent $10,000 to the church in Davis to carry on religious work, espeically for students and noted there was more if needed. He asked me to attend the meeting in Davis to discuss how the money might well be spent. They discussed trips to jails, and to see how the poor lived, but finally agreed that trips to Woodland to sit through trials and see how the courts were hard on the poor was probably best. Lowell was interested in Christian Endeavor, Young Couples, Vacation Camp for religious thought and devotion, but such projects were not suggested. This was how the times were in the churches. Lowell lost all interest.

A Japanese men's musical group came to Sacramento sponsored by the YMCA. We hosted the leader and one other man for two days. We still get cards.

October 24 we dedicated Callison College at UOP. Students specialized in international understanding and spent the sophomore year abroad first at the University in Bangalore, India, and later at a university in Japan.

In November we went to San Francisco to see Harold Wadsworth off on an extended tour on the "President Wilson," the ship I had had a gala dinner and dance on in Brest, France, in 1919.

On November 6 the Libyan contract was signed by Dick Vaughan and myself and approved by our board.

December 10-14 was the annual AFBF meeting held in Chicago. Afterward I visited the farm in Champaign County, seeing Mr. Hartman, tenant, and Mr. Johnson, manager for $120. per year, $1.50 per acre.

We spent a good deal of time with Occidental Petroleum winding up the Libya project, getting the camper to them, and other things.

We held a number of meetings trying to get support for building an international lounge and meeting rooms for international students at Cal State University, Sacramento. Also worked on U.C. Davis Alumni Foundation, Farm Bureau and other activities as well as Slough House. But most of my time was spent on how to get a good operation going for TWAD Co., studying many projects.

Development and Resources wanted me to go on a trip they were planning for businessmen to explore the possibilities in Iran. We were not ready yet for that, but Iran seemed to have the most stable government, most money, most desire to build its production of any country we considered.

†1968

Dr. Hammer said Oxy was delayed in going ahead in Libya, so we felt that it might take all of 1968 to get ready to start there in 1969. Hop Merwin and I met with Mr. Macy, vice president of Porter International, in relation to developing a rice project in the west bulge of Africa. Glen Harris went to Colombia to look at a project there.

King Idris was very popular with the people of Libya, and highly respected worldwide, but he was getting old and needed to come to the United States on account of eye trouble. He arranged for several of the Generals to take over in his absence as he had no heir apparent. Colonel Kadafee knew of the plan so he stepped in, captured and killed the Generals, and he took over. Of course this caused further confusion and delay.

I studied the development of the Dez River Project in Iran. Both Leo Anderson and Fred Hotes had worked on the project and were familiar with it.

I was working long hours, day and night, drawing up plans, cash flows, capital costs of a three-thousand hectare project in that area. It seemed to be about the minimum size farm to carry the overhead for a project so far away.

Top, landing at Kufra in the Libyan Sahara in the Occidental Petroleum plane we flew from Los Angeles to Libya. Ctr. typical Sahara Oasis. Below left, reception lunch in Kufra; right, an overland traveler from sudan to Tripoli.

16

ADVENTURE IN IRAN

1968, continued

On July 7, I set out for Iran to see what might be good for us, stopping in Washington and New York. We looked over the project west of Tehran which had been recommended, but it did not seem attractive. I then went down to the Dez project. It was very similar to Imperial Valley. The water is better and the land equal or better. The Khuzistan is five times the size of the Imperial Valley and has five live rivers running across it. Much of it is extremely hot, quite alkaline, and sometimes floods from the rivers so no land is visible for many miles around, but the area of the Dez project is higher, cooler and free from floods.

The Experiment Station on the project grows good cotton, rice, beets, alfalfa, peanuts and other crops and vegetables. The orchard looked good and they raise and feed cattle for meat and milk, and fat-tail sheep. There were at least one-hundred villages on the project, most enclosed by a high wall to protect the people and livestock at night.

The dam and concrete water distribution system is just as modern and quite similar to the irrigation projects in California. The town of Sush, or Susan in the bible, was on the project. It is where Queen Esther's palace of bible times was located with the marble columns and foundation of the palace still there. Here Daniel was cast in the lion's den. His grave is a holy place visited by many worshippers. Many sleep and eat there for a week or two at a time coming from long distances to worship. The area is enclosed by a high wall. Around the inside wall are open compartments about 10'x10' where a family can live for a week or more.

At Hafe Tape (seven hills) is a large sugar cane plantation and mill. The Hawai–

355

ians say it is one of the top sugar cane producers in the world. Here are also many archaeological diggings.

Tehran is a large city. The principal streets are very wide and very busy. They had running water in the gutters, the way Salt Lake used to have. It is a combination of very new and very old. The people are interested in Americans and very friendly.

The Shah says the first sugar produced in the world was produced on the new irrigation project we were interested in. Maps two-thousand years old show the area as Khuzestan, which means "sugar land," so I assume this was true. I saw maps over two-thousand years old which showed the main irrigation canals almost the same as the present newly built system.

Local folklore says that the early shepherds stopped there and planted wild wheat and barley and then harvested it for themselves and the sheep. So, ten thousand years ago farming started there on the Dez River in Mesopotamia.

At this time one of the first considerations where we might start a project was the economic and political stability of the country, and all our studies and discussions with government people and others led to the conclusion that Iran was probably the most stable, economically and politically, of all the third-world countries. Time has proven how wrong one can be.

On Thursday, October 24, Bella and I flew to Rome where we met Ken and Joyce Reynolds, Mike Merachini and his wife, then on to Tehran at 9:30 p.m. Lots of people, but few taxis, but Mrs. Ditto, wife of the Pan Am manager, got us a taxi to the hotel.

We all went out to take a more thorough look at the project. They, of course, knew desert farming better than I did, and it was planned that if the project looked good enough, Ken would be project manager, Mike the farm manager, and Ken Brown the project engineer in charge of land layout, survey, land leveling, etc. Each man was tops in his field. We were concerned with the water, soil, availability of labor, supplies, and, of course, markets.

Saturday, October 26, was the birthday and first anniversary of the coronation of the Shah, so a big holiday. The John Deere men had lunch with us. They took Ken, Mike and me to see a project near Karaj, west of Tehran.

We stopped at the Shah's sisters' dairy and farm. The Holstein cattle were from Holland. The alfalfa, melons and beets were fine, still being irrigated. We stopped on our return at Danir, a large very modern poultry plant with large freezers, as modern as in the U.S.

The religious holiday there is Friday. We visited Al Gross, Bank of America representative, and Mr. Sagatalian, President of the Foreign Trade Bank. He was a very distinguished gentleman, very friendly, but gave us every reason why we coult not succeed. It was just a different world than we knew. The rules would be changed often. You just can't succeed. Other large organizations spending millions had given up or failed. We were confident and determined. Met Nader Saleh who ran his office like an American. He imported frozen and fresh meat, mostly sheep. Would receive 1,000 tons from Uruguay the next day. The men went to Dr. Rouhani's office. He was very cooperative and happy to see us, interested in the Dez project, instructed his men to arrange for us at the project.

356

We were up at 4 a.m. October 27 to fly to Isfahan. At 7:05 we went to Shah Abbas Hotel, the finest and most beautiful of any I have seen. We had breakfast and Mr. Borovmand came for us. We went to his farm ten miles north. He had attended Cal Poly SLO for five years. Some of his farm is modern, some ancient. He feeds silage to dairy cows and sheep, harvests pistachios and melons. Red beets are dug, put in small pits, and covered with dirt until used in the winter. They hold lambs in corrals in the day while ewes pasture, then in the sheep corral is a runway going down to underground pens with chimneys for ventilation where they used to hold all the sheep at night to protect them from robbers. Now they use it for some of the sheep. They also have beautiful inside sheep pens built of brick; each pen has a domed roof and chimney for ventilation. They are cool in summer and warm in winter. These pens were real works of art. He took us to his new ranch house for tea.

We visited the Plaza and the shops. Then on to Bouramond's city house for a family dinner, three families and the U.S. Consul and Vice Consul—fifteen in all. We had informal snacks, steak and chicken.

We went to Abadan and were met by Kulpa, director and head of National Iranian Oil Co. We then went to Khoramshah for dinner. We met Nadar Saleh who was there awaiting a shipment of mutton. He had two very large refrigerator trucks. There was much activity in the Port shown us by the Port Manager, then we were off to Ahwaz. There were many date palms on both sides of the river, but the road was bare desert to about ten miles south of Ahwaz, then villages, poor at first, then better. Ahwaz is the state capitol—about 200,000 people. We drove out of Ahwaz to the club for a nice lunch for us with top KWPA people and Governor Nasser of the state and others.

After a two-hour drive to Andimeshk we were received by the KWPA and D&R people. Bella and I stayed with McKeags. We had a nice dinner at Pollards with top Dez, Irrigation Project, and D&R people.

On the 30th we went to see DRIP.* Dug many holes. Many rice fields planted in early August are now harvested. Large villages spread rice on hard ground and thresh with a tractor. Rice is cut by hand and moved to threshing floors on donkeys. Women and children sort it, putting heads in one direction, and sorting out water grass. They then put it in a circle and tractors or donkeys or, in small lots, people tramp it out The straw is thrown out, the rice and chaff is piled and then winnowed out.

After a sack lunch we saw the trial farm. The cotton looked very good. The alfalfa, yellow corn, milo, peanuts and tomatoes all looked good.

The next day at the trial farm we looked over sheep and equipment. It rained some. We went to the Dez Bench, which is higher ground not deep but very good soil. We then saw a leveling job by KWPA—several D8's on scrapers, graders, ditchers, JD5020 with small scrapers and harrows . Plenty of equipment but job a disappointment and ground rough and poorly laid out. We went to see the Dam.

November 1 we met with consultants on cost of production time of each farming operation, tractors to be used, etc. After lunch we went to see the land east of the Dez River. Crossed to Haft Tapeih and up to Shush.

On the 2nd John McKeog gave us all the figures on temperature, ground water

*Dez River Irrigation Project.

357

level, etc. for '67-'68. We had a session discussing lands available to us, villages to be kept, people needed, etc. We suggested setting aside 500H or so for villager's sheep pasture, and ½H garden space for each family in the village.

On the 4th I went early to the Dezful slaughter house. The house gets head, hide, liver and offal. They can kill 50 head per day. They kill 100 head of sheep in 3-4 hours. They cut a hole in the shank and blow into to skin the sheep. Three-wheeled motorcycles distribute the meat to the retailers.

Ken, Mike and their wives left for home.

Some villages were Arab, some Persian. The Arabs are second-rate citizens. The Arabs are excellent irrigators and also stay out later in the evening with the sheep and are willing to irrigate through the night. The Persian villages are walled with walls 10-12 feet high for safety; the Arab villages are not walled.

We returned to Tehran. We saw Dr. Rouhani, and he said they would finish all the land purchases for Lat. 9 south. They would put in a new bridge at Dezful, heavy and wide enough to carry our traffic, large equipment, beets, etc. in, and build four modern villages for our workers.

Mr. Pritchard of D&R took us to dinner. Mr. Pritchard said our project had been a subject of constant discussion at the World Bank meeting in Washington.

On the 10th we saw Dr. Allen again. We should join Half Topeh in setting up Aqua Ammonia plant for both. It was raining and we needed a taxi to the hotel. I tried a while, then a policeman flagged one down for me. He didn't want to take me and started on, but the police whistled him back and told him to take me to the Park Hotel, which he did, reluctantly.

We had lunch at the Park Hotel with Mr. Sephapour, Dr. Allen, Dr. Phillips and Sam Nager. Mr. Sephapour received a medal from the Shah that morning for outstanding work. He is developing a 10,000 H farm on the Caspian for the War Department. He will raise 30,000 head of sheep and several thousand cattle for beef plus several thousand for milk, plus clover, fruits and other crops His family milk 6,000 cows for the Tehran market. The World Bank wants a complete copy of our proposal. We left for home feeling we had a good project and that we were wanted. Soil, climate, water and markets also seemed attractive.

The cane sugar refinery north of Ahwaz was being remodeled to handle beets. Iran was importing much of its food, with Kuwait and other high-priced markets close by. All factors seemed favorable. I had developed detailed charts and planting schedules, crop yields, income costs with several groupings of crops, but the Bank of America insisted we must have a consulting firm draw up a whole feasibility study as to cropping procedures, equipment and other costs, cash flow, capital needs and all. Fred Hotes recommended a mid-Western company which had use of computers to do the work for $36,000. This was done, but it cost $60,000 for checking my work. But that is an essential part of a project and probably desirable. Vol. I of the study was 270 pages; Vol II, 450 pages, mostly tables.

TWAD Company board moved that we proceed with the Dez Irrigation Project. It was still day-and-night work with all the plans necessary to proceed with the project. I took many trips to San Francisco to meet Bank of America people while working out all the details of financing, marketing, production, and so forth. I had to justify every detail. This was a division of Bank of America set up to handle foreign loans. They were as new at it as we were, and sometimes seemed quite unreasonable and slow. I surely had to put in long hours.

By February the study was about complete and action was taken to set up the Iranian company. This was to be made up of Mr. Talighani, who had formerly been both Secretary of State and Secretary of Agriculture for the government of Iran but was now connected with a large American engineering company. He had his own engineering company in Iran. They had constructed many of the dams in the northern part of Iran as well as bridges and roads on other projects. A very close friend of the Shah, he accompanied the Shah on many of his trips. He was interested in the development of the Khuzestan and seemed happy to take stock in our company.

†1969

The year 1969 started off with lots of activity with trips down to San Francisco to meet with Bank of America. Grafland for John Deere came to Sacramento on February 8 and I spent the day with him when we worked out most of our relationships and a good deal of the problems of securing the farm equipment. Met with Fred Frick on the 17th and right after that went to Iran to select land, to develop the lease and the general agreement.

I stayed at the Hilton Hotel on the top floor. Outside of my room, every other room on that floor was taken by a Sheik from Saudi Arabia who had his whole crowd up there. They had their own dining room, their own cooks, their own big cars sitting out front. It was quite a group.

His Excellency, Sadul Ebtahaj, invited me to his house for lunch where he had quite a group of very prominent people in Iran to receive the Vice President of the National City Bank which was the correspondent of Mr. Eptahaj's "Iranian's Bank." Mr. Ebtahaj was one of the real characters of Iran. He had been somewhat critical of the Shah in earlier days and was put in jail, presumably for a rather serious offense, where he stayed for some months, insisting all the time that he was not guilty and should be released. Finally the government decided to release him but he refused to leave the jail until they had published a complete repudiation of all their accusations against him and held him completely free from any anti-governmental activities. This made him quite prominent in Iran; very much the leader of independent thought there. He likewise was one of the first to take an early interest in the Khuzistan Desert and its development. At a meeting in Europe he met Mr. Lillianthal, President of Development and Resources Corporation, who was in the business of developing projects of that type and he induced the government of Iran to have Mr. Lillianthal come over and make a proposition on the Khuzistan and then develop the area. So, it was kind of Mr. Ebtahaj's "baby" in a way, and he was particularly delighted to see somebody, we being the first to come in to start the development of a real farming operation in the area.

I met with Mr. Rouhani, Minister of Water and Power, on many, many meetings, working out the general agreement and the lease. Other people, including Mr. Naraghi, had indicated definite interest in the project and had indicated that they would be interested in coming in. We were the first to actually come so the whole operation determining what should be the type of lease and what the general agreement should say and include was left up to the Minister of Water and Power, Mr. Rouhani, and me, with his people, to work out. This meant many, many days; to which Mr. Rouhani devoted his own time up until 9 or 10 or sometimes later in the evening. I employed Mr. Westerberg as our attorney to work with us on these matters and others where we needed an attorney. He had had quite a long experience as attorney for the "AID" program of the United States in Tehran, so that he knew most of the people in the government, they knew him and had considerable respect for him and his viewpoint which was a big help to us.

We finished our general outline, you might call it, with the Minister and then it was to be turned over to his staff people to work out all the details. We had started working on it, but it was quite apparent that it would take a matter of at least one week, and there was an **extended** religious holiday when it was customary to be happy, have quite a vacation. In order to not lose any time, the Minister had all of his people and me move down to the project in Andemesk and continue our activities down there. This was considered quite a desirable thing to do at this time of year when the weather was beautiful down there and often not so beautiful in Tehran, so that they were happy to go down and we spent a full week pretty well working out the programs. By March 19 we had a tentative program worked out and I went on down to the Khusistan again to start employing people or selecting people for employment and working out a little more detail as to what crops we might grow and how we would go about it.

On March 26 down there they had a birthday party for me which was a very interesting occasion. It began to be an annual affair as the next three birthdays were spent there, and always with a party.

While all of the D&R people employed at Andermesk were friendly, the John McKeogs' were particularly friendly to us. Bella and I went there often, and I stayed with them when I was alone. We really enjoyed the hospitality they extended to us. John, unfortunately, died not too long after that. Mrs. McKeog is living in Sacramento and we see her occasionally.

I went back up to Tehran where I got in touch with Mr. Telegani, the Minister of course, and Mr. Ameri of the Agricultural Development Fund who would be a part of the Iranian Company and also the supplier of farm credit for us. We spent four days steady with Minister Rouhani in finalizing the general agreement and lease, as these things were rather new to them and required a tremendous amount of detailed discussion to make sure they were drawing up a contract fair to them as well as to us.

Ken Reynolds came over and he, John Grafland, John Deere, Mr. Roughani, Mr. Ameri, and Mr. Gross of Bank of America had lunch together and wound up most of the matters that were hanging fire at that time and the next day I left for home, stopping in Washington, seeing the World Bank people there and a number of other people that we needed to contact and then of course many meetings with the Bank of America, equipment people, D & R and so forth after we returned.

I went down to Imperial to see our members down there and make sure that everything was all right with them as they were to be the actual operators of the project, manager, farmer and engineer.

On May 13 I went to Moline, Illinois. The John Deere headquarters there is exceedingly interesting. It is a large steel building in which you see many girders exposed but the building is quite attractive as well as unusual. It sits astride a small creek which comes down through a forest area so that you have the feeling of being completely away from urbanization when you get in there. It is very modern. Certainly their dining room for the officials is one of the fanciest I have seen anywhere. Large menus which look like New York's finest, and the meals were quite outstanding. The view through the large windows was down to the park area, with the stream running through it. I asked John Grafland how they liked it compared to Chicago. He said it was tremendous, that everybody loved it, that they could be on the golf course within five minutes of the time they left the office. I told him I wasn't particularly interested in that, I wondered how John Deere Company was doing. He said, "Oh, far, far better than we did in the old headquarters in Chicago. There we had visitors running through all the time, day after day, leaving very small orders, but here they call up for you to get them a reservation at the motel, they stay all night, they look over everything and when they leave, you have a far bigger order than we ever got in Chicago...." I comment on this because this movement from the big cities to the rural areas is maybe slowly but still gradually expanding with more and more companies making this move and finding it beneficial to the company as well as pleasant to the staff.

It was necessary, of course, to go over our general agreement and lease with the Bank people a good deal which we did, and then we got into the detail of exactly what crops we would be planting and exactly what the financial responsibilities and outcome would be. This took a great deal of time.

I went to Midland, Michigan for a meeting with W. W. Allen of Dow Chemical, somewhat comparable with the one in Moline, except that Dow was more interested in being accepted as one of our partners with no immediate responsibilities other than financing, but still it was necessary to work out our relationships as we felt they would be as we got going along further.

Maybe I should just comment on the livestock symposium in Fresno. This was an activity of the Bank of America in which they invited in speakers from all over the United States, in fact, from all over the world to speak on livestock subjects. The group then was divided up into cattle, beef and milk, sheep, hogs and later horses. This is the outstanding symposium of the country and many people come from very considerable distances. They go to great extent, such as freezing an entire carcass of a prime steer then cutting it up into its various parts frozen so that you can see each of the separate parts just as it is normally prepared in the market. An advisory group was set up to spend the year planning next year's symposium.

July 8, 1969, I spent with Bank of America, then on to Washington and Tehran to again go over a lot of the same material and some of the legal requirements of organization in Iran and developing the Iranian Company. Next I went down to the project for four days to pull what I could together there, coming back on the 9th to initial the agreements with the Minister of Water and Power and then flew home to New York and then to Moline to see John Deere and then back to Sacramento. We of course had Trans World meetings, then right after that to approve of actions taken.

One of the projects which Dow Chemical was particularly interested in was in our setting up an affiliate to freeze fruits, vegetables and so on in Iran and we made a study of that at U.C. Davis, in the Department of Food Technology, where they gave us a great deal of assistance.

We again had a meeting of John Deere, Bank of America, and Dow Chemical at the airport in Chicago to pull the whole thing together which I think was pretty well done at that time so that we could go ahead in Iran.

Mr. Ameri came over here and we again had meetings in San Francisco with the Bank of America folks and him in working out more details of the financing of the project. I spent a day with Doyle Reed, economist at Davis, who specializes in crop yields and all to go over our crop estimates and make sure we had our estimated yields within reason.

In October I spent three days in Washington with Gwen Garnett, the World Bank, Bank of America, John Deere and others, these being the people who would have some part in the program that we should become more familiar with. Amazing how much time it takes on things of this kind, but the facts were that not only were we new at this business at that time but so were all the rest of the people with whom we were involved, although they had international organization and the appearance of international working. Groups like John Deere had unquestionably exported a great deal of farm commodities; at the same time they didn't have much experience in a program of this kind so that all of us were getting acquainted with the requirements and what we might be up against.

I then went on to Washington and had lunch there with David Lillienthal who I have always looked up to very highly as a great American, but he certainly has a knowledge of the world in his travels to find out where are the possibilities for development. His feeling was that it wasn't ready for development yet for political reasons, but that the Mekong Delta was the largest and potentially most productive in the world not now being developed. This was somewhat of a surprise to me as I had assumed there was a large population in the Mekong Delta, but he said "Not at all, that it is very sparsely populated and as soon as they can get political stability, that that will be a tremendously rich development...."

†1970

My records for 1970 indicate that it was a great deal like 1969 with a tremendous amount of planning and getting ready for the operation which by now had enlarged to 25,000 acres for thirty years with a lease which was partly based on yields but was designed to pay about six dollars per acre. Of course, this sounds quite low but we were doing all of the development work, the land levelling, the buildings and all that kind of thing would be at our expense, in addition to the rentals to be paid. I think it was a program very fair to both sides.

Our thought, of course, in setting up Trans World was that we would set up a project of this kind and then follow it with others and we had a good deal of talk about projects in the northwest part of Africa, so we had a meeting in relation to the development of a thousand-acre rice project in Ghana and Nigeria.

By this time we had gotten to a place where we needed an office here at home, so we set one up in West Sacramento with Bob Hartsell as our office manager/assistant secretary and, of course, he had a secretary.

362

One of our principal jobs then was to find a well-qualified auditing firm acquainted with the laws and customs of Iran to audit our ICC books and, hopefully get us an accountant to handle books for the company. This proved to be one of our most difficult jobs. It was not only difficult to keep books in both Persian and English and with Iranian and American money, but there just didn't seem to be people over there who were qualified or willing to handle our books. There are businesses over there who do, of course, keep books, but somehow they would tell us they would help us but we never did get a satisfactory bookkeeper. Even including several we sent from the United States who seemed to be very able in handling dollars but when it came to doing the job in rials and doing it according to the customs of the country, this was one of our biggest stumbling blocks.

Our Iranian Company was set up as Iran/California Company with two directors from Trans World, one from Bank of America, one from John Deere and Dow, and two from the Iranian investors, primarily Mr. Talagani and the agricultural development fund of Iran. We set up with an office in Tehran and a general manager there which is the office through which we dealt primarily with the Bank and other governmental institutions. Of course our office for the farming operation was in Andemeshk.

One of the interesting incidents was that we dealt with Mr. Hossien Mirdamad, who was the Mack truck distributor in Iran. They import what they call the essential parts—engines, frames, brakes, transmissions and so forth, from the Mack factory in the United States, so the other parts were made there in Iran. This included the cab and fenders which were made of fiberglass. There were two representatives of the Mack Company in the United States to see that the quality of the trucks was maintained. But there seemed to be little question but that the fiberglass fenders and cabs were better than the American steel. This was quite a large operation and I found that it was true of many companies such as Caterpillar which assembles through its Iranian Company all of the parts from the United States, but the assembly plant is reqlly quite a large industrial operation and I know the caterpillar service organization in Ahwaz was certainly better than any agency I have seen in the United States. Better equipped, very large, all air-conditioned, including all the shop. They had computerized programs whereby you went to a big book in the lobby to pick out the part you wished and pressed a button and it would tell you just what bin in the warehouse the part was in, and how many of them they had on hand, so that it was very easy to order your parts and know right away whether they were available. In fact, you could get delivery much more quickly than you ordinarily can here.

One evening, Mr. Miramad invited me to their home for dinner. There were about thirty people around the dinner table which seemed to be the normal group and we had a very fine meal. After dinner he pointed out a young man and said, "You see that young fellow over there? He is my son-in-law. He is one of a family of thirty-five, all of them university graduates and all of them doing well...." This is the Farman-Farmian family. They are rather well-known in government, business, farming, everything else in Iran. They had five different mothers but still, for one family of thirty-five, all of them to be college graduates and all of them do well is a most unusual circumstance. Even if you were only figureing the average of seven to a mother, it would still be an outstanding performance.

In the Imperial Valley during April of this year Mike Merachini was turning his land over to his partner, preparing to leave soon for Iran as farm manager. Ken Reynolds was delayed so we were having Dean Pryor fill in that post until Ken could leave. Dean and I went to Tehran to meet people, locate the equipment, employ four good Iranian employees from KWPA, Khuzistan Water and Power Company. We got word that Mike Marachini had cancer and died in just a few days. This, of course, was a very serious blow to our operation.

We rented several houses from KWPA for our people in the compound at Andimeshk until we could build our own.

On April 29, our project engineer, Ken Brown, was on the project to set up his survey-leveling program. We employed Joe Flamming as assistant engineer. He supervised the land leveling and trained the drivers. Joe's father had been a land leveler in Imperial for many years, one of the very best. Joe was raised around and on the equipment and knew it very well He had graduated from Cal Poly and was "raring to go."

May 7 was a big day as we opened our West Sacramento office for TWAD Co. and John Deere said they would order the equipment shipped to Iran.

On May 13 we left for Iran. Dean and I met Stan Kapon in London. He had worked for Development and Resources as the accountant in the Khuzistan and was accustomed to Iran, doing accounting in rials as well as dollars and knew all the people, the climate, and so forth. I was very happy when he agreed to come with us. Leo Anderson had recommended him as one of the best.

In Iran the Iran/California Board met and seemed to be falling in line.

On May 20 we took the plane to Andemesk. Ken Brown, the engineer, was very enthusiastic about his work and the prospects for the future, but he had a rather bad headache. The next day we got a doctor and decided to send him to the hospital in Tehran. Our reports were that he was improving in the hospital. I went to Tehran on June 7 and went directly to the hospital to check on "Brownie" whose doctor was educated in the United States. He said "Brownie" had a brain tumor and should go to the United States for an operation. I thought the doctor was very good. He said he could operate on him, but the hospital there didn't have the trained nurses, the instruments, the lights, and all the other things that are needed as aides in a serious operation. He said "Brownie" had gotten up and had his shower that morning without any aid at all and could easily travel home alone. The nurse said the same. I didn't talk to him until 11 o'clock, then came back again at 1 o'clock. I felt he was not getting better, so I looked up the doctor. He, by then, was not sure that "Brownie" could travel alone, so I thought I'd have to go with him. I went to see the Pan Am manager in Tehran to arrange tickets which often is rather difficult on such short notice. We talked for some time about it, then he said, "Let's do this thing right; let's call the Pan Am doctor so he can look for himself at "Brownie" and see what he thinks...." He did come and he approved

364

the flight home. We needed to leave the hospital in an ambulance at 1:30 a.m. to get the flight. To get all arranged, I was going as fast as I could without stopping to eat. Pan Am had a roll-away cot, everything ready to help including a registered nurse when we arrived at the airport. They had just called us to get on the plane early when the incoming passengers were coming in and there was young Joe Flamming. I told Joe that I knew he was tired too, but I wished that he would go back with "Brownie" as a good friend of his. It was a great relief to me. A bed was made up for "Brownie" and also another patient who had a woman doctor attending him. She said she would look after "Brownie" also. They got to London and a doctor there said "Brownie" should be moved to a hospital for further observation before crossing the Atlantic. Joe stayed with him for about two weeks until his wife and sister, both of them nurses, came and took him home for an operation. They got to San Diego and "Brownie" was operated on, but it was too late. His passing was a real blow to us.

Our Iranian partners proposed Iraj Sepapuar for the general manager of the company, to be headquartered in an office in Tehran. He and his brother had a dairy farm west of Tehran. He had been employed by the Agricultural Development Fund of Iran where I had met him. He seemed to be quite able. He told me that some years before they had a bad drought in that area so the government had a relief program of selling cattle feed to the farmers at a low price per ton and a low interest rate with payments starting in ten years. They signed up for carloads of corn which they then sold for a high price and invested in farm land and imported dairy cattle, so now they are quite well off. They are one of the old families of Iran.

The problem was that the Iranians in the company always seemed to feel that I should be able to come up with similar deals.

In June Ambassador and Mrs. MacArthur (a cousin of the General—not with the military, but he stood, looked, moved, and spoke very much like the General) invited me to a reception at the Embassy. Their home is in the trees northeast of the office building. I met there many whom I had earlier met or had dealings with and many who I had heard of but not met before. The Embassy was beautifully designed for entertainment of large groups without seeming crowded.

Bella and I attended a reception there later.

July 15 Capon, our new accountant, and I took the train to Andremesk where he got set up in a house and office. Al Gross, Bank of America in Iran, and Iraj Sepapuar came down to see the project. It was very hot. Al brought a plastic hat and left it on the shelf behind the back seat of the car. It melted and so did Al. They were surprised and amazed by the land leveling and the progress made, but they never forgot the heat. We got a desert cooler for the office, which helped.

We had men on hand and the planting program all drawn up. The land had been purchased from the farmers and they paid, so we were anxious both to get started and to give the local people something to do. Motorcycles began to appear on the road as the land was paid for. We wanted to have at least some of the people employed and happy, but none of our equipment had arrived. KWPA had lots of equipment which they had rented to farmers. They agreed to sell us what we wanted, so we selected what we could use including small tractor discs, planters, cultivators, etc. Before we could get it much was moved to another farm, so we were still very short but we used what we could get and got some crops in.

The D&R engineer covering land leveling and water distribution was Hack Smith from Imperial Valley. He had been on the job about six years and was almost finished. They had returned to Imperial on leave. We got him to check up on the latest ideas in Imperial Valley and then return as our engineer. He was very valuable in that he knew the people and the land and rapidly had land prepared for leveling. He continued as our engineer all through the project with George Flamming acting as his assistant handling the leveling operations and later the shop.

We left August 11 for Tehran and home, stopping in Rome. We went to the Outdoor Opera at the Roman Baths. We spent a busy month at home locating men and equipment for Iran. We attended TWAD Board meeting, D&R meeting, etc., and were back in Iran September 25.

Capon left to take a more responsible position which was another blow to us. He said he had enough pioneering his first stint there and did not want to start again.

Our agreement with the Ministry of Water and Power was called the General Agreement. There were over 60 pages covering most of the agreement and plan for farming the land. There was a long lease document covering the A area and then the B-C area.

There was also "The Law Covering Establishment of Companies for the Development of Lands Downstream of Dams." Also the Law Concerning the Attraction and Protection of Foreign Investment in Iran.

The 1970 list of crops planted were:

250 acres of beets—most looked good.
250 acres of berseem clover for sheep feed and seed.
100 acres of vegetables—tomatoes, carrots, onions, celery, lettuce.
 57 acres of sudan pasturing 200 sheep.
250 acres of wheat, Inia 66 for seed for Department of Agriculture.
1000 acres of wheat was ready to plant.

Five John Deere paddle-wheel scrapers had started leveling. Other John Deere equipment arrived November 30. Four Hancock scrapers were still on the docks.

We were in new offices in Andemeshk, six rooms. The President of Asgrow International was in Iran in October studying the seed growing potential and a 50-50 joint seed company with our company. Bill Allen of Dow and Bob Hartzell have completed phase 1 of a study of freezing and dehydration of vegetables on our project.

On October 7, Mr. Trambuste of the World Bank looked us over and was very complimentary, saying they would like to be stockholders in the project. Shell Cotts came in about this time to farm the land north of us up to Mr. Narghi's area. Shell was Shell Oil Company—Cotts was Mitchell and Cotts, a part of the old "East India" company still farming in India, Africa and other countries as well as owning steamships, railroads and office buildings around the world.

They built nice residences, had a full staff of people, and had much better land than our A area. It was land held out by the Government of Iran for the Government of Yugoslavia and then given up. We had many troubles, but they had more. We enjoyed them as neighbors and met socially but we all had problems.

Iraj Sephapour, our Tehran Office Manager, was employed to handle problems with the Government of Iran, importation of seeds and equipment, and other relations with government offices.

Our farm equipment was in port, but we could not get it released. He employed a friend of his to get it released, but no progress, only excuses. Finally, I went down to Khorramshahr. An Iranian friend who spoke good English came into the hotel that evening and went with me to the port the next day. We found our equipment and got busy on getting it out, signing lots of papers in different places. At lunchtime, we were about done, but not quite. We paid the man to work through lunch hour and got it all loaded that afternoon. The railroad yard in Andemeshk let us use the railroad cranes to unload and assemble the scrapers and other equipment. Then on a rainy day, we took it all across the Dezful bridge to our new shop on the project and started moving dirt.

I had gone earlier to Lubbock, Texas, and ordered five Hancock scrapers to be pulled by John Deere tractors, and they had started moving them when a flood covered the factory area five feet deep. The damage prevented start-up any time soon, so they found some for us which had been used but overhauled (one more delay).

We could buy Allis Chalmer scrapers from the dealer in Tehran—tractor and scraper a single unit. We were about to order when John Deere said they had a very fine similar unit at less money. I hesitated, but felt John Deere were our partners and would have a full supply of parts handy. About the time to order, A.C. cut their price to John Deere's, and I was surely tempted but felt I should stay with our partner.

We used both the Hancock and John Deere scrapers and moved dirt ahead of schedule, then the John Deeres started to break down. The big drive wheels cracked at the hubs and the rims, so they laid up the whole machine and there were no spares in Iran. We then learned that we faced real trouble.

We asked John Deere into the project because they had a broad line of tractors and farm equipment. They were building a large factory and assembly plant at Arak, an industrial city on the railroad about half-way between Tehran and Andemeshk. They agreed they would set up a branch in Andemeshk or make us distributors of John Deere equipment and parts.

They had a distributor who had exclusive distribution in Iran, but he had not made any sales effort and they could easily buy him out and have full control for themselves, they said.

The construction of the factory in Arak was well along. Their distributor had few parts and we had bought direct from John Deere so he had no interest in us. We found that he was expanding his showrooms, he was not bought out, and before long, we found he owned the new factory at Arak and John Deere was out. I believe they lost all they had in Iran and we lost lots of time and money with long delays in getting parts, having land levelers and farm equipment held up for months waiting for repair parts, and we never got the mechanics they were to provide. I had had all my dealings with John Grafland, I am sure a very fine, conscientious man who expected to provide all he talked of, but he was elevated to being in charge of all John Deere manufacturing and sales in Canada, so I never had a chance to talk to him and get our problems cared for.

There are many sugar beet factories in Iran, but none around Khuzestan except the sugar cane plant in Ahwaz now being overhauled to refine both cane and beet sugar. The raw cane sugar came from Russia, India and many other areas of the world for refining and use in Iran. It was a good modern plant.

Growing beets was new to all the people in the area. The small plantings so far were pretty poor; often the seed had been just scattered, and the beets raised out of the ground with a spade. We, of course, planted in rows and cultivated and thinned as here. They did a remarkably good job of planting fairly straight rows for us. The first year we only had local 2-row planters so it was more difficult. They were thinned by the women and girls. We paid by the 100 meters of row. They were very conscientious and did a good job. We paid them individually; I often wished I could see just what happened when the women came home with that much cash; temporary, but their own.

At harvest time, the men topped and pulled the beets and then hand-loaded them into trucks with high sides. To load them, they would throw them in over the sides, then when the truck was half to two-thirds full, the men on the ground piled the beets into a woven basket and threw them up for the men in the truck to catch the basket, empty it, throw it back. This sometimes got to be hilarious fun and the next year we had beet harvesters as we use here. The first-year yields were not great, but they were far the best in the area and they kept the sugar factory going which it never could have done without our beets.

We were so busy that we hadn't paid much attention to the articles in national and international papers about our project in Iran. Some were short and some quite lengthy, but I was surprised and interested when Mr. Rasern, photographer for Fortune, wanted pictures and a story.

It was a very interesting day. He had travelled widely. He carried three cameras all ready for quick action. A real interesting shot would call for all three cameras, and every shot was automatically three full exposures.

When he finished a roll in his camera, he put new film in all three far faster than I could refill one. The children fascinated him and we had lots of fun with them putting on great shows for him.

The story came out in the November 1970 issue of Fortune as "Oil and Water Rebuild an Ancient Land." There were many other articles in Newsweek, Business Week, U.S. News & World Report, and many other national and international magazines. The project was more newsworthy than I had imagined, or maybe I should say was more broadly recognized than I had expected.

On December 2, 1970, I arrived back in New York and went up to Connecticut to see my nephew Gilbert Scott, Vice President of Associated Seed Company. We were considering setting up a joint venture with them. We to grow seed, and they to market it in that part of the world.

To get to the offices, one left the freeway, drove back maybe one-half mile through the timber, then entered a meadow and there they were, all alone. Good access, beauty, quiet, and they loved it.

I ordered seed for the crop year. We considered the joint venture further, but climate, weed, insect and a disease conditions were not well enough known to really start seed production.

Legal problems were arising here and in Iran, so we got Frank Richardson as our attorney. He had travelled widely, was active in the World Affairs Council, later served as justice California Supreme Court, Regent of University of Pacific, and is now helping in the U.S. State Department, Washington D.C.

†1971

On January 30 I arrived in Iran to work with Dean on the project. Wayne Weeks arrived February 13. Wayne had been Farm Advisor, Director of Agricultural Extension Service in California, now manager of the Bowles Farming Company of Los Banos. His advice was excellent. He should have been our Project Manager.

The John Deere beet harvester was about ready for use and the grain harvester was in Iran. The grain harvester came from John Deere in Germany as it was closer, cheaper, and stronger, as Europe has far more rain than Western U.S. so they harvest damper grain. In fact, they ship the German-made harvester to the U.S. as a rice harvester.

Glen Harris had been in Ghana and Nigeria for us to study a rice project. There was lots of land and lots of water for rice on the Accra Plain north of the city and west of the river. It looked good, and we spent a good deal of time studying the project and working with Kaiser Aluminum who had a large plant there and a good deal of say in use of the water.

Land next to the KWPA housing was allocated to us for housing and we had developed plans for building 12 houses nicely landscaped and all. The International Finance Corporation said they would like to have a $250,000 equity with us.

On April 25 I flew to Washington D.C. and consulted with the World Bank and others, and on to Andemeshk on the 28th.

It seemed now that Ken Reynolds would not be available soon, so I had Bob Thomason come over from the Kufra project in Lybia. He was a real good man, I am sure, but he wanted more salary than we could offer, and he said he was very happy where he was. I increased our offer, but he did not want to leave Kufra. Dean asked me if we were looking for a new man. I told him we were looking for a man to fill the position we had planned for Ken Reynolds, overall manager and vice president of Trans World.

Ken and I went to Tehran. I returned to Andemeshk on May 26, 1971. Dean had received a message saying his father, who was sick, was sinking, so he left early that morning before I arrived.

Our Iran-California Board was disturbed that we had no manager on the ground, so I promised to stay until we got one; they to pay me per diem for travel, dining, hotel, etc. so I would not be on the payroll, or have to get work permits, pay taxes, etc., so I settled in for a full schedule of keeping the project moving ahead and Bob Hartzell and Glen Harris looking out for TWAD Company in Sacramento and finding a good manager, bookkeeper, and two farmers to assure a good job in Iran.

I drew up the budget for 700 Hectares in the B-C area to be planted on, land-planed but not leveled, 300 Hectares = 660 acres for beets and 370 Hectares wheat and 30 Hectares for vegetables.

369

The manager of the supermarket in Tehran said they would have five stores in operation soon so they could use all the vegetables we could raise and more. It looked like I might be in Iran for some time, so Bella came over.

The B-C area is better land than the A area. It is on the main highway, Tehran to the Persian Gulf. It is much better for selling vegetables or other produce to passing trucks going north or south and many people see the crops and the benefit of better farming, that better crops can be a reality, not just a dream.

On June 1 we took delivery of two new GMC trucks, one to be a service truck to fuel, grease, clean and otherwise service equipment in the field. The other was for general hauling.

Mr. Stephanides, agricultural attache for Tehran, and Mr. Clements, U.S. Consul for Korramshah, spent the day of June 23 looking over the operation. Both were fine officials who spent a good deal of time in the farming areas of Iran. They were well-informed of progress anywhere in Iran.

On July 29 Bella left for Dick's wedding to Arline Morse, a young widow with two sons, Tim and Kevin, and a daughter, Kirsti, living on Bruceville Road, Elk Grove. Bella returned pleased by the wedding and seeing all the family friends at home.

We bought sheep to pasture the areas not farmed, and grazed the sudan, corn stubble and other feed available. We had the sheep tatooed but never were quite sure just when and how sheep joined or left the bands. I am sure we needed them, but not so sure that we received most of the income.

Our real pest was wild hogs in the corn. It would look like a cyclone had hit, but the hoof marks told the story. The first crop of milo was a disappointment, some would be beautiful and look like a bumper crop, and then turn dry and produce little. We should have had an entomologist. It would have paid big.

I had been in Iran as long as my visa was good. I was called before a police court. I had to wait a long while when an officer came by. I had a copy of our general agreement with me, signed by Minister Rouhani. I showed it to him. He brought it back with smiles and bows and took me to a judge who very graciously told me he would gladly omit the fine if I would leave within five days for Kuwait, get a new visa and return. I left our house at 3:30 a.m. for a flight from Abadan at 7:20 a.m., flying low over the Arabian Gulf, seeing the sailing boats called Dhows, which looked just like the Bible days. A few were equipped with refrigeration to carry vegetables, milk or other cargo needing to be cold *A two-hour flight. The airport at Kuwait was large and modern as was the city. Lots of shade trees and some of the roads very wide with large lawns and gardens. I found it very interesting to sit in a big chair in the large lobby of the hotel and watch the Sheiks in long flowing robes slowly seem to slide along on the marble floors seeming to watch and be watched. The evidence of money was everywhere. I met the owner of the supermarket. His market was good. He had been manager of a large supermarket in the Boston area for seven years. It looked quite U.S.A. He took me to the vegetable market; much came from Italy, Turkey and other areas by air and was of excellent quality.

The truck road from Iran to Kuwait is good through Iraq if too much red tape doesn't stop you.

370

We set up an electric generator with floodlights on high masts and started night land leveling to make up for tractor failure and parts delays. Our harvester did all right in the wheat, milo, and corn, but we had to get grain cleaners to clean out fine and coarse material.

I wrote many appeals for a vegetable man to grow our vegetables and help with the other farming, but never got one over, so we never did well enough to sell many marketable vegetables. I did get an Iranian, Iraj Fohootan, who had gone to the Ahwaz Agricultural College, and he did very well with the field crops. Glen Harris, Jerry Fielder and Fred Frick had several meetings with George "Bud" Hobbs. He was the type of man we needed. He had managed the Bud Antle Vegetable Company in Salinas, one of the large ones, handling growing, packing and sales for the company.

They offered $50,000 salary, $12,500 deferred compensation, $1,250 each for children's schooling, 1-5% of the net profit of the company and up to 25,000 shares of TWAD Company stock at $1.00 to $3.00 per share in the first five years. This was more compensation than we had planned, but still reasonable for an able executive which we needed. Bud Hobbs met the Bank of America folks August 9 and they were well impressed.

On September 7, Glen Harris, Fred Frick and Bud Hobbs arrived in Andemeshk for a look around. We went into all aspects of the operation. He seemed to be challenged by the project. We met further with the ICC directors in Tehran and on the 10th relaxed and talked more on a trip to the Caspian Sea, going the northeast road and returning the south road. It is a beautiful trip. Very steep mountains; a tea, rice, tobacco, and vacation area.

I felt we were pretty well set for success with Bud Hobbs at the wheel. I am sure he could have pleased the Iranians, but they do not like to decide quickly and delayed outright approval, and Bud decided he should have a year or two guaranteed salary in case of failure or replacing him. He wanted Bank of America to guarantee his salary, which they could not do. He now is a successful Salinas Valley grower, shipping on his own.

Mr. Ameri of the Agricultural Development Fund of Iran, our financier, was giving us lots of trouble in getting money to farm with. We were not getting the hoped-for yield. We did not have accurate cost and income figures. Our budgets were based on Ken Reynolds, Mike Marrachini, and Brownie being on the ground handling the operation and John Deere having adequate equipment and repairs readily available to us.

In the planning stage, Grafland of Deere felt we should put in $1.00 of capital for $4.00 borrowing from the Agricultural Development Fund, ADFI. The Bank of America thought $1.00 for $3.00 borrowed. I used $3.00 in all budgets which were approved by the Minister of Water and Power and the Council of Ministers but Mr. Ameri of the Fund required that we use part of our capital first and then ruled that he would only advance us $1.00 of loan for $1.00 of capital. I insisted on using the 3 to 1 included in the plan, approved by the Council of Ministers, but got no help from either Bank of America or John Deere. Each cash advance would be so delayed that plantings were delayed and yields reduced.

We said in our plan and proposed to the Minister of Water and Power that we would precision-level the land. None of the other agricultural industry leases had that

371

provision, but Mr. Ameri got the idea that that would be the dominant factor and he would only loan us money according to the hectares of land precision-leveled. This meant that when we got an advance, much of the money had to go into leveling instead of crop production but, of course, if he had to foreclose on us, he could show all the land he had precision-leveled at a very low cost to the government of Iran.

He told me that our loan was larger than all the previous loans combined. Mr. Ameri came to the U.S. in September, 1971, and expressed his displeasure with the job we were doing. The Bank of America found over two million dollars in errors in the figures he was using. During that time, we should have been busy planting, but couldn't get money until he returned, and then so late that yields were reduced materially.   I am sure my figures were reasonable for a going farming operation with land, water, and sun as they have in Iran and with the management team we thought would be in charge.

I spent a good deal of time getting good designs for houses for our people. The Iranians do not do much in convenient design for houses for employees, but they do have very positive and good ideas on avoiding the heat of the sun, adequate south overhang. No windows on west side of house, etc.

Sephapour left the Tehran office to go into business for himself. Mr. Yassif Rad took his place. Rad was manager of the government-owned supermarket and seems a good man. It was sometimes unbelievable how difficult it was to import insecticide, pure seeds, etc. We finally had to import Vitavax from Canada to be shipped by air, but they sent it by water. This would take months and be too late to use effectively.

We were fighting on all fronts, it seemed every day, hoping to get Hobbs or someone over here, trying to get bookkeepers to get the books in order, and continually improve the land preparation, the accuracy of the planting and cultivation.

Vegetable seeds arrived late, some too late to plant. We had no idea seed would be so difficult to get in, and thought we had that problem covered in the general agreement, but such an agreement approved by the Council of Ministers of Iran does not outrank the bureaucracies.

In October I was still hoping for Bud Hobbs or another General Manager and also one or two good farmers to arrive soon. On November 26 Dick Ward came over to look over the position of Project Manager. He was known by several of our members. His dad had owned and operated the Clearlake Water Company, furnishing irrigation, water to much of Yolo County, and was liked by the farmers. Dick had followed his father in that position and also managed a large ranch in Arizona, and then gone to CAL for a Master of Business Administration which he just completed. He signed up for the position and was leaving for home.

A new farmer, Lee Dudley and his wife, also arrived to replace Dave Nelson.

By December 1   we had had over 4" of rain and a little clear weather for three weeks. Very bad for the weeds and late beets; all were thinned by now and most were cultivated and weeded. We have 1250 acres of beets in. Most people think they are fantastic. We have 2700 acres of wheat planted and 500 more to plant in the next ten days.

On December 4 I went to see Mr. Rouhani, now Minister of Agriculture, and told him we were having trouble getting our money from ADFI. We had a new man coming as Project Manager and he must have money on time if we expect him to do well. Mr. Rouhani said not to worry, he would see that we got the money we needed for Dick Ward.

Mr. Teleghani planned to be on the project December 17, 1971, with the Shah who was to come down to dedicate the new Dezful Bridge. He will at least fly over our project in the helicopter. I feel sure we will be better cared for if the Shah lands and looks over the fields.

Dick Ward arrived December 22 as Project Manager, and I had the best night's sleep in a long while. Dick had Christmas dinner with us, turkey and all. There was lots to do acquainting Dick with the people and the project.

†1972

On January 2 Dick went to Tehran with us. We met with the ICC Board and met many people to introduce Dick and on January 6, left Tehran for Washington D.C. where we reported to World Bank, I.F.C. and others and joyfully came home to see the family.

Our Secretary-Treasurer, Jerry Fielder, had been appointed Director of Agriculture by Governor Reagan. He had been attending a series of meetings throughout the state using his own plane for transportation. A heavy windy electrical storm came up as he was approaching the landing at Executive Airport when his plane apparently exploded and he was killed on landing. This was a great loss to his family, the state, and TWAD Co.

February 25 we went to Monterey and the Bay Area to study freezing equipment and methods for use in Iran. We went on south to see my sister, Ethel, who was in a convalescent home doing well but needing family and friends, then on to see Eleanor and Mary, Isabelle's sisters, and on to Imperial to see Ken Reynolds, then Ensenada to see Tom and Dorothy Robertson.

We attended the El Dorado Cattlemen's Association meeting at El Dorado Royal Country Club On March 16 was Dick's birthday dinner.

TWAD Co. applied for a state permit to sell stock. We got Tony Kennedy as attorney and spent long hours getting all the statistical data together to sell the stock.

March 22 we went to see Pat, Wes and the girls.

April 5 we joined the University Club in Sacramento, at first they were on the second floor on K Street, but it was a nice place to meet, visit and eat. They then moved to an old Victorian home on H Street. They had the whole house here. It was very nice for lunches, dinners, etc. I was meeting quite regularly with a group of 8-10 men who ate and talked on Monday noons. I found it a social group; we met for several years until the club was not able to keep up the payments on the house.

For quite a few years, the Wells Fargo Bank gave cash and other awards to FFA members in this district, 4 or 5 counties to the members doing best in several categories. They had a big dinner, first at the Sutter Club, then at El Macero Country Club. I sopke at, at least, one dinner, but was invited and went for many years. They showed colored slides of each person's project, had some entertainment and a speaker. They were very inspirational and I enjoyed them.

May 26 was the inauguration of Stan McCaffrey as President of the University of the Pacific. A short time before this, we attended the inauguration of Dr. Hitch, President of University of California at the UCLA campus. It, too, was quite a formal affair, but I am quite sure there were more formal representatives from other universities at Stan's inaugural than I saw at Hitch's. Maybe that is because there are more of the smaller and middle-sized universities. That evening there was a dinner meeting of the Alumni Foundation Board at Chancellor Meyer's in Davis.

On June 22 we left for Iran with Glen Harris. We had an ICC Board Meeting and flew to Ahwaz. We were met by Dick Ward and the accountant. We stayed at the Imperial Hotel in Andemeshk.

Some things looked better. The morale of the employees and all we saw and heard seemed to justify the rumors we had been hearing that Dick Ward would like to operate directly with ICC and have TWAD Co. out of the picture. He had learned in the MBA course how to gain control and profit for himself. This did not dominate all things in the beginning, but it made it more difficult for both of us and both of us were the losers. We had another ICC board meeting on July 1 and left Tehran July 5, returning over the pole. I spoke at Rotary on the 13th.

Much of the time was spent getting all the data on TWAD Co. and the Iranian operation in proper form for a prospectus to sell stock in TWAD Co. and getting the permit from the California Corporation Commissioner who it seemed made the problem more difficult and then the Governor appointed a new Commissioner and we had to do much of it all over for him, which took a lot of time when we were in need of money, as our payment from Iran was terribly delayed.

One of our principal jobs then was to find a well-qualified auditing firm acquainted with the laws and customs of Iran to audit our ICC books and, hopefully, get us an accountant to handle books for the company. This proved to be one of our most difficult jobs. It was not only difficult to keep books in both Persian and English and with Iranian and American money, but there just didn't seem to be people over there who were qualified or willing to handle our books. There are businesses over there who do, of course, keep books, but somehow they would tell us they would help us but we never did get a satisfactory bookkeeper. Even including several we sent from the United States who seemed to be very able in handling dollars, but when it came to doing the job in rials and doing it according to the customs of the country, this was one of our biggest stumbling blocks.

As I write this story in May, 1985, I have read over some of the letters to me from our American staff in Andemeshk, and in them are plainly spelled out how Dick Ward was doing all he could to discredit TWAD Co. and claimed the management agreement should be with him and ICC rather than between TWAD Co. and ICC. He claimed he could do better and save the ICC lots of money.

Apparently at the time, we were so sure that the land, water, sunshine, the local workers, and the market were so good that the project had to succeed, and we failed to believe the reports we were receiving from our local staff who were warning us of difficulties. Soon after this, Mr. Ameri of the Agricultural Development Fund of Iran, who

374

was financing us, said he would not advance any more money until we agreed to a revision of the management agreement and fees. We opposed the changes he wanted, but agreed to some. I am sure that, at the time, we felt our problem was Ameri, who we felt was trying to be sure he protected his own position if he had losses on his loans to the foreign agricultural industry companies in Khuzestan.

In our struggle for finances as budgeted on time and retaining management control, we never thought of us having an internal problem to make our collection of our management fee more difficult. By now, John Deere was in greater financial trouble than we were, so they could not be of much help. The Bank of America representative in Iran had many more projects in which he was interested, so he sided, most of the time, with the Iranians. The Bank of America officials in San Francisco always said they wanted TWAD to retain management, but they were not in Iran to help us.

What I am saying mainly is that a person or group can be so sure that their overall project is so good that it cannot be lost, and fail to face up to some of the problems that work against one.

On September 15, I spoke at the West Sacramento Rotary Club. On October 2 I see I had joined the Comstock Club in Sacramento which is a small edition of the Commonwealth in San Francisco.

I went to the TWAD Co. office in West Sacramento every day or so, looking up equipment, seed, chemicals or something for Iran, or seeing Bank of America people, or our present or prospective members.

I went to the Sloughhouse Ranch, usually just to look around, but sometimes to sell or gather cattle or work on a reservoir or other project.

On December 10 we attended the AFBF annual meeting in Los Angeles. Lawrence Welk and his group entertained for the banquet and then for the dance.

†1973

Glen Harris was now President of TWAD Co. and I Senior Vice-President, but Glen still had farming at home so I still did much of the routine office work.

Glen was in Iran March 20-April 9, 1973. Mr. Famshid Medhat was overall manager of ICC as Carl Williams, one of our four TWAD Co. shareholders from Imperial, was advising on the farming operation for a few months. The wheat looked good; some of the beets were grassy as the hoeing crew was laid off for lack of finances. Glen felt Mr. Medhat was doing well at the ICC board meeting. Ameri agreed to advance $200,000 on the old loan, but Ward figured they would need $300,000 through May 21, 1973, when they hoped to get the IFC (International Finance Corporation) loan.

It had been this way from the first; advances always late and too small so crop income was drastically reduced from late planting, shortage of chemicals, and hoeing and other practices delayed. Ward resigned.

In June, Bob Hartzell resigned to accept the position as Assistant Director for the State Department of Agriculture. Al McKee, a brilliant young fellow from Bank of America and a friend of ours, contacted a friend of his from Chase Manhattan Bank, who were financing part of Hawaiian Agronomics about financing and managing our operation. He felt it might be a good idea, but right then, they were having too many birth pains and had not yet gotten any of their money from ADFI. Also, Chase Manhattan Bank had pledged one-third of their shares as security to the ADFI loan and that Mitsui, Diamond A Cattle Company, belonging to Anderson of ARCO, Hawaiian Agronomics, and Azod of the Ahwaz Sugar Company had pledged 100% of their shares for 10 years.

We could easily see signs that before long, ADFI would require that we pledge part or all of our stock in ICC to them in order to be financed. Of course, if we did and failed to pay off the loan on schedule, the project would belong to ADFI and we would be out.

Mardom, the minor political party in Iran, was quite minor. The shah felt it would be better to have it more of a "loyal opposition" party and suggested it be revitalized, so Nasser Ameri was elected as new head of the party and they were quite active in the next election.

Mr. and Mrs. Raymond had given their ranch, a little above Knights Landing, to the University of Pacific, about 620 acres in rice in Natomas District, and about 3030 acres in the Bypass subject to floods. The Bypass was leased to seven tenants who had farmed it for many years and still had leases. No one on the university staff was really experienced in farm management, so they felt it best to sell the property, if possible.

I spent a great deal of time digging out the records of each tenant, crops raised, yields, prices, rent received by UOP, and costs to UOP. Jack Anderson of Davis, a very prosperous young farmer, made a proposal, so I spent all of my time completing my analysis and I found that there were two or three crops of milo in storage at Adams Grain which had not been sold and had never gotten onto the university accounts. When this was added to the income, it made it look a good deal better. Mrs. Raymond had plenty of money for her limited needs, so she did not keep track of details of sales and the executors were not pressed for funds, so the crops of milo were not missed, hence the relatively low return sent to the university. It looked like Jack Anderson's offer was better for the university than holding the land and having the expense of repairing the damage of frequent floods. We sold the land and since then, the floods have been very few so really I was sorry we let it go.

Jack became very wealthy in farm land, tomato cannery, and through large nonfarm investments. The saving or accumulation of wealth is largely a matter of hard work and effort, but also of time, weather and conditions over which we have little control.

UOP had received a fine bequest from Grace A. Covell including securities, city and farm real estate, and also a 17,000 acre cattle ranch in S.W. Stanislaus County being leased by Fred Freitas and his brother, on which they ran cattle from October to May and then moved them to Tule Lake country or river bottom land along the San Joaquin River. The ranch was quite steep and very short of water, either drilled or good locations for building ponds large enough to carry through the summer. In fact, they had a tank truck to bring in drinking water in the fall for the cattle. It had real good grass in season on soil that was good quality and deep.

On August 20 I had Rube Abaugh, from the U.C. Davis Agricultural Extension Service, spend the day with Mr. Freitas and me on the ranch and write up a report and appraisal which he did very well. His value was $1,184,000. His son is a coach in the Athletic Department at UOP. We elected to hold it about two years and got a materially better price for it, $2,950,000.

Sunday, September 9, 1973, I flew to San Diego and met Mark and his friend. We traveled in Mark's station wagon, stopping at Tom and Dorothy Robertson's. We went to a new hotel near Sky Ranch, but $30. each sent us onto the beach. It was overcast, but warm all night. We had coffee with Senora Espinosa. She says the new road is a mixed blessing; too many people of all kinds. Five miles below Puerta Prieta we stopped for the night.

We arrived at Guerro Negro and found the Cesano store, but Cipriano had died about two months before, of ulcers and water in the blood. I was surely sorry to have missed him.

We looked over the salt works and saw many old friends in the office. They seemed as glad to see me as I was to enjoy their company for a while. They were delivering 20,000 tons of salt per day, 500,000 per month. They pulled three long 20-ton trailers. They were tremendous. Mitsubishi had management of the project, but they were in Mexico City and the old crew was still running the operation.

There are several hotels in Guerro Negro and the new government hotel is being built on the state-territory boundary.

We stopped in Ejido Viscaino, just north of Rancho Margarita. They have new shops, a dehydrator, and packing shed for figs and raisins, packed dried in 5-gallon cans, 900 hectares of cotton sprinkler irrigated, 200 hectares of figs very good, 100 hectares of grapes drip irrigated. There are 150 brick houses for the families, all from the mainland. They had a "fair" two weeks before. There is a large church with service each Sunday.

Each Ejido is 10 hectares and each lives on his own 10 hectares, but most of the land is farmed by the corporation and each works at least 50 days per year for the corporation and the other time on his own place.

Rancho Margarita was all in tomatos, in rows 2 meters (6½ feet) apart. They say they fill the rows. They go to the U.S. They were building a new packing shed including refrigeration.

Our house was neat and clean, but no flowers; it had tile and cement floors.

We looked around St. Ignacio for an hour and saw some old friends. It is just one hour from St. Ignacio to Santa Rosalia. Some grades steep, but the road is good. We had dinner and rooms at the Central Hotel. Everything started at 6 a.m. We walked around town and bought ferry tickets from La Paz to Guaymas, then arrived Mulege at 11:15 a.m., on to Loreto where we visited the old church, ate at Hotel Mission on the waterfront. We visited a dairy farm and then the creamery in Constitucion. There was lots of cotton, some very good, some short of water, several cotton gins, some oranges looked very good.

Constitucion is now quite a city, wide streets, a mile or more of fancy street lights, etc. Cat, IHC, and Ford all have agencies.

We arrived at La Paz at 7:30 p.m. Tremendous growth. We went to La Perla Hotel and met the present owner of Rancho Margarita, Manuel Y. Borguin. His brother bought it from Alberto, then the brother was killed in an auto accident. We had breakfast with him. He said we were welcome to have all the land we wanted to build a house on the place for free. I told him Mark might like to, but I was too old for that now.

South of La Paz, the landscape, trees and flora are greener and more tropical in nature. The hotels are more luxurious with air strips for most of the guests.

We arrived in Cabo San Lucas at noon. We stopped at a beautiful beach south of Tados Santos for an hour of swimming and relaxation alone with the fish and birds. Back to black-top 83 miles north of Cabo San Lucas. Boarded the ferry in La Paz in the evening and got off at Guaymas at 7:30 a.m.

We put oil in the VW in Guaymas, then 2 miles out 2 quarts; 35 miles more, another 2 quarts; 12 miles more, 2 quarts; 7 miles more 1 quart; 2 miles 1 quart. Mark made a gasket of cardboard, but it still leaked. Found a parts store and a VW gasket and permatex just right for 20 pesos and had the gasket on at 10:50 a.m.

The grass was very good from Hermosillo to Santa Anna, the cattle fat and some land being plowed for cotton.

We left Santa Anna at 1:50 p.m. We siphoned one gallon of gas from a car at the custom stop to get to Sonoita. We gave him the last of our sack of onions. Mexicali 526K at 8:15 p.m. The town was sure bright and alive. Left Mexicali at 10:30 p.m. the boys had to get back for school Monday. I called Bella.

We drove to Brawley and had a good supper at the Truckadero, leaving at midnight. I drove to Colony House on I-5 west of Bakersfield, arrived at 5:45 a.m. Cook not up yet, so we had coffee and doughnuts, left at 6:45 a.m. with Mark driving 259 miles to home.

In October, Mr. Medhat, manager of ICC in Iran, came to California to meet our people, buy some equipment and see California agriculture. I drove him 1565 miles south through Salinas to Los Angeles and Imperial Valley then north through the San Joaquin Valley to Fresno where we had a TWAD Co. board meeting with him. Our waiters at the lunch were Iranians. He said he would like to meet the other Iranians working with the hotel, and 14 came in to meet him.

Mr. Medhat also visited Wayne Weeks operation in Los Banos, John Gebhardt in Sanger, and David Wilson's in Clarksburg, also the University of California Davis where he had been a student. He assured us that TWAD Co. would receive considerable money due us.

At the project, the canals were now finished and Bonifico, the Italian contractor, was leaving, so ICC bought for $60,000 their headquarters, shops, office, housing, water system adjacent to KWPA housing at Amdineshk.

After the ICC board meeting, the Bank of America people, Foreign Trade Bank of Iran, and Mr. Medhat along with Glen and I took the train to the project and looked it all over and left feeling quite optimistic.

Ameri resigned as President of ADFI to devote full time to the Mardon party. The political campaign in Iran was over. The government party won big, but the opposition under Ameri was very active. I was told by a friend of Ameri's that the party leaders met in his home and after a lively meeting, someone cut Ameri's throat and they took him out and set him in his car and pushed it against a tree. The morning papers told of his death when he ran his car into the tree.

While we had many problems in 1973, still it seemed we were farming better and progress was really being made. The International Finance Corp. of Washington D.C. thought we were doing a fine job and wanted to buy stock and make us a loan of $1,250,000, which with a loan of $1,000,000 from ADFI would care for our needs.

On October 20 Mr. Medhi Samii was appointed head of ADFI. Mr. Samii had twice been governor for the Central Bank of Iran and also was director of the Plan Organization and played a leading part in the early development of ADFI.

We got a call from ICC for increased capital payment without a statement of why it was needed or for what it would be used. The TWAD Co. Board felt we should go to Iran, find out what was going on and protect our interest, so on February 10, 1974, Glen Harris and I left for Iran.

We had planned on a fairly good return from the 1973 crops of sugar beets, wheat, etc. Our sugar contract called for the sugar company paying all hauling costs, all insecticide and seed costs. The Ministry of Agriculture announced a bonus payment on all sugar beets grown in Iran. We were paid the bonus, but the hauling, insecticides and seed were deducted, amounting to 18,053,593 riales or $243,967.

We had leveled land in Iran at 10 riales per M^3. We contracted leveling by the hour at a cost of 12–14 R/M^3. In Imperial Valley, it costs 17R/M^3. Cost to Hawaiian Agronomics with own equipment and including administrative and allocated costs is 17–18R/M^3. The ICC Board, without our approval, contracted leveling in A area, much easier to work, at 36R/M^3. The ADB of Iran was deadset on precision leveling, a maximum acreage under Hach Smith's layout and direction. The daily papers were full of stories saying the government would pay up to 80% for the cost of land leveling, but we never got a cent.

†1974

We needed to build about twelve homes for our staff, but we needed what money we received on loan from ADFI for farming. The American Agricultural Attache suggested to me that we use some of the counterpart funds from sales, under Public Law 480, where we sold commodities to foreign countries at a concessionary price to be paid for largely in the funds of the recipient country. Those funds were left in the recipient country but could be used by the embassy to buy items they needed, or in some cases, by U.S. companies to be used in the host country. He said they were definitely available to us to build homes with Iranian men and materials and would be administered by the ADFI. In fact, at one time, the ADFI suggested use of the funds, but said no when we suggested it again.

They supported sale of stock to International Finance Corporation and dividing the financing of ICC with them. The IFC people thought we were doing an excellent job under the conditions and wanted to help us. The ADFI stalled for a long while and then did not want IFC in the picture. We could see all these things happening, but still we knew they needed us to properly carry out the farming and we felt they would recognize that and all would be well.

On February 11 Glen Harris and I left for a very important ICC board meeting in Tehran. Bank of America sent Walt Minger and two others. We left Sacramento at 7:30 a.m. for Salt Lake City, New York, Rome, Beirut. Arrived at Tehran at 6:55 p.m., February 11. Went to a party at Medhats. Snow was falling as I got to bed at 12:30 a.m. I was up at 5:45 a.m., wrote a letter home, and had breakfast with Staller.

Lunched with Dick Burgess of Deere. Hosepian, the Deere dealer they were supposed to buy out, now owns 65% of the Iran Deere stock, the new factory at Arak, and all. He is Managing Director of Deere in Iran and Burgess is leaving with no replacement.

The papers were featuring big aids to agriculture in Iran. The Journal of Business reports the government program on long-term loans for seeds, pesticides, etc. and large subsidies of 80% on costly outlays as land leveling irrigation and new construction. The government is extremely anxious to encourage large-scale mechanized farming.

The principal daily paper, Kayhan, says an investor can get almost total refund on feasibility and project studies, over 50% of expense on land leveling, irrigation and drainage. They will play the role in agriculture the IMDBI (the Development Bank of Iran) played in industry. The government of Iran wants 9 million Has (22,500,000 our acres) irrigated against the present 3.5 million Has. Reading all these things in the Iranian papers gives one a certain confidence that we will be reasonably financed.

On the 16th I met with Mr. Samii, the new head of the ADFI. He seemed able and said, "Many of the matters I raised he had never heard of before...we must get the folks involved together and straighten them out." He left the city and I had to leave before his return.

Following Mr. Samii's appointment as Governor of the ADFI, he had an analysis made of the Agra-industry farming groups including ICC and decided we should raise another $2,000,000 as capital and ADFI would loan $2,000,000 to ICC. There was no analysis to support the figures, so we could not see how the figures were arrived at. He just came to the meeting and they authorized the call.

We analyzed what figures we had, and what they gave us and we could not see any reason for any immediate call, at least that much. They owed us about $200,000. If that was paid, it would have been easy for us to meet our share, but they ruled the matters were not related and they would not pay us until we had paid our share of the call.

The underpayment of about $250,000 on our sugar beet crop also made the picture look bad. ICC wouldn't even consider the reduced payment on beets and demand an accounting from the sugar company. It may be that the Ahwaz Sugar Company belonging to the Pahleri Foundation made a difference (the Shah's family).

Figures recorded this month show:

Acreage planted:		3,999 Has.	Yield
Alfalfa	382		
Sugar beets	667		47 T. per Has.
Wheat	2,640		3.5
Corn	132		
Vegetables	175		

Income for beets and wheat should be $1,900,000, or equal to ADFI estimates for total production.

*Above, signing the general agreement; l-r Rohani, Wilson, Emerson (of Bank of America).
Below, Dean Pryor and I in Libya as pictured in Fortune Magazine, November 1970.*

The Shah of Iran visiting our ranch, here shaking hands with Hack Smith, our engineer. Ctr, beet field in Iran. Below, honored by a visit from David Lilienthal.

Top, preparing rice for threshing in Iran. Ctr, native plowing in Iran. Below left, Baktari tent made of black goat skins; right, Daniel's tomb in Susa (the biblical Shushan).

17

MORE TRAVELS, AT HOME AND ABROAD

On March 28 we went to Sparks to the Rotary District Annual Meeting, then on to Austin, Nevada, a small mining town to visit Sandy and Anne Cutting at the Goldfield Mine. It was crude and dusty outside, but cheerful and beautiful inside as usual, then on to see Pat, Wes and the girls in Texas.

In June I had considerable correspondence with Edwin M. Martin, Department of State Leader of U.S. Mission to the FAO meeting in Rome. I tried to get discussion on restraints to production, more consideration for producers of raw materials, remove restraints to production, etc. His replies were always constructive and in agreement, but he wrote me after the conference saying the great majority of participants wanted to spend money to feed people with little other interest.

On June 20 we drove up to Seattle and took the boat trip to Alaska, much as we had 25 years before with Pat, Dorothy and Mary Hill. It was beautiful and relaxing, as before. The biggest surprise was the long distance, 2-3 miles the glaciers had receded in that time. We stopped at Vancouver Island and then back to the U.S. to Port Angeles, then west and down Pacific Highway 1. The forests were as beautiful to me as the Buschart Gardens of Vancouver, and that is saying a good deal.

We spent a good deal of time on a proposed Ghana Rice growing project with Kaiser Engineers of Oakland. There was a large Accra plain east of Accra, which was quite level and had lots of water available from the river. We held several meetings with Kaiser folks, but they were not able to finalize agreement with Ghana.

In October and up to November 7 I was again in Iran with Glen. We were very active with B-C area where the land was much better in quality, but on the north edge, the good soil was somewhat shallow over gravel. These areas were best adapted to sprinkler irrigation and the cost of sprinkler equipment was somewhat less than precision leveling and the land could be planted to profitable crops about two years sooner, so we proposed adding sprinkler pipe pumping out of the irrigation canal.

They seemed agreeable at first, then decided they did not want the sprinklers, especially if it might mean we would not level the land later. They seemed to have developed a mania for precision leveling at our expense.

†1975

During 1975, I still worked on TWAD Co. affairs a good deal, but not as regular as I had been. Mark was working on the Sloughhouse ranch. He and Godfry Saner, who had been ranch manager since 1942, when I bought the ranch from his mother, were working on the roof of a feeding shed when Godfry stepped on a loose board, fell through and broke his hip. He was in Mercy Hospital some weeks, and then to Mercy Convalescent for a while. He walked with a limp and did not do heavy work after that, so much of it was up to Mark.

On January 25 I went to Lovelock, Nevada, to see the cattle on feed, and then to Susanville to see land owned by UOP, which we later sold.

On February 25, 1975, I went to Methodist Hospital. Dr. Primasing and the other doctors said I had water in my lungs and other things, I don't know what. They used a machine to pump medicated vapor into my lungs pretty often with a therapist to handle the machine. I was released on March 11, 1975, but was returned for more observation and treatment until April 8, 1975. It was my first hospital experience after 83 years of life. It wasn't bad. I was glad to be cared for and Dr. Primasing was great.

We visited him at his home some months ago. He did the gardening and a few other things. He said, "You know, in our days, we didn't have so many medicines and wonder drugs as we have today, and a doctor did the best he could with the drugs and aids we had, then he just had to give a part of himself." That is what he did. The Sacramento doctors all recognized him as one of the best.

In July we weaned 267 calves at Sloughhouse.

September 6 was Farm Bureau Day at the new State Fair grounds. We had a good Farm Bureau barbeque lunch with our young Governor, Jerry Brown, and also with our Director of Agriculture, now well known as Chief Justice of the California Supreme Court, Rose Bird. The lunch was in the natural area along the river.

Mark and I went to Fallon and Lovelock on September 10 to see the cattle on feed. They looked good in both places. Fallon was a small yard, but they did very well. On the 11th I bought a mobile home for Mark. We located it on a south slope overlooking the natural and irrigated pastures. He worked up a good vegetable garden and from then on, he was his own cook and housekeeper. He seemed to thrive on it.

On November 1 Ken Reynolds and I went to Bank of America for a meeting with all the involved Bank of America people. Ken would go to Iran with a representative of Bank of America, analyze the whole situation, propose a plan where we would cut the farming the first year to 2,500 acres, hold up on leveling, increase another 2,500 acres for the second year with two more Americans. Then, 2,500 acres the third year with two more U.S. farmers. Fourth year, level more land as practical.

Glen Harris wished to resign as President. Glen had done a great job but needed more time at home. Ken Reynolds was elected President and authorized to go to Iran to get approval of his plan. He asked that David Wilson go with him and that was agreed to and carried out. Glen continued on as Chairman of the Board.

A letter outlining the history of the project and its many problems was drafted and sent to Prime Minister Hoveyda, ICC, Teleghani, and officials in Washington. Bernell and Ken Reynolds were in Washington, D.C. and saw Dr. Steele, Department of Ag. Commission for Cooperation U.S. and Iran. He had received 75 letters of complaints from Americans doing business in Iran with experiences like TWAD Co. Bernell and Ken saw the World Bank about financing us, but Iran is on the World Bank's no loan list.

November 29, 1975, was Debbie and Bob Rose's wedding.

The U.S. State Department has recently sent an agriculture, commercial, and one other attache to Iran expecially to help Americans in trouble as we were.

†1976

On January 9 we had a TWAD Co. board meeting at the Sacramento Airport.

David and Ken felt we had a good man managing the farming on the B-C area. David said Mr. Samii was very angry about our letter outlining the history of the Project and problems encountered. David said, as he traveled in Europe, he met several people doing business in Iran. All of them had difficulties like ours and were in trouble.

Bank of America said they would urge ICC to pay TWAD Co. money owed, $109,000. at the end of agreement, would be $260,000., but none was paid.

Between April 5-14, we drove to Rancho Margarita, San Ignacio, and back home.

On May 7 we celebrated our 55th anniversary, April 17, and took the family, or they took us, to Folsom for dinner and then the melodrama.

Most of May and June was spent assembling the files for the OPIC claim.

On October 17, David gave the message at the Clarksburg Community Church and did very well.

On December 1 I realized my financial advisor, Ken Ratto, was using my account for his advantage and not mine. I reported him to Payne-Webber, who had introduced me to him with high recommendation, but they would not believe me, so I went back to Dean Witter. Ken Ratto was soon on the front page of the newspaper for gipping several ladies out of several hundred thousand.

On December 19 we left for Hereford, Texas for Christmas. David, Dick, and Dorothy all had grandchildren, so they liked to have Christmas at their homes.

†1977

On January 5 we flew to Hawaii for an American Farm Bureau Federation Annual Meeting and visited with Debbie and Bob. Allan Grant was now the American Farm Bureau Federation President.

We had very good visits with Charlie Shuman of Illinois, former President of American Farm Bureau Federation, and with Mrs. Schuman and Roger Fleming, former Secretary-Treasurer of American Farm Bureau Federation, now Manager of the North East Farm Bureau Insurance Co., and many other old timers. It was great to see them and get their ideas on present day issues.

On January 15 we flew to Hilo to see Debbie and Bob. They were well situated, Bob with Brewer Sugar Co. He had worked over the old chain-driven harvesters into hydraulic-driven, lightened up the equipment and speeded up the harvest, so he was getting more responsibility and pay. We went up to the volcano, which was still active, then home.

On January 31 I leased the Pierson Ranch to the Johnson Brothers. I bought 125 tons of hay from Lentz for $85. in the barn at Sloughhouse. It was a terrible dry fall and winter with very little grass coming, so cattle had to be sold or fed.

March 15 Glen Harris and Fred Frick and I went to Washington and employed top flight attorneys to get compensation from OPIC. Insurances on account of creeping expropriation of our operation in Iran.

On August 20 Bella and I sat as hosts at the Locke Chinese Gambling Museum. It was interesting to talk to the more than 100 people who came from far and wide.

September 19 we left for a tour of the British Isles with Farm Bureau Tours. It was a pleasure to be with Frank Pierce again for a while. We saw Ireland first, then Scotland, Wales, and England. Of course, we only saw limited areas, but it was beautiful and interesting. We ate in ancient style in ancient castles with ancient entertainment, also with a Lord and Lady in their manor as well as many farmers along the way.

Most farms are small, old, in delightful settings. Several large modern, highly technical farms have pigs, cattle, beets, potatoes, grass, etc. They get very high capital investment income tax credits, so some were modernizing rapidly.

October 23, Mr. Tom Long, of Long Drug Stores and a regent of UOP, had purchased the old Feather River Inn, built by the railroad as a vacation spot for Easterners to ride the Pullman cars for a vacation in California summer or winter. The old Inn and some of the cottages were being used by Feather River School for boys through high school. One of the Long boys was a student there. Tom Long gave 100 acres including the Inn and its 9-hole golf course to UOP to give the school more prestige and supervision. We went up several times to see how we should handle it. It is doing well in a beautiful area to get an education and training.

On November 5 we attended the annual meeting and dinner of Amador-Sacramento Cattlemen Association at Amador Fairgrounds. It gave Mark a chance to meet many of the cattlemen of the area.

Herbert "Hop" Merwin, one of the somewhat younger men, started farming in the Holland land soon after we did. He married Daisy King, had a fine family and was one of the outstanding men in the district. He got cancer, and the memorial service was December 3, 1977, in our church. It was a loss to us, his family, and the community.

†1978

January 20 Mark and I went to the Red Bluff Bull sale. This is the best screened and graded bull sale in the country. Then on January 31, 1978, we went to the Nevada-California Beef Conference and Bull Sale in Sparks, Nevada.

Sandra and Gavin were married May 20 on the lawn at David's house. His parents came from South Africa for the event as well as his sister, husband, and three children from Kentucky.

On June 10 a new well at Sloughhouse tested 1200 gallons.

June 29 Rotary Demotion was at Ed Willey's in a beautiful setting between the house and the river and across the river from the monument. His father, who had been active in Farm Bureau affairs, was there and I was happy to see him again.

July 2 David and Mark put on the church service and did very well.

July 4 the Clarksburg Parade was quite an event. David had an entry with large blown-up pictures of all the folks on Wilson Farms.

On August 12 Helen Ably married Leslie Nelson.

September 28 B. P. Singh was at the house overnight, and I took him to Davis next day. We had met and spent several days with him in India in '56, then he was here with the party of Indians in '57 and attended Dorothy's wedding.

He told me then that he was going back to India to set up a farm organization for the benefit of farmers. He tried it and Indira Ghandi put him in jail for it. No charges, no trial. The Supreme Court of India released him, but she put him back in, still with no charges or trial. Desaii was in with him, so when Indira Ghandi's party lost the election and Desaii was made Prime Minister, he appointed B. P. as his Minister of Agriculture and Irrigation.

He had never been active in politics, so he hardly knew where to start, but India had a law that no one could move farm products from one district of India to another without a government permit. He thought that was not right, so he had the law rescinded and there was a terrible howl in the city papers and elsewhere, but within a year, people were asking what he had done for the fruit and vegetables were fresher, better, and cheaper than ever before. A natural result of farmer's ability to sell where the demand is best.

One does not have to explain to California farmers what would happen to this state if we could not freely ship across state lines. Many countries today have similar laws.

October 16 Reuben Albaugh, Mark and I drove up to Conways in Grass Valley to buy five bulls from cows of U.C. Davis breeding. They were excellent bulls. This morning, November 1, 1985, as I write this, we are staying at Murphys Inn, a bed and breakfast place in Grass Valley. I must look up Mr. Conway while we are here.

†1979

Scud Marshall had joined us in inviting the Alpha Zeta Honorary Fraternity for Agriculture to hold a meeting and have dinner on our patio. Scud did the barbeque. There were more girls than boys and the outgoing and incoming chief officers were girls. They were a fine group of young people, but I hadn't realized agriculture had become so feminized.

On May 1 we were invited to Future Farmer's of America annual dinner in the high school cafeteria. The top officer was Martha Hernandez, a girl of Mexican descent whose family lived in our old house on the ranch, where her father, Victor, was foreman.

May 13 the family picnicked on Deer Creek on the Sloughhouse Ranch. We ate, swam and played. Those picnics were always pleasant occasions. The Boy Scouts and Camp Fire Girls also make good use of the facilities.

May 19 was the Cattlemen's Picnic on the Cosumnes River at Van Vleck Park, a little east of Rancho Murrieta.

July 13 Roger, John, Mark and I weaned calves.

July 31 our B. H. Crocheron Committee met in Berkeley. The California Farm Bureau Federation was building a new building and moving to Sacramento.

We decided that to help maintain the tie between Farm Bureau and the Ag Extension Service and Education, it would be well to have a good artist paint a picture of B. H. Crocheron to hang in the new Farm Bureau building; the picture was financed by his admirers in Farm Bureau and the Extension Service.

I had been having very severe pain in my left leg. I thought it was arthritis, and I could take it until it went away, but they got worse and I couldn't walk a block without sitting down and rubbing my leg.

I went to Dr. Go. There was little pulse in my right ankle or foot, and none in the left, so they decided it was clogged arteries and I went into Dr. Norman S. Lovell, a fine fellow. He told me I could probably ride it out for three or four years, then it would get me or there was a new operation. He had never done one, or seen it done, but I could try it. He thought it was worth a try.

He told me to be in Mercy Hospital Monday morning for an operation that afternoon, then called me and said make it Tuesday. I was in Tuesday. They said they had never heard of me or my operation by Dr. Lovell, and they couldn't take me, but I said he told me to be there and I was going to stay until I heard from him, so they finally gave me a bed. Then they set it for Wednesday morning, then Wednesday at 5 p.m. They had me in the operating room at 6 p.m. with two anesthesiologists, but Drs. Go and Lovell showed up at 8:30 p.m. I woke up about 1 a.m. feeling like a million dollars. I really felt good.

I think Dr. Lovell had been very busy figuring how the operation should be carried out or talking to U.C. Davis doctors or reading their reports. I read soon after that, UCD doctors had performed three such operations, but would not try another until they saw how the ones done had worked out.

They made an incision on the shin, opened up the artery, inserted a catheter with a little balloon on the upper end, pushed it up the artery as far as they care to, blew up the balloon and pulled it out, bringing with it all the material clogging the

386

artery. He did it a number of times. I do not know how many. Then he opened up the groin, reached back to the backbone and cut a nerve controlling the expansion and contraction of the capillary blood vessels, letting the blood flow through the capillaries a little more easily.

For at least four years after the operation, the left foot was hot almost all the time. After six years, I would say the operation was almost perfect.

I went home about September 10 and found I had to learn to walk straight almost like a baby would. Twenty-four days later, we left with a Commonwealth group for a cruise of the Black Sea and Greek Islands. Our immediate group were Knowles and Edith Ryerson, Beryl and Horace Strong, and Elsie and Hilton Richardson. We flew to London and Athens, staying at the very modern Hilton Hotel and seeing some of Athens, then boarding the Viking Star, a beautiful modern ship.

†††Trip to Greece

We got our table setting and it was not with the rest of the Commonwealth group, so I told the dining room steward that there must be an error as we are with the Commonwealth group. He said he would appreciate it if we sat as assigned the first meal at least. Of course, I agreed, and at the first meal found ourselves at the Chief Engineer's table. The Captain had his wife on this trip, so they ate in their quarters. Also at the table were David McMillan and his wife from Vero Beach, Florida, and a well-built elderly Swedish woman who always spoke out with the unexpected. The Chief Engineer was a most hospitable gentleman, so the meals were most pleasant and entertaining occasions. The McMillans were outstanding and became very good friends. We still hear from them at Christmas at least.

Our first stop was Varna, Bulgaria. They appear to be real friends of Russia, to feel that Russia helped get their freedom, but they did not appear to be a happy people or to have much ambition. We stopped at three Russian ports, Odessa, Yalta and Sochia. These were Mediterranean vacation spots. The people were better dressed and more ambitious than in Bulgaria. Some of the newest and best buildings were controlled by the labor unions for the pleasure of their members on vacation. The only spots not government-owned were little irregular spots of land still farmed by the owner, barber shop and other shops large or small were government-owned and operated. On the street, we felt no ill will, but neither was there any feeling of mutual kinship.

Police and local administrators were numerous in cars or on motorcycles. As they approached or stopped, the women streetsweepers and the other workers would speed up noticeably and as they left, the workers slowed down or sought a bench. The climate was delightful and the views inspiring as any Mediterranean area. In Yalta, the Commonwealth Club had arranged a meeting with a group similar to our City Council in their Council Chambers. They were very courteous and seemed very anxious to please us, giving us pins with the city coat of arms.

We stopped in Istanbul for a day, always beautiful and interesting, much like San Francisco.

We then visited the Greek Islands in the Mediterranean, much as they were in Bible times. They collect a tourist tax and the local government sees that all the houses are whitewashed or painted white to maintain a clean attractive appearance.

We then boarded the buses and toured Greece for a week, seeing many of the historic places and seeing the Museum of Ancient Greece.

Everywhere we stopped, we would meet people who had lived much of their lives in the United States and then returned to Greece to retire. They were anxious to get the latest word from the United States.

We saw the field where the first Olympic games were played. Edith Ryerson and others ran the original 100-meter track.

Any trip to Greece means lots of climbing and I was a little doubtful, as I left home, if I would see many places on account of my leg operation. But, I saw every place except the last leg of our trip on the islands where everyone rode a donkey.

I think I was better off for having taken the trip, as I was forced to do a great deal of walking and climbing, which was good for me.

†††Back in Clarksburg

On November 13 we had a program and hung the picture of Prof. B. H. Crocheron in the new Farm Bureau Building.

It was interesting that the artist would do the painting for $3,000. without showing his hands or $5,000 with the hands showing. He recommended the latter and we approved, I think correctly. I always check a portrait now to see if the hands show; it is much better if they do.

On November 19 the Delta Historical Society met in the Dutra home in Rio Vista. It is a home, but also a fine museum of the origin and development of dredges used to reclaim the Sacramento and other deltas. The models are accurate, some large and working, and there are many fine plans and pictures. The Dutra's are most hospitable and helpful in describing the exhibits.

The new California Farm Bureau Federation Building was dedicated in Sacramento on December 2. We had the usual speakers and program for such an occasion, and in addition, I had arranged to get the UOP Acapella Choir and their orchestra under the leadership of Professor Denning. They did a beautiful job and helped give real class to the occasion.

The moveable office walls were not yet in place, so we had the whole second floor wide open for seating a large crowd.

†1980

The year started off on January 5 with Mark and Cathy's wedding at the Wilton Bible Church. Mark was running the Sloughhouse Ranch and Cathy had graduated from Fresno State with honors, in addition to winning awards in snaffle bit horse shows.

We drove into Phoenix in the evening for the AFBF Annual Meeting and found our "Roadway Inn" was thirteen miles out of Phoenix. Allen Grant, President, had a good convention.

†††Foreign Service Schooling

One of the principal results of my contacts with U.S. embassies in many parts of the world was a feeling that now, as world leaders, we must reassess our position in the world and qualify our foreign service to meet that need. In 1970, we had had a top-level commission in the State Department subdivided into many small groups studying the

388

many phases of our worldwide contacts.

About 600 recommendations for improvements were adopted to prepare to meet our responsibilities in the 70s. I have been told on various occasions that practically none of the improvements have been adopted, but the needs in the 80s are even greater and more complex. So it seemed to me that the best course would be for us to turn to a university to give young people special training to meet the needs of our State Department as representative of a world leader. They would be trained to help write in bold, but simple and concise terms, our foreign policies, simple enough for all to understand, and sound enough so we will not revise them in the near future. This takes a broad study of just "What does the U.S. stand for in the world?"

The world grew for many years under English Foreign Policy, basically cheap food, cheap labor, cheap raw materials, and freedom of the seas to permit free movement of food and raw materials and distribution throughout the world of manufactured products. Control of piracy on the seas was an important policy; we need an answer for control of modern piracy or tyranny due to political, religious or social fantasies. We need laws not only covering the surface of the seas, but also subsurface travel, fish, minerals or other things of value on the floor of the seas. We need laws for the sky and all it contains for millions of miles. We have tried making international law covering human rights, but the subject, and even our American understanding of what is meant, are too broad to issue a statement for the world to follow. We are not sure what we mean by "human rights" except those we list as "God-given rights." If we could determine what caused hundreds of millions of people of all classes to seek a life in the U.S., maybe that could be the basis of a universal statement of what we stand for in human relations. Many suggest that the millions came to our shores seeking "equality of opportunity."

During the century or more when England largely dictated world law and policy, it was not necessary for us to maintain embassy staffs to know the thinking and living of the whole population of the nation. Neither is it adequate for us to depend on a CIA or such groups to keep us informed of the thinking of people in the world. The presence of many U.S. companies in manufacturing and trade throughout the world, and now the presence of many truly international companies, opens a wholesnew field of understanding and assistance by our embassy staffs.

The field of U.S. representation abroad is so varied and the areas of specialization so broad that it is difficult to say what courses a young person should take in the university to prepare for such a career. Still, a broad understanding of history, government, languages, business, anthropoligy is basic, and further specialization may come later.

Education, as practiced in our high schools and universities, is a matter of passing from one generation to the next the sum total of information now available. State Department people need all they can get of such information. They also need intuition, an understanding of the feelings of the world's people. Millions who never learned to read or write are still net producers of goods and services (wealth), or net consumers of useful goods and services (poverty), and may be either a constructive stabilizing force in the world or a destructive force.

The United States is not only the new world leader, but its concept of "equality of opportunity for all people" and "government for the benefit of all people" is a new concept, difficult to administer at home and far more difficult for the world. We need a foreign service qualified to understand the peoples of the world and to help them understand us.

At home, we studied our personal financial situation as a family and decided we could meet our needs during my lifetime and provide adequately for the family without the Pearson 366 acres. I discussed our situation and our wishes with President Stan McCaffry and he felt UOP could start work on such a project for $250,000, the net value of the ranch. Later, I saw it would cost more, but the market price of the ranch had risen to $350,000, which seemed OK. In November, 1978, we gave the UOP the eastern portion of the ranch, then in June 1981 we gave them the western portion of the acreage. Land values were still going up, too high to last.

The university authorized George Dahlgren to find a buyer at $4,000 per acre. He found a buyer, Charles M. Tin. We authorized the sale at a price to net over $1 million to the university and completed the sale at the very peak of farmland prices.

About this time, England had almost dropped any effort to be the peacekeeper in the world, and we had to pick up the role, ready or not. We found we were dealing with nations, societies, peoples about whom we knew little. It was our desire to maintain peace and stability. Henry Kissinger became a world figure with his shuttle diplomacy, and he did well, but he seemed to be all we had in that field.

American policy and world desire for peace seemed to dictate that we should set up in the State Department various teams of experts trained in principal subjects of dispute, but mainly in the art of negotiation, so the State Department would be our first line of defense, using skilled and experienced teams to negotiate solutions to problems that are acceptable to all. We would call in the military only as a last resort if negotiations failed. Conflict management would be one of the prominent courses provided. One of the advantages of such a course is that expertise in that field is a universal need. Whether it be industrial relations, commerce, or family life, negotiation of differences is of vital concern.

We appointed a committee to help us plan such a school for foreign service: Dr. Harry Wellman, former acting President of U.C.; Allen Grant, former President California Farm Bureau Federation and American Farm Bureau Federation; Eyvan Faye, former President of Sun Sweet and several other California cooperatives; Gordon Van Vleck, former President California Cattlemen, American National Cattlemen, California State Chamber of Commerce, and now in Governor Deukmejian's cabinet as Director of Natural Resources.

One of the big nights of the year in Clarksburg is the Old Timers Dinner in March, cooked and served by volunteer firemen at the firehouse. The equipment is shined and driven outside. Lots of old-time pictures decorate the walls, tables hold popcorn and soft drinks, plenty for everyone. After an hour of yarn-swapping, a deluxe dinner is served, The volunteer firemen fight the fires and operate the ambulance, the heart machine, and the "jaws of life." They're a great group whom we all appreciate and honor, and they honor the old-timers on this night. It is about the only time we meet during the year. Honor to them.

390

On June 5, on our patio at home, we entertained 35 Ag Attaches from foreign countries. They were seeing the U.S. as guests of the AFBF with an AFBF staff leader and some California and local Farm Bureau people. It was a good evening and a good project. We should have more like it.

The California Beet Growers' Association Board held its summer Director's Meeting in July at San Luis Bay Inn at Avila Beach, southwest of San Luis Obispo.

At 5:45 p.m., 1½ miles north of Kings City, we were cruising along at about 55 mph when all of a sudden a car appeared in our lane coming north. It looked for a second like he might swing left and miss us, then he turned back and came at us, I presume at about 55 mph; he in a heavy Mercury weighing the same as our heavy old Cad. We sure stopped quick. We both had our seat belts on, but Bella had a pain in her neck and head. The police were there in no time. They put Bella to bed right away. They said they had no bed for me, but finally let me sleep on the couch in the Chapel for two or three nights.

The other driver had been in a diabetic coma. He left his work at 5 pm to drive about five miles south to his turnoff for home, but he did not turn off. The bridge, the river, or Kings City caused him to turn around for home and he turned north in the southbound lane. For at least 35 minutes, he was driving that car in a diabetic coma. My first thought as I saw the enmeshed cars ahead of me was, "Boy, it is good to have lots of steel around you."

We got total coverage from the Farm Bureau Insurance Company as well as part of the hospital. The move to smaller cars was on in January, 1981, but we still wanted as heavy a car as feasible for safety, so we got a 1977 Cadillac.

Sandra and Gavin's twin boys, David and Phillip, were baptized August 3 in our church. The next day we went to Incline Village, Lake Tahoe, and spent several days in a nice house David rented for the summer for Wilson Farm employees.

Sacramento Rotary Club had a meeting October 30 with lunch and an inspection of the new California Farm Bureau Federation building across from the State Fair entrance. The building had the latest in heating, cooling and lighting, and it has proven good, as the utility bills are far below similar older buildings.

I had not been actively interested in selling the Sloughhouse Ranch, but I was getting older. We were not sure what Mark would like to do, and for several years the ranch had not been profitable for us. I did not really think of selling, but an agent wanted me to set a price on it and let her sell it for us. I told her no, but if she offered more than I thought it was worth, I would consider her offer. She had a number of offers, but none seemed advantageous to us. Finally, a group from Spain looked it over and talked of buying; we looked over the ranch and then had lunch for 13 at Rancho Murrieta. They were going back to Spain and would be ready to buy on their return. I told Lucille to forget it, then George Dahlgren showed up with a young couple. It was then December; the tax would be over $200,000 if we sold, so I said we would only consider a trade with no capital gains tax involved. George Dahlgren was an old hand at that.

The young folks said they liked the ranch, so we talked price. I didn't want to have the job of selling the cattle or equipment as separate items or have them left over, so I gave a price for us to just walk off, leaving cattle and equipment just as was. Dahlgren looked for a trade at about the same price and came up with the

Hanks' Ranch. One proviso of Hanks was that the sale must be completed and the cash due them paid by December 31, 1980. This gave only a few days, but George Dahlgren said he could do it and he did, so January 1, 1981, we were out of the cattle business and had a 660-acre crop ranch on I-5 and the Sacramento River, with a five-year lease back to Hanks' family.

†1981

We flew on the 10th to New Orleans for an AFBF meeting. The hall there is tremendous; the feature of the banquet was many folks and groups associated with the Mardi Gras throwing out candies, strings of beads, and all sorts of trinkets, some of which I brought home and still have. We took a trip up the Mississippi River and saw all the shipping and harbor facilities. They export much of the midwest grain.

The UOP Alumni Fellows lunch was March 4. This is getting a little larger each year. The Old-Timers Firehouse Dinner was March 21.

In April I spent a day, as I had many others, trying to get a permit to sell Bob and Debbie the house and 2.2 acrea in the Pearson District.

On April 17 we had our 60th-wedding anniversary reception in the patio and yard with a large tent erected by Bob Cole. The children put the party on and all were present: Gilbert and Wilma Scott came down from Oregon, Stan and Beth McCaffry and Cliff and Doris Hand from UOP, Mary Hill, Bella's sister, and all her family. It was a delightful day, long to remember. Pat, Wes and the girls came and brought us beautiful handmade quilts. Bob and Debbie gave us a fine family tree with all the pictures on it. We are indeed blessed with a wonderful loving family.

We left in June for two weeks vacation on the UCSB campus for UC alumni, located on the coast. We had two rooms in a dorm, good dining room meals, games, talks and other entertainment, a day in S.B., and just relaxation. There were many children. There was shuffleboard and other games as well as ball games, tennis matches, etc.

We flew up to San Francisco June 25 to attend a luncheon at the Bohemian Club given by Steve Bechtel, Sr. and his wife for Stan and Beth McCaffry before they started their year as President of Rotary International.

We left UCSB July 4, visited with Estelle and Eleanore and attended the Dunne wedding in North Ridge.

Elizabeth Meadows flew in August 21. Her husband, Alger, a great fellow among rich or poor, great or humble, had some time before ridden with a friend to play golf when a driver came in from a side road, ran into them midway of the car and killed him. Elizabeth seemed to crave friendship and companionship with relatives, so we had four very pleasant days and considerable rest and relaxation for her, but she was leaving for Dallas to be back in San Francisco for a party in a few days and then parties, parties, parties as far as she could see. She loved it, but still she was a slave to it.

I paid Lovell $1,500 for trying to get the right for us to sell Bob and Debbie 2.2 acres of land in Pearson. All he got was the right to make the sale, if I would agree to sign a contract with the Sacramento County Board of Supervisors that I would not build anything on the remaining land ever. I could not, in conscience, sign such a contract even though I knew I was giving the remainder of the land to the UOP very shortly. Now, in 1985, having given all the rest of the land (366 acres) to UOP, the 2.2 acres is all we own. I am expecting to have the papers ready for our signature to sell Bob and Debbie the 2.2 acres, the house, barn and all without interference from the County.

Alex Spanos had given much of the money to build the Alex Spanos Center, a beautiful complex for basketball, volleyball, banquets, distinguished speakers, conventions or university convocations. Much of the money was contributed by citizens of Stockton, as a meeting center the whole community might enjoy. Some of the leading couples of Stockton and UOP organized a dinner-dance to dedicate the building for community use and demonstrate its usefulness. They surely went all out. It was December 4, so some of the principal stores loaned reindeer and many other Christmas decorations for the occasion. There were evergreen trees in tubs, the table linen fit the occasion, and we had the UOP jazz band. It was a breathtaking occasion. The service of that large a hot meal was difficult but well done.

We drove to Pomona to see Estell December 5, then to Redland Cherry Valley to CFBF meeting in Palm Springs, where Henry Voss was elected President of CFBF. I spoke to Sacramento Rotary Club December 10. On the 29th, we bought three oriental rugs—one for the day room, a small one for the boy's room, and a large one for the dining room.

† 1982

Darius Rouhami, son of the Minister of Water and Power and later of Agriculture in Iran, came to the house to see us. He was married to an American girl and she talked him into dropping the final "i" from his name so it would not sound so Iranian. He told me his family was on vacation in Switzerland when Khomani came back to Iran. Most of the family did not want to return, but the father said, "Iran will need us now more than ever," so we must go back and help all we can.

His father was the second one shot right after Prime Minister Hoveyda. They took the Prime Minister out seven mornings in succession, blindfolded him, and had the firing squad use blank cartridges. Then on the eighth morning, the cartridges were real. Young Darius was living in Walnut Creek. He had had a business consulting firm in Teheran with 40 employees, but hadn't gotten a job here yet. I went to Walnut Creek and picked him up to go over to see Walt Minger, Vice-President of Bank of America.

Both Walt and I were a little surprised to hear that he did not just want a job, he wanted to analyze the Bank of America to see where improvements might be made. Walt said later that he was not sure whether the Bank employed him, but he later saw the name Rouhan on the list of bank staff. We met two other Iranians on the street. They said many were in the U.S., a lot in San Francisco and more in Los Angeles, and practically all seemed to be employed.

Cliff Hand was acting President of UOP while Stan was on leave to Rotary International as President. Cliff invited us to his home in May for a small dinner before the commencement along with the speaker E. P. James, a UOP alumnus and now seeking out the best men for appointment to important offices in the Reagan government. I sat next to him and found him very interesting.

We flew to Dallas June 5 as a delegate from Sacramento Club to Rotary International. Stan and Beth McCaffry were there and did a great job of presiding over the meeting. There was lots of color and excitement at every turn.

One of the original attractions for going to Dallas was to see my cousin, Elizabeth Meadows, but just about a week before we left, we got word that she had passed on. We were pleased to visit her son, Franklin, and his family, who live quite modestly and seemed to have little interest in his mother's estate or money in general. He has several farms in Illinois of his own and he seemed to follow those quite closely and have a very good idea of seed improvement, fertilizers, insecticides, herbicides and so on, as well as prices of corn, beans, oats, etc. We flew to Amarillo to see Pat and Wes for a few days and then on home.

We went to Knowles Ryerson's 90th birthday party October 17 in Berkeley. It was a great day and a great party. Few men of 90 could muster such a group of devoted friends. It, of course, mirrored Knowles honesty and loyalty to people of all ages over a period of many years. So many people wanted to talk to Knowles that I thought maybe it was too much for him, but he just thrives on it and gets younger by the year.

The Golden Society of U.C. Davis had a dinner October 22 with Lysle Leach as the honoree and then went over for the dedication of the Lysle Leach Hall. Lysle is a great example of loyal dedication to several causes which go way beyond the line of duty. It is men like Lysle who advance human knowledge in the world. We all owe them a great debt of gratitude.

†1983

California Beet Growers' Association Annual Meeting was February 15-19 in San Diego. We took a trip to Tijuana by bus with the beet growers. We went to a very modern museum built by the government, probably better by now, though it was excellent then. There were nearly a million residents in Tijuana, larger than San Diego. The stores in the middle of Tijuana are very modern and complete.

I knew something was stirring, as a girl came down to interview me and photographers came down to take pictures. We were to go to the Sacramento Metropolitan Chamber of Commerce Annual Dinner. David, Dick and Dorothy's families were there, so I felt sure something was going to happen. I read the program over several times, but I didn't see anything to include me. The program was about over and they announced the Sacramento Metropolitan Man of the Year, and it was I. I was completely surprised, as it had been many years since I used to go to the agricultural committee meetings with Gus Olson. I could hardly believe I would be selected for such an honor by the city folks. My remarks were well received and that was it. The only responsibilities were to join the past "Men of the Year" in selecting the man or woman for the following year and then introducing the new "Man of the Year" at next year's dinner.

At a luncheon on March 2 with the UOP alumni who were speaking at classes, Stan McCaffry formally announced the setting up of a new organization of "UOP Alumni Fellows," to include all the alumni who had been invited back to speak to the classes.

My hearing was gradually deteriorating, so I signed up for classes in lip reading, Tuesday and Thursday, at 2 pm at Sacramento State University. The classes were four or five persons so we had individual attention from the senior students who taught the course under the direction of a regular professor. I went for two semesters. I am sure it helped a little, but I do not read lips.

The Governor's Prayer Breakfast was April 12, with Governor Deukmejian in office and Judge Tom McBride chief organizer. The breakfast was dignified and inspiring, with a packed room of nearly nine hundred people.

We left home July 21 for a trip to Baja California with Cathy, stopping in Riverside and Cherry Valley, then on to San Diego, where Mark parked his car and joined us. We stopped at Tom and Dorothy's, but it seemed awfully hollow with Tom and Dorothy not there and the grandson away on business. We stopped at the Government Hotel on the beach at San Quintin. They had had a storm with high tide, so the waves broke out the first-floor windows. The landscaping was washed out and the swimming pool full of sand, but the beds were good and also the meals.

We stopped in El Rosario July 22 for gas and coffee with Mrs. Espinosa. We bought snacks and a few items at the new mini-supermarket, then went southeast down the ridge of the peninsula to the Bahia de Los Angeles turn off. We didn't have time so on to the El Presidente Hotel on the stateline out of Guirrero Negro. We looked over the town; it had grown a good deal.

The next day we drove about 50 miles southeast to our old road into Ejido Vezcaino, drove all through the farmed area. It looked good. We stopped at a house where they welcomed us most cordially. We had watermelon, figs, other fruit and a very pleasant half-hour, then went to Rancho Margarita. Being Sunday, they were all enjoying a siesta under the trees.

They had planted about 80 acres of grapes. They were very cordial and seemed glad to see us. The citrus was doing well, the jajoba not much, and the date palms just fair. The farm seemed, however, to be a successful operation.

We then went on to San Ignacio for lunch at the Presidente amidst the date palms, visited the City Square and the old Mission and the old graveyard, then 45 miles on to Sta Rosalia, a five-hour drive, at best, from San Ignacio in our day down there.

Monday we drove up the river to Muleje, the hotel on top of the hill, the mission and the town and penitentiary, where the inmates are free to work in the area, but spend the night in the cell.

The ride along Bahia Conception is one of the beautiful spots of the world. We stayed at the Hotel Presidente on the coast in Loreto. Mark and Cathy saw some of the town in the evening and found where they could buy a handmade cowhide riato, which they got in the rain the next morning. We all looked over the church and museum. The Mission was the Mother of all the missions in California, north or south.

Tuesday we went down the coast, then over the mountains to the valley of Constitution. As we came down on the Pacific Ocean side, the farms started and soon we saw irrigation and dairies. Mark was interested in the dairy, the medication, etc., so the owner showed him a well-run dairy. As we were approaching Ciudad Constitution, we all went through a modern creamery. The city is still growing rapidly.

We had reservations at a very nice hotel north of the center of La Paz. We checked in and went 10 miles further north to the ferry landing for Guaymos and then home up the east side of the Gulf, but we could not get reservations on the ferry, so we stayed in La Paz.

Wednesday we saw some of La Paz, shopped, and headed north for Loreto. Probably six miles south of Loreto was a sign to a Presidente Hotel. We went in and found, on the Gulf shore, a fine new expansive hotel with golf, large swimming pools, horses, fishing boats, and a large area for vacation homes. A complete resort area, beautiful and comfortable. It rained, but we set off very nicely in the morning; we got to Purissama Creek and it was boiling. Several cars were ahead of us, some small trucks very cautiously made it across, a VW got through with boys pushing it ahead and on the side to keep it from floating down the stream. The big diesel tankers just plower right through. It was a flash flood and in an hour or so it was down enough to make it through and we headed on for Sta Rosalia. We rolled along to Arroya Santa Aqueda and cars were backed up a long way. It was too deep and too fast to try. There was the old road crossing about a half-mile down the Arroya where some cars and trucks were making it across, but on the highway, it was wide, deep and rapid, not safe to try. For the first hour or two, not even the big diesels could make it, so we watched, talked to the people, and wondered when. We found a level place off the road, fairly dry. We had a tarpaulin and blankets and air mattress; Mark and Cathy spread those. We fixed a dinner. They went to sleep under the stars hoping for a dry night and Bella and I each had a seat in the car. About 3 am, the water had receded some and they began crossing with lots of yelling, screaming and luck. By about 4 am they had all crossed. It was getting light, so we made it without incident.

We had lunch at Catavina. The car was getting hot and the air conditioning was off. A little further on, we found a mechanic of sorts, at least he had tools. He and Mark got it running, provided we went slow. At night we kept going as Mark must be on the job. We got the battery charged some, but the lights were dim, so a Mexican friend went slow ahead of us to El Rosario. We got the lights fixed better and set out again at about 10 pm.

We went through San Quintin about 11 pm and saw more people and life there than I had expected. We arrived at Ensenada at 2 am, where we had rooms reserved at the La Pinta Hotel, but at 2 am we had no rooms. North of Ensenada we found a motel, many other noisy Americanos checking in. We got an apartment and a good night's sleep, then across the border, got Mark's car in San Diego and drove on up to Anaheim in sight of Disneyland for a good night's sleep.

After breakfast, Mark was on his way selling vet supplies and Cathy brought us home. An interesting trip with some of the old West.

At the Clarksburg Community Church Annual Meeting November 13, we had Rev. Garry Putnam, Chaplain at UOP. He told the old bible stories we all knew,

396

but never before had heard them told in such an interesting way. It reminded me of the old story teller I had heard at the Shah Abbas Hotel in Isphaham, Iran. The people loved it.

†1984

We went to Stan and Beth McCaffry's home at 5:30 pm on January 4 for a small reception for Wes Shelton and his wife, President of Rotary International. They were delightful folks; then we went over to the Spanos Center for a big dinner for all Rotarians in the nearby districts.

The Sacramento Metropolitan Chamber of Commerce Annual Dinner was held January 27 at the Red Lion Inn where I introduced Ed Lammering as Man of the Year for 1984. It is amazing to me how much good work many of our private citizens have accomplished for public welfare and done it joyfully, asking so little in return.

We arrived at the Del Monte in Monterey February 7 for the Beet Growers' Annual Meeting. It was a little late, so we called Ralph and told him we would visit them in the morning. We hadn't left the hotel yet when Corrine called to say they had been out working in the yard and Ralph had gone in the house. She went in maybe twenty minutes later and Ralph was sitting in his chair with his bottle of nitroglycerine pills in his hand. We went down to their home, but there was little we could do. The church people and many friends turned out for a memorial service for Ralph. The people showed a real appreciation of Ralph's many actions to help the church and people.

In March we had a committee at UOP working on setting up the courses in International Studies to start under the leadership of Dr. Elliot Kline, Dean of the School of Business and Public Administration, with Professor Don Halper chairing the committee. They planned three meetings to explore do's and don'ts and appropriate courses of study to qualify students for work in the international field.

Pam and Steve Roberts were the new pastors at Clarksburg Community Church, starting May 6. They are young, just out of seminary, seem full of vim and vigor and we have great hope for the place of the church in the community.

We attended the UOP Football Hall of Fame Dinner on May 8 at the Stockton Country Club, a beautiful setting. I mention this because I heard that night some of the finest testamonials about the role of football in filling out the educational process among college students, and equally important was the place of the humanities in properly preparing a young person for life. I was sorry more professors of the humanities were not present to hear these "he-men" of brawn, and now some fat, extoll the importance of the humanities.

We flew to Pat and Wes's October 23 just to see them and the girls. Phil and Lyn flew over from Arkansas and Nancy and Jack Denison and daughter (5) and their baby, Drew, drove up from Brownsfield, Texas. Wes had enjoyed probably the best year of potato production and sales they have seen, and he was fully enjoying his experiences as Mayor of Hereford.

On church clean-up day, November 3, I used pruning shears almost steadily from 8 am to 12:30 pm, much of it reaching high up. I thought I would be sore, but I wasn't. I guess picking up walnuts has strengthened the old back.

On December 14 I talked with Dave Newsom about how we could best set up an effective school to train students for foreign service. I had met Dave in Pakistan in '49, in Manilla in '54 and in Libya in '67. In each place, he was doing a good job for the U.S. He is a good friend of Stan's and is now in the School of Foreign Service at Georgetown University.

On December 26 we gave UOP $15,000 for faculty enrichment. We would add another $10,000 to it if UOP raised a matching amount. The goal was to set up a program of faculty enrichment of at least $1 million, a portion of the amount raised could be used currently and a part set aside to build an endowment fund.

†1985

We had planned on attending the Beet Growers' Annual Meeting in Long Beach. Bill Mack, Bella's brother, had been in the hospital for a while. The doctor told him he was improved enough to move to a nursing home. What Bill thought, no one knows, but very shortly, they found Bill had passed on, so we drove south, visited Eleanor, and went to Bill's memorial service on January 28. There were a good group of the family and friends there, and we stayed with Mary and the Pickets. Mike had done a beautiful job glassing in the whole front porch, two stories high, for a large enclosed solarium.

Bella and I drove to Palm Springs and leisurely drove through the area of the large beautiful homes and gardens. It was a revelation as we had always stayed on the highways before.

We went to Pomona January 31 to Estelle's where Beryl and Martha were visiting, so we had lunch and a good visit in the afternoon.

February 1 we went to Apple Valley and visited my nephew, Walter Scott and Ida. They had moved out there after his life work with General Electric, after graduating from USC in Electrical Engineering.

We visited Oliver and Marie Johnston overnight February 2-3. He still has his locomotives, cars and tracks all around his property and the natural growth of trees and shrubs. It is a beautiful area.

We arrived in Long Beach February 4 and visited the Spruce Goose and the Queen Mary, both interesting. We did not see the hotel part of the Queen Mary; what we saw was the size of the ship and its engines and accommodations as it finished its record as a troop ship. Interesting, but not beautiful.

The Spruce Goose was there in all its glory. It is tremendous and inspiring to think that a man could visualize such an aircraft and then go ahead and build it during wartime when scarce metals and materials were not available to him and then have the confidence to go ahead and fly it. It is a monument to American genius.

Attended the Beet Growers' Meeting February 5-10 and drove home.

We gave $1,260 to His Farm, a home for wayward boys on Eagle Nest Road between Sacramento and Sloughhouse.

March 28-30 we held our second meeting of consultants to advise us in setting up our School of Foreign Service. These were 14 well-selected representatives of government agencies and international business, representing about all phases of international activities, very conscientious and innovative in giving us their best suggestions:

398

1. Faculty must learn to think as other cultures do if we are to understand them.
2. We must be sure we prepare students for future, not past foreign service needs.
3. Overriding all are the skills of coping with uncertainty and creative problem solving.
4. Currently, business spends over 50 billion dollars for reeducating its executives.
5. Have students understand that rules which apply in the U.S. may not apply everywhere.
6. First, motivate the faculty to be internationalized.
7. Make use of foreign instructors to help internationalize the material, and other instructors.
8. Students should have an applied research program, such as analyzing the laws that restrict production in various countries.
9. Several suggested an "International Fellows" program.
10. Should have an International Program Coordinator to develop the program and coordinate into University dimensions of the programs. He should have wide experience in international affairs, fund-raising ability, and enthusiasm and energy, not over one or two classes of teaching.

We spent a few days in April at Little River Inn in Mendocino County relaxing and exploring the surrounding area by car and on foot.

We went to Picnic Day in Davis April 20 to see the parade and Harry Wellman, Knowles Ryerson, Emil Mrak, their wives and all the other old friends on the campus. Lunched with Chancellor Meyers at his home, which was built and landscaped by Knowles when he was chancellor at Davis.

May 3-5 was 519 Rotary District Conference in Sacramento for the first time in many years. Bill Smith, District Governor, and his wife, Alice, had finished a great year of building Rotary in District 519 and organized an outstanding conference to wind up the year. Sacramento proved a good conference location.

I went to Cosumnes River College May 7 to hear an Agricultural Extension Economist talk on "The Future of Farming." We started late, I guess, because one other man, I think a student at Cosumnes, and I were the only attendants not on the program. The presentation was a statement of the past and present in agriculture and all our problems. There was nothing about the future.

At the close of the meeting, I couldn't help telling the speaker that I had come to hear about the future of farming. He said, "What future? Agriculture doesn't have a future." I said I was thinking of that as I was driving over and decided today is the best time for a young man to start farming that I have seen in the last twenty-five years.

Even five years ago, it was very difficult and expensive to enter farming, either as an owner or as a tenant. Today, there is lots of land for lease on good terms, lots to buy and far cheaper than five years ago, lots of farm machinery of all sorts for sale, cheap and easy terms. There will be a tendency to lower total farm production for a while, which should help strengthen prices. The next few years may be difficult, but history says the next few years will lay the foundation for many farm fortunes. Why do economists say of farming, "There is no future"?

The Rotary lunch and dedication of the Rotary Grove was held May 23 in the Discovery Park area. Don Hess, Dean of the College of Agriculture in Davis, was the speaker. Several months ago, Rotary planted 450 trees in the grove, one for each member; some day they will be a great asset to the park.

We had dinner May 24 in the Regents dining room with Dr. Bell, recent Secretary of the U.S. Department of Education, a fine gentleman and proven educator. We all sat on the stage as he gave the commencement address.

I spent an hour May 30 with George Anderson, General Agent of the Farm Credit District in their fine Sacramento offices. I am very fearful of a group trying to centralize the Farm Credit Banks in Washington D.C., so it would no longer be farmer-owned, farmer-controlled, or operated in the long-time interest of farmers.

A major function of Congress during the first 200 years, especially 150 years, was disposal of the public domain into private hands, now a group seems determined to get all the land, water and power back into the hands of government, under the guise of efficiency and public welfare.

I felt George Anderson and the District Farm Credit Board realized the danger and will try to prevent such action, but it will take eternal vigilance and support of the public to keep Farm Credit localized.

Bella and I spent several pleasant days during July in David's rented house at Incline Village, Lake Tahoe. One day we leisurely drove all around the lake, including Fallen Leaf Lake.

The Hernandez wedding took place August 3 at 3:30 pm in the Cathedral in Sacramento. They had 14 ushers and 14 bridesmaids, and each one had a part in the ceremony, which was beautifully done. A big dinner followed, with several hundred guests and a very good mariachi orchestra throughout the dinner and dance.

The Reamer wedding was August 24 on the lawn southeast of Howard and Helen's home at the east of the grove of natural trees. It was about sunset and it was beautiful, the sunset on the sprinklers and broad expanse of grass pasture with the horses grazing in the shade.

A new gas well with the Christmas tree on it was just east of the house, another with Christmas tree south of the house. I believe we have a 1/16th interest on this well dug by Occidental. The wells are not producing yet, but they are putting in the pipeline going across the deep-water channel and the Bypass to hook into a line Sacramento-Rio Vista. They drilled a dry hole on the Harter land, just east of our Spangaard 47 acres. They drilled nine holes in that immediate area with five good ones.

On September 11 Bill Dunlap of Clarksburg put a new roof on our house, after 50 years, replacing the old roof of shingles. It hadn't leaked yet, but it was showing signs of wear and weather.

18
LOOKING BACK TO LOOK AHEAD

All my life, or at least since fifth grade, I wanted to be a farmer like Grandpa Boggs. In 1922, when I moved to our farm, I became interested in Yolo County farmers. As I became more involved with the California Farm Bureau Federation, my interest extended to California farmers, growing to include all America in the 1930s, and the farmers of the world in the 1940s.

Seventy-three years ago, as a student assistant, I helped write a bulletin, "How to Organize a County Farm Bureau." Since then, Farm Bureau has been an important part of my life. We had monthly Farm Center and County Board meetings, plus regional, state, and national meetings. I consider Farm Bureau the greatest adult education organization in the nation. Issues were discussed, debated, and decided at those monthly meetings. When our county and state directors faced the issues, they had already heard them discussed; they knew what the membership thought, and could respond quickly and decisively. Now we have given up most of the membership meetings, and most members today have little feel for the power they once generated. Our directors now face the issues with little input from members. Perhaps we need some review and self-analysis; many groups in our society — big business, big labor, commerce — have found it helpful to look back and analyze where they got off the track. Farm Bureau is an ideal organization to keep ground-level issues before legislators, helping them make ground-level decisions; we need to restore Farm Bureau to its former place.

My years in Farm Bureau brought me into contact with farmers and states-men all over the world. I have slept in some very pleasant beds and some very uncomfortable beds in farm homes in various countries, but regardless of the beds, there was always hospitality. Most of the world's people have great respect, often love, for Americans, and they wish us to succeed -- it is difficult to see why we do some of the things we do.

One unworthy attitude held by too many people is prejudice toward some countries because of their leadership. The people of the world are our friends, and we should not, in most cases, blame the people for the sins of their leaders. Our State Department should get to know the people, not just the leaders whose objectives may or may not be to advance the welfare of their own people.

Libya is a good example. Most desert people have little contact with the outside world, and have little formal education. King Idris was our friend and he planned a quiet change to an elected government as soon as possible. Khadafi came along and took power by assassination. The people had no part in selecting their leader, but we feel inclined to punish all Libyans. The same is somewhat true of Iran. The people are mostly the same people we recently considered friends. Their government has changed, but not the people. In World War I we made it quite plain we were fighting the Kaiser, not necessarily the people. It is in our power to keep the people as friends, or turn them against us by penalizing them for the crimes of those who dominate them.

Perhaps the most universal problem affecting farm production is excess -- and often unwise -- government. In our own country, the current farm depression can be traced to some of the farm programs started in 1936. At that time, President Roosevelt had Congress pass the National Industrial Recovery Act (NIRA), setting up many codes of procedure for labor, industry, commerce. The act was declared unconstitutional by the Supreme Court as not within the power of Congress or the President. The Agricultural Adjustment Act (AAA) was also declared by the Supreme Court as not within the limited powers of the federal government. The President then tried to stack the Supreme Court with young, venturesome judges to carry out his wishes. During the twelve years of his presidency, the people became accustomed to the assumption by the federal government of powers not assigned to it by the Constitution. Our U.S. Constitution with its Bill of Rights stated clearly the powers of the federal government. Powers not specifically delegated to the federal government are reserved to the states or people.

Throughout high school and college I was taught that people were governed best where the problem was financed and administered by the level of government closest to the problem. Grade schools are governed by school boards from city or county; local roads and local crime are controlled by cities and counties; state highways and universities by the state, with limited powers assigned by the Constitution to the federal government.

As population increased, complexity and overlapping increased costs of government. Districts, cities, counties, and states used up their sources of income. In contrast, the federal government seemed to have unlimited income plus methods of hiding costs. Also, legislators had discovered that giving out money to the voting public was an effective way of being reelected. People and courts took the easy path and let the federal government perform many duties not authorized by the Constitution. The federal government now exercises powers in areas such as public welfare and education never given to it by the Constitution.

One program that has become a detriment to farming is the farm subsidy. An earlier example of the detrimental effect of subsidies can be found in our own Merchant Marine. The first act of the first U.S. Congress was to create a subsidy to assure the success of the Merchant Marine. This has now become a deterrent to U.S. export, and it has become a deterrent to the Merchant Marine itself. After receiving subsidies for over 200 years, today we have one of the weakest Merchant Marines of any country, and the most expensive rates! The high rates and the requirement for shipping a specified percentage of farm export in American ships is squeezing farm sales and is one cause of the current farm depression. Nobody wins. Ironically, the two most successful U.S. shipping companies (one of these is Ludwig) did not accept subsidies. Neither industry nor farming thrives for long on subsidies.

Another universal detriment -- and another form of excess government -- is retraints to trade. Many of these restraints were set up for a seemingly good reason, and many worked for a time, but outlived their usefulness. Restraints to trade are often written into laws, and laws tend to remain in force whether they serve a useful purpose or not. Restraints to trade usually translate into curtailed compensation to the farmer. The farmer then curtails production, as he cannot operate long at a loss.

In discussing the issue of restraints to trade, people often ask, "What restraints? Name some." These restraints have become so much a part of our lives that we accept them as an essential part of trade. Tariffs and export fees, for example, can discourage production of useful goods and services.

India raises quite a few peanuts, or groundnuts, but the growers say that every year the buyers come at harvest saying they are so sorry, but there are too many peanuts. The government will not give them export permits, so the price is low; then, when the peanuts are in buyer's warehouses, the government gives export permits and the price bounces up. But the producer has already sold, so he never gets the benefit of his production. The economic advisors to the government of India said this is necessary to assure there are plenty of nuts for India, before they allow export. They don't look ahead to see that if they do run short of nuts, they could use the income from them to buy more wheat, rice, and other foods.

India was divided by law into 12-15 districts. The law provided one could not ship food from one district to another without a government permit. This reduced both the volume and value of food available to many willing buyers in other districts. When B. P. Singh became Minister of Agriculture, he had the law repealed, in spite of terrible cries from the cities. Within a year, city people were asking him what he had done, as fruits and vegetables in city stores were fresher, better, and cheaper than ever before. The farmers were happy, as they were selling more produce, because they were able to sell wherever the market was best and for a longer period of time. Almost anyone can imagine what would happen to agriculture in California if we could not ship our production across state lines at will. We would not be the most populous state in the

Union, nor enjoy the quality of life we are used to.

The Indian farmer does not have to know how to read or write to know that when PL480 rice is shipped into Karella at harvest time, it comes in for one purpose only -- to reduce the price of rice to the Indian farmer. If it came to reduce the price to the city consumers, it would have arrived at Bombay or Calcutta.

Many well-intentioned American people do not understand that their shipments of PL480 wheat and rice to poverty-stricken areas of the world have been misused to lower the prices to the farmers of India and other areas, which in turn limits his production and finally increases his poverty. Dr. Ted Schultz, a Nobel-prize winner in Agricultural Economics, says "There is no question that India produced less wheat and rice because of our shipments. The only question was 'did the people of India have less wheat and rice to eat because of our shipment'?"

When I was in Pakistan as a member of President Eisenhower's Agricultural Trade Mission to Asia, the first thing the government people said to us was, they had a drought in 1948 and a short crop of wheat, so they asked for PL480 wheat from the U.S. It was promised. Two shipments arrived and more was due soon, but they wanted us to divert the rest to some other country because when word got out that the U.S. wheat had arrived, the price dropped, and far more Pakistani wheat showed up in the market. Later shipments dropped the price further, so they believed the Pakistani farmers would not plant in the face of low prices, creating a shortage of wheat for the next year. They were thinking smarter than some of our educated theoretical economists. PL480 did some good, but needs careful handling.

Many laws or commercial practices restraining trade end up keeping millions of people in poverty, doing little for them or their children. These laws or practices may be supported by good people with good intentions who have not analyzed the effects. It is important to study the cause and effect of production failure when supplying goods or services to people.

Farm losses end up as a loss for everyone, for without income, the farmer cannot buy the production of others, and world trade stagnates. When Henry Ford saw his cars rolling off the assembly line 70 years ago, he wondered who in the world would buy them. Ford said, "The thing won't work unless the men who build the cars can afford to buy them." So he announced, out of a clear sky, that he would pay $5 per day for an 8-hour day instead of the usual $2.50 per 10-hour day. The press called him wild, crazy-mad, but the next year he raised wages to $6 per day, then $7, then $8. He found it worked or he would not have kept raising wages.

If the production of useful goods and services constitutes wealth, then it is also true that restraints to the production of such goods and services diminish wealth. Ford saw clearly that if he was to succeed, his workers also needed to succeed; by enriching them, he enriched himself. What worked for Ford will work for the world's farmers. Restraints to farm income means the farmer cannot buy the production of others, and world trade suffers.

With useless restraints removed, millions can earn for themselves a higher place in society, and this automatically creates a larger demand for goods and services from the more developed world. A good thesis subject might be "Restraints which discourage production of useful goods and services among people of low production." Students could gain much knowledge of value in international activities. Both business and government could gain a picture of the situation as it is and a guide to what it should be. The U.S. will never do as well as it should in world leadership until more of our young people travel in useful pursuits all over the world and get better acquainted with the world's people. We will like them; they will like us; and we will all be winners.

Another factor detrimental to farmers everywhere is a mistaken attitude toward farmers. Some people relegate farmers to a lower social strata. Rural areas tend to get poorer roads, fewer schools and communications, so it is easy for city dwellers to look on farmers as ignorant, uneducated, or lazy, born in poverty and expected to live in poverty. But farm people around the world are neither lazy nor dumb. They may be unschooled, but they are not uneducated. They may not read, but they can count. They may lack formal education, but they use their natural senses better than most; they see, hear, feel, and smell things that many university graduates never see, feel, or hear. Many have learned well the answers to life's problems. After visiting with farmers large and small, rich and poor, in their homes and in the fields, in most of the countries of the world, I have confidence in them.

In recent years, people around the world have surprised us and even surpassed us with ingenious solutions and ambitious successes. My generation had learned to respect the Japanese as thrifty, hard workers, but we were not prepared to see them challenge us so successfully in automobiles and banking. We were unprepared to see South Korea compete with us in heavy construction or shipbuilding, as well as many smaller products. The farmers of the Sahara and other deserts know much we do not about the use of water to produce crops.

The farmers of the world have a unique and necessary talent. They are truly the "heart of the earth," the ones who keep all of us alive, and not everyone can do what they do. In the Depression in our country in the 20s and 30s, moneylenders and bankers foreclosed on farms, and they assumed they could "do it better," but soon found they could not. In our recent agricultural depression, lenders and bankers may take title to the land and equipment, but they make every effort to get the farmer to continue to farm the land.

The question is still, how do we change the world situation so millions can become economic producers and have the ability to buy 21st-century miracles? They want to produce. They want to improve their lives and their children's future. They want the products of the high-tech world, and they want to work to gain them. But restraints to production and free movement are so great, they must sit on the sidelines. We need these potential buyers as much as they need us.

Where do we start to change the present world scene? I was talking with an Indian from India during an election campaign. He said, "Some people are promising our people 'equality.' It doesn't mean a thing, not a thing. Now you Americans talk about 'equality of opportunity,' that means something." I have asked many people why they believed hundreds of millions of people of all social and economic classes left their homeland, often at great risk, to come to America. "Equality of opportunity" seems to be the popular opinion.

Millions of people came to America seeking equality of social and economic opportunity. They knew it was not conquest, but the production of useful goods and services which constitute wealth, and through hard work, we became a wealthy nation.

If opportunity drew millions to our shores, why isn't our goal for all people in the world "equality of opportunity"? If this is a valid goal to strength and wealth, why do we not set as our first goal equality of opportunity for the world's people, and especially for the world's farmers -- those who stand at the center and make the earth produce a livelihood for everyone? Education, better roads, and other infrastructure all help. . .but these things come easily when farm people prosper.

Some people fear increased world farm production. I do not. As people prosper, they want to go from roots to rice, to wheat, to vegetables and fruits and meat, and many will buy more of our farm and industrial production. The production of useful goods and services constitutes wealth, and the world never got poorer by the production of more wealth.

PROLOGUE

My 94th birthday was March 26, 1986, and Bella's 85th was March 31. Our 65th wedding anniversary (April 17) was celebrated with a reception from 2-5 at El Macero Country Club on Sunday, April 13th. Our first plan was to have the family and a few close friends, but the list grew longer and longer. Even then, we realized there were others whom we wished we had invited. We had our UOP friends, our UC friends, Rotary Club, Bella's PEO and Card Club, our relatives and our Clarksburg neighbors. About 300 were present, a great group of wonderful people. We had a buffet lunch with tables for all who wanted to sit. Many guests met old friends they hadn't seen for years. Everyone seemed to really enjoy the occasion.

About 4 o'clock David made a very nice statement for the family, followed by remarks by Dick and Dorothy. Pat and Wes had been here in January and hope to return this summer, but could not come at this time. A very nice letter from Nancy and Ronald Reagan was read and much appreciated. David then introduced Stan McCaffrey, President of UOP. Stan announced that, as part of our 65th wedding anniversary, we were giving a Conservatory Grand Piano to the School of Music at UOP.

The University had already awarded a UOP chair to me. Now they awarded a chair to Isabelle in honor of our 65th wedding anniversary, April 17, 1986.

Stan introduced the harpist, Cynthia Dodge, with pianist Ken Kugelman, and the beautiful vocalist, Elena Duarte, all from the UOP Conservatory of Music. Dr. Nosse of the Conservatory of Music had kindly provided background music, and all our guests really enjoyed the outstanding music program.

I wish to note, among the other guests, Knowles Ryerson, a friend during my Berkeley days 1911-15 and ever since; Harry Wellman, Ag-Economist, 1925; Emil Mrak, Chancellor at UC Davis for many years; and Dick Owens of Farm Bureau days. I could go on, as everyone were old friends who honored and pleased us by their attendance. All seemed to have a very pleasant afternoon meeting many old-time friends they had not seen for years.

The many letters we received after the reception made us feel very humble and most grateful for so many true and outstanding friends, and we were most thankful for our fine, loving family who arranged the party for us.

The day, the flowers, the friends were all beautiful. It was a heartwarming day.